Give Me Five! ENGLISH 1

BASICS

TEACHER'S BOOK

Donna Shaw • Joanne Ramsden

macmillan education

Macmillan Education
4 Crinan Street
London N1 9XW
A division of Springer Nature Limited

Companies and representatives throughout the world

Teacher's Book 1 Basics 978-1-380-02546-3
Teacher's Book 1 Basics Pack 978-1-380-02487-9

This edition published 2018
First edition entitled *High Five! English* published 2014 by Springer Nature Limited

Original series concept design by Tom Cole
Page make-up by emc design limited
Illustrated by Ángeles Peinador
Cover design by Bigtop Design Limited
Cover photograph by Tom Dick and Debbie Productions

Authors' acknowledgments
The authors would like to thank everyone at Macmillan who has given help and advice throughout this project. Special thanks from Jo to Carlos, Daniel and Alex for their patience and support during this process. Special thanks from Donna to José, Elisa, Teresa and Marina for their encouragement and enthusiasm.

The publishers would like to thank Amanda Morrison Prince, Colegio El Parque, La Navata, Madrid; Amaya Carrera García, Colegio Santa Teresa de Jesús, Valladolid; Ana Isabel Fernández Sáez, CEIP La Encina, Las Rozas, Madrid; Aránzazu Sánchez Rodríguez, CEIP Rosa Luxemburgo, Madrid; Beatriz García Vaquero, CEIP Mariano José de Larra, Madrid; Carme Tena, Col·legi Sagrada Familia, Tortosa, Tarragona; Carmen María Largo Muñoz, CEIP Federico García Lorca, Colmenar Viejo, Madrid; Cristina Nieto Ruiz de Gaona, CEIP Margarita Salas, Arroyo de la Encomienda, Valladolid; David García Martínez, CEIP Amador de los Ríos, Madrid; Estíbaliz Medina Martín, CEIP Virgen de Navalazarza, San Agustín de Guadalix, Madrid; Francisco Javier Navarro Pineda, Colegio Tajamar, Madrid; Iratxe Zabaleta Zendagorta, Ikastola San Fidel, Guernica, Vizcaya; Jesús Javier de Andrés Urraca, CEIP Esperanza, Madrid; Juana Rego Freire, CEIP Padre Poveda, Madrid; Judith Muñoz Díaz, CEIP Rodríguez Sahagún, Madrid; Lucía Manso Estébanez, CEIP Ciudad de Guadalajara, Madrid; Lucía López Sánchez, CEIP San Juan de la Cruz, Madrid; Lucía Soria García, CEIP Alberto Alcocer, Madrid; María Jesús Pérez Pérez, CEIP Alberto Alcocer, Madrid; Mario Merino Fernández, CEIP María Martín, Madrid; Marta Moreno Arroyo, CEIP Vicente Aleixandre, Móstoles, Madrid; Miren Itziar Ispizua Mintegui, CEIP Ramiro de Maetzu, Madrid; Paula Reyes García, CEIP Alberto Alcocer, Madrid; Susana Espinel Beneitez, Colegio Grazalema, El Puerto de Santa María, Cádiz; Susana García Pizarro, Ateneu Instructiu, Sant Joan Despí, Barcelona; Virginia Escalona Monreal, CEIP La Encina, Las Rozas, Madrid.

Commissioned photography by Lisa Payne p14, Redhill Media Ltd p21 (br) and Tom Dick and Debbie Productions p16

Full acknowledgments for illustrations and photographs in the facsimile pages can be found in the Pupil's Book 1 Basics ISBN 978-1-380-01356-9, the Activity Book 1 Basics ISBN 978-1-380-01376-7.

Printed and bound in Brazil

2022
13

Give Me Five!

BASICS 1

TEACHER'S BOOK

Syllabus

Unit	Key Competences and Key Learning Outcomes	Contents
		Lexis
Starter Unit Hello, friends!	• Ask for someone's name and give your name (Lesson 1) • Say the vocabulary chant (Lesson 1) • Identify and say the numbers 1–10 (Lesson 1) • Ask and answer the question *What's this?* (Lesson 2) • Identify and say colours (Lesson 3) • Ask and answer the question *What day is it today?* (Lesson 4) • Identify and say five shapes (Lesson 2) • Use the Pupil's App on Navio • Make a cut-out and evaluate your learning (Lesson 4) • Get to know your teacher and classmates (Lesson 1) • Work with a Talk Partner to practise and reinforce learning (all lessons) • Sing a song (Lesson 1 and 4) • Read, listen and understand a story about a magic bike (Lesson 3)	**Core vocabulary** • *goodbye, hello* • numbers 1–10 (words and figures) • shapes (*circle, oval, rectangle, square, triangle*) • colours (*blue, brown, green, orange, red, yellow*) • days of the week (*Monday, Tuesday, Wednesday, Thursday, Friday, Saturday, Sunday*) • *balloons, balls, bananas, bike, books, dogs, hats, socks* **Extension vocabulary (optional)** • *black, grey, pink, purple, white* **Other vocabulary** • *bell, clean, children, idea, fantastic, magic bike, ring, surprise*
Unit 1 Ready for school!	• Identify and say ten classroom objects (Lesson 1) • Say the vocabulary chant (Lesson 1) • Use *Where's? …* and *here …* in a conversation (Lesson 2) • Ask and answer the question *Where's my pen?* (Lesson 2) • Understand and give instructions using prepositions (Lesson 4) • Watch and understand a video about what children do at school (Video and 21st Century Skills) • Use the Pupil's App on Navio • Practise spelling (Lesson 1) • Say a tongue twister to practise the 'r' sound (Lesson 5) • Review language in the unit and reflect on own learning (Lesson 8) • Understand the importance of keeping the classroom tidy (Lesson 3) • Read and understand classroom rules (Lesson 7) • Understand the importance of being organised (Video and 21st Century Skills) • Work with a Talk Partner to practise and reinforce learning (all lessons) • Play a communication game about classroom objects (Lesson 5) • Sing three songs (Lessons 1, 4 and 8) • Understand and act out a story (Lesson 3) • Read about school assemblies in Britain (Lesson 6) • Think about what you do at school (Lesson 6)	**Core vocabulary** • *book, computer, crayon, pen, pencil, pencil case, rubber, ruler, school bag, sharpener* • *bin, board, chair, cupboard, desk, shelf* **Extension vocabulary (optional)** • *file, glue, notebook, paintbrush, paper, scissors; bookcase, door, floor, window* **Other vocabulary** • *floor, good work, poster, rules, school assembly, white* **Recycled vocabulary** • Numbers 1–10 • Colours • Days of the week
Unit 2 Happy birthday!	• Identify and say ten toys (Lesson 1) • Say the vocabulary chant (Lesson 1) • Use *What is it? Is it a …? Yes, it is. / No, it isn't.* in a conversation. (Lesson 2) • Ask and answer questions about your favourite toys (Lesson 4) • Describe your favourite toy (Lesson 4) • Watch and understand a video about ranking favourite toys (Video and 21st Century Skills) • Say what your favourite toys are (Video and 21st Century Skills) • Understand why forms of transport go fast or slow (Lesson 3) • Order things (Video and 21st Century Skills) • Use the Pupil's App on Navio • Practise spelling (Lesson 1) • Say a tongue twister to practise the 's' sound (Lesson 5) • Review language in the unit and reflect on own learning (Lesson 8) • Understand the importance of saying 'thank you' (Lesson 3) • Understand the importance of sharing (Lesson 5) • Work with a Talk Partner to practise and reinforce learning (all lessons) • Play a communication game about toys (Lesson 5) • Sing four songs (Lessons 1, 4, 5, and 8) • Understand and act out a story (Lesson 3) • Read about birthday parties in Britain (Lesson 6) • Read, understand and design a birthday card (Lesson 7)	**Core vocabulary** • *ball, car, computer game, dinosaur, doll, kite, robot, scooter, teddy, train* • *big, fast, new, old, slow, small* **Extension vocabulary (optional)** • *bat, board game, boat, football, monster, skateboard; loud, quiet, long, short* **Other vocabulary** • *balloons, birthday cake, birthday card, candles, costume, fancy dress, party, party games, present* • *wheels* • *To …, Lots of love …, From …* **Recycled vocabulary** • Numbers 1–10 • Colours • *book, computer, crayon, pen, pencil, pencil case, rubber, ruler, school bag, sharpener*

Competence in linguistic communication | Competence in mathematics, science and technology | Digital competence | Learning to learn | Social and civic competences | Sense of initiative and entrepreneurship | Cultural awareness and expression

Contents					Cross-curricular links
Structures	**Phonics**	**Sociocultural aspects**	**British Culture and Literacy**	**21st Century Skills**	
Core structures • *What's your name? I'm (Jake).* • *What's this? It's a (bike).* • *What colour is it? It's (green).* • *What day is it today? It's (Thursday).* **Other structures** • *Ring the bell again. Let's (clean the bike). The (bike) is (green). It's a (bike). Good idea! This magic bike is fantastic!*		**Cooperative learning** **Skills** • Listening to your classmates (Lesson 1) • Learning to learn (Lesson 2) • Turn taking (Lesson 4)			**Link to Science** **Physical characteristics** • Counting the boys and girls in the class. **Arts and Crafts** **Art is everywhere** • Understanding that artists find inspiration in the world around them; thinking about what inspires you.
Core structures • *Where's my (pen)? It's here.* • *Where's my (purple) (pencil case). It's in / on / under the (desk). Put the (pencil case) on / in / under (the desk).* **Other structures** • *I'm ready for school. Let's tidy up. We (sit on the floor / listen to the head teacher / sing songs / clap our hands). Listen to others. Put your hand up to speak. Work quietly. Sit down on your chair. Walk in the classroom. Tidy up your things. Find the (computer on the desk). Point to the (pencil).* **Recycled structures** • *What's this? It's (a pen). What colour is it? It's (purple).*	• Consonant sound 'r' (**r**ed, **r**abbit, **r**uler)	**Cooperative learning** **Song** • *Well Done!* (Lesson 8) **Skills** • Think-Pair-Share (Lesson 1) • Listening to others (Lesson 2) • Developing a positive classroom atmosphere (Lesson 6) • Behaving well in class (Lesson 7) **Values** • Keeping the classroom tidy	**British Culture** • School assembly **Literacy** **Text type** • A classroom poster (instructional text) **Reading skills** • Reading for specific information	**21st Century Skills** • **Ways of working:** being organised	**Links to Science** **My school** • Identifying classroom equipment and materials and keeping them tidy • Being aware that there are different school subjects • Behaving correctly in class and around the school **Arts and Crafts** **Lines and shapes** • Identifying lines and shapes in Art and around school • Using lines and shapes to represent your school
Core structures • *What is it?* • *Is it a (bike)? Yes, it is. No, it isn't.* • *What's your favourite toy? My favourite toy is a (ball). It's (old). My favourite toy is (old).* • *My (scooter) is (slow).* **Other structures** • *Happy birthday. Here's (a present for you). It's a fantastic present. Thank you (for my present). I've got a (birthday cake).* • *I have (a party). I play (party games). I wear (fancy dress). How old are you? I'm (six). What is it? It's a (motor). It's (good fun).* **Recycled structures** • *It's (red). Put (the car) (in the cupboard).*	• Consonant sound 's' (**s**ix, **s**nakes, **s**low, **s**cooter)	**Cooperative learning** **Songs** • *Sharing is a good thing to do* (Lesson 5) • *Well Done!* (Lesson 8) **Skills** • Working together and supporting each other (Lesson 1) • Listening to others (Lesson 2) • Developing a positive classroom atmosphere (Lessons 4 and 7) **Values** • The importance of saying 'thank you'	**British Culture** • Birthday parties **Literacy** **Text type** • A birthday card (text to express) **Reading skills** • Using pictures • Reading for specific information	**21st Century Skills** • **Ways of thinking:** learn to order your favourite things	**Link to Science** **The senses** • Using adjectives to describe touch (*hard, soft, rough, smooth*), sight (*colours*) and sounds (*loud, quiet*) **Arts and Crafts** **Patterns** • Identifying patterns in Art and in the environment • Using lines, shapes and colours to create patterns

Syllabus

Unit	Key Competences and Key Learning Outcomes	Contents Lexis
Unit 3 At the circus	• Identify and say ten parts of the body (Lesson 1) • Say the vocabulary chant (Lesson 1) • Use *I've got …* in a conversation (Lesson 2) • Make statements about your body (Lesson 2) • Describe a friend's hair and eyes (Lesson 4) • Watch and understand a video about the circus (Video and 21st Century Skills) • Count the parts of the body (Lesson 1) • Use the Pupil's App on Navio • Practise spelling (Lesson 1) • Say a tongue twister to practise the 'h' sound (Lesson 2) • Review language in the unit and reflect on own learning (Lesson 8) • Understand the importance of riding a bike safely (Lesson 3) • Describe your feelings (Lesson 7) • Identify different feelings (Lesson 7) • Understand the importance of working together (Video and 21st Century Skills) • Work with a Talk Partner to practise and reinforce learning (all lessons) • Play a communication game describing people (Lesson 5) • Sing four songs (Lessons 1, 4, 7 and 8) • Understand and act out a story (Lesson 3) • Read about 'Circus Day' in British schools (Lesson 6) • Think about a circus where you live (Lesson 6) • Understand and act out an action rhyme (Lesson 7)	**Core vocabulary** • *arms, ears, eyes, feet, fingers, head, legs, mouth, nose, toes* • *black hair, blonde hair, brown hair, long hair, red hair, short hair* **Extension vocabulary (optional)** • *back, bottom, hand, knee, shoulder, stomach; curly, spiky, straight, wavy* **Other vocabulary** • *acrobat, circus, clown* • *juggle scarves, ride a special bike, spin a plate, walk on stilts* • *angry, sad, happy, tired* • *cry, go to sleep, laugh, sit, smile, stamp my feet* **Recycled vocabulary** • Numbers 1–10 • *ball, car, computer game, dinosaur, doll, kite, robot, scooter, teddy, train; big, small; hand*
My project 1: Family	• Identify and talk about family members (Lesson 1) • Ask and answer questions about family members (Lesson 1) • Present a class tree display (Lesson 2) • Understand and complete a simple graph about family members (Lesson 1) • Prepare to make a family leaf (Lesson 1) • Think about your project (Lesson 2) • Work together to make a class display (Lesson 2) • Sing a cooperative learning song (Lesson 2) • Listen to others (Lesson 2) • Respect different types of families (Lesson 2) • Follow instructions to make a family leaf (Lesson 2)	**Core vocabulary** • *aunt, brother, cousin, family, father, grandfather, grandmother, mother, sister* • *copy, decorate, fold, leaf, photo, stick, tree* **Other vocabulary** • *coloured pencils and crayons, glue, scissors, star* • *help, like, make an effort, plan, share, work together* **Recycled vocabulary** • *big, small; colour, listen*
Unit 4 Fantastic food!	• Identify and say ten items of food (Lesson 1) • Say the vocabulary chant (Lesson 1) • Use *like*, *don't like* and *love* (Lesson 2) • Understand and act out a conversation (Lesson 2) • Ask and answer questions to find out what fruit people like (Lesson 4) • Read and draw a lunch menu (Lesson 7) • Watch and understand a video about school lunches (Video and 21st Century Skills) • Identify healthy / unhealthy food (Lessons 3 and 7) • Use the Pupil's App on Navio • Practise spelling (Lesson 1) • Say a tongue twister to practise the 'j' sound (Lesson 5) • Review language in the unit and reflect on own learning (Lesson 8) • Understand the importance of eating healthy food (Lesson 3 and Video and 21st Century Skills) • Work with a Talk Partner to practise and reinforce learning (all lessons) • Play a communication game about food (Lesson 5) • Sing four songs (Lessons 1, 4, 5 and 8) • Understand and act out a story (Lesson 3) • Read about a traditional English breakfast (Lesson 6) • Think about what you have for breakfast (Lesson 6) • Draw healthy food for your lunch box (Video and 21st Century Skills)	**Core vocabulary** • *cake, chicken, chips, eggs, fish, fruit, ice cream, meat, rice, salad* • *cherry, coconut, grape, lemon, mango, peach* **Extension vocabulary (optional)** • *burger, juice, lemonade, milk, pie, water; kiwi, pear, strawberry, watermelon* **Other vocabulary** • *bread, breakfast, cereal, food, fruit juice, fruit salad, jelly, orange juice, pasta, soup, toast, vegetables* • *cook the food, cut the tomatoes, make the toast, mix the eggs, prepare the tray* **Recycled vocabulary** • *arms, ears, eyes, feet, fingers, head, legs, mouth, nose, toes; bananas; juggle; toy* • Days of the week

Competence in linguistic communication | Competence in mathematics, science and technology | Digital competence | Learning to learn | Social and civic competences | Sense of initiative and entrepreneurship | Cultural awareness and expression

Contents					Cross-curricular links
Structures	**Phonics**	**Sociocultural aspects**	**British Culture and Literacy**	**21st Century Skills**	
Core structures • *I've got (a big nose).* • *I've got (small eyes).* • *My friend has got (long hair).* • *He's / She's got (blue eyes).* **Other structures** • *This is me. This is my body. Count with me. He's / She's got (blue eyes). Let's make (a circus). How are you today? I'm (sad). When I'm (happy), I (smile). What colour is (your hair)? My (hair) is (black). What colour are (your eyes)? My (eyes) are (brown). He's / She's fantastic. We're (different). We're (friends). We're (in the garden). We can do it. My clown has got (a big nose). My clown has got (red hair).* **Recycled structures** • *I've got (a friend called Beth).*	• Consonant sound 'h' (**H**elen, **h**appy, **h**ippo, **h**ops)	**Cooperative learning** **Songs** • *We can do it!* (Lesson 7) • *Well Done!* (Lesson 8) **Skills** • Working together (Lesson 1) • Working together to complete a task (Lesson 2) • Developing a positive classroom atmosphere (Lesson 4) • Think-Pair-Share (Lesson 8) **Values** • Understanding the importance of riding a bike safely	**British Culture** • 'Circus Day' **Literacy** **Text type** • An action rhyme (text to express) **Reading skills** • Using visual clues • Reading for specific information	**21st Century Skills** • **Ways of working:** learn to work together	**Links to Science** **The human body** • The main parts of the body and adjectives to describe the face • Similarities and differences in what the body can do • Action, movement and body joints • Recognising and expressing emotion and feelings **Arts and Crafts** **Lines and colours** • Identifying primary and secondary colours in Art and in the environment • Using lines, shapes and colours to represent the human body
Core structures • *Have you got (a brother)? Yes, I have. / No, I haven't.* • *This is my (mother). (His / Her) name is …* • *This is my family. My family is great.* **Other structures** • *How many people are in your family?* **Recycled structures** • *I've got (one sister). I've got a (big) family. I've got a (small) family.*		**Cooperative learning** **Song** • *It's fun to work together.* (Lesson 2) **Skill** • Working together (Lessons 1 and 2)			**Links to Science** **Families** • Small and big families • Respecting different types of family **Arts and Crafts** **Art in my home** • Identifying lines, shapes, colours and patterns in Art and in the home • Using lines, shapes, colours and patterns to decorate a room
Core structures • *I like (fruit).* • *I love (ice cream).* • *I don't like (cake).* • *Do you like (fruit)? Yes, I do. No, I don't.* **Other structures** • *I'm hungry. It's my favourite. Eating fruit is fun to do. What's for lunch on (Monday)? We've got (meat and vegetables) on (Monday). I (mix the eggs). We (prepare the tray). I have (eggs). Calm down.* **Recycled structures** • *I've got (rice and eggs). What about you? What's your favourite (food)? It's (ice cream).*	• Consonant sound 'j' (**J**im, **j**uggles, **j**am, **j**uice, **j**elly)	**Cooperative learning** **Songs** • *Calm down* (Lesson 5) • *Well Done!* (Lesson 8) **Skills** • Working together and supporting each other (Lesson 1) • Discovering similarities (Lesson 2) **Values** • Understanding the importance of eating healthy food	**British Culture** • A traditional English breakfast **Literacy** **Text type** • A lunch menu (informative text) **Reading skills** • Relating pictures to new vocabulary • Reading for specific information	**21st Century Skills** • **Living in the world:** learn to eat healthily	**Links to Science** **Food** • Recognising that food can be hot or cold • Identifying food that is good for you and food that is not good for you • Reviewing vegetables • Reviewing the meals of the day **Arts and Crafts** **Texture** • Identifying texture in Art • Using fruit and vegetables to create a collage

Syllabus

Unit	Key Competences and Key Learning Outcomes	Contents Lexis
Unit 5 **Fun on the farm**	• Identify and say ten farm animals (Lesson 1) • Say the vocabulary chant (Lesson 1) • Use *Can you …?* and *Yes, I can. No, I can't.* in a conversation. (Lesson 2) • Say what animals can and can't do (Lesson 4) • Read and say an animal riddle (Lesson 7) • Watch and understand a video about farm animals (Video and 21st Century Skills) • Identify two-legged and four-legged animals (Lesson 7) • Put things in groups (Video and 21st Century Skills) • Use the Pupil's App on Navio • Practise spelling (Lesson 1) • Say a tongue twister to practise the 'sh' sound (Lesson 5) • Review language in the unit and reflect on own learning (Lesson 8) • Understand the importance of washing your hands after touching animals (Lesson 3) • Draw animals according to the group they belong to (Video and 21st Century Skills) • Work with a Talk Partner to practise and reinforce learning (all lessons) • Make a cut-out and play a game about what animals can do (Lesson 5) • Sing four songs (Lessons 1, 4, 5 and 8) • Understand and act out a story (Lesson 3) • Read about urban farms in Britain (Lesson 6) • Think about farms where you live (Lesson 6)	**Core vocabulary** • *bird, cat, chicken, cow, duck, frog, goat, horse, mouse, sheep* • *climb, fly, jump, run, swim, walk* **Extension vocabulary (optional)** • *bee, bull, cockerel, donkey, rabbit, spider; crawl, dive, hop, talk* **Other vocabulary** • *animals, carrots, farm, feed, interesting, lamb, shop, shout, stop!, touch, park, pet shop, zoo* **Recycled vocabulary** • Colours • Numbers 1–10 • *big, small; cake, chicken, chips, eggs, fish, fruit, grapes, ice cream, meat, rice, salad, vegetables; delicious; ruler, rubber; doll, robot; ear, toes; garden; juggle; ride a bike*
Unit 6 **A day in the park**	• Identify and say ten park objects (Lesson 1) • Say the vocabulary chant (Lesson 1) • Use *Where …?* and prepositions to find out where people are (Lessons 2 and 4) • Understand and act out a conversation (Lesson 2) • Watch and understand a video about playgrounds (Video and 21st Century Skills) • Read and draw instructions for growing flowers (Lesson 7) • Use the Pupil's App on Navio • Practise spelling (Lesson 1) • Say a tongue twister to practise the sound /w/ (Lesson 5) • Review language in the unit and reflect on own learning (Lesson 8) • Understand the importance of respecting signs (Lesson 3) • Understand the importance of being careful in the playground (Video and 21st Century Skills) • Work with a Talk Partner to practise and reinforce learning (all Lessons) • Play a communication game about finding people (Lesson 5) • Sing four songs (Lessons 1, 4, 5 and 8) • Understand and act out a story (Lesson 3) • Read about activities you can do in the park in Britain (Lesson 6) • Think about parks where you live (Lesson 6) • Think about what you do in the playground (Video and 21st Century Skills)	**Core vocabulary** • *climbing frame, roundabout, see-saw, slide, swing* • *bush, flower, grass, rock, tree* • *behind, between, in front of, near, next to* **Extension vocabulary (optional)** • *bench, fountain, playhouse, sandpit, trampoline, wall; ground, plant, pond, shell* **Other vocabulary** • *playground, sign* • *cricket, park, picnic, zip wire* • *grow, plants, pot, seeds, soil, sun, sunny place, watch, water* **Recycled vocabulary** • *climb, jump, run; bird, cat, cow, dog, duck, frog, goat, horse, sheep; brother, sister; big; in, on, under; long; train, ball; finger; flowers, garden; bin, books, chair, computer, pencil, rubber, ruler, school bag* • Colours

Competence in linguistic communication | Competence in mathematics, science and technology | Digital competence
Learning to learn | Social and civic competences | Sense of initiative and entrepreneurship | Cultural awareness and expression

Contents					Cross-curricular links
Structures	**Phonics**	**Sociocultural aspects**	**British Culture and Literacy**	**21st Century Skills**	
Core structures • *Can you see (a cow)? Yes, I can. No, I can't.* • *(Cats) can (climb). (Cats) can't (swim).* • *Can you (swim)? Yes, I can. No, I can't* **Other structures** • *It's my turn now. I'm (small). This (sheep) can climb trees. I can (feed them). We can see (chickens on the farm). What can (Peter) see? This is a (cow).* **Recycled structures** • *I've got (two legs). Is it a (cow)? Yes, it is. I love (the goats). I like (the garden). What am I? It's (green).*	• Consonant sound 'sh' (**sh**ush, **sh**out, **sh**eep)	**Cooperative learning** **Songs** • *Let's take turns* (Lesson 5) • *Well done!* (Lesson 8) **Skill** • Working together and supporting each other (Lesson 1) **Values** • Understanding the importance of washing your hands after touching animals	**British Culture** • Urban farms **Literacy** **Text type** • Animal riddles (text to entertain) **Reading skills** • Using visual clues • Reading for specific information • Speculating	**21st Century Skills** • **Ways of thinking:** learn to put things in groups	**Links to Science** **Animals** • (Domestic animals) pets and farm animals • The different ways that animals move • Farm animals and wild animals **Arts and Crafts** **Forms** • Identifying 3D forms in Art and in the environment • Using shapes and forms to represent animals
Core structures • *Where's my brother / sister? He's / She's (on the swing).* • *Where are (Beth and Molly)? They're (behind) the (tree).* **Other structures** • *We can (climb). We can play on the (slide). The park is fun. It's fun in the park. Where's (my sister)? She's (on the swing). Where are (Jake and Molly)? They're (behind) the (tree). Where's (Toby)? I don't know. He isn't (under the bush). Ready or not, here I come. Let's play (hide and seek). You can / can't (play in here). We love (the playground). We play (cricket on the grass). We (feed the ducks / ride on the train). Put the (pot in a sunny place). Push the seeds (into the soil). Water the seeds.* **Recycled structures** • *I can (see) (six flowers). Put the (pen near the computer).*	• Consonant sound 'w' (**W**ally, **w**orm, **w**ashes, **w**indows)	**Cooperative learning** **Songs** • *Listen to others* (Lesson 5) • *Well done!* (Lesson 8) **Skills** • Working together and supporting each other (Lesson 1) • Being aware of others (Lesson 2) **Values** • Understanding the importance of respecting signs in public places	**British Culture** • Parks **Literacy** **Text type** • Instructions (instructional text) **Reading skills** • Using visual clues • Relating new vocabulary to pictures • Reading for specific information	**21st Century Skills** • **Living in the world:** learning to be careful in the playground	**Links to Science** **Plants** • Identifying living and non-living things • The importance of sunlight, water and soil for plants to survive **Arts and Crafts** **Shapes** • Identifying and distinguishing between geometric and organic shapes in Art and in the environment • Using geometric and natural shapes to represent a garden

Syllabus

Unit	Key Competences and Key Learning Outcomes	Contents Lexis
My project 2: Spring	• Identify and talk about spring animals and plants (Lesson 1) • Present a class spring display (Lesson 2) • Count items in a picture (Lesson 1) • Identify weather conditions in spring (Lesson 1) • Find pictures on the Internet (Lesson 1) • Prepare to make a class spring wall display (Lesson 1) • Follow instructions (Lesson 2) • Think about your project (Lesson 2) • Sing a cooperative learning song (Lesson 2) • Work together to make a display (Lesson 2) • Make a spring animal (Lesson 2)	**Core vocabulary** • *butterflies, chicks, lambs, rabbits, spring* • *cloudy, rainy, snowy, stormy, sunny, windy* • *paint, wall display* **Extension vocabulary** • *cold, cool, foggy, hot, warm* **Other vocabulary** • *tissue paper* **Recycled vocabulary** • Colours • Numbers 1–10 • *animal, birds, bushes, flowers, trees; ears*
Unit 7 Let's explore my town!	• Identify and say ten places in town (Lesson 1) • Say the vocabulary chant (Lesson 1) • Use *There's …* and *There are …* in a conversation (Lesson 2) • Recognise and say different forms of transport (Lesson 4) • Watch and understand a video about transport (Video and 21st Century Skills) • Recognise and use numbers up to 20 (Lesson 4) • Ask and say how many objects there are (Lesson 4) • Use the Pupil's App on Navio • Read and understand digital maps (Video and 21st Century Skills) • Practise spelling (Lesson 1) • Say a tongue twister to practise the sound /z/ (Lesson 5) • Review language in the unit and reflect on own learning (Lesson 8) • Understand the importance of taking care when crossing the road (Lesson 3) • Draw, say and write what places are near to where you live (Video and 21st Century Skills) • Work with a Talk Partner to practise and reinforce learning (all lessons) • Play a communication game about transport (Lesson 5) • Sing three songs (Lessons 1, 4 and 8) • Understand and act out a story (Lesson 3) • Read about cycling in Britain (Lesson 6) • Think about how you travel where you live (Lesson 6) • Read and understand a fable (Lesson 7)	**Core vocabulary** • *bookshop, café, cinema, hospital, restaurant, supermarket, sweet shop, swimming pool, toyshop, zoo* • *boat, bus, helicopter, lorry, motorbike, train* **Extension vocabulary (optional)** • *bus stop, crossing, pavement, roundabout, square, street; metro, plane, ship, taxi* **Other vocabulary** • *bone, count, cross the road, steps, sweets, treasure map* • *bad, cheese, country, fantastic, life, quiet* • *by bike, by bus, by car, on foot, on the metro* • Numbers 1–20 (in words and figures) **Recycled vocabulary** • *bush, flower, grass, tree; playground, rock, roundabout, seesaw, slide, swing; animal, cats; bike, scooter; town; wheels; cake, ice cream; delicious; cousin* • Days of the week • Numbers 1–10
Unit 8 Camping fun!	• Identify and say ten items of clothing (Lesson 1) • Say the vocabulary chant (Lesson 1) • Ask and say what people are wearing (Lessons 1 and 2) • Use present continuous in a conversation (Lesson 2 and Lesson 4) • Read and complete a postcard (Lesson 7) • Watch and understand a video about camping (Video and 21st Century Skills) • Say what the weather is like (Video and 21st Century Skills) • Recognise which clothes we wear when it's hot or cold (Lesson 2) • Use the Pupil's App on Navio • Practise spelling (Lesson 1) • Say a tongue twister to practise the 'v' sound (Lesson 5) • Review language in the unit and reflect on own learning (Lesson 8) • Understand the importance of safety near water (Lesson 3) • Understand the importance of thinking before choosing (Video and 21st Century Skills) • Work with a Talk Partner to practise and reinforce learning (all lessons) • Play a communication game about what people are doing (Lesson 5) • Sing four songs (Lessons 1, 4, 6 and 8) • Understand and act out a story (Lesson 3) • Read about camping in Britain (Lesson 6) • Sing and enjoy a traditional camp song (Lesson 6) • Think about what activities you do (Lesson 6)	**Core vocabulary** • *shirt, shoes, shorts, skirt, sun hat, sweater, swimsuit, trainers, trousers, T-shirt* • *play the guitar, play volleyball, ride a horse, sail a boat, sing songs* **Extension vocabulary (optional)** • *dress, coat, jacket, jeans, scarf, tracksuit; draw a picture, play games on my tablet, play the piano, watch television* **Other vocabulary** • *dangerous, flag, forest, lake* • *camel, camp, funny, ghost stories, go camping, hump, scary, sea, sleeping bag, tent* • *beautiful, campsite, postcard* • *paint a picture* **Recycled vocabulary** • *bookshop, café, cinema, hospital, restaurant, supermarket, sweet shop, toyshop, zoo; fun, lake, swim*

Competence in linguistic communication | Competence in mathematics, science and technology | Digital competence
Learning to learn | Social and civic competences | Sense of initiative and entrepreneurship | Cultural awareness and expression

Contents					Cross-curricular links
Structures	Phonics	Sociocultural aspects	British Culture and Literacy	21st Century Skills	
Core structures • *How many (lambs) can you see? I can see (three lambs).* • *What's the weather like today? It's (windy).* • *Is it (rainy) today? Yes, it is. No, it isn't.* • *It's got (big ears).* **Recycled structures** • *This is my (butterfly). It's (blue). My (bird) is near a (bush).*		**Cooperative learning Songs** • *What do I need to do?* (Lesson 2) • *Well done!* (Lesson 2) **Skills** • Listening to instructions (Lesson 2) • Working together (Lessons 1 and 2)			**Link to Science** **Living things** • Review farm animals **Arts and Crafts** **Art in My World** • Using lines, shapes, colours, patterns, textures and forms make an outdoor scene and create a spring animal
Core structures • *There's a (zoo) in my town.* • *There are (two cafés).* • *How many (cars) are there? There are (ten) cars.* **Other structures** • *Let's go (to town). Welcome to (my town). Stand up. Sit down. There's a (tree) next to the (swimming pool). There are (two rocks) / in front of the (zoo). How many (cars) are there? There are (20) cars. I live in the (country). I eat (apples) and (cheese). Where is (Nick)? He's in the (bookshop). How do you go to school? I go to school (by car). Where do you live? I live in (Madrid). How many (girls) are there in your class? There are (twelve) (girls).* **Recycled structures** • *I love (sweets). I don't like (cats). I like (a quiet life).*	• Consonant sound 'z' (la**z**y, **z**ebra, **z**oo)	**Cooperative learning Song** • *Well done!* (Lesson 8) **Skills** • Working together and supporting each other (Lesson 1) • Discovering similarities • Listening to others (Lesson 4) • Think-Pair-Share (Lesson 8) **Values** • Understanding the importance of crossing the road safely	**British Culture** • Cycling **Literacy** **Text type** • A fable (text to entertain and educate) **Reading skills** • Using visual clues • Understanding the order of events • Extracting key information • Understanding the moral of a story	**21st Century Skills** • **Digital skills:** learn to read digital maps	**Links to Science** **My neighbourhood** • Features in their neighbourhood • The importance of road safety rules • Identifying and categorising types of transport **Arts and Crafts** **Buildings** • Identifying symmetry in architecture and in the environment • Using symmetry to create a neighbourhood
Core structures • *What are you wearing? I'm wearing (shorts) and (a T-shirt).* • *What is he / she wearing? He / She is wearing (a T-shirt).* • *What's he / she doing? He's / She's (sailing a boat).* **Other structures** • *He's / She's (riding a horse). It's dangerous. I'm sorry. He's having fun! Camping is great. We sleep in our sleeping bags. We camp in the garden. We sing songs. We tell ghost stories.* **Recycled structures** • *Let's (swim in the lake). You can / can't (swim today).There are (lots of fun activities). There's a (lake). What colour (is / are) your (sweater / trousers)? (It / They) (is / are) purple. Where (is the dog)? It's (near the tree). How many (flowers) are there? There are (five flowers).*	• Consonant sound 'v' (**V**icky, **v**et, lo**v**es, **v**olleyball)	**Cooperative learning** **Song** • *Well done!* (Lesson 8) **Skills** • Working together and supporting each other (Lesson 1) • Raising your hand (Lesson 4) • Think-Pair-Share (Lesson 8) **Values** • Understanding the importance of safety near water	**British Culture** • Camping in the garden **Literacy** **Text type** • A postcard (text to express) **Reading skills** • Using visual clues • Reading for specific information	**21st Century Skills** • **Ways of thinking:** learn to think before you choose	**Links to Science** **Landscapes** • Human and physical elements in the environment • The importance of suitable clothing in different weather **Arts and Crafts** **Landscapes** • Identifying background, middle ground and foreground in Art and in the environment • Creating landscapes

Syllabus

Unit	Key Competences and Key Learning Outcomes	Contents Lexis
Unit 9 Day and night	• Identify and say ten daily routines (Lesson 1) • Say the vocabulary chant (Lesson 1) • Use present simple in a conversation (Lesson 2) • Identify and say the three meals a day (Lesson 4) • Say when you have meals (Lesson 4) • Watch and understand a video about teeth (Video and 21st Century Skills) • Draw and say what you do to look after your teeth (Video and 21st Century Skills) • Think about what you can see in the day or at night (Lesson 7) • Use the Pupil's App on Navio • Practise spelling (Lesson 1) • Say a tongue twister to practise the 'th' sound (Lesson 5) • Review language in the unit and reflect on own learning (Lesson 8) • Understand the importance of looking after your teeth (Lesson 3 Video and 21st Century Skills) • Work with a Talk Partner to practise and reinforce learning (all lessons) • Play a communication game about daily routines (Lesson 5) • Sing three songs (Lessons 1, 4 and 8) • Understand and act out a story (Lesson 3) • Read about the Tooth Fairy in Britain (Lesson 6) • Think about what happens to teeth where you live (Lesson 6) • Read and understand a poem (Lesson 7)	**Core vocabulary** • *brush my teeth, comb my hair, get dressed, get up, go to bed, go to school, have a shower, make my bed, sleep, wash my face* • *breakfast in the morning, lunch in the afternoon, dinner in the evening, a snack at night* **Extension vocabulary (optional)** • *do my homework, get undressed, have a bath, put my pyjamas on, read a book, wake up; fork, knife, plate, spoon* **Other vocabulary** • *breakfast, dinner* • *champion, incredible, magic, pillow, tomorrow, wobbly tooth* • *hungry* • *garden, letter, lunch, money, pillow, Tooth Fairy* • *children, cockerel, moon, owl, stars in the day* • *animal noises* **Recycled vocabulary** • *shirt, shoes, skirt, sun hat, sweater, swimsuit, T-shirt, trainers, trousers; play; sleep; sun* • Days of the week
My project 3: Holidays	• Identify and talk about holiday places and objects (Lesson 1) • Describe holiday clothes and holiday things (Lesson 2) • Present the holiday list (Lesson 2) • Identify places in the world around us (Lesson 1) • Use a computer to make a holiday list and create a class display (Lesson 2) • Prepare to make a holiday list (Lesson 1) • Think about your project (Lesson 2) • Work together to make a list (Lesson 2) • Sing a cooperative learning song (Lesson 2)	**Core vocabulary** • *beach, city, desert, jungle* • *boots, camera, map, sunglasses, torch, water* **Other vocabulary** • *place* **Recycled vocabulary** • *shorts, sun hat, swimsuit, trainers, T-shirt; country; mountain; sweets*
Festivals: Bonfire Night	• Say and do a firework action rhyme • Read about Bonfire Night in Britain • Think about fireworks in your country • Make a firework	**Core vocabulary** • *bonfire, Bonfire Night, firework, toffee apple* **Recycled vocabulary** • *blue, brown, orange, purple, red, yellow, sky, stars*
Festivals: Valentine's Day	• Read about Valentine's Day • Think and write about the people you love • Think about Valentine's Day in your country • Make a Valentine's Day card	**Core vocabulary** • *I love (my mother). She (helps me).* **Recycled vocabulary** • *aunt, brother, cousin, family, father, grandfather, grandmother, mother, sister, uncle*

Competence in linguistic communication · Competence in mathematics, science and technology · Digital competence
Learning to learn · Social and civic competences · Sense of initiative and entrepreneurship · Cultural awareness and expression

Contents					Cross-curricular links
Structures	**Phonics**	**Sociocultural aspects**	**British Culture and Literacy**	**21st Century Skills**	
Core structures • *I (brush my teeth) every day. Me, too.* • *I (have breakfast) every (morning).* **Other structures** • *It's a beautiful day. I (wash my face). What's the matter? I've got (a wobbly tooth). Are you hungry (in the morning)? Yes, I am. The Tooth Fairy (comes at night). I put the box (under my pillow). I find (a letter).* **Recycled structures** • *Are you ready? Yes, I am. Me, too. Let's play. Can you (see my tooth)? No, I can't. Have you got (a wobbly tooth)? Yes, I have. No, I haven't. Yes, that's right. That isn't right. My turn.*	• Consonant sound 'th' (**th**ree, **th**in, ba**th**, **Th**ursday)	**Cooperative learning** **Song** • *Well done!* (Lesson 8) **Skill** • Working together and supporting each other (Lesson 1) **Values** • Understanding the importance of looking after your teeth	**British culture** The Tooth Fairy **Literacy** **Text type** • A poem (text to express) **Reading skills** • Using visual clues • Reading for specific information • Using rhyme when reading	**21st Century Skills** • **Living in the world:** learn to look after your teeth	**Links to Science** **The Sun** • Daytime and night-time activities • Elements seen in the sky and during the day • Understanding that the pattern of day and night affects some animals **Arts and Crafts** **Colours** • Identifying warm and cool colours in Art and in the environment • Using warm and cool colours to represent day and night
Core structures • *I go to the (beach). It's hot there. I've got a (swimsuit) on my list.* **Other structures** • *Have a nice holiday!* **Recycled structures** • *What's your favourite place? My favourite place is (the mountains). I've got (a map and boots).*		**Cooperative learning** **Songs** • *Sharing is a good thing to do* (Lesson 2) • *Well done!* (Lesson 2) **Skills** • Sharing classroom equipment and turn taking (Lesson 2) • Working together (Lessons 1 and 2)			**Link to Science** **Continents and oceans** • Identifying cardinal points; continents and oceans **Arts and Crafts** **Recycled Art** • Observing and using recycled materials to create a toy
Core structures • *I can see (fireworks).* • *They're (red and yellow).* **Other structures** • *I eat (a toffee apple). It's delicious.*					
Core structures • *I love (my mother).* • *She (helps me).* **Other structures** • *(Her) name is (Anna).*					

Introduction to *Give Me Five! Basics*

Give Me Five! 1 Basics is part of a six-level course for pupils who have an extended English timetable and are being taught at a faster pace. It is designed to develop pupils' communicative competences in a systematic and comprehensive manner and to provide a basis for life-long learning.

With *Give Me Five! 1 Basics*, pupils …

- **identify language patterns** and be creative with grammar.
- **use new technologies and multimedia** as tools for learning.
- **develop 21st Century Skills** through engaging and real-world videos to explore ways of thinking, ways of working and living in the world.
- **develop their social and civic competences** through cooperative learning projects, songs and activities.
- **develop literacy skills** through a range of enjoyable and motivating real-world texts.
- **communicate confidently and fluently** through well-supported speaking tasks.
- **participate fully** in fun and engaging activities such as songs, stories, games and chants.
- **prepare for external exams** through the systematic integration of exam practice material in each unit.
- **develop their thinking skills and multiple intelligences** through challenging activities.
- **become independent and reflective learners** through the integration of learning-to-learn strategies and activities.
- **develop reading, writing, listening and speaking** in a balanced and integrative manner.
- **learn about British culture** and think about their own culture through lively culture lessons.
- **develop clear and natural pronunciation** through the systematic practice of tricky consonant sounds.
- **link their learning to other subjects in the curriculum** such as Science and Arts and Crafts.

Meet the characters in *Give Me Five! 1 Basics*

Molly and **Jake** are brother and sister. They are six years old and have got a mischievous dog called **Toby**. They are the lucky owners of a magic bike. Their bike looks like a normal tandem, but when they ring the bell amazing things happen!

Beth is Jake and Molly's friend, and she's six years old, too. She uses her scooter to accompany her friends on their adventures.

Alex and **Lucy** are two British children who introduce us to their favourite traditions and cultural activities.

Cooperative learning

Give Me Five! 1 Basics incorporates a variety of **cooperative learning tasks and strategies** which require the pupils to work together in a structured way. Working in pairs and small groups has many benefits. The pupils are prepared to spend more time on the tasks, are motivated to produce more language and are more likely to use creative and logical thinking. Cooperative learning also helps develop a positive classroom environment as the pupils have a greater sense of belonging and learn to understand and value all the members of the group. Finally, cooperative tasks require the pupils to be active and more independent learners, building their self-confidence and their ability to cope with uncertainty and unpredictability.

Give Me Five! 1 Basics makes use of common and well-researched cooperative learning strategies. The pupils are taught how to work with **Talk Partners,** learning that the Talk Partners Task flashcard means they should turn to the person sitting next to them and form a pair. The teacher then sets the task, e.g. practising a question and answer exchange or saying a tongue twister together. Alternatively, during **Think-Pair-Share** activities, learners listen to a question, think about it individually, discuss the answer with a partner and then share their ideas with the rest of the class. In addition to these strategies, the Teacher's Book lesson plans provide a selection of **easy-to-use cooperative learning activities** which require no or minimal preparation. There is also a simple, clearly-staged **cooperative project** at the end of each term where the pupils plan, create and then evaluate a piece of work in groups and as a class.

In order for cooperative learning to be successful, the pupils need to learn and practise interpersonal skills such as turn taking, listening to others and sharing. *Give Me Five! 1 Basics* provides an **innovative cooperative learning songs bank** which supports the teacher in this task. The ***Well Done!* song** is introduced at the end of Unit 1 and is played at the end of each unit. Other cooperative songs are presented in the following units in Terms 1 and 2, and can be reused throughout the year when needed.

Cooperative learning songs bank

Well Done!
Well done!
Well done!
Well done everyone!
Let's do a high five!
Well done everyone!
(Repeat)

Sharing is a good thing to do
Pencils, rubbers, scissors, too.
You share with me,
I share with you.
Sharing is a good thing to do.
Yes! Sharing is a good thing to do.
(Repeat)

We can do it!
We can do it!
We can do it!
Yeah!
We can do it!
We can do it!
Yeah!
Come on everybody!
Come on everybody!
We can do it!
We can do it!
Yeah!

It's fun to work together
Together, together,
It's fun to work together.
You and me,
Me and you.
It's fun to work together.
(Repeat)

Calm down
Let's calm down.
Let's calm down.
Breathe in,
Breathe out.
Now let's count.
One, two, three, four, five
Let's calm down.

Let's take turns!
Let's take turns.
Let's take turns.
Come on everybody.
Let's take turns.
It's my turn.
It's your turn.
Let's have fun!
(Repeat)

Listen to others
Listen to others.
Listen, please.
Listen with your ears.
Listen, please.
Listen to others.
Listen, please.
Listen, everybody.
(Repeat)

What do I need to do?
What do I need to do?
What do I need to do?
Read instructions,
They help you.
What do I need to do?
What do I need to do?
Listen to instructions,
They help you.

21st Century learning

Give Me Five! 1 Basics and 21st Century learning

Today's learners are growing up in a complex, changing world where an enormous amount of information is available at the touch of a button and where social media allows them to communicate with people all around the world. Technology is transforming the way we live and the way we learn. A key objective of *Give Me Five! 1 Basics* is to support learners in developing the necessary skills for the digital age. Apart from using digital technology, skills such as communicating and collaborating with others, thinking creatively and critically, and working to become a caring global citizen are an essential part of this course.

Give Me Five! 1 Basics takes an integrated approach to the use of digital technology and the teaching of **digital skills**. In each unit there is a comprehensive set of digital practice material for the learner, helping them to become autonomous and digitally confident. Pupils are also supported in developing specific ICT skills. There are tips on how to use the Internet to find, select and present information, and there is a selection of projects with digital outcomes.

There are multiple opportunities for **communication** and **collaboration** in *Give Me Five! 1 Basics*. Learners are encouraged to work together to discover and build knowledge through quizzes and questionnaires, whole-class discussions and a wide range of *Talk Partner* activities. Pupils also work with *Writing Partners* to plan, write and evaluate pieces of written work, and are encouraged to work cooperatively to review learning and reflect on progress at the end of each unit. Finally, there are structured cooperative projects which by providing opportunities for authentic communication, they encourage the development of interpersonal skills and enable learners to celebrate achievement.

Each unit of *Give Me Five! 1 Basics* provides a range of tasks to build the pupil's **critical and creative thinking skills**. These include problem-solving, evaluating, and using imaginative thinking. The Video and 21st Century Skills lessons also focus on a selection of discrete thinking skills. They provide practical tips and thinking strategies.

The interconnectivity of the 21st century and the increasing diversity of our communities mean that pupils need to learn how to respect and value other cultures. *Give Me Five! 1 Basics* provides learners with historical, geographical and cultural information about the UK. This rich content provides opportunities for **intercultural learning**, where learners identify cultural differences and similarities and build a positive attitude toward their own and other cultures. Finally, a dedicated *Values* section in each unit supports learners in developing their **social and civic competencies** and helps them to make a positive difference in the world.

Video and 21st Century Skills lessons

Video generates interest and supports learners' listening skills by providing a clear visual context and model to practise speaking. It is also a flexible tool, allowing teachers to pause the recording or turn off the sound, and can be used as a stimulus for thinking, language practice and communication. Each unit in *Give Me Five! 1 Basics* concludes with a Video and 21st Century Skills lesson. These video lessons help to build key 21st century skills, develop visual literacy and provide a springboard for authentic communication.

The stars of the videos are the children Sophie and Tom, and the adult Abby, who are the presenters of *Channel 21*. They begin each programme by introducing a new topic and then share a selection of related video clips that they have gathered. These visually rich videos bring images of the world into the classroom and offer insights into British culture. The children and the adult then discuss the clips and highlight a 21st century skill in the material. This serves to contextualise the 21st century skill and show the learner how it is relevant in their learning and in their lives.

The 21st Century Skills selected for this level are the following:

Ways of thinking: these skills focus on critical and creative thinking and include ordering things (Unit 2), putting things in groups (Unit 5) and thinking before your choose (Unit 8).

Ways of working: these skills focus on collaboration organisation and communication and include being organised (Unit 1) and working together (Unit 3).

Digital skills: these skills focus on evaluating information and using digital technology and include reading digital maps (Unit 7).

Living in the world: these skills focus on values, responsibility and cultural awareness and include eating healthily (Unit 4), being careful in the playground (Unit 6) and looking after your teeth (Unit 9).

Multiple Intelligences

According to this theory, each human being possesses a set of intelligences. Some of these may be more dominant than others, but all of them can be nurtured and developed. In *Give Me Five!*, seven key intelligences are highlighted:

Linguistic intelligence

The pupils are supported on their journey to becoming confident and **accurate speakers**, listeners, readers and writers of the English language through a wide variety of activities. The **four language skills** are carefully integrated into the material and the pupils are given opportunities to use this language in familiar communicative contexts.

Visual-spatial intelligence

The engaging **artwork** in *Give Me Five!* helps the pupils to visualise contexts for language. **Graphic organisers**, such as simple charts, help the pupils form their own conceptual links and order new information.

Musical intelligence

The pupils are exposed to **songs, chants, tongue twisters, rhymes, riddles** and **poems**. These help them to appreciate and produce natural-sounding rhythm, stress and intonation.

Logical-mathematical intelligence

The pupils' understanding of **numbers, shapes and space** is reinforced. The pupils are encouraged to notice and use the **rules and patterns** of language.

Bodily-kinaesthetic intelligence

The pupils are encouraged to use **mime, gesture** and **acting out**. They develop their fine motor skills through **projects, games** and **cut-out activities**.

Interpersonal intelligence

The Values sections give the pupils the opportunity to reflect on their relationship with people around them. **Cooperative learning songs and activities** reinforce positive classroom behaviour such as sharing.

Intrapersonal intelligence

The pupils are encouraged to think about their feelings and beliefs through questionnaires and discussion questions. The pupils are also encouraged to **reflect on their learning and progress** throughout the course.

Tips for teaching pupils with Special Educational Needs

Setting up the class and working together

- Change the groupings regularly to make sure the SEN pupils have an opportunity to work with all their classmates. Check *Give Me Five! 1 Basics Teacher's Book* for pair and group work suggestions.
- Keeping routines is highly important for SEN pupils. Use visuals to reinforce rules and routines and the task cards to show different parts of the lesson.
- Make instructions clear and on a step-by-step basis. Check understanding by giving an example and getting an example from the pupils.
- Use positive classroom language. Say what you want pupils to do, not what you don't want them to do. For example, say ***Look at the board*** not ***Don't keep turning round***.
- Develop a peer mentoring system to encourage pupils to help each other and share skills.

Hearing Impaired (HI) pupils

- Write instructions on the board or highlight them on the IWB. Make sure you have your pupil's attention before you read out the instructions or speak.
- Seat your hearing impaired (HI) pupil facing you to make lip reading and following instruction gestures easier.
- Assign a volunteer helper or note-taker depending on the level. The helper can point out the instructions in the Pupil's Book and a note-taker can take note of the key ideas of a listening to support the hearing impaired pupil.

Visually Impaired (VI) learners

- Say every word you write on the board and use realia to teach vocabulary. Realia allows the visually impaired pupils to use all their senses.
- *Give Me Five! 1 Basics* offers plenty of songs, stories and dialogues with lesson tips on how to include total physical response (TPR) activities.
- Encourage other pupils to describe experiences to give plenty of exposure to personal and shared interests and create an active and engaging learning environment.

Dyslexic learners

- Provide enough scaffolding in every lesson. For brainstorming activities, do the first few examples with the class. Ask the pupils to do the first part of an activity and check their answers before moving on to the next part. For writing activities, provide the pupils with a model which can be done as a whole class first.
- If pupils can't write in their books, provide photocopies to allow pupils with dyslexia to mark the text or cut it and move it around. This allows for information to be processed in manageable chunks.

Key Competences and Key Learning Outcomes

The **Key Competences and Key Learning Outcomes** outline the **knowledge**, **skills** and **behaviour** that the pupils need to develop in order to achieve their full personal potential, participate in an effective and constructive way in society and become responsible and autonomous life-long learners.

Competence in linguistic communication: the ability to use language to express and interpret concepts, facts, feelings and ideas.

Cultural awareness and expression: the ability to understand and appreciate different art and cultural forms.

Competence in mathematics, science and technology: the ability to apply mathematical thinking to solve everyday problems and to use scientific knowledge to explain the natural world and understand the consequences of human action.

Sense of initiative and entrepreneurship: the ability to apply qualities and skills such as creativity, critical thinking and perseverance, and to plan and manage projects.

Digital competence: the ability to use digital technology confidently, critically and responsibly.

Social and civic competences: the ability to understand and appreciate diversity in society and to develop personal and interpersonal competences.

Learning to learn: the ability to organise one's own learning and work efficiently and autonomously as an individual or in a group.

How *Give Me Five! 1 Basics* develops the Key Competences and Key Learning Outcomes

Competence in linguistic communication

Give Me Five! Basics 1 develops the pupils' linguistic skills in a systematic and integrative manner. The pupils learn to identify the meaning, sounds and rhythms of words and phrases through **songs, chants** and **stories**. The use of short **listening texts** helps them develop the ability to understand simple communicative messages in everyday contexts. There is systematic practice of tricky sounds which helps the pupils develop clear and natural pronunciation. In addition, the structured use of **games**, **personalisation activities** and simple **dialogues** provide the pupils with the opportunity to practise real-world exchanges in the classroom and express their feelings and opinions in English.

A clearly structured **cooperative project** each term involving pair or group work further develops the pupils' speaking skills and also their presentation skills, as they share their completed work with the class.

Give Me Five! 1 Basics also helps support the pupils' **emergent reading and writing** by systematically focusing on **key letter sounds** in English and their different **spelling patterns**. In the **Literacy Lessons**, the pupils have the opportunity to read a variety of rich and engaging real-world texts, while the Activity Book provides ample opportunities for **written production** through a range of guided tracing and writing activities in the third term.

Competence in mathematics, science and technology

In *Give Me Five! 1 Basics*, mathematical competence is developed in a number of ways. **Language patterns** are highlighted. Activities and tasks that require the pupils to use **mathematical and logical thinking skills** are integrated into the material. These include sequencing, counting, finding differences and solving riddles. Each unit of *Give Me Five! 1 Basics* is **linked to an area of learning in Science**, reinforcing key concepts and language across the curriculum. In addition, **real-world factual texts**, such as a fact file or a lunch menu, introduce the pupils to different ways of presenting and processing information. The pupils are also given the opportunity to work with simple **charts, diagrams** and **graphic organisers**.

Digital competence

Give Me Five! 1 Basics uses digital resources as tools to support learning, familiarising the pupils with computer technology and showing them how technology can be used for learning purposes. The **Pupil's App on Navio** serves to consolidate classwork and allows the pupils to work independently outside the classroom. Within the classroom, the Teacher's Resource Bank provides enhanced digital resources for presentation and practice, integrated audio and phonics videos and interactive activities.

Learning to learn

Give Me Five! 1 Basics introduces a variety of **learning strategies** to help the pupils become more independent and reflective learners. Learning objectives are set at the beginning and reviewed at the end of each lesson using **Task flashcards**. The pupils are encouraged to reflect on their learning and progress at the end of each unit through the use of a **self-evaluation traffic light cut-out.**

The pupils also use the **Look-Read-Trace strategy** (Units 1–6) and the **Look-Copy-Cover-Write strategy** (Units 7–9) **to practise spelling** ten core vocabulary words.

Social and civic competences

Developing the ability to understand how somebody else is feeling and knowing how to respond appropriately is an important objective of *Give Me Five! 1 Basics*, and emphasis is placed on **cooperative learning** and **positive classroom behaviour**.

A bank of **cooperative learning songs** is provided to teach and reinforce the importance of active participation, cooperation and respect and support for others in the classroom. In addition, each unit of the Teacher's Book suggests one or more easy-to-use **cooperative learning activities**.

A **Values** section in each unit encourages the pupils to reflect on their natural, social and cultural environment, integrating topics such as road safety, the need to respect and care for animals and the importance of hygiene and healthy habits.

Sense of initiative and entrepreneurship

Give Me Five! 1 Basics develops a sense of initiative and entrepreneurship through the inclusion of a **cooperative project** in each term. These require the pupils to work in groups to successfully plan and complete a task, such as designing and making a class wall display or a group poster. Working together to complete a task helps the pupils to take responsibility for their work and gain confidence in their abilities.

Regular **Talk Partner** activities and a **communicative game using a cut-out** in each unit offer the pupils the opportunity to practise speaking in pairs, personalise the language and work independently. Initiative is also encouraged through regular **personalisation activities**, as well as activities which encourage the pupils to be creative and use their imagination.

Cultural awareness and expression

In *Give Me Five! 1 Basics*, the pupils are introduced to **British culture** through lively and age-appropriate culture lessons. These help the pupils understand and respect different customs. A **Think about your culture** section encourages the pupils to reflect on their own culture and have a clearer idea of their own cultural identity.

Give Me Five! 1 Basics also provides the opportunity to experience and appreciate a range of **art forms** such as poems, songs, stories, craft activities, miming and performance and encourages the pupils to express their ideas, experiences and emotions through these mediums.

Give Me Five! 1 Basics Pupil's components

Pupil's Book

This is a 120-page, full-colour, write-in book that contains a Starter Unit and nine thematic units, each with ten photographic stickers. It also comprises three fun and easy-to-use projects and two festivals sections. Each unit is divided into eight lessons and provides vocabulary input and practice, a short conversation to contextualise and practise chunks of language and a double-page story for language input and consolidation. It also contains a humorous tongue twister to practise a tricky consonant sound, a photographic British culture lesson, an engaging real-world literacy text and a unit review. At the end of each unit there is a Video and 21st Century Skills lesson, and at the back of the book there is practice material for Cambridge English Young Learners exams.

Activity Book

This 120-page write-in book works in tandem with the Pupil's Book to reinforce and practise the unit language and to develop the pupil's literacy, listening and speaking skills. Guided tracing/writing activities provide the support the pupils need at the start of their first year of Primary with the level of challenge progressing gradually through the book. Each unit comprises a variety of activities which are devised to engage and challenge the pupils, activate different intelligences, encourage creativity and allow the pupils to use language in a personal and meaningful way. At the end of each unit there is a spelling page. At the back of the Activity Book there is a practice material for Cambridge English Young Learners exams and vocabulary review section.

Pupil's App on Navio

Powered By NAVIO

The Pupil's App on Navio is designed to accompany the course and provide extra practice in class or at home. Pupils can create avatars and then explore Navio's immersive worlds. Pupils complete game-based activities designed to practise and review the language and content learnt in class. As they do so, they earn rewards, points and badges. The App tracks pupils' progress so the teacher can see how they are doing and provide extra support where it is needed. The App also includes all the songs, stories and animations from the course so that pupils can review them at home and share them with their family. The access code for the Pupil's App can be found inside the front cover of the Pupil's Book.

PERFECT PARTNERS WITH

BY ME

Social Science Primary 1 **Natural Science Primary 1**

Arts and Crafts Primary 1

Grammar Goals 1

Give Me Five! 1 Basics Teacher's components

Teacher's Book

This user-friendly, spiral-bound book provides teachers with as much or as little support as they need. The At a Glance Lesson Plans, illustrated with images of the Pupil's Book and Activity Book, clearly highlight the learning aims, key language, materials required, learning routines, key activities and a range of optional extra activities, including Links to Science and cooperative learning activities. These are accompanied by Detailed Lesson Plans which provide complete and concise teaching notes for each activity and answer keys. Full audioscripts can be found at the back of the book. In addition, there is a Reflective Teacher page at the end of each unit for documenting learning, noting ideas and planning actions.

Teacher's App on Navio

The Teacher's App on Navio offers one-stop access to all the many resources which accompany the course. **Tap and Teach Lessons** with **integrated audio and video** ensure that everything you need to teach each lesson is in one place. You can use the **Classroom Management tool** to award points for good behaviour or success in class, and track your pupils' marks and progress using the **Progress Tracker**. You'll find additional photocopiable resources in the **Teacher's Resource Bank** (see opposite) and **Test Generator**. For Levels 1–2 you'll also have access to additional phonics activities on Magic Phonics.

Powered By NAVIO

Class CDs

Four class CDs provide all the recorded material for the Pupil's Book and Activity Book: songs, chants, dialogues, listening tasks, stories, games, tongue twisters, culture lessons, literacy texts, review material 21st Century Skills lessons and Cambridge Young Learner Exams practice material. They also include recordings of the cooperative learning songs and a karaoke version of the Lesson 1 song in each unit.

Flashcards

A set of 110 full-colour flashcards with photographic images of the key vocabulary from Lesson 1 of each unit. Suggestions for using the flashcards are given in the Detailed Lesson Plans and in the Flashcards games bank on page 23.

Teacher's Resource Bank: Course Resources

The **Teacher's Resource Bank**, located within the Teacher's App on Navio, contains a wealth of resources that complement *Give Me Five! Basics*. In addition to providing downloads for all class audio and video, the resource bank contains:

- **Letters to parents:** an introductory letter, followed by a letter to present each unit.
- **Task flashcards:** a set of 19 cards showing a word and a picture to support the pupils' understanding of key activity instructions.

- **Vocabulary and Grammar worksheets:** to reinforce and extend the vocabulary and grammar syllabus.
- **Evaluation Rubrics:** one grid per unit to evaluate pupils' level of achievement of the Key Learning Outcomes and Key Competences, as well as their cooperative learning skills.
- **Tests:** a Diagnostic Test, Unit Tests, Term Tests and an End-of-Year Test with audio and Teacher's Notes. Each test has a standard and a higher level version.

- **Word cards:** a set of 110 word cards, written in handwriting font. Suggestions for using the word cards can be found in the Detailed Lesson Plans and in the Word cards games bank on page 23.

Teacher's Resource Bank: External Exams Resources

This section supports teachers who are preparing their pupils for the ***Trinity Graded Exam in Spoken English*** (Grades 2 and 3) or the ***Cambridge English Young Learners Starters Test***. These resources contain the following:

- **Videos** of children doing speaking practice.
- **Teacher's Notes** on how to exploit these videos in the classroom and tips for teachers.
- **Trinity Exams Practice Worksheets**.
- Extra Cambridge Exams **practice material** and **practice tests**.
- A set of **Trinity Exams Practice cards** for optional Trinity-type speaking practice at the start of each lesson.

Teacher's and Pupil's Apps on Navio

The Navio app which accompanies this course offers one-stop access to the huge range of resources that come with *Give Me Five! 1 Basics*. **Tap and Teach Lessons** enable you to move seamlessly between the book and digital components, and you can track your pupils' marks and review their progress using the **Progress Tracker**, and find additional resources in the **Resource Bank** and **Test Generator**.

Accessing the app

To access Navio:

1. Go to www.MacmillanNavio.com/givemefive
2. Follow the onscreen instructions

If you haven't got a Macmillan Education account, you need to create a profile. Then you can enter your access code and download the app for your device (see System Requirements: www.macmillannavio.com/system-requirements).

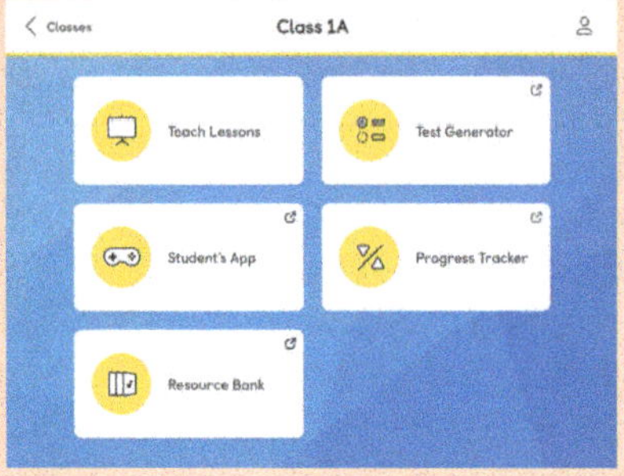

Setting up a class

You, or your school administrator, will need to set up a class and register pupils with their names and the email address of their parents or guardians. Once the class is created, login details can be given to parents. Parents can then log in to the Pupil's App and enter the access code from the inside cover of the Pupil's Book to access the 3D worlds and practise content.

Managing your downloads

Navio makes it easy to manage the storage space on your device, as you can control how much material you download at one time. Navio makes it clear how much storage space your chosen content will need. You can download the complete Teacher's and Pupil's Apps at once, or, if your device has limited storage capacity, you can choose to download only one or two units. And after you finish a unit, you can safely delete the content from your device. You won't lose your pupils' data, as this information is stored online.

Using the Progress Tracker

All the work your pupils complete in the app is recorded in the **Progress Tracker**. You can monitor the progress of a whole class or any individual pupil. Every activity in the App is mapped against the course Learning Outcomes and Skills, so you can easily identify where your pupils need extra support.

Teaching a lesson

Navio makes it easy to plan and teach your lessons with fully interactive **Tap and Teach Lessons** for every lesson in *Give Me Five! Basics 1*. Go to your Class Dashboard and choose Teach Lessons. Find the lesson you want to teach and click to open it. Click on the Toolbar along the bottom of the screen to expand it to Thumbnail view. The Toolbar also contains the Tap and Teach tools you need to teach heads-up, whole-class activities, including a Timer, Pen tool and Mask tool.

Lessons follow the lesson plans in the Teacher's Book, and provide everything you need to teach from your device in one place. They include digital versions of all the activities in the Pupil's Book, Activity Book and Basics Activity Book, with their answer keys. They also include all the audio and video you need for the lesson, as well as some extra tools such as digital Flashcards. All relevant pages from all three books are also provided so that you can project them in class, to help your pupils and to encourage heads-up participation.

When you teach, move through the lesson slide by slide using the arrows, or double click on a thumbnail to jump straight to a particular activity. If you prefer, you can **Filter activities** to customise the lesson so it includes only the content you want to teach.

Using the Rewards tool

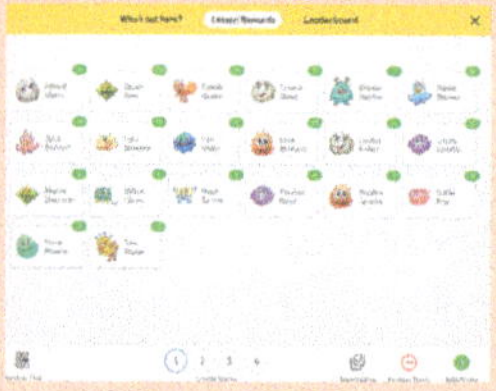

Navio's new **Rewards tool** is a great way to keep your pupils engaged in class. Much more than just a record of attendance, you can also use it to award points for good behaviour or success in activities. You can even organise your class into teams, and you can award points to individuals, groups or the whole class at any time. When pupils earn points, they appear in the Pupil's App next time they log in, so parents can see their performance.

Pupil's App

As a teacher you can also access a version of the Pupil's App from the Class Dashboard. This has all the same content that your pupils can access at home, but your version is set in **Teacher Mode**. This means that all the activities and worlds are already unlocked, and the App does not record any marks to the Progress Tracker.

We recommend using Teacher Mode when pupils share devices to avoid mixing up pupils' grades and progress. However, if pupils have individual devices or are using the app at home, they should always log in with their own username and password. In this way they can earn points and badges, set up and customise their avatar and build a record of their progress in the Progress Tracker.

Flashcards and Word cards games bank

Flashcard games

1 Fast finger

Stick the flashcards in a row on the board and quickly review the vocabulary items. Then ask the pupils **Where's the (tree)?** Move your finger quickly along the row of cards. The pupils should say *Stop!* when you touch the corresponding card. Repeat the procedure, speeding up your finger each time. Invite a confident pupil to take your role.

2 Here!

Stick the flashcards in a row on the board and quickly review the vocabulary items. Then invite two pupils to the board. Ask **Where's the (sweetshop)?** The two pupils should find and point to the card as quickly as possible, and say *Here!* Repeat with other pairs of pupils. As a variation, invite two pupils to come to the board. One pupil asks the question and the other points and says *Here!*

3 Memory!

Show a flashcard to the pupils and ask them to name the object. Stick the card face down on the board and write the number 1 above it. Repeat the procedure with the other cards, writing the next number above each one. Then ask **Where's the (rubber)?** The pupils say *It's number (1).* Turn over the card and show it to the pupils. If they answered incorrectly, elicit further ideas. Repeat the procedure with the other vocabulary items.

4 Silent words

Hold up a flashcard so that the pupils can't see the picture. Ask **What's this?** and mouth the word silently. The pupils try to identify the word. When the pupils have guessed correctly, show them the card and repeat the word as a class. Repeat the procedure with the other cards.

5 Slowly, slowly

Hold up a flashcard, but cover the picture with a piece of paper so the pupils can't see it. Slowly slide the covering paper down to show a section of the picture and ask **What is it?** If a pupil guesses correctly, remove the paper and say **Yes, it's a (plane). Well done!** If the guess is incorrect, say **No, it isn't a (plane).** Continue revealing more of the picture and repeat the question until a pupil guesses correctly. Then repeat the procedure with the remaining cards.

6 What is it?

Hold up a flashcard so that the pupils can't see the picture. Ask **What is it?** The pupils try to guess, for example *Is it a (bike)?* You can prompt the class by describing the object on the card. When the class successfully guess the picture, show it to them and ask them to repeat the word. Repeat the procedure with all the flashcards. The pupils can do a similar activity with their Talk Partner using the stickers along the bottom of Lessons 1 and 2 of each unit: one pupil chooses a vocabulary item, the other pupil asks questions to guess what it is.

7 What's missing?

Stick six flashcards in a row on the board and quickly review the vocabulary items. Then say the items in order, deliberately missing one of them out. The pupils should identify the missing word. Repeat the procedure several times, missing out a different item each time. When the pupils are confident, remove the cards and repeat the activity. The pupils should try to identify the missing item, but this time from memory.

8 Disappearing flashcards

Stick ten flashcards in a row or in a grid on the board. Point to each card and elicit the word. Repeat until the pupils are saying the words in a fluent and rhythmical manner. Then remove one of the cards. Point to the nine remaining cards and the empty space in order and prompt the class to say the ten words again. Continue removing the cards until there are no cards on the board and the class are chanting the words in order from memory.

9 How many can you remember?

Stick ten flashcards on the board. Give the class one minute to look at the pictures and then remove the cards. Organise the class into their Talk Partners. The pupils work together to remember and name the ten items. You can set a time limit for this if you wish. Check the activity as a class.

Word card games

1 Stop!

Say one of the words from the lexical set that you want to practise, for example **skirt.** Then hold up the clothes words cards one by one, allowing enough time for the pupils to read each word. The pupils should say *Stop!* when you hold up the corresponding card.

2 Clever parrots

Hold up a word card and say a word. The pupils should repeat the word if it is the same as the word on the card. If it isn't the same, the pupils should stay silent. To add an element of fun to the game, encourage the class to do a mime or make a noise (e.g. imitate a squawking parrot) when they repeat the word.

3 Bit by bit

Cover a word card with a piece of paper. Then slide the paper to reveal the word's first letter. Ask **Which word is it?** The pupils say the words they know starting with that letter. Continue revealing more letters, one by one, until the pupils guess the word.

4 Splat!

Stick the word cards on the board in random order. Invite two pupils to the board and say one of the words. The pupils point to the corresponding word card as quickly as possible. Repeat the procedure with different pupils. To add an element of fun, give each pupil a plastic fly swatter to 'swat' the corresponding card.

5 Board pelmanism

Stick a set of flashcards and the corresponding word cards face down on the board in random order. Number all the cards. Then divide the class into two teams. The teams take turns to choose two numbers. The teacher turns over the corresponding cards each time. If the cards match, the teacher removes them from the board and awards the team a point. If the cards do not match, the teacher returns them face down to their original positions. Encourage the class to try to remember where the different cards are located. The team with the most points, when all the cards have been removed, is the winner.

Using the Pupil's Book and Activity Book

Lessons 1 and 2

Ten items of vocabulary are introduced and practised using **photographic flashcards**.

Attractive artwork engages the pupils and helps contextualise language.

A **fun and easy-to-sing song** builds fluency and makes language more memorable.

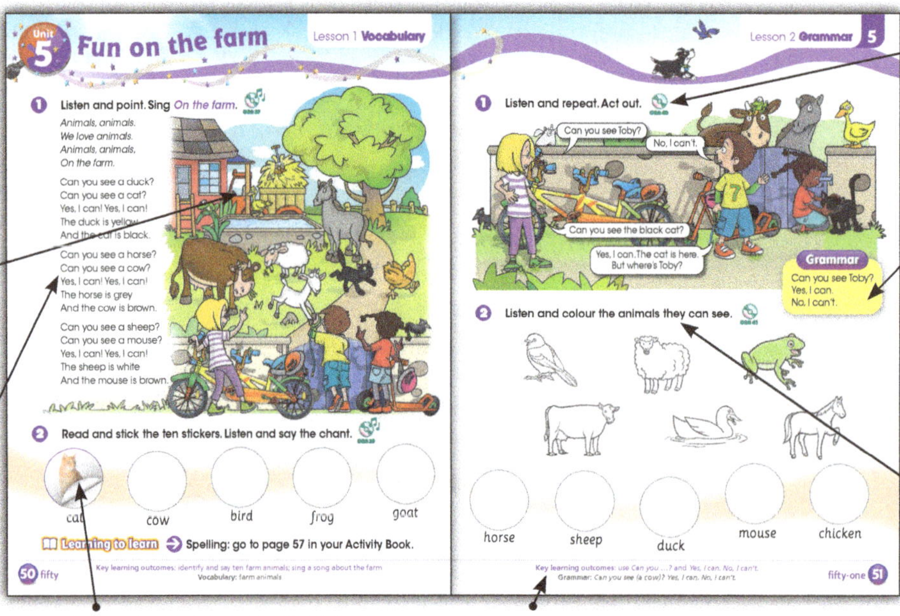

A short conversation places grammar in a fun and familiar context.

Key language is highlighted in the **grammar box**.

A variety of **engaging listening tasks** build the pupils' confidence in understanding the new language. All the audioscripts can be found at the back of the Teacher's Book.

The pupils use **real-world photographic stickers** to create a record of the vocabulary across the bottom of the spread. The pupils then say a **catchy vocabulary chant**.

The key learning outcomes and the key language are given at the bottom of the page.

Activities are devised to engage the pupils and provide practice in reading the new vocabulary items.

Fun, game-like activities motivate the pupils to learn and practise the new vocabulary.

The pupils **review and recycle** an item of vocabulary at the bottom of each Activity Book page.

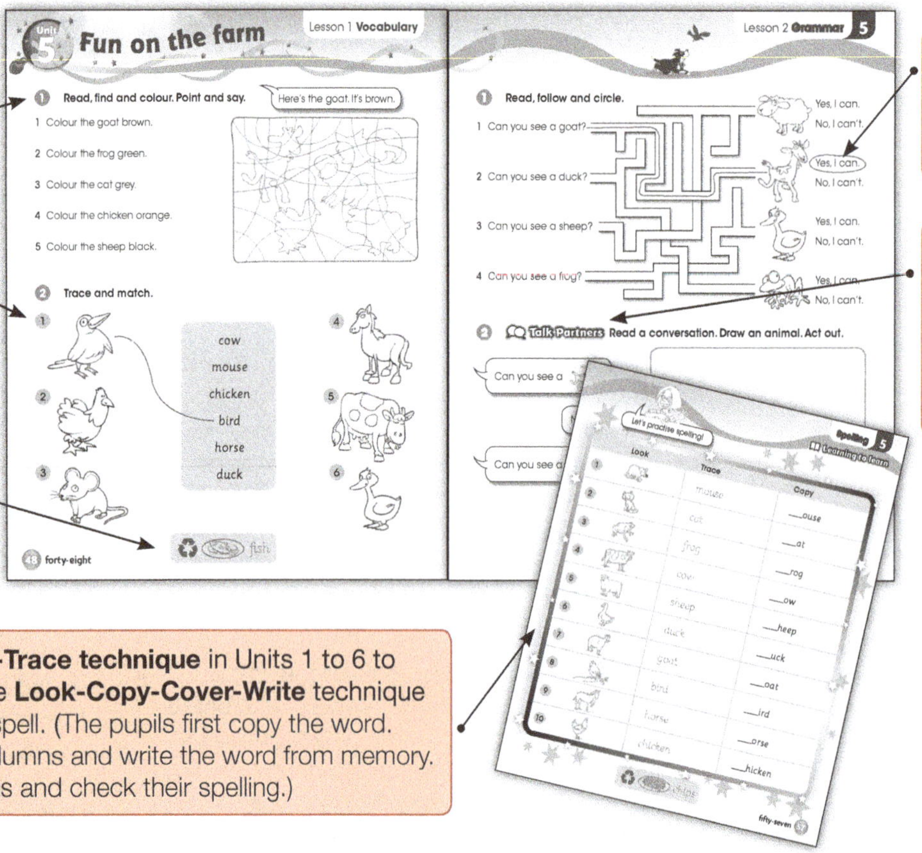

A range of activities give the pupils practice in reading the new grammar.

Talk Partners icon indicates when the pupils have the opportunity to practise speaking in pairs.

The pupils use the **Look-Read-Trace technique** in Units 1 to 6 to practise forming letters and the **Look-Copy-Cover-Write** technique in Units 7 to 9 to learn how to spell. (The pupils first copy the word. Then they cover the first two columns and write the word from memory. Finally, they uncover the columns and check their spelling.)

Digital resources

Teacher's Digital: Don't forget you can teach these lessons using the Teacher's App on Navio.

Pupil's Digital: Encourage your pupils to use the Pupil's App on Navio to practise the vocabulary from these lessons.

Powered By NAVIO

Lesson 3

A pre-reading task helps prepare the pupils for reading and listening to the story.

In each unit, the pupils enjoy a **magical adventure** with Molly, Jake, Beth, Toby the dog and their magic bike. A list of frame-by-frame comprehension questions for each story are provided in the Detailed Lesson Plan in the Teacher's Book.

Attractive and humorous pictures and an **exciting audio recording** support the pupils' understanding of the narrative.

Pupils watch an **exciting, animated video** to consolidate their understanding of the story.

The story reinforces language introduced in Lessons 1 and 2 and previews language from Lesson 4.

The ***Give Me Five! Basics* Values** section uses photos to encourage the pupils to reflect on the story and relate a personal, social or civic value to their own lives.

A wide range of engaging story activities reinforce and check the pupils' understanding of the story and encourage them to use key language from it.

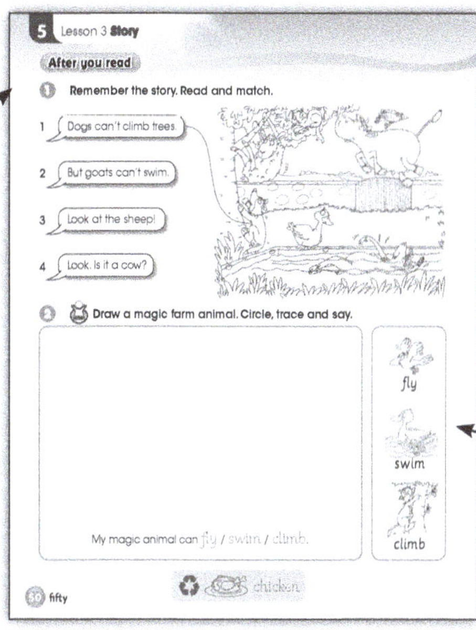

The activities encourage the pupils to respond to the story in a **personal and creative way**.

Digital resources

Teacher's Digital: Don't forget you can teach this lesson using the Teacher's App on Navio.

Pupil's Digital: Encourage your pupils to use the Pupil's App on Navio to practise the vocabulary from these lessons.

Powered By NAVIO

Using the Pupil's Book and Activity Book

Lessons 4 and 5

Four–six new items of vocabulary are introduced and practised, using **photos or colourful illustrations**.

The **Toby's tongue twister** section gives the pupils practice in recognising and producing tricky consonant sounds. These are sounds that are often mispronounced due to mother-tongue interference.

A **lively song or chant** gives further practice of the vocabulary and introduces additional grammar.

Simple **games** allow the pupils to practise the new language and encourage them to work independently.

A listening task prepares the pupils for a communicative game. The pupils listen to children playing the game.

Cooperative learning songs are introduced to teach and practise interpersonal skills. In this example, the pupils are reminded to listen to others.

Talk Partners icons indicate when the pupils have the opportunity to practise speaking in pairs. These activities build confidence, encourage cooperative learning and ensure full participation.

The pupils make one **cut-out** in each unit and play a **communicative game** in pairs. These cut-outs can be found in the Teacher's Resource Bank.

The pupils enjoy a **full page of phonics** activities to practise reading, tracing letters, writing and saying the key grapheme.

Listening activities have a clear and meaningful purpose. In this activity, the pupils listen to check their answers.

An enjoyable range of tracing and writing activities encourage the pupils to **notice and play with language patterns**.

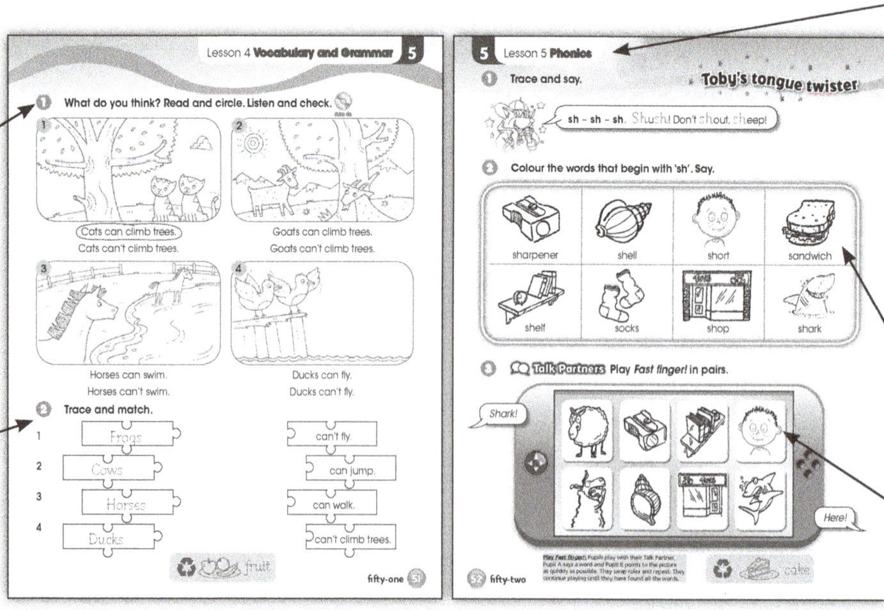

The activities use recycled words to build the pupils' confidence and link new information to existing knowledge.

The pupils play simple **phonics games** with their Talk Partner.

Digital resources

Teacher's Digital: Don't forget you can teach these lessons using the Teacher's App on Navio.

Pupil's Digital: Encourage your pupils to use the Pupil's App on Navio to practise the vocabulary from these lessons.

Powered By NAVIO

Lessons 6 and 7

The pupils are introduced to **interesting and age-appropriate cultural content** through two British children, Alex and Lucy.

Photos of the Culture Kids doing **real-world cultural activities** really bring the culture to life. This helps foster a positive attitude towards British culture and English language learning.

Think about your culture encourages the pupils to identify similarities and differences between the two cultures and to begin to form their own cultural identity.

The **Before you read activities** help prepare the pupils to read. These include activating the pupils' existing knowledge, exploiting visuals, asking questions to raise interest and making predictions.

The pupils are introduced to a **wide range of text types**. These are selected to reflect the interests and experiences of the age group and have an **authentic appearance** that will appeal to learners.

All texts are supported by an audio recording.

The pupils are directed to the **After you read activities** in the Activity Book.

Understanding of the cultural content is consolidated through a listening activity.

A question asked by Alex or Lucy encourages the pupils to think more about their own culture.

Me icons indicate when the pupils have the opportunity to use language to talk and draw or write about themselves and their lives. These **personalisation tasks** help make language more meaningful and memorable.

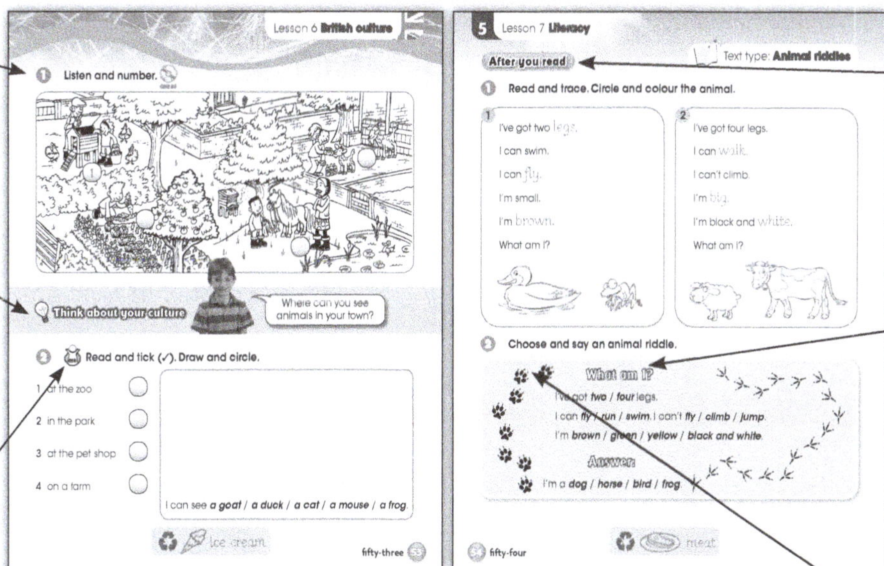

A range of **After you read activities** reinforce and check the pupils' understanding of the literacy text.

A variety of **enjoyable tracing and writing activities** allow the pupils to respond to the text in a personal and creative way.

The pupils have the opportunity to **create their own text**, through tracing in Units 1 to 6 and writing in Units 7 to 9, similar to the texts in the Pupil's Book. This writing activity is very guided to help ensure success.

Digital resources

Teacher's Digital: Don't forget you can teach these lessons using the Teacher's App on Navio.

Pupil's Digital: Encourage your pupils to use the Pupil's App on Navio to practise the vocabulary from these lessons.

Powered By NAVIO

Using the Pupil's Book and Activity Book

Lesson 8 Review and 21st Century Skills video lesson

A **full-page review** in both the Pupil's Book and the Activity Book checks and reinforces all of the unit vocabulary and grammar.

Review activities develop **thinking skills** such as logical thinking. In this activity, the pupils read the questions, find the animal and complete the answers.

Achievement is recognised by singing a ***Well done!* cooperative learning song** and sticking the ***Give Me Five!* sticker**.

The children introduce the video lesson and spark the pupils' interest in a wide range of topics.

The pupils watch an engaging **video** related to the topic of the unit and 21st Century Skills.

Pupils are set fascinating tasks to promote the skills needed in the modern world.

The Activity Book Review activities help to reinforce reading, tracing and writing of the unit vocabulary and grammar.

The pupils use the **traffic light cut-out** in the Teacher's Resource Bank at the end of each Activity Book Review to **reflect and feed back on their learning** in the unit. The teacher reads each statement in turn (from the 'Key' box at the bottom of the page) and the pupils point to the colour / face that best describes how they feel.

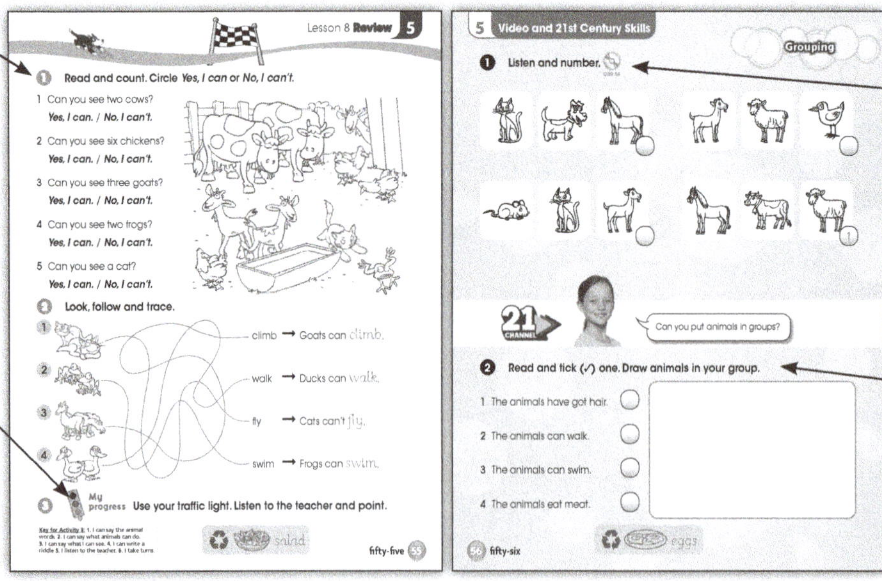

The pupils do a **listening task** to further develop their understanding of the 21st Century Skill.

The pupils do a personalised **21st Century Skills** task.

Digital resources

Teacher's Digital: Don't forget you can teach these lessons using the Teacher's App on Navio.

Pupil's Digital: Encourage your pupils to use the Pupil's App on Navio to practise the vocabulary from these lessons.

Powered By NAVIO

Using the projects

Give Me Five! 1 Basics provides three fun and highly doable **projects**. These provide an opportunity for the pupils to **work cooperatively** and develop their speaking skills in a structured way, building autonomy and promoting creativity.

Each project introduces a **new lexical set,** while also **recycling vocabulary** from earlier units. All new vocabulary is recorded on the Class audio.

Listening and speaking activities **introduce the topic** of the project by **recycling** vocabulary and grammar from previous units.

Pupils are encouraged to do further Internet research by answering a question.

Enjoyable hands-on activities develop pupils's fine motor skills and encourage creativity.

Cooperative learning songs develop interpersonal skills and group work skills.

An **attractive final class or group display** creates a sense of achievement and builds confidence.

The project is broken down into stages and pupils follow a step-by-step guide to complete it.

Simple instructions guide pupils in the preparation of their project highlighting the importance of planning and preparing their work.

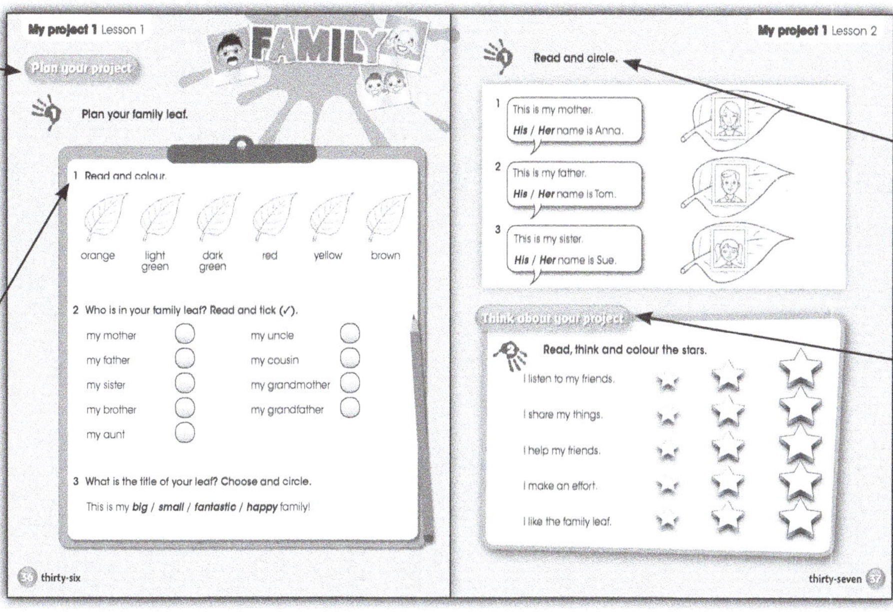

These activities provide a model for the pupils' own writing in the project.

The pupils **reflect on their cooperative skills and their work.**

Digital resources

Teacher's Digital: Don't forget you can teach these lessons using the Teacher's App on Navio.

Pupil's Digital: Encourage your pupils to use the Pupil's App on Navio to practise the vocabulary from these lessons.

Powered By NAVIO

Using the Exams Practice

The Cambridge Exams Practice section at the end of both the Pupil's Book and Activity Book introduces the pupils to the activity types found in the different Parts of the three papers of the Cambridge English Young Learners Starter Tests: Listening, Reading and Writing and Speaking.

The Cambridge Exams Practice pages at the back of the Pupil's Book will help the pupils to **develop the necessary** skills to do the Listening and Speaking papers.

The **shield** highlights **the skill** practised in each activity.

An **engaging, achievable listening** activity, requiring a non-linguistic response. Pupils, typically, demonstrate their understanding by **colouring or ticking**.

After listening, the pupils, with their Talk Partners, have the opportunity to **activate the production** of the core vocabulary and grammar.

For further practice, watch the **External Exams Video** which you can find in the Teacher's Resource Bank.

The **key learning outcomes** and **parts of the exam** practised are given at the bottom of the page.

The Cambridge Exams Practice pages at the back of the Activity Book will help the pupils to **develop the necessary** skills to do the Reading and Writing papers.

These activities focus on the **vocabulary from the unit**. **Clear visual cues** provide support and **guide** the pupils' reading and writing.

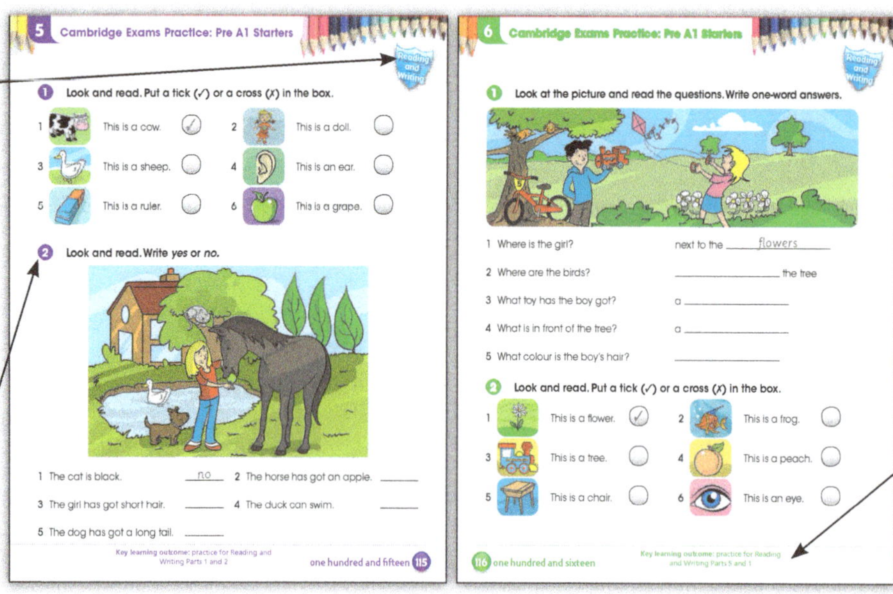

The **key learning outcomes** and **parts of the exam** practised are given at the bottom of the page.

Digital resources

Teacher's Digital: Don't forget you can teach these lessons using the Teacher's App on Navio.

Pupil's Digital: Encourage your pupils to use the Pupil's App on Navio to practise the vocabulary from these lessons.

Powered By NAVIO

Exams Practice

Give Me Five! 1 Basics and the external exams

Give Me Five! 1 Basics provides a wide range of materials to support teachers who are preparing their pupils for the ***Cambridge English Young Learners Starters Test***. Reading, writing and listening activity types found in the ***Cambridge English Young Learners Starters Tests*** are integrated into the material and each book ends with Cambridge Exams Practice lessons in the Pupil's Book and Activity Book. This material is adapted to match the linguistic and cognitive level of the pupils, and language is systematically extended as the course progresses.

There are also the **External Exams Resources** which contain videos of children doing speaking exams, and provide Teacher's Notes on how to exploit these videos in the classroom. The resources, which are part of the Teacher's Resource Bank, also includes additional External Exams material and practice tests, for both the *Cambridge English Young Learners Starters* and the *Trinity Graded Exam in Spoken English* (Elementary Stage, Grades 2 and 3), material focused on developing specific exam related skills and a set of **Trinity Exam Practice cards**.

Trinity Exam Practice cards

The **Trinity Exam Practice cards** are a set of photocopiable cards. They can be used to build the pupils' confidence in asking and answering questions. On each card is a question based on the ***Trinity Graded Exam in Spoken English*** syllabus (Grades 2 and 3). Some cards may also contain other language from *Give Me Five! Basics*. These cards should be printed out, laminated if possible and filed by unit. They can then be used during the Starting the lesson stage, which systematically recycles language, transferring it to the pupils' long-term memory. For the Trinity Exam Practice cards routine, the teacher selects several cards from previous units. The teacher should choose a different set of cards for each lesson, and tricky questions and recent topics should be revisited more frequently. The teacher then uses the cards to practise asking and answering questions by doing one of the following suggested activities:

Trinity Exam Practice cards activity bank

1 *Ask and answer in Talk Partners*

Point to the Talk Partners Task flashcard and ask the class to get into their pairs. Then hold up one of the selected Trinity Exam Practice cards and ask the class the question. Invite a pupil to answer and repeat their answer for the class. The pupils then ask and answer the same question with their Talk Partner. Repeat the procedure with other cards.

2 *Question bounce*

Select a Trinity Exam Practice card, read out the question and ask the class to think of an answer. Then point around the room, finally choosing one pupil. This pupil should answer the question. If the pupil answers correctly, he / she should take another card and ask the question to the class. Once again, the class should think of the answer and then the pupil with the card selects another pupil to answer. Repeat the procedure as many times as you wish, ensuring that the questions are 'bounced' to a range of pupils in the class.

3 *Walking questions*

Select six to eight Trinity Exam Practice cards. Drill each question as a class and invite a different pupil to answer each time. Hand out the cards to different pupils. These pupils must move around the class and ask their question to five other pupils. When they have asked five pupils, they should return to their seats. When all the pupils have returned to their seats, hand out the cards to six different pupils and repeat the procedure.

4 *Pass the questions around the circle*

Organise the class so that the pupils are sitting in a circle. Hold up a Trinity Exam Practice card and ask the question to the pupil on your left. Once the pupil has answered, give him / her the card. The pupil then turns to his / her left and asks the next pupil the same question. The card gets passed around the circle. As the pupils become more confident, introduce more cards.

5 *Pass the questions around the circle (variation)*

Organise the class so that the pupils are sitting in a circle. Then drill each question as a class and invite a different pupil to answer each time. Play some music and have the pupils pass several cards around the circle at the same time. Use the pause button to stop the music. When the music stops, the pupils with the cards ask the question they are holding to the pupil on their right. Play the music again and repeat the procedure.

6 *Bag and ball*

For this game you need a bag containing a selection of Trinity Exam Practice cards and a soft ball. Organise the class so that the pupils are sitting in a circle. Then play some music. The pupils pass the bag and ball around the circle separately while the music is playing. When the music stops, the pupil holding the bag takes out and reads a question. The pupil holding the ball should answer the question. Play the music again and repeat the procedure.

7 *Snakes and ladders*

Draw a simple snakes and ladders board on the board and draw a question mark in eight to ten of the squares. Divide the class into two teams and ask each team to throw the dice. The team with the highest number should begin the game. The teams take turns to throw the dice and move along the board. When a team lands on a question mark, read out one of the Trinity Exam Practice cards. The team has to answer correctly to stay on the square. If they don't answer correctly, they move back to their last square. The game continues until a team reaches the 'finish' square.

8 *Card race*

Select two sets of five questions and stick them face down on the board in two 'lanes', with a flag or 'finish' line drawn at the end. Divide the class into two teams. Invite a pupil from Team A to come to the board, turn over the first card and read the question to his / her team. If Team A answers the question correctly, the card remains face up. If the team answers incorrectly, the card is turned face down again and must be repeated on the next turn. Then invite a pupil from Team B to come up and do the same. The team that turns over all the cards first, reaching the 'finish' flag or line, is the winner.

Using the Teacher's Book

The Teacher's Notes have a clear, user-friendly design, offering both an **At a Glance Lesson Plan** and a **Detailed Lesson Plan**. These mirror each other, enabling teachers to move between the two lesson plans with ease.

This box clearly shows the learning objectives, key active language and materials required for the lesson. The lesson objectives are mapped to the **Key Competences and Key Learning Outcomes**.

The **At a Glance Lesson Plan** provides a brief overview of all the activities in the lesson, including **Starting** and **Ending the lesson activities**, and **Extra activities**. Class audio references are also provided.

Fast Forward icons indicate the **fast route** through the lesson for teachers who have shorter lessons or fewer hours of English.

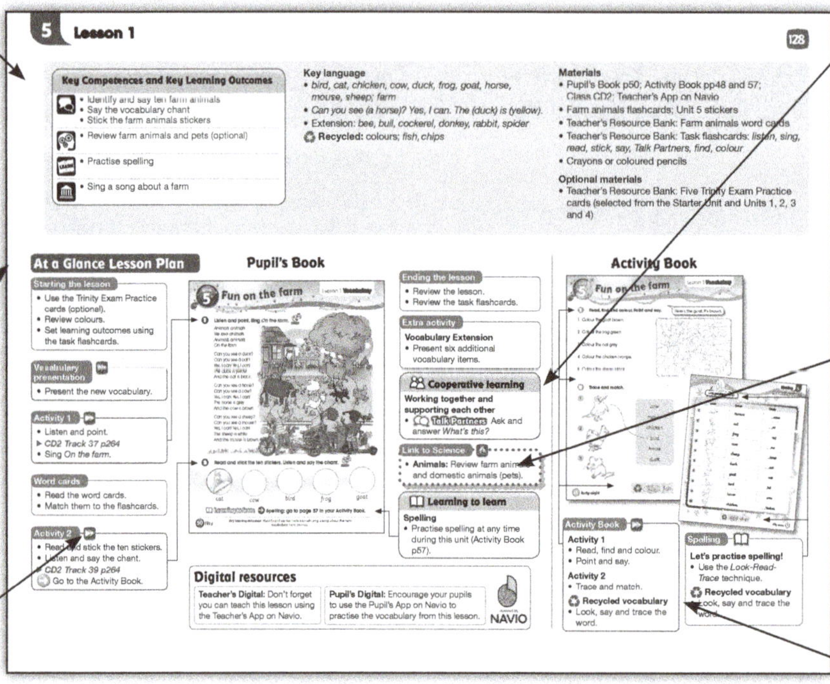

Each unit includes a number of enjoyable **Cooperative learning activities**, which require no or minimal preparation.

Optional **Link to Science** activities in each unit review and reinforce learning from the Science curriculum.

There is also a brief overview of the Activity Book activities.

The **Detailed Lesson Plan** provides more detailed **step-by-step instructions** for each activity.

The activities for **Starting the lesson** include optional use of the **Trinity Exam Practice cards** (see page 31) and the **Task flashcards** (see page 21) to give the pupils a clear idea of what they are going to do in the lesson.

Activity Book teaching notes always appear in a shaded box so they can be easily identified.

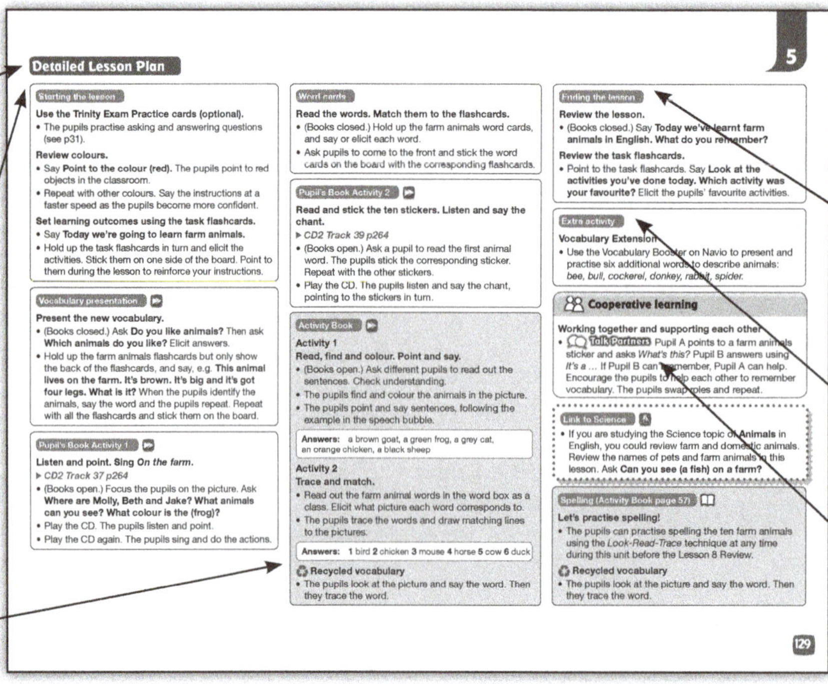

The activities for **Ending the lesson** include reviewing the lesson objectives using the **Task flashcards**.

Each lesson includes optional **Extra activities** to reinforce and extend learning.

Talk Partner activities are clearly signposted.

Starter Unit Hello, friends!

Unit overview

Key Competences and Key Learning Outcomes

- Ask for someone's name and give your name (Lesson 1)
- Say a chant (Lesson 1)
- Identify and say the numbers 1–10 (Lesson 1)
- Ask and answer the question *What's this?* (Lesson 2)
- Identify and say colours (Lesson 3)
- Say the days of the week (Lesson 4)
- Ask and answer the question *What day is it today?* (Lesson 4)

- Identify and say five shapes (Lesson 2)

- Use the Pupil's App on Navio

- Make a cut-out and evaluate your learning (Lesson 4)

- Get to know your teacher and classmates (Lesson 1)

- Work with a Talk Partner to practise and reinforce learning (all lessons)

- Sing a song (Lesson 1 and 4)
- Read, listen and understand a story about a magic bike (Lesson 3)

Vocabulary

Core vocabulary
goodbye, hello; numbers 1–10 (words and figures); shapes (*circle, oval, rectangle, square, triangle*); colours (*blue, brown, green, orange, red, yellow*); days of the week (*Monday, Tuesday, Wednesday, Thursday, Friday, Saturday, Sunday*); *balloons, balls, bananas, bike, books, dogs, hats, socks*

Extension vocabulary (optional)
black, grey, pink, purple, white

Other vocabulary
bell, clean, children, idea, fantastic, magic bike, ring, surprise

Structures

Core structures
What's your name? I'm (Jake).
What's this? It's a (bike).
What colour is it? It's (green).
What day is it today? It's (Thursday).

Other structures
Ring the bell again. Let's (clean the bike). The (bike) is (green). It's a (bike). Good idea! This magic bike is fantastic!

Cooperative learning

Skills: Listening to your classmates (Lesson 1); Learning to learn (Lesson 2); Turn taking (Lesson 4)

Cross-curricular links

Links to Science
Counting the boys and girls in the class.

Suggested Arts and Crafts concepts
Understanding that artists find inspiration in the world around them; thinking about what inspires you.

Key Competences and Key Learning Outcomes

- Ask for someone's name and give your name
- Say the vocabulary chant
- Identify and say the numbers 1–10
- Count the boys and girls in the class (optional)
- Get to know your teacher and classmates
- Sing a song

Key language
- *goodbye, hello; balloons, balls, bananas, bike, books, dogs, hats, socks;* numbers 1–10
- *What's your name? I'm (Jake).*
- Extension: *black, grey, pink, purple, white*

Materials
- Pupil's Book p4; Activity Book p2; Class CD1; Teacher's App on Navio
- Character flashcards; numbers and colours balloon flashcards
- Teacher's Resource Bank: Numbers word cards
- Teacher's Resource Bank: Task flashcards: *listen, sing, Talk Partners, say, find, write, read, match, think*

At a Glance Lesson Plan

Starting the lesson
- Set learning outcomes using the task flashcards.

Vocabulary presentation
- Present the characters using the flashcards.

Activity 1
- Listen and point.
- ▶ ***CD1 Track 1 p256***
- Sing *What's your name?*
- Talk Partners Ask and answer in pairs.

Activity 2
- Say *The ten balloons* chant.
- ▶ ***CD1 Track 3 p256***

Activity 3
- Find, count and write.
- Go to the Activity Book.

Word cards
- Read the word cards.
- Match them to the flashcards.

Pupil's Book

Ending the lesson
- Review the lesson.
- Review the task flashcards.

Extra activities

Reinforcement
- Act out *The ten balloons* chant.

Vocabulary Extension
- Present five additional vocabulary items.

Cooperative learning

Listening to your classmates
- Do a counting chain.

Link to Science
- **Physical characteristics:** Count the boys and girls in the class.

Digital resources

Teacher's Digital: Don't forget you can teach this lesson using the Teacher's App on Navio.

Pupil's Digital: Encourage your pupils to use the Pupil's App on Navio to practise the vocabulary from this lesson.

Powered By NAVIO

Activity Book

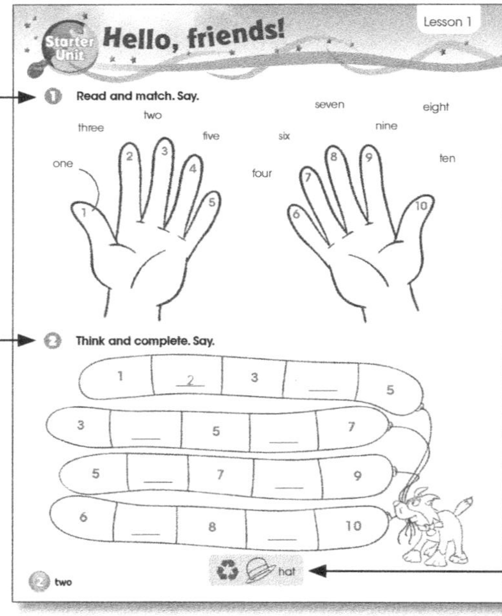

Activity Book

Activity 1
- Read and match.
- Talk Partners Say.

Activity 2
- Think and complete.
- Talk Partners Say.

Recycled vocabulary
- Look, remember and say the word.

Detailed Lesson Plan

Starting the lesson

Set learning outcomes using the task flashcards.

- Say **Today we're going to learn how to say hello to friends.**
- Hold up the task flashcards for the lesson in turn and teach the activities. Stick them on one side of the board. Point to them and say the action during the lesson to reinforce your instructions.

Vocabulary presentation

Present the characters using the flashcards.

- (Books closed.) Greet the class. Hold up the flashcard of Jake and say **This is Jake. Say *Hello* to Jake.** The children greet the character. Repeat with the flashcards of the other characters. Stick the flashcards on one side of the board.

Pupil's Book Activity 1

Listen and point. Sing *What's your name?*

▶ *CD1 Track 1 p256*

- (Books open.) The pupils find and point to the four characters in the scene.
- Play the CD. Listen and point to the characters.
- Ask pupils **What's your name?** and elicit *I'm (Paula)*.
- Play the CD again. The pupils sing and do the actions.
  Talk Partners The pupils ask *What's your name?* and answer *I'm (David)* with a Talk Partner.

Pupil's Book Activity 2

Say *The ten balloons* chant.

▶ *CD1 Track 3 p256*

- (Books open.) Hold up the numbers and colours balloon flashcards. Say or elicit each number in turn. Say **One!** Stick the flashcard on the board. The pupils repeat the number. Repeat with the other numbers.
- Play the CD and do the actions. The pupils listen and watch you do the actions.
- Play the CD again. The pupils say the chant and do the actions.

Pupil's Book Activity 3

Find, count and write.

- Point to the picture in Activity 1. Ask **Can you see the balloons?**
- Say **Let's count! One, …** The pupils count the balloons with you.
- Say **Let's count the balls.** The pupils find, count and write the number of balls in the circle.
- Repeat for the other objects.

Answers: 10 balloons, 8 bananas, 7 balls, 5 hats, 4 socks, 7 books, 3 dogs, 1 bike

Word cards

Read the word cards. Match them to the flashcards.

- (Books closed.) Hold up the numbers word cards in turn, and say or elicit each word. The pupils repeat.
- Invite different pupils to the front to stick each word card on the board with the corresponding balloon flashcard.
- Point to each word card in turn and elicit the numbers.

Activity Book

Activity 1

Read and match. Say.

- Ask the pupils to count to ten.
- Focus the pupils on Activity 1. They read and draw lines to match the numbers.
- **Talk Partners** The pupils point to the fingers and say the numbers with a Talk Partner.

Activity 2

Think and complete. Say.

- Read out the numbers on the balloons. Elicit the missing numbers. The pupils write the missing numerals.
- **Talk Partners** The pupils point to and say the number sequences with a Talk Partner.

Answers: 2, 4; 4, 6; 6, 8; 7, 9

Recycled vocabulary

- The pupils look at the picture and say the word.

Ending the lesson

Review the lesson.

- (Books closed.) Say **Today we've learnt numbers. What numbers do you remember?** Elicit the numbers.

Review the task flashcards.

- Point to the task flashcards. Say **Look at the activities you've done today. Which activity was your favourite?** Elicit the pupils' favourite activities.

Extra activities

Reinforcement

- The pupils act out *The ten balloons* chant. Give ten pupils a numbers and colours balloon flashcard. They stand up when they hear their number. Repeat several times with different pupils.

Vocabulary Extension

- Use the Vocabulary Booster on Navio to present and practise five additional words to describe colours: *black, grey, pink, purple, white*

Cooperative learning

Listening to your classmates

- Do a counting chain with the class. Go round the class and each child says a number.
- Start again when you reach number ten.

Link to Science

- If you are studying the Science topic of **Physical characteristics** in English, you could encourage the pupils to give more personal information, e.g. *I'm a (boy)*. Ask them to review and extend numbers by counting the number of boys and girls in the class to investigate and compare how many of each there are.

Key Competences and Key Learning Outcomes

- Ask and answer the question *What's this?*
- Identify and say five shapes
- Listen for specific information

Key language

- shapes *(circle, oval, rectangle, square, triangle)*
- *What's this? It's a (bike).*
- Recycled: *balloons, bananas, bikes, books, dogs, hats, socks*

Materials

- Pupil's Book p5; Activity Book p3; Class CD1; Teacher's App on Navio
- Character flashcards; numbers and colours balloon flashcards
- Teacher's Resource Bank: Task flashcards: *listen, sing, act out, Talk Partners, say, find, read, circle*

At a Glance Lesson Plan

Starting the lesson

- Review the *What's your name?* song.
- ▶ ***CD1 Track 1 p256***
- ▶ ***CD1 Track 2 p256 (optional karaoke version)***
- Review *The ten balloons* chant.
- ▶ ***CD1 Track 3 p256***
- Set learning outcomes using the task flashcards.

Activity 1

- Listen and repeat.
- ▶ ***CD1 Track 4 p256***
- Act out.

Activity 2

- Listen and find.
- ▶ ***CD1 Track 5 p256***
- Point.

Activity 3

- Point.
- Talk Partners Ask and answer.

Pupil's Book

Activity 4

- Find these shapes in the picture.
- Go to the Activity Book.

Ending the lesson

- Review the lesson.
- Review the task flashcards.

Extra activities

Reinforcement

- Play *Magic finger*.
- Play *What's missing?*
- Play *Guess the shape.*

Cooperative learning

Learning to learn

- Use the teacher as a resource.

Digital resources

Teacher's Digital: Don't forget you can teach this lesson using the Teacher's App on Navio.

Pupil's Digital: Encourage your pupils to use the Pupil's App on Navio to practise the vocabulary from this lesson.

Powered By NAVIO

Activity Book

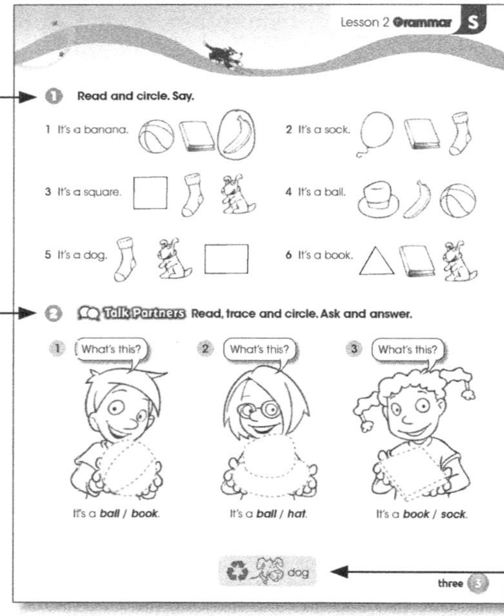

Activity Book

Activity 1

- Read and circle.
- Say.

Activity 2

- Talk Partners Read, trace and circle.
- Ask and answer.

Recycled vocabulary

- Look, remember and say the word.

Starting the lesson

Review the *What's your name?* song.

▶ ***CD1 Track 1 p256***

▶ ***CD1 Track 2 p256 (optional karaoke version)***

- Hold up the character flashcards and ask **Who's this?**
- Play the CD. The pupils sing and do the actions.

Review *The ten balloons* chant.

▶ ***CD1 Track 3 p256***

- Use the numbers and colours balloon flashcards to review the numbers. Give the flashcards to ten pupils.
- Play the CD.
- The pupils sing and hold up their number when it appears in the song.
- The pupils swap flashcards. Repeat the procedure.

Set learning outcomes using the task flashcards.

- Say **Today we're going to learn the question *What's this?***
- Stick the task flashcards for the lesson on one side of the board. Point to them and say the action during the lesson to reinforce your instructions.

Pupil's Book Activity 1

Listen and repeat. Act out.

▶ ***CD1 Track 4 p256***

- (Books open.) Focus the class on the picture. Point to Dad and say **This is Dad. Let's listen**.
- Play the CD. The pupils listen and read.
- Play the CD again. Pause the CD after each sentence and the pupils repeat.
- Ask pairs of pupils to act out the conversation.

Pupil's Book Activity 2

Listen and find. Point.

▶ ***CD1 Track 5 p256***

- Focus on the people in the picture on Pupil's Book pages 4 and 5.
- Play the CD, pausing after each conversation. The pupils point to the people and say the object they are talking about.

Answers: **1** a balloon **2** a hat **3** a banana **4** a book

Pupil's Book Activity 3

Point. Ask and answer.

- Hold up your Pupil's Book pages 4 and 5 and point to different objects as you ask **What's this?** The pupils answer *It's a (balloon)*.
- Review all the vocabulary from page 4.
- Talk Partners The pupils ask and answer with a Talk Partner.

Pupil's Book Activity 4

Find these shapes in the picture.

- Focus the pupils' attention on the shapes and say the names of each one. The pupils repeat.
- Say **Can you find a red circle?** Once the pupils have located the circle in the picture, encourage them to find the other shapes hidden in the picture.

Answers: Red circle is one of the juggler's balls. Orange rectangle on the ice cream stall. Blue square on the car. Yellow triangle on the clothes stall. Green oval on the fruit stall.

Activity Book

Activity 1

Read and circle. Say.

- (Books open.) Ask a confident pupil to read the first sentence. Point to the correct picture. Repeat with other pupils.
- The pupils read the sentences and circle the objects.

Answers: **1** third picture **2** third picture **3** first picture **4** third picture **5** second picture **6** second picture

Activity 2

Read, trace and circle. Ask and answer.

- Focus the pupils on Activity 2. Ask for volunteers to read the question then the words in the word box.
- The pupils trace over the objects, read the sentences and circle the correct word.
- Talk Partners The pupils ask and answer the questions with a Talk Partner.

Answers: **1** ball **2** hat **3** book

Recycled vocabulary

- The pupils look at the picture and say the word.

Ending the lesson

Review the lesson.

- (Books closed.) Say **Today we've learnt a question. What was the question?** Elicit the question and some possible answers from the pupils.

Review the task flashcards.

- Point to the task flashcards. Say **Look at the activities you've done today. Which activity was your favourite?** Elicit the pupils' favourite activities.

Extra activities

Reinforcement

- Play *Magic finger* to review vocabulary items that pupils know (numbers, *banana*). The pupils point to the number or object in the Pupil's Book.
- Play *What's missing?* (see p23) with the numbers and colours balloon flashcards.
- Play *Guess the shape*. Ask a pair of pupils to come to the front of the class. Pupil A draws a shape on Pupil B's back. Pupil B guesses the shape and says *It's a (circle)*. They swap places and repeat. Repeat the activity with different pairs of pupils. If you have a confident class, the pupils could then play the game in pairs.

Cooperative learning

Learning to learn

- Help pupils to understand that you are an important resource for learning English. Encourage the pupils to touch different objects in the classroom and ask the question *What's this, please?* Tell them the name of the object in English.

Key Competences and Key Learning Outcomes

- Identify and say colours
- Read, listen and understand a story about a magic bike

Key language

- Colours: *blue, brown, green, grey, orange, red, yellow*
- *What colour is it? It's (green). The (bike) is (green). Ring the bell again. Let's (clean the bike). This magic bike is fantastic! Good idea!*

Recycled: *banana*

Recycled: *What's this? It's a (bike).*

Materials

- Pupil's Book p6; Activity Book p4; Class CD1; Teacher's App on Navio
- Numbers and colours balloon flashcards
- Teacher's Resource Bank: Numbers and colours word cards
- Teacher's Resource Bank: Task flashcards: *listen, read, act out, colour, Talk Partners*
- Teacher's Resource Bank: Starter Unit Lesson 3 Animated Story
- Crayons or coloured pencils

At a Glance Lesson Plan

Starting the lesson

- Review vocabulary from Lessons 1 and 2.
- Set learning outcomes using the task flashcards.

Before you read

- Present and practise the colours.
- Explain the story title.

Activity 1

- Listen and read.

▶ *CD1 Track 6 p256*

- Act out.

Now watch the animated story!

Go to the Activity Book.

Pupil's Book

Ending the lesson

- Review the lesson.
- Review the task flashcards.

Extra activity

Vocabulary Extension

- *Pink, purple, black, white.*
- Play *Memory!* with ten flashcards (see p23).

Digital resources

Teacher's Digital: Don't forget you can teach this lesson using the Teacher's App on Navio.

Pupil's Digital: Encourage your pupils to use the Pupil's App on Navio to practise the vocabulary from this lesson.

Powered By NAVIO

Activity Book

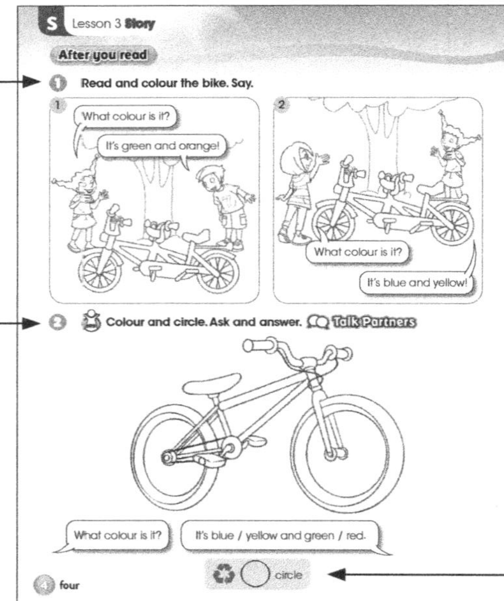

Activity Book

After you read: Activity 1

- Read and colour the bike.
- Talk Partners Say.

Activity 2

- Colour and circle.
- Talk Partners Ask and answer.

Recycled vocabulary

- Look, remember and say the word.

Detailed Lesson Plan

Starting the lesson

Review vocabulary from Lessons 1 and 2.

- Review objects from the previous lessons. Mime peeling and eating a banana. Ask **What's this?** Repeat with other key vocabulary, e.g. a balloon, a ball, a hat, a sock, a book and a bike.

Set learning outcomes using the task flashcards.

- Explain the aims of the lesson. Say **Today we're going to learn the colours**.
- Stick the task flashcards for the lesson on one side of the board. Point to them and say the action during the lesson to reinforce your instructions.

Before you read

Present and practise the colours.

- Hold up the number one balloon flashcard. Ask **What number is it?** Point to the colour of the balloon. Ask **What colour is it?** *(Red.)* Say **Point to something (red) in the class.** Stick the flashcard on the board and repeat with the other colours.
- Hold up the word card for the colour (red) and say the word. A pupil sticks the word card on the board next to the corresponding flashcard. Repeat with the other word cards and colours.

Explain the story title.

- (Books open.) Focus on the story title. Mime being very surprised.
- Ask **What's the surprise in the story?**
- The pupils guess and then scan the story to check.
- Point to frame 1 and ask **Who's this? Is it Molly? What's this?**

Pupil's Book Activity 1

Listen and read. Act out.

▶ *CD1 Track 6 p256*

- The pupils place their 'magic finger' (i.e. their index finger) on the first frame of the story.
- Play the CD. The pupils point to the different frames as the story progresses. Pause the CD after each frame to check that all the pupils are following.
- Play the CD again. If necessary, ask questions about each story frame to help and check understanding.

Suggested comprehension questions

- Frame 1: **What's this?** (*A bike.*) **Are Jake and Molly happy with the bike?** (*Yes.*)
- Frame 2: **What do the children clean?** Mime cleaning the bike. (*The bike and the bell.*)
- Frame 3: **Is the bike special?** (*Yes.*) **What colour is the bike now?** (*Green and red.*)
- Frame 4: **Who rings the bell?** (*Beth.*) **What colour is the bike now?** (*Green, red and orange.*)
- Frame 5: **What colour is it now?** (*Green, red, orange and blue.*)
- Frame 6: **What colour is it now?** (*Green, red, orange, blue, brown and yellow.*) **Are Jake and Molly happy with the bike now?** (*Yes.*)
- Finally, ask the pupils **Is this a good story?** The pupils give their opinion through gesture (thumbs up / down) or orally (*yes / no*).
- Organise the class into three groups (Beth, Molly and Jake). You can say Dad's two lines at the start of the story.
- Play the CD. Each group joins in when their character speaks. If necessary, pause the CD after each sentence for the pupils to repeat.
- The groups swap roles, and repeat several times.

▶ ***Now watch the animated story***

Activity Book

Activity 1: After you read.

Read and colour the bike. Say.

- (Books open.) Ask the pupils to read out the speech bubbles. Check comprehension using the numbers and colours flashcards.
- The pupils colour the bikes.
- **Talk Partners** The pupils say the conversation with a Talk Partner.

Activity 2 (me)

Colour and circle. Ask and answer.

- Focus the class on Activity 2. Ask a volunteer to read out the question.
- The pupils colour their bike in two different colours: the first colour should be blue or yellow and the second colour green or red. Then they circle the different colours they have used for their bike.

Talk Partners The pupils ask and answer with a Talk Partner using the text in the speech bubbles.

Recycled vocabulary

- The pupils look at the picture and say the word.

Ending the lesson

Review the lesson.

- (Books closed.) Say **Today we've learnt the colours. What colours do you know?** Elicit the colours.

Review the task flashcards.

- Point to the task flashcards. Say **Look at the activities you've done today. Which activity was your favourite?** Elicit the pupils' favourite activities.

Extra activity

Vocabulary Extension

- Use the numbers and colours flashcards to teach 'pink', 'purple', 'black' and 'white'. Then play *Memory!* with ten flashcards (see p23).

Key Competences and Key Learning Outcomes

- Say the days of the week
- Ask and answer the question *What day is it today?*
- Make the traffic light cut-out and evaluate your learning
- Sing a song

Key language

- days of the week: *Monday, Tuesday, Wednesday, Thursday, Friday, Saturday, Sunday*
- *What day is it today? It's (Thursday).*

Recycled: *ball*

Materials

- Pupil's Book p7; Activity Book p5; Class CD1; Teacher's App on Navio
- Numbers and colours balloon flashcards
- Teacher's Resource Bank: Days of the week word cards
- Teacher's Resource Bank: Traffic light cut-out, scissors, red, yellow and green crayons or coloured pencils
- Teacher's Resource Bank: Task flashcards: *listen, sing, Talk Partners, read, cut out, colour, think*
- Teacher's Resource Bank: Starter unit Lesson 4 Activity 3 cut-outs

At a Glance Lesson Plan

Pupil's Book

Starting the lesson

- Review the colours.
- Set learning outcomes using the task flashcards.

Vocabulary presentation

- Present the new vocabulary using the word cards.

Activity 1

- Listen and sing *Seven days a week.*
- ▶ *CD1 Track 7 p256*

Activity 2

- Listen.
- ▶ *CD1 Track 8 p256*
- Talk Partners Ask and answer.

Go to the Activity Book.

Ending the lesson

- Review the task flashcards.

Cooperative learning

Turn taking

- Play *Your turn!*

Activity Book

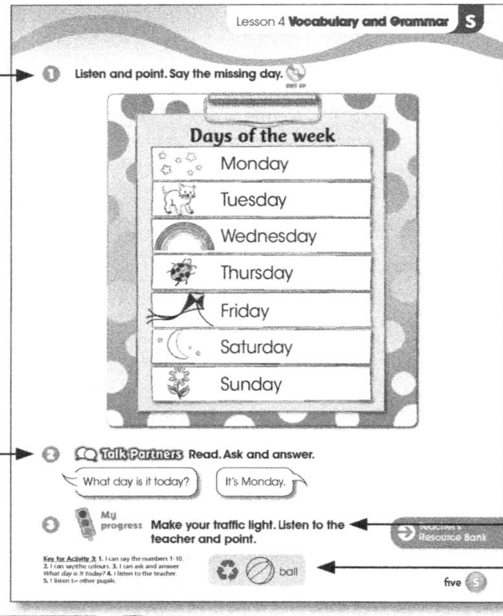

Activity Book

Activity 1

- Listen and point.
- ▶ *CD1 Track 9 p256*
- Say the missing day.

Activity 2

- Read.
- Talk Partners Ask and answer.

Activity 3 My progress

- Make your traffic light. Listen to the teacher and point.

Go to the Teacher's Resource Bank.

Recycled vocabulary

- Look, remember and say the word.

Digital resources

Teacher's Digital: Don't forget you can teach this lesson using the Teacher's App on Navio.

Pupil's Digital: Encourage your pupils to use the Pupil's App on Navio to practise the vocabulary from this lesson.

Powered By NAVIO

Detailed Lesson Plan

Starting the lesson

Review the colours.

- Revise the colours with the numbers and colours balloon flashcards. Hold up one of the flashcards so the pupils can't see it and ask **What colour is it?** The pupils guess the colour of the flashcard. Repeat with the other flashcards. Different pupils come to the front of the class and take your role.

Set learning outcomes using the task flashcards.

- Say **Today, we're going to sing a song**.
- Stick the task flashcards for the lesson on one side of the board. Point to them and say the action during the lesson to reinforce your instructions.

Vocabulary presentation

Present the new vocabulary using the word cards.

- (Books closed.) Point to the class calendar and say **Today is (Monday).**
- Show the pupils the days of the week word cards and they say the words.
- Stick the word cards on the board in order. Say the seven days of the week and the class repeats.

Pupil's Book Activity 1

Listen and sing *Seven days a week.*

▶ *CD1 Track 7 p256*

- (Books closed.) Point to the days of the week word cards on the board and ask **How many days are there?** Say **Seven days is one week**. Show the pupils one week on the class calendar.
- Play the CD. The pupils listen and do the actions.
- (Books open.) Ask **What can you see?** *(Jake and Molly on the magic bike.)*
- Play the CD. The pupils listen and watch your actions.
- Play the CD again. The pupils sing the song and do the actions.

Pupil's Book Activity 2

Listen. Ask and answer.

▶ *CD1 Track 8 p256*

- (Books open.) Ask **What can you see?**
- Play the CD. The pupils listen.
- Play the CD again. The pupils repeat.
- Point to the class calendar or the date written on the board. Ask **What day is it today?**
- **Talk Partners** The pupils ask and answer the question with a Talk Partner.

Activity Book

Activity 1

Listen and point. Say the missing day.

▶ *CD1 Track 9 p256*

- (Books open.) Say the seven days of the week with the pupils.
- Tell the class they are going to listen to the days of the week, but one day is missing each time.
- Play the CD, pausing after each day for the pupils to point to the day as they hear it. Elicit the missing day each time.

Answers: **1** Friday **2** Tuesday **3** Saturday **4** Thursday **5** Sunday **6** Wednesday

Activity 2

Read. Ask and answer.

- Ask two pupils to read the question and answer in the speech bubble.
- **Talk Partners** The pupils take turns to point to a day of the week in Activity 1 and ask and answer with a Talk Partner.

Activity 3 My progress

Make your traffic light. Listen to the teacher and point.

- The pupils cut out the traffic light.

Go to the Teacher's Resource Bank.

- Point to each circle and ask **What colour is it?** (*Red, yellow, green.*) The pupils colour their traffic light.
- (Books closed.) Say **Let's think about our work in this unit.** Point to the green circle, nod your head, smile a lot, and say **I can say the colours in English. Yes, I can do this very well.** Point to the yellow circle, move your head a little and smile a little and say **Yes, I can do this.** Then point to the red circle, shake your head and say **No, I can't do this.**
- Read the different statements. For each one, the pupils point to the colour on their traffic light that shows how they feel about their own learning.

Self-assessment statements

1. I can say the numbers 1–10.
2. I can say the colours.
3. I can ask and answer *What day is it today?*
4. I listen to the teacher.
5. I listen to other pupils.

Recycled vocabulary

- The pupils look at the picture and say the word.

Ending the lesson

Review the task flashcards.

- Point to the task flashcards. Say **Look at the activities you've done today. Which activity was your favourite?** Elicit the pupils' favourite activities.

Cooperative learning

Turn taking

- Active listening is essential for communication. The pupils need practice in focussing on the speaker and turn taking.
- The pupils work with a Talk Partner to play *Your turn!* They take turns to read or say the days of the week, e.g. Pupil A: *Monday*. Pupil B: *Tuesday*.
- The pupils repeat the game with the colours and then numbers.

Date: ____________________ Unit: __________

1 What did my pupils learn in this unit?

____

____

____

____

2 How did my pupils work? (✓)

individually ☐ in pairs ☐ in small groups ☐

in large groups ☐ as a class ☐

3 Which key competences did my pupils develop?

- Competence in linguistic communication ☐
- Competence in mathematics, science and technology ☐
- Digital competence ☐
- Learning to learn ☐
- Social and civic competences ☐
- Sense of initiative and entrepreneurship ☐
- Cultural awareness and expression ☐

4 Which lessons / activities were the most successful and why?

____

____

____

____

5 Which lessons / activities did my pupils find the most difficult and why?

____

____

____

____

6 What did I try in the classroom for the first time? How did it go?

____

____

____

____

7 Which resources did I find most useful? (including webpages)

____

____

____

____

____

____

8 What could I do differently next time I teach this unit?

____

____

____

____

Unit 1

Ready for school!

Unit overview

Key Competences and Key Learning Outcomes

- Identify and say ten classroom objects (Lesson 1)
- Say the vocabulary chant (Lesson 1)
- Use *Where's …?* and *here* in a conversation (Lesson 2)
- Ask and answer the question *Where's my pen?* (Lesson 2)
- Understand and give instructions using prepositions (Lesson 4)
- Watch and understand a video about what children do at school (Video and 21st Century Skills)

- Use the Pupil's App on Navio

- Practise spelling (Lesson 1)
- Say a tongue twister to practise the 'r' sound (Lesson 5)
- Review language in the unit and reflect on own learning (Lesson 8)
- Practise activity types found in the Cambridge English Young Learners Exams: Pre A1 Starters

- Understand the importance of keeping the classroom tidy and putting rubbish in the bin (Lesson 3)
- Read and understand a classroom rules poster (Lesson 7)
- Understand the importance of being organised (Video and 21st Century Skills)

- Work with a Talk Partner to practise and reinforce learning (all lessons)
- Play a communication game about classroom objects (Lesson 5)

- Sing three songs (Lessons 1, 4, and 8)
- Understand and act out a story (Lesson 3)
- Read about school assemblies in Britain (Lesson 6)
- Think about what you do at school (Lesson 6)

Vocabulary

Core vocabulary
book, computer, crayon, pen, pencil, pencil case, rubber, ruler, school bag, sharpener; bin, board, chair, cupboard, desk, shelf

Extension vocabulary (optional)
file, glue, notebook, paintbrush, paper, scissors; bookcase, door, floor, window

Other vocabulary
floor, good work, poster, rules, school assembly, white

Recycled vocabulary
numbers 1–10; colours; days of the week

Structures

Core structures
Where's my (pen)? It's here.
Where's my (purple) (pencil case)?
It's in / on / under the (desk).
The (pencil case) is (on the shelf).
Put the (pencil case) on / in / under (the desk).

Other structures
I'm ready for school. Let's tidy up. We (sit on the floor / listen to the head teacher / sing songs / clap our hands). Listen to others. Put your hand up to speak. Work quietly. Sit down on your chair. Walk in the classroom. Tidy up your things. Find the (computer on the desk). Point to the (pencil).

Recycled structures
What's this? It's (a pen). What colour is it? It's (purple).

Phonics

Consonant sound 'r' (red, rabbit, ruler)

British Culture

School assembly

Literacy

Text type: a classroom poster (instructional text)
Reading skill: reading for specific information

21st Century Skills

Ways of working: being organised

Cooperative learning

Song: *Well done!* (Lesson 8)
Skills: **Think-Pair-Share** (Lesson 1); Listening to others (Lesson 2); Developing a positive classroom atmosphere (Lesson 6); Behaving well in class (Lesson 7)

Values

Keeping the classroom tidy

Cross-curricular links

Links to Science
My school: identifying classroom equipment and materials and keeping them tidy; being aware that there are different school subjects; behaving correctly in class and around the school

Suggested Arts and Crafts concepts
Lines and shapes: identifying lines and shapes in Art and around school; using lines and shapes to represent your school

Key Competences and Key Learning Outcomes

- Identify and say ten classroom objects
- Say the vocabulary chant
- Stick the classroom objects stickers

- Practise spelling
- Review classroom objects

- Sing a song about school

Key language
- *book, computer, crayon, pen, pencil, pencil case, rubber, ruler, school bag, sharpener*
- *I'm ready for school.*
- Extension: *file, glue, notebook, paintbrush, paper, scissors*

Recycled: *eight, five*

Materials
- Pupil's Book p8; Activity Book pp6 and 15; Class CD1; Teacher's App on Navio
- Numbers and colours flashcards; classroom objects flashcards; Unit 1 stickers
- Teacher's Resource Bank: Classroom objects word cards
- Teacher's Resource Bank: Task flashcards: *listen, sing, read, match, stick, say, colour, Talk Partners*

Optional materials
- Teacher's Resource Bank: Five Trinity Exam Practice cards (selected from the Starter Unit)

At a Glance Lesson Plan

Starting the lesson
- Use the Trinity Exam Practice cards (optional).
- Review numbers and colours.
- Set learning outcomes using the task flashcards.

Vocabulary presentation
- Present the new vocabulary.

Activity 1
- Listen and point.
- ▶ *CD1 Track 10 p256*
- Sing *I'm ready for school!*

Word cards
- Read the word cards.
- Match them to the flashcards.

Activity 2
- Read and stick the ten stickers.
- Listen and say the chant.
- ▶ *CD1 Track 12 p256*

Go to the Activity Book.

Pupil's Book

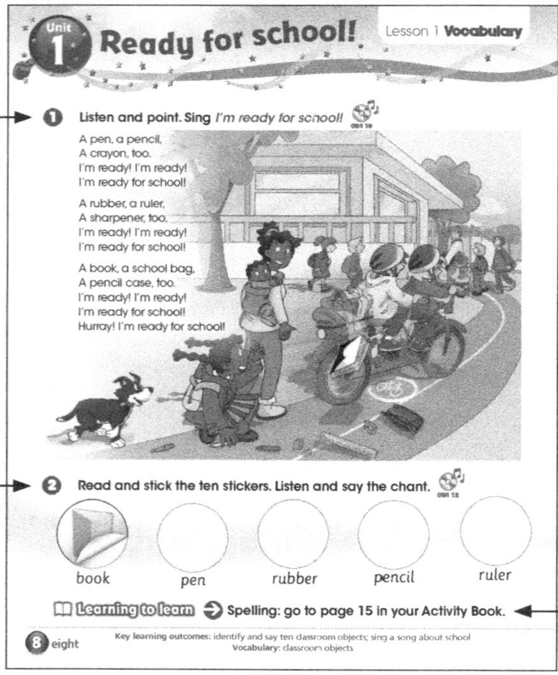

Ending the lesson
- Review the lesson.
- Review the task flashcards.

Extra activity

Vocabulary Extension
- Present six additional vocabulary items.

Cooperative learning

Think-Pair-Share
- Review classroom objects.

Learning to learn

Spelling
- Practise spelling at any time during this unit (Activity Book p15).

Digital resources

Teacher's Digital: Don't forget you can teach this lesson using the Teacher's App on Navio.

Pupil's Digital: Encourage your pupils to use the Pupil's App on Navio to practise the vocabulary from this lesson.

Powered By NAVIO

Activity Book

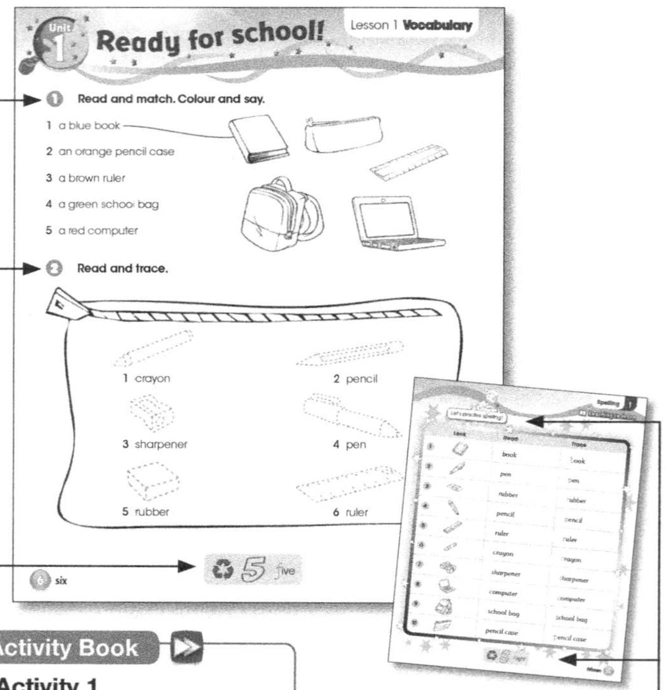

Activity Book

Activity 1
- Read and match.
- Colour and say.

Activity 2
- Read and trace.

Recycled vocabulary
- Look, say and trace the letter.

Spelling

Let's practise spelling!
- Use the *Look-Read-Trace* technique.

Recycled vocabulary
- Look,say and trace the letter.

Detailed Lesson Plan

Starting the lesson

Use the Trinity Exam Practice cards (optional).

- The pupils practise asking and answering questions (see p31).

Review numbers and colours.

- Review numbers and colours using the numbers and colours balloons flashcards.

Set learning outcomes using the task flashcards.

- Say **Today we're going to learn the names of classroom objects.**
- Hold up the task flashcards in turn and elicit the activities. Stick them on one side of the board. Point to them during the lesson to reinforce your instructions.

Vocabulary presentation

Present the new vocabulary.

- (Books closed.) Draw a large school bag on the board.
- Play *Slowly, slowly* to introduce each classroom objects flashcard (see p23). Then stick it inside the school bag.
- Point to each classroom objects flashcard in turn and say the words with the pupils.
- Then play *What's missing?* (see p23).

Pupil's Book Activity 1

Listen and point. Sing *I'm ready for school!*

▶ *CD1 Track 10 p256*

- (Books open.) Focus the pupils on Activity 1. Ask **What classroom objects can you see? Who can you see?**
- Play the CD. The pupils listen and point to the objects on the page.
- Play the CD again. The pupils sing and do the actions. Stick the classroom objects flashcards on the board in the order of the song, if necessary.

Word cards

Read the word cards. Match them to the flashcards.

- (Books closed.) Hold up the classroom objects word cards in turn, and say or elicit each word.
- Ask different pupils to come to the front and stick each word card on the board with the corresponding flashcard.
- Point to each word card in turn and elicit the words.

Pupil's Book Activity 2

Read and stick the ten stickers. Listen and say the chant.

▶ *CD1 Track 12 p256*

- (Books open.) Ask a pupil to read the first classroom object word. The pupils stick the corresponding sticker. Repeat with the other stickers.
- Play the CD. The pupils listen and say the chant, pointing to the stickers in turn.

Activity Book

Activity 1

Read and match. Colour and say.

- Ask different pupils to read out the phrases. The pupils draw a line to match them to the objects.
- Then they colour the classroom objects and say what each object is.

Activity 2

Read and trace.

- Focus the pupils on Activity 2. Ask different pupils to read out the classroom words.
- The pupils trace the classroom objects and say the correct words under the pictures.

Recycled vocabulary

- The pupils look at the number and say the word. Then they trace the first letter of the word.

Ending the lesson

Review the lesson.

- (Books closed.) Say **Today we've learnt the names of classroom objects. What classroom objects do you know?** Elicit the classroom objects.

Review the task flashcards.

- Point to the task flashcards. Say **Look at the activities you've done today. Which activity was your favourite?** Elicit the pupils' favourite activities.

Extra activity

Vocabulary Extension

- Use the Vocabulary Booster on Navio to present and practise six additional words to describe classroom objects: *file, glue, notebook, paintbrush, paper, scissors.*

Cooperative learning

Think-Pair-Share

- Ask **Can you remember the ten classroom objects?** The class think silently on their own for one minute.
- Talk Partners Then the pupils work with a Talk Partner to name all ten items. Ask a pair to say one of the objects. Praise them for their good memory. Hold up the corresponding flashcard and prompt the class to repeat the word.
- Finally, repeat, asking different pairs of pupils each time, until all ten classroom objects have been named.

Spelling (Activity Book p15)

Let's practise spelling!

- The pupils can practise spelling the ten classroom objects using the *Look-Read-Trace* technique at any time during this unit before the Lesson 8 Review.

Recycled vocabulary

- The pupils look at the number and say the word. Then they trace the first letter of the word.

Key Competences and Key Learning Outcomes

- Use *Where's …?* and *here* in a conversation
- Ask and answer the question *Where's my (pen)?*

- Listen for specific information

Key language

- *Where's my (pen)? It's here.*

Recycled: *book, computer, crayon, pen, pencil, pencil case, rubber, ruler, sharpener, school bag; six*

Materials

- Pupil's Book p9; Activity Book p7; Class CD1; Teacher's App on Navio
- Classroom objects flashcards
- Teacher's Resource Bank: Task flashcards: *listen, act out, find, circle, read, follow, draw, Talk Partners*

Optional materials

- Teacher's Resource Bank: Five Trinity Exam Practice cards (selected from the Starter Unit)

At a Glance Lesson Plan

Starting the lesson

- Use the Trinity Exam Practice cards (optional).
- Review classroom objects.
- Review the *I'm ready for school!* song.
- ▶ ***CD1 Track 10 p256***
- ▶ ***CD1 Track 11 p256 (optional karaoke version)***
- Set learning outcomes using the task flashcards.

Activity 1

- Listen and repeat.
- ▶ ***CD1 Track 13 p256***
- Act out.

Activity 2

- Listen and find.
- ▶ ***CD1 Track 14 p257***
- Circle.

Go to the Activity Book.

Pupil's Book

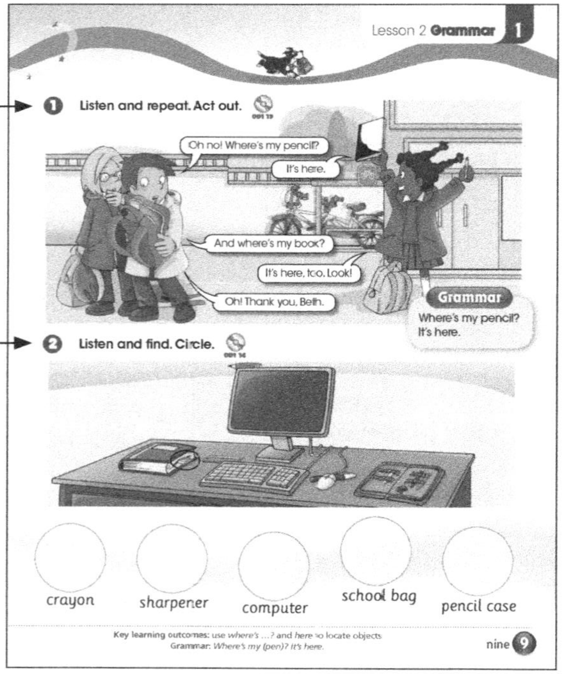

Ending the lesson

- Review the lesson.
- Review the task flashcards.

Extra activities

Reinforcement

- Practise asking questions.
- **Talk Partners** Play a guessing game.

Cooperative learning

Listening to others

- Play the *Secret message* game.

Activity Book

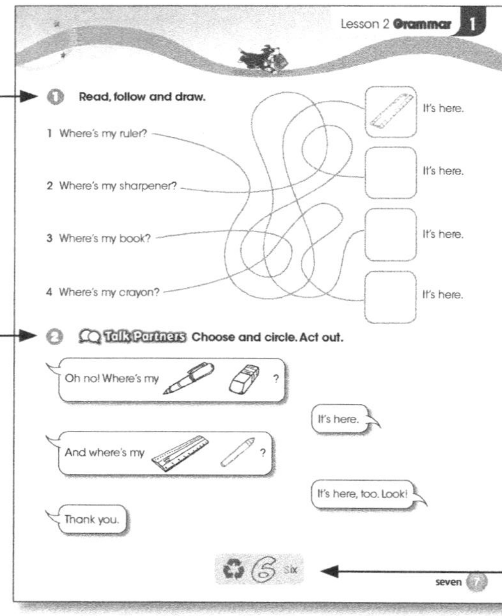

Activity Book

Activity 1

- Read, follow and draw.

Activity 2

- Choose and circle.
- **Talk Partners** Act out.

Recycled vocabulary

- Look, say and trace the letter.

Digital resources

Teacher's Digital: Don't forget you can teach this lesson using the Teacher's App on Navio.

Pupil's Digital: Encourage your pupils to use the Pupil's App on Navio to practise the vocabulary from this lesson.

Powered By NAVIO

Starting the lesson

Use the Trinity Exam Practice cards (optional).

- The pupils practise asking and answering questions (see p31).

Review classroom objects.

- Use the classroom objects flashcards to review the vocabulary. Invite a pupil to the front of the class. The pupil holds up one of the flashcards and asks *What's this?* Another pupil answers and says *It's a (book).* Repeat with different pupils.

Review the *I'm ready for school!* song.

▶ *CD1 Track 10 p256*

▶ *CD1 Track 11 p256 (optional karaoke version)*

- Invite three pupils to the front of the class and give each one the flashcards that correspond to a verse of *I'm ready for school!* Place a school bag on the desk at the front of the classroom.
- Play the CD (or the karaoke version) and prompt the class to sing. The pupils hold up their flashcards and place them in the school bag when their verse is sung. Repeat with three other pupils.

Set learning outcomes using the task flashcards.

- Say **Today we're going to learn a new question.**
- Hold up the task flashcards in turn and elicit the activities. Stick them on one side of the board. Point to them during the lesson to reinforce your instructions.

Pupil's Book Activity 1

Listen and repeat. Act out.

▶ *CD1 Track 13 p256*

- (Books open.) The pupils look at the picture. Ask **What can you see?**
- Play the CD. The pupils listen and read the conversation. Ask **Who has got the pencil? Who has got the book?**
- Play the CD again, pausing after each sentence for the pupils to repeat.
- Ask different pupils to come to the front and act out the conversation.

Pupil's Book Activity 2

Listen and find. Circle.

▶ *CD1 Track 14 p257*

- Focus the pupils on Activity 2. Ask **What can you see?** The pupils name the objects on the desk.
- Say **Let's listen.** Play the CD, pausing after each conversation.
- The pupils listen and find the classroom objects. They circle the objects.
- Play the CD again. The pupils listen and point to the object and say *It's here*.

Answers: **1** a rubber **2** a pencil **3** a pen **4** a ruler

Activity Book

Activity 1

Read, follow and draw.

- (Books open.) Read out the first question. The pupils follow the path with their finger. Repeat with the other questions.
- The pupils work on their own. They follow the lines and draw the correct classroom objects.

Answers: ruler, book, sharpener, crayon

Activity 2

Choose and circle. Act out.

- (Books open). Read the speech bubbles, pausing before the pictures to elicit the vocabulary.
- Practise the conversation as a class.
- **Talk Partners** When the pupils are confident with the language, they work in pairs to choose and circle an object for each question. They ask and answer with their partner.
- Invite different pairs of pupils to act out their conversations.

Recycled vocabulary

- The pupils look at the number and say the word. Then they trace the first letter of the word.

Ending the lesson

Review the lesson.

- (Books closed.) Say **Today we've learnt a new question. What question is it?** Elicit the question and answers from the pupils.

Review the task flashcards.

- Point to the task flashcards. Say **Look at the activities you've done today. Which activity was your favourite?** Elicit the pupils' favourite activities.

Extra activities

Reinforcement

- Put the class into a circle. Give the *ruler* flashcard to one pupil. Ask **What's this?** The pupil answers (*It's a ruler.*) then turns to the pupil on his/her left and asks the same question. That pupil answers, and so on.
- Repeat several times with different classroom objects flashcards.
  Talk Partners The pupils play a guessing game with a Talk Partner. Pupil A has his/her eyes closed. Pupil B gives him/her a classroom object and asks *What's this?* Pupil A guesses what it is. The pupils repeat several times, changing roles.

Cooperative learning

Listening to others

- Raise the pupils' awareness of the importance of listening to their classmates by playing the *Secret message* game (Chinese whispers).
- Stick the classroom objects flashcards on the board and organise the class into a line. Whisper the name of a classroom object to the pupil at the end of the line. This pupil whispers the same word to the pupil in front of them. The whispering continues along the line until it arrives at the pupil at the front. This pupil points to the correct flashcard on the board.

Key Competences and Key Learning Outcomes

- Read, listen and understand a story about Toby in school
- Read the story with some fluency
- Become familiar with the story through a pre-reading task
- Understand the importance of keeping the classroom tidy and putting rubbish in the bin
- Understand and act out the story
- Give an opinion on the story

Key language
- *black, pink, purple, white*
- *The (pencil case) is (on the shelf). Put the (pencil case) (on the desk).*

Recycled: *one*
Recycled: *Where's my (purple) (pencil case)?*

Materials
- Pupil's Book pp10–11; Activity Book p8; Class CD1; Teacher's App on Navio
- Classroom objects flashcards
- Teacher's Resource Bank: Task flashcards: *think, read, listen, act out, circle, number, colour*
- Teacher's Resource Bank: Unit 1 Lesson 3 Animated Story
- Crayons or coloured pencils

Optional materials
- Teacher's Resource Bank: Five Trinity Exam Practice cards (selected from the Starter Unit)

At a Glance Lesson Plan

Pupil's Book

Starting the lesson
- Use the Trinity Exam Practice cards (optional).
- Review the language from Lesson 2.
- Set learning outcomes using the task flashcards.

Before you read
- Explain the story title.
- Read and answer the question.

Activity 1
- Listen and read.
- ▶ *CD1 Track 15 p257*
- Act out.
- *Now watch the animated story!*

After you read: Activity 2
- Go to page 8 in your Activity Book.
- Values: Read and circle.

Ending the lesson
- Review the lesson.
- Review the task flashcards.

Activity Book

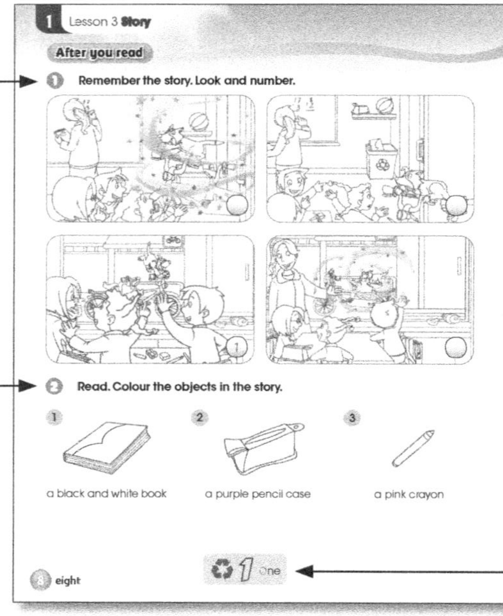

Activity Book

After you read: Activity 1
- Remember the story. Look and number.

Activity 2
- Read.
- Colour the objects in the story.

Recycled vocabulary
- Look, say and trace the letter.

Digital resources

Teacher's Digital: Don't forget you can teach this lesson using the Teacher's App on Navio.

Pupil's Digital: Encourage your pupils to use the Pupil's App on Navio to practise the vocabulary from this lesson.

Powered By NAVIO

Detailed Lesson Plan

Starting the lesson

Use the Trinity Exam Practice cards (optional).

- The pupils practise asking and answering questions (see p31).

Review the language from Lesson 2.

- Play *Memory!* (see p23) to review language from Lesson 2.

Set learning outcomes using the task flashcards.

- Say **Today we're going to listen to a story**.
- Hold up the task flashcards in turn and elicit the activities. Stick them on one side of the board. Point to them during the lesson to reinforce your instructions.

Before you read

Explain the story title.

- (Books open.) Focus on the story title. Ask **Do you go to school? Do boys and girls go to school? Do dogs go to school?**

Read and answer the question.

- Read the speech bubble. The pupils scan the story to find the different classroom objects.

Answers: a book, a pencil case, crayons, pencils, rubbers, a sharpener, school bags

Pupil's Book Activity 1

Listen and read. Act out.

▶ ***CD1 Track 15 p257***

- The pupils place their 'magic finger' on the first frame of the story.
- Play the CD. The pupils point to the different frames as the story progresses. Pause the CD after each frame to check that all the pupils are following.
- Play the CD again. Ask questions about each story frame to help and check understanding.
- Play the CD one more time, pausing it so the pupils can repeat.

Suggested comprehension questions

- Frame 1: **Is Toby happy?** (*No.*) **Why is he sad?** (*Dogs don't go to school.*)
- Frame 2: **Where is Toby now?** (*On the bike.*)
- Frame 3: **Where is Toby now?** (*In the classroom.*)
- Frame 4: **Is the book on the table?** (*No.*) **Are the crayons on the table?** (*Yes.*)
- Frame 5: **Is Molly looking for her book?** (*No.*) **Is she looking for her purple pencil case?** (*Yes.*)
- Frame 6: **Where's the black and white book?** (*In the bin.*) **Where's the purple pencil case?** (*On the shelf.*)
- Frame 8: **Where's the purple pencil case now?** (*On the desk.*) **Is the teacher happy?** (*Yes.*)
- Finally, ask the pupils **Is this a good story?** The pupils give their opinion through gesture (thumbs up / down) or orally (*yes* / *no*).
- Organise the class into three groups (Beth, Molly and Jake).
- Play the CD. Each group joins in when their character speaks. The groups swap roles and repeat several times.

Now watch the animated story

After you read

Go to page 8 in your Activity Book.

Activity Book

After you read: Activity 1

Remember the story. Look and number.

- (Books open.) Ask **Which frame is number 1?**
- The pupils remember the story and answer.
- Then they number the rest of the frames.

Answers: **1** third picture **2** first picture **3** second picture **4** fourth picture

Activity 2

Read. Colour the objects in the story.

- (Books open.) Focus the pupils on Activity 2. Point to each object in turn and read out the sentences. Ask **What colour is the (book)?**
- The pupils read the sentences again, colour the objects and say the sentences.

Answers: **1** a black and white book **2** a purple pencil case **3** a pink crayon

Recycled vocabulary

- The pupils look at the number and say the word. Then they trace the first letter of the word.

Pupil's Book Activity 2

Values: Read and circle.

- The pupils look at the photo on the right. Read out the first sentence in the speech bubble and prompt the class to tell you which is the correct object to put in the bin.
- Explain the importance of keeping the classroom (and rooms at home) tidy.
- Encourage the pupils to think about how to keep places tidy and what they should put in the bin.

Answer: rubbish

Ending the lesson

Review the lesson.

- (Books closed.) Say **Today we've listened to a story about a dog.** Ask **What happened in the story?** Elicit the story from the pupils.
- Then say **Today you've learnt that we put rubbish in the bin and we keep the classroom tidy.**

Review the task flashcards.

- Point to the task flashcards on the board. Say **Look at the activities you've done today. Which activity was your favourite?** Elicit the pupils' favourite activities.

Key Competences and Key Learning Outcomes

- Name more classroom objects
- Use the prepositions *in, on* and *under*
- Give and follow instructions

- Understand the importance of keeping classroom equipment tidy (optional)

- Sing a song

Key language

- *bin, board, chair, cupboard, desk, shelf*
- *Let's tidy up!*
- *Put the (paper in the bin).*
- Extension: *bookcase, door, floor, window*

Recycled: *nine*

Recycled: *Put the (book) in / on / under the (desk).*

Materials

- Pupil's Book p12; Activity Book p9; Class CD1; Teacher's App on Navio
- Teacher's Resource Bank: Task flashcards: *listen, sing, think, Talk Partners, tick, read, draw*

Optional materials

- Teacher's Resource Bank: Five Trinity Exam Practice cards (selected from the Starter Unit).
- A ruler, a screwed-up piece of paper, a book
- A4 paper, scissors, coloured pencils or crayons

At a Glance Lesson Plan

Starting the lesson

- Use the Trinity Exam Practice cards (optional).
- Review the Lesson 3 story.
- Set learning outcomes using the task flashcards.

Vocabulary presentation

- Present the new vocabulary.

Activity 1

- Listen, point and say.

▶ *CD1 Track 16 p257*

Activity 2

- Listen and point.
- Sing *Let's tidy up.*

▶ *CD1 Track 17 p257*

Activity 3

- Listen and repeat.

▶ *CD1 Track 18 p257*

- Talk Partners Play a game.

Go to the Activity Book.

Pupil's Book

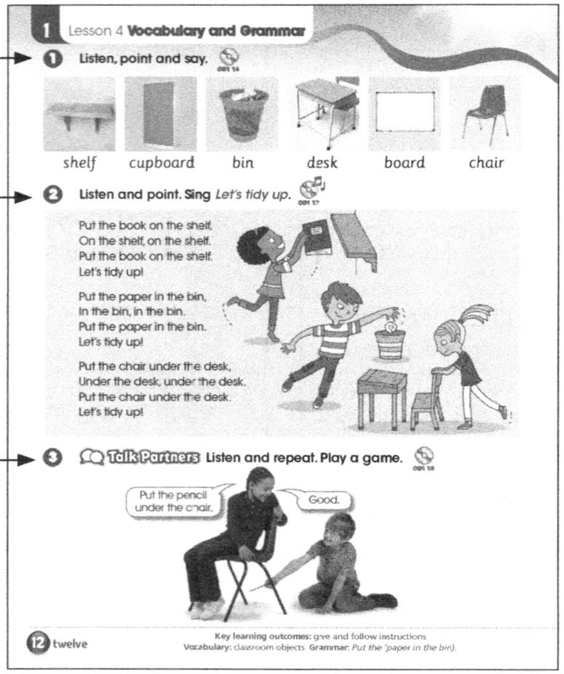

Ending the lesson

- Review the lesson.
- Review the task flashcards.

Extra activity

Vocabulary Extension

- Present four additional vocabulary items.

Link to Science

- **My school:** Review classroom equipment and materials and the importance of keeping them tidy.

Digital resources

Teacher's Digital: Don't forget you can teach this lesson using the Teacher's App on Navio.

Pupil's Digital: Encourage your pupils to use the Pupil's App on Navio to practise the vocabulary from this lesson.

Powered By NAVIO

Activity Book

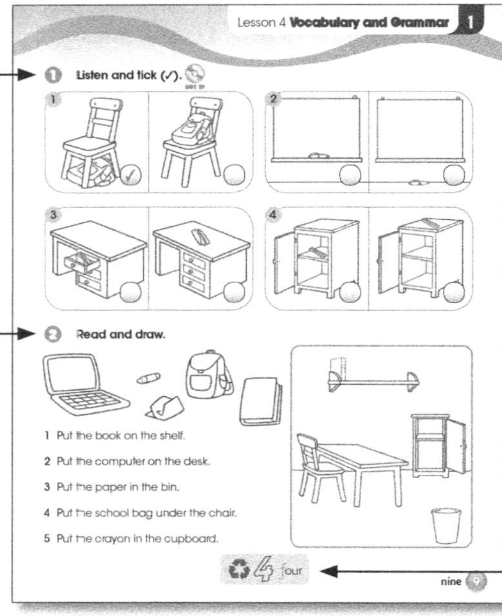

Activity Book

Activity 1

- Listen and tick (✓).

▶ *CD1 Track 19 p257*

Activity 2

- Read and draw.

Recycled vocabulary

- Look, say and trace the letter.

Detailed Lesson Plan

Starting the lesson

Use the Trinity Exam Practice cards (optional).
- The pupils practise asking and answering questions (see p31).

Review the Lesson 3 story.
- Give the pupils two minutes to look at the story. Then say **One, two, three, I can see a (pencil case). Where is it?** The pupils scan the story and point to the object. Repeat with other things in the story.

Set learning outcomes using the task flashcards.
- Say **Today we're going to learn some more classroom objects**.
- Hold up the task flashcards in turn and elicit the activities. Stick them on one side of the board. Point to them during the lesson to reinforce your instructions.

Vocabulary presentation

Present the new vocabulary.
- (Books open.) Point to the first photo and read the word. Ask **Is there a shelf in the classroom?** Ask a pupil to find a shelf.
- Repeat with the other photos on Pupil's Book page 12 (Activity 1).

Pupil's Book Activity 1

Listen, point and say.
▶ *CD1 Track 16 p257*
- (Books open.) Say **Let's listen and repeat the words.**
- Play the CD. The pupils repeat the words and point to the photos.

Pupil's Book Activity 2

Listen and point. Sing *Let's tidy up.*
▶ *CD1 Track 17 p257*
- Use classroom objects to introduce the prepositions 'on', 'in' and 'under'. Say **Put the (ruler) on the chair.** Show a pupil how to do this. Repeat with other actions.
- Place a book and a screwed up piece of paper on the floor, and move a chair away from a desk. Say **Oh dear. Let's tidy up.**
- Play the CD. The class listen and watch you tidy up. Invite three pupils to the front of the class.
- Play the CD again. These pupils do the actions while the rest of the class sing. Repeat.

Pupil's Book Activity 3

Listen and repeat. Play a game.
▶ *CD1 Track 18 p257*
- Play the CD. The pupils listen and repeat.
- The pupils take out their pencils and follow instructions. Say **Put the pencil on the desk. Put the pencil in the desk. Put the pencil under the desk.**
  Talk Partners The pupils practise giving and following instructions with a Talk Partner.

Activity Book

Activity 1
Listen and tick (✓).
▶ *CD1 Track 19 p257*
- (Books open.) The pupils say where the school bag is in the first pair of pictures.
- Play the CD, pausing after each conversation. The pupils listen and tick the correct picture.

Answers: **1** under the chair **2** on the board **3** on the desk **4** in the cupboard

Activity 2
Read and draw.
- Focus on the activity. Ask **What can you see?**
- Ask different pupils to read the instructions. Check comprehension.

- The pupils draw the five objects in the correct places in the picture.

Recycled vocabulary
- The pupils look at the number and say the word. Then they trace the first letter of the word.

Ending the lesson

Review the lesson.
- (Books closed.) Say **Today we've sung a song. What classroom objects were in the song?** Elicit the classroom objects from the pupils.

Review the task flashcards.
- Point to the task flashcards. Say **Look at the activities you've done today. Which activity was your favourite?** Elicit the pupils' favourite activities.

Extra activity

Vocabulary Extension
- Use the Vocabulary Booster on Navio and present and practise four additional words to describe classroom objects: *bookcase, door, floor, window.*
- Say instructions and the pupils do the actions.
- Play the game *Simon says* with the classroom instructions. Give an instruction to the class. If you say 'Simon says' before the action, the pupils do the action. However, if you don't say 'Simon says' before the action, they do nothing. Say **Simon says 'Stand up!'** The pupils stand up. Say **Sit down!** They remain standing.

Link to Science

- If you are studying the Science topic of **My school** in English, you could review the importance of a tidy classroom and identify classroom equipment and materials.
- Make classroom labels for the different materials and areas of the classroom. The pupils can colour and decorate these classroom labels for you.

Key Competences and Key Learning Outcomes

- Say a tongue twister with the 'r' sound
- Listen for specific information
- Play a communication game about classroom objects

Key language

- *Where's the (sharpener)? It's in / on / under the (desk).*

Recycled: *bin, board, chair, computer, cupboard, desk, pencil, school bag, sharpener, shelf; four*

Materials

- Pupil's Book p13; Activity Book p10; Class CD1; Teacher's App on Navio
- Teacher's Resource Bank: Task flashcards: *listen, say, match, cut out, Talk Partners, colour*
- Teacher's Resource Bank: Unit 1 Lesson 5 Activity 3 cut-outs
- Scissors and crayons or coloured pencils

Optional materials

- Teacher's Resource Bank: Five Trinity Exam Practice cards (selected from the Starter Unit)
- Different coloured paper

At a Glance Lesson Plan

Pupil's Book

Starting the lesson

- Use the Trinity Exam Practice cards (optional).
- Review the vocabulary from Lesson 4.
- Set learning outcomes using the task flashcards.

Activity 1

- Listen and say.

▶ *CD1 Track 20 p257*

Go to Magic Phonics.

Go to the Activity Book.

Activity 2

- Listen and match.

▶ *CD1 Track 21 p257*

Activity 3

- Make and play the game.

Talk Partners

Ending the lesson

- Review the lesson.
- Review the task flashcards.

Extra activity

Reinforcement

- Make a pronunciation wall display.

Activity Book

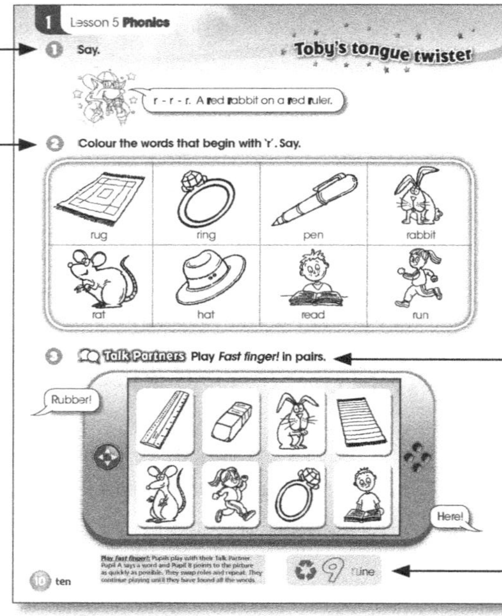

Activity Book

Activity 1

- Say.

Activity 2

- Colour the words that begin with 'r'. Say.

Go to Magic Phonics.

Activity 3

- Talk Partners

Play *Fast finger!* in pairs.

Recycled vocabulary

- Look, say and trace the letter.

Digital resources

Teacher's Digital: Don't forget you can teach this lesson using the Teacher's App on Navio.

Pupil's Digital: Encourage your pupils to use the Pupil's App on Navio to practise the vocabulary from this lesson.

Powered By NAVIO

Starting the lesson

Use the Trinity Exam Practice cards (optional).

- The pupils practise asking and answering questions (see p31).

Review the vocabulary from Lesson 4.

- Ask a pupil to come to the front of the class. Say **You are a robot. Put the (crayon) on the (desk).** The pupils moves like a robot and does the actions.
- Repeat with different pupils and the prepositions 'in' and 'under'.

Set learning outcomes using the task flashcards.

- Say **Today we're going to practise saying a tongue twister and make and play a speaking game.**
- Hold up the task flashcards in turn and elicit the activities. Stick them on one side of the board. Point to them during the lesson to reinforce your instructions.

Pupil's Book Activity 1

Listen and say.

▶ *CD1 Track 20 p257*

- (Books open.) Write the target 'r' sound on the board and say it. The pupils repeat.
- Say **It's time for Toby's tongue twister. What can you see here? Can you see a rabbit? What colour is the ruler?**
- Play the CD. The pupils listen and repeat the target sound, then the words and then the entire tongue twister, faster and faster.

Go to Magic Phonics.

Activity Book

Activity 1

Say.

- (Books open.) Read out the tongue twister for the pupils to repeat.
- The pupils say the tongue twister to their partner, saying it faster and faster each time.

Activity 2

Colour the words that begin with 'r'. Say.

- Ask the pupils to colour the words that begin with 'r'.
- The pupils say the words.

Answers: rug, ring, rabbit, rat, read, run

Go to Magic Phonics.

Activity 3

Play *Fast finger!* in pairs.

- Demonstrate the activity. Say a word and the pupils point to the picture representing the object as quickly as possible. Repeat with several words.

  Talk Partners The pupils take turns to play the game with a Talk Partner. One pupil says a word and the other needs to point to the picture representing that object as quickly as possible. They continue playing until they've found all the words in the game.

Recycled vocabulary

- The pupils look at the number and say the word. Then they trace the first letter of the word.

Pupil's Book Activity 2

Listen and match.

▶ *CD1 Track 21 p257*

- Focus the pupils on Activity 2. Ask **What can you see?**
- Play the CD, pausing after the first conversation so the pupils can match the classroom objects to the main picture.
- Play the rest of the CD. The pupils listen and match.

Answers: **1** in the cupboard **2** on the shelf
3 under the chair **4** under the desk

Pupil's Book Activity 3

Make and play the game.

- Focus the pupils on Activity 3. Tell the class that they are going to play the game.
- The pupils cut out and colour the cards and place them on their desk.
- Demonstrate the activity. A volunteer asks *Where's the (pencil)?* Answer the question **It's (on the desk)**. The pupils put the (pencil on the desk).
- Ask a pupil to take your part. The rest of the class asks him / her questions.

  Talk Partners The pupils play the game with a Talk Partner.

Ending the lesson

Review the lesson.

- (Books closed.) Say **Today we've practised a tongue twister.** Elicit the tongue twister from the pupils.

Review the task flashcards.

- Point to the task flashcards. Say **Look at the activities you've done today. Which activity was your favourite?** Elicit the pupils' favourite activities.

Extra activity

Reinforcement

- Make a pronunciation wall display. Cut out the letter 'r' in coloured paper. Stick it onto a piece of differently coloured paper to make a wall display. Elicit words that begin with that letter and write them on the wall display.
- Encourage the pupils to add new words beginning with the letter 'r' during the year. They can either tell you the new word for you to add or write the word themselves if they can.

Key Competences and Key Learning Outcomes

- Review school subjects (optional)
- Listen for general information
- Read about school assemblies in Britain
- Think about what you do at school

Key language

- *We sit on the floor. We listen to the head teacher. We play music. We sing songs. We clap our hands.*
- *floor, good work, school, assembly*

Recycled: *two*

Materials

- Pupil's Book p14; Activity Book p11; Class CD1; Teacher's App on Navio
- Teacher's Resource Bank: Task flashcards: *listen, read, think, number, tick, draw*

Optional materials

- Teacher's Resource Bank: Five Trinity Exam Practice cards (selected from the Starter Unit)
- A camera, pieces of A4 paper

At a Glance Lesson Plan

Starting the lesson

- Use the Trinity Exam Practice cards (optional).
- Talk Partners Review Toby's tongue twister.
- ▶ *CD1 Track 20 p257*
- Set learning outcomes using the task flashcards.

Activity 1

- Listen and read.
- ▶ *CD1 Track 22 p257*
- Answer.

Think about your culture

- What do you do every day at school?

Go to the Activity Book.

Pupil's Book

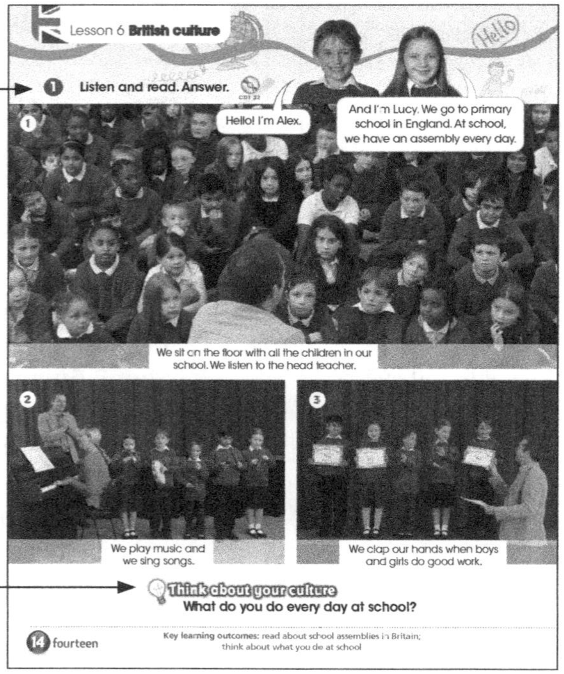

Ending the lesson

- Review the lesson.
- Review the task flashcards.

Extra activities

Reinforcement

- Play an assembly game.

Extension

- Make a class wall display.

Cooperative learning

Developing a positive classroom atmosphere

- Set up an assembly in the classroom.

Link to Science

- **School subjects:** Review school subjects.

Digital resources

Teacher's Digital: Don't forget you can teach this lesson using the Teacher's App on Navio.

Powered By NAVIO

Activity Book

Activity Book

Activity 1

- Listen and number.
- ▶ *CD1 Track 23 p257*
- Say.

Activity 2: Think about your culture

- Read and tick (✓).
- Draw and say.

Recycled vocabulary

- Look, say and trace the letter.

Starting the lesson

Use the Trinity Exam Practice cards (optional).

- The pupils practise asking and answering questions (see p31).

Review Toby's tongue twister.

▶ *CD1 Track 20 p257*

- Ask **What sound did you practise in Toby's tongue twister? Can you remember the tongue twister?** (*A red rabbit on a red ruler.*)
- Play the CD. Practise the tongue twister as a class. **Talk Partners** The pupils practise saying the tongue twister as fast as possible with a Talk Partner. Choose a fast pair to say it for the class.

Set learning outcomes using the task flashcards.

- Say **Today we're going to learn about assemblies in Britain.**
- Hold up the task flashcards in turn and elicit the activities. Stick them on one side of the board. Point to them during the lesson to reinforce your instructions.

Pupil's Book Activity 1

Listen and read. Answer.

▶ *CD1 Track 22 p257*

- (Books open.) Focus attention on the photos at the top of the page and ask **What can you see?** *(A boy and girl.)* Say **Their names are Alex and Lucy. They are ready for school.** Focus the class on the other photos and ask **What can you see?** Then say **Let's read and listen.**
- Play the CD. Pause the CD after the first piece of information. Ask **Do Alex and Lucy sit on a chair in assembly?** *(No.)* **Do they sit on the floor?** *(Yes.)* Highlight that the whole school sits on the floor in assembly every morning. Repeat with the other photos, pausing to check comprehension each time.
- Ask the pupils to mime the actions to show they understand.

Pupil's Book Think about your culture

What do you do every day at school?

- Read out the question. The pupils answer.
- Ask questions, e.g. **Do you have an assembly every day? Do you (sing songs / sit on the floor / play music)? Do you listen to the head teacher?**

Activity Book

Activity 1

Listen and number. Say.

▶ *CD1 Track 23 p257*

- (Books open.) Tell the pupils they are going to listen to a teacher and children in a school assembly.
- Play the CD, pausing after the first section. Ask **What do the children do?** The pupils point to the correct box.
- Repeat with all four sections of the audio. The pupils write the numbers in the correct boxes.

Answers: **1** We listen to the head teacher. **2** We clap our hands. **3** We sing songs. **4** We play music.

Activity 2: Think about your culture

Read and tick (✓). Draw and say.

- Read out the question in the speech bubble. Elicit the pupils' answers.
- Read the four sentences. The pupils tick the things they do at school.
- The pupils draw themselves doing one of the actions.
- Invite different pupils to show the class their drawings and say what they do.

Recycled vocabulary

- The pupils look at the number and say the word. Then they trace the first letter of the word.

Ending the lesson

Review the lesson.

- (Books closed.) Say **Today we've talked about what you do at school. What do you remember?** Elicit the activities from the pupils.

Review the task flashcards.

- Point to the task flashcards. Say **Look at the activities you've done today. Which activity was your favourite?** Elicit the pupils' favourite activities.

Extra activities

Reinforcement

- Say **Let's play an assembly game.** Say **Sit on the floor.** Prompt the children to do the action. Repeat the procedure with the other actions: **Listen to a story. Sing a song. Play music. Think. Clap your hands.** Repeat the instructions in a random order. The pupils listen and do the action each time.

Extension

- Work together as a class to make a display of what the pupils do at school. Take photos of the pupils doing daily tasks and stick them on a piece of paper. Display the photos.
- The pupils take turns to point to the photos and say what activities they do at school, for example *I sing songs. I write. I speak English.*

Cooperative learning

Developing a positive classroom atmosphere

- Set up an assembly in the classroom to develop a positive classroom atmosphere. Decide what activities to do in the assembly such as reading a book, singing a song or playing music.
- The pupils sit on the floor in a circle. Ask the pupils to perform the activities.
- Praise good behaviour. Remind the pupils that they should listen when somebody is speaking.

Link to Science

- If you are studying the Science topic of **My school** in English, you could review the different subjects (Music, Science, Art and PE) and activities (read, write, draw, sing, think, speak English) that they do at school.

Key Competences and Key Learning Outcomes

- Review how to line up correctly (optional)

- Read and understand a classroom rules poster
- Think about good behaviour in the classroom and class rules

Key language

- *poster, rules*
- *Listen to others. Put your hand up to speak. Work quietly. Sit down on your chair. Walk in the classroom. Tidy up your things.*

Recycled: *ten*

Materials

- Pupil's Book p15; Activity Book p12; Class CD1; Teacher's App on Navio
- Teacher's Resource Bank: Task flashcards: *think, circle, listen, read, number, colour*

Optional materials

- Teacher's Resource Bank: Five Trinity Exam Practice cards (selected from the Starter Unit)

At a Glance Lesson Plan

Starting the lesson

- Use the Trinity Exam Practice cards (optional).
- Review the culture lesson.
- Set learning outcomes using the task flashcards.

Before you read

- Talk about good behaviour.

Activity 1

- Who are the good children?
- Circle.

Activity 2

- Listen and read the classroom poster.

▶ *CD1 Track 24 p257*

After you read

Go to page 12 in your Activity Book.

Pupil's Book

Ending the lesson

- Review the lesson.
- Review the task flashcards.

Extra activities

Extension

- Decide on the most important class rule.
- Make a classroom poster.

Cooperative learning

Behaving well in class

- Talk about rules.

Link to Science

- **My school:** Review how to line up correctly.

Activity Book

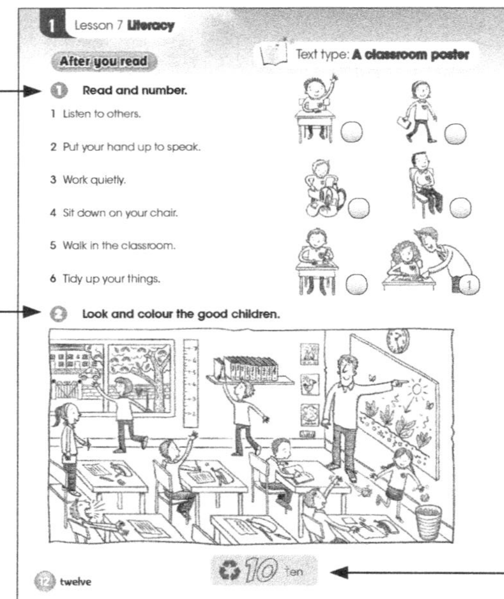

Activity Book

After you read: Activity 1

- Read and number.

Activity 2

- Look and colour the good children.

Recycled vocabulary

- Look, say and trace the letter.

Digital resources

Teacher's Digital: Don't forget you can teach this lesson using the Teacher's App on Navio.

Pupil's Digital: Encourage your pupils to use the Pupil's App on Navio to practise the vocabulary from this lesson.

Powered By NAVIO

Detailed Lesson Plan

Starting the lesson

Use the Trinity Exam Practice cards (optional).
- The pupils practise asking and answering questions (see p31).

Review the culture lesson.
- Review the actions that British children do in an assembly. Use mime to elicit the different activities. (*Listen to the head teacher. Sing songs. Play music. Clap our hands.*)
- Repeat the instructions. The pupils listen and do the actions.

Set learning outcomes using the task flashcards.
- Say **Today we're going to read a classroom poster.**
- Hold up the task flashcards in turn and elicit the activities. Stick them on one side of the board. Point to them during the lesson to reinforce your instructions.

Before you read

Talk about good behaviour.
- Ask the children to give examples of good behaviour (being polite, listening to others, following rules, etc.).

Pupil's Book Activity 1

Who are the good children? Circle.
- (Books open.) Point to an illustration and say **Look at the boys and girls. Where are they?** (*In the classroom.*) Point to the first picture and ask **Is this good (behaviour) or bad (behaviour) in the classroom?** (*Good.*) Say **Yes, it's good. Is the teacher happy with this (boy)?** (*Yes.*) Repeat with the other illustrations, prompting the pupils to say 'good' or 'bad' each time.
- The pupils circle the good children.

Answers: first, third and sixth pictures

Pupil's Book Activity 2

Listen and read the classroom poster.

▶ *CD1 Track 24 p257*
- Focus the class on the poster and say **Here are the class rules.** Explain that the rules tell the pupils what is good (behaviour) in the class. Ask **How many rules are on the poster?** (*Six.*)
- Play the CD. The pupils listen and read.
- Play the CD again, pausing after each class rule. The pupils point to the corresponding illustrations.
- Ask different pupils to read the rules. Encourage the pupils to do the actions.

Activity Book

After you read: Activity 1

Read and number.
- (Books open.) Read the first classroom rule. Ask **What's the picture?**
- Repeat with all the rules.
- The pupils read and write the numbers.

Answers: **1** sixth picture **2** first picture **3** fifth picture **4** fourth picture **5** second picture **6** third picture

Activity 2

Look and colour the good children.
- Focus the pupils on Activity 2. The pupils look and colour the six good children.
- Circulate, helping where necessary.

Answers: Boy with hand up / Boy working quietly / Boy sitting on his chair / Boy listening to the teacher / Girl putting rubbish in the bin / Boy putting a book on the shelf

Recycled vocabulary
- The pupils look at the number and say the word. Then they trace the first letter of the word.

Ending the lesson

Review the lesson.
- (Books closed.) Say **Today we've read a classroom poster in English. What did it say?** Elicit the class rules from the pupils.

Review the task flashcards.
- Point to the task flashcards. Say **Look at the activities you've done today. Which activity was your favourite?** Elicit the pupils' favourite activities.

Extra activities

Extension
- Have a class discussion about which class rule the pupils think is the most important, and why.
- Write the most important classroom rules they say on the board.
- The pupils make a classroom poster of good behaviour, drawing pictures to illustrate the rules.

Cooperative learning

Behaving well in class
- Ask the pupils if class rules are a good idea. Explain that rules are important for children to work together and learn.

Link to Science

- If you are studying the Science topic of **My school** in English, you could review how to line up correctly.
- Practise lining up quickly and quietly with the class. Repeat the language that they know (*Line up. One behind the other. Hands down. Mouth closed. Don't push.*) Ask five different pupils to line up each time and at the end of the activity decide which group lined up the best.

Key Competences and Key Learning Outcomes

- Review language in the unit
- Reflect on own learning
- Sing a cooperative learning song

Key language

Recycled: *book, computer, crayon, pen, pencil, pencil case, rubber, ruler, sharpener, school bag; bin, board, chair, cupboard, desk, shelf; three*

Recycled: *Where's my (book)? The (rubber) is in / on / under the (chair).*

Materials

- Pupil's Book p16; Activity Book p13; Class CD1; Teacher's App on Navio
- Classroom objects flashcards
- Teacher's Resource Bank: Task flashcards: *listen, number, read, sing, stick, draw, match, think*
- Teacher's Resource Bank: Traffic light cut-out
- *Give Me Five!* sticker

Optional materials

- Teacher's Resource Bank: Five Trinity Exam Practice cards (selected from the Starter Unit)

At a Glance Lesson Plan

Starting the lesson

- Use the Trinity Exam Practice cards (optional).
- Review the unit vocabulary.
- Set learning outcomes using the task flashcards.

Activity 1

- Listen and number.
- ▶ ***CD1 Track 25 p258***
- Say.

Activity 2

- Look, read and circle.

Activity 3 Cooperative learning

- Sing *Well done!*
- ▶ ***CD1 Track 26 p258***

Stick the *Give Me Five!* sticker.

Go to the Activity Book.

Pupil's Book

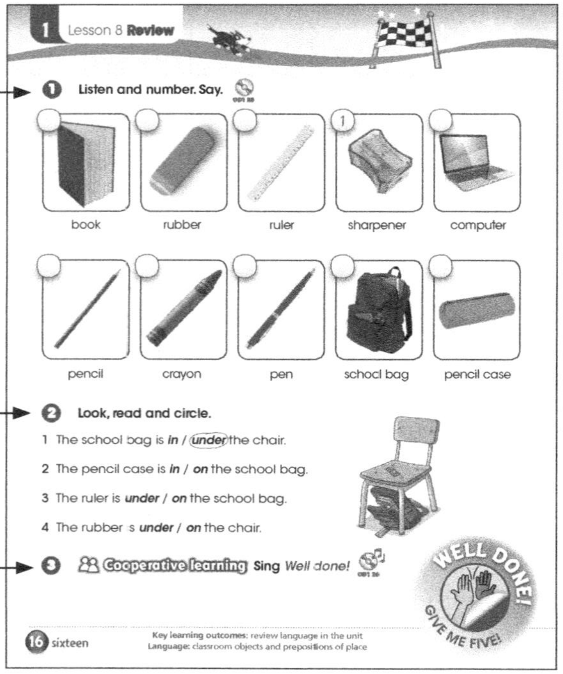

Ending the lesson

- Review the task flashcards.

Activity Book

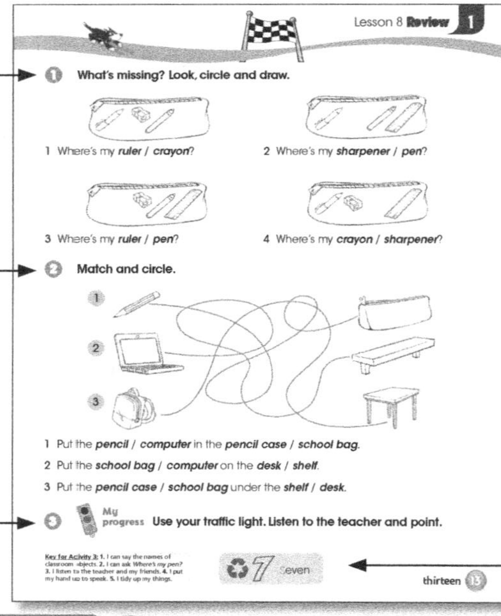

Activity Book

Activity 1

- What's missing?
- Look, circle and draw.

Activity 2

- Match and circle.

Activity 3 My progress

- Use your traffic light. Listen to the teacher and point.

Recycled vocabulary

- Look,say and trace the letter.

Digital resources

Teacher's Digital: Don't forget you can teach this lesson using the Teacher's App on Navio.

Pupil's Digital: Encourage your pupils to use the Pupil's App on Navio to practise the vocabulary from this lesson.

Powered By NAVIO

Detailed Lesson Plan

Starting the lesson

Use the Trinity Exam Practice cards (optional).
- The pupils practise asking and answering questions (see p31).

Review the unit vocabulary.
- Hold up a classroom objects flashcard and elicit the word. Stick the flashcards face down on the board. Repeat until all the flashcards are on the board.
- Ask **Where's the (ruler)?** Ask a pupil to turn over one of the flashcards. If it's the correct flashcard, he/she says *It's here*. If it isn't the correct flashcard, another pupil has a go. Repeat with different words.
- Variation: Play the game in two teams. The teams take it in turns to remember the classroom objects.

Set learning outcomes using the task flashcards.
- Say **Today we're going to remember what we've learnt in Unit 1.**
- Hold up the task flashcards in turn and elicit the activities. Stick them on one side of the board. Point to them during the lesson to reinforce your instructions.

Pupil's Book Activity 1

Listen and number. Say.
▶ *CD1 Track 25 p258*
- (Books open.) Point to the pictures and ask different pupils to name the classroom objects.
- Play the CD, pausing after each conversation. The pupils point to the object.
- Play the CD again. The pupils write the correct number for each picture.
- The pupils say the words under each picture.

Answers: **1** sharpener **2** book **3** pencil **4** rubber **5** pen **6** ruler **7** school bag **8** pencil case **9** crayon **10** computer

Pupil's Book Activity 2

Look, read and circle.
- Focus the pupils on the picture in Activity 2. Ask **What can you see? Where's the (rubber)?**
- Read out the sentences, saying both prepositions, and elicit the correct word.
- The pupils circle the correct prepositions.

Answers: **1** under **2** in **3** under **4** on

Pupil's Book Activity 3: Cooperative learning

Sing *Well done!*
▶ *CD1 Track 26 p258*
- Praise the pupils for their hard work and play the *Well done!* song. The pupils sing and do the actions.

Stick the *Give Me Five!* sticker.
- The pupils stick the *Give Me Five!* sticker on the Pupil's Book page.
- Variation: Sing the *Well done!* song and stick the *Give Me Five!* sticker after the pupils have also completed the Activity Book Lesson 8 Review.

Activity Book

Activity 1

What's missing? Look, circle and draw.
- (Books open.) Elicit what's missing from each pencil case.
- Read out the questions with both objects and elicit the correct classroom object.
- The pupils draw the objects and circle the correct word in each question.

Answers: **1** ruler **2** sharpener **3** pen **4** crayon

Activity 2

Match and circle.
- Focus the pupils on Activity 2. Ask **Where do I put the pencil?**
- The pupils follow the lines to match the objects. They circle the correct objects in each sentence.

Answers: **1** pencil / pencil case **2** computer / shelf **3** school bag / desk

Activity 3: My progress

My progress

Use your traffic light. Listen to the teacher and point.
- (Books closed.) Ask the pupils to take out their traffic light cut-out. Say **Let's think about our work in this unit.** Point to the green circle, nod your head, smile a lot, and say **I can ask *Where's my (pen):* Yes, I can do this very well.** Point to the yellow circle, move your head a little, smile a little and say **Yes, I can do this.** Then point to the red circle, shake your head and say **No, I can't do this.**
- Read the different statements. For each one, the pupils point to the colour on their traffic light that shows how they feel about their own learning.

Self-assessment statements
1. I can say the names of the classroom objects.
2. I can ask *Where's my pen?*
3. I listen to the teacher and my friends.
4. I put my hand up to speak.
5. I tidy up my things.

Recycled vocabulary
- The pupils look at the number and say the word. Then they trace the first letter of the word.

Ending the lesson

Review the task flashcards.
- Point to the task flashcards. Say **Look at the activities you've done today. Which activity was your favourite?** Elicit the pupils' favourite activities.

Key Competences and Key Learning Outcomes

- Watch and understand a video about what children do at school
- Identify what's in your school bag
- Understand the importance of being organised

Key language

- *ball, book, box, classroom, desk, pencil case, ruler, run, school bag, sing songs, snack, water*

Materials

- Pupil's Book p17; Activity Book p14; Class CD1; Video; Teacher's App on Navio
- Teacher's Resource Bank: Task flashcards: *number, listen, Talk Partners, draw, think, say, tick, circle*
- Classroom objects flashcards

Optional materials

- Teacher's Resource Bank: Trinity Exam Practice cards (selected from Unit 1)

At a Glance Lesson Plan

Starting the lesson

- Use the Trinity Exam Practice cards (optional).
- **Think-Pair-Share** Review school rules.
- Set learning outcomes and use the task flashcards.

Pre-watching activity

- Play *Here!* to review classroom objects.
- Look at the photo and talk about what the pupils do at school.

Activity 1

- Watch the video.
  Unit 1 video p277
- Number the pictures.

Activity 2

- Watch the video again.
  Unit 1 video
- Read and tick (✓) or cross (✗).

Pupil's Book

Activity 3

- Read and circle.
- Go to the Activity Book.

Ending the lesson

- Review the lesson.
- Review the task flashcards. Elicit the pupils' favourite activities at school.

Extra activity

- Pupils make a daily tick chart to remind them what to put in their school bag.

Cooperative learning

- Talk about being organised.

Activity Book

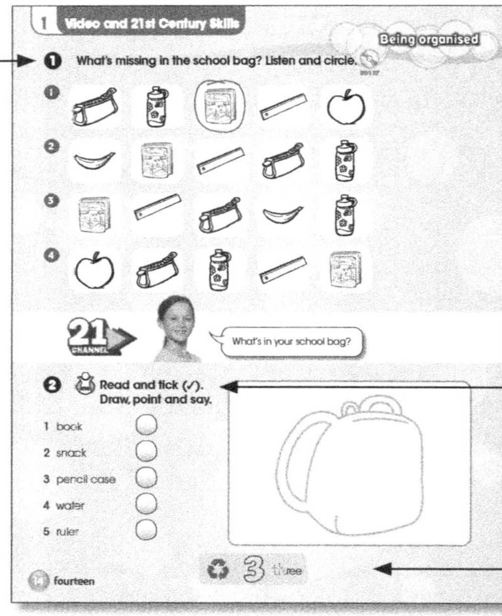

Activity Book

Activity 1

- What's missing in the school bag? Listen and circle.
- ▶ *CD1 Track 27 p258*

Activity 2

- Read and tick (✓). Draw, point and say.

Recycled vocabulary

- Look, say and trace the letters.

Digital resources

Teacher's Digital: Don't forget you can teach this lesson using the Teacher's App on Navio.

Pupil's Digital: Encourage your pupils to use the Pupil's App on Navio to practise the vocabulary from this lesson.

Powered By NAVIO

Detailed Lesson Plan

Starting the lesson

Use the Trinity Exam Practice cards (optional).

- The pupils practise asking and answering questions.
  Think-Pair-Share Review class rules.
- Ask **Can you remember the six class rules?**
  Talk Partners The pupils work with a Talk Partner to name the rules. Invite different Talk Partners to say a different rule. Write the rule on the board.

Set learning outcomes and use the task flashcards.

- Say **Today we're going to watch a video and then ask and answer questions about school**.
- Explain to pupils that each video will cover a different topic. Point to the task flashcards throughout to elicit activities and reinforce your instructions.

Pre-watching activity

- Play *Here!* with the classroom objects flashcards (see p23).
- Look at the photo of Abby, Sophie and Tom and explain that these are the presenters of Channel 21. Ask **What do you do at school?** Elicit responses.

Pupil's Book Activity 1

Watch the video. Number the pictures? *p277*

- Ask **What is the video about?** Play Part 1, pausing after Sophie says, *Today's programme is about our school*.
- Ask **Where are the children? What are they doing? What can you see?** Then say **Let's watch and listen.**
- Play Part 2 of the video pausing after the first video still. Ask the pupils to point to the corresponding photo in their book.
- Play the rest of Part 2 for pupils to write the numbers in order of the photos.
- Ask **What do Sophie and Tom do at school? What do they take to school?**

Answers: 3, 2 ,4, 1

Pupil's Book Activity 2

Watch the video again. Read and tick (✓) or cross (✗).

- Play Part 2 again. Pause after Sophie says, *This is our classroom*. Read out the first sentence in Activity 2. Ask **Is the desk green?** Show the tick in the circle.
- Play Part 2. Pupils tick or cross the sentences.
- Ask general questions to check understanding.
  When do the children put their hands up? *(To speak.)*
  What do the children do at home time? *(Tidy the classroom.)*
  Is Sophie ready for school? *(Yes.)* **Why?** *(Her things are in her school bag.)*
  Is Tom ready for school? *(No.)* **Why not?** *(His things aren't in his school bag.)*

Answers: **1** ✓ **2** ✓ **3** ✗ **4** ✗

Pupil's Book Activity 3

Read and circle.

- Point to the pictures to elicit the vocabulary.
- Read out number one, including the circled word.
- The pupils read the other sentences and circle the words.
  Think-Pair-Share Ask **Why is it important to prepare your school bag? When do you prepare your school bag? Who prepares your school bag?**

Answers: **1** ruler **2** pencil case **3** book **4** snack

Activity Book

Activity 1

What's missing in the school bag? Listen and circle.

▶ *CD1 Track 27 p258*

- Ask **What can you see?**
- Play the first exchange on the CD. Ask **What's missing?** Play the rest of the CD, pausing for pupils to circle the missing object.

Answers: **1** book **2** water **3** ruler **4** pencil case

Activity 2

Read and tick (✓). Draw, point and say.

- Ask a few pupils **What's in your school bag?** The pupils tick the things they have got in their school bag and then draw them.
  Talk Partners In pairs, pupils take turns to ask and answer What's in your school bag?

Recycled vocabulary

- The pupils look at the number and say the word. Then they trace the first two letters of the word.

Ending the lesson

Review the lesson.

- Ask **Which activity was easy / difficult?**

Review the task flashcards.

- Say **Look at the activities you've done today. Which activity was your favourite?**

Extra activity

Extension

- On the board draw a table with five columns. Number the columns one to five, and tell the pupils that one is Monday, two is Tuesday, etc.
- Ask the pupils to copy the table into their notebooks. In the first column, tell them to draw a list of things they have to put in their school bag on Monday. Tell them to do the same for the other four days.
- Explain that every day they check their list and tick the things they put in their school bag.

Cooperative learning

Being organised

- Ask the pupils to tell you other times that it's important to be organised. For example, keeping the classroom tidy, doing their homework or packing a suitcase for a holiday.

Date: ____________________ Unit: __________

1 What did my pupils learn in this unit?

2 How did my pupils work? (✓)

individually ☐ in pairs ☐ in small groups ☐

in large groups ☐ as a class ☐

3 Which key competences did my pupils develop?

- Competence in linguistic communication ☐
- Competence in mathematics, science and technology ☐
- Digital competence ☐
- Learning to learn ☐
- Social and civic competences ☐
- Sense of initiative and entrepreneurship ☐
- Cultural awareness and expression ☐

4 Which lessons / activities were the most successful and why?

5 Which lessons / activities did my pupils find the most difficult and why?

6 What did I try in the classroom for the first time? How did it go?

7 Which resources did I find most useful? (including webpages)

8 What could I do differently next time I teach this unit?

Unit 2

Happy birthday!

Unit overview

Key Competences and Key Learning Outcomes

- Identify and say ten toys (Lesson 1)
- Say the vocabulary chant (Lesson 1)
- Use *What is it?*, *Is it a …?*, *Yes, it is.* / *No, it isn't.* in a conversation (Lesson 2)
- Ask and answer questions about favourite toys (Lesson 4)
- Describe your favourite toy (Lesson 4)
- Watch and understand a video about ranking favourite toys (Video and 21st Century Skills)

- Understand why forms of transport go fast or slow (Lesson 3)
- Order things (Video and 21st Century Skills)

- Use the Pupil's App on Navio

- Practise spelling (Lesson 1)
- Say a tongue twister to practise the 's' sound (Lesson 5)
- Review language in the unit and reflect on own learning (Lesson 8)
- Practise activity types found in the Cambridge English Young Learners Exams: Pre A1 Starters

- Understand the importance of saying 'thank you' (Lesson 3)
- Understand the importance of sharing (Lesson 5)

- Work with a Talk Partner to practise and reinforce learning (all lessons)
- Play a communication game about toys (Lesson 5)

- Sing four songs (Lessons 1, 4, 5, and 8)
- Understand and act out a story (Lesson 3)
- Read about birthday parties in Britain (Lesson 6)
- Think about your birthday party (Lesson 6)
- Read, understand and design a birthday card (Lesson 7)

Vocabulary

Core vocabulary
ball, car, computer game, dinosaur, doll, kite, robot, scooter, teddy, train; big, fast, new, old, slow, small

Extension vocabulary (optional)
bat (i.e. sports equipment), *board game, boat, football, monster, skateboard; loud, quiet, long, short*

Other vocabulary
balloons, birthday cake, birthday card, candles, costume, fancy dress, party, party games, present; wheels; To … , Lots of love … , From …

Recycled vocabulary
numbers 1–10; colours; *book, computer, crayon, pen, pencil, pencil case, rubber, ruler, school bag, sharpener*

Structures

Core structures
What is it? Is it a (bike)? Yes, it is. No, it isn't.
What's your favourite toy? My favourite toy is a (ball). It's (old).
My favourite toy is (old).
My (scooter) is (slow).

Other structures
Happy birthday. Here's (a present for you). It's a fantastic present. Thank you (for my present). I've got a (birthday cake). I have (a party). I play (party games). I wear (fancy dress). How old are you? I'm (six). What is it? It's a (motor). It's (good fun).

Recycled structures
It's (red). Put (the car) (in the cupboard).

Phonics

Consonant sound 's' (**s**ix, **s**nake**s**, **s**low, **s**cooter)

British Culture

Birthday parties

Literacy

Text type: a birthday card (text to express)
Reading skills: using pictures; reading for specific information

21st Century Skills

Ways of thinking: learn to order your favourite things

Cooperative learning

Songs: *Sharing is a good thing to do* (Lesson 5); *Well done!* (Lesson 8)
Skills: Working together and supporting each other (Lesson 1); Listening to others (Lesson 2); Developing a positive classroom atmosphere (Lesson 4, Lesson 7)

Values

The importance of saying 'thank you' when you receive a present or when someone helps you

Cross-curricular links

Link to Science

The Senses: using adjectives to describe touch (*hard, soft, rough, smooth*), sight (*colours*) and sounds (*loud, quiet*)

Suggested Arts and Crafts concepts

Patterns: identifying patterns in Art and in the environment; using lines, shapes and colours to create patterns

Key Competences and Key Learning Outcomes

- Identify and say ten toys
- Say the vocabulary chant
- Stick the toys stickers

- Practise spelling

- Sing a song about a birthday present

Key language
- *ball, car, computer game, dinosaur, doll, kite, robot, scooter, teddy, train*
- *Happy birthday! Here's a present (for you). Is it a (ball)?*
- Extension: *bat* (i.e. sports equipments), *board game, boat, football, monster, skateboard*

Recycled: classroom objects; colours

Materials
- Pupil's Book p18; Activity Book pp16 and 25; Class CD1; Teacher's App on Navio
- Toys flashcards; Unit 2 stickers
- Teacher's Resource Bank: Toys word cards
- Teacher's Resource Bank: Task flashcards: *listen, sing, read, match, stick, say, find, colour, circle, Talk Partners*
- Crayons or coloured pencils

Optional materials
- Teacher's Resource Bank: Five Trinity Exam Practice cards (selected from the Starter Unit and Unit 1)
- A selection of real toys and a (non-transparent) 'feely' bag
- A scarf

At a Glance Lesson Plan

Pupil's Book

Starting the lesson
- Use the Trinity Exam Practice cards (optional).
- Review colours and classroom objects.
- Set learning outcomes using the task flashcards.

Vocabulary presentation
- Present the new vocabulary.

Activity 1
- Listen and point.
- ▶ *CD1 Track 28 p258*
- Sing *Happy birthday!*

Word cards
- Read the word cards.
- Match them to the flashcards.

Activity 2
- Read and stick the ten stickers.
- Listen and say the chant.
- ▶ *CD1 Track 30 p258*

Go to the Activity Book.

Ending the lesson
- Review the lesson.
- Review the task flashcards.

Extra activities

Reinforcement
- Play *What toy is it?*

Vocabulary Extension
- Present six additional vocabulary items.

Cooperative learning

Working together and supporting each other
- Talk Partners Ask and answer *What's this?*

Learning to learn

Spelling
- Practise spelling at any time during this unit (Activity Book p25).

Digital resources

Teacher's Digital: Don't forget you can teach this lesson using the Teacher's App on Navio.

Pupil's Digital: Encourage your pupils to use the Pupil's App on Navio to practise the vocabulary from this lesson.

Powered By NAVIO

Activity Book

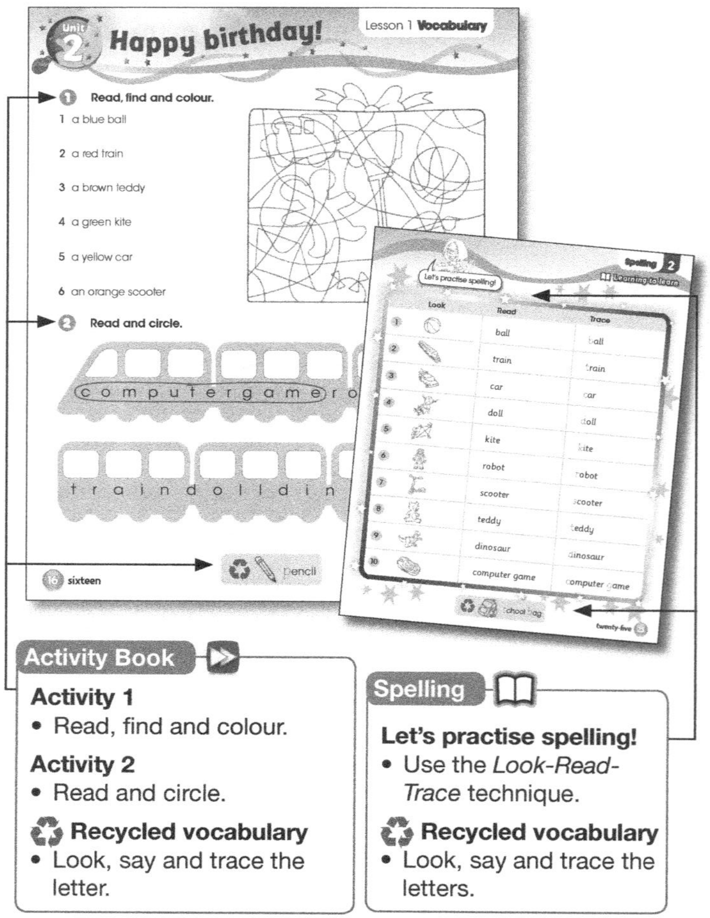

Activity Book

Activity 1
- Read, find and colour.

Activity 2
- Read and circle.

Recycled vocabulary
- Look, say and trace the letter.

Spelling

Let's practise spelling!
- Use the *Look-Read-Trace* technique.

Recycled vocabulary
- Look, say and trace the letters.

Detailed Lesson Plan

Starting the lesson

Use the Trinity Exam Practice cards (optional).
- The pupils practise asking and answering questions (see p31).

Review colours and classroom objects.
- Say **A (blue crayon). A (blue crayon). One, two, three … Show it to me!** Any pupil who has that object should hold it up. Repeat with other colours and classroom objects.

Set learning outcomes using the task flashcards.
- Say **Today we're going to learn the names of toys.**
- Hold up the task flashcards in turn and elicit the activities. Stick them on one side of the board. Point to them during the lesson to reinforce your instructions.

Vocabulary presentation

Present the new vocabulary.
- (Books closed.) Draw a large cupboard on the board. Say **This is a toy cupboard.** Ask **What's in the cupboard?**
- Play *Slowly, slowly* to introduce the toys flashcards (see p23). Then stick the flashcards inside the cupboard.
- Point to each flashcard in turn. Say the words together.

Pupil's Book Activity 1

Listen and point. Sing *Happy birthday!*

▶ *CD1 Track 28 p258*
- (Books open.) Say **It's Beth's birthday. How old is she? What colour is her present?** Elicit the toys the pupils can see.
- Play the CD. The pupils listen and point to the toys.
- Play the CD again. The pupils sing and do the actions.
- Ask **What is the present?** Elicit ideas.

Word cards

Read the word cards. Match them to the flashcards.
- (Books closed.) Hold up the toys word cards in turn, and say or elicit each word.
- Different pupils come to the front and stick the word cards with the corresponding flashcards.

Pupil's Book Activity 2

Read and stick the ten stickers. Listen and say the chant.

▶ *CD1 Track 30 p258*
- (Books open.) Ask a pupil to read the first toy word. The pupils stick the corresponding sticker. Repeat with the other stickers.
- Play the CD. The pupils listen and say the chant, pointing to the stickers in turn.

Activity Book

Activity 1

Read, find and colour.
- Ask different pupils to read out the phrases. The pupils find and colour each toy.

Activity 2

Read and circle.
- Ask a pupil to find one of the toys in the text. Tell the class to circle the word.
- The pupils find and circle the rest of the words in the trains.

Answers: **1** computer game **2** robot **3** car **4** train **5** doll **6** dinosaur

Recycled vocabulary
- The pupils look at the picture and say the word. Then they trace the first letter.

Ending the lesson

Review the lesson.
- (Books closed.) Say **Today we've learnt the names of toys. What toys do you know?** Elicit the toys.

Review the task flashcards.
- Point to the task flashcards. Say **Look at the activities you've done today. Which activity was your favourite?** Elicit the pupils' favourite activities.

Extra activities

Reinforcement
- Take out your 'feely' bag with real toys inside. Invite a pupil to come to the front and blindfold him / her. Put one of the toys in his / her hands. Ask **What toy is it?** The pupil guesses using *Is it a …?*
- Repeat with different pupils and toys.

Vocabulary Extension
- Use the Vocabulary Booster on Navio to present and practise six additional words: *bat* (i.e. sports equipment), *board game, boat, football, monster, skateboard*

Cooperative learning

Working together and supporting each other

Talk Partners Pupil A checks the learning of Pupil B by pointing to a toy sticker and asking *What's this?* Pupil B answers using *It's a …* If Pupil B can't remember, Pupil A helps him / her.
- When Pupil B has named the ten toys, they swap roles.

Spelling (Activity Book page 25)

Let's practise spelling!
- The pupils can practise spelling the ten toys using the *Look-Read-Trace* technique at any time during this unit before the Lesson 8 Review.

Recycled vocabulary
- The pupils look at the picture and say the word. Then they trace the first letters of each word.

Key Competences and Key Learning Outcomes

- Use *What is it?*, *Is it a …?*, *Yes, it is. / No, it isn't.*
- Complete and practise a conversation
- Listen for specific information

Key language

- *What is it? Is it a (bike)? Yes, it is. / No, it isn't. It's a fantastic present. Thank you.*

Recycled: *ball, car, computer game, dinosaur, doll, kite, robot, scooter, teddy, train; ruler*

Materials

- Pupil's Book p19; Activity Book p17; Class CD1; Teacher's App on Navio
- Toys flashcards
- Teacher's Resource Bank: Task flashcards: *listen, act out, find, circle, read, follow, draw, Talk Partners*

Optional materials

- Teacher's Resource Bank: Five Trinity Exam Practice cards (selected from the Starter Unit and Unit 1)

At a Glance Lesson Plan

Starting the lesson

- Use the Trinity Exam Practice cards (optional).
- **Think-Pair-Share** Review the toys.
- Review the *Happy birthday!* song.
- ▶ ***CD1 Track 28 p258***
- ▶ ***CD1 Track 29 p258 (optional karaoke version)***
- Set learning outcomes using the task flashcards.

Activity 1

- Listen and repeat.
- ▶ ***CD1 Track 31 p258***
- Act out.

Activity 2

- Listen and circle.
- ▶ ***CD1 Track 32 p258***
- Go to the Activity Book.

Pupil's Book

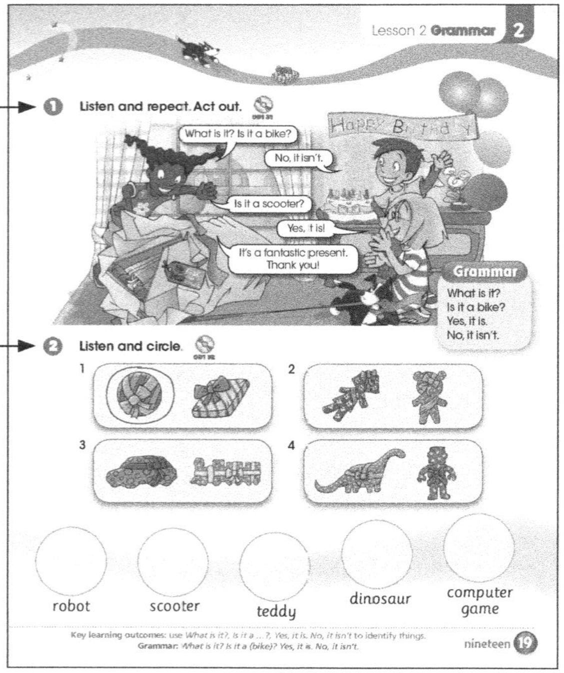

Ending the lesson

- Review the lesson.
- Review the task flashcards.

Cooperative learning

Listening to others

- Play the *Secret message* game.

Digital resources

Teacher's Digital: Don't forget you can teach this lesson using the Teacher's App on Navio.

Pupil's Digital: Encourage your pupils to use the Pupil's App on Navio to practise the vocabulary from this lesson.

Powered By NAVIO

Activity Book

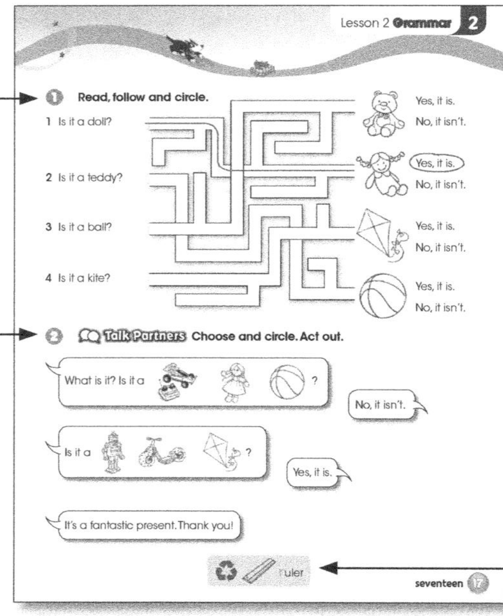

Activity Book

Activity 1

- Read, follow and circle.

Activity 2

- Choose and circle.
- Act out.

Talk Partners

Recycled vocabulary

- Look, say and trace the letter.

Detailed Lesson Plan

Starting the lesson

Use the Trinity Exam Practice cards (optional).

- The pupils practise asking and answering questions (see p31).

Think-Pair-Share Review the toys.

- Ask **Can you remember the ten toys?** The class thinks silently for a minute.
  Talk Partners Then the pupils work with a Talk Partner to name the toys.
- Invite different pairs to say a different toy. Hold up the corresponding flashcard and prompt the class to repeat the word.
- Finally, repeat the procedure, asking different pairs of pupils each time, until all ten toys have been named.

Review the *Happy birthday!* song.

▶ *CD1 Track 28 p258*

▶ *CD1 Track 29 p258 (optional karaoke version)*

- Put the toys flashcards on the board in the order they appear in the song. Divide the class into two groups. Play the CD. Group A sings the chorus and mimes giving a present. The pupils in Group B sing the two verses and shrugs their shoulders to indicate uncertainty for each line. They then swap roles and repeat.

Set learning outcomes using the task flashcards.

- Say **Today we're going to practise asking and answering two questions.**
- Hold up the task flashcards in turn and elicit the activities. Stick them on one side of the board. Point to them during the lesson to reinforce your instructions.

Pupil's Book Activity 1

Listen and repeat. Act out.

▶ *CD1 Track 31 p258*

- (Books open.) The pupils look at the picture. Ask **What can you see?**
- Play the CD. The pupils listen and read the conversation.
- Ask **What's Beth's present?** (a scooter)
- Play the CD again, pausing after each sentence for the pupils to repeat.
- Invite different pairs of pupils to come to the front and act out the story with your help or while the CD is playing.

Pupil's Book Activity 2

Listen and circle.

▶ *CD1 Track 32 p258*

- Point to the first present and ask **What's this present?** The pupils give ideas using *It's a …* Repeat for the other presents.
- Say **Let's listen and find out.** Play the CD, pausing after each conversation. The pupils listen and circle the correct present.
- Play the CD again pausing it after each conversation to check the answers.

Answers: **1** a ball **2** a teddy **3** a train **4** a dinosaur

Activity Book

Activity 1

Read, follow and circle.

- Read out the first question. The pupils follow the path with their finger through the maze. Elicit the correct answer option. Repeat for the other questions, inviting different pupils to read out the questions.
- The pupils work on their own to draw the paths and circle the correct answers.

Answers: **1** Yes, it is. **2** No, it isn't. **3** No, it isn't. **4** Yes, it is.

Activity 2

Choose and circle. Act out.

- (Books open.) Read the speech bubbles, pausing before the pictures to elicit the vocabulary.
- Practise the conversation as a class.
- **Talk Partners** When the pupils are confident with the language, they work in pairs to choose and circle an object for each question. They ask and answer with their partner.
- Invite different pairs of pupils to act out their conversations.

Recycled vocabulary

- The pupils look at the picture and say the word. Then they trace the first letter.

Ending the lesson

Review the lesson.

- (Books closed.) Say **Today we've asked and answered questions about toys. What questions and answers do you remember?** Elicit the questions and answers from the pupils.

Review the task flashcards.

Point to the task flashcards. Say **Look at the activities you've done today. Which activity was your favourite?** Elicit the pupils' favourite activities.

Cooperative learning

Listening to others

- Raise the pupils' awareness of the importance of listening to their classmates by playing the *Secret message* game (Chinese whispers).
- Stick the toys flashcards on the board and organise the class into a line. Whisper the name of a toy to the pupil at the end of the line. This pupil whispers the same word to the pupil in front of them. The whispering continues along the line until it arrives at the pupil at the front. This pupil points to the correct flashcard on the board.

Key Competences and Key Learning Outcomes

- Read, listen and understand a story about a new toy
- Read the story with some fluency
- Understand why forms of transport go fast or slow
- Become familiar with the story through a pre-reading task
- Understand the importance of saying 'thank you'
- Understand and act out the story
- Give an opinion on the story

Key language
- *big, fast, slow, small, wheels*
- *What is it? It's a (motor). My (scooter) is (slow).*

Recycled: *rubber*

Materials
- Pupil's Book pp20–21; Activity Book p18; Class CD1; Teacher's App on Navio
- Toys flashcards
- Teacher's Resource Bank: Toys word cards
- Teacher's Resource Bank: Task flashcards: *think, listen, read, act out, circle, match*
- Teacher's Resource Bank: Unit 2 Lesson 3 Animated Story

Optional materials
- Teacher's Resource Bank: Five Trinity Exam Practice cards (selected from the Starter Unit and Unit 1)

At a Glance Lesson Plan

Pupil's Book

Starting the lesson
- Use the Trinity Exam Practice cards (optional).
- Review toys.
- Set learning outcomes using the task flashcards.

Before you read
- Explain the story title.
- Read and answer the question.

Activity 1
- Listen and read.
- ▶ *CD1 Track 33 p258*
- Act out.
- *Now watch the animated story!*

After you read: Activity 2
- Go to page 18 in your Activity Book.
- Values: Read and circle.

Ending the lesson
- Review the lesson.
- Review the task flashcards.

Activity Book

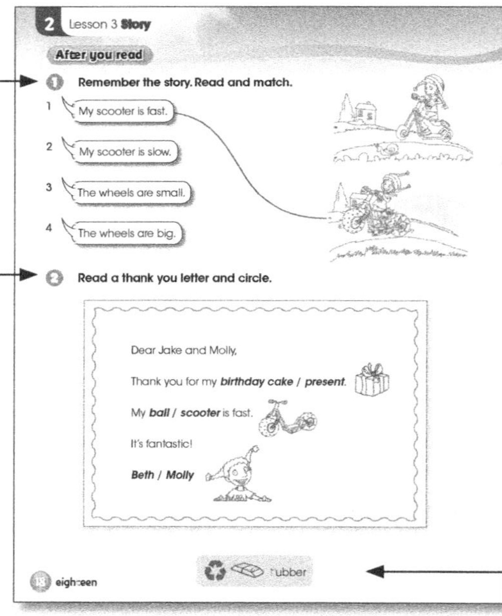

Activity Book

After you read: Activity 1
- Remember the story. Read and match.

Activity 2
- Read a thank you letter and circle.

Recycled vocabulary
- Look, say and trace the letter.

Digital resources

Teacher's Digital: Don't forget you can teach this lesson using the Teacher's App on Navio.

Pupil's Digital: Encourage your pupils to use the Pupil's App on Navio to practise the vocabulary from this lesson.

Powered By NAVIO

Detailed Lesson Plan

Starting the lesson

Use the Trinity Exam Practice cards (optional).

- The pupils practise asking and answering questions (see p31).

Review toys.

- Play *What is it?* with the toys flashcards or word cards (see p23).

Set learning outcomes using the task flashcards.

- Say **Today we're going to listen to a story**.
- Hold up the task flashcards in turn and elicit the activities. Stick them on one side of the board. Point to them during the lesson to reinforce your instructions.

Before you read

Explain the story title.

- (Books open.) Focus on the story title. Demonstrate what a race is. Ask two pupils to race from the back of the class to the board. Start the race by saying **Ready, steady … go!**

Read and answer the question.

- Read the speech bubble. The pupils scan the story to find the different toys.

Answers: bike, scooter, ball, car, kite

Pupil's Book Activity 1

Listen and read. Act out.

▶ ***CD1 Track 33 p258***

- The pupils place their 'magic finger' on the first frame of the story.
- Play the CD. The pupils point to the different frames as the story progresses. Pause the CD after each frame to check that all the pupils are following.
- Play the CD again. Ask questions about each story frame to check understanding.

Suggested comprehension questions

- Frame 1: **Who is on the scooter?** *(Beth.)* **Who is on the bike?** *(Jake and Molly.)* **Is it a race?** *(Yes.)*
- Frame 2: **Are Jake and Molly happy?** *(Yes.)* **Is Beth's scooter slow?** *(Yes.)* Mime moving slowly.
- Frame 3: **Is Beth happy with the scooter?** *(No.)* **Look at the wheels. Are they big or small?** *(Small.)* Explain that the scooter is slow because the wheels are small.
- Frame 4: **Where is the magic?** *(In the bell.)*
- Frame 5: **Are the wheels big or small now?** *(Big.)*
- Frame 6: **Does Molly like the motor?** *(Yes.)*
- Frame 7: **Is the scooter slow now?** *(No.)*
- Frame 8: **Who is the winner?** *(Beth.)* **Is Beth happy?** *(Yes.)*
- Finally, ask the pupils **Is this a good story?** The pupils give their opinion through gesture (thumbs up / down) or orally (*yes / no*).
- Organise the class into three groups (Beth, Molly and Jake).
- Play the CD. Each group joins in when their character speaks. If necessary, pause the CD after each sentence for the pupils to repeat. The groups swap roles, and repeat once or twice.

Now watch the animated story

After you read

Go to page 18 in your Activity Book.

Activity Book

After you read: Activity 1

Remember the story. Read and match.

- Read out the first speech bubble and elicit if the sentence describes the first or second scooter. The pupils draw the matching line. Repeat with the other speech bubbles.

Answers: **1** second scooter **2** first scooter **3** first scooter **4** second scooter

Activity 2

Read a thank you letter and circle.

- Focus the pupils on the thank you letter. Elicit what the pictures are.
- Read out the thank you letter with both words and elicit the correct word.
- The pupils circle the correct words in the letter.

Answers: present, scooter, Beth

Recycled vocabulary

- The pupils look at the picture and say the word. Then they trace the first letter.

Pupil's Book Activity 2

Values: Read and circle.

- The pupils look at the photo on the right. Read out the sentence in the speech bubble and elicit the correct answer.
- Explain that the words 'thank you' are very important and we should use them every time a person helps us or gives us something such as a present.
- Encourage the class to say the names of people at school and at home who help them.

Answer: thank you

Ending the lesson

Review the lesson.

- (Books closed.) Say **Today we've listened to a story about a scooter.** Ask **What happened in the story?** Elicit the story.
- Then say **Today you've learnt some very important words. What do you say when someone helps you / gives you a present?** Elicit *thank you* from the pupils.

Review the task flashcards.

- Point to the task flashcards on the board. Say **Look at the activities you've done today. Which activity was your favourite?** Elicit the pupils' favourite activities.

Key Competences and Key Learning Outcomes

- Ask and answer questions about favourite toys
- Describe your favourite toy
- Review adjectives to describe the senses (optional)
- Listen for specific information
- Sing a song

Key language

- *new, old*
- *What's your favourite toy? My favourite toy is a (ball).*
- Extension: *loud, quiet, long, short*
- **Recycled:** *computer; big, fast, slow, small*

Materials

- Pupil's Book p22; Activity Book p19; Class CD1; Teacher's App on Navio
- Teacher's Resource Bank: Task flashcards: *listen, sing, Talk Partners, match, draw*

Optional materials

- Teacher's Resource Bank: Five Trinity Exam Practice cards (selected from the Starter Unit and Unit 1)
- A piece of poster paper, coloured crayons
- A selection of real toys

At a Glance Lesson Plan

Starting the lesson

- Use the Trinity Exam Practice cards (optional).
- Review the Lesson 3 story.
- Set learning outcomes using the task flashcards.

Vocabulary presentation

- Present the new vocabulary.

Activity 1

- Listen, point and say.

▶ *CD1 Track 34 p259*

Activity 2

- Listen and point.
- Sing *My favourite toy*.

▶ *CD1 Track 35 p259*

Activity 3

- Listen and repeat.
- Talk Partners Ask and answer.

▶ *CD1 Track 36 p259*

Go to the Activity Book.

Pupil's Book

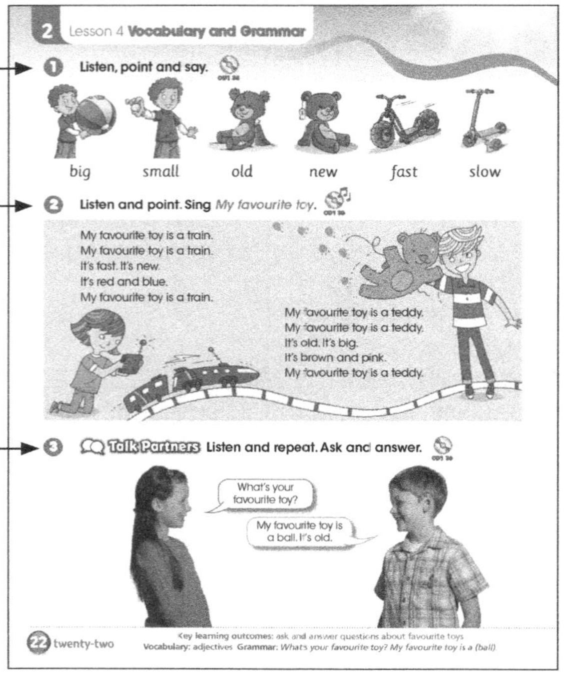

Ending the lesson

- Review the lesson.
- Review the task flashcards.

Extra activities

Reinforcement

- Do a 'favourite toy' class survey.

Vocabulary Extension

- Present four additional vocabulary items.

Cooperative learning

Developing a positive classroom atmosphere

- Play *Me too!*

Link to Science

- **The senses:** Review adjectives to describe touch, sight and sound.

Activity Book

Activity Book

Activity 1

- Listen and match.

▶ *CD1 Track 37 p259*

Activity 2

- Read and circle.
- Draw.

- Talk Partners Ask and answer.

Recycled vocabulary

- Look, say and trace the letter.

Digital resources

Teacher's Digital: Don't forget you can teach this lesson using the Teacher's App on Navio.

Pupil's Digital: Encourage your pupils to use the Pupil's App on Navio to practise the vocabulary from this lesson.

Powered By NAVIO

Detailed Lesson Plan

Starting the lesson

Use the Trinity Exam Practice cards (optional).

- The pupils practise asking and answering questions (see p31).

Review the Lesson 3 story.

- Give the pupils two minutes to look at the story. Then say **One, two, three, I can see a (scooter). Where is it?** The pupils scan the story and point to it. Repeat with other things.

Set learning outcomes using the task flashcards.

- Say **Today we're going to sing a song and talk about our favourite toys.**
- Hold up the task flashcards in turn and elicit the activities. Stick them on one side of the board. Point to them during the lesson to reinforce your instructions.

Vocabulary presentation

Present the new vocabulary.

- (Books open.) Point to the first picture on Pupil's Book page 22. Say **Look at the ball. It's big.** Pretend to carry a large ball. The class names something big, e.g. *a car*. Repeat for the other adjectives.

Pupil's Book Activity 1

Listen, point and say.

▶ *CD1 Track 34 p259*

- Play the CD. The pupils listen, point to the pictures and repeat the words.
- Play the CD again if needed.
- Play *What's missing?* (without flashcards) Read out the adjectives in the same order as they appear in the Pupil's Book, but miss one of them out, e.g. **big, small, old, …, fast, slow.** The pupils listen and say the missing word. *(New.)*
- Repeat with different missing adjectives.

Pupil's Book Activity 2

Listen and point. Sing *My favourite toy.*

▶ *CD1 Track 35 p259*

- Ask questions such as **What can you see? Is the train (old)? Is the teddy (new)?** etc.
- Play the CD. The pupils listen and point.
- Play the CD again. The pupils sing and do the actions.

Pupil's Book Activity 3

Listen and repeat. Ask and answer.

▶ *CD1 Track 36 p259*

- (Books open.) Play the CD. The pupils listen and read.
- Play the CD again. The pupils repeat the question and answer.
- Invite a pupil to come to the front. The class asks him / her the question in chorus. He / She answers.
- Talk Partners The pupils ask and answer.

Activity Book

Activity 1

Listen and match.

▶ *CD1 Track 37 p259*

- Ask the pupils to name and describe the first toy. (*It's a ball. It's big.*) Repeat with the other toys.
- Play the CD. The pupils listen and draw a matching line. Pause after the first conversation to check the answer. Repeat with the other conversations.

Answers: **1** a big ball **2** a fast bike **3** a small dinosaur **4** an old doll

Activity 2

Read and circle. Draw. Ask and answer.

- Read out the question. The pupils circle their favourite toy, and whether it is big or small.
- The pupils draw their favourite toy.
- Talk Partners The pupils ask and answer the question and show each other their drawings.

Recycled vocabulary

- The pupils look and say the word. Then they trace the first letter.

Ending the lesson

Review the lesson.

- (Books closed.) Say **Today we've talked about our favourite toys. What words can we use to describe our favourite toys?** Elicit the adjectives.

Review the task flashcards.

- Point to the task flashcards. Say **Look at the activities you've done today. Which activity was your favourite?** Elicit the pupils' favourite activities.

Extra activities

Reinforcement

- Do a 'favourite toy' class survey. Ask each pupil **What's your favourite toy?** Record all the answers in a table on the board.

Vocabulary Extension

- Use the Vocabulary Booster on Navio and present and practise four additional words to describe a toy: *long, loud, short, quiet*

Cooperative learning

Developing a positive classroom atmosphere

- Discovering similarities helps to develop a positive classroom atmosphere. Play *Me too!* Invite a pupil to come to the front. Ask **What's your favourite toy?** When he / she answers, everyone who has the same opinion shouts out *Me too!*
- Extend this activity with other questions, e.g. **What's your favourite (colour / day / number)?**

Link to Science

- If you are studying the Science topic of **The senses** in English, you could review adjectives to describe touch (*hard, soft, rough, smooth*), sight (colours) and sound (*loud, quiet*). Ask **Is a (teddy) (soft)?**
- Provide a selection of real toys and give groups of pupils several toys to describe.

Key Competences and Key Learning Outcomes

- Say a tongue twister with the 's' sound
- Listen for specific information
- Sing a cooperative learning song
- Understand the importance of sharing
- Play a communication game about toys

Key language
- *My favourite toy is (old).*

Recycled: *big, fast, new, old, small, slow; ball, bike, car, computer game, dinosaur, doll, kite, robot, scooter, teddy, train; pen; six*

Recycled: *Is it a (scooter)? Yes, it is. No, it isn't.*

Materials
- Pupil's Book p23, Activity Book p20; Class CD1; Teacher's App on Navio
- Teacher's Resource Bank: Task flashcards: *listen, say, number, sing, cut out, think, Talk Partners, colour*
- Teacher's Resource Bank: Unit 2 Lesson 5 Activity 3 cut-outs

Optional materials
- Teacher's Resource Bank: Five Trinity Exam Practice cards (selected from the Starter Unit and Unit 1)
- Coloured paper, scissors; coloured pencils or crayons

At a Glance Lesson Plan

Starting the lesson
- Use the Trinity Exam Practice cards (optional).
- Review the vocabulary from Lesson 4.
- Review *My favourite toy* song.
- ▶ *CD1 Track 35 p259*
- Set learning outcomes using the task flashcards.

Activity 1
- Listen and say.
- ▶ *CD1 Track 38 p259*
- Go to Magic Phonics.
- Go to the Activity Book.

Activity 2
- Listen and number.
- ▶ *CD1 Track 39 p259*

Pupil's Book

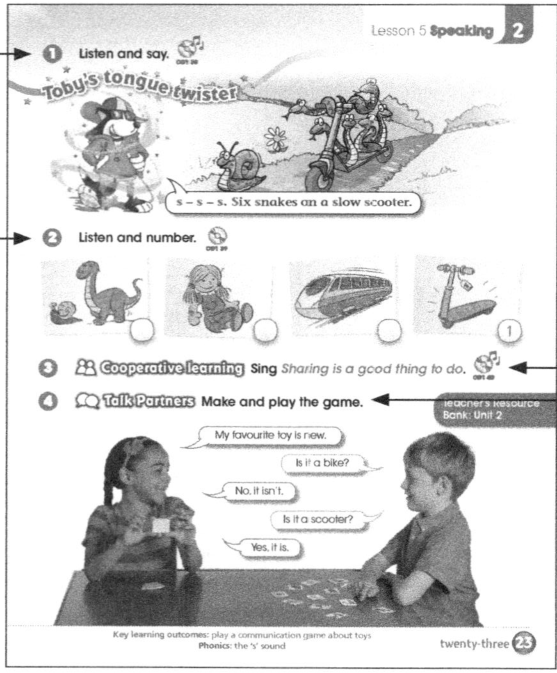

Activity 3 Cooperative learning
- Sing *Sharing is a good thing to do.*
- ▶ *CD1 Track 40 p259*

Activity 4
- Make and play the game.
- Talk Partners
- Go to the Activity Book.

Ending the lesson
- Review the lesson.
- Review the task flashcards.

Extra activity
Reinforcement
- Continue the pronunciation wall display.

Digital resources

Teacher's Digital: Don't forget you can teach this lesson using the Teacher's App on Navio.

Pupil's Digital: Encourage your pupils to use the Pupil's App on Navio to practise the vocabulary from this lesson.

Powered By NAVIO

Activity Book

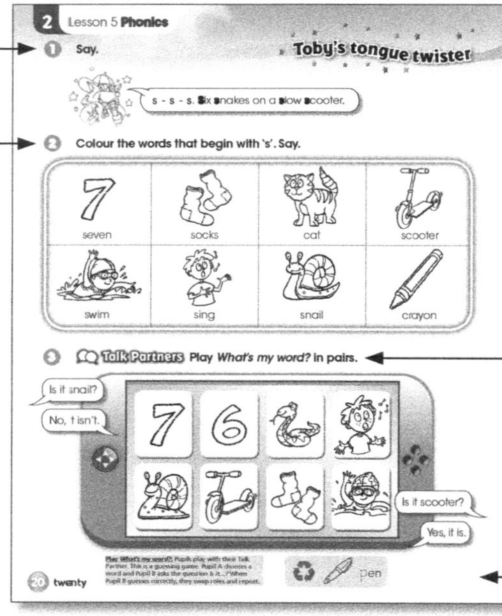

Activity Book

Activity 1
- Say.

Activity 2
- Colour the words that begin with 's'. Say.
- Go to Magic Phonics.

Activity 3
- Talk Partners
  Play *What's my word?* in pairs.

Recycled vocabulary
- Look, say and trace the letter.

Detailed Lesson Plan

Starting the lesson

Use the Trinity Exam Practice cards (optional).

- The pupils practise asking and answering questions (see p31).

Review the vocabulary from Lesson 4.

- Ask a pupil **What's your favourite toy? Is it (old)?** Repeat with different pupils and adjectives.

Review *My favourite toy* song.

- Play the CD. The pupils sing along.

▶ *CD1 Track 35 p259*

Set learning outcomes using the task flashcards.

- Say **Today we're going to practise saying a tongue twister and make and play a speaking game.**
- Hold up the task flashcards in turn and elicit the activities. Stick them on one side of the board. Point to them during the lesson to reinforce your instructions.

Pupil's Book Activity 1

Listen and say.

▶ *CD1 Track 38 p259*

- (Books open.) Write the target 's' sound on the board, and say it for the pupils. The pupils repeat.
- Say **It's time for Toby's tongue twister. How many snakes can you see?**
- Play the CD. The pupils listen and repeat the target sound, then the words and then the entire tongue twister, faster and faster.

Go to Magic Phonics.

Activity Book

Activity 1

Say.

- (Books open.) Read out the tongue twister for the pupils to repeat.
- The pupils say the tongue twister to their partner, saying it faster and faster each time.

Activity 2

Colour the words that begin with 's'. Say.

- Ask the pupils to say the words that begin with 's'. The pupils colour and say these words.

Answers: seven, socks, scooter, swim, sing, snail

Go to Magic Phonics.

Activity 3

Play *What's my word?* in pairs.

- Point to each picture and elicit the word.
- Demonstrate the game. Think of one of the objects and ask **What's my word?** The pupils ask questions to guess your word.
  Talk Partners The pupils play the game with a Talk Partner.

Recycled vocabulary

- The pupils look at the picture and say the word. Then they trace the first letter.

Pupil's Book Activity 2

Listen and number.

▶ *CD1 Track 39 p259*

- Point to the pictures and ask the class to name and describe the toys, e.g. *a new scooter*.
- Play the CD, pausing after the first conversation to check that the pupils understand.
- Play the other conversations. The pupils write the numbers.

Answers: **1** a new scooter **2** a fast train **3** a slow dinosaur **4** an old doll

Pupil's Book Activity 3: Cooperative learning

Sing *Sharing is a good thing to do.*

▶ *CD1 Track 40 p259*

- Highlight the importance of sharing our things with other people.
- Point to yourself and say **Me.** Point to the class and say **You.** Play the CD. The pupils do the actions when they hear these words.
- Play the CD again. The pupils sing and do the actions.

Pupil's Book Activity 4

Make and play the game.

- Tell the class that they are going to play the game.
- The pupils cut out and colour the cards.
- Demonstrate the activity. Take a card and say **My favourite toy is (old).** The pupils guess the toy. *Is it a (teddy)?*
- Ask a pupil to take your role. The rest of the class asks him / her questions.
  Talk Partners The pupils play the game with a Talk Partner.

Ending the lesson

Review the lesson.

- (Books closed.) Say **Today we've practised a tongue twister and played a game.** Elicit the tongue twister.

Review the task flashcards.

- Point to the task flashcards. Say **Look at the activities you've done today. Which activity was your favourite?** Elicit the pupils' favourite activities.

Extra activity

Reinforcement

- Continue with the pronunciation wall display. Cut out the letter 's' in coloured paper. Stick it on a piece of differently coloured paper to make a wall display. Elicit words that begin with that letter and write them on the wall display.
- Encourage the pupils to add new words beginning with the letter 's' during the year. They can either tell you the new word for you to add or write the word themselves if they can.

Key Competences and Key Learning Outcomes

- Listen for general information

- Read about birthday parties in Britain
- Answer questions about a birthday party
- Think about your birthday party

Key language

- *birthday cake, birthday card, candles, fancy dress, party, party games, presents*
- *I've got a (birthday cake). I have (a party). I play (party games). I wear (fancy dress). It's (good fun).*

Recycled: *sharpener*

Materials

- Pupil's Book p24; Activity Book p21; Class CD1; Teacher's App on Navio
- Toys flashcards
- Teacher's Resource Bank: Task flashcards: *listen, read, think, circle, tick, draw*

Optional materials

- Teacher's Resource Bank: Five Trinity Exam Practice cards (selected from the Starter Unit and Unit 1)

At a Glance Lesson Plan

Starting the lesson

- Use the Trinity Exam Practice cards (optional).
- Talk Partners Review Toby's tongue twister.

▶ *CD1 Track 38 p259*

- Review the *Happy birthday!* song.

▶ *CD1 Track 28 p258*

▶ *CD1 Track 29 p258 (optional karaoke version)*

- Set learning outcomes using the task flashcards.

Activity 1

- Listen and read.

▶ *CD1 Track 41 p259*

- Answer.

Think about your culture

- Do you have a party on your birthday?

Go to the Activity Book.

Pupil's Book

Ending the lesson

- Review the lesson.
- Review the task flashcards.

Extra activity

Extension

- Play a traditional party game.

Digital resources

Teacher's Digital: Don't forget you can teach this lesson using the Teacher's App on Navio.

Powered By NAVIO

Activity Book

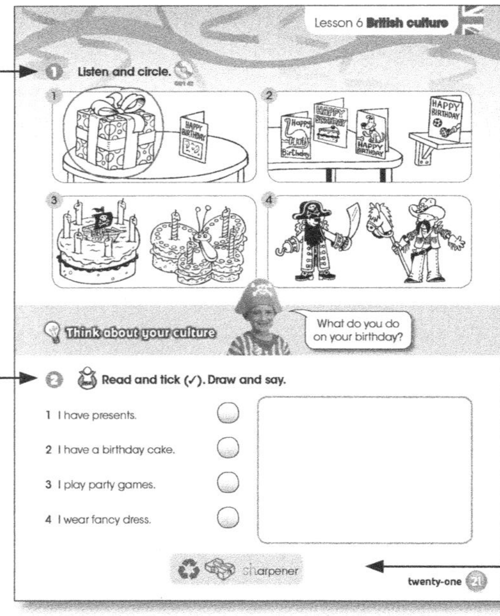

Activity Book

Activity 1

- Listen and circle.

▶ *CD1 Track 42 p259*

Activity 2: Think about your culture

- Read and tick (✓).
- Draw and say.

Recycled vocabulary

- Look, say and trace the letters.

Detailed Lesson Plan

Starting the lesson

Use the Trinity Exam Practice cards (optional).

- The pupils practise asking and answering questions (see p31).

Review Toby's tongue twister.

▶ *CD1 Track 38 p259*

- Ask **What sound did you practise in Toby's tongue twister? Can you remember the tongue twister?** (*Six snakes on a slow scooter.*) Play the CD. Practise the tongue twister as a class.
  Talk Partners The pupils practise saying the tongue twister as fast as possible with a Talk Partner. Choose a fast pair to say it for the class.

Review the *Happy birthday!* song

▶ *CD1 Track 28 p258*

▶ *CD1 Track 29 p258 (optional karaoke version)*

- Put the toys flashcards on the board in the order they appear in the song. Divide the class into two groups. Play the CD (or use the karaoke version). Group A sings the chorus and mimes giving a present. The pupils in Group B sing the two verses and shrugs their shoulders for each line. They swap roles.

Set learning outcomes using the task flashcards.

- Say **Today we're going to learn about birthday parties in Britain.**
- Hold up the task flashcards in turn and elicit the activities. Stick them on one side of the board. Point to them during the lesson to reinforce your instructions.

Pupil's Book Activity 1

Listen and read. Answer.

▶ *CD1 Track 41 p259*

- (Books open.) The pupils look at the photos. Ask **Where are the children? What can you see?** Elicit the things in the pictures (balloons, cake, etc.).
- Play the CD. Pause after each text. Ask questions to check understanding.

Suggested comprehension questions

- Photo 1: **The children have got costumes. Are the children princesses?** (*No.*) **Are they football players?** (*No.*) **Are they pirates?** (*Yes.*)
- Photo 2: **Has the boy got a birthday cake?** (*No.*) **Has the boy got birthday cards?** (*Yes.*) **Is he happy?** (*Yes.*)
- Photo 3: **The children are playing games. Are they playing the games in the house?** (*No.*) **Where are they playing games?** (*In the garden.*)
- Photo 4: **What is on the birthday cake?** (*Candles.*) **How many can you see?** (*Seven.*)

Pupil's Book Think about your culture

Do you have a party on your birthday?

- Read out the question.
- Encourage the pupils to tell you about birthday parties in their country.
- Ask questions, e.g. **Do you have presents / a birthday cake / birthday cards? Do you play party games? Do you wear a costume?**

Activity Book

Activity 1

Listen and circle.

▶ *CD1 Track 42 p259*

- (Books open.) Play the CD, pausing after each text. The pupils circle the object they hear.
- Repeat with the other pictures.

Answers: **1** big present **2** birthday card on the shelf **3** cake with six candles **4** cowboy costume

Activity 2: Think about your culture

Read and tick (✓). Draw and say.

- Read out the question in the speech bubble. Elicit the pupils' answers.
- Read out the first sentence. The pupils tick the box if they have presents on their birthday. Repeat with the other sentences.
- The pupils draw the things they have and do on their birthday.
- Invite different pupils to show the class their drawings and say what they do.

Recycled vocabulary

- The pupils look at the picture and say the word. Then they trace the first two letters.

Ending the lesson

Review the lesson.

- (Books closed.) Say **Today we've learnt about birthdays in Britain. What do children do at birthday parties in Britain?** Elicit the activities from the pupils.

Review the task flashcards.

- Point to the task flashcards. Say **Look at the activities you've done today. Which activity was your favourite?** Elicit the pupils' favourite activities.

Extra activity

Extension

- Play a traditional party game. Invite a confident pupil to come to the front of the class and place a blindfold or scarf over his / her eyes. Then silently choose another pupil to stand in front of him / her. Carefully place the blindfolded pupil's hands on the second pupil's head and prompt him / her to make a guess. *Is it (Paula)?* The rest of the class chorus their response *Yes, it is / No, it isn't.* The pupil with the blindfold has three attempts to guess their classmate. Repeat the game with different pairs of pupils.

Key Competences and Key Learning Outcomes

- Read for specific information

- Read and understand a birthday card
- Design a birthday card

Key language

- *balloons*
- *To … , Lots of love, From …*
- *Have a (fantastic party with your friend).*

Recycled: *bike, dinosaur, kite, scooter; birthday cake, present; crayon, dog, six*

Recycled: *Happy birthday*

Materials

- Pupil's Book p25; Activity Book p22; Class CD1; Teacher's App on Navio
- Teacher's Resource Bank: Task flashcards: *think, circle, listen, read, draw*

Optional materials

- Teacher's Resource Bank: Five Trinity Exam Practice cards (selected from the Starter Unit and Unit 1)
- Plain card, coloured crayons
- A selection of birthday cards

At a Glance Lesson Plan

Starting the lesson

- Use the Trinity Exam Practice cards (optional).
- Review the culture lesson.
- Set learning outcomes using the task flashcards.

Before you read

- Look at and talk about some real birthday cards.

Activity 1

- What can you see on the birthday card?
- Circle and say.

Activity 2

- Listen and read the birthday card.

▶ *CD1 Track 43 p259*

After you read

Go to page 22 in your Activity Book.

Pupil's Book

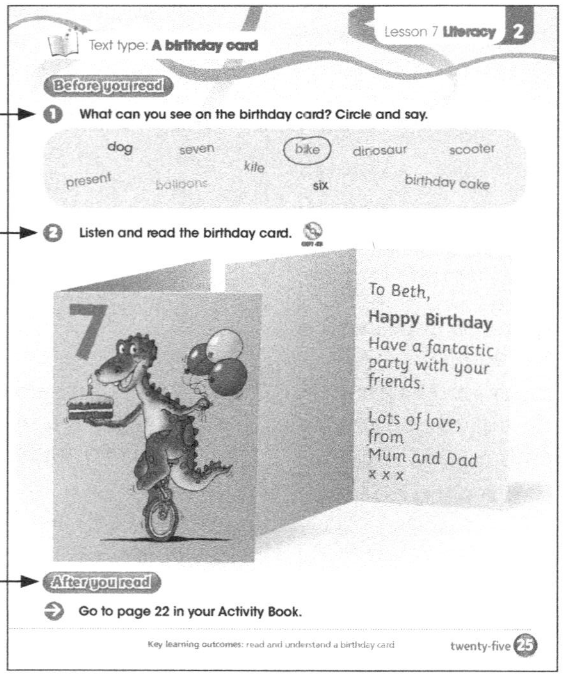

Ending the lesson

- Review the lesson.
- Review the task flashcards.

Extra activity

Extension

- Make a birthday card.

Cooperative learning

Developing a positive classroom atmosphere

- Establish a classroom birthday routine.

Digital resources

Teacher's Digital: Don't forget you can teach this lesson using the Teacher's App on Navio.

Pupil's Digital: Encourage your pupils to use the Pupil's App on Navio to practise the vocabulary from this lesson.

Activity Book

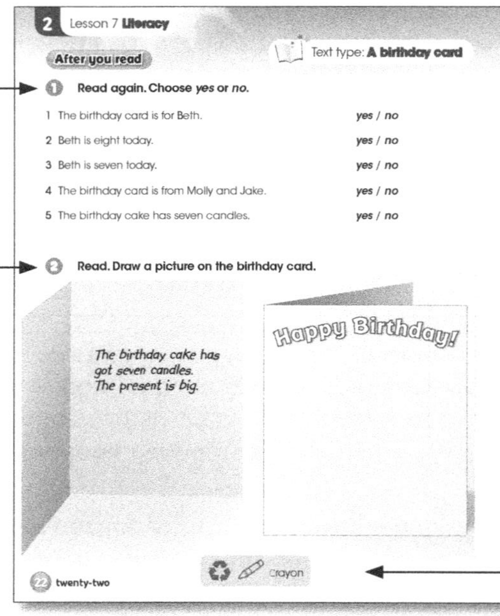

Activity Book

After you read: Activity 1

- Read again.
- Choose *yes* or *no*.

Activity 2

- Read.
- Draw a picture on the birthday card.

Recycled vocabulary

- Look, say and trace the letter.

Detailed Lesson Plan

Starting the lesson

Use the Trinity Exam Practice cards (optional).

- The pupils practise asking and answering questions (see p31).

Review the culture lesson.

- Review birthday party activities from Lesson 6. Draw a birthday cake on the board and ask **What's this?** Say **Blow out the candles on the birthday cake.** The pupils do the action.
- Repeat with a present, a birthday card and a pirate costume. The pupils mime the actions. Say **Open the present, Write inside the birthday card** and **Be a pirate**.

Set learning outcomes using the task flashcards.

- Say **Today we're going to read a birthday card.**
- Hold up the task flashcards in turn and elicit the activities. Stick them on one side of the board. Point to them during the lesson to reinforce your instructions.

Before you read

Look at and talk about some real birthday cards.

- (Books closed.) If you have some birthday cards, show the first card to the class and ask **What's this?** (If you don't have cards, you can find some examples online instead.)
- Ask questions about the card, e.g. **What's this? What colour is the …? How many … can you see?** Repeat with the other cards. Ask the class **Which is your favourite birthday card?**

Pupil's Book Activity 1

What can you see on the birthday card? Circle and say.

- Point to the birthday card in the Pupil's Book and ask **What's this?**
- Read out the instructions to Activity 1. Focus on the example answer that is circled. Ask **Is there a (bike) on the birthday card?** Invite different pupils to read out the other words and elicit from the class if they can see each object on the card. The pupils circle all the things that appear on the card.

Answers: bike, seven, balloons, dinosaur, birthday cake

Pupil's Book Activity 2

Listen and read the birthday card.

▶ *CD1 Track 43 p259*

- Say **Let's listen and read the birthday card**. Play the CD.
- Ask **Is the birthday card for Beth?** (Yes.) **Is she six today?** (No.) **Is the card from Jake and Molly?** (No.) **How many kisses are on the card?** (Three.)
- Play the CD again, pausing after each section. The class repeats the sentences.
- Cultural information: In Britain, people often write kisses at the end of personal emails, letters and cards. These are represented by the letter X.

Activity Book

After you read: Activity 1

Read again. Choose yes or *no*.

- The pupils read the birthday card again.
- Read out the first sentence and elicit the answer. Repeat with the other sentences. Alternatively, invite different pupils to read out and answer each sentence.
- The pupils circle *yes* or *no*.

Answers: **1** yes **2** no **3** yes **4** no **5** no

Activity 2

Read. Draw a picture on the birthday card.

- Read out the description of the birthday card for the pupils to follow.
- The pupils read the description again and draw the picture on the front of their card.
- Encourage individual pupils to show their card to the rest of the class and say who it's for.

Recycled vocabulary

- The pupils look at the picture and say the word. Then they trace the first letter.

Ending the lesson

Review the lesson.

- (Books closed.) Say **Today we've read a birthday card in English. What message do we put in a birthday card?** Elicit the message from the pupils.

Review the task flashcards.

- Point to the task flashcards. Say **Look at the activities you've done today. Which activity was your favourite?** Elicit the pupils' favourite activities.

Extra activity

Extension

- The pupils make a birthday card.
- Hand out card and ask the pupils to fold it in half. Then they draw a picture on the front.
- Go round the class and write *Happy Birthday* on their cards.

Cooperative learning

Developing a positive classroom atmosphere

- Celebrating birthdays helps build a positive classroom atmosphere as pupils feel included and valued. A birthday routine can be as simple as singing *Happy Birthday* in English or adding birthday news to a class notice board. You could encourage the pupils to make birthday cards for each other in English.

Key Competences and Key Learning Outcomes

- Review language in the unit
- Reflect on own learning
- Sing a cooperative learning song

Key language

Recycled: *ball, car, computer game, dinosaur, doll, kite, robot, scooter, teddy, train; big, fast, new, old, slow, small; book*

Recycled: *Is it a (ball)? Yes, it is. No, it isn't. My favourite toy is (old and brown).*

Materials

- Pupil's Book p26; Activity Book p23; Class CD1; Teacher's App on Navio
- Toys flashcards
- Teacher's Resource Bank: Task flashcards: *listen, number, read, sing, think, stick*
- Teacher's Resource Bank: Traffic light cut-out
- *Give Me Five!* sticker

Optional materials

- Teacher's Resource Bank: Five Trinity Exam Practice cards (selected from the Starter Unit and Unit 1)

At a Glance Lesson Plan

Starting the lesson

- Use the Trinity Exam Practice cards (optional).
- Review the unit vocabulary.
- Set learning outcomes using the task flashcards.

Activity 1

- Listen and number.
- ▶ ***CD1 Track 44 p260***
- Say.

Activity 2

- Look, read and circle.

Activity 3 Cooperative learning

- Sing *Well done!*
- ▶ ***CD1 Track 45 p260***
- Stick the *Give Me Five!* sticker.
- Go to the Activity Book.

Pupil's Book

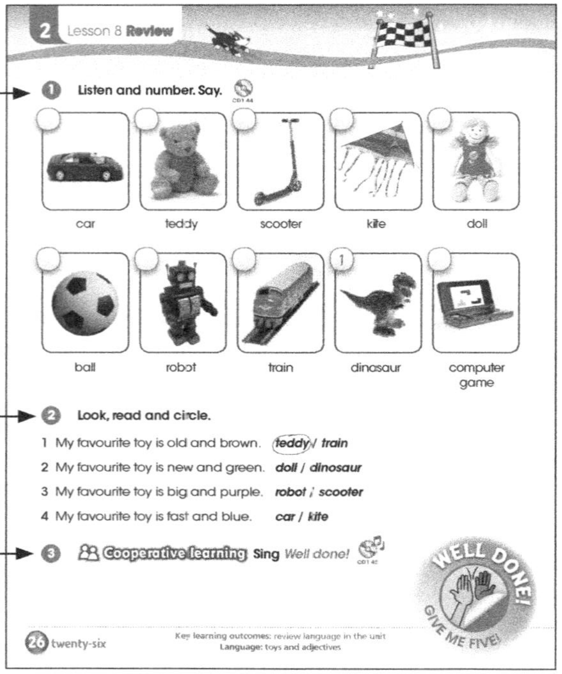

Ending the lesson

- Review the task flashcards.

Activity Book

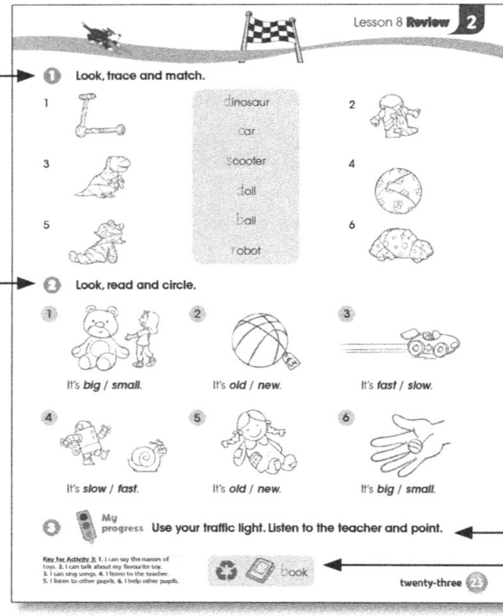

Activity Book

Activity 1

- Look, trace and match.

Activity 2

- Look, read and circle.

Activity 3 My progress

- Use your traffic light. Listen to the teacher and point.

Recycled vocabulary

- Look, say and trace the letter.

Digital resources

Teacher's Digital: Don't forget you can teach this lesson using the Teacher's App on Navio.

Pupil's Digital: Encourage your pupils to use the Pupil's App on Navio to practise the vocabulary from this lesson.

Powered By NAVIO

Detailed Lesson Plan

Starting the lesson

Use the Trinity Exam Practice cards (optional).

- The pupils practise asking and answering questions (see p31).

Review the unit vocabulary.

- Review the unit vocabulary using the toys flashcards. Hold up a flashcard and elicit the word. Stick the flashcard face down on the board. Repeat until all the flashcards are on the board.
- Ask **Where's the (ball)?** Ask a pupil to come to the front and turn over one of the flashcards. If it's the correct card, he / she says *It's here*. If it isn't the correct flashcard, another pupil has a go. Repeat with different words.
- Variation: Play the game in two teams. The teams take it in turns to remember the toys.

Set learning outcomes using the task flashcards.

- Say **Today we're going to remember what we've learnt in Unit 2.**
- Hold up the task flashcards in turn and elicit the activities. Stick them on one side of the board. Point to them during the lesson to reinforce your instructions.

Pupil's Book Activity 1

Listen and number. Say.

▶ *CD1 Track 44 p260*

- (Books open.) Point to the pictures and ask different pupils to name the toys.
- Play the CD, pausing after each conversation. The pupils point to the toys.
- Play the CD again. The pupils write the correct number for each picture.
- The pupils say the words under each picture.

Answers: **1** dinosaur **2** computer game **3** doll **4** car **5** train **6** teddy **7** scooter **8** ball **9** robot **10** kite

Pupil's Book Activity 2

Look, read and circle.

- Ask a pupil to read out the first description. Point to the pictures in Activity 1 and ask **Which toy is it?** Repeat with the other sentences.
- The pupils read the sentences again and circle the correct word.

Answers: **1** teddy **2** dinosaur **3** scooter **4** car

Pupil's Book Activity 3: Cooperative learning

Sing *Well done!*

▶ *CD1 Track 45 p260*

- Praise the pupils for their hard work and play the *Well done!* song. The pupils sing and do the actions.

Stick the *Give Me Five!* sticker.

- The pupils stick the *Give Me Five!* sticker on the Pupil's Book page.
- Variation: Sing the *Well done!* song and stick the *Give Me!* sticker after the pupils have also completed the Activity Book Lesson 8 Review.

Activity Book

Activity 1

Look, trace and match.

- (Books open.) Read out the words in the box.
- The pupils trace the first letter of each word.
- Say the words for the pupils to point to the pictures.
- The pupils draw a matching line from the pictures to the correct word.

Answers: **1** scooter **2** robot **3** dinosaur **4** ball **5** doll **6** car

Activity 2

Look, read and circle.

- Focus the pupils on Activity 2. Ask the pupils to describe each picture.
- Read out the sentences, saying both adjectives to elicit the correct one.
- The pupils read the sentences again and circle the correct adjectives.

Answers: **1** big **2** new **3** fast **4** slow **5** old **6** small

Activity 3: My progress My progress

Use your traffic light. Listen to the teacher and point.

- (Books closed.) Ask the class to take out their traffic light cut-out. Say **Let's think about our work in this unit.** Point to the green circle, nod your head, smile a lot, and say **I can sing songs in English. Yes, I can do this very well.** Point to the yellow circle, move your head a little, smile a little and say **Yes, I can do this.** Then point to the red circle, shake your head and say **No, I can't do this.**
- Read out the statements. For each one, the pupils point to the colour on their traffic light that shows how they feel about their own learning.

Self-assessment statements

1. I can say the names of toys.
2. I can talk about my favourite toy.
3. I can sing songs.
4. I listen to the teacher.
5. I listen to other pupils.
6. I help other pupils.

Recycled vocabulary

- The pupils look at the picture and say the word. Then they trace the first letter.

Ending the lesson

Review the task flashcards.

- Point to the task flashcards. Say **Look at the activities you've done today. Which activity was your favourite?** Elicit the pupils' favourite activities.

Key Competences and Key Learning Outcomes

- Watch and understand a video about ranking favourite toys
- Say what your favourite toys are
- Order things

Key language

- *ball, dinosaur, fast, kite, new, old, robot, scooter, slow, teddy, train, video game*

Materials

- Pupil's Book p27; Activity Book p24; Class CD1; Video; Teacher's App on Navio
- Teacher's Resource Bank: Task flashcards: *tick, read, circle, think, number, listen, Talk Partners, draw, say*
- Toy flashcards

Optional materials

- Teacher's Resource Bank: Trinity Exam Practice cards (selected from Unit 2)

At a Glance Lesson Plan

Starting the lesson

- Use the Trinity Exam Practice cards (optional).
- **Think-Pair-Share** Review toy vocabulary.
- Set learning outcomes and use the task flashcards.

Pre-watching activity

- Look at the photo and talk about favourite toys.

Activity 1

- Watch the video.
  Unit 2 video p277
- Tick (✓) or cross (✗). Are these toys in the video?

Activity 2

- Watch the video again.
  Unit 2 video
- Read and circle.

Pupil's Book

Activity 3

- Read and think. Write *1*, *2*, and *3*.
- Go to the Activity Book.

Ending the lesson

- Review the lesson.
- Review the task flashcards. Elicit the pupils' favourite activities.

Activity Book

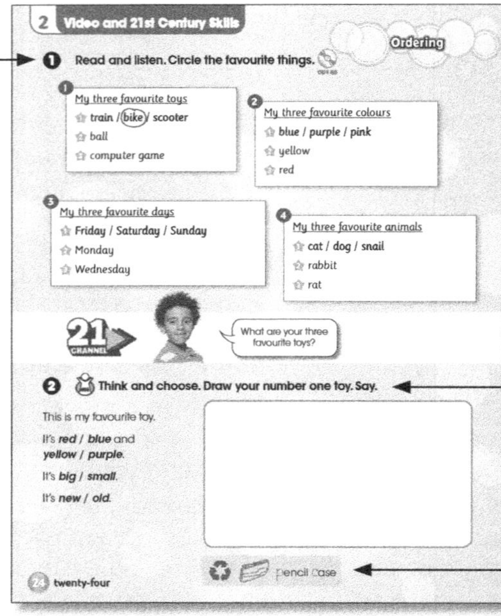

Activity Book

Activity 1

- Read and listen.
- *CD1 Track 46 p260*
- Circle the favourite things.

Activity 2

- Think and choose. Draw your number one toy. Say.

Recycled vocabulary

- Look, say and trace the letters.

Digital resources

Teacher's Digital: Don't forget you can teach this lesson using the Teacher's App on Navio.

Pupil's Digital: Encourage your pupils to use the Pupil's App on Navio to practise the vocabulary from this lesson.

Powered By NAVIO

Detailed Lesson Plan

Starting the lesson

Use the Trinity Exam Practice cards (optional).

- The pupils practise asking and answering questions.

Review toys vocabulary.

Think-Pair-Share Ask How many toys from Unit 2 can you remember? The class thinks silently for a minute.

Talk Partners The pupils work with a Talk Partner to name as many toys as they can in two minutes.

- Invite different Talk Partners to say how many toys they remembered.

Set learning outcomes and use the task flashcards.

- Say **Today we're going to watch a video and then ask and answer questions about favourite toys**.
- Point to the task flashcards throughout to elicit activities and reinforce your instructions.

Pre-watching activity

- Ask **What do you think the video is about this week?**
- Look at the photo. Ask **What's your favourite toy?** Elicit responses from a number of pupils.

Pupil's Book Activity 1

Watch the video. Tick (✓) or cross (✗). Are these toys in the video? *p277*

- Ask **How many favourite toys are in the video?** Play Part 1, pausing after Tom says, *It's about five favourite toys*.
- On the board stick four toy flashcards. Tell the pupils to listen and tell you which toy you don't say and come to the board and write a cross under it. Repeat with different toy flashcards.
- Focus the pupils on the video stills. Ask **What can you see?** Encourage full sentences for example A red robot. Then say **Let's watch and listen**.
- Explain that the pupils cross the toy that is not in the video. Play Part 2 of the video. Pause after the first video still. Ask the pupils to point to the corresponding photo. Play Part 2 for pupils to point to the photos in the order they see the toys.
- Play Part 2 again for pupils to write the cross. The pupils then tick the toys that are in the video.
- Ask **What is the number one favourite toy? Describe it?** (It's a video game. It's fun. It's about cars).

Answers: ✓, ✗, ✓, ✓

Pupil's Book Activity 2

Watch the video again. Read and circle.

- Play Part 1 and Part 2 again. Pause after Sophie says, *This teddy is cute*. Read out the first sentence in Activity 2. Ask **Is the teddy grey or red?** Show *grey* circled.
- Play the video all the way through. Ask **Which toy is the number one favourite toy? Why?**
- Ask general questions to check understanding.
  What colour is the teddy? *(Grey.)*
  Are the dinosaurs big or small? *(Small.)*
  What can the red robot do? *(Walk and turn around.)*
  What colour are the scooters? *(Pink and green.)*
  Does everyone have the same favourite toy? *(No, we are all different.)*

Answers: **1** grey **2** small **3** fast **4** kite

Pupil's Book Activity 3

Read and think. Write *1*, *2* and *3*.

- Copy the smiley face key onto the board. To demonstrate the activity, stick three of the toy flashcards on the board. Write one, two or three under each one. Ask **Which toy is my favourite? How do you know?** Explain the ranking order. Ask volunteers to come to the board and rank the toys for themselves. Read out the speech bubble. The pupils look at the pictures and rank the toys one to three.
- Say **My number one favourite teddy is orange. My number one favourite robot is green.** Ask a couple of pupils, **What's your number one favourite teddy / robot?** Encourage full answers.
  Think-Pair-Share The pupils compare their ranking with their Talk Partner. Ask **Are your answers the same or different? Is it OK to be different? Why?**

Activity Book

Activity 1

Read and listen. Circle the favourite things.

▶ *CD1 Track 46 p260*

- Play the CD, pausing after each topic to elicit the answer.
- On the board write *1 train, bike* and *scooter*. Ask **Which toy – train, bike or scooter – is the number one favourite thing?** Circle bike. Read out the four rankings and play the rest of the track, pausing for pupils to circle the number one favourite thing.

Answers: **1** bike **2** blue **3** Sunday **4** a dog

Activity 2

Think and choose. Draw your number one toy. Say.

- Ask a few pupils, **What are your three favourite toys?**
- Read out the sentences for the pupils to follow.
- The pupils read the sentences again, then choose and circle the colours and adjectives.
- The pupils draw their number one toy.
  Talk Partners In pairs, pupils take turns to tell their partner about their favourite toy.

Recycled vocabulary

- The pupils look at the picture and say the word. Then they trace the first letter of each word.

Ending the lesson

Review the lesson.

- Say **What did we learn about ranking favourite things?** (How to rank them. We are all different and that's OK).

Review the task flashcards.

- Say **Look at the activities you've done today. Which activity was your favourite?**

Date: ______________ Unit: __________

1 What did my pupils learn in this unit?

2 How did my pupils work? (✓)

individually ☐ in pairs ☐ in small groups ☐

in large groups ☐ as a class ☐

3 Which key competences did my pupils develop?

- Competence in linguistic communication ☐
- Competence in mathematics, science and technology ☐
- Digital competence ☐
- Learning to learn ☐
- Social and civic competences ☐
- Sense of initiative and entrepreneurship ☐
- Cultural awareness and expression ☐

4 Which lessons / activities were the most successful and why?

5 Which lessons / activities did my pupils find the most difficult and why?

6 What did I try in the classroom for the first time? How did it go?

7 Which resources did I find most useful? (including webpages)

8 What could I do differently next time I teach this unit?

Unit 3

At the circus

Unit overview

Key Competences and Key Learning Outcomes

- Identify and say ten parts of the body (Lesson 1)
- Say the vocabulary chant (Lesson 1)
- Use *I've got …* in a grammar conversation (Lesson 2)
- Make statements about your body (Lesson 2)
- Describe a friend's hair and eyes (Lesson 4)
- Watch and understand a video about the circus (Video and 21st Century Skills)

- Count the parts of the body (Lesson 1)

- Use the Pupil's App on Navio

- Practise spelling (Lesson 1)
- Say a tongue twister to practise the 'h' sound (Lesson 2)
- Review language in the unit and reflect on own learning (Lesson 8)
- Practise activity types found in the Cambridge English Young Learners Exams: Pre A1 Starters

- Understand the importance of riding a bike safely (Lesson 3)
- Describe your feelings (Lesson 7)
- Identify different feelings (Lesson 7)
- Understand the importance of working together (Video and 21st Century Skills)

- Work with a Talk Partner to practise and reinforce learning (all lessons)
- Play a communication game describing people (Lesson 5)

- Sing four songs (Lessons 1, 4, 7 and 8)
- Understand and act out a story (Lesson 3)
- Read about 'Circus Day' in British schools (Lesson 6)
- Think about a circus where you live (Lesson 6)
- Understand and act out an action rhyme (Lesson 7)

Vocabulary

Core vocabulary
arms, ears, eyes, feet, fingers, head, legs, mouth, nose, toes; black hair, blonde hair, brown hair, long hair, red hair, short hair

Extension vocabulary (optional)
back, bottom, hand, knee, shoulder, stomach; curly, spiky, straight, wavy

Other vocabulary
acrobat, circus, clown; juggle scarves, ride a special bike, spin a plate, walk on stilts; angry, happy, sad, tired; cry, go to sleep, laugh, sit, smile, stamp my feet

Recycled vocabulary
numbers 1–10; *ball, car, computer game, dinosaur, doll, kite, robot, scooter, teddy, train; big, small; hand*

Structures

Core structures
I've got (a big nose). I've got (small eyes). My friend has got (long hair). He's / She's got (blue eyes).

Other structures
This is me. This is my body. Count with me. Let's make (a circus). How are you today? I'm (sad). When I'm (happy), I (smile). What colour is (your hair)? My (hair) is (black). What colour are (your eyes)? My (eyes) are (brown). He's / She's fantastic. We're different. We're friends. We're (in the garden). We can do it. My clown has got (a big nose). My clown has got (red hair).

Recycled structures
I've got (a friend called Beth).

Phonics

Consonant sound 'h' (**H**elen, **h**appy, **h**ippo, **h**ops)

British Culture

'Circus Day'

Literacy

Text type: an action rhyme (text to express)
Reading skills: using visual clues; reading for specific information

21st Century Skills

Ways of working: learn to work together

Cooperative learning

Songs: *We can do it!* (Lesson 7); *Well Done!* (Lesson 8)
Skills: Working together (Lesson 1); Working together to complete a task (Lesson 2); Developing a positive classroom atmosphere (Lesson 4); Think-Pair-Share (Lesson 8)

Values

Understanding the importance of riding a bike safely

Cross-curricular links

Links to Science

The human body: the main parts of the body: bones joints and muscles; adjectives to describe the face; action, movement and body joints; recognising and expressing emotion and feelings

Suggested Arts and Crafts concepts

Lines and colours: using lines, shapes and colours to represent the human body

Key Competences and Key Learning Outcomes

- Identify and say ten parts of the body
- Say the vocabulary chant
- Stick the parts of the body stickers

- Count the parts of the body
- Review main parts of the body and face (optional)

- Practise spelling

- Sing a song about the body

Key language
- *arms, ears, eyes, feet, fingers, head, legs, mouth, nose, toes*
- *This is me. This is my body. Count with me.*
- Extension: *back, bottom, hand, knee, shoulder, stomach*

Recycled: numbers 1–10; *car; train*

Materials
- Pupil's Book p28; Activity Book pp26 and 35; Class CD1; Teacher's App on Navio
- Parts of the body flashcards; Unit 3 stickers
- Teacher's Resource Bank: Parts of the body word cards
- Teacher's Resource Bank: Task flashcards: *listen, sing, read, match, stick, say*

Optional materials
- Teacher's Resource Bank: Five Trinity Exam Practice cards (selected from the Starter Unit and Units 1 and 2)

At a Glance Lesson Plan

Pupil's Book

Starting the lesson
- Use the Trinity Exam Practice cards (optional).
- Review classroom instructions.
- Set learning outcomes using the task flashcards.

Vocabulary presentation
- Present the new vocabulary.

Activity 1
- Listen and point.
- ▶ *CD1 Track 47 p260*
- Sing *This is me.*

Word cards
- Read the word cards.
- Match them to the flashcards.

Activity 2
- Read and stick the ten stickers.
- Listen and say the chant.
- ▶ *CD1 Track 49 p260*
- Go to the Activity Book.

Ending the lesson
- Review the lesson.
- Review the task flashcards.

Extra activity

Vocabulary Extension
- Present six additional vocabulary items.

Link to Science
- **The human body:** Review the main parts of the body and face.

Cooperative learning

Working together
- Play a mirror game.

Learning to learn

Spelling
- Practise spelling at any time during this unit (Activity Book p35).

Digital resources

Teacher's Digital: Don't forget you can teach this lesson using the Teacher's App on Navio.

Pupil's Digital: Encourage your pupils to use the Pupil's App on Navio to practise the vocabulary from this lesson.

Powered By NAVIO

Activity Book

Activity Book

Activity 1
- Read and match.
- Say.

Activity 2
- Count and tick (✓) or cross (✗).

Recycled vocabulary
- Look, say and trace the letter.

Spelling

Let's practise spelling!
- Use the *Look-Read-Trace* technique.

Recycled vocabulary
- Look, say and trace the letter.

Detailed Lesson Plan

Starting the lesson

Use the Trinity Exam Practice cards (optional).
- The pupils practise asking and answering questions (see p31).

Review classroom instructions.
- Say **Point to the (board). Touch (the chair). Stand up. Sit down. Put your hands up.** The pupils do the actions.

Set learning outcomes using the task flashcards.
- Say **Today we're going to learn the parts of the body.**
- Hold up the task flashcards in turn and elicit the activities. Stick them on one side of the board. Point to them during the lesson to reinforce your instructions.

Vocabulary presentation

Present the new vocabulary.
- (Books closed.) Touch your head and say **This is my head. Touch your head.** The pupils do the actions. Repeat with other parts of the body.
- Hold up each part of the body flashcard and ask **What's this?** Say the words and the pupils repeat.
- Put the flashcards on the board. Point to them in turn. The pupils say the word and touch their body.
- Point out that the plural of 'foot' is 'feet'.

Pupil's Book Activity 1

Listen and point. Sing *This is me.*
▸ *CD1 Track 47 p260*
- (Books open.) Say **Look! Two clowns. This clown is touching her …** (*nose*)**. This clown is pointing to his …** (*legs*)**.**
- Play the CD. The pupils point to the parts of their body.
- Play the CD again. The pupils sing and do the actions.

Word cards

Read the word cards. Match them to the flashcards.
- (Books closed.) Hold up the parts of the body word cards in turn, and say or elicit each word.
- Invite different pupils to come to the front and stick each word card on the board with the flashcard.

Pupil's Book Activity 2

Read and stick the ten stickers. Listen and say the chant.
▸ *CD1 Track 49 p260*
- (Books open.) Ask a pupil to read the first part of the body. The pupils stick the corresponding sticker. Repeat with the other stickers.
- Play the CD. The pupils listen and say the chant, pointing to the stickers in turn.

Activity Book

Activity 1

Read and match. Say.
- (Books open.) Review the numbers one to ten.
- Ask **How many (arms) have you got?**
- The pupils match the numbers and body parts.
- Ask different pupils to read out the parts of the body.

Answers: **One:** head, nose, mouth **Two:** legs, feet, arms, ears, eyes **Ten:** toes, fingers

Activity 2

Count and tick (✓) or cross (✗).
- Read out the body parts and numbers. Say **Let's count. How many (heads) can you see?**
- Read out number one and ask if it's correct (*yes*). Tell the pupils to tick number 1.
- The pupils read the rest of the phrases, look at the picture and tick or cross.
- Ask the pupils to correct the phrases they crossed.

Answers: **1 ✓ 2 ✗** six hands **3 ✓ 4 ✓ 5 ✗** ten legs

Recycled vocabulary
- The pupils look at the picture and say the word. Then they trace the first letter.

Ending the lesson

Review the lesson.
- (Books closed.) Say **Today we've learnt the parts of the body in English. What words do you remember?** Elicit the words from the pupils.

Review the task flashcards.
- Point to the task flashcards. Say **Look at the activities you've done today. Which activity was your favourite?** Elicit the pupils' favourite activities.

Extra activity

Vocabulary Extension
- Use the Vocabulary Booster on Navio to present and practise six additional words describing body parts: *back*, *bottom*, *hand*, *knee*, *shoulder*, *stomach*.

Link to Science

- If you are studying the Science topic of the **Human body** in English, you could review the vocabulary for the main parts of the body and the face before the pupils play the mirror game.

Cooperative learning

Working together
- Play a mirror game. Organise the class into pairs and ask them to stand in front of each other. Pupil A touches a part of his / her body and says a word (*nose*). Pupil B copies the action and repeats the word. After a few turns the pupils swap roles.

Spelling (Activity Book page 35)

Let's practise spelling!
- The pupils can practise spelling the ten parts of the body using the *Look-Read-Trace* technique at any time during this unit before the Lesson 8 Review.

Recycled vocabulary
- The pupils look at the picture and say the word. Then they trace the first letter.

Key Competences and Key Learning Outcomes

- Use *I've got …*
- Complete and practise a conversation
- Describe parts of the face (optional)
- Listen for specific information

Key language

- *I've got a (big nose). I've got (small eyes). I'm a (clown).*

Recycled: *arms, ears, eyes, feet, fingers, head, legs, mouth, nose, toes; doll*

Materials

- Pupil's Book p29; Activity Book p27; Class CD1; Teacher's App on Navio
- Parts of the body flashcards
- Teacher's Resource Bank: Task flashcards: *think, listen, act out, draw, read, colour, Talk Partners*
- Coloured pencils or crayons

Optional materials

- Teacher's Resource Bank: Five Trinity Exam Practice cards (selected from the Starter Unit and Units 1 and 2)

At a Glance Lesson Plan

Starting the lesson

- Use the Trinity Exam Practice cards (optional).
- **Think-Pair-Share** Review the parts of the body.
- Review the *This is me* song.
- ▶ ***CD1 Track 47 p260***
- ▶ ***CD1 Track 48 p260 (optional karaoke version)***
- Set learning outcomes using the task flashcards.

Activity 1

- Listen and repeat.
- ▶ ***CD1 Track 50 p260***
- Act out.

Activity 2

- Listen and draw.
- ▶ ***CD1 Track 51 p260***

Go to the Activity Book.

Pupil's Book

Ending the lesson

- Review the lesson.
- Review the task flashcards.

Extra activity

Reinforcement

- Play *What's this?*

Cooperative learning

Working together to complete a task

- Make a body sculpture.

Link to Science

- **The human body:** Describe parts of the face by adding adjectives.

Digital resources

Teacher's Digital: Don't forget you can teach this lesson using the Teacher's App on Navio.

Pupil's Digital: Encourage your pupils to use the Pupil's App on Navio to practise the vocabulary from this lesson.

Powered By NAVIO

Activity Book

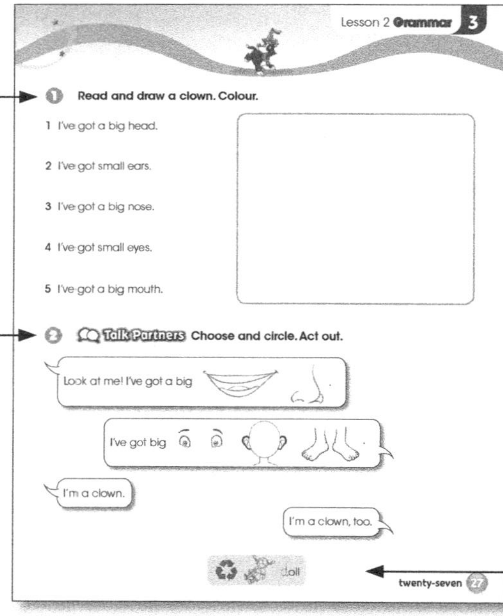

Activity Book

Activity 1

- Read and draw a clown.
- Colour.

Activity 2

- Choose and circle.
- **Talk Partners** Act out.

Recycled vocabulary

- Look, say and trace the letter.

Starting the lesson

Use the Trinity Exam Practice cards (optional).

- The pupils practise asking and answering questions (see p31).

Think-Pair-Share Review the parts of the body.

- Ask **Can you remember the ten parts of the body?** The class thinks silently for a minute.
- **Talk Partners** Then the pupils work with a Talk Partner to name the parts of the body.
- Invite different pairs to say a different part of the body. Hold up the corresponding flashcard and prompt the class to repeat the word.
- Repeat, asking different pairs each time, until all ten parts of the body have been named.

Review the *This is me* song.

▶ *CD1 Track 47 p260*

▶ *CD1 Track 48 p260 (optional karaoke version)*

- Play the song from Lesson 1 (or use the karaoke version). The pupils sing and do the actions.

Set learning outcomes using the task flashcards.

- Say **Today we're going to be clowns and practise talking about parts of the body.**
- Hold up the task flashcards in turn and elicit the activities. Stick them on one side of the board. Point to them during the lesson to reinforce your instructions.

Pupil's Book Activity 1

Listen and repeat. Act out.

▶ *CD1 Track 50 p260*

- (Books open.) The pupils look at the picture. Ask **What can you see?**
- Play the CD. The pupils listen and read the conversation. Ask **Who has got a red nose? Who has got big ears?**
- Play the CD again, pausing after each sentence for the pupils to repeat.
- Ask different pupils to come to the front and act out the conversation with your help or playing the CD.

Pupil's Book Activity 2

Listen and draw.

▶ *CD1 Track 51 p260*

- Say **Look at the girl. What's missing? Is her nose big or small? Let's listen.**
- Play the CD, pausing after each piece of information. The pupils listen and draw the missing body parts.
- Finally, point to your eyes and say **I've got small eyes. I've got a small nose.** Encourage the class to describe their eyes and noses.

Answers: **1** a big nose **2** a small mouth **3** big eyes **4** big ears

Activity Book

Activity 1

Read and draw a clown. Colour.

- (Books open.) Read out the first sentence. The pupils draw the clown's head.
- Ask different pupils to read the other sentences.
- The pupils draw the clown's face. Then they colour it.

Activity 2

Choose and circle. Act out.

- Read the speech bubbles, pausing before the pictures to elicit the vocabulary.
- Practise the conversation as a class.
- **Talk Partners** When the pupils are confident with the language, they work in pairs to choose and circle an object for each sentence. They ask and answer with their partner.
- Invite different pairs of pupils to act out their conversations.

Recycled vocabulary

- The pupils look at the picture and say the word. Then they trace the first letter.

Ending the lesson

Review the lesson.

- (Books closed.) Say **Today we've drawn a clown. What parts of the body did we draw? Is your drawing good?** Elicit answers from the pupils.

Review the task flashcards.

- Point to the task flashcards. Say **Look at the activities you've done today. Which activity was your favourite?** Elicit the pupils' favourite activities.

Extra activity

Reinforcement

- Play *Here!* with the parts of the body flashcards (see p23).

Cooperative learning

Working together to complete a task

- Raise the pupils' awareness of the importance of working together to do an activity. Tell the class they are going to make a group sculpture.
- The pupils form a circle. Say **Leg to leg**. The pupils have to join these parts of the body together with the person on their left and right.
- Repeat the procedure with other parts of the body, e.g. fingers to fingers, feet to feet.

Link to Science

- If you are studying the Science topic of the **Human body** in English, you could review the names of other parts of the face. With the help of the class, draw a clown's face on the board and describe it in more detail. Say **I'm a clown. I've got (big, red nose)**.

Key Competences and Key Learning Outcomes

- Read, listen and understand a story about a circus
- Read the story with some fluency
- Become familiar with the story through a pre-reading task
- Understand the importance of riding a bike in a safe and responsible manner
- Understand and act out the story
- Give an opinion on the story

Key language

- *acrobat, circus, clown*
- *He's got (purple hair). Let's make (a circus). Here's (Molly the clown). She's (fantastic).*

Recycled: *teddy; ball*

Recycled: *I've got (big feet).*

Materials

- Pupil's Book pp30 and 31; Activity Book p28; Class CD1; Teacher's App on Navio
- Teacher's Resource Bank: Task flashcards: *think, listen, read, act out, circle, match*
- Teacher's Resource Bank: Unit 3 Lesson 3 Animated Story

Optional materials

- Teacher's Resource Bank: Five Trinity Exam Practice cards (selected from the Starter Unit and Units 1 and 2)

At a Glance Lesson Plan

Starting the lesson

- Use the Trinity Exam Practice cards (optional).
- Review the parts of the body.
- Set learning outcomes using the task flashcards.

Before you read

- Explain the story title.
- Read and answer the question.

Activity 1

- Listen and read.
- ▶ *CD1 Track 52 p260*
- Act out.
- ***Now watch the animated story!***

After you read: Activity 2

- Go to page 28 in your Activity Book.
- Values: Read and circle.

Pupil's Book

Ending the lesson

- Review the lesson.
- Review the task flashcards.

Digital resources

Teacher's Digital: Don't forget you can teach this lesson using the Teacher's App on Navio.

Pupil's Digital: Encourage your pupils to use the Pupil's App on Navio to practise the vocabulary from this lesson.

Powered By NAVIO

Activity Book

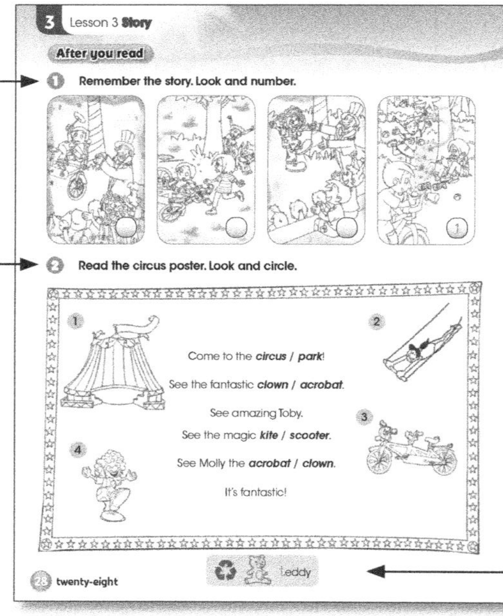

Activity Book

After you read: Activity 1

- Remember the story. Look and number.

Activity 2

- Read the circus poster.
- Look and circle.

Recycled vocabulary

- Look, say and trace the letter.

Detailed Lesson Plan

Starting the lesson

Use the Trinity Exam Practice cards (optional).

- The pupils practise asking and answering questions (see p31).

Review the parts of the body.

- Play *True or false* to practise the parts of the body vocabulary. Say a statement about your body. If the sentence is true the pupils stand up and if it is false, the pupils remain seated. Say **I've got two ears.** (The pupils stand up.) **I've got nine toes.** (The pupils sit down.) Encourage confident pupils to take your role and say a sentence.

Set learning outcomes using the task flashcards.

- Say **Today we're going to listen to a story in English**.
- Hold up the task flashcards in turn and elicit the activities. Stick them on one side of the board. Point to them during the lesson to reinforce your instructions.

Before you read

Explain the story title.

- (Books open.) Focus on the story title. Ask **What can you see at the circus? Is a circus fun?**

Read and answer the question.

- The pupils scan the story to find the clown (in frame 4).

Pupil's Book Activity 1

Listen and read. Act out.

▶ *CD1 Track 52 p260*

- The pupils place their 'magic finger' on the first frame of the story.
- Play the CD. The pupils point to the different frames as the story progresses. Pause the CD after each frame to check that all the pupils are following.
- Play the CD again. Ask questions about each story frame to help and check understanding.

Suggested comprehension questions

- Frame 1: **Where are the children?** (*In the garden.*) **What do they want to make?** (*A circus.*)
- Frame 2: **Where are the children now?** (*At a circus.*) **Are they surprised?** (*Yes.*) Mime being surprised.
- Frame 3: **Who can they see?** (*An acrobat.*)
- Frame 4: **Who can they see now?** (*Molly. / A clown.*) **What colour is the clown's hair?** (*Purple.*)
- Frame 5: **Who can they see now?** (*Toby.*)
- Frame 6: **Who can they see now?** (*Jake.*) **Where is Jake?** (*On the magic bike.*)
- Frame 7: **Is Jake an acrobat?** (*No.*)
- Frame 8: **Has the magic finished?** (*Yes.*) **Where are the children now?** (*In the garden.*) **Are they happy?** (*Yes.*)
- Finally, ask the pupils **Is this a good story?** The pupils give their opinion through gesture (thumbs up / down) or orally (*yes / no*).
- Organise the class into four groups (Beth, Molly, Jake and the circus ringmaster).
- Play the CD. Each group joins in when their character speaks. If the pupils need extra support, pause the CD after each sentence for the pupils to repeat. The groups swap roles and repeat several times.

Now watch the animated story

After you read

Go to page 28 in your Activity Book.

Activity Book

After you read: Activity 1

Remember the story. Look and number.

- (Books open.) Ask **Which picture is number 1?**
- The pupils remember the story and number the frames.

Answers: **1** fourth picture **2** third picture **3** first picture **4** second picture

Activity 2

Read the circus poster. Look and circle.

- Read out the circus poster, pausing before the two options to elicit the correct word.
- The pupils read the poster again and circle the correct word in each sentence.
- Fast finishers can colour the poster.

Answers: circus, acrobat, bike, clown

Recycled vocabulary

- The pupils look at the picture and say the word. Then they trace the first letter.

Pupil's Book Activity 2

Values: Read and circle.

- The pupils look at the photo on the right. Read out the sentence in the speech bubble and prompt the class to tell you the correct thing to do when you ride a bike.
- Explain that it is important to ride a bike in a safe and responsible manner.
- Encourage the pupils to say if they wear a helmet when they ride their bikes and if they use two hands.

Answer: hands

Ending the lesson

Review the lesson.

- (Books closed.) Say **Today we've listened to a story about a circus.** Ask **What happened in the story?** Elicit the story from the pupils.
- Then say **Today you've learnt how to be careful when you ride a bike.**

Review the task flashcards.

- Point to the task flashcards. Say **Look at the activities you've done today. Which activity was your favourite?** Elicit the pupils' favourite activities.

Key Competences and Key Learning Outcomes

- Describe a friend's hair and eyes
- Focus on similarities and differences in people's appearances (optional)
- Listen for specific information
- Sing a song

Key language

- *black hair, blonde hair, brown hair, long hair, red hair, short hair*
- *My friend has got (long) hair. He's / She's got (blue) eyes.*
- Extension: *curly, spiky, straight, wavy*

Recycled: *computer game; eyes, hair*

Materials

- Pupil's Book p32; Activity Book p29; Class CD2; Teacher's App on Navio
- Character flashcards *Beth* and *Jake*
- Teacher's Resource Bank: Task flashcards: *listen, sing, Talk Partners, think, draw, colour*
- Crayons or coloured pencils

Optional materials

- Teacher's Resource Bank: Five Trinity Exam Practice cards (selected from the Starter Unit and Units 1 and 2)
- Pieces of A4 paper, card

At a Glance Lesson Plan

Starting the lesson

- Use the Trinity Exam Practice cards (optional).
- Review the Lesson 3 story.
- Set learning outcomes using the task flashcards.

Vocabulary presentation

- Present the new vocabulary.

Activity 1

- Listen, point and say.

▶ ***CD2 Track 1 p261***

Activity 2

- Sing *My friend.*
- Listen and point.

▶ ***CD2 Track 2 p261***

Activity 3

- Listen and repeat.
- Talk Partners Talk about your friend.

▶ ***CD2 Track 3 p261***

Go to the Activity Book.

Pupil's Book

Ending the lesson

- Review the lesson.
- Review the task flashcards.

Extra activities

Reinforcement

- Make a class graph of eye colour.

Vocabulary Extension

- Present four additional vocabulary items.

Cooperative learning

Developing a positive classroom atmosphere

- Play *Me too!*

Link to Science

- **The human body:** Focus on similarities and differences in people's appearances.

Digital resources

Teacher's Digital: Don't forget you can teach this lesson using the Teacher's App on Navio.

Pupil's Digital: Encourage your pupils to use the Pupil's App on Navio to practise the vocabulary from this lesson.

Powered By NAVIO

Activity Book

Activity Book

Activity 1

- Listen and colour.

▶ ***CD2 Track 4 p261***

Activity 2

- Draw and colour a friend.
- Circle and say.

Talk Partners Talk about your friend.

Recycled vocabulary

- Look, say and trace the letters.

Detailed Lesson Plan

Starting the lesson

Use the Trinity Exam Practice cards (optional).
- The pupils practise asking and answering questions (see p31).

Review the Lesson 3 story.
- Give the pupils two minutes to look at the story. Then say **One, two, three, I can see a (clown). Where is it?** The pupils find and point to it. Repeat with other things.

Set learning outcomes using the task flashcards.
- Say **Today we're going to sing a song and talk about friends.**
- Hold up the task flashcards in turn and elicit the activities. Stick them on one side of the board. Point to them during the lesson to reinforce your instructions.

Vocabulary presentation

Present the new vocabulary.
- (Books open.) Point to the first photo in Activity 1 and read the words. Say **Stand up if you've got long hair.**
- Repeat with the other photos.

Pupil's Book Activity 1

Listen, point and say.
▶ *CD2 Track 1 p261*
- (Books open.) The pupils look at the photos. Say **Let's listen and say the words.**
- Play the CD. The pupils point and say the words.

Pupil's Book Activity 2

Listen and point. Sing *My friend.*
▶ *CD2 Track 2 p261*
- Hold up the *Beth* flashcard and ask **Who's this? Has she got short hair?** Repeat with other adjectives and then with the *Jake* flashcard.
- Play the CD. The pupils point to the characters.
- Play the CD again. The pupils sing the song.

Pupil's Book Activity 3

Listen and repeat. Talk about your friend.
▶ *CD2 Track 3 p261*
- Play the CD. The pupils listen.
- Play the CD again. The pupils listen and repeat.
- Ask different pupils to point to a friend in the class and describe his / her hair and eyes.
  Talk Partners The pupils practise talking about their friends with a Talk Partner.

Activity Book

Activity 1
Listen and colour.
▶ *CD2 Track 4 p261*
- (Books open.) Play the CD, pausing after each description. The pupils listen and colour.

Answers: **1** brown hair, green eyes **2** red hair, blue eyes **3** black hair, brown eyes **4** black hair, blue eyes

Activity 2
Draw and colour a friend. Circle and say.
- Ask the pupils to think about a friend. They draw their friend in the box and then colour the picture.
- The pupils read the sentences and circle the adjective and colour that describes their friend.
  Talk Partners The pupils show their partner their drawings and read the sentences.

Recycled vocabulary
- The pupils look at the picture and say the word. Then they trace the first letter of each word.

Ending the lesson

Review the lesson.
- Say **Today we've sung a song. Who is in the song? What parts of the body are in the song?** Elicit the answers from the pupils.

Review the task flashcards.
- Point to the task flashcards. Say **Look at the activities you've done today. Which activity was your favourite?** Elicit the pupils' favourite activities.

Extra activities

Reinforcement
- Draw a large, simple eye on the board. The pupils copy it and then colour it to match their own eye colour.
- Write the different eye colours along the bottom of the board.
- The pupils come up to the front one by one, show their drawing and say **I've got (brown) eyes.** Then they stick their drawing on the board above the corresponding colour. Finally, count the eyes together and say **(Ten) children have got (brown) eyes.**

Vocabulary Extension
- Use the Vocabulary Booster on Navio and present and practise four additional words to describe hair: *curly, spiky, straight, wavy.*

Cooperative learning

Developing a positive classroom atmosphere
- Discovering similarities helps to develop a positive classroom atmosphere. Play *Me too!* Ask a pupil to come to the front. He / She says *I've got (brown) hair.* Everyone who has similar colour hair shouts out *Me too!*

Link to Science

- If you are studying the Science topic of the **Human body** in English, you could review that we are all the same, but all different. Focus the pupils' attention on what is the same (we have all got two eyes) and what is different (some people have got blue eyes and others have got green or brown eyes).

Key Competences and Key Learning Outcomes

- Say a tongue twister with the 'h' sound
- Listen for information and write the numbers
- Play a communication game describing people

Key language

- *My clown has got a (big nose). My clown has got (red hair).*
- **Recycled:** *eyes, hair, mouth, nose; kite*
- **Recycled:** *He's got (big eyes).*

Materials

- Pupil's Book p33; Activity Book, p30, Class CD2; Teacher's App on Navio
- Teacher's Resource Bank: Task flashcards: *listen, say, number, cut out, colour, Talk Partners*
- Scissors and crayons or coloured pencils
- Teacher's Resource Bank: Unit 3 Lesson 5 Activity 3 cut-outs

Optional materials

- Teacher's Resource Bank: Five Trinity Exam Practice cards (selected from the Starter Unit and Units 1 and 2)
- Coloured paper

At a Glance Lesson Plan

Starting the lesson

- Use the Trinity Exam Practice cards (optional).
- Review the vocabulary from Lesson 4.
- Set learning outcomes using the task flashcards.

Activity 1

- Listen and say.
- ▶ *CD2 Track 5 p261*
- Go to Magic Phonics.
- Go to the Activity Book.

Activity 2

- Listen and number.
- ▶ *CD2 Track 6 p261*

Activity 3

- Make and play the game. Talk Partners

Pupil's Book

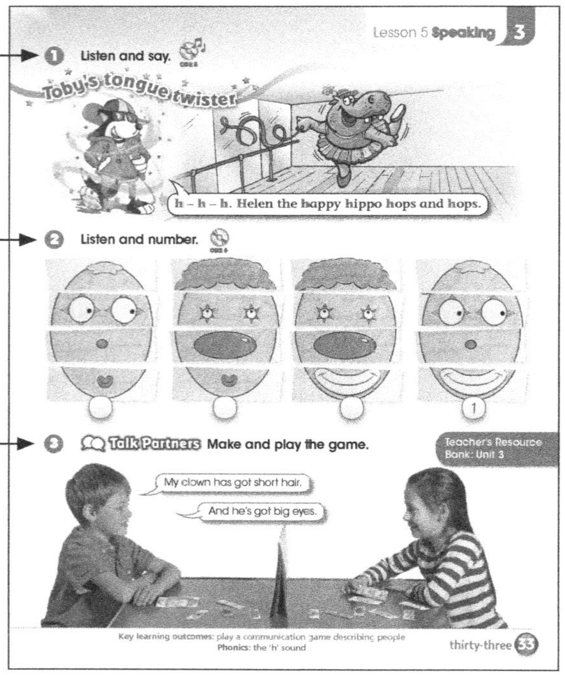

Ending the lesson

- Review the lesson.
- Review the task flashcards.

Extra activity

Reinforcement

- Continue the pronunciation wall display.

Activity Book

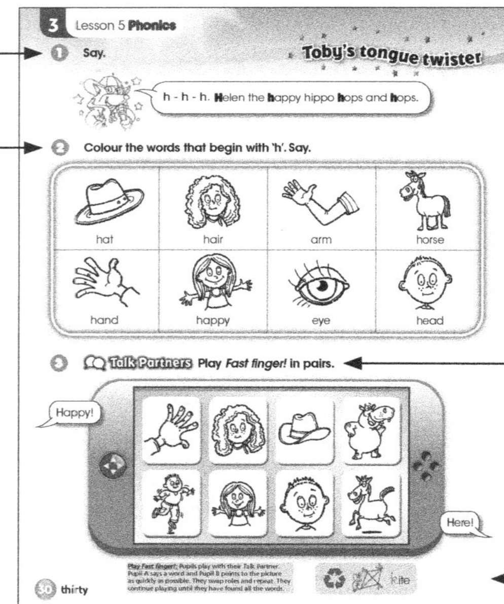

Activity Book

Activity 1

- Say.

Activity 2

- Colour the words that begin with 'h'.
- Say.
- Go to Magic Phonics.

Activity 3

- Talk Partners Play *Fast finger!* in pairs.

Recycled vocabulary

- Look, say and trace the letter

Digital resources

Teacher's Digital: Don't forget you can teach this lesson using the Teacher's App on Navio.

Pupil's Digital: Encourage your pupils to use the Pupil's App on Navio to practise the vocabulary from this lesson.

Powered By NAVIO

Starting the lesson

Use the Trinity Exam Practice cards (optional).

- The pupils practise asking and answering questions (see p31).

Review the vocabulary from Lesson 4.

- The pupils form a circle. Point to the pupil on your left and say **He's / She's got (brown) hair.** That pupil then says a sentence about the pupil on his / her left.
- Continue around the circle until each pupil has said a sentence.

Set learning outcomes using the task flashcards.

- Say **Today we're going to practise saying a tongue twister and make and play a speaking game.**
- Hold up the task flashcards in turn and elicit the activities. Stick them on one side of the board. Point to them during the lesson to reinforce your instructions.

Pupil's Book Activity 1

Listen and say.

▶ *CD2 Track 5 p261*

- (Books open.) Write the target 'h' sound in letters on the board, and say it for the pupils. The pupils repeat.
- Say **It's time for Toby's tongue twister. What can you see here? Is the hippo happy or sad?** Demonstrate the word 'hop'. The pupils do the action.
- Play the CD. The pupils listen and repeat the target sound, then the words and then the entire tongue twister, faster and faster.

Go to Magic Phonics.

Activity Book

Activity 1

Say.

- (Books open.) Read out the tongue twister for the pupils to repeat.
- The pupils say the tongue twister to their partner, saying it faster and faster each time.

Activity 2

Colour the words that begin with 'h'. Say.

- Ask the pupils to look and say the words that begin with 'h'. The pupils colour and say these words.

Answers: hat, hair, horse, hand, happy, head

Go to Magic Phonics.

Activity 3

Play *Fast finger!* in pairs.

- **Talk Partners** The pupils take turns to play with a Talk Partner. One pupil says a word and the other needs to point to the picture representing that object as quickly as possible. They continue playing until they've found all the words in the game.

Recycled vocabulary

- The pupils look at the picture and say the word. Then they trace the first letter.

Pupil's Book Activity 2

Listen and number.

▶ *CD2 Track 6 p261*

- Focus the pupils on Activity 2. Ask **What can you see in the pictures?**
- Tell the pupils that they are going to listen to children playing a game.
- Play the CD, pausing after each conversation so the pupils can point to the correct picture.
- Play the CD again. The pupils listen and write the numbers.

Answers: **1** fourth picture **2** third picture **3** first picture **4** second picture

Pupil's Book Activity 3

Make and play the game.

- Tell the class that they are going to play the game.
- The pupils cut out and colour the cards and place them on their desk.
- Demonstrate the activity with the class. Create a clown's face and describe the four parts. The pupils 'make' the face with their cards.
- Ask a pupil to take over your role. The rest of the class 'makes' the clown that is being described.
- **Talk Partners** The pupils play the game with a Talk Partner.

Ending the lesson

Review the lesson.

- (Books closed.) Say **Today we've practised a tongue twister and played a game in pairs.** Elicit the tongue twister from the pupils.

Review the task flashcards.

- Point to the task flashcards. Say **Look at the activities you've done today. Which activity was your favourite?** Elicit the pupils' favourite activities.

Extra activity

Reinforcement

- Continue the pronunciation wall display. Cut out the letter 'h' in coloured paper. Stick it on a piece of differently coloured paper to make a wall display. Elicit words that begin with that letter and write them on the wall display.
- Encourage the pupils to add new words beginning with the letter 'h' during the year. They can either tell you the new word for you to add or write the word themselves if they can.

Key Competences and Key Learning Outcomes

- Review what the body can do (optional)
- Listen for general information
- Read about 'Circus Day' in British schools
- Think about a circus where you live

Key language

- *circus; face*
- *I juggle scarves. I ride a special bike. I spin a plate. I walk on stilts.*

Recycled: *robot; feet, hand, legs; birthday party*

Materials

- Pupil's Book p34; Activity Book p31; Class CD2; Teacher's App on Navio
- Teacher's Resource Bank: Task flashcards: *listen, read, think, circle, match, tick, draw*

Optional materials

- Teacher's Resource Bank: Five Trinity Exam Practice cards (selected from the Starter Unit and Units 1 and 2)
- Face paints

At a Glance Lesson Plan

Pupil's Book

Starting the lesson

- Use the Trinity Exam Practice cards (optional).
- Talk Partners Review Toby's tongue twister.

▶ *CD2 Track 5 p261*

- Set learning outcomes using the task flashcards.

Activity 1

- Listen and read.

▶ *CD2 Track 7 p261*

- Answer.

Think about your culture

- Do you go to the circus with your family?

Go to the Activity Book.

Ending the lesson

- Review the lesson.
- Review the task flashcards.

Link to Science

- **The human body:** Review what the body can do: actions, movement and joints.

Extra activities

Reinforcement

- Play a 'Circus Day' mime game.

Extension

- Do a face painting activity.

Activity Book

Activity Book

Activity 1

- Listen and number.

▶ *CD2 Track 8 p261*

Activity 2: Think about your culture

- Read and tick (✓).
- Draw and say.

Recycled vocabulary

- Look, say and trace the letter.

Digital resources

Teacher's Digital: Don't forget you can teach this lesson using the Teacher's App on Navio.

Powered By NAVIO

Detailed Lesson Plan

Starting the lesson

Use the Trinity Exam Practice cards (optional).

- The pupils practise asking and answering questions (see p31).

Review Toby's tongue twister.

▶ *CD2 Track 5 p261*

- Ask **What sound did you practise in Toby's tongue twister? Can you remember the tongue twister?** Play the CD. Practise the tongue twister as a class. (*Helen the happy hippo hops and hops.*)
- Talk Partners The pupils practise saying the tongue twister as fast as possible with a Talk Partner. Choose a fast pair to say it for the class.

Set learning outcomes using the task flashcards.

- Say **Today we're going to learn about circus activities in Britain.**
- Hold up the task flashcards in turn and elicit the activities. Stick them on one side of the board. Point to them during the lesson to reinforce your instructions.

Pupil's Book Activity 1

Listen and read. Answer.

▶ *CD2 Track 7 p261*

- (Books open.) Focus the pupils on the photos. Ask **What can you see?** Explain that Lucy and Alex sometimes do circus activities at school. Say **Let's find out what activities they do.**
- Play the CD, pausing after each activity mentioned to check understanding.
- Ask **What do Lucy and Alex do on Circus Day? Do they (spin a plate)?** Mime the action and encourage the pupils to mime to show understanding. Repeat with the other activities.

Pupil's Book Think about your culture

Do you go to the circus with your family?

- Read out the question. The pupils answer.
- Ask additional questions, e.g. **Do you like the circus? What can you see at a circus in your country?**

Activity Book

Activity 1

Listen and number.

▶ *CD2 Track 8 p261*

- (Books open.) Focus the pupils on the pictures.
- Play the CD, pausing after the first part describing stilt-walking. Ask pupils to look at the image labelled 1 and elicit that this is the first image being described.
- Tell the pupils they need to number the images according to the order they are heard on the CD.
- Play the CD, pausing after each description for pupils to number the correct image.

Answers: (left to right) 4, 2, 5, 1, 3

Activity 2: Think about your culture

Read and tick (✓). Draw and say.

- Read out the question in the speech bubble. Elicit the pupils' answers.
- Read out the first phrase. The pupils tick the box if they paint their faces at a birthday party.
- Repeat with the other phrases.
- Then the pupils draw their painted face. They can be clowns, monsters or animals.
- Invite different pupils to show the class their drawing and describe it, e.g. *I've got a green and white face.*

Recycled vocabulary

- The pupils look at the picture and say the word. Then they trace the first letter.

Ending the lesson

Review the lesson.

- (Books closed.) Say **Today we've talked about 'Circus Days' in British schools. What activities do Alex and Lucy do on 'Circus Day'?** Elicit activities from the pupils, with mime if necessary.

Review the task flashcards.

- Point to the task flashcards. Say **Look at the activities you've done today. Which activity was your favourite?** Elicit the pupils' favourite activities.

Link to Science

- If you are studying the Science topic of the **Human body** in English, you could review what we can do with our bodies (*run*, *skip*, *jump*, etc.), and the parts of the body we use for each action. Review the joints we use to do different movements when you play the Circus Day mime game.

Extra activities

Reinforcement

- Say **Let's play a Circus Day mime game. Listen and do the action.** Then say **Spin a plate.** Prompt the pupils to do the action. Repeat with other actions: *juggle balls*, *paint your face*, *walk on stilts*. Repeat the instructions in a random order. The pupils listen and do the corresponding action each time.

Extension

- Use face paints to do a simple face painting activity. Encourage the pupils to ask **Can I have a (red nose) please?** At the end of each turn, each pupil points to his / her face and says *Look at me. I've got a (big mouth). I'm a clown.*

Key Competences and Key Learning Outcomes

- Sing a cooperative learning song
- Understand the importance of a positive attitude
- Identify different feelings
- Read and understand an action rhyme

Key language

- *angry, happy, sad, tired; cry, go to sleep, laugh, sit, smile, stamp my feet*
- *How are you today? I'm (sad). When I'm (happy), I (smile). We can do it.*

Recycled: *ball*

Materials

- Pupil's Book p35; Activity Book p32; Class CD2; Teacher's App on Navio
- Teacher's Resource Bank: Task flashcards: *think, circle, listen, read, act out, sing, draw*

Optional materials

- Teacher's Resource Bank: Five Trinity Exam Practice cards (selected from the Starter Unit and Units 1 and 2)
- Teacher's Resource Bank: Parts of the body word cards
- A large piece of paper

At a Glance Lesson Plan

Starting the lesson

- Use the Trinity Exam Practice cards (optional).
- Review the culture lesson.
- Set learning outcomes using the task flashcards.

Before you read

- Look at the pictures and talk about feelings.

Activity 1

- How are you today?
- Circle.

Activity 2

- Listen and read the rhyme.

▶ *CD2 Track 9 p261*

Activity 3 Cooperative learning

- Sing *We can do it!*

▶ *CD2 Track 10 p261*

Pupil's Book

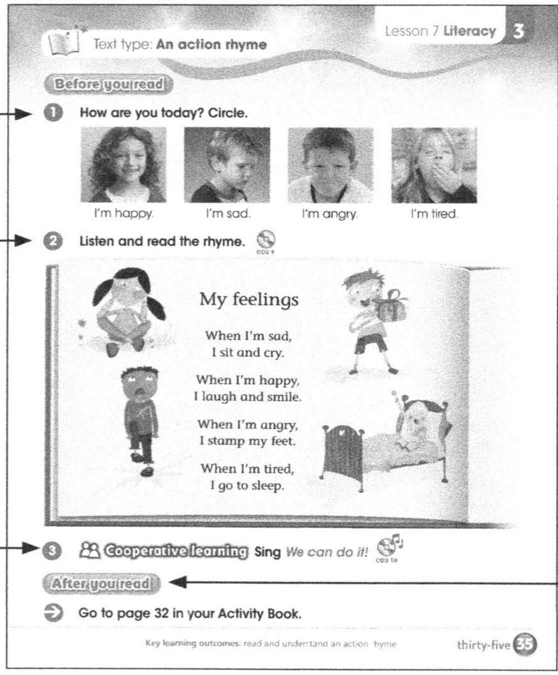

After you read

- Go to page 32 in your Activity Book.

Ending the lesson

- Review the lesson.
- Review the task flashcards.

Extra activities

Reinforcement

- Perform the rhyme in groups of four.
- Make a class body poster.

Link to Science

- **The human body:** Review the importance of recognising and expressing emotions and feelings.

Digital resources

Teacher's Digital: Don't forget you can teach this lesson using the Teacher's App on Navio.

Pupil's Digital: Encourage your pupils to use the Pupil's App on Navio to practise the vocabulary from this lesson.

Activity Book

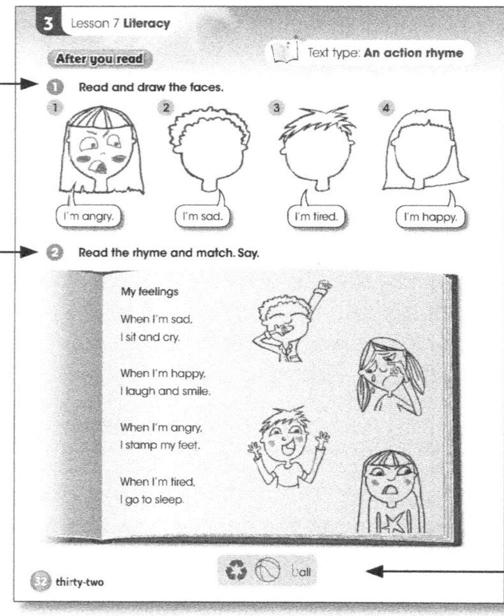

Activity Book

After you read: Activity 1

- Read and draw the faces.

Activity 2

- Read the rhyme and match.
- Say.

Recycled vocabulary

- Look, say and trace the letter.

Detailed Lesson Plan

Starting the lesson

Use the Trinity Exam Practice cards (optional).
- The pupils practise asking and answering questions (see p31).

Review the culture lesson.
- Review the circus activities that British children do at school.
- Elicit the activities *spin a plate, juggle scarves, ride a special bike, walk on stilts.*
- Say the activities in random order. The pupils listen and do the actions.

Set learning outcomes using the task flashcards.
- Say **Today we're going to read an action rhyme.**
- Hold up the task flashcards in turn and elicit the activities. Stick them on one side of the board. Point to them during the lesson to reinforce your instructions.

Before you read

Look at the pictures and talk about feelings.
- (Books open.) Focus the pupils on the pictures and elicit possible situations for each feeling (e.g. happy – It's my birthday!; sad – I fell out with my friend.; angry – My brother keeps taking my things.; tired – I went to bed too late.).

Pupil's Book Activity 1

How are you today? Circle.
- (Books open.) Ask **How are you today?** Point to the first photo and ask **Hands up if you're happy today.** Encourage the pupils to do the action and say the sentence *I'm happy.*
- Repeat with all the photos.
- The pupils circle how they are feeling today.

Pupil's Book Activity 2

Listen and read the rhyme.
▶ *CD2 Track 9 p261*
- Focus the pupils on the rhyme in Activity 2.
- Play the CD. The pupils listen and read the rhyme and point to the correct pictures.
- Play the CD again, pausing after each line. The class repeats and does the action.
- Ask different pupils to read the verses with the CD.
- Ask the class **Is it a good rhyme?** Elicit their opinions.
- Slowly say **Cry. Smile.** Ask the class to repeat the two words and explain that they rhyme. Ask **Can you see two more words that rhyme?** (*Feet. Sleep.*)

Pupil's Book Activity 3: Cooperative learning

Sing *We can do it!*
▶ *CD2 Track 10 p261*
- It can be difficult for young learners to sustain concentration and motivation, especially when a task is challenging. In a cooperative classroom, children help, support and encourage each other as they learn. Use the *We can do it!* chant when you see that the class or individual members are finding or are going to find a task difficult.
- Play the CD. The pupils listen and do the actions with you.
- Play the CD again and encourage the pupils to sing and do the actions.

Activity Book

After you read: Activity 1
Read and draw the faces.
- (Books open.) Ask the class if they liked the rhyme in the Pupil's Book.
- Read the first speech bubble. The pupils mime the emotion.
- Repeat with all the speech bubbles.
- The pupils read the speech bubbles again and draw the correct emotion on the faces.

Activity 2
Read the rhyme and match. Say.
- Focus the pupils on Activity 2. The pupils look at the pictures and read the rhyme.
- The pupils read the rhyme again and match the verses to the pictures.
- The pupils take turns to say the rhyme to their partner.

Answers: **verse one:** first girl **verse two:** second boy **verse three:** second girl **verse four:** first boy

Recycled vocabulary
- The pupils look at the picture and say the word. Then they trace the first letter.

Ending the lesson

Review the lesson.
- (Books closed.) Say **Today we've read an action rhyme in English and sung a song. What feelings were in the rhyme?** Elicit the adjectives from the pupils.

Review the task flashcards.
- Point to the task flashcards. Say **Look at the activities you've done today. Which activity was your favourite?** Elicit the pupils' favourite activities.

Extra activities

Reinforcement
- Make a class body poster. A pupil lies on a large piece of paper. Trace his / her outline.
- Hold up the parts of the body word cards one by one, and ask different pupils to put them in the correct place on the poster.

Link to Science

- If you are studying the Science topic of the **Human body** in English, you could review the importance of recognising and expressing emotions and feelings. Encourage the class to talk about when they experience the different emotions in the rhyme.

Key Competences and Key Learning Outcomes

- Review language in the unit
- Reflect on own learning
- Sing a cooperative learning song

Key language

Recycled: *arms, ears, eyes, feet, fingers, head, legs, mouth, nose, toes; black, blue, blonde, brown, green, long, red, short; dinosaur*

Recycled: *I've got (one mouth). He's / She's got (long hair). He's / She's got (brown eyes). (Molly) has got (blue eyes).*

Materials

- Pupil's Book p36; Activity Book p33; Class CD2; Teacher's App on Navio
- Parts of the body flashcards
- Teacher's Resource Bank: Task flashcards: *listen, number, read, sing, think, stick, draw*
- Teacher's Resource Bank: Traffic light cut-out
- *Give Me Five!* sticker

Optional materials

- Teacher's Resource Bank: Five Trinity Exam Practice cards (selected from the Starter Unit and Units 1 and 2)
- Pieces of A4 paper, coloured pencils or crayons

At a Glance Lesson Plan

Starting the lesson

- Use the Trinity Exam Practice cards (optional).
- Review the unit vocabulary.
- Set learning outcomes using the task flashcards.

Activity 1

- Listen and number.
- ▶ ***CD2 Track 11 p261***
- Say.

Activity 2

- Read and circle *A* or *B*.

Activity 3 Cooperative learning

- Sing *Well done!*
- ▶ ***CD2 Track 12 p261***
- Stick the *Give Me Five!* sticker.
- Go to the Activity Book.

Pupil's Book

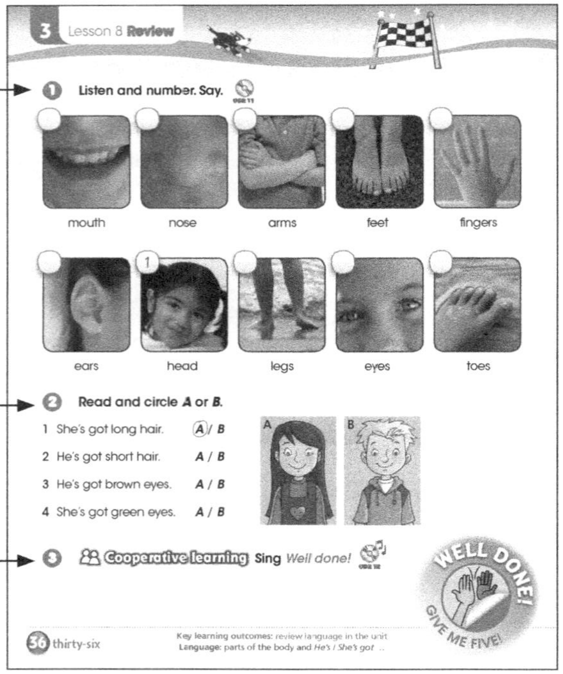

Ending the lesson

- Review the task flashcards.

Extra activities

Reinforcement

- Play *Silent words*.

Cooperative learning

- **Think-Pair-Share**
  Review parts of the body.

Digital resources

Teacher's Digital: Don't forget you can teach this lesson using the Teacher's App on Navio.

Pupil's Digital: Encourage your pupils to use the Pupil's App on Navio to practise the vocabulary from this lesson.

Powered By NAVIO

Activity Book

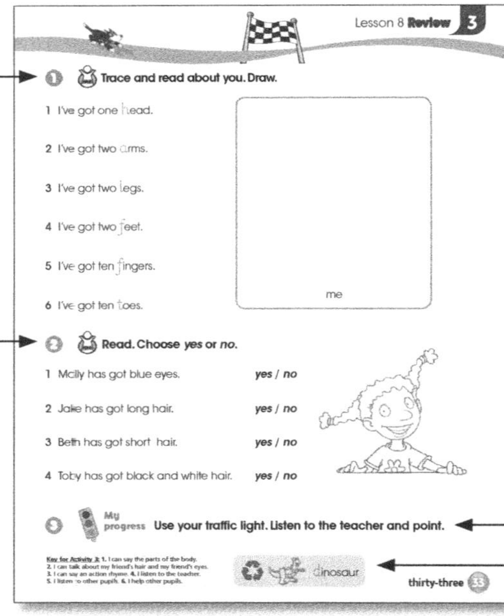

Activity Book

Activity 1

- Trace and read about you.
- Draw.

Activity 2

- Read.
- Choose *yes* or *no*.

Activity 3 My progress

- Use your traffic light. Listen to the teacher and point.

Recycled vocabulary

- Look, say and trace the letter.

Starting the lesson

Use the Trinity Exam Practice cards (optional).
- The pupils practise asking and answering questions (see p31).

Review the unit vocabulary.
- Hold up a parts of the body flashcard and elicit the word. Stick the flashcard face down on the board. Repeat until all the flashcards are on the board.
- Ask **Where's the (head)?** Ask a pupil to turn over a flashcard. If it's correct, he / she says *It's here*. If it isn't correct, another pupil has a turn. Repeat with different words and pupils.

Set learning outcomes using the task flashcards.
- Say **Today we're going to remember what we've learnt in Unit 3.**
- Hold up the task flashcards in turn and elicit the activities. Stick them on one side of the board. Point to them during the lesson to reinforce your instructions.

Pupil's Book Activity 1

Listen and number. Say.
▶ *CD2 Track 11 p261*
- (Books open.) Point to the pictures and ask different pupils to name the parts of the body.
- Play the CD, pausing after each sentence. The pupils point to the parts of the body.
- Play the CD again. The pupils write the correct number for each picture.
- The pupils say the words under each picture.

Answers: **1** head **2** legs **3** feet **4** mouth **5** nose **6** fingers **7** ears **8** arms **9** eyes **10** toes

Pupil's Book Activity 2

Read and circle *A* or *B*.
- Focus on Activity 2. Ask **What can you see?**
- Read the first sentence. Ask **Who is it: A or B?**
- Repeat with the other sentences. Elicit the answers.
- The pupils read again and circle *A* or *B*.

Answers: **1** A **2** B **3** B **4** A

Pupil's Book Activity 3: Cooperative learning

Sing *Well done!*
▶ *CD2 Track 12 p261*
- Praise the pupils for their hard work and encourage them to praise each other. Play the *Well done!* song. The pupils sing and do the actions.

Stick the *Give Me Five!* sticker.
- The pupils stick the *Give Me Five!* sticker on the Pupil's Book page.
- Variation: Sing the *Well done!* song and stick the *Give Me Five!* sticker after the pupils have also completed the Activity Book Lesson 8 Review.

Activity Book

Activity 1
Trace and read about you. Draw.
- (Books open.) Read out the sentences for the pupils to follow.
- The pupils read the sentences and trace the first letter of the body parts words.
- The pupils draw a picture of themselves.

Activity 2
Read. Choose *yes* or *no*.
- Read out the sentences one by one and ask **Yes or no?**
- The pupils read the sentences again and circle *yes* or *no*.

Answers: **1** yes **2** no **3** no **4** yes

Activity 3: My progress My progress
Use your traffic light. Listen to the teacher and point.
- (Books closed.) Ask the pupils to take out their traffic light cut-out. Say **Let's think about our work in this unit.** Point to the green circle, nod your head, smile a lot, and say **I can say the parts of the body in English. Yes, I can do this very well.** Point to the yellow circle, move your head a little, smile a little and say **Yes, I can do this.** Then point to the red circle, shake your head and say **No, I can't do this.**
- Read the different statements. For each one, the pupils point to the colour on their traffic light that shows how they feel about their own learning.

Self-assessment statements
1. I can say the parts of the body.
2. I can talk about my friend's hair and my friend's eyes.
3. I can say an action rhyme.
4. I listen to the teacher.
5. I listen to other pupils.
6. I help other pupils.

Recycled vocabulary
- The pupils look at the picture and say the word. Then they trace the first letter.

Ending the lesson

Review the task flashcards.
- Point to the task flashcards. Say **Look at the activities you've done today. Which activity was your favourite?** Elicit the pupils' favourite activities.

Extra activities

Reinforcement
- Play *Silent words* (see p23) with the parts of the body flashcards.

Cooperative learning

Think-Pair-Share
- Ask **Can you remember the ten parts of the body?** The class think on their own for one minute.
- Talk Partners The pupils work with a Talk Partner to name all ten items.
- Ask a pair to say one of the parts of the body. Hold up the corresponding flashcard and prompt the class to repeat the word.
- Finally, repeat, asking different pairs of pupils each time, until all ten parts of the body have been named.

Key Competences and Key Learning Outcomes

- Watch and understand a video about the circus
- Identify and say what activities you do with your friends
- Understand the importance of working together

Key language

- *circus, clean the car, draw, football, head, juggle, music, plates, sing songs, spins, tidy up, work together, write, video games*

Materials

- Pupil's Book p37; Activity Book p34; Class CD2; Video; Teacher's App on Navio
- Teacher's Resource Bank: Task flashcards: *number, read, tick, circle, listen, draw*

Optional materials

- Teacher's Resource Bank: Trinity Exam Practice cards (selected from Unit 3)

At a Glance Lesson Plan

Starting the lesson

- Use the Trinity Exam Practice cards (optional).
- **Think-Pair-Share** Review the *My feelings* rhyme.

▶ *CD2 Track 9 p261*

- Set learning outcomes and use the task flashcards.

Pre-watching activity

- Talk about what skills they can see at a circus.

Activity 1

- Watch the video.

Unit 3 video p277

- Number the pictures.

Activity 2

- Watch the video again.

Unit 3 video

- Read and tick (✓) or cross (✗).

Pupil's Book

Activity 3

- Read and circle.

Go to the Activity Book.

Ending the lesson

- Review the lesson.
- Review the task flashcards. Elicit the pupils' favourite activities.

Extra activity

- Pupils work together in groups to do an activity.

Activity Book

Activity Book

Activity 1

- Listen and number.

▶ *CD2 Track 13 p262*

Activity 2

- Read and tick (✓). Draw you and your friends.

Recycled vocabulary

- Look, say and trace the letter.

Digital resources

Teacher's Digital: Don't forget you can teach this lesson using the Teacher's App on Navio.

Pupil's Digital: Encourage your pupils to use the Pupil's App on Navio to practise the vocabulary from this lesson.

Powered By NAVIO

Detailed Lesson Plan

Starting the lesson

Use the Trinity Exam Practice cards (optional).

- The pupils practise asking and answering questions.

Review the *My feelings* rhyme.

▶ *CD2 Track 9 p262*

- Tell the pupils they are going to listen and mime to the *My feelings* rhyme from Lesson 7. Play the track and mime the actions with the pupils. Then mime the actions yourself and encourage the pupils to say the rhyme.
- Divide the class into four groups. Each group takes a turn to mime a verse while the rest of the class say the verse.

Set learning outcomes and use the task flashcards.

- Say **Today we're going to watch a video and then ask and answer questions about the circus**.
- Point to the task flashcards throughout to elicit activities and reinforce your instructions.

Pre-watching activity

- **Think-Pair-Share** Ask the pupils what activities and people they can see in a circus. Write their answers on the board.

Pupil's Book Activity 1

Watch the video. Number the pictures. *p277*

- Play Part 1. Ask What has Sophie got? (big eyes, red nose) What has Tom got? (yellow hair, big mouth)
- Focus the pupils' attention on the video stills. Ask **What are the people doing?**
- Play Part 2, pausing after the first video still. Ask the pupils to point to the corresponding photo.
- Play the rest of the video for pupils to point to the photos in order. Play Part 2 again for pupils to write the numbers in order of the photos.
- Ask **What circus skills do the children learn on the video? Which skills would you like to learn?**

Answers: 3, 4, 2, 1

Pupil's Book Activity 2

Watch the video again. Read and tick (✓) or cross (✗).

- Play Part 2 again. Pause after Sophie says, *The circus is blue and yellow.* Ask **Is the circus blue and yellow?** Show the tick in the circle.
- Play the video. Pupils tick or cross the sentences.
- Ask general questions to check understanding.
  Who has long legs? *(Two girls on stilts.)*
  Which skills are better when the children work together? *(Cycle and juggling.)*
  Can Tom and Sophie juggle when they work together? *(Yes.)*

Answers: 1 ✓ 2 ✗ 3 ✓ 4 ✓

Pupil's Book Activity 3

Read and circle.

- Point to the pictures to elicit the activities vocabulary. Read out number one, including the circled word.
- Pupils circle the words to complete the sentences.
- **Think-Pair-Share** Say **Abby says *It's good to work together*.** Read out the speech bubble. Explain that some activities and tasks are easier when you work together too.
- Ask **What activities do you do that are better when you work together?**

Answers: **1** video games **2** draw pictures **3** sing songs **4** clean the car

Activity Book

Activity 1

Listen and number.

▶ *CD2 Track 13 p262*

- The pupils look at the pictures. Ask **What can you see?**
- Play the first exchange on the CD. Ask **Which picture?** Play the rest of the CD, pausing for pupils to number the pictures.

Answers: **1** juggle **2** play music **3** play football **4** tidy up

Activity 2

Read and tick (✓). Draw you and your friends.

- Ask a few pupils **What do you do with your friends?** Read out the sentences for the pupils to follow. The pupils tick the things they do with their friends and then draw themselves and their friends.
  Talk Partners Pupils take turns to point to their pictures and tell their partner what they do with their friends.

Recycled vocabulary

- The pupils look at the picture and say the word. Then they trace the first letter.

Ending the lesson

Review the lesson.

- Ask **Which activity was easy / difficult?**

Review the task flashcards.

- Say **Look at the activities you've done today. Which activity was your favourite?**

Extra activity

Extension

- Divide the class into small groups. Ask each group to think of an activity they can do together to show the rest of the class for example, sing a song, draw a picture, play a game, juggle. Give the groups a few minutes to think about and practise what they are going to do. The groups take turns to show their activity to the class. After each group has demonstrated their activity ask, **How did you feel about working together?**

My project 1: Family

Key Competences and Key Learning Outcomes

- Identify and talk about family members
- Ask and answer questions about family members
- Understand and complete a simple graph about family members
- Prepare to make a family leaf

Key language

- *aunt, brother, cousin, family, father, grandfather, grandmother, mother, sister*
- *Have you got (a brother)? Yes, I have. No, I haven't.*

Recycled: *big, small*

Recycled: *I've got (one sister). I've got a (big) family.*

Materials

- Pupil's Book p38; Activity Book p36; Class CD2; Teacher's App on Navio
- Teacher's Resource Bank: Task flashcards: *listen, think, colour, Talk Partners, read, plan, tick*
- Coloured pencils or crayons

Optional materials

- Teacher's Resource Bank: Five Trinity Exam Practice cards (selected from the Starter Unit and Units 1, 2 and 3).

At a Glance Lesson Plan

Starting the lesson

- Use the Trinity Exam Practice cards (optional).
- Review family members.
- Set learning outcomes using the task flashcards.

Learn: Activity 1

- Listen and point.
- ▶ *CD2 Track 14 p262*
- Say.

Activity 2

- Listen.
- ▶ *CD2 Track 15 p262*
- Talk Partners Ask and answer.
- Write the numbers.

Pupil's Book

My project 1 Lesson 1

FAMILY

Make a class family tree display

Learn

1 Listen and point. Say.

1 grandmother
2 grandfather
3 father
4 mother
5 uncle
6 aunt
7 brother
8 sister
9 cousins

2 Talk Partners Listen. Ask and answer. Write the numbers.

Have you got a brother?

Yes, I have. I've got two brothers.

Have you got a sister?

No, I haven't.

	brothers	sisters	aunts	uncles	cousins
my friend					

Plan your project

Prepare to make a family leaf.
Go to page 36 in your Activity Book.

Digital tip!
Look for pictures of leaves on the Internet. What colours can you see?

38 thirty-eight

Plan your project

- Prepare to make a family leaf. Go to page 36 in your Activity Book.

Ending the lesson

- Review the lesson.
- Review the task flashcards.

Extra activity

Reinforcement

- Practise describing family members.

Activity Book

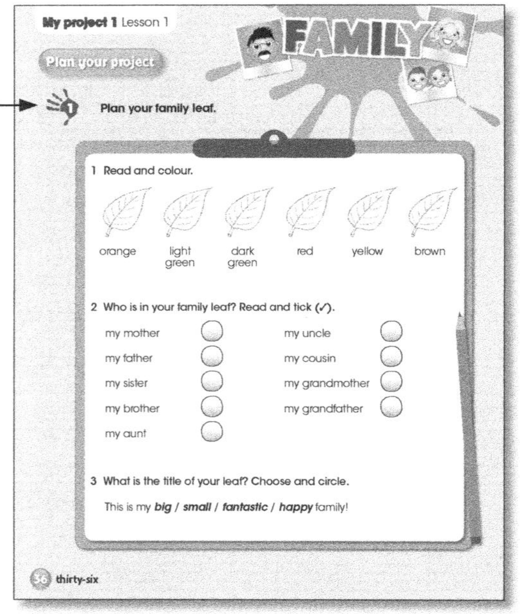
My project 1 Lesson 1

Plan your project

FAMILY

1 Plan your family leaf.

1 Read and colour.

orange, light green, dark green, red, yellow, brown

2 Who is in your family leaf? Read and tick (✓).

my mother, my father, my sister, my brother, my aunt, my uncle, my cousin, my grandmother, my grandfather

3 What is the title of your leaf? Choose and circle.

This is my *big* / *small* / *fantastic* / *happy* family!

36 thirty-six

Activity Book: Plan your project

Activity 1

- Plan your family leaf.

Digital resources

Teacher's Digital: Don't forget you can teach this lesson using the Teacher's App on Navio.

Pupil's Digital: Encourage your pupils to use the Pupil's App on Navio to practise the vocabulary from this lesson.

Powered By NAVIO

Detailed Lesson Plan

Starting the lesson

Use the Trinity Exam Practice cards (optional).

- The pupils practise asking and answering questions (see p31).

Review family members.

- If the class already knows some family vocabulary, quickly review these words.

Set learning outcomes using the task flashcards.

- Say **Today we're going to learn about families.**
- Hold up the task flashcards in turn and elicit the activities. Stick them on one side of the board. Point to them during the lesson to reinforce your instructions.

Learn: Pupil's Book Activity 1

Listen and point. Say.

▶ *CD2 Track 14 p262*

- (Books open.) Focus the pupils on the picture in Activity 1. Say **Let's listen and learn the family members.** Play the CD. The pupils listen.
- Play the CD again, pausing after each family member. The pupils repeat the words and point.
- Ask the pupils to use their 'magic finger'. Say different family members at random. The pupils point and say *Here!*
- Talk Partners The pupils play the same game with a Talk Partner.

Pupil's Book Activity 2

Listen. Ask and answer. Write the numbers.

▶ *CD2 Track 15 p262*

- (Books open.) Focus the pupils on the speech bubbles.
- Play the CD. The pupils listen and follow the conversation.
- Play the CD again, pausing after each sentence for the pupils to repeat.
- Draw the table on the board. Complete the first row with your information, saying the sentences each time, e.g. **I've got (two) brothers. I've got (one) sister**.
- The pupils complete the first row of their tables.
- Choose a pupil and ask **Have you got a brother?** Write the number of brothers in the second row of your chart on the board. Repeat with the other columns.
- Talk Partners The pupils ask and answer with a Talk Partner and complete their tables.

Digital tip!

- Ask the pupils to look for pictures of leaves on the Internet. Elicit the colours.

Activity Book: Plan your project

Activity 1

Plan your family leaf.

- (Books open.) Explain to the pupils that they are going to plan a family leaf. Read out the first sentence and go through the colours with the class. Explain that they need to read and colour the leaves.
- Read the second sentence. The pupils tick all of the people in their family.
- Read the third sentence. Tell pupils to choose and circle an adjective that describes their family.

- Tell the pupils to bring in a photo of their family to the next lesson to go on the front of their leaf. If possible, bring in some of your own family photos to go through the family members with the pupils at the start of the next lesson.

Ending the lesson

Review the lesson.

- (Books closed.) Say **Today we've learnt about families. Have you got a big family or a small family?** Elicit answers from the pupils.

Review the task flashcards.

- Point to the task flashcards on the board. Say **Look at the activities you've done today. Which activity was your favourite?** Elicit the pupils' favourite activities.

Extra activity

Reinforcement

- Practise describing family members. Describe a member of your family to the class, for example **My sister has got long hair. She's got brown eyes.** Encourage the pupils to do the same.

My project 1: Family

Key Competences and Key Learning Outcomes

- Make a family leaf
- Present a class tree display

- Think about your project

- Work together to make a class display
- Sing a cooperative learning song
- Listen to others
- Respect different types of families

- Follow instructions to make a family leaf

Key language

- *copy, decorate, fold, stick; family leaf, photo, tree*
- *This is my (mother). Her name is (Marta).*

Recycled: *aunt, brother, cousin, family, father, grandfather, grandmother, mother, sister;*

Recycled: *I've got a (small) family.*

Materials

- Pupil's Book p39; Activity Book p37; Class CD2; Teacher's App on Navio
- Teacher's Resource Bank: Task flashcards: *read, stick, write, listen, Talk Partners, sing, draw, think, circle, colour*
- Teacher's Resource Bank: My project 1 cut-out
- A4 coloured card, card for large family tree display, scissors, glue, coloured pencils/crayons, family photos, white paper

Optional materials

- Teacher's Resource Bank: Five Trinity Exam Practice cards (selected from the Starter Unit and Units 1, 2 and 3)

At a Glance Lesson Plan

Starting the lesson

- Use the Trinity Exam Practice cards (optional).
- Review family members.
- Set learning outcomes using the task flashcards.

Create: Activity 1

- Read.
- Make a family leaf.

Show and tell: Activity 2 Cooperative learning

- Sing *It's fun to work together.*
- ▶ *CD2 Track 16 p262*

Activity 3

- Make a family tree with the class.
- Listen.
- ▶ *CD2 Track 17 p262*
- Tell the class about your family.

Pupil's Book

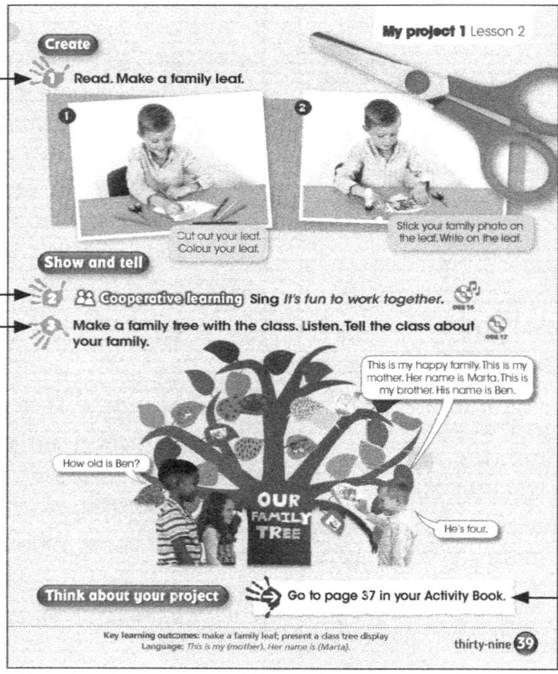

Think about your project

- Go to page 37 in your Activity Book.

Link to Science

- **Families:** Different types of family.

Ending the lesson

- Review the lesson.
- Sing *Well done!*
- ▶ *CD2 Track 12 p261*

Digital resources

Teacher's Digital: Don't forget you can teach this lesson using the Teacher's App on Navio.

Pupil's Digital: Encourage your pupils to use the Pupil's App on Navio to practise the vocabulary from this lesson.

Activity Book

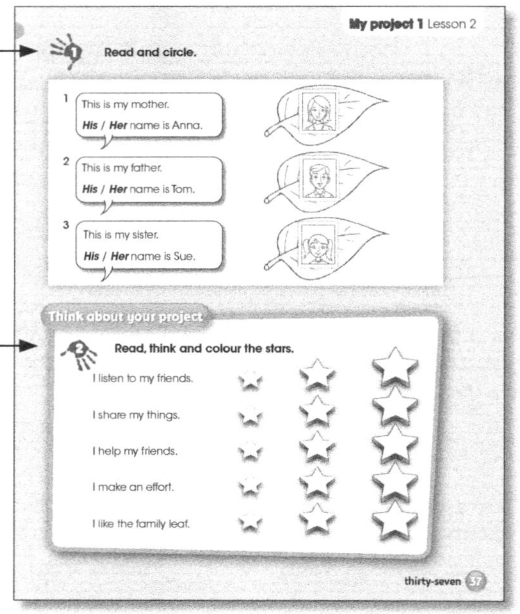

Activity Book

Activity 1

- Read and circle.

Activity 2: Think about your project

- Read, think and colour the stars.

Starting the lesson

Use the Trinity Exam Practice cards (optional).

- The pupils practise asking and answering questions (see p31).

Review family members.

- If you have brought photos of your family to the class, show them to the pupils. Tell them who the different family members are. The pupils repeat.

Set learning outcomes using the task flashcards.

- Say **Today we're going to make a family leaf.**
- Hold up the task flashcards in turn and elicit the activities. Stick them on one side of the board. Point to them during the lesson to reinforce your instructions.

Create: Pupil's Book Activity 1

Read. Make a family leaf.

- (Books open.) Focus the pupils on the photos. Read out the instructions. The pupils follow the text.
- Hand out the scissors and coloured pencils. The pupils cut out their leaf and colour it, then stick their family photo to it and write on it. (If any of the pupils haven't brought in a photo, give them a sheet of white paper for them to draw and colour a picture of their family.)

Show and tell: Pupil's Book Activity 2:
Cooperative learning

Sing *It's fun to work together!*

▶ *CD2 Track 16 p262*

- In order to build a positive classroom atmosphere, all of the pupils need to participate and contribute to the lesson. Play the *It's fun to work together!* song whenever you want to remind the pupils of the importance of joining in.
- Play the CD. The pupils do the actions with you.
- Play the CD again. The pupils sing and do the actions.

Pupil's Book Activity 3

Make a family tree with the class. Listen. Tell the class about your family.

▶ *CD2 Track 17 p262*

- Ask **What can you see?** Elicit answers.
- Play the CD. The pupils listen and read the speech bubble.
- Ask **What two family members does the boy talk about?**
- Explain that the class is going to make a similar tree. Make a simple tree trunk shape on the classroom wall using pieces of large card. Hold up your family leaf and tell the class about your family, then stick your leaf on the tree. Each pupil comes to the front, tells the class about his / her family, and then sticks his / her leaf on the tree.

Link to Science

- If you are studying the Science topic of **My family** in English, you could remind pupils that each family structure is different and it is important to respect this. This will have been reinforced when pupils showed their family leaves to the class.

Activity Book

Activity 1

Read and circle.

- (Books open.) If necessary, use this activity to reinforce the new language. Read out the sentences as a class and decide on the correct possessive adjective. The pupils circle the correct word each time.

Answers: **1** Her **2** His **3** Her

Activity 2: Think about your project

Read, think and colour the stars.

- Say **Let's think about how we work together.** Read out each sentence. The pupils think about how they work together and colour the corresponding star (small star: sometimes; medium-sized star: usually; big star: always).

Ending the lesson

Review the lesson.

- (Books closed.) Say **Today we've worked together. What have we made?** Elicit answers. Praise the pupils for their effort.

Sing *Well done!*

▶ *CD2 Track 12 p261*

- (Books closed.) Praise the class for working together and for following instructions well. Play the CD. The pupils sing and do the actions.

Date: ______________ Unit: ______________

1 **What did my pupils learn in this unit?**

____

____

____

____

2 **How did my pupils work? (✓)**

individually ☐ in pairs ☐ in small groups ☐

in large groups ☐ as a class ☐

3 **Which key competences did my pupils develop?**

- Competence in linguistic communication ☐
- Competence in mathematics, science and technology ☐
- Digital competence ☐
- Learning to learn ☐
- Social and civic competences ☐
- Sense of initiative and entrepreneurship ☐
- Cultural awareness and expression ☐

4 **Which lessons / activities were the most successful and why?**

____

____

____

____

5 **Which lessons / activities did my pupils find the most difficult and why?**

____

____

____

____

6 **What did I try in the classroom for the first time? How did it go?**

____

____

____

____

7 **Which resources did I find most useful? (including webpages)**

____

____

____

____

____

____

8 **What could I do differently next time I teach this unit?**

____

____

____

____

Unit 4

Fantastic food!

Unit overview

Key Competences and Key Learning Outcomes

- Identify and say ten items of food (Lesson 1)
- Say the vocabulary chant (Lesson 1)
- Use *like*, *don't like* and *love* (Lesson 2)
- Understand and act out a conversation (Lesson 2)
- Ask and answer questions to find out what fruit people like and don't like (Lesson 4)
- Read and draw a lunch menu (Lesson 7)
- Watch and understand a video about school lunches (Video and 21st Century Skills)

- Identify healthy / unhealthy food (Lessons 3 and 7)

- Use the Pupil's App on Navio

- Practise spelling (Lesson 1)
- Say a tongue twister to practise the 'j' sound (Lesson 5)
- Review language in the unit and reflect on own learning (Lesson 8)
- Practise activity types found in the Cambridge English Young Learners Exams: Pre A1 Starters

- Understand the importance of eating healthy food (Lesson 3 and Video and 21st Century Skills)

- Work with a Talk Partner to practise and reinforce learning (all lessons)
- Play a communication game about food (Lesson 5)

- Sing four songs (Lessons 1, 4, 5 and 8)
- Understand and act out a story (Lesson 3)
- Read about a traditional English breakfast (Lesson 6)
- Think about what you have for breakfast (Lesson 6)
- Draw healthy food for your lunch box (Video and 21st Century Skills)

Vocabulary

Core vocabulary
cake, chicken, chips, eggs, fish, fruit, ice cream, meat, rice, salad; cherry, coconut, grape, lemon, mango, peach

Extension vocabulary (optional)
burger, juice, lemonade, milk, pie, water; kiwi, pear, strawberry, watermelon

Other vocabulary
bread, breakfast, cereal, food, fruit juice, fruit salad, jelly, orange juice, oranges, pasta, soup, toast, vegetables; delicious, healthy; cook the food, cut the tomatoes, make the toast, mix the eggs, prepare the tray

Recycled vocabulary
arms, bananas, ears, eyes, feet, fingers, head, legs, mouth, nose, toes; juggle, toy; days of the week

Structures

Core structures
I like (fruit). I love (ice cream). I don't like (cake).
Do you like (fruit)? Yes, I do. No, I don't.

Other structures
I'm hungry. It's my favourite. Eating fruit is fun to do. What's for lunch on (Monday)? We've got (meat and vegetables) on (Monday). I (mix the eggs). We (prepare the tray). I have (eggs). Calm down.

Recycled structures
I've got (rice and eggs). What about you? What's your favourite (food)? It's (ice cream).

Phonics

Consonant sound 'j' (**J**im, **j**uggles, **j**am, **j**uice, **j**elly)

British Culture

A traditional English breakfast

Literacy

Text type: a lunch menu (information text)
Reading skills: relating pictures to new vocabulary; reading for specific information

21st Century Skills

Living in the world: learn to eat healthily

Cooperative learning

Songs: *Calm down* (Lesson 5); *Well done!* (Lesson 8)
Skills: Working together and supporting each other (Lesson 1); Discovering similarities (Lesson 2)

Values

Understanding the importance of eating healthy food

Cross-curricular links

Links to Science

Food: recognising that food can be hot or cold; identifying food that is good for you and food that is not good for you; reviewing vegetables; reviewing the meals of the day

Suggested Arts and Crafts concepts

Texture: identifying texture in Art; using fruit and vegetables to create a collage

Key Competences and Key Learning Outcomes

- Identify and say ten items of food
- Stick the food stickers
- Say the vocabulary chant
- Talk about hot and cold food (optional)
- Practise spelling
- Sing a song about food

Key language
- *cake, chicken, chips, eggs, fish, fruit, ice cream, meat, rice, salad; delicious, food*
- Extension: *burger, juice, lemonade, milk, pie, water*
- **Recycled:** *eyes, head*
- **Recycled:** *I've got (fish and chips).*

Materials
- Pupil's Book p40; Activity Book p38 and 47; Class CD2; Teacher's App on Navio
- Food flashcards; Unit 4 stickers
- Teacher's Resource Bank: Food word cards
- Teacher's Resource Bank: Task flashcards: *listen, sing, read, stick, say, Talk Partners, match*

Optional materials
- Teacher's Resource Bank: Five Trinity Exam Practice cards (selected from the Starter Unit and Units 1, 2 and 3)

At a Glance Lesson Plan

Starting the lesson
- Use the Trinity Exam Practice cards (optional).
- Review parts of the body.
- Set learning outcomes using the task flashcards.

Vocabulary presentation
- Present the new vocabulary.

Activity 1
- Listen and point.
- ▶ *CD2 Track 18 p262*
- Sing *Delicious food.*

Word cards
- Read the word cards.
- Match them to the flashcards.

Activity 2
- Read and stick the ten stickers.
- Listen and say the chant.
- ▶ *CD2 Track 20 p262*
- Go to the Activity Book.

Pupil's Book

Ending the lesson
- Review the lesson.
- Review the task flashcards.

Extra activity

Vocabulary Extension
- Present six additional vocabulary items.

Cooperative learning

Working together and supporting each other
- Talk Partners Ask and answer *What's this?*

Link to Science
- **Food:** Talk about hot and cold food. Play the *Hot / cold game*.

Learning to learn

Spelling
- Practise spelling at any time during this unit (Activity Book p47).

Activity Book

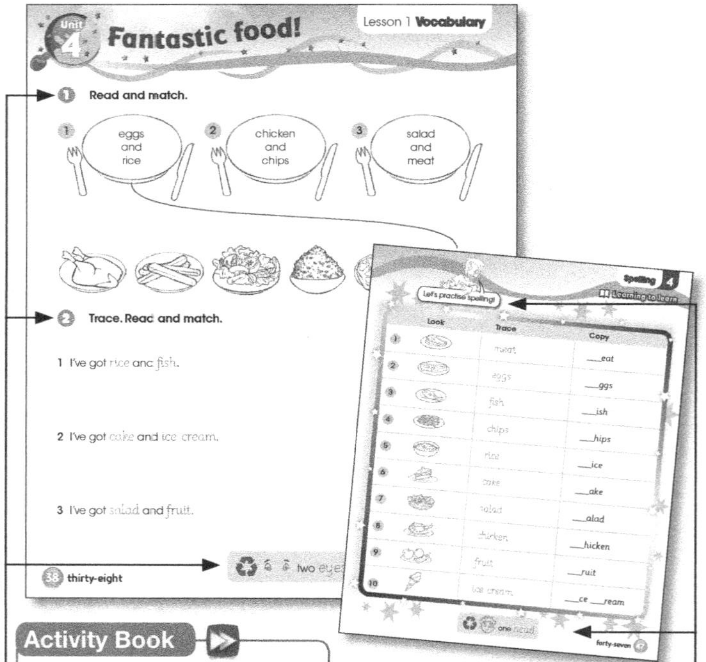

Activity Book

Activity 1
- Read and match.

Activity 2
- Trace.
- Read and match.

Recycled vocabulary
- Look, say and trace the word.

Spelling

Let's practise spelling!
- Use the *Look-Read-Trace* technique.

Recycled vocabulary
- Look, say and trace the word.

Digital resources

Teacher's Digital: Don't forget you can teach this lesson using the Teacher's App on Navio.

Pupil's Digital: Encourage your pupils to use the Pupil's App on Navio to practise the vocabulary from this lesson.

Powered By NAVIO

Detailed Lesson Plan

Starting the lesson

Use the Trinity Exam Practice cards (optional).

- The pupils practise asking and answering questions (see p31).

Review parts of the body.

- Say **Touch your (eyes).** The pupils do the actions.
- Repeat with other parts of the body.

Set learning outcomes using the task flashcards.

- Say **Today we're going to learn food words.**
- Hold up the task flashcards in turn and elicit the activities. Stick them on one side of the board. Point to them during the lesson to reinforce your instructions.

Vocabulary presentation

Present the new vocabulary.

- (Books closed.) Rub your stomach and say **I'm hungry.** Then ask the class **Are you hungry?**
- Hold up the food flashcards and say **I've got lots of delicious food here.** Play *Slowly, slowly* to practise the words (see p23).

Pupil's Book Activity 1

Listen and point. Sing *Delicious food*.

▶ *CD2 Track 18 p262*

- (Books open.) Focus the pupils on the picture. Ask **Where are Molly and Jake? Is the café special?**
- Play the CD. The pupils listen and point to the different food items in the picture.
- Play the CD again. The pupils sing and do the actions.

Word cards

Read the word cards. Match them to the flashcards.

- (Books closed.) Hold up the food word cards in turn, and say or elicit each word.
- Ask different pupils to come to the front and stick each word card on the board with the corresponding flashcard.

Pupil's Book Activity 2

Read and stick the ten stickers. Listen and say the chant.

▶ *CD2 Track 20 p262*

- (Books open.) Ask a pupil to read the first food item. The pupils stick the corresponding sticker. Repeat with the other stickers.
- Play the CD. The pupils listen and say the chant, pointing to the stickers in turn.

Activity Book

Activity 1

Read and match.

- (Books open.) The pupils look at the pictures. Say the foods as a class.
- Say the words on the first plate rhythmically. Encourage the pupils to join in. Repeat with the other two plates.
- The pupils match the food pictures with the plates.

Activity 2

Trace. Read and match.

- Focus the pupils on Activity 2. Point to the pictures and elicit the food items on each plate.
- The pupils trace the words in the sentences.
- The pupils read the sentences and draw matching lines to the correct plates of food.

Answers: **1** second plate **2** third plate **3** first plate

Recycled vocabulary

- The pupils look at the picture and say the words. They trace the second word.

Ending the lesson

Review the lesson.

- (Books closed.) Say **Today we've learnt the names of food. What words do you remember?**

Review the task flashcards.

- Point to the task flashcards. Say **Look at the activities you've done today. Which activity was your favourite?** Elicit the pupils' favourite activities.

Extra activity

Vocabulary Extension

- Use the Vocabulary Booster on Navio to present and practise six additional words describing food and drink: *burger*, *juice*, *lemonade*, *milk*, *pie*, *water*.

Cooperative learning

Working together and supporting each other

- Encourage the pupils to help each other to remember vocabulary.
- **Talk Partners** Pupil A points to a food sticker and asks *What's this?* Pupil B answers using *It's a …* If Pupil B can't remember, Pupil A helps him / her.
- When Pupil B has named the ten food items, the pupils swap roles and repeat.

Link to Science

- If you are studying the Science topic of **Food** in English, you could play the *Hot / cold game* to review different types of food. Draw two circles on the board and label them 'hot' and 'cold'. Use mime to aid understanding. Invite two pupils to come to the board. Say **ice cream.** The pupils touch the 'cold' circle. Some of the food may be eaten hot or cold. In these cases, the pupils touch both circles. The pupil who touches the circle first, wins a point.

Spelling (Activity Book page 47)

Let's practise spelling!

- Pupils can practise spelling the ten food words using the *Look-Read-Trace* technique at any time during this unit before the Lesson 8 Review.

Recycled vocabulary

- The pupils look at the picture and say the words. They trace the second word.

Key Competences and Key Learning Outcomes

- Use *like*, *don't like* and *love*
- Complete and practise a conversation
- Listen for specific information

Key language

Recycled: *cake, chicken, chips, eggs, fish, fruit, ice cream, meat, rice, salad; nose*

Recycled: *I like (fruit). I love (ice cream). I don't like (cake). What about you?*

Materials

- Pupil's Book p41; Activity Book p39; Class CD2; Teacher's App on Navio
- Food flashcards
- Teacher's Resource Bank: Task flashcards: *listen, act out, draw, match, think, Talk Partners*

Optional materials

- Teacher's Resource Bank: Five Trinity Exam Practice cards (selected from the Starter Unit and Units 1, 2 and 3)

At a Glance Lesson Plan

Pupil's Book

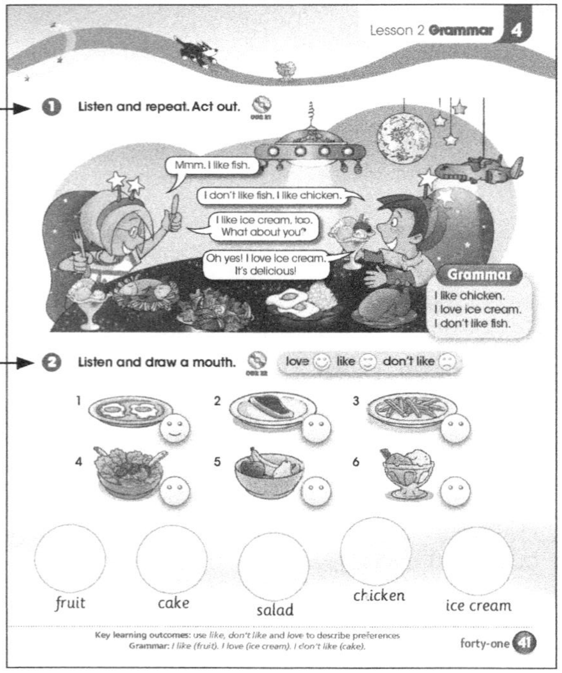

Starting the lesson

- Use the Trinity Exam Practice cards (optional).
- **Think-Pair-Share** Review food words.
- Review the *Delicious food* song.
- ▶ ***CD2 Track 18 p262***
- ▶ ***CD2 Track 19 p262 (optional karaoke version)***
- Set learning outcomes using the task flashcards.

Activity 1

- Listen and repeat.
- ▶ ***CD2 Track 21 p262***
- Act out.

Activity 2

- Listen and draw a mouth.
- ▶ ***CD2 Track 22 p262***
- Go to the Activity Book.

Ending the lesson

- Review the lesson.
- Review the task flashcards.

Extra activities

Reinforcement

- Create and say a food rhyme.
- Play a moving game.

Cooperative learning

Discovering similarities

- Play *Me too!*

Activity Book

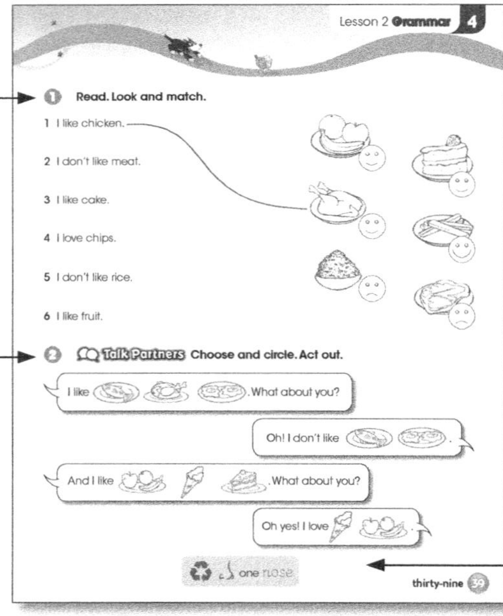

Activity Book

Activity 1

- Read.
- Look and match.

Activity 2

- Choose and circle.
- **Talk Partners** Act out.

Recycled vocabulary

- Look, say and trace the word.

Digital resources

Teacher's Digital: Don't forget you can teach this lesson using the Teacher's App on Navio.

Pupil's Digital: Encourage your pupils to use the Pupil's App on Navio to practise the vocabulary from this lesson.

Powered By NAVIO

Detailed Lesson Plan

Starting the lesson

Use the Trinity Exam Practice cards (optional).

- The pupils practise asking and answering questions (see p31).
- **Think-Pair-Share** Review food words.
- Ask **Can you remember the ten food words?** The class thinks silently for a minute.
- **Talk Partners** Then the pupils work with a Talk Partner to name the food words.
- Invite different pairs to say a different food word. Hold up the corresponding flashcard and prompt the class to repeat the word.
- Finally, repeat the procedure, asking different pairs of pupils each time, until all ten food words have been named.

Review the *Delicious food* song.

▶ *CD2 Track 18 p262*

▶ *CD2 Track 19 p262 (optional karaoke version)*

- Ask three pupils to come to the front of the class. Give each pupil the food flashcards that correspond to a verse. Play the CD (or use the karaoke version). The pupils hold up the flashcards when they hear the words. Repeat several times.

Set learning outcomes using the task flashcards.

- Say **Today we're going to talk about food we like, love and don't like.**
- Hold up the task flashcards in turn and elicit the activities. Stick them on one side of the board. Point to them during the lesson to reinforce your instructions.

Pupil's Book Activity 1

Listen and repeat. Act out.

▶ *CD2 Track 21 p262*

- (Books open.) The pupils look at the picture. Ask **Where are Jake and Molly? What food has Molly got? What food has Jake got?**
- Play the CD. The pupils listen and read the conversation.
- Ask **Does Molly like fish? Does Jake like fish?**
- Play the CD again, pausing after each sentence for the pupils to repeat.
- When the pupils are confident with the language, invite different pairs of pupils to act out their conversations with your help.

Pupil's Book Activity 2

Listen and draw a mouth.

▶ *CD2 Track 22 p262*

- Focus the pupils on Activity 2. Point to the food items and elicit what is in each picture. Explain the key.
- Play the CD, pausing after each sentence to allow the pupils time to draw. The pupils draw the mouths to represent the children's likes and dislikes.
- Play the CD again. The pupils repeat the sentences.

Answers: **1** like **2** don't like **3** love **4** don't like **5** like **6** love

Activity Book

Activity 1

Read. Look and match.

- (Books open.) Elicit what the pupils can see in the pictures. Check that they know what the smiley and unhappy faces mean.
- Ask a volunteer to read out the first sentence and follow the matching line to the food item.
- The pupils complete the activity on their own. Then ask the pupils to read out the sentences.

Activity 2

Choose and circle. Act out.

- (Books open.) Read the speech bubbles, pausing before the pictures to elicit the vocabulary.
- Practise the conversation as a class.
- **Talk Partners** When the pupils are confident with the language, they work in pairs to choose and circle an object for each speech bubble. They ask and answer with their partner.
- Invite different pairs of pupils to act out their conversations.

Recycled vocabulary

- The pupils look at the picture and say the words. Then they trace the second word.

Ending the lesson

Review the lesson.

- (Books closed.) Say **Today we've acted out a conversation together. Did you work well?** Elicit answers from the pupils.

Review the task flashcards.

- Point to the task flashcards. Say **Look at the activities you've done today. Which activity was your favourite?** Elicit the pupils' favourite activities.

Extra activities

Reinforcement

- Stick the meat flashcard on the board and ask the pupils to say the word with you. Then stick the eggs flashcard next to it and say in a rhythmic manner **meat and eggs**. Repeat until there are four cards on the board *(meat and eggs and fish and chips)*. Finally, remove the flashcards and ask the pupils to say the food rhyme from memory. Repeat with different food cards.
- Play a moving game with the class. The pupils form a line in front of you.
- Show them a food flashcard and say the word. The pupils jump to the left if they like the food and jump to the right if they don't. They stay in the line if they love the food.
- Repeat several times. If the class is confident with the vocabulary, play the game without the flashcards, just by saying the words.

Cooperative learning

Discovering similarities

- Discovering similarities helps develop a positive classroom atmosphere.
- Invite a pupil to come to the front of the class. He / She says a food item he / she likes, e.g. *I like fruit.*
- The pupils who feel the same say *Me too!*
- The pupils repeat with other food items and with the structure *I love …*

Key Competences and Key Learning Outcomes

- Read, listen and understand a story about a magic restaurant
- Read the story with some fluency
- Identify food which is / isn't good for you (optional)
- Become familiar with the story through a pre-reading task
- Understand the importance of eating healthy food
- Understand and act out the story
- Give an opinion on the story

Key language

- *fruit juice, grapes, oranges, peach*
- *I'm hungry. It's my favourite. Do you like (peaches)? Yes, I do. No, I don't.*

Recycled: *cake, fruit, ice cream, meat; fingers*

Recycled: *I love (cake). I like (ice cream). I don't like (oranges).*

Materials

- Pupil's Book pp42–43; Activity Book p40; Class CD2; Teacher's App on Navio
- Food flashcards
- Teacher's Resource Bank: Task flashcards: *think, listen, read, act out, circle, draw*
- Teacher's Resource Bank: Unit 4 Lesson 3 Animated Story

Optional materials

- Teacher's Resource Bank: Five Trinity Exam Practice cards (selected from the Starter Unit and Units 1, 2 and 3)

At a Glance Lesson Plan

Starting the lesson

- Use the Trinity Exam Practice cards (optional).
- Review the language from Lesson 2.
- Set learning outcomes using the task flashcards.

Before you read

- Explain the story title.
- Read and answer the question.

Activity 1

- Listen and read.
- ▶ *CD2 Track 23 p262*
- Act out.
- *Now watch the animated story!*

After you read: Activity 2

- Go to page 40 in your Activity Book.
- Values: Read and circle.

Pupil's Book

Ending the lesson

- Review the lesson.
- Review the task flashcards.

Link to Science

- **Food:** Identify food which is good for you and not good for you.

Activity Book

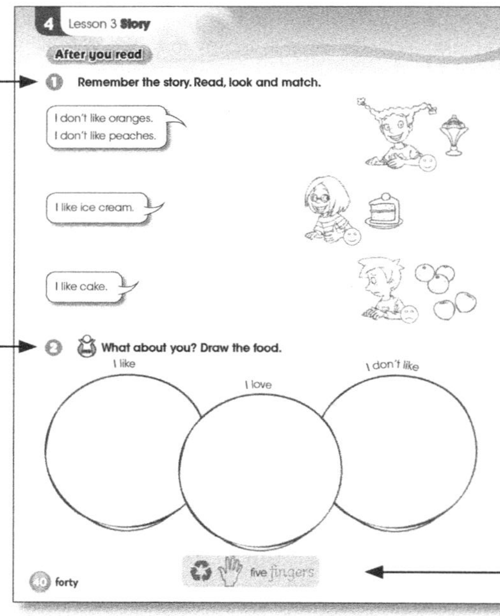

Activity Book

After you read: Activity 1

- Remember the story. Read, look and match.

Activity 2

- What about you?
- Draw the food.

Recycled vocabulary

- Look, say and trace the word.

Digital resources

Teacher's Digital: Don't forget you can teach this lesson using the Teacher's App on Navio.

Pupil's Digital: Encourage your pupils to use the Pupil's App on Navio to practise the vocabulary from this lesson.

Powered By NAVIO

Detailed Lesson Plan

Starting the lesson

Use the Trinity Exam Practice cards (optional).

- The pupils practise asking and answering questions (see p31).

Review the language from Lesson 2.

- Take a food flashcard but don't show it to the pupils. Say **I (like) this food. What is it?** The pupils guess the food. Repeat several times.
- Ask the more confident pupils to come to the front of the class and take over your role.

Set learning outcomes using the task flashcards.

- Say **Today we're going to listen to a story**.
- Hold up the task flashcards in turn and elicit the activities. Stick them on one side of the board. Point to them during the lesson to reinforce your instructions.

Before you read

Explain the story title.

- (Books open.) Focus on the story title. Rub your stomach and say **I'm hungry!** The pupils do the same. Ask what food they like to eat when they are hungry.

Read and answer the question.

- Read the speech bubble. The pupils scan the story to find the food.

Answers: rice, fruit, eggs, fish, chicken, cake, ice cream

Pupil's Book Activity 1

Listen and read. Act out.

▶ *CD2 Track 23 p262*

- The pupils place their 'magic finger' on the first frame of the story.
- Play the CD. The pupils point to the different frames as the story progresses. Pause the CD after each frame to check that all the pupils are following.
- Play the CD again. Ask questions about each story frame to help and check understanding.
- Play the CD one more time, pausing it so the pupils can repeat.

Suggested comprehension questions

- Frame 1: **Where are the children?** (*In the garden.*) **What has Beth got?** (*Some food.*)
- Frame 2: **Are the children happy?** (*No.*) **What do they do?** (*Ring the bell.*) Mime ringing the bell.
- Frame 3: **Look at the food now. Is it toy food?** (*No.*) Point to the robot and ask **Who's this?** (*The waiter.*)
- Frame 4: **What food have Molly and Beth got?** (*Ice cream and cake.*) **Do they like the food?** (*Yes.*)
- Frame 5: **What food has the robot got for Jake?** (*An orange.*) **Does Jake like oranges?** (*No.*)
- Frame 6: **Does Jake like peaches?** (*No.*)
- Frame 7: **Are the children happy?** (*Yes.*)
- Frame 8: **Does Jake like the fruit juice?** (*Yes.*)
- Finally, ask the pupils **Is this a good story?** The pupils give their opinion through gesture (thumbs up / down) or orally (*yes* / *no*).
- Organise the class into four groups (Beth, Molly, Jake and the robot).
- Play the CD. Each group joins in when their character speaks. If the pupils need extra support, pause the CD after each sentence for the pupils to repeat.

Now watch the animated story

After you read

Go to page 40 in your Activity Book.

Activity Book

After you read: Activity 1

Remember the story. Read, look and match.

- (Books open.) Ask **Do you remember the story?**
- Ask different pupils to read out the speech bubbles.
- The pupils remember the story and match the sentences to the pictures.

Answers: **Jake:** I don't like oranges. I don't like peaches.
Beth: I like ice cream.
Molly: I like cake.

Activity 2

What about you? Draw the food.

- Focus the pupils on the three circles.
- Tell the pupils to think about food they like, love and don't like. They draw pictures of the food in the correct circle for them.
- Ask volunteers to read out their likes and dislikes.

Recycled vocabulary

- The pupils look at the picture and say the words. Then they trace the second word.

Pupil's Book Activity 2

Values: Read and circle.

- The pupils look at the photo on the right. Read out the sentence in the speech bubble and prompt the class to tell you the correct answer. The pupils circle the correct answer.
- Encourage the pupils to tell you other food it is important to eat every day.

Answer: fruit

Ending the lesson

Review the lesson.

- (Books closed.) Say **Today we've listened to a story.** Ask **What happened in the story?** Elicit the story.
- Then say **Today you've learnt that it's important to eat fruit every day.**

Review the task flashcards.

- Point to the task flashcards. Say **Look at the activities you've done today. Which activity was your favourite?** Elicit the pupils' favourite activities.

Link to Science

- If you are studying the Science topic of **Food** in English, you could review what food is good for you and what food is not good for you. Play a game. Say a food item and the pupils stand up if it's good for you and stay seated if it isn't.

Key Competences and Key Learning Outcomes

- Identify and name different fruit
- Ask and answer questions to find out what fruit people like and don't like

- Review vegetables (optional)

- Sing a song

Key language
- *cherry, coconut, grape, lemon, mango, peach*
- *Eating fruit is fun to do.*
- Extension: *kiwi, pear, strawberry, watermelon*

Recycled: *toes*

Recycled: *Do you like (grapes)? Yes, I do. No, I don't. What about you?*

Materials
- Pupil's Book p44; Activity Book p41; Class CD2; Teacher's App on Navio
- Food flashcards
- Teacher's Resource Bank: Task flashcards: *think, listen, sing, Talk Partners, tick, circle*

Optional materials
- Teacher's Resource Bank: Five Trinity Exam Practice cards (selected from the Starter Unit and Units 1, 2 and 3)

At a Glance Lesson Plan

Pupil's Book

Starting the lesson
- Use the Trinity Exam Practice cards (optional).
- Review the Lesson 3 story.
- Set learning outcomes using the task flashcards.

Vocabulary presentation
- Present the new vocabulary.

Activity 1
- Listen, point and say.
- ▶ *CD2 Track 24 p263*

Activity 2
- Listen and point.
- ▶ *CD2 Track 25 p263*
- Sing *Do you like fruit?*

Activity 3
- Listen and repeat.
- ▶ *CD2 Track 26 p263*
- Talk Partners Ask and answer.

Go to the Activity Book.

4 Lesson 4 Vocabulary and Grammar

1 Listen, point and say.

mango grape peach cherry lemon coconut

2 Listen and point. Sing *Do you like fruit?*

I like grapes.
What about you?
Do you like grapes?
Do you like fruit?
I like grapes.
Yes, I do.
Eating fruit is fun to do.

I like peaches.
What about you?
Do you like peaches?
Do you like fruit?
I like peaches.
Yes, I do.
Eating fruit is fun to do.

3 Talk Partners Listen and repeat. Ask and answer.

Do you like grapes?
Yes, I do. What about you?
No, I don't. I don't like grapes.

44 forty-four

Ending the lesson
- Review the lesson.
- Review the task flashcards.

Extra activities

Reinforcement
- Play *Disappearing flashcards*.

Vocabulary Extension
- Present four additional vocabulary items.

Link to Science
- **Food:** Review vegetables.

Digital resources

Teacher's Digital: Don't forget you can teach this lesson using the Teacher's App on Navio.

Pupil's Digital: Encourage your pupils to use the Pupil's App on Navio to practise the vocabulary from this lesson.

Powered By NAVIO

Activity Book

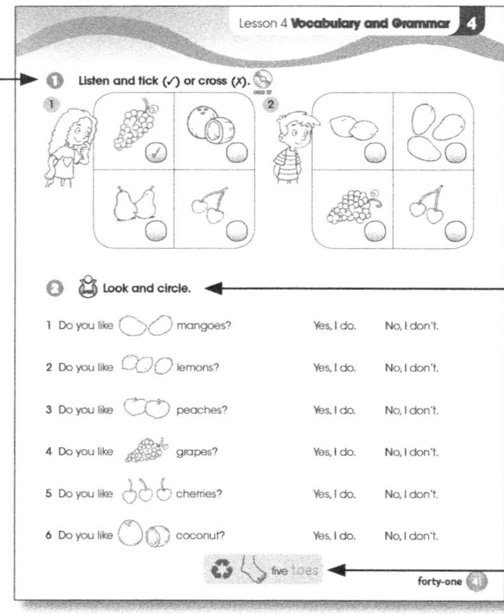

Lesson 4 Vocabulary and Grammar 4

1 Listen and tick (✓) or cross (✗).

2 Look and circle.

1 Do you like mangoes? Yes, I do. No, I don't.
2 Do you like lemons? Yes, I do. No, I don't.
3 Do you like peaches? Yes, I do. No, I don't.
4 Do you like grapes? Yes, I do. No, I don't.
5 Do you like cherries? Yes, I do. No, I don't.
6 Do you like coconut? Yes, I do. No, I don't.

five toes

forty-one 41

Activity Book

Activity 1
- Listen and (✓) tick or cross (✗).
- ▶ *CD2 Track 27 p263*

Activity 2
- Look and circle.

Recycled vocabulary
- Look, say and trace the word.

Detailed Lesson Plan

Starting the lesson

Use the Trinity Exam Practice cards (optional).

- The pupils practise asking and answering questions (see p31).

Review the Lesson 3 story.

- Give the pupils two minutes to look at the story. Then read out one of the speech bubbles, e.g. **Thank you. I like ice cream.** The pupils scan the story and point to the correct frame. Do the same with other speech bubbles.

Set learning outcomes using the task flashcards.

- Say **Today we're going to sing a song and ask questions about the food we like and don't like.**
- Hold up the task flashcards in turn and elicit the activities. Stick them on one side of the board. Point to them during the lesson to reinforce your instructions.

Vocabulary presentation

Present the new vocabulary.

- (Books open.) Point to the first photo in Activity 1 and read the word. Say **What colour is it? Is it delicious?** Say **I like mangoes.**
- Repeat with the other photos.

Pupil's Book Activity 1

Listen, point and say.

▶ *CD2 Track 24 p263*

- Say **Let's listen and repeat the words.**
- Play the CD. The pupils point to the photos and say the words.
- Play *What's missing?* with the photos (not the flashcards).

Pupil's Book Activity 2

Listen and point. Sing *Do you like fruit?*

▶ *CD2 Track 25 p263*

- Elicit the two fruits in the song.
- Play the CD. The pupils listen to the song and point to the fruit on the page.
- Divide the class into two groups. Play the CD again and one group sings the first verse and the second group sings the second verse.
- Play the CD again. The pupils swap roles.

Pupil's Book Activity 3

Listen and repeat. Ask and answer.

▶ *CD2 Track 26 p263*

- Play the CD. The pupils look and listen.
- Play the CD again. The pupils listen and repeat.
- Invite a volunteer to come to the front. The pupils ask the question and the volunteer answers.
- **Talk Partners** The pupils ask and answer questions with a Talk Partner.
- Invite volunteers to demonstrate the conversation.

Activity Book

Activity 1

Listen and tick (✓) or cross (✗).

▶ *CD2 Track 27 p263*

- (Books open.) Tell the pupils they are going to listen to two children talking about the fruit they like and don't like.
- Play the CD, pausing it after each fruit mentioned in the conversations. The pupils listen and tick or cross.

Answers: **1** grapes ✓ coconuts ✗ pears ✓ cherries ✓
2 lemons ✗ mangoes ✓ grapes ✓ cherries ✓

Activity 2

Look and circle.

- Read out the questions for the pupils to follow.
- Then read out the first question again. The pupils circle the answer that is correct for them.
- The pupils complete the rest of the questions and circle the answers on their own.

Answers: Pupils' own answers

Recycled vocabulary

- The pupils look at the picture and say the words. Then they trace the second word.

Ending the lesson

Review the lesson.

- (Books closed.) Say **Today we've sung a song and asked questions about fruit.**

Review the task flashcards.

- Point to the task flashcards. Say **Look at the activities you've done today. Which activity was your favourite?** Elicit the pupils' favourite activities.

Extra activities

Reinforcement

- Play *Disappearing flashcards* (see p23) with the food flashcards.

Vocabulary Extension

- Use the Vocabulary Booster on Navio and present and practise four additional words to describe fruit: *kiwi, pear, strawberry, watermelon.*

Link to Science

- If you are studying the Science topic of **Food** in English, you could review the vegetables that pupils know. Make a list on the board. The pupils say if they like or don't like each vegetable.

Key Competences and Key Learning Outcomes

- Review the meals of the day (optional)
- Say a tongue twister with the 'j' sound
- Listen for specific information
- Sing a cooperative learning song
- Understand the importance of keeping calm
- Play a communication game about food

Key language

- *Calm down*

Recycled: *banana, cake, chicken, fruit, ice cream; legs*

Recycled: *Do you like (chicken)? Yes, I do. No, I don't.*

Materials

- Pupil's Book p45; Activity Book p42; Class CD2; Teacher's App on Navio
- Teacher's Resource Bank: Task flashcards: *listen, say, match, cut out, think, Talk Partners, sing, colour*
- A ball
- Scissors, crayons or coloured pencils
- Teacher's Resource Bank: Unit 4 Lesson 5 Activity 3 cut-outs

Optional materials

- Teacher's Resource Bank: Five Trinity Exam Practice cards (selected from the Starter Unit and Units 1, 2 and 3)
- Coloured paper

At a Glance Lesson Plan

Starting the lesson

- Use the Trinity Exam Practice cards (optional).
- Review the vocabulary from Lesson 4.
- Review the *Do you like fruit?* song.

▶ *CD2 Track 25 p263*

- Set learning outcomes using the task flashcards.

Activity 1

- Listen and say.

▶ *CD2 Track 28 p263*

Go to Magic Phonics.

Go to the Activity Book.

Activity 2

- Listen and match.

▶ *CD2 Track 29 p263*

Activity 3

- Make and play the game Talk Partners

Pupil's Book

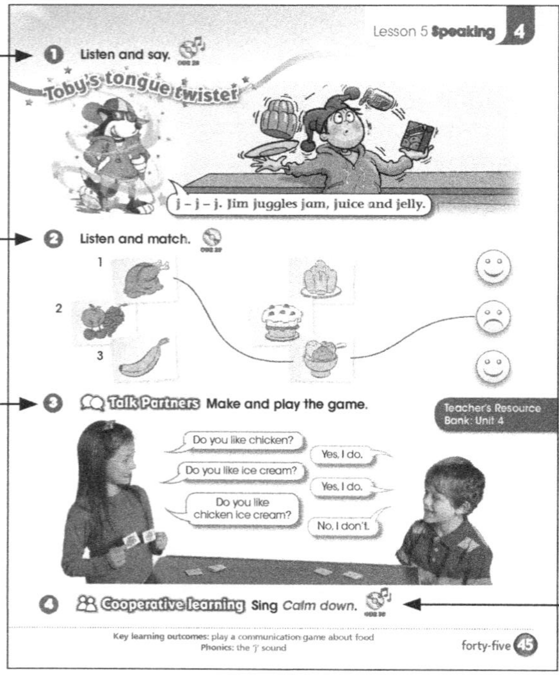

Activity 4 Cooperative learning

- Sing *Calm down.*

▶ *CD2 Track 30 p263*

Ending the lesson

- Review the lesson.
- Review the task flashcards.

Extra activity

Reinforcement

- Continue the pronunciation wall display.

Digital resources

Teacher's Digital: Don't forget you can teach this lesson using the Teacher's App on Navio.

Pupil's Digital: Encourage your pupils to use the Pupil's App on Navio to practise the vocabulary from this lesson.

Powered By NAVIO

Activity Book

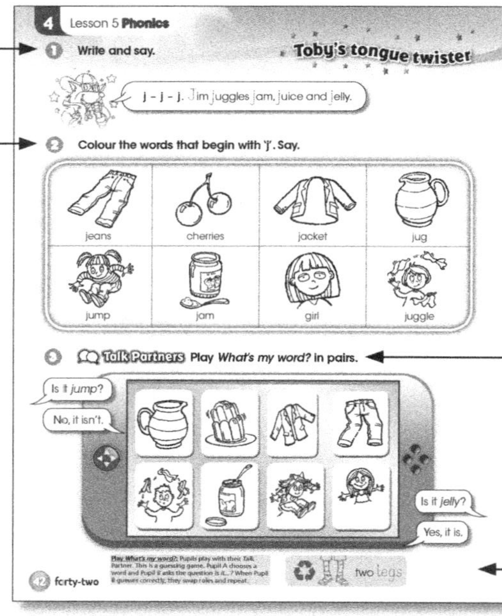

Activity Book

Activity 1

- Trace and say.

Activity 2

- Colour the words that begin with 'j'. Say.

Go to Magic Phonics.

Activity 3

- Talk Partners Play *What's my word?* in pairs.

Recycled vocabulary

- Look, say and trace the word.

Detailed Lesson Plan

Starting the lesson

Use the Trinity Exam Practice cards (optional).
- The pupils practise asking and answering questions (see p31).

Review the vocabulary from Lesson 4.
- The pupils form a circle. Gently throw a ball to a pupil and ask **Do you like (coconuts)?** The pupil answers.
- That pupil then asks a question about fruit and throws the ball to another pupil. Continue around the circle.

Review the *Do you like fruit?* song.

▶ *CD2 Track 25 p263*
- Play the CD. The pupils sing along.

Set learning outcomes using the task flashcards.
- Say **Today we're going to practise saying a tongue twister and make and play a speaking game.**
- Stick the task flashcards on one side of the board. Point to them during the lesson to reinforce your instructions.

Pupil's Book Activity 1

Listen and say.

▶ *CD2 Track 28 p263*
- (Books open.) Write the target 'j' sound on the board and say it. The pupils repeat.
- Say **It's time for Toby's tongue twister! What food can you see here?** (*Jam, juice and jelly.*)
- Play the CD. The pupils listen and repeat the target sound, then the words and then the entire tongue twister, faster and faster.

Go to Magic Phonics.

Activity Book

Activity 1

Trace and say.
- (Books open.) The pupils trace the letter 'j' in the tongue twister. Remind them that the first one is a capital 'J' for Jim's name, and the others are lower case.
- The pupils say the tongue twister to their partner, saying it faster and faster each time.

Activity 2

Colour the words that begin with 'j'. Say.
- Ask pupils to say the words that begin with 'j'. The pupils colour and say these words.

Answers: jeans, jacket, jug, jump, jam, juggle

Go to Magic Phonics.

Activity 3

Play *What's my word?* in pairs.
- Focus the pupils on Activity 3. Say the words.
- Think of a word and the pupils guess the word you are thinking of. Read the speech bubbles to demonstrate.
- Talk Partners The pupils play the game with a Talk Partner.

Recycled vocabulary
- The pupils look at the picture and say the words. Then they trace the second word.

Pupil's Book Activity 2

Listen and match.

▶ *CD2 Track 29 p263*
- Ask **What food can you see in the pictures?**
- Play the CD, pausing after each conversation so the pupils can point to the correct picture.
- Play the CD again. The pupils listen and draw matching lines to the faces.

Answers: **1** chicken ice cream, unhappy face **2** fruit jelly, happy face **3** banana cake, happy face

Pupil's Book Activity 3

Make and play the game.
- The pupils cut out and colour the cards and place them on their desks.
- Demonstrate the activity. Place the cards face down on your desk in two piles. Then pick one card from one pile and one from the second pile. Ask the corresponding questions, based on the model conversation.
- Repeat. Then ask a pupil to take your part.
- Talk Partners The pupils play the game with a Talk Partner.

Pupil's Book Activity 4: Cooperative learning

Sing *Calm down*.

▶ *CD2 Track 30 p263*
- Explain that everyone can feel excited but it's important to stay calm.
- Play the CD. The pupils listen and do the actions with you.
- Play the CD again. The pupils sing and do the actions.

Ending the lesson

Review the lesson.
- (Books closed.) Say **Today we've practised a tongue twister and played a game in pairs.** Elicit the tongue twister.

Review the task flashcards.
- Point to the task flashcards. Say **Look at the activities you've done today. Which activity was your favourite?** Elicit the pupils' favourite activities.

Extra activity

Reinforcement
- Continue the pronunciation wall display. Cut out the letter 'j' in coloured paper. Stick it on a piece of differently coloured paper to make a wall display. Elicit words that begin with that letter and write them on the wall display.
- Encourage the pupils to add new words beginning with the letter 'j' during the year. They can either tell you the new word for you to add or write the word themselves if they can.

Key Competences and Key Learning Outcomes

- Review healthy food (optional)

- Listen for general information
- Answer questions about a traditional English breakfast

- Read about a traditional English breakfast
- Think about what you have for breakfast

Key language

- *baked beans, bread, breakfast, cereal, eggs, mushrooms, orange juice, tomatoes; cook the food, cut the tomatoes, make the toast, mix the eggs, prepare the tray*
- *I (mix the eggs). We (prepare the tray). I have (eggs).*

Recycled: *feet*

Materials

- Pupil's Book p46; Activity Book p43; Class CD2; Teacher's App on Navio
- Food flashcards
- Teacher's Resource Bank: Task flashcards: *listen, read, think, number, circle, tick, draw*

Optional materials

- Teacher's Resource Bank: Five Trinity Exam Practice cards (selected from the Starter Unit and Units 1, 2 and 3)

At a Glance Lesson Plan

Starting the lesson

- Use the Trinity Exam Practice cards (optional).
- **Talk Partners** Review Toby's tongue twister.
- ▶ *CD2 Track 28 p263*
- Review the *Delicious food* song.
- ▶ *CD2 Track 18 p262*
- ▶ *CD2 Track 19 p262 (optional karaoke version)*
- Set learning outcomes using the task flashcards.

Activity 1

- Listen and read.
- ▶ *CD2 Track 31 p263*
- Answer.

Think about your culture

- What do you have for breakfast?

Go to the Activity Book.

Pupil's Book

Ending the lesson

- Review the lesson.
- Review the task flashcards.

Extra activity

Reinforcement

- Play *How many can you remember?*

Link to Science

- **Food:** Review the meals of the day.

Digital resources

Teacher's Digital: Don't forget you can teach this lesson using the Teacher's App on Navio.

Powered By NAVIO

Activity Book

Activity Book

Activity 1

- Listen and number.
- ▶ *CD2 Track 32 p263*
- Circle the breakfast you like.

Activity 2: Think about your culture

- Read and tick (✓).
- Draw.

Recycled vocabulary

- Look, say and trace the word.

Starting the lesson

Use the Trinity Exam Practice cards (optional).

- The pupils practise asking and answering questions (see p31).

Review Toby's tongue twister.

▶ *CD2 Track 28 p263*

- Ask **What sound did you practise in Toby's tongue twister? Can you remember the tongue twister?** (*Jim juggles jam, juice and jelly.*) Play the CD. Practise the tongue twister as a class.
- Talk Partners The pupils practise saying the tongue twister as fast as possible with a Talk Partner. Choose a fast pair to say it for the class.

Review the *Delicious food* song.

▶ *CD2 Track 18 p262*

▶ *CD2 Track 19 p262 (optional karaoke version)*

- Put the food flashcards on the board in the order they appear in the song. Divide the class into three groups. Play the CD (or use the karaoke version). Each group sings one verse. They change roles and repeat.

Set learning outcomes using the task flashcards.

- Say **Today we're going to learn about a traditional English breakfast in Britain.**
- Hold up the task flashcards in turn and elicit the activities. Stick them on one side of the board. Point to them during the lesson to reinforce your instructions.

Pupil's Book Activity 1

Listen and read. Answer.

▶ *CD2 Track 31 p263*

- (Books open.) Read the speech bubble and then focus the pupils on the pictures.
- Ask the class to tell you the food they can see in the photos.
- Play the CD, pausing to check understanding. The pupils listen and read.
- Play the CD again. Ask questions to check comprehension.

Suggested comprehension questions

- Photo 1: **What food can you see?** (*Eggs, mushrooms, baked beans, tomatoes, bread.*)
- Photo 2: **Who makes the toast?** (*Lucy.*) **Who cuts the tomatoes?** (*Dad.*) **Who mixes the eggs?** (*Alex.*)
- Photo 3: **Who cooks the food?** (*Dad.*)
- Photo 4: **Who's in bed?** (*Mum.*) **Is she happy?** (*Yes.*)

Pupil's Book Think about your culture

What do you have for breakfast?

- Read out the question.
- The pupils tell you what they have for breakfast.
- Ask additional questions, e.g. **Do you make your breakfast? Do you make breakfast for your mum / dad / brother / sister?**

Activity Book

Activity 1

Listen and number. Circle the breakfast you like.

▶ *CD2 Track 32 p263*

- (Books open.) Focus the pupils on the pictures.
- Play the CD, pausing after each text. The pupils listen and number the pictures.
- The pupils circle the breakfast they like. Ask volunteers to say which they prefer.

Answers: 4, 3, 2, 1

Activity 2: Think about your culture

Read and tick (✓). Draw.

- Tell the pupils what you have for breakfast.
- Read out the first sentence. The pupils tick the box if they have eggs for breakfast.
- Repeat with the other sentences.
- The pupils draw the breakfast they have.
- Invite different pupils to show the class their drawings and to say what they have for breakfast.

Recycled vocabulary

- The pupils look at the picture and say the words. They trace the second word.

Ending the lesson

Review the lesson.

- (Books closed.) Say **Today we've talked about a traditional English breakfast. Do you like it?** Elicit opinions from the pupils.

Review the task flashcards.

- Point to the task flashcards. Say **Look at the activities you've done today. Which activity was your favourite?** Elicit the pupils' favourite activities.

Extra activity

Reinforcement

- Play *How many can you remember?* (see p23) with the food flashcards.

Link to Science

- If you are studying the Science topic of **Food** in English, you could review the meals of the day in English. Ask the pupils to tell you what they normally eat for each meal.

Key Competences and Key Learning Outcomes

- Read and understand a lunch menu
- Draw a lunch menu

- Read for specific information

Key language

- *fruit salad, pasta, soup, vegetables; healthy*
- *What's for lunch on (Monday)? We've got (meat and vegetables) on (Monday).*

Recycled: *cake, chicken, fruit, ice cream, jelly, meat and vegetables*

Materials

- Pupil's Book p47; Activity Book p44; Class CD1 and 2; Teacher's App on Navio
- Teacher's Resource Bank: Task flashcards: *think, read, circle, listen, Talk Partners*

Optional materials

- Food flashcards
- Teacher's Resource Bank: Five Trinity Exam Practice cards (selected from the Starter Unit and Units 1, 2 and 3).

At a Glance Lesson Plan

Starting the lesson

- Use the Trinity Exam Practice cards (optional).
- Review the culture lesson.
- Review the days of the week.
- ▶ *CD 1 Track 7 p256*
- Set learning outcomes using the task flashcards.

Before you read

- Elicit healthy food.

Activity 1

- Read, look and circle.
- How many days is the menu for?

Activity 2

- Listen and read the lunch menu.
- ▶ *CD2 Track 33 p263*

After you read

Go to page 44 in your Activity Book.

Pupil's Book

Ending the lesson

- Review the lesson.
- Review the task flashcards.

Extra activities

Reinforcement

- Play *Stop!*

Extension

- Establish a *What's for lunch?* routine.

Link to Science

- **Food:** Review healthy food.

Digital resources

Teacher's Digital: Don't forget you can teach this lesson using the Teacher's App on Navio.

Pupil's Digital: Encourage your pupils to use the Pupil's App on Navio to practise the vocabulary from this lesson.

Powered By NAVIO

Activity Book

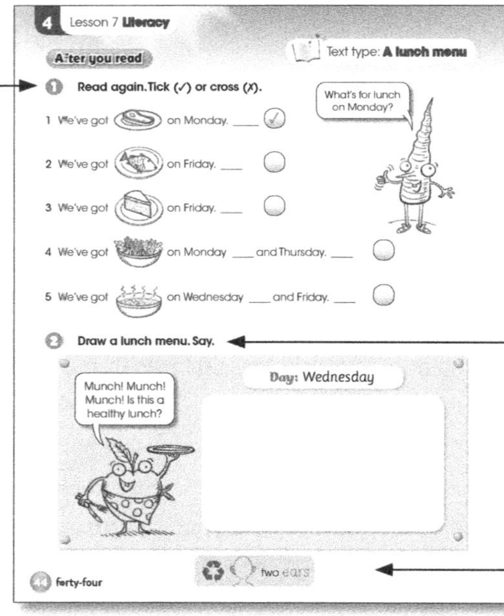

Activity Book

After you read: Activity 1

- Read again.
- Tick (✓) or cross (✗).

Talk Partners
Say the sentences in pairs.

Activity 2

- Draw a lunch menu.
- Say.

Recycled vocabulary

- Look, say and trace the word.

Detailed Lesson Plan

Starting the lesson

Use the Trinity Exam Practice cards (optional).
- The pupils practise asking and answering questions (see p31).

Review the culture lesson.
- Ask the pupils if they can remember what foods are in a traditional English breakfast.

Review the days of the week.
▶ *CD 1 Track 7 p256*
- Use the word cards to review the days of the week. Ask the class to put the cards in order and say each day.
- Play the *Seven days a week* chant. The pupils sing along and do the actions.

Set learning outcomes using the task flashcards.
- Say **Today we're going to read a lunch menu.**
- Hold up the task flashcards in turn and elicit the activities. Stick them on one side of the board. Point to them during the lesson to reinforce your instructions.

Before you read

Elicit healthy food.
- (Books open.) Focus the pupils on the speech bubble at the top of the page. Read it aloud. The pupils repeat.
- Elicit the meaning of 'healthy'. Ask the pupils what healthy food they know.

Pupil's Book Activity 1

Read, look and circle. How many days is the menu for?
- Read out the question. Give the pupils time to look at the menu and think. Elicit the answer.

Answer: five days

Pupil's Book Activity 2

Listen and read the lunch menu.
▶ *CD2 Track 33 p263*
- Say **Yum, salad!** Nod your head as you point to the first picture.
- Say **Hands up if you like salad.** The pupils respond. Repeat with all the pictures.
- Play the CD. The pupils listen, read the lunch menu and point to the correct picture as they hear it.
- Play the CD again, pausing after each sentence. The class repeats.

Activity Book

After you read: Activity 1
Read again. Tick (✓) or cross (✗).
- (Books open.) Focus the pupils on Activity 1. Ask **What's for lunch on Monday?** Read out the first sentence.
- The pupils look at the menu in the Pupil's Book to find the day they have fish. Repeat with the other sentences.
- The pupils work on their own to tick or cross the days. **Talk Partners** The pupils say the sentences with a Talk Partner.

Answers: 2 ✓ 3 ✓ 4 ✓ 5 ✓

Activity 2
Draw a lunch menu. Say.
- Focus the pupils on Activity 2. The pupils draw a lunch menu for one day of the week.
- Ask different pupils to show their pictures and talk about their menu to the class. Then ask **Is this a healthy lunch?** The rest of the class decides.

Recycled vocabulary
- The pupils look at the picture and say the words. Then they trace the second word.

Ending the lesson

Review the lesson.
- (Books closed.) Say **Today we've read and drawn a lunch menu. What food was on the menu in your Pupil's Book?** Elicit some food items that appear on the menu.

Review the task flashcards.
- Point to the task flashcards. Say **Look at the activities you've done today. Which activity was your favourite?** Elicit the pupils' favourite activities.

Extra activities

Reinforcement
- Play *Stop!* (see p23) with the food flashcards.

Extension
- If there's a canteen in your school, establish a *What's for lunch?* routine.
- In each lesson a different pupil reads the menu for the day and tells the class, e.g. *We've got (soup) for lunch today.*

Link to Science

- If you are studying the Science topic of **Food** in English, you could reinforce how to identify healthy food.
- Encourage the class to tell you what they have got for lunch today and if it is healthy or not.

Key Competences and Key Learning Outcomes

- Review language in the unit
- Reflect on own learning

- Sing a cooperative learning song

Key language

Recycled: *cake, cherries, chicken, chips, coconuts, eggs, fish, fruit, grapes, ice cream, mangoes, meat, rice, salad, soup; mouth*

Recycled: *I like (ice cream). I love (salad). I don't like (cake). Do you like (fruit)?*

Materials

- Pupil's Book p48; Activity Book p45; Class CD2; Teacher's App on Navio
- Food flashcards
- Teacher's Resource Bank: Task flashcards: *listen, number, think, sing, stick, tick, Talk Partners*
- Teacher's Resource Bank: Traffic light cut-out
- *Give Me Five!* sticker

Optional materials

- Teacher's Resource Bank: Five Trinity Exam Practice cards (selected from the Starter Unit and Units 1, 2 and 3)

At a Glance Lesson Plan

Starting the lesson

- Use the Trinity Exam Practice cards (optional).
- Review the unit vocabulary.
- Set learning outcomes using the task flashcards.

Activity 1

- Listen and number.
- ▶ *CD2 Track 34 p263*
- Say.

Activity 2

- Read and circle for you.

Activity 3 Cooperative learning

- Sing *Well done!*
- ▶ *CD2 Track 35 p264*
- Stick the *Give Me Five!* sticker.
- Go to the Activity Book.

Pupil's Book

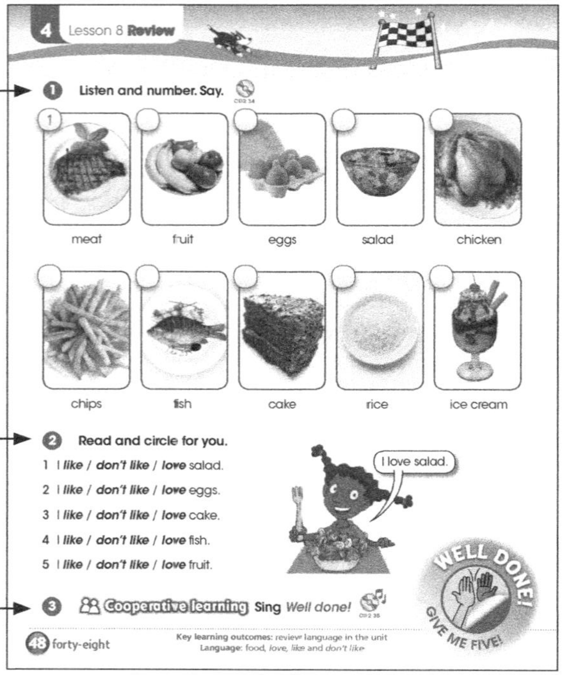

Ending the lesson

- Review the task flashcards.

Extra activity

Reinforcement

- Play *Match the word and flashcard.*

Activity Book

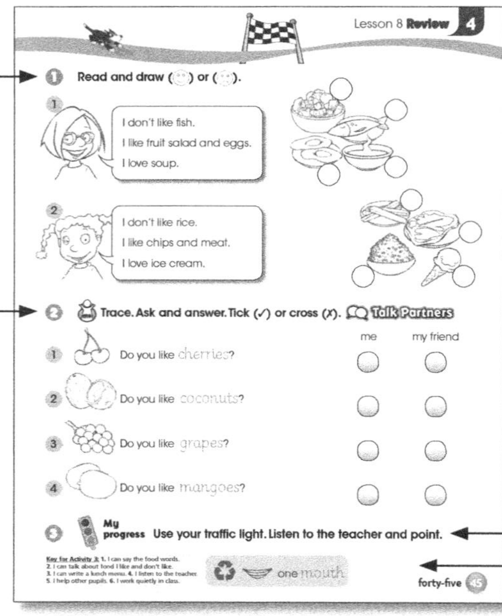

Activity Book

Activity 1

- Read and draw (☺) or (☹).

Activity 2

- Trace.
- Talk Partners Ask and answer.
- Tick (✓) or cross (✗).

Activity 3 My progress

- Use your traffic light. Listen to the teacher and point.

Recycled vocabulary

- Look, say and trace the word.

Digital resources

Teacher's Digital: Don't forget you can teach this lesson using the Teacher's App on Navio.

Pupil's Digital: Encourage your pupils to use the Pupil's App on Navio to practise the vocabulary from this lesson.

Powered By NAVIO

Detailed Lesson Plan

Starting the lesson

Use the Trinity Exam Practice cards (optional).

- The pupils practise asking and answering questions (see p31).

Review the unit vocabulary.

- Stick the food flashcards face down on the board. Ask **Where's the (ice cream)?** Ask a pupil to come to the front and turn over one of the flashcards. If it's the correct flashcard, he / she says *It's here.* If it isn't the correct flashcard, another pupil has a turn. Repeat with different words and different pupils.

Set learning outcomes using the task flashcards.

- Say **Today we're going to remember what we've learnt in Unit 4.**
- Hold up the task flashcards in turn and elicit the activities. Stick them on one side of the board. Point to them during the lesson to reinforce your instructions.

Pupil's Book Activity 1

Listen and number. Say.

▶ *CD2 Track 34 p263*

- (Books open.) Point to the pictures and ask different pupils to name the food.
- Play the CD, pausing after each sentence. The pupils point to the food items.
- Play the CD again. The pupils write the correct number for each picture.
- The pupils say the words under each picture.

Answers: **1** meat **2** chicken **3** ice cream **4** salad **5** fish **6** rice **7** cake **8** fruit **9** chips **10** eggs

Pupil's Book Activity 2

Read and circle for you.

- Focus the pupils on the sentences in Activity 2.
- The pupils think about the foods.
- The pupils choose and circle *like*, *don't like* or *love* for themselves.
- Ask different pupils to read out their sentences.

Pupil's Book Activity 3: Cooperative learning

Sing *Well done!*

▶ *CD2 Track 35 p264*

- Praise the pupils for their hard work and encourage them to praise each other.
- Play the *Well done!* song. The pupils sing and do the actions.

Stick the *Give Me Five!* sticker.

- The pupils stick the *Give Me Five!* sticker on the Pupil's Book page.
- Variation: Sing the *Well done!* song and stick the *Give Me Five!* sticker after the pupils have also completed the Activity Book Lesson 8 Review.

Activity Book

Activity 1

Read and draw (☺) or (☹).

- (Books open.) The pupils look at the food items in Activity 1. Elicit the food words. Remind them that the smiley and unhappy faces mean 'like', 'love' and 'don't like'.
- The pupils read the speech bubbles and draw the correct faces next to the food items.
- **Talk Partners** The pupils point to the food items and say the sentences with a Talk Partner.

Answers: fish ☹; fruit salad, eggs, soup ☺; rice ☹; chips, meat, ice cream ☺

Activity 2

Trace. Ask and answer. Tick (✓) or cross (*x*).

- Focus the pupils on Activity 2. The pupils trace the words.
- Read out the first question. The pupils write a tick in the 'me' column if they like cherries and a cross if they don't.
- The pupils write a tick or a cross to answer the rest of the questions for themselves.
- **Talk Partners** The pupils ask and answer with a Talk Partner.
- The pupils write a tick or a cross for their friend.

Activity 3: My progress

Use your traffic light. Listen to the teacher and point.

- (Books closed.) Ask the pupils to take out their traffic light cut-out. Say **Let's think about our work in this unit.** Point to the green circle, nod your head, smile a lot, and say **I can say the food words. Yes, I can do this very well.** Point to the yellow circle, move your head a little, smile a little and say **Yes, I can do this.** Then point to the red circle, shake your head and say **No, I can't do this.**
- Read the different statements. For each one, the pupils point to the colour on their traffic light that shows how they feel about their own learning.

Self-assessment statements

1. I can say the food words.
2. I can talk about food I like and don't like.
3. I can write a lunch menu.
4. I listen to the teacher.
5. I help other pupils.
6. I work quietly in class.

Recycled vocabulary

- The pupils look at the picture and say the words. Then they trace the second word.

Ending the lesson

Review the task flashcards.

- Point to the task flashcards. Say **Look at the activities you've done today. Which activity was your favourite?** Elicit the pupils' favourite activities.

Extra activity

Reinforcement

- Play *Match the word and flashcard* with the food flashcards and word cards.

Key Competences and Key Learning Outcomes

- Watch and understand a video about school lunches
- Choose and draw healthy food for your lunch box
- Understand the importance of eating healthily

Key language

- *cake, chicken, fruit, healthy, lunch, pasta, spaghetti, vegetables, water*

Materials

- Pupil's Book p49; Activity Book p46; Class CD2; Video; Teacher's App on Navio
- Teacher's Resource Bank: Task flashcards: *tick, read, circle, think, listen, number, draw, Talk Partners*
- Teacher's Resource Bank: Food flashcards

Optional materials

- Teacher's Resource Bank: Trinity Exam Practice cards (selected from Unit 4)

At a Glance Lesson Plan

Pupil's Book

Starting the lesson

- Use the Trinity Exam Practice cards (optional).
- Play a game to review food vocabulary.
- Set learning outcomes and use the task flashcards.

Pre-watching activity

- Look at the photo and talk about a healthy lunch.

Activity 1

- Watch the video.
  Unit 4 video p278
- Tick (✓) or cross (✗). Are these lunches in the video?

Activity 2

- Watch the video again.
  Unit 4 video
- Read and circle.

Activity 3

- Read and think. Tick (✓) or (✗).
- Go to the Activity Book.

Ending the lesson

- Review the lesson.
- Review the task flashcards.

Activity Book

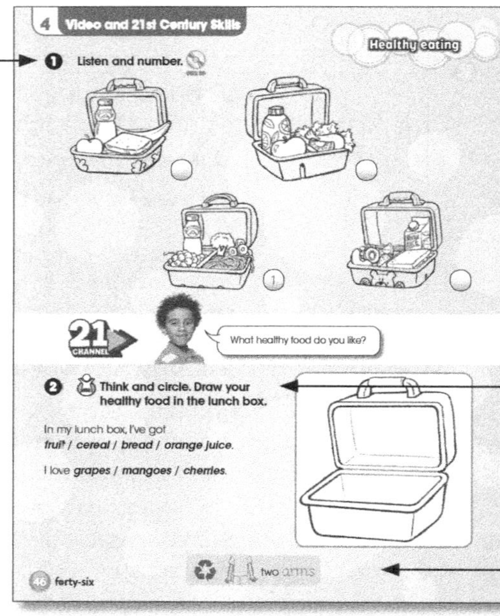

Activity Book

Activity 1

- Listen and number.
- ▶ *CD2 Track 36 p264*

Activity 2

- Think and circle. Draw your healthy food in the lunch box.

Recycled vocabulary

- Look, say and trace the word.

Digital resources

Teacher's Digital: Don't forget you can teach this lesson using the Teacher's App on Navio.

Pupil's Digital: Encourage your pupils to use the Pupil's App on Navio to practise the vocabulary from this lesson.

Powered By NAVIO

Detailed Lesson Plan

Starting the lesson

Use the Trinity Exam Practice cards (optional).

- The pupils practise asking and answering questions.
- Give out the food flashcards and word cards to different pupils. Tell them to hold the cards up so you can see them. Tell them when you say a food word that corresponds to their card, they stand up. When they hear it again, they sit down. Do a couple of examples and then say the words faster and faster. Vary the game by explaining if you say *I like (chicken)* they stand up and if you say *I don't like (rice)* they sit down. You could also ask different pupils to lead the activity.

Set learning outcomes and use the task cards.

- Say **Today we're going to watch a video and then ask and answer questions about school lunches**.
- Point to the task flashcards throughout to elicit activities and reinforce your instructions.

Pre-watching activity

- Look at the photo and read the speech bubble to pupils. Ask **Do you have a healthy lunch?** Elicit responses from a number of pupils.

Pupil's Book Activity 1

Watch the video. Tick (✓) or cross (✗). Are these lunches in the video? *p278*

- Play Part 1, pausing after Abby says *Yes, I am*. Ask **Is Abby hungry?**
- On the board stick four food flashcards. Tell the pupils to listen and tell you which food you don't say. Say three of the foods. Ask a pupil to come to the board and write a cross under the food flashcard you didn't say. Repeat with different food flashcards.
- Focus the pupils on the video stills. Ask **What can you see?** Then say **Let's watch and listen**.
- Explain that the pupils cross the food that is not in the video like the previous flashcard activity. Play Part 2 of the video. Pause the video after the first video still. Ask the pupils to point to the corresponding photo in their book.
- Play the rest of Part 2 for pupils to point to the photos in the order they see the food.
- Play Part 2 again for pupils to write the cross. The pupils then tick the food that is in the video.
- Ask **What is in Abby's healthy lunch box?** (A sandwich and an apple).

Answers: ✓, ✗, ✓, ✓

Pupil's Book Activity 2

Watch the video again. Read and circle.

- Play Part 1 and Part 2 again. Pause after Abby says, *The children like the lunch*. Read out the first sentence in Activity 2. Ask **Do the children like the lunch?** Show 'like' circled.
- Play the video all the way through for pupils to circle the words. Ask **Which lunch in the video do you like? Why?**
- Ask general questions to check understanding.
  Do the children eat on their own? *(No, together.)*
  What food makes the happy face? *(Spaghetti.)*
  What animals did you see? *(A rabbit, a teddy, a bear, a bird.)*
  What colour hair does the face sandwich have? *(Green and orange.)*
  What unhealthy lunch does Abby have? *(Biscuits, crisps and chocolate.)*

Answers: **1** like **2** bird **3** small **4** is

Pupil's Book Activity 3

Read and think. Tick (✓) or cross (✗).

- Point to the pictures and elicit the vocabulary. Read out the first sentence and ask if the sentence is true or false. Read out the other sentences for the pupils to follow in their books.
- **Think-Pair-Share** After completing the activity individually, the pupils compare their answers with their Talk Partner. Ask **Are your answers the same or different?**

Answers: **1** ✓ **2** ✗ **3** ✓ **4** ✓

Activity Book

Activity 1

Listen and number.

▶ *CD2 Track 36 p264*

- Play the first exchange on the CD. Ask **Which lunch box are they talking about?** Show the number one in the circle. Play the rest of the track, pausing after each exchange, for pupils to number the lunch boxes.
- Ask **Which lunch boxes are healthy? Why?**

Answers: Top row from left to right: 3, 2
Bottom row left to right: 1, 4

Activity 2

Think and circle. Draw your healthy food in the lunch box.

- Read out the speech bubble. Ask a few pupils, **What healthy food do you like?**
- The pupils read the sentences. They circle the food items that are in their lunch box, and the food they love.
- Then they draw the food in the box.
- Say **What's in your lunch box?** for the pupils to repeat the sentences, saying the answers that are correct for them.
- **Talk Partners** In pairs, pupils take turns to ask and answer *What's in your lunch box?* Encourage the pupils to answer in full, for example, *In my lunch box I've got (fruit).*

Recycled vocabulary

- The pupils look at the picture and say the words. Then they trace the second word.

Ending the lesson

Review the lesson.

- Say **What did we learn today about school lunches? Do you think it is important to have a healthy lunch? Why?** (Yes, it is. To be healthy our lunch needs fruit, vegetables, water or juice. Crisps, chocolate, biscuits and cake are not healthy.)

Review the task flashcards.

- Say **Look at the activities you've done today. Which activity was your favourite?**

Date: ____________ Unit: ____________

1 What did my pupils learn in this unit?

2 How did my pupils work? (✓)

individually ☐ in pairs ☐ in small groups ☐

in large groups ☐ as a class ☐

3 Which key competences did my pupils develop?

- Competence in linguistic communication ☐
- Competence in mathematics, science and technology ☐
- Digital competence ☐
- Learning to learn ☐
- Social and civic competences ☐
- Sense of initiative and entrepreneurship ☐
- Cultural awareness and expression ☐

4 Which lessons / activities were the most successful and why?

5 Which lessons / activities did my pupils find the most difficult and why?

6 What did I try in the classroom for the first time? How did it go?

7 Which resources did I find most useful? (including webpages)

8 What could I do differently next time I teach this unit?

Unit 5

Fun on the farm

Unit overview

Key Competences and Key Learning Outcomes

- Identify and say ten farm animals (Lesson 1)
- Say the vocabulary chant (Lesson 1)
- Use *Can you …?* and *Yes, I can. No, I can't.* in a conversation (Lesson 2)
- Say what animals can and can't do (Lesson 4)
- Read and say an animal riddle (Lesson 7)
- Watch and understand a video about farm animals (Video and 21st Century Skills)

- Identify two-legged and four-legged animals (Lesson 7)
- Put things in groups (Video and 21st Century Skills)

- Use the Pupil's App on Navio

- Practise spelling (Lesson 1)
- Say a tongue twister to practise the 'sh' sound (Lesson 5)
- Review language in the unit and reflect on own learning (Lesson 8)
- Practise activity types found in the Cambridge English Young Learners Exams: Pre A1 Starters

- Understand the importance of washing your hands after touching animals (Lesson 3)
- Draw animals according to their group (Video and 21st Century Skills)

- Work with a Talk Partner to practise and reinforce learning (all lessons)
- Play a communication game about what animals can do (Lesson 5)

- Sing four songs (Lessons 1, 4, 5 and 8)
- Understand and act out a story (Lesson 3)
- Read about urban farms in Britain (Lesson 6)
- Think about farms where you live (Lesson 6)

Vocabulary

Core vocabulary
bird, cat, chicken, cow, duck, frog, goat, horse, mouse, sheep; climb, fly, jump, run, swim, walk

Extension vocabulary (optional)
bee, bull, cockerel, donkey, rabbit, spider; crawl, dive, hop, talk

Other vocabulary
animals, carrots, farm, feed, interesting, lamb, shop, shout, stop!, touch, park, pet shop, zoo

Recycled vocabulary
colours; numbers 1–10; *big, small; cake, chicken, chips, eggs, fish, fruit, grapes, ice cream, meat, rice, salad, vegetables; delicious; ruler, rubber; doll, robot; ear, toes; garden; juggle; ride a bike*

Structures

Core structures
Can you see (a cow)? Yes, I can. No, I can't.
(Cats) can (climb). (Cats) can't (swim).
Can you (swim)? Yes, I can. No, I can't.

Other structures
It's my turn now. I'm (small). This (sheep) can climb trees. I can (feed them). We can see (chickens on the farm). What can (Peter) see? This is a (cow).

Recycled structures
I've got (two legs). Is it a (cow)? Yes, it is. I love (the goats). I like (the garden). What am I? It's (green).

Phonics

Consonant sound 'sh' (**sh**ush, **sh**out, **sh**eep)

British Culture

Urban farms

Literacy

Text type: animal riddles (text to entertain)
Reading skills: using visual clues; reading for specific information; speculating

21st Century Skills

Ways of thinking: learn to put things in groups

Cooperative learning

Songs: *Let's take turns* (Lesson 5); *Well done!* (Lesson 8)
Skill: Working together and supporting each other (Lesson 1)

Values

Understanding the importance of washing your hands after touching animals

Cross-curricular links

Links to Science

Animals: (domestic animals) pets and farm animals; the different ways that animals move; farm animals and wild animals

Suggested Arts and Crafts concepts

Forms: identifying 3D forms in Art and in the environment; using shapes and forms to represent animals

Key Competences and Key Learning Outcomes

- Identify and say ten farm animals
- Say the vocabulary chant
- Stick the farm animals stickers
- Review farm animals and pets (optional)
- Practise spelling
- Sing a song about a farm

Key language
- *bird, cat, chicken, cow, duck, frog, goat, horse, mouse, sheep; farm*
- *Can you see (a horse)? Yes, I can. The (duck) is (yellow).*
- Extension: *bee, bull, cockerel, donkey, rabbit, spider*
- **Recycled:** colours; *fish, chips*

Materials
- Pupil's Book p50; Activity Book pp48 and 57; Class CD2; Teacher's App on Navio
- Farm animals flashcards; Unit 5 stickers
- Teacher's Resource Bank: Farm animals word cards
- Teacher's Resource Bank: Task flashcards: *listen, sing, read, stick, say, Talk Partners, find, colour*
- Crayons or coloured pencils

Optional materials
- Teacher's Resource Bank: Five Trinity Exam Practice cards (selected from the Starter Unit and Units 1, 2, 3 and 4)

At a Glance Lesson Plan

Starting the lesson
- Use the Trinity Exam Practice cards (optional).
- Review colours.
- Set learning outcomes using the task flashcards.

Vocabulary presentation
- Present the new vocabulary.

Activity 1
- Listen and point.
- ▶ *CD2 Track 37 p264*
- Sing *On the farm.*

Word cards
- Read the word cards.
- Match them to the flashcards.

Activity 2
- Read and stick the ten stickers.
- Listen and say the chant.
- ▶ *CD2 Track 39 p264*
- Go to the Activity Book.

Pupil's Book

Ending the lesson
- Review the lesson.
- Review the task flashcards.

Extra activity

Vocabulary Extension
- Present six additional vocabulary items.

Cooperative learning

Working together and supporting each other
- Talk Partners Ask and answer *What's this?*

Link to Science
- **Animals:** Review farm animals and domestic animals (pets).

Learning to learn

Spelling
- Practise spelling at any time during this unit (Activity Book p57).

Digital resources

Teacher's Digital: Don't forget you can teach this lesson using the Teacher's App on Navio.

Pupil's Digital: Encourage your pupils to use the Pupil's App on Navio to practise the vocabulary from this lesson.

Powered By NAVIO

Activity Book

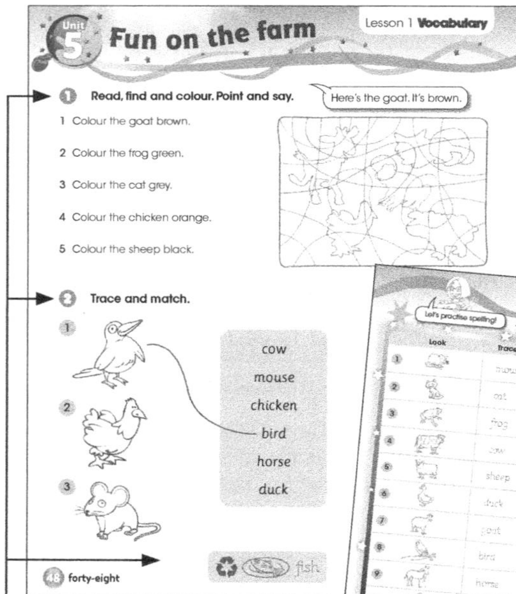

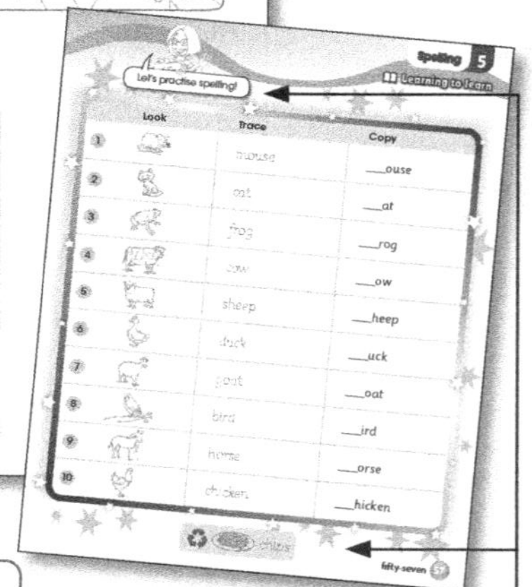

Activity Book

Activity 1
- Read, find and colour.
- Point and say.

Activity 2
- Trace and match.

Recycled vocabulary
- Look, say and trace the word.

Spelling

Let's practise spelling!
- Use the *Look-Read-Trace* technique.

Recycled vocabulary
- Look, say and trace the word.

Detailed Lesson Plan

Starting the lesson

Use the Trinity Exam Practice cards (optional).

- The pupils practise asking and answering questions (see p31).

Review colours.

- Say **Point to the colour (red).** The pupils point to red objects in the classroom.
- Repeat with other colours. Say the instructions at a faster speed as the pupils become more confident.

Set learning outcomes using the task flashcards.

- Say **Today we're going to learn farm animals.**
- Hold up the task flashcards in turn and elicit the activities. Stick them on one side of the board. Point to them during the lesson to reinforce your instructions.

Vocabulary presentation

Present the new vocabulary.

- (Books closed.) Ask **Do you like animals?** Then ask **Which animals do you like?** Elicit answers.
- Hold up the farm animals flashcards but only show the back of the flashcards, and say, e.g. **This animal lives on the farm. It's brown. It's big and it's got four legs. What is it?** When the pupils identify the animals, say the word and the pupils repeat. Repeat with all the flashcards and stick them on the board.

Pupil's Book Activity 1

Listen and point. Sing *On the farm*.

▶ *CD2 Track 37 p264*

- (Books open.) Focus the pupils on the picture. Ask **Where are Molly, Beth and Jake? What animals can you see? What colour is the (frog)?**
- Play the CD. The pupils listen and point.
- Play the CD again. The pupils sing and do the actions.

Word cards

Read the words. Match them to the flashcards.

- (Books closed.) Hold up the farm animals word cards, and say or elicit each word.
- Ask pupils to come to the front and stick the word cards on the board with the corresponding flashcards.

Pupil's Book Activity 2

Read and stick the ten stickers. Listen and say the chant.

▶ *CD2 Track 39 p264*

- (Books open.) Ask a pupil to read the first animal word. The pupils stick the corresponding sticker. Repeat with the other stickers.
- Play the CD. The pupils listen and say the chant, pointing to the stickers in turn.

Activity Book

Activity 1

Read, find and colour. Point and say.

- (Books open.) Ask different pupils to read out the sentences. Check understanding.
- The pupils find and colour the animals in the picture.
- The pupils point and say sentences, following the example in the speech bubble.

Answers: a brown goat, a green frog, a grey cat, an orange chicken, a black sheep

Activity 2

Trace and match.

- Read out the farm animal words in the word box as a class. Elicit what picture each word corresponds to.
- The pupils trace the words and draw matching lines to the pictures.

Answers: **1** bird **2** chicken **3** mouse **4** horse **5** cow **6** duck

Recycled vocabulary

- The pupils look at the picture and say the word. Then they trace the word.

Ending the lesson

Review the lesson.

- (Books closed.) Say **Today we've learnt farm animals in English. What do you remember?**

Review the task flashcards.

- Point to the task flashcards. Say **Look at the activities you've done today. Which activity was your favourite?** Elicit the pupils' favourite activities.

Extra activity

Vocabulary Extension

- Use the Vocabulary Booster on Navio to present and practise six additional words to describe animals: *bee, bull, cockerel, donkey, rabbit, spider.*

Cooperative learning

Working together and supporting each other

- **Talk Partners** Pupil A points to a farm animals sticker and asks *What's this?* Pupil B answers using *It's a …* If Pupil B can't remember, Pupil A can help. Encourage the pupils to help each other to remember vocabulary. The pupils swap roles and repeat.

Link to Science

- If you are studying the Science topic of **Animals** in English, you could review farm and domestic animals. Review the names of pets and farm animals in this lesson. Ask **Can you see (a fish) on a farm?**

Spelling (Activity Book page 57)

Let's practise spelling!

- The pupils can practise spelling the ten farm animals using the *Look-Read-Trace* technique at any time during this unit before the Lesson 8 Review.

Recycled vocabulary

- The pupils look at the picture and say the word. Then they trace the word.

Key Competences and Key Learning Outcomes

- Use *Can you ...?* and *Yes, I can. No, I can't.*
- Complete and practise a conversation
- Listen for specific information

Key language

- *Can you see (a cow)? Yes, I can. No, I can't.*

Recycled: *bird, cat, chicken, cow, duck, frog, goat, horse, mouse, sheep; rice*

Materials

- Pupil's Book p51; Activity Book p49; Class CD2; Teacher's App on Navio
- Farm animals flashcards
- Teacher's Resource Bank: Task flashcards: *think, listen, act out, colour, read, follow, circle, draw, Talk Partners*
- Coloured pencils or crayons

Optional materials

- Teacher's Resource Bank: Five Trinity Exam Practice cards (selected from the Starter Unit and Units 1, 2, 3 and 4)

At a Glance Lesson Plan

Starting the lesson

- Use the Trinity Exam Practice cards (optional).
- **Think-Pair-Share** Review farm animals.
- Review the *On the farm* song.
- ▶ ***CD2 Track 37 p264***
- ▶ ***CD2 Track 38 p264 (optional karaoke version)***
- Set learning outcomes using the task flashcards.

Activity 1

- Listen and repeat.
- ▶ ***CD2 Track 40 p264***
- Act out.

Activity 2

- Listen and colour the animals they can see.
- ▶ ***CD2 Track 41 p264***
- Go to the Activity Book.

Pupil's Book

Ending the lesson

- Review the lesson.
- Review the task flashcards.

Extra activity

Reinforcement

- Play a farm animals flashcard game.

Activity Book

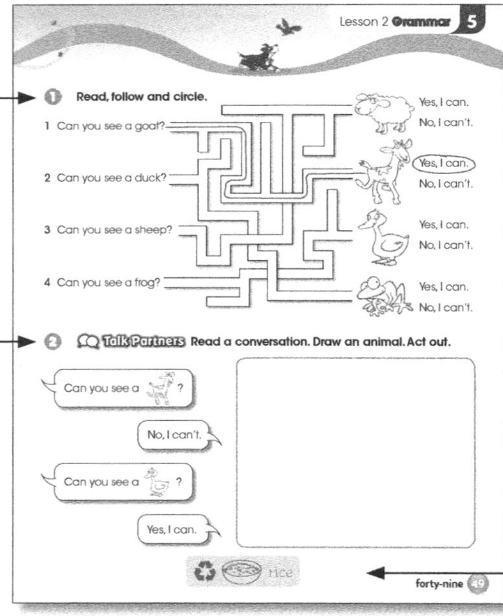

Activity Book

Activity 1

- Read, follow and circle.

Activity 2

- Read a conversation.
- Draw an animal.
- **Talk Partners** Act out.

Recycled vocabulary

- Look, say and trace the word.

Digital resources

Teacher's Digital: Don't forget you can teach this lesson using the Teacher's App on Navio.

Pupil's Digital: Encourage your pupils to use the Pupil's App on Navio to practise the vocabulary from this lesson.

Powered By NAVIO

Starting the lesson

Use the Trinity Exam Practice cards (optional).

- The pupils practise asking and answering questions (see p31).
  Think-Pair-Share Review farm animals.
- Ask **Can you remember the ten farm animals?** The class thinks silently for a minute.
- **Talk Partners** Then the pupils work with a Talk Partner to name the farm animals.
- Invite different pairs to say a different farm animal. Hold up the corresponding flashcard and prompt the class to repeat the word.
- Repeat the procedure, asking different pairs of pupils each time, until all ten farm animals have been named.

Review the *On the farm* song.

▶ *CD2 Track 37 p264*

▶ *CD2 Track 38 p264 (optional karaoke version)*

- Invite six pupils to come to the front of the class and mime being one of the animals in the song. Play the CD (or use the karaoke version). The rest of the class sing the song and point to each animal in turn as it appears in the song.

Set learning outcomes using the task flashcards.

- Say **Today we're going to talk about farm animals.**
- Hold up the task flashcards in turn and elicit the activities. Stick them on one side of the board. Point to them during the lesson to reinforce your instructions.

Pupil's Book Activity 1

Listen and repeat. Act out.

▶ *CD2 Track 40 p264*

- (Books open.) The pupils look at the picture. Ask **What animals can you see?**
- Play the CD. The pupils listen and read the conversation.
- Ask **Can Molly see Toby? Can Jake see Toby? Can Molly see the black cat? Can Jake see the black cat?**
- Play the CD again, pausing after each sentence for the pupils to repeat.
- When the pupils are confident with the language, ask different pairs of pupils to come to the front and act out the conversation.

Pupil's Book Activity 2

Listen and colour the animals they can see.

▶ *CD2 Track 41 p264*

- Focus the pupils on Activity 2. Point to the farm animals and elicit what's in each picture.
- Say **Let's listen. What can they see?**
- Play the CD, pausing after each conversation to give the pupils time to colour the animals. The pupils listen and colour each animal.

Answers: **1** a green frog **2** a black and white cow **3** (horse uncoloured) **4** a yellow bird **5** a black sheep **6** (duck uncoloured)

Activity Book

Activity 1

Read, follow and circle.

- (Books open.) Read out the first question. Follow the path to the answer and the pupils do the same.
- The pupils work on their own to follow the paths and circle the answers.

Answers: **1** Yes, I can. **2** No, I can't. **3** Yes, I can. **4** No, I can't.

Activity 2

Read a conversation. Draw an animal. Act out.

- Read the speech bubbles, pausing before the pictures to elicit the vocabulary.
- Practise the conversation as a class.
- The pupils draw a different farm animal in the box.
- **Talk Partners** When the pupils are confident with the language, they work in pairs to practise their conversations. They draw the animal that is in their conversation in the box.
- Invite different pairs of pupils to act out their conversations.

Recycled vocabulary

- The pupils look at the picture and say the word. Then they trace the word.

Ending the lesson

Review the lesson.

- (Books closed.) Say **Today we've talked about farm animals and we've acted out a conversation together. Did you work well?** Elicit answers from the pupils.

Review the task flashcards.

- Point to the task flashcards. Say **Look at the activities you've done today. Which activity was your favourite?** Elicit the pupils' favourite activities.

Extra activity

Reinforcement

- Play a flashcard game to reinforce the farm animals vocabulary. Invite a pupil to the front of the class and secretly show him / her a farm animal flashcard. Ask the pupil to mime being the animal and then ask the rest of the class **What animal can you see?** Prompt the class to say the animal. Repeat with the other farm animals cards.

Key Competences and Key Learning Outcomes

- Read, listen and understand a story about a magic farm
- Read the story with some fluency
- Become familiar with the story through a pre-reading task
- Understand the importance of washing your hands after touching animals
- Understand and act out the story
- Give an opinion on the story

Key language:
- *climb, fly, swim*
- *(Cows) can't (fly). This (sheep) can (climb trees). Is it a (cow)? Yes, it is. Stop!*

Recycled: *chicken; face, feet, hands*
Recycled: *Can you see (a cat)? Yes, I can.*

Materials
- Pupil's Book pp52–53; Activity Book p50; Class CD2; Teacher's App on Navio
- Farm animals flashcards
- Teacher's Resource Bank: Task flashcards: *think, listen, read, act out, circle, match, draw*
- Teacher's Resource Bank: Unit 5 Lesson 3 Animated Story

Optional materials
- Teacher's Resource Bank: Five Trinity Exam Practice cards (selected from the Starter Unit and Units 1, 2, 3 and 4)

At a Glance Lesson Plan

Pupil's Book

Starting the lesson
- Use the Trinity Exam Practice cards (optional).
- Review the language from Lesson 2.
- Set learning outcomes using the task flashcards.

Before you read
- Explain the story title.
- Read and answer the question.

Activity 1
- Listen and read.
- ▶ *CD2 Track 42 p264*
- Act out.
- *Now watch the animated story!*

After you read: Activity 2
- Go to page 50 in your Activity Book.
- Values: Read and circle.

Ending the lesson
- Review the lesson.
- Review the task flashcards.

Activity Book

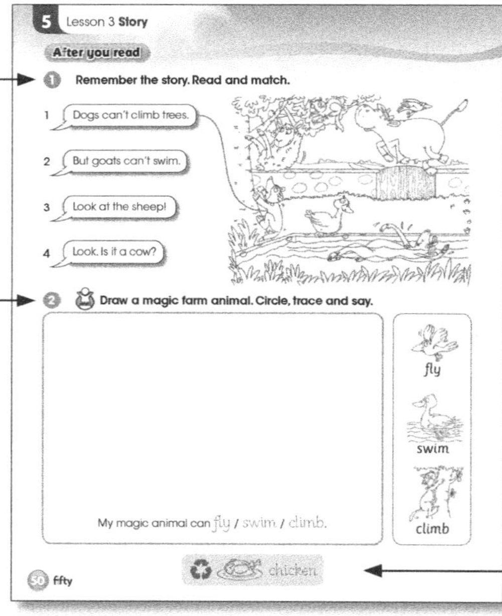

Activity Book

After you read: Activity 1
- Remember the story. Read and match.

Activity 2
- Draw a magic farm animal.
- Circle, trace and say.

Recycled vocabulary
- Look, say and trace the word.

Digital resources

Teacher's Digital: Don't forget you can teach this lesson using the Teacher's App on Navio.

Pupil's Digital: Encourage your pupils to use the Pupil's App on Navio to practise the vocabulary from this lesson.

Powered By NAVIO

Detailed Lesson Plan

Starting the lesson

Use the Trinity Exam Practice cards (optional).
- The pupils practise asking and answering questions (see p31).

Review the language from Lesson 2.
- Ask a pupil to come to the front of the class. He / She takes a farm animals flashcard. Ask **Can you see a (frog)?** The pupil answers *Yes, I can* or *No, I can't* according to what's on the flashcard. Prompt the class to ask similar questions until someone guesses correctly.
- Repeat with different flashcards and different pupils.

Set learning outcomes using the task flashcards.
- Say **Today we're going to listen to a story**.
- Hold up the task flashcards in turn and elicit the activities. Stick them on one side of the board. Point to them during the lesson to reinforce your instructions.

Before you read

Explain the story title.
- (Books open.) Focus on the story title. Read it out and ask **Where's the magic?** The pupils say where the magic is and think about what's going to happen.

Read and answer the question.
- Read the speech bubble. The pupils scan the story to find the animals.

Answers: a dog, a cat, a cow, a bird, a frog, a goat, a sheep

Pupil's Book Activity 1

Listen and read. Act out.

▶ *CD2 Track 42 p264*
- The pupils place their 'magic finger' on the first frame of the story.
- Play the CD. The pupils point to the different frames as the story progresses. Pause the CD after each frame to check that all the pupils are following.
- Play the CD again. Ask questions about each story frame to help and check understanding.
- Play the CD one more time, pausing it so the pupils can repeat.

Sugggested comprehension questions
- Frame 1: **What can Toby see?** (*A cat.*) **Does Toby like cats?** (*No.*)
- Frame 2: **Where is the cat?** (*On the magic bike.*)
- Frame 3: **It's magic! What can the cow in the story do?** (*Fly.*) **Can cows normally fly?** (*No.*)
- Frame 4: **It's magic! What can the goat in the story do?** (*Swim.*) **Can goats normally swim?** (*No.*)
- Frame 5: **It's magic! What can the sheep in the story do?** (*Climb trees.*) **Can sheep normally climb trees?** (*No.*)
- Frame 6: **Do the children stop the magic?** (*Yes.*)
- Frame 7: **Can Molly see the cat now?** (*Yes.*) **Where is it?** (*In the tree.*)
- Frame 8: **Is Toby happy?** (*No.*) **Why not?** (*He can't climb trees.*)
- Finally, ask the pupils **Is this a good story?** The pupils give their opinion through gesture (thumbs up / down) or orally (*yes* / *no*).
- Organise the class into three groups (Beth, Molly and Jake).
- Play the CD. Each group joins in when their character speaks. If the pupils need extra support, pause the CD after each sentence for the pupils to repeat.
- The groups swap roles, and repeat several times.

Now watch the animated story

After you read

Go to page 50 in your Activity Book.

Activity Book

After you read: Activity 1

Remember the story. Read and match.
- (Books open.) Ask **Do you remember the story?**
- Ask different pupils to read out the speech bubbles.
- The pupils match the speech bubbles to the pictures.

Answers: **1** Toby climbing a tree **2** a swimming goat **3** a sheep climbing a tree **4** a flying cow

Activity 2

Draw a magic farm animal. Circle, trace and say.
- Elicit what animals appear in the story and what they can do. The pupils say the words in the word box.
- The pupils draw a magic farm animal. They read the sentence, circle the action the animal can do and trace the word.
- Ask volunteers to show the class their pictures and to read out their sentences.

Recycled vocabulary
- The pupils look at the picture and say the word. Then they trace the word.

Pupil's Book Activity 2

Values: Read and circle.
- The pupils look at the photo on the right. Read out the sentence in the speech bubble and prompt the class to tell you the correct answer.
- Highlight the importance of washing your hands after touching animals.

Answer: hands

Ending the lesson

Review the lesson.
- (Books closed.) Say **Today we've listened to a story about magic farm animals.** Ask **What happened in the story?** Elicit the story from the pupils.
- Then say **Today you've learnt that it's important to wash your hands after touching animals.**

Review the task flashcards.
- Point to the task flashcards. Say **Look at the activities you've done today. Which activity was your favourite?** Elicit the pupils' favourite activities.

Key Competences and Key Learning Outcomes

- Say what animals can and can't do
- Listen to a conversation and play a game
- Review that animals move in different ways (optional)
- Sing a song

Key language

- *climb, fly, jump, run, swim, walk; cats, cows, ducks, frogs, goats, horses*
- *(Birds) can (fly).*
- Extension: *crawl, dive, hop, talk*

Recycled: *fruit*

Recycled: *(Cows) can't (climb).*

Materials

- Pupil's Book p54; Activity Book p51; Class CD2; Teacher's App on Navio
- Teacher's Resource Bank: Task flashcards: *listen, sing, Talk Partners, read, think, circle*

Optional materials

- Teacher's Resource Bank: Five Trinity Exam Practice cards (selected from the Starter Unit and Units 1, 2, 3 and 4)

At a Glance Lesson Plan

Starting the lesson

- Use the Trinity Exam Practice cards (optional).
- Review the Lesson 3 story.
- Set learning outcomes using the task flashcards.

Vocabulary presentation

- Present the new vocabulary.

Activity 1

- Listen, point and say.

▶ ***CD2 Track 43 p264***

Activity 2

- Listen and point.
- Sing *Cats can't fly.*

▶ ***CD2 Track 44 p265***

Activity 3

- Listen and repeat.
- Talk Partners Play a game.

▶ ***CD2 Track 45 p265***

Go to the Activity Book.

Pupil's Book

Ending the lesson

- Review the lesson.
- Review the task flashcards.

Extra activities

Reinforcement

- Practise hearing and saying *can* and *can't*.
- Talk Partners Say sentences.

Vocabulary Extension

- Present four additional vocabulary items.

Link to Science

- **Animals:** Review that animals move in different ways.

Digital resources

Teacher's Digital: Don't forget you can teach this lesson using the Teacher's App on Navio.

Pupil's Digital: Encourage your pupils to use the Pupil's App on Navio to practise the vocabulary from this lesson.

Powered By NAVIO

Activity Book

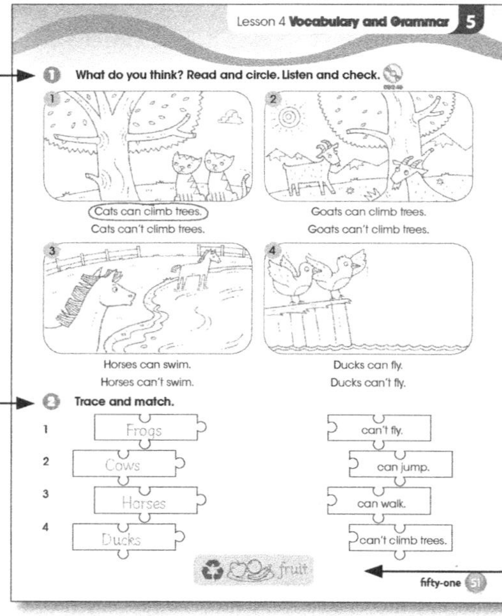

Activity Book

Activity 1

- What do you think? Read and circle.
- Listen and check.

▶ ***CD2 Track 46 p265***

Activity 2

- Trace and match.

Recycled vocabulary

- Look, say and trace the word.

Detailed Lesson Plan

Starting the lesson

Use the Trinity Exam Practice cards (optional).
- The pupils practise asking and answering questions (see p31).

Review the Lesson 3 story.
- Give the pupils two minutes to look at the story. Then describe one of the frames, e.g. **In this picture, there's a goat and a frog.** The pupils scan the story to find the frame (frame 4).
- Repeat with other frames from the story.

Set learning outcomes using the task flashcards.
- Say **Today we're going to sing a song and talk about actions that animals can do.**
- Hold up the task flashcards in turn and elicit the activities. Stick them on one side of the board. Point to them during the lesson to reinforce your instructions.

Vocabulary presentation

Present the new vocabulary.
- (Books open.) Point to the first photo in the Pupil's Book and read the word. Say **Look at the bird. It can fly.** Repeat the verb and mime the action. Encourage the class to do the same.
- Repeat with the other verbs.

Pupil's Book Activity 1

Listen, point and say.
▶ *CD2 Track 43 p264*
- (Books open.) The pupils look at the photos. Say **Let's listen and repeat the words.**
- Play the CD. The pupils point to the photos and say the words.
- Play *What's missing?* (without the flashcards). Read out the words but miss one out each time. Elicit the missing verb. Repeat for other words.

Pupil's Book Activity 2

Listen and point. Sing *Cats can't fly.*
▶ *CD2 Track 44 p265*
- Focus the pupils on Activity 2 and identify the animals in the pictures. Ask **Can cats fly? Can frogs run? Can cows talk?**
- Play the CD. The pupils listen and point to the animals. Then read the song line by line and the pupils repeat.
- Play the CD again. The pupils sing and do the actions.

Pupil's Book Activity 3

Listen and repeat. Play a game.
▶ *CD2 Track 45 p265*
- Focus pupils on the activity and play the CD. The pupils look and listen.
- Play the CD again. The pupils listen and repeat.
- **Talk Partners** The pupils ask and answer with a Talk Partner.

Activity Book

Activity 1

What do you think? Read and circle. Listen and check.
▶ *CD2 Track 46 p265*
- (Books open.) Read out the sentences and elicit which ones are correct. The pupils circle the correct answers.
- Play the CD, pausing after each sentence to check the pupils' answers.
- Play the CD again and the pupils repeat. Make sure they are distinguishing between 'can' and 'can't'.

Answers: **1** Cats can climb trees. **2** Goats can't climb trees. **3** Horses can swim. **4** Ducks can fly.

Activity 2

Trace and match.
- The pupils trace the farm animal words.
- Ask different pupils to read out the words to make sentences.
- The pupils draw matching lines to make sentences.

Answers: **1** Frogs can jump. **2** Cows can't fly. **3** Horses can run. **4** Ducks can walk.

Recycled vocabulary
- The pupils look at the picture and say the word. Then they trace the word.

Ending the lesson

Review the lesson.
- (Books closed.) Say **Today we've sung a song and talked about the actions animals can do. Can you say the actions?** Elicit the actions from the pupils.

Review the task flashcards.
- Point to the task flashcards. Say **Look at the activities you've done today. Which activity was your favourite?** Elicit the pupils' favourite activities.

Extra activities

Reinforcement
- Distinguish between 'can' and 'can't'. Write the numbers *1* and *2* on the board. Under number 1 write *I can swim* and under number 2 write *I can't swim.* Say different sentences at random with 'can' or 'can't' and the pupils listen and say *1* or *2*.
- **Talk Partners** The pupils say sentences with a Talk Partner.

Vocabulary Extension
- Use the Vocabulary Booster on Navio and present and practise four additional words to describe actions: *crawl, dive, hop, talk.*

Link to Science

- If you are studying the Science topic of **Animals** in English, you could remind the pupils that animals move in different ways. Review the ways of moving that pupils know. Say **Jump like a (frog / tiger). Slither like a (snake / snail). Swim like (a fish / an octopus).** The pupils do the actions.

Key Competences and Key Learning Outcomes

- Say a tongue twister with the 'sh' sound
- Listen for specific information
- Sing a cooperative learning song
- Understand the importance of taking turns
- Play a communication game about what animals can do

Key language
- *It's my turn now.*

Recycled: *cat, cow, frog, horse; fly, jump, run, swim; cake*

Recycled: *(Cats) can (swim). (Frogs) can't (fly).*

Materials
- Pupil's Book p55; Activity Book p52; Class CD2; Teacher's App on Navio
- Farm animals flashcards
- Teacher's Resource Bank: Task flashcards: *listen, say, colour, Talk Partners, tick, sing, cut out*
- Scissors, crayons or coloured pencils
- Teacher's Resource Bank: Unit 5 Lesson 5 Activity 3 cut-outs

Optional materials
- Teacher's Resource Bank: Five Trinity Exam Practice cards (selected from the Starter Unit and Units 1, 2, 3 and 4)
- Coloured paper
- A spinner (prepared in advance)

At a Glance Lesson Plan

Pupil's Book

Starting the lesson
- Use the Trinity Exam Practice cards (optional).
- Review the vocabulary from Lesson 4.
- Review the *Cats can't fly* song.

▶ ***CD2 Track 44 p265***
- Set learning outcomes using the task flashcards.

Activity 1
- Listen and say.

▶ ***CD2 Track 47 p265***

Go to Magic Phonics.

Go to the Activity Book.

Activity 2
- Listen.

▶ ***CD2 Track 48 p265***
- Tick or cross *can* (✓) *can't* (✗)

Activity 3 Cooperative learning

Sing *Let's take turns.*

▶ ***CD2 Track 49 p265***

Activity 4
- Make and play the game Talk Partners

Ending the lesson
- Review the lesson.
- Review the task flashcards.

Extra activity

Reinforcement
- Continue the pronunciation wall display.

Activity Book

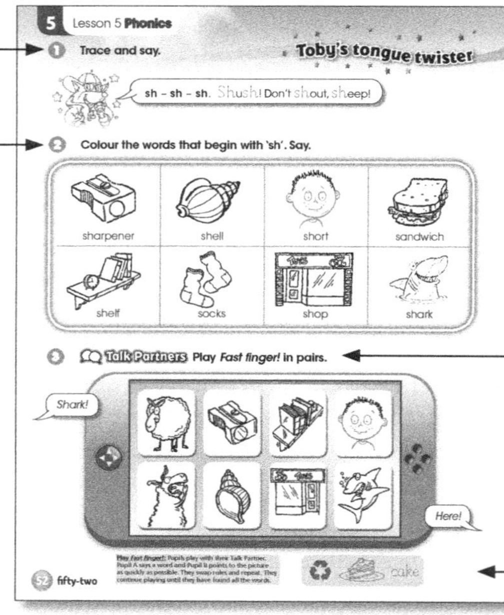

Activity Book

Activity 1
- Trace and say.

Activity 2
- Colour the words that begin with 'sh'.
- Say.

Go to Magic Phonics.

Activity 3
- Talk Partners

Play *Fast finger!* in pairs.

Recycled vocabulary
- Look, say and trace the word.

Digital resources

Teacher's Digital: Don't forget you can teach this lesson using the Teacher's App on Navio.

Pupil's Digital: Encourage your pupils to use the Pupil's App on Navio to practise the vocabulary from this lesson.

Powered By NAVIO

Detailed Lesson Plan

Starting the lesson

Use the Trinity Exam Practice cards (optional).
- The pupils practise asking and answering questions (see p31).

Review the vocabulary from Lesson 4.
- Hold one of the farm animals flashcards behind your back and say what the animal can and can't do. Say **This animal can (fly).** The pupils guess the animal.
- Ask different pupils to come to the front and take over your role. Repeat several times.

Review the *Cats can't fly* song.
▶ *CD2 Track 44 p265*
- Play the CD. The pupils sing and do the actions.

Set learning outcomes using the task flashcards.
- Say **Today we're going to practise saying a tongue twister and make and play a speaking game.**
- Hold up the task flashcards in turn and elicit the activities. Stick them on one side of the board. Point to them during the lesson to reinforce your instructions.

Pupil's Book Activity 1

Listen and say.
▶ *CD2 Track 47 p265*
- (Books open.) Write the target 'sh' sound on the board. Ask the pupils if they know what sound this makes. Put your fingers to your lips and say the sound. The pupils repeat.
- Say **It's time for Toby's tongue twister.**
- Play the CD. The pupils listen and repeat the target sound, then the words and then the entire tongue twister, faster and faster.

Go to Magic Phonics.

Activity Book

Activity 1
Trace and say.
- (Books open.) The pupils trace the letters 'sh' in the tongue twister. Remind them that the first one is a capital 'S' for the start of the sentence, and the others are lower case.
- The pupils say the tongue twister to their partner, saying it faster and faster each time.

Activity 2
Colour the words that begin with 'sh'. Say.
- Ask pupils to say the words that begin with 'sh'. The pupils colour and say these words.

Answers: sharpener, shell, short, shelf, shop, shark

Go to Magic Phonics.

Activity 3
Play *Fast finger!* in pairs.
- Demonstrate the activity. Say one of the objects. The pupils point to the correct picture as quickly as possible. Repeat several times with different words.
- **Talk Partners** The pupils play the game with a Talk Partner.

Recycled vocabulary
- The pupils look at the picture and say the word. Then they trace the word.

Pupil's Book Activity 2

Listen. Tick or cross. *can* (✓) *can't* (✗)
▶ *CD2 Track 48 p265*
- Ask **What can you see in the pictures?**
- Tell the pupils they are going to listen to children playing a game using spinners. If you have made a spinner, show the pupils.
- Play the CD, pausing after each conversation so the pupils can point to the correct picture.
- Play the CD again. The pupils listen and tick or cross the pictures.

Answers: 1 ✓ 2 ✗ 3 ✓ 4 ✗

Pupil's Book Activity 3: Cooperative learning

Sing *Let's take turns*.
▶ *CD2 Track 49 p265*
- The pupils need to learn how to wait and take their turn, especially for pair and group work. Sing *Let's take turns* when you want to remind them to take turns.
- Play the CD. The pupils listen and do the actions.
- Play the CD again. The pupils sing and do the actions.

Pupil's Book Activity 4

Make and play the game.
- Ask volunteers to read out the speech bubbles.
- Tell the pupils that they are going to make their own spinners and play the same game.
- The pupils cut out and colour the spinners.
- Show the pupils how to push a pencil through the middle and demonstrate how the spinners work. Spin one spinner and then the other. Make a sentence with an animal and a verb.
- **Talk Partners** The pupils play the game with a Talk Partner. Encourage them to make ten sentences.

Ending the lesson

Review the lesson.
- (Books closed,) Say **Today we've practised a tongue twister and played a game**. Elicit the tongue twister.

Review the task flashcards.
- Point to the task flashcards. Say **Look at the activities you've done today. Which activity was your favourite?** Elicit the pupils' favourite activity.

Extra activity

Reinforcement
- Add to the pronunciation wall display. Cut out the letters 'sh'. Stick them on a piece of differently coloured paper to make a wall display. Elicit words that begin with that sound and write them on the wall display. Ask the pupils to write a word beginning with 'sh'.
- Encourage the pupils to add new words beginning with 'sh' during the year. They can either tell you the new word for you to add or write the word themselves if they can.

Key Competences and Key Learning Outcomes

- Observe similarities and differences between animals
- Listen for general information
- Read about urban farms in Britain
- Answer questions about an urban farm
- Think about farms where you live

Key language
- *carrots, garden, park, pet shop, zoo*
- *I can (feed them). We can see (chickens on the farm).*

Recycled: *delicious; garden, farm; chicken, goat, horse; eggs, fruit, ice cream, vegetables*

Recycled: *I love (the goats). I like (the garden).*

Materials
- Pupil's Book p56; Activity Book p53; Class CD2; Teacher's App on Navio
- Farm animals flashcards
- Teacher's Resource Bank: Task flashcards: *listen, read, think, number, tick, draw*

Optional materials
- Teacher's Resource Bank: Five Trinity Exam Practice cards (selected from the Starter Unit and Units 1, 2, 3 and 4)
- Coloured card, plasticine, plastic animals

At a Glance Lesson Plan

Starting the lesson
- Use the Trinity Exam Practice cards (optional).
- **Talk Partners** Review Toby's Tongue Twister.
- ▶ ***CD2 Track 47 p265***
- Review the *On the farm* song.
- ▶ ***CD2 Track 37 p264***
- ▶ ***CD2 Track 38 p264 (optional karaoke version)***
- Set learning outcomes using the task flashcards.

Activity 1
- Listen and read.
- ▶ ***CD2 Track 50 p265***
- Answer.

Think about your culture
- Can you visit a farm in your country?

Go to the Activity Book.

Pupil's Book

Ending the lesson
- Review the lesson.
- Review the task flashcards.

Extra activities

Reinforcement
- Play *Splat!*

Extension
- Make a model farm as a class.

Link to Science
- **Animals:** Observe the similarities and differences between farm animals and wild animals.

Activity Book

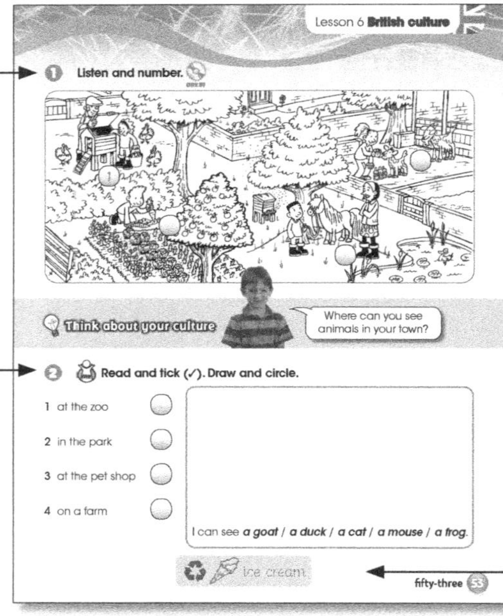

Activity Book

Activity 1
- Listen and number.
- ▶ ***CD2 Track 51 p265***

Activity 2: Think about your culture
- Read and tick (✓).
- Draw and circle.

Recycled vocabulary
- Look, say and trace the word.

Digital resources

Teacher's Digital: Don't forget you can teach this lesson using the Teacher's App on Navio.

Powered By NAVIO

Starting the lesson

Use the Trinity Exam Practice cards (optional).

- The pupils practise asking and answering questions (see p31).

Review Toby's tongue twister.

▶ *CD2 Track 47 p265*

- Ask **What sound did you practise in Toby's tongue twister? Can you remember the tongue twister?** (*Shush! Don't shout, sheep!*) Play the CD. Practise the tongue twister as a class.
- Talk Partners The pupils practise saying the tongue twister as fast as possible with a Talk Partner. Choose a pair to say it for the class.

Review the *On the farm* song.

▶ *CD2 Track 37 p264*

▶ *CD2 Track 38 p264 (optional karaoke version)*

- Put the farm animals flashcards on the board in the order they appear in the song. Divide the class into three groups. Play the CD (or use the karaoke version). Each group sings a verse and they all sing the chorus. They then swap verses and repeat.

Set learning outcomes using the task flashcards.

- Say **Today we're going to learn about urban farms in Britain.**
- Hold up the task flashcards in turn and elicit the activities. Stick them on one side of the board. Point to them during the lesson to reinforce your instructions.

Pupil's Book Activity 1

Listen and read. Answer.

▶ *CD2 Track 50 p265*

- (Books open.) Focus the pupils on the photos. Ask **What can you see?** Read the speech bubble.
- Play the CD, pausing after each photo to check understanding.
- Play the CD again. The pupils listen and look at the photos.

Suggested comprehension questions:

- Photo 1: **What's this?** (*A goat.*) **Can the children feed the goat?** (*Yes.*)
- Photo 2: **What's this?** (*A horse.*) **Is it big or small?** (*Small.*)
- Photo 3: **Who can you see here?** (*The farmer.*) **What animals can you see?** (*Chickens.*)
- Photo 4: **What grows in the garden?** (*Fruit and vegetables.*) **What vegetables have they got?** (*Carrots.*)

Pupil's Book Think about your culture

Can you visit a farm in your country?

- Read out the question. Encourage the pupils to tell you if they have visited a farm.
- Ask additional questions, e.g. **What farm did you visit? What animals did you see? Did you like it?**

Activity Book

Activity 1

Listen and number.

▶ *CD2 Track 51 p265*

- (Books open.) Focus the pupils on the picture. Ask **What can you see?** Say **Let's listen to some children on a farm. What activities do they do?**
- Play the CD, pausing after each conversation. The pupils listen and number the different activities.
- Play the CD again to check the pupils' answers.

Answers: **1** collect the eggs **2** look at the horse **3** pick fruit and vegetables **4** feed the goat

Activity 2: Think about your culture

Read and tick (✓). Draw and circle.

- Read out the question in the speech bubble. Elicit the pupils' answers.
- Read out the places where you can see animals. The pupils choose one of the places in their town and tick it.
- The pupils draw the place where they can see animals in their town and then circle the animals they can see there.
- Invite different pupils to show the class their drawings and to read their sentences.

Recycled vocabulary

- The pupils look at the picture and say the word. Then they trace the word.

Ending the lesson

Review the lesson.

- (Books closed.) Say **Today we've learnt about an urban farm in Britain. Do you like this farm?** Elicit opinions from the pupils.

Review the task flashcards.

- Point to the task flashcards. Say **Look at the activities you've done today. Which activity was your favourite?** Elicit the pupils' favourite activities.

Extra activity

Reinforcement

- Play *Splat!* (see p23) with the animal word cards.

Extension

- The class works together and makes a model farm. Use coloured card for the scene and plasticine for the trees and bushes.
- Encourage the pupils to bring in plastic animals from home. Alternatively, use plasticine for the animals.
- Encourage the class to talk about their model. *I can see (six cows). I can see (two goats).*
- Leave the farm on a table at the side of the class with a sign *What can you see on the farm?* Remember to change the display each day by removing / adding animals or changing their positions. Fast finishers can go to the display in pairs and ask and answer the question together.

Link to Science

- If you are studying the Science topic of **Animals** in English, you could review the wild animals the pupils know. Help them to observe the similarities and differences between farm animals and wild animals. Say **A (cow) has four legs. Does a (tiger) have four legs?**

Key Competences and Key Learning Outcomes

- Read and understand animal riddles
- Say a riddle
- Brainstorm two-legged and four-legged farm animals
- Review wild animals (optional)

Key language
- *What am I? I can't (climb).*

Recycled: *bird, chicken, cow, dog, duck, horse; climb, fly, swim, walk; big, small; meat;* colours; numbers 1–10

Recycled: *I've got (two legs). I can (swim). I'm (small).*

Materials
- Pupil's Book p57; Activity Book p54; Class CD2; Teacher's App on Navio
- Farm animals flashcards
- Teacher's Resource Bank: Task flashcards: *think, listen, read, colour, Talk Partners*

Optional materials
- Teacher's Resource Bank: Five Trinity Exam Practice cards (selected from the Starter Unit and Units 1, 2, 3 and 4)
- Pieces of A4 paper
- Crayons or coloured pencils

At a Glance Lesson Plan

Starting the lesson
- Use the Trinity Exam Practice cards (optional).
- Review farm animals vocabulary.
- Set learning outcome using the task flashcards.

Before you read
- Identify two-legged and four-legged farm animals.

Activity 1
- Think and draw.
- Tell your partner.

Activity 2
- Listen and read.
- ▶ *CD2 Track 52 p265*
- Answer the riddles.

After you read
- Go to page 54 in your Activity Book.

Pupil's Book

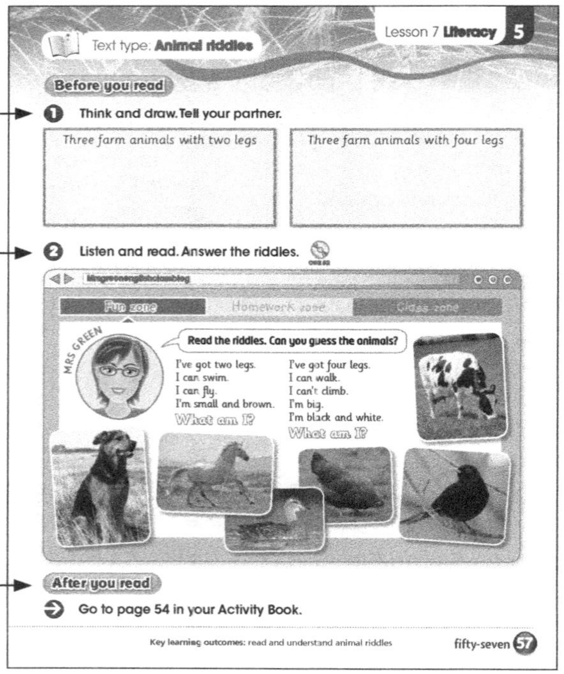

Ending the lesson
- Review the lesson.
- Review the task flashcards.

Extra activity

Extension
- Make a class riddles display.

Link to Science
- **Animals:** Identify and draw animals from a riddle.

Digital resources

Teacher's Digital: Don't forget you can teach this lesson using the Teacher's App on Navio.

Pupil's Digital: Encourage your pupils to use the Pupil's App on Navio to practise the vocabulary from this lesson.

Powered By NAVIO

Activity Book

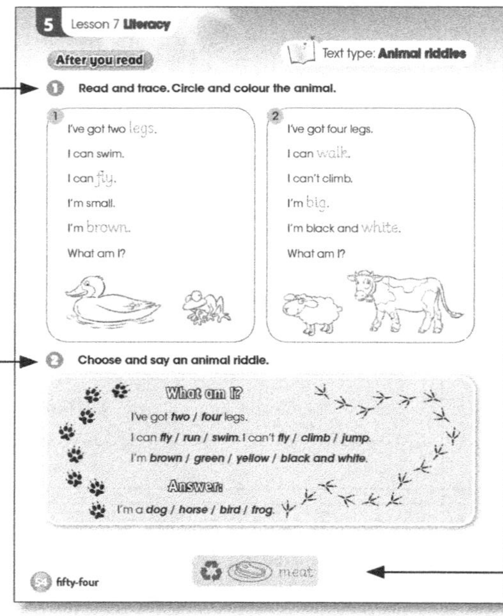

Activity Book

After you read: Activity 1
- Read and trace.
- Circle and colour the animal.

Activity 2
- Choose and say an animal riddle.

Recycled vocabulary
- Look, say and trace the word.

Starting the lesson

Use the Trinity Exam Practice cards (optional).

- The pupils practise asking and answering questions (see p31).

Review the farm animals vocabulary.

- Use the farm animals flashcards to review vocabulary. Hold up a flashcard and ask the class to tell you the word. Then stick the card face down on the board. Repeat until all the cards are on the board. Then ask **Where's the (chicken)?** Invite a pupil to turn over one of the cards. If it's the correct card, the pupil says *It's here*. If it isn't the correct card, invite another pupil to come to the board and have a turn. Repeat with different flashcards.
- To finish, ask **Where can you see these animals? What activities can you do on a farm?**
- **Option:** Play the game in two teams. The teams take it in turns to remember the words.

Set learning outcomes using the task flashcards.

- Say **Today we're going to read some animal riddles.**
- Hold up the task flashcards in turn and elicit the activities. Stick them on one side of the board. Point to them during the lesson to reinforce your instructions.

Before you read

Identify two-legged and fourlegged farm animals.

- (Books open.) Focus the pupils on the photos and elicit examples of farm animals with two legs. Then elicit some with four legs.

Pupil's Book Activity 1

Think and draw. Tell your partner.

- Ask the class to tell you all the farm animals they know with two legs (*bird, duck, chicken*) and four legs (*cow, horse, goat, cat, sheep, dog*). Allow them to look back through the unit if necessary. Write their suggestions on the board.
- The pupils choose three farm animals with two legs and three with four legs and draw them in the boxes.
- The pupils show their partner their pictures and tell them about the animals.

Pupil's Book Activity 2

Listen and read. Answer the riddles.

▶ *CD2 Track 52 p265*

- Focus the pupils on Activity 2. Say **Let's listen and read some animal riddles. Can you guess the answers?**
- Play the CD, pausing after each riddle. The pupils read the riddles and point to the correct pictures.
- Play the CD again, pausing after each line. The class repeats.
- Ask volunteers to read out the riddles to the class.

Answers: a duck, a cow

Activity Book

After you read: Activity 1

Read and trace. Circle and colour the animal.

- (Books open.) Focus the pupils on Activity 1. The pupils trace the words in the riddles.
- Read out the first riddle for the pupils to follow. The pupils circle the correct picture of the animal and colour it in. Repeat with the second riddle.

Answers: **1** a duck **2** a cow

Activity 2

Choose and say an animal riddle.

- Focus the pupils on Activity 2. Read out the riddle, including all the options.
- The pupils read the sentences again. They choose and circle one of the words for each option.
- Ask a pupil to read out their riddle without naming the animal. Ask **What animal is it?** The rest of the class answers.
- Repeat with different pupils.

Recycled vocabulary

- The pupils look at the picture and say the word. Then they trace the word.

Ending the lesson

Review the lesson.

- (Books closed.) Say **Today we've read and said animal riddles in English. What animal riddle did you choose?** Elicit the animal riddles from the pupils.

Review the task flashcards.

- Point to the task flashcards. Say **Look at the activities you've done today. Which activity was your favourite?** Elicit the pupils' favourite activities.

Extra activity

Extension

- Make a class riddles display. Copy the three riddles from the Activity Book onto large pieces of paper.
- Ask the pupils to choose one of the riddles and to draw a picture of the animal.
- Display the animal pictures next to the riddles.

Link to Science

- If you are studying the Science topic of **Animals** in English, you could review wild animals. Elicit the wild animals they know and write them on the board.
- The pupils can say another riddle about a wild animal by following the model in Activity Book Activity 2.

Key Competences and Key Learning Outcomes

- Review language in the unit
- Reflect on own learning

- Sing a cooperative learning song

Key language

- *What can (Peter) see? This is a (cow).*

Recycled: *chicken, cow, frog; rubber, ruler; doll, robot; ear, toes; grape; jump, fly, ride a bike, swim; juggle*

Recycled: *Can you (swim)? Yes, I can. No, I can't. I can see (a robot).*

Materials

- Pupil's Book p58; Activity Book p55; Class CD2; Teacher's App on Navio
- Farm animals flashcards
- Teacher's Resource Bank: Task flashcards: *listen, number, read, sing, stick, Talk Partners, follow*
- Teacher's Resource Bank: Traffic light cut-out
- *Give Me Five!* sticker

Optional materials

- Teacher's Resource Bank: Five Trinity Exam Practice cards (selected from the Starter Unit and Units 1, 2, 3 and 4)

At a Glance Lesson Plan

Starting the lesson

- Use the Trinity Exam Practice cards (optional).
- Review the unit vocabulary.
- Set learning outcomes using the task flashcards.

Activity 1

- Listen and number.
- ▶ ***CD2 Track 53 p265***
- Say.

Activity 2

- Look at the pictures.
- Circle the animal.

Activity 3 Cooperative learning

- Sing *Well done!*
- ▶ ***CD2 Track 54 p266***
- Stick the *Give Me Five!* sticker.
- Go to the Activity Book.

Pupil's Book

Ending the lesson

- Review the task flashcards.

Extra activity

Reinforcement

- Play *Board pelmanism.*

Activity Book

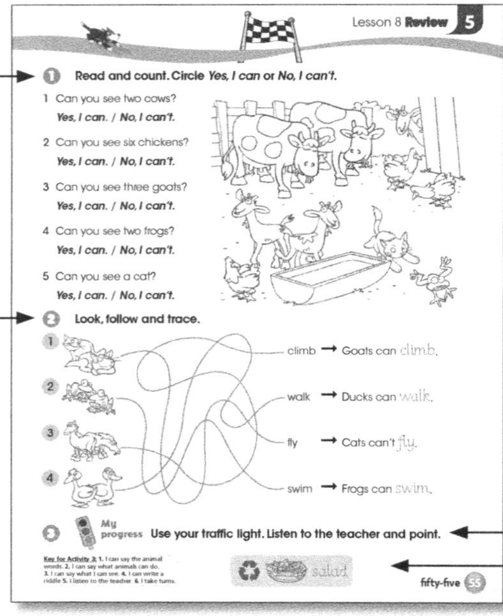

Activity Book

Activity 1

- Read and count.
- Circle *Yes, I can* or *No, I can't.*

Talk Partners Ask and answer.

Activity 2

- Look, follow and trace.

Activity 3 My progress

- Use your traffic light. Listen to the teacher and point.

Recycled vocabulary

- Look, say and trace the word.

Digital resources

Teacher's Digital: Don't forget you can teach this lesson using the Teacher's App on Navio.

Pupil's Digital: Encourage your pupils to use the Pupil's App on Navio to practise the vocabulary from this lesson.

Powered By NAVIO

Starting the lesson

Use the Trinity Exam Practice cards (optional).

- The pupils practise asking and answering questions (see p31).

Review the unit vocabulary.

- Hold up a farm animals flashcard and elicit the word. Stick the flashcard face down on the board. Repeat until all the flashcards are on the board.
- Ask **Where's the (chicken)?** Ask a pupil to come to the front and turn over one of the flashcards. If it's the correct flashcard, he / she says *It's here.* If it isn't the correct flashcard, another pupil has a go. Repeat with different words and different pupils.
- Variation: Play the game in two teams. The teams take it in turns to remember the farm animals.

Set learning outcomes using the task flashcards.

- Say **Today we're going to remember what we've learnt in Unit 5.**
- Hold up the task flashcards in turn and elicit the activities. Stick them on one side of the board. Point to them during the lesson to reinforce your instructions.

Pupil's Book Activity 1

Listen and number. Say.

▶ *CD2 Track 53 p265*

- (Books open.) Point to the pictures and ask different pupils to name the farm animals.
- Play the CD, pausing after each conversation. The pupils point to the farm animals.
- Play the CD again. The pupils write the correct number for each picture.
- The pupils say the words under each picture.

Answers: **1** chicken **2** bird **3** frog **4** horse **5** duck **6** cow **7** cat **8** mouse **9** sheep **10** goat

Pupil's Book Activity 2

Look at the pictures. Circle the animal.

- Focus the pupils on the pictures in Activity 1 again. Read out the first sentence in Activity 2. Elicit the answer.
- Repeat with the other sentences.
- The pupils circle the answers on their own in their books.

Answers: **1** frog **2** bird **3** sheep **4** duck **5** cat **6** horse

Pupil's Book Activity 3: Cooperative learning

Sing *Well done!*

▶ *CD2 Track 54 p266*

- Praise the pupils for their hard work and encourage them to praise each other. Play the *Well done!* song. The pupils sing and do the actions.

Stick the *Give Me Five!* sticker.

- The pupils stick the *Give Me Five!* sticker on the Pupil's Book page.
- Variation: Sing the *Well done!* song and stick the *Give Me Five!* sticker after the pupils have also completed the Activity Book Lesson 8 Review.

Activity Book

Activity 1

Read and count. Circle *Yes, I can* or *No, I can't.*

- (Books open.) Read out each question. The pupils count the animals in the scene. Elicit the answers.
- The pupils circle the answers on their own.
- **Talk Partners** The pupils ask and answer with a Talk Partner.

Answers: **1** Yes, I can. **2** No, I can't. **3** Yes, I can. **4** No, I can't. **5** Yes, I can.

Activity 2

Look, follow and trace.

- Focus the pupils on Activity 2. The pupils follow the line from the cat to the verb.
- Read out the sentence at the end of the line **Cats can't fly.**
- Repeat with the other animals. The pupils trace the verbs in the sentences.

Answers: **1** Cats can't fly. **2** Frogs can swim. **3** Horses can't climb. **4** Ducks can walk.

Activity 3: My progress My progress

Use your traffic light. Listen to the teacher and point.

- (Books closed.) Ask the pupils to take out their traffic light cut-out. Say **Let's think about our work in this unit.** Point to the green circle, nod your head, smile a lot, and say **I can say the animal words. Yes, I can do this very well.** Then point to the yellow circle, move your head a little, smile a little and say **Yes, I can do this.** Then point to the red circle, shake your head and say **No, I can't do this.**
- Read the different statements. For each one, the pupils point to the colour on their traffic light that shows how they feel about their own learning.

Self-assessment statements

1. I can say the animal words.
2. I can say what animals can do.
3. I can say what I can see.
4. I can write a riddle.
5. I listen to the teacher.
6. I take turns.

Recycled vocabulary

- The pupils look at the picture and say the word. Then they trace the word.

Ending the lesson

Review the task flashcards.

- Point to the task flashcards. Say **Look at the activities you've done today. Which activity was your favourite?** Elicit the pupils' favourite activities.

Extra activity

Reinforcement

- Play *Board pelmanism* (see p23) with the animals flashcards and word cards.

Key Competences and Key Learning Outcomes

- Watch and understand a video about farm animals
- Draw animals according to the group they belong to

- Put things in groups

Key language

- *cat, chicken, climb, cow, dog, duck, fly, goat, horse, lamb, mouse, sheep; tired*

Materials

- Pupil's Book p59; Activity Book p56; Class CD2; Video; Teacher's App on Navio
- Teacher's Resource Bank: Task flashcards: *number, read, tick, listen, draw*

Optional materials

- Teacher's Resource Bank: Trinity Exam Practice cards (selected from Unit 5)

At a Glance Lesson Plan

Starting the lesson

- Use the Trinity Exam Practice cards (optional).
- Play a guessing game to review animals.
- Set learning outcomes and use the task flashcards.

Pre-watching activity

- Predict what animals they are going to see.

Activity 1

- Watch the video.
  Unit 5 video p278
- Number the pictures.

Activity 2

- Watch the video again.
  Unit 5 video
- Read and tick (✓) or cross (✗).

Activity 3

- Read and tick (✓).
  Go to the Activity Book.

Pupil's Book

Ending the lesson

- Review the lesson.
- Review the task flashcards. Elicit the pupils' favourite activities.

Extra activity

- Pupils work together in groups to do an activity.

Digital resources

Teacher's Digital: Don't forget you can teach this lesson using the Teacher's App on Navio.

Pupil's Digital: Encourage your pupils to use the Pupil's App on Navio to practise the vocabulary from this lesson.

Powered By NAVIO

Activity Book

Activity Book

Activity 1

- Listen and number.
- ▶ *CD2 Track 55 p266*

Activity 2

- Read and tick (✓) one. Draw animals in your group.

Recycled vocabulary

- Look, say and trace the word.

Starting the lesson

Use the Trinity Exam Practice cards (optional).

- The pupils practise asking and answering questions.

Review farm animals.

- Hold up one of the farm animal flashcards facing you so the pupils can't see it. Ask **What animal am I?** Describe the animal, colour, number of legs, big or small ears, eyes etc., for pupils to guess.
- Divide the class into eight teams. Give each group an animal flashcard and give them a couple of minutes to think how to describe it. The teams take turns to describe their animal.

Set learning outcomes and use the task flashcards.

- Say **Today we're going to watch a video and then ask and answer questions about farm animals.**
- Point to the task flashcards throughout to elicit activities and reinforce your instructions.

Pre-watching activity

- **Think-Pair-Share** Ask the pupils what animals they can see on a farm. Write their answers on the board.

Pupil's Book Activity 1

Watch the video. Number the pictures. *p278*

- Focus the pupils' attention on the video stills. Ask **What animals can you see?** Ask **Are they similar to the animals on the board?**
- Play Part 1 again. Pause after Sophie says, *I love ducks*. Ask **What is Tom / Sophie's favourite animal?**
- Play Part 2, pausing after the first video still. Ask the pupils to point to the corresponding photo in their book.
- Play the rest of Part 2 for pupils to point to the photos in order.
- Play the video again for pupils to write the numbers in order of the photos.
- Ask **Which animals make a noise? What noise do they make?**

Answers: 2, 4, 3, 1

Pupil's Book Activity 2

Watch the video again. Read and tick (✓) or cross (✗).

- Read out the sentences checking the vocabulary. Ask if the pupils can tell you what a lamb is and to mime the word *tired*. Ask the pupils if they can fly and to mime fly.
- The pupils draw a tick or a cross next to the sentences. Play Part 2 for the pupils to check their answers.
- Ask general questions to check understanding.

  What do the horse and cow eat? *(Grass.)*

  Can you describe the sheep? *(It's white. It's got long ears and a long nose.)*

  Can a chicken / duck fly? *(No / Yes.)*

  Which animal can swim? *(A duck.)*

  What's the name for a baby duck? *(Duckling.)*

  Why are a chicken, a duck and a bird similar? *(They've got two legs.)*

Answers: **1 ✗ 2 ✓ 3 ✓ 4 ✗**

Pupil's Book Activity 3

Read and tick (✓).

- Stick the frog, dog, horse, chicken, goat and cat flashcards on the board. Ask the pupils to describe each animal. Ask **What can each animal do?**
- Read out the sentences to check vocabulary. Ask the pupils to jump and to mime climb.
- Explain that the animals are in groups and the pupils have to read the sentences and decide which sentence fits all three animals in the circle.
- Read out the speech bubble. Explain, also, that grouping things can help pupils remember new vocabulary and think about similarities and differences.
- Ask **What other things can you group? How?** (Food – vegetables, meat, sweet things, healthy things. Toys – with wheels, big, small, electronic).

Answers: **1** They can jump. **2** They have got a tail.

Activity Book

Activity 1

Listen and number.

▶ *CD2 Track 55 p266*

- The pupils look at the pictures. Ask **How is each group of animals similar?** Elicit pupils' answers.
- Ask the pupils to number the pictures in the order they hear them. Play the first exchange on the CD. Ask **Which picture?** (One) **Why?** (They all eat grass).
- Play the rest of the CD, pausing after each exchange, for pupils to number the pictures.

Answers: Top row left to right: 2, 3
Bottom row left to right: 4, 1

Activity 2

Read and tick (✓) one. Draw animals in your group.

- Read out the sentences for the pupils to follow. The pupils choose and tick one sentence. The pupils draw the animals for the group they chose.
- **Talk Partners** Pupils take turns to point to their pictures and tell their partner about their animal group.

Recycled vocabulary

- The pupils look at the picture and say the word. Then they trace the word.

Ending the lesson

Review the lesson.

- Ask **Which activity was easy / difficult today?**

Review the task flashcards.

- Say **Look at the activities you've done today. Which activity was your favourite?**

Extra activity

Extension

- On the board write *Toys, Food, School objects*. Divide the class into small groups. Ask each group to choose a topic. The groups work together to choose four things from their topic that they can group together. They draw the things in their grouping. The groups take turns to present their pictures and explain why they grouped them together.

Date: ____________ Unit: ________

1 **What did my pupils learn in this unit?**

2 **How did my pupils work? (✓)**

individually ☐ in pairs ☐ in small groups ☐

in large groups ☐ as a class ☐

3 **Which key competences did my pupils develop?**

- Competence in linguistic communication ☐
- Competence in mathematics, science and technology ☐
- Digital competence ☐
- Learning to learn ☐
- Social and civic competences ☐
- Sense of initiative and entrepreneurship ☐
- Cultural awareness and expression ☐

4 **Which lessons / activities were the most successful and why?**

5 **Which lessons / activities did my pupils find the most difficult and why?**

6 **What did I try in the classroom for the first time? How did it go?**

7 **Which resources did I find most useful? (including webpages)**

8 **What could I do differently next time I teach this unit?**

Unit 6

A day in the park

Unit overview

Key Competences and Key Learning Outcomes

- Identify and say ten park objects (Lesson 1)
- Say the vocabulary chant (Lesson 1)
- Use *Where…?* and prepositions to find out where people are (Lessons 2 and 4)
- Understand and act out a grammar conversation (Lesson 2)
- Watch and understand a video about playgrounds (Video and 21st Century Skills)

- Read and draw instructions for growing flowers (Lesson 7)

- Use the Pupil's App on Navio

- Practise spelling (Lesson 1)
- Say a tongue twister to practise the sound /w/ (Lesson 5)
- Review language in the unit and reflect on own learning (Lesson 8)
- Practise activity types found in the Cambridge English Young Learners Exams: Pre A1 Starters

- Understand the importance of respecting signs (Lesson 3)
- Understand the importance of being careful in the playground (Video and 21st Century Skills)

- Work with a Talk Partner to practise and reinforce learning (all lessons)
- Play a communication game about finding people (Lesson 5)

- Sing four songs (Lessons 1, 4, 5 and 8)
- Understand and act out a story (Lesson 3)
- Read about activities you can do in the park in Britain (Lesson 6)
- Think about parks where you live (Lesson 6)
- Think about what you do in the playground (Video and 21st Century Skills)

Vocabulary

Core vocabulary
climbing frame, roundabout, see-saw, slide, swing; bush, flower, grass, rock, tree; behind, between, in front of, near, next to

Extension vocabulary (optional)
bench, fountain, playhouse, sandpit, trampoline, wall; ground, plant, pond, shell

Other vocabulary
playground, sign; cricket, park, picnic, zip wire; grow, plants, pot, seeds, soil, sun, sunny place, watch, water

Recycled vocabulary
climb, jump, run; bird, cat, cow, dog, duck, frog, goat, horse, sheep; brother, sister; big; in, on, under; long; train, ball; finger; flowers, garden, bin, books, chair, computer, pencil, rubber, ruler, school bag; colours

Structures

Core structures
Where's my brother / sister? He's / She's (on the swing).
Where are (Beth and Molly)? They're (behind) the (tree).

Other structures
We can (climb). We can play on the (slide). The park is fun. It's fun in the park. Where's (my sister)? She's (on the swing). Where are (Jake and Molly)? They're (behind) the (tree). Where's (Toby)? I don't know. He isn't (under the bush). Ready or not, here I come. Let's play (hide and seek). You can / can't (play in here). We love (the playground). We play (cricket on the grass). We (feed the ducks / ride on the train). Put the (pot in a sunny place). Push the seeds (into the soil). Water the seeds.

Recycled structures
I can (see) (six flowers). Put the (pen near the computer).

Phonics

Consonant sound 'w' (**W**ally, **w**orm, **w**ashes, **w**indows)

British Culture

Parks

Literacy

Text type: instructions (instructional text)
Reading skills: using visual clues; relating new vocabulary to pictures; reading for specific information

21st Century Skills

Living in the world: learning to be careful in the playground

Cooperative learning

Songs: *Listen to others* (Lesson 5); *Well done!* (Lesson 8)
Skills: Working together and supporting each other (Lesson 1); Being aware of others (Lesson 2)

Values

Understanding the importance of respecting signs in public places

Cross-curricular links

Links to Science

Plants: identifying living and non-living things; the importance of sunlight, water and soil for plants to survive

Suggested Arts and Crafts concepts

Shapes: identifying and distinguishing between geometric and organic shapes in Art and in the environment

Key Competences and Key Learning Outcomes

- Identify and say ten park objects
- Say the vocabulary chant
- Stick the stickers
- Identify living and non-living things (optional)
- Practise spelling
- Sing a song about playing in the park

Key language
- *climbing frame, roundabout, seesaw, slide, swing; bush, flower, grass, rock, tree; play*
- *We can (climb). We can play on the (slide). The park is fun. It's fun in the park.*
- Extension: *bench, fountain, playhouse, sandpit, trampoline, wall*

Recycled: *climb, jump, run; cat*
Recycled: *I can see (six flowers).*

Materials
- Pupil's Book p60; Activity Book pp58 and 67; Class CD3; Teacher's App on Navio
- Playground objects and nature flashcards; Unit 6 stickers
- Teacher's Resource Bank: Playground objects and nature word cards
- Teacher's Resource Bank: Task flashcards: *listen, sing, read, match, stick, say, colour, Talk Partners*
- A music CD
- Crayons or coloured pencils

Optional materials
- Teacher's Resource Bank: Five Trinity Exam Practice cards (selected from the Starter Unit and Units 1, 2, 3, 4 and 5)

At a Glance Lesson Plan

Starting the lesson
- Use the Trinity Exam Practice cards (optional).
- Review the action words.
- Set learning outcomes using the task flashcards.

Vocabulary presentation
- Present the new vocabulary.

Activity 1
- Listen and point.
- ▶ *CD3 Track 1 p266*
- Sing *It's fun in the park.*

Word cards
- Read the word cards.
- Match them to the flashcards.

Activity 2
- Read and stick the ten stickers.
- Listen and say the chant.
- ▶ *CD3 Track 3 p266*
- Go to the Activity Book.

Learning to learn

Spelling
- Practise spelling at any time during this unit (Activity Book p67).

Pupil's Book

Ending the lesson
- Review the lesson.
- Review the task flashcards.

Extra activity

Vocabulary Extension
- Present six additional vocabulary items.

Cooperative learning

Working together and supporting each other
- Talk Partners Ask and answer *What's this?*

Link to Science
- **Plants:** Identify living and non-living things and review what plants need to survive.

Digital resources

Teacher's Digital: Don't forget you can teach this lesson using the Teacher's App on Navio.

Pupil's Digital: Encourage your pupils to use the Pupil's App on Navio to practise the vocabulary from this lesson.

Powered By NAVIO

Activity Book

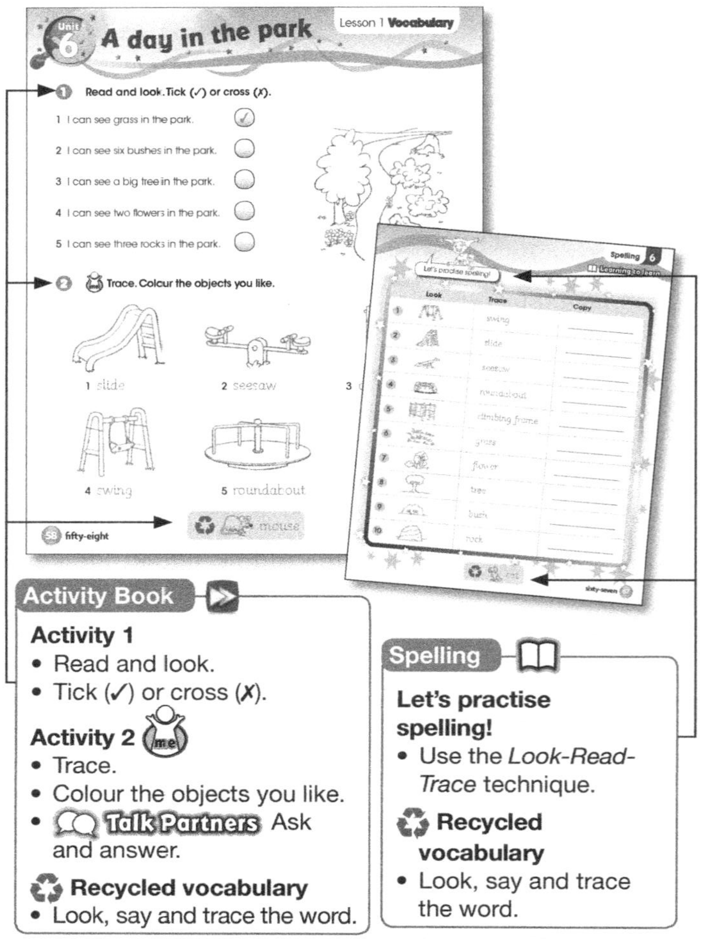

Activity Book

Activity 1
- Read and look.
- Tick (✓) or cross (✗).

Activity 2
- Trace.
- Colour the objects you like.
- Talk Partners Ask and answer.

Recycled vocabulary
- Look, say and trace the word.

Spelling

Let's practise spelling!
- Use the *Look-Read-Trace* technique.

Recycled vocabulary
- Look, say and trace the word.

Starting the lesson

Use the Trinity Exam Practice cards (optional).
- The pupils practise asking and answering questions (see p31).

Review the action words.
- Play some music from a CD and say one of the action words *walk, fly, jump, swim, run, climb*. The pupils do the action. Stop the music and the pupils freeze like statues. Repeat several times.

Set learning outcomes using the task flashcards.
- Say **Today we're going to learn playground objects and nature words.**
- Hold up the task flashcards and elicit the activities. Stick them on one side of the board. Point to them during the lesson to reinforce your instructions.

Vocabulary presentation

Present the new vocabulary.
- (Books closed.) Ask **Do you like going to the park? What can you see at the park?** Elicit the names of natural and man-made things.
- Hold up the playground objects and nature flashcards and say the word. The class repeats. Stick the flashcards on the board. Point to them in turn. The pupils say the words.

Pupil's Book Activity 1

Listen and point. Sing *It's fun in the park.*

▸ *CD3 Track 1 p266*
- (Books open.) Focus the pupils on the picture. Ask **Where are Molly, Beth, Toby and Jake? What can they do in the park?**
- Play the CD. The pupils point to the objects.
- Play the CD again. The pupils sing and do the actions. Stick the playground objects and nature flashcards on the board in the order of the song, if necessary.

Word cards

Read the word cards. Match them to the flashcards.
- (Books closed.) Hold up the playground objects and nature word cards in turn, and say or elicit each word.
- Ask different pupils to come and stick each word card on the board with the corresponding flashcard.

Pupil's Book Activity 2

Read and stick the ten stickers. Listen and say the chant.

▸ *CD3 Track 3 p266*
- (Books open.) Ask a pupil to read the first word. The pupils stick the corresponding sticker. Repeat with the other stickers.
- Play the CD. The pupils listen and say the chant, pointing to the stickers in turn.

Activity Book

Activity 1

Read and look. Tick (✓) or cross (✗).
- (Books open.) Ask different pupils to read out the sentences. Check understanding.
- The pupils work on their own. They look at the picture, read the sentences and tick or cross what they can see in the picture.

Answers: 1 ✓ 2 ✗ 3 ✓ 4 ✗ 5 ✓

Activity 2

Trace. Colour the objects you like.
- Read out the park objects as a class.
- The pupils trace the park objects words under the pictures. Then they colour the park objects they like.
- **Talk Partners** Read the speech bubbles. The pupils ask and answer with a Talk Partner.

Recycled vocabulary
- The pupils look at the picture and say the word. Then they trace the word.

Ending the lesson

Review the lesson.
- (Books closed.) Say **Today we've learnt playground objects and nature words. What words do you remember?** Elicit the words from the pupils.

Review the task flashcards.
- Point to the task flashcards. Say **Look at the activities you've done today. Which activity was your favourite?** Elicit the pupils' favourite activities.

Extra activity

Vocabulary Extension
- Use the Vocabulary Booster on Navio to present and practise six additional words describing playground objects: *bench, fountain, playhouse, sandpit, trampoline, wall.*

Cooperative learning

Working together and supporting each other
- **Talk Partners** Pupil A checks the learning of Pupil B by pointing to a park object sticker and asking *What's this?* Pupil B answers using *It's (a) ...* If Pupil B can't remember, Pupil A helps him / her. They swap roles and repeat.

Link to Science

- If you are studying the Science topic of **Plants** in English, review living and non-living things with the objects on the opening spread. Then review what all plants need to survive (air, water and sunlight).

Spelling (Activity Book page 67)

Let's practise spelling!
- The pupils can practise spelling the ten playground objects and nature words using the *Look-Read-Trace* technique at any time during this unit before the Lesson 8 Review.

Recycled vocabulary
- The pupils look at the picture and say the word. Then they trace the word.

Key Competences and Key Learning Outcomes

- Use *Where...?* and prepositions to find out where people are
- Complete and practise a conversation
- Listen for specific information

Key language

- *Where's (Beth)? She's (on the swing). Where's (Jake)? He's (on the slide).*

Recycled: *climbing frame, roundabout, seesaw, slide, swing; bush, flower, grass, rock, tree; park; brother, sister; big; duck*

Materials

- Pupil's Book p61; Activity Book p59; Class CD3; Teacher's App on Navio
- Playground objects and nature flashcards
- Teacher's Resource Bank: Task flashcards: *listen, act out, match, read, follow, think, Talk Partners*

Optional materials

- Teacher's Resource Bank: Five Trinity Exam Practice cards (selected from the Starter Unit and Units 1, 2, 3, 4 and 5)
- A scarf

At a Glance Lesson Plan

Starting the lesson

- Use the Trinity Exam Practice cards (optional).
- Talk Partners Review the playground objects and nature vocabulary.
- Review the *It's fun in the park* song.
- ▶ ***CD3 Track 1 p266***
- ▶ ***CD3 Track 2 p266 (optional karaoke version)***
- Set learning outcomes using the task flashcards.

Activity 1

- Listen and repeat.
- ▶ ***CD3 Track 4 p266***
- Act out.

Activity 2

- Listen and match.
- ▶ ***CD3 Track 5 p266***
- Go to the Activity Book.

Pupil's Book

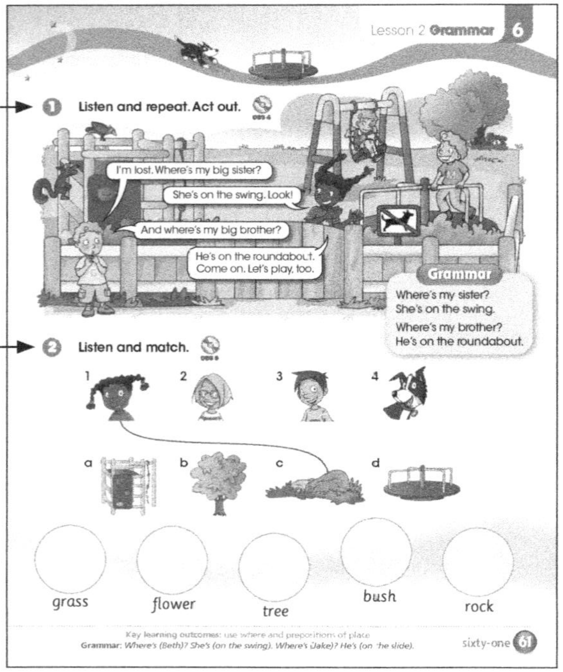

Ending the lesson

- Review the lesson.
- Review the task flashcards.

Extra activity

Reinforcement

- Play *Fast finger*.

Cooperative learning

Being aware of others

- Play a class game.

Activity Book

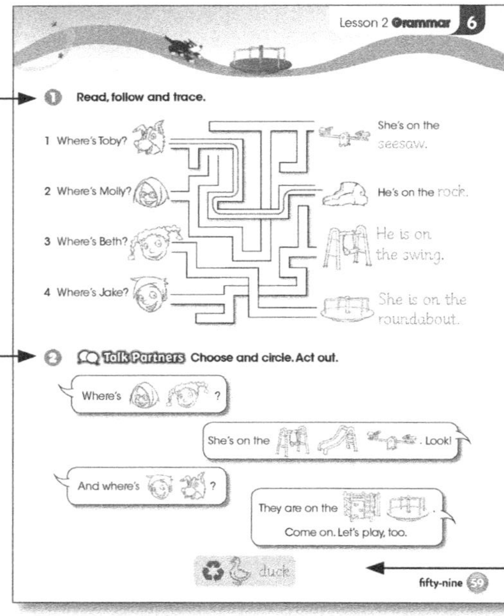

Activity Book

Activity 1

- Read, follow and trace.

Activity 2

- Choose and circle.
- Talk Partners Act out.

Recycled vocabulary

- Look, say and trace the word.

Digital resources

Teacher's Digital: Don't forget you can teach this lesson using the Teacher's App on Navio.

Pupil's Digital: Encourage your pupils to use the Pupil's App on Navio to practise the vocabulary from this lesson.

Powered By NAVIO

Starting the lesson

Use the Trinity Exam Practice cards (optional).
- The pupils practise asking and answering questions (see p31).

Review the playground objects and nature vocabulary.
- Talk Partners The pupils work with a Talk Partner to remember and name the playground objects and nature vocabulary. Ask a pair to say a playground objects and nature word and hold up the corresponding flashcard. The class repeats the word. Repeat for all the playground objects and nature flashcards, asking different pairs of pupils each time.

Review the *It's fun in the park* song.
▶ *CD3 Track 1 p266*
▶ *CD3 Track 2 p266 (optional karaoke version)*
- Use the playground objects flashcards to quickly review the ten items in the park. Then, stick the flashcards in different places around the classroom. Ask **Where's the slide?** The pupils face and point to the corresponding flashcard. Repeat with the other flashcards. As the pupils become more confident, increase the speed of your delivery.
- Play the CD (or use the karaoke version). The class sings the song and points to the flashcards when they are mentioned in the song.

Set learning outcomes using the task flashcards.
- Say **Today we're going to talk about boys and girls in the park.**
- Hold up the task flashcards in turn and elicit the activities. Stick them on one side of the board. Point to them during the lesson to reinforce your instructions.

Pupil's Book Activity 1

Listen and repeat. Act out.
▶ *CD3 Track 4 p266*
- (Books open.) The pupils look at the picture. Ask **Where's Beth?** Point to the small boy. Ask **Is he big or small? Is he happy or sad?**
- Play the CD. The pupils listen and read the conversation. Ask **What's the matter with the small boy? Where are his brother and sister?**
- Play the CD again, pausing after each sentence for the pupils to repeat.
- Ask different pupils to come to the front and act out the conversation.

Pupil's Book Activity 2

Listen and match.
▶ *CD3 Track 5 p266*
- Name the characters and the objects in Activity 2.
- Then say **Let's listen and match.**
- Play the CD. The pupils listen and draw matching lines. Pause the CD after each conversation to allow the pupils time to match the characters and the park objects.
- Play the CD again and check the answers.

Answers: **1** c **2** a **3** d **4** b

Activity Book

Activity 1
Read, follow and trace.
- (Books open.) Read out the first question in Activity 1. Tell the pupils to follow the path to the answer with their finger.
- Ask a volunteer to read the second question. The pupils follow the path with their finger. Elicit the answer.
- The pupils draw the paths and trace the answers.

Answers: **1** He's on the rock. **2** She's on the seesaw. **3** She's on the roundabout. **4** He's on the swing.

Activity 2
Choose and circle. Act out.
- Demonstrate the activity to the class. Read the first speech bubble, adding either *Molly* or *Beth*, and say a playground object from the second bubble.
- Repeat with the third speech bubble, adding *Jake* or *Toby*, and a different playground object from the fourth bubble.
- Practise the conversation as a class.
- Talk Partners When the pupils are confident with the language, they work in pairs to choose and circle a character and object in each bubble. They ask and answer with their partner.
- Invite different pairs of pupils to act out their conversations.

Recycled vocabulary
- The pupils look at the picture and say the word. Then they trace the word.

Ending the lesson

Review the lesson.
- (Books closed.) Say **Today we've talked about boys and girls and we've acted out a conversation together. Remember we use 'he' for boys and 'she' for girls. Did you work well today?** Elicit responses from the pupils.

Review the task flashcards.
- Point to the task flashcards. Say **Look at the activities you've done today. Which activity was your favourite?** Elicit the pupils' favourite activities.

Extra activity

Reinforcement
- Play *Fast finger* (see p23) with the playground objects and nature flashcards.

Cooperative learning

Being aware of others
- Ask the class to look carefully at where the other pupils are sitting.
- Invite one pupil to the front and cover his / her eyes with a blindfold. Ask **Where's (Patricia)?** The pupil points to where his / her classmate is sitting.
- Repeat with other pupils.

Key Competences and Key Learning Outcomes

- Read, listen and understand a story about a game of hide and seek
- Read the story with some fluency
- Become familiar with the story through a pre-reading task
- Understand the importance of respecting signs
- Understand and act out the story
- Give an opinion on the story

Key language

- *behind; playground, sign*
- *Where are (Jake and Molly)? They're (behind) the (tree). Where's Toby? He's (on the slide). He isn't (under the bush). Ready or not, here I come. Let's play (hide and seek). You can / can't (play in here).*

Recycled: *in, on, under; tree, bush, grass; slide; long; play; chicken*

Recycled: *Thank you.*

Materials

- Pupil's Book pp62–63; Activity Book p60; Class CD3; Teacher's App on Navio
- Teacher's Resource Bank: Playground objects and nature word cards
- Teacher's Resource Bank: Task flashcards: *think, listen, read, act out, circle, tick, match*
- Teacher's Resource Bank: Unit 6 Lesson 3 Animated Story

Optional materials

- Teacher's Resource Bank: Five Trinity Exam Practice cards (selected from the Starter Unit and Units 1, 2, 3, 4 and 5).

At a Glance Lesson Plan

Starting the lesson

- Use the Trinity Exam Practice cards (optional).
- Review the language from Lesson 2.
- Set learning outcomes using the task flashcards.

Before you read

- Explain the story title.
- Read and answer the question.

Activity 1

- Listen and read.
- ▶ *CD3 Track 6 p266*
- Act out.
- *Now watch the animated story!*

After you read: Activity 2

- Go to page 60 in your Activity Book.
- Values: Read and circle.

Ending the lesson

- Review the lesson.
- Review the task flashcards.

Pupil's Book

Activity Book

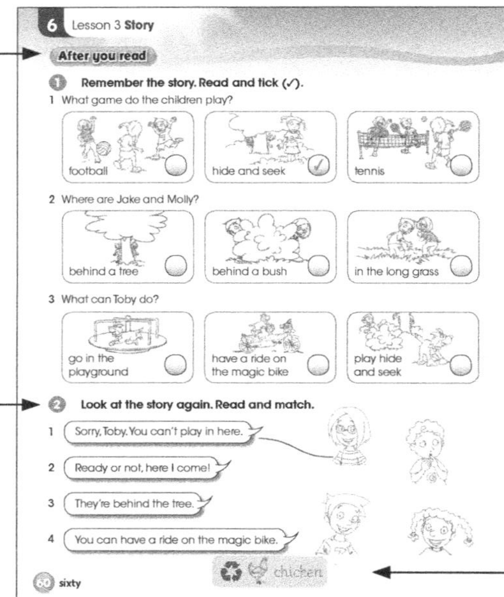

Activity Book

After you read: Activity 1

- Remember the story. Read and tick (✓).

Activity 2

- Look at the story again. Read and match.

Recycled vocabulary

- Look, say and trace the word.

Digital resources

Teacher's Digital: Don't forget you can teach this lesson using the Teacher's App on Navio.

Pupil's Digital: Encourage your pupils to use the Pupil's App on Navio to practise the vocabulary from this lesson.

Powered By NAVIO

Detailed Lesson Plan

Starting the lesson

Use the Trinity Exam Practice cards (optional).

- The pupils practise asking and answering questions (see p31).

Review the language from Lesson 2.

- Play *Clever parrots* (see p23) to review the playground objects and nature vocabulary from Lesson 2 using the corresponding word cards.

Set learning outcomes using the task flashcards.

- Say **Today we're going to listen to a story.**
- Hold up the task flashcards in turn and elicit the activities. Stick them on one side of the board. Point to them during the lesson to reinforce your instructions.

Before you read

Explain the story title.

- (Books open.) Focus on the story title. Read it aloud and ask **Do you know this game?** Count to ten and hide to demonstrate the game, if necessary.

Read and answer the question.

- Read the speech bubble. The pupils scan the story to find the playground objects.

Answers: a slide, a swing, a climbing frame, a roundabout, a seesaw

Pupil's Book Activity 1

Listen and read. Act out.

▶ *CD3 Track 6 p266*

- The pupils place their 'magic finger' on the first frame of the story.
- Play the CD. The pupils point to the different frames as the story progresses. Pause the CD after each frame to check that all the pupils are following.
- Play the CD again. Ask questions about each story frame to help and check understanding.
- Play the CD one more time, pausing it so the pupils can repeat.

Suggested comprehensive questions

- Frame 1: **Where are the children?** (*At the park.*) **What game do they play?** (*Hide and seek.*) **Can Toby play?** (*No.*)
- Frame 2: **What numbers does Beth count?** (*8, 9, 10.*)
- Frame 3: **Can the boy see Jake and Molly?** (*Yes.*) **Where are they?** (*Behind the tree.*)
- Frame 4: **Does Beth find Jake and Molly?** (*Yes.*)
- Frame 5: **Can the children see Toby?** (*No.*) **Are they happy?** (*No.*)
- Frame 6: **Can the children see Toby now?** (*No.*) **What can help them?** (*The magic bike.*)
- Frame 7: **Can Molly see Toby?** (*Yes.*) **Where is he?** (*On the slide.*)
- Frame 8: **Can Toby play in the playground?** (*No.*) **Can Toby have a ride on the magic bike?** (*Yes.*)
- Finally, ask the pupils **Is this a good story?** The pupils give their opinion through gesture (thumbs up / down) or orally (*yes / no*).
- Organise the class into four groups (Beth, Molly, Jake and the small boy).
- Play the CD. Each group joins in when their character speaks. If the pupils need extra support, pause the CD after each sentence for the pupils to repeat.
- The groups swap roles, and repeat several times.

Now watch the animated story

After you read

Go to page 60 in your Activity Book.

Activity Book

After you read: Activity 1

Remember the story. Read and tick (✓).

- (Books open.) Ask **Do you remember the story?**
- Ask different pupils to read out the questions.
- The pupils remember the story and tick the correct pictures.
- To check the answers, ask the pupils to read out the questions with their answers.

Answers: **1** hide and seek **2** behind a tree **3** have a ride on the magic bike

Activity 2

Look at the story again. Read and match.

- Read the story again, then focus the pupils on Activity 2. Read out the speech bubbles as a class.
- The pupils match them to the characters.

Answers: **1** Molly **2** Beth **3** boy **4** Jake

Recycled vocabulary

- The pupils look at the picture and say the word. Then they trace the word.

Pupil's Book Activity 2

Values: Read and circle.

- The pupils look at the photo on the right. Read out the sentence in the speech bubble and prompt the class to tell you the correct answer.
- Highlight the importance of respecting signs.

Answer: Respect

Ending the lesson

Review the lesson.

- (Books closed.) Say **Today we've listened to a story about the game *Hide and seek*.** Ask **What happened in the story?** Elicit the story from the pupils.
- Then say **Today you've learnt that it's important to respect the signs around you.**

Review the task flashcards.

- Point to the task flashcards. Say **Look at the activities you've done today. Which activity was your favourite?** Elicit the pupils' favourite activities.

Key Competences and Key Learning Outcomes

- Ask and answer questions to find out where people are
- Sing a song

Key language
- *between, in front of, near, next to*
- Extension: *ground, plant, pond, shell*

Recycled: *bush, flowers, grass, rocks, tree; dogs, horse; behind; big, small, long*

Recycled: *Ready or not, here I come. Where are (Jake and Molly)? They're (next to) (the tree).*

Materials
- Pupil's Book p64; Activity Book p61; Class CD3; Teacher's App on Navio
- Teacher's Resource Bank: Task flashcards: *listen, sing, Talk Partners, tick, read*

Optional materials
- Teacher's Resource Bank: Five Trinity Exam Practice cards (selected from the Starter Unit and Units 1, 2, 3, 4 and 5)

At a Glance Lesson Plan

Starting the lesson
- Use the Trinity Exam Practice cards (optional).
- Review the Lesson 3 story.
- Set learning outcomes using the task flashcards.

Vocabulary presentation
- Present the new vocabulary.

Activity 1
- Listen, point and say.
- ▶ *CD3 Track 7 p266*

Activity 2
- Listen and point.
- Sing *Hide and seek.*
- ▶ *CD3 Track 8 p266*

Activity 3
- Listen and repeat.
- ▶ *CD3 Track 9 p267*
- Talk Partners Ask and answer.

Go to the Activity Book.

Pupil's Book

Ending the lesson
- Review the lesson.
- Review the task flashcards.

Extra activities

Reinforcement
- Review prepositions of place.

Vocabulary Extension
- Present four additional vocabulary items.

Digital resources

Teacher's Digital: Don't forget you can teach this lesson using the Teacher's App on Navio.

Pupil's Digital: Encourage your pupils to use the Pupil's App on Navio to practise the vocabulary from this lesson.

Powered By NAVIO

Activity Book

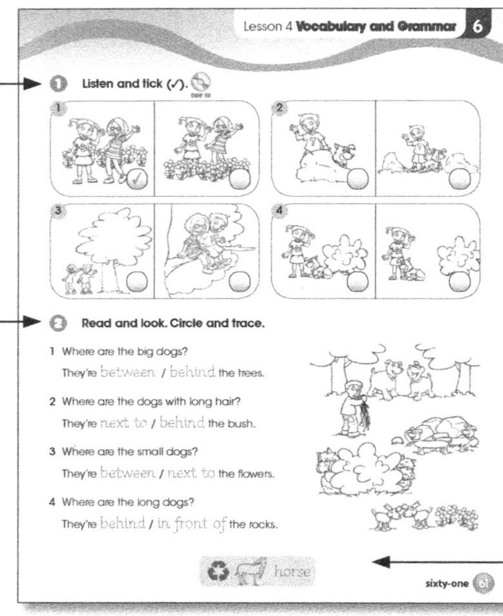

Activity Book

Activity 1
- Listen and tick (✓).
- ▶ *CD3 Track 10 p267*

Activity 2
- Read and look.
- Circle and trace.

Recycled vocabulary
- Look, say and trace the word.

Detailed Lesson Plan

Starting the lesson

Use the Trinity Exam Practice cards (optional).

- The pupils practise asking and answering questions (see p31).

Review the Lesson 3 story.

- Read out the story. The pupils follow in their Pupil's Books. When you come to a key word, make a beep sound instead of saying the word. The pupils say the missing word.

Set learning outcomes using the task flashcards.

- Say **Today we're going to learn to say where things are and sing a song.**
- Hold up the task flashcards in turn and elicit the activities. Stick them on one side of the board. Point to them during the lesson to reinforce your instructions.

Vocabulary presentation

Present the new vocabulary.

- (Books open.) Point to the first picture and read the caption. Say **Look at Toby. He's behind the tree.** Repeat the preposition and place your hands behind your back. Prompt the class to repeat the preposition and do the same action. Repeat with the other prepositions (in front of: hands in front of you; next to: hands touching your side; near: hands stretched out and circling around you; between: hands between your knees).

Pupil's Book Activity 1

Listen, point and say.

▶ *CD3 Track 7 p266*

- (Books open.) The pupils look at the pictures. Say **Let's listen and say the words.**
- Play the CD. The pupils say the words and point to the pictures.
- Point to different pictures and ask the pupils where Toby is. The pupils answer using the prepositions.

Pupil's Book Activity 2

Listen and point. Sing *Hide and seek.*

▶ *CD3 Track 8 p266*

- Ask **What game are the children playing?**
- Play the CD. The pupils listen to the song and point to the correct pictures.
- Divide the class into three groups.
- Play the CD again. Each group sings a verse and the whole class sings the chorus and does the actions.

Pupil's Book Activity 3

Listen and repeat. Ask and answer.

▶ *CD3 Track 9 p267*

- Focus the pupils on the activity and read out the two speech bubbles.
- Play the CD. The pupils listen and read.
- Play the CD again. The pupils listen and repeat the question and the answer.
- Ask two pupils to come to the front and stand in front of your desk. Ask **Where are (Sara and David)?** The other pupils answer.
- **Talk Partners** Repeat with different pupils in different places. The pupils ask and answer each question with a Talk Partner.

Activity Book

Activity 1

Listen and tick (✓).

▶ *CD3 Track 10 p267*

- (Books open.) The pupils look at the first two pictures and say where Molly and Beth are. Continue with all the pictures.
- Play the CD, pausing after each conversation. The pupils tick the correct pictures.

Answers: **1** They're in front of the flowers. **2** They're between the rocks. **3** They're next to the tree. **4** They're near the bush.

Activity 2

Read and look. Circle and trace.

- Ask **What can you see in the picture?**
- Read out the first question and elicit the correct preposition in the sentence. The pupils circle the preposition and trace the word.
- The pupils complete the rest of the sentences on their own.
- Ask different pupils to ask and answer the questions.

Answers: **1** between **2** behind **3** next to **4** in front of

Recycled vocabulary

- The pupils look at the picture and say the word. Then they trace the word.

Ending the lesson

Review the lesson.

- (Books closed.) Say **Today we've sung a song and talked about where things are. Can you remember the different places?** Elicit the prepositions.

Review the task flashcards.

- Point to the task flashcards. Say **Look at the activities you've done today. Which activity was your favourite?** Elicit the pupils' favourite activities.

Extra activities

Reinforcement

- Repeat the preposition activity from the vocabulary presentation, encouraging the pupils to repeat the prepositions and do the actions (behind: hands behind your back; in front of: hands in front of you; next to: hands touching your side; near: hands stretched out and circling around you; between: hands between your knees).

Vocabulary Extension

- Use the Vocabulary Booster on Navio and present and practise four additional words to describe nature: *ground, plant, pond, shell.*

Key Competences and Key Learning Outcomes

- Say a tongue twister with the 'w' sound
- Listen for specific information
- Sing a cooperative learning song
- Play a communication game about finding people

Key language

Recycled: *bush, flower, grass, rock, tree; behind, between, in front of, near, next to; sheep*

Recycled: *Where are (Molly and Toby)? They're (between the bushes). Where's (Jake)? He's (next to the tree). Where's (Beth)? She's (in front of the flowers).*

Materials

- Pupil's Book p65; Activity Book p62; Class CD3; Teacher's App on Navio
- Playground objects and nature flashcards
- Teacher's Resource Bank: Task flashcards: *listen, say, write, colour, think, Talk Partners, match, cut out*
- Scissors, crayons or coloured pencils
- Teacher's Resource Bank: Unit 6 Lesson 5 Activity 3 cut-outs

Optional materials

- Teacher's Resource Bank: Five Trinity Exam Practice cards (selected from the Starter Unit and Units 1, 2, 3, 4 and 5)
- Coloured paper

At a Glance Lesson Plan

Pupil's Book

Starting the lesson

- Use the Trinity Exam Practice cards (optional).
- Review prepositions of place.
- Set learning outcomes using the task flashcards.

Activity 1

- Listen and say.

▶ *CD3 Track 11 p267*

Go to Magic Phonics.

Go to the Activity Book.

Activity 2

- Listen and match.

▶ *CD3 Track 12 p267*

Activity 3 Cooperative learning

Sing *Listen to others.*

▶ *CD3 Track 13 p267*

Activity 4

- Talk Partners Make and play the game.

Ending the lesson

- Review the lesson.
- Review the task flashcards.

Extra activity

Reinforcement

- Continue the pronunciation wall display.

Activity Book

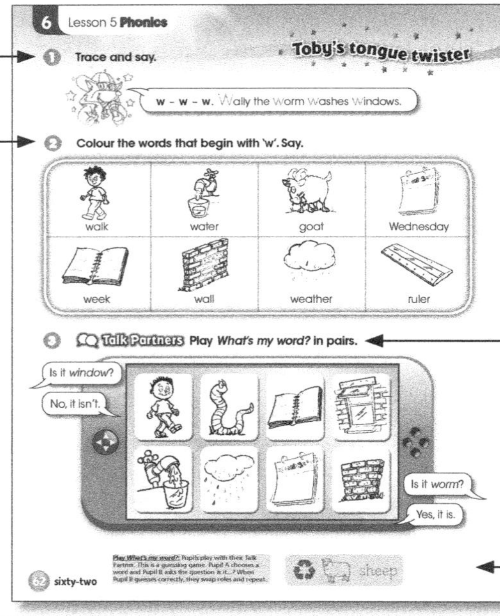

Activity Book

Activity 1

- Trace and say.

Activity 2

- Colour the words that begin with 'w'. Say.

Go to Magic Phonics.

Activity 3

- Talk Partners Play *What's my word?* in pairs.

Recycled vocabulary

- Look, say and trace the word.

Digital resources

Teacher's Digital: Don't forget you can teach this lesson using the Teacher's App on Navio.

Pupil's Digital: Encourage your pupils to use the Pupil's App on Navio to practise the vocabulary from this lesson.

Powered By NAVIO

Detailed Lesson Plan

Starting the lesson

Use the Trinity Exam Practice cards (optional).

- The pupils practise asking and answering questions (see p31).

Review the prepositions of place.

- Invite two to four pupils to come to the front of the class and give them instructions. Say **Stand (in front of) the (board). Stand (behind) (Maria).** The pupils listen and do the actions. Repeat with different groups of pupils.

Set learning outcomes using the task flashcards.

- Say **Today we're going to practise saying a tongue twister and make and play a speaking game.**
- Hold up the task flashcards in turn and elicit the activities. Stick them on one side of the board. Point to them during the lesson to reinforce your instructions.

Pupil's Book Activity 1

Listen and say.

▶ *CD3 Track 11 p267*

- (Books open.) Write the target 'w' sound on the board. Ask the pupils if they know what sound this letter makes. Say the sound and the pupils say it with you. Make sure they are saying the sound correctly.
- Say **It's time for Toby's tongue twister.**
- Play the CD. The pupils listen and repeat the target sound, then the words and then the entire tongue twister, faster and faster.

Go to Magic Phonics.

Activity Book

Activity 1

Trace and say.

- (Books open.) The pupils trace the letter 'w' in the tongue twister. Remind them that the first one is a capital 'W' for Wally's name, and the others are lower case.
- The pupils say the tongue twister to their partner, saying it faster and faster each time.

Activity 2

Colour the words that begin with 'w'. Say.

- Ask the pupils to say the words that begin with the 'w' sound. The pupils colour and say these words.

Answers: walk, water, Wednesday, week, wall, weather

Go to Magic Phonics.

Activity 3

Play *What's my word?* in pairs.

- Point to each picture and elicit the words.
- Think of an object on the page and ask **What's my word?** The pupils guess your word.
- Talk Partners The pupils play the game with a Talk Partner.

Recycled vocabulary

- The pupils look at the picture and say the word. Then they trace the word.

Pupil's Book Activity 2

Listen and match.

▶ *CD3 Track 12 p267*

- Ask **What can you see in the pictures?**
- Play the CD. The pupils listen to find out where the characters are.
- Play the CD again, pausing after each conversation so the pupils can draw lines from the characters to the place.

Answers: **1** Molly and Toby are between the bushes. **2** Jake is near the roundabout. **3** The Magic Bike is next to the tree. **4** Beth is in front of the flowers.

Pupil's Book Activity 3: Cooperative learning

Sing *Listen to others*.

▶ *CD3 Track 13 p267*

- Remind the class that it's important to listen to each other and take turns. Teach the *Listen to others* song.
- Play the CD. The pupils listen and do the actions.
- Play the CD again. The pupils sing and do the actions.

Pupil's Book Activity 4

Make and play the game.

- Explain to the class that they are going to make the game. Ask them to place the scene and the cards on the table in front of them.
- Prompt a pupil to ask you where one of the characters is, *Where's (Beth)*? Decide on a place in the scene and give the answer. Say **She's (next to) the tree.** All the pupils place the card in the scene. Repeat with the other cards, using the prepositions from Lesson 4 and recycling 'in', 'on' or 'under'. Continue playing until the class is confident with the language and the activity.
- Talk Partners The pupils play the game.

Ending the lesson

Review the lesson.

- (Books closed.) Elicit the tongue twister from the pupils.

Review the task flashcards.

- Point to the task flashcards. Say **Look at the activities you've done today. Which activity was your favourite?** Elicit the pupils' favourite activities.

Extra activity

Reinforcement

- Continue the pronunciation wall display. Cut out the letter 'w' in coloured paper. Stick it on a piece of differently coloured paper. Elicit words that begin with 'w' and write them on the wall display.
- Encourage the pupils to add new words beginning with the letter 'w' during the year. They can either tell you the new word for you to add or write the word themselves if they can.

Key Competences and Key Learning Outcomes

- Listen for general information

- Read about parks in Britain
- Think about parks where you live

Key language
- *cricket, picnic, zip wire*
- *We love (the playground). We play (cricket on the grass). We (feed the ducks). We (ride on the train).*

Recycled: *goat; train, ball; play, grass, park, playground; big*

Recycled: *I can (hit the ball).*

Materials
- Pupil's Book p66; Activity Book p63; Class CD3; Teacher's App on Navio
- Playground objects and nature flashcards
- Teacher's Resource Bank: Task flashcards: *listen, read, think, match, tick, draw*

Optional materials
- Teacher's Resource Bank: Five Trinity Exam Practice cards (selected from the Starter Unit and Units 1, 2, 3, 4 and 5).

At a Glance Lesson Plan

Starting the lesson
- Use the Trinity Exam Practice cards (optional).
- Talk Partners Review Toby's tongue twister.
- ▶ *CD3 Track 11 p267*
- Review the *It's fun in the park* song.
- ▶ *CD3 Track 1 p266*
- ▶ *CD3 Track 2 p266 (optional karaoke version)*
- Set learning outcomes using the task flashcards.

Activity 1
- Listen and read.
- ▶ *CD3 Track 14 p267*
- Answer.

Think about your culture
- What do you do at the park?
- Go to the Activity Book.

Pupil's Book

Ending the lesson
- Review the lesson
- Review the task flashcards.

Extra activities
Reinforcement
- Play *Clever parrots*.

Extension
- Investigate a local park.

Digital resources

Teacher's Digital: Don't forget you can teach this lesson using the Teacher's App on Navio.

Powered By NAVIO

Activity Book

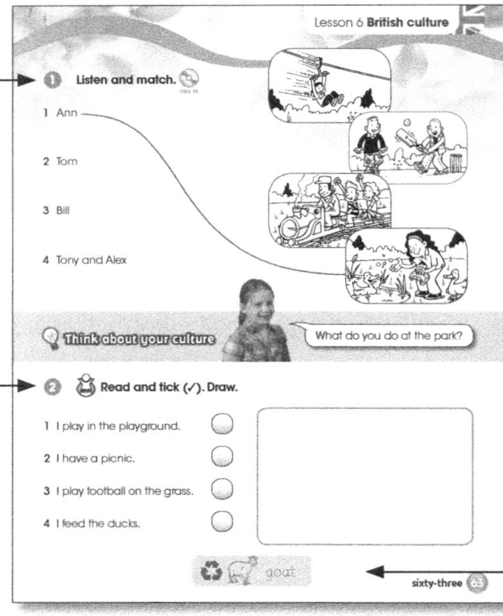

Activity Book

Activity 1
- Listen and match.
- ▶ *CD3 Track 15 p267*

Activity 2: Think about your culture
- Read and tick (✓).
- Draw.

Recycled vocabulary
- Look, say and trace the word.

Starting the lesson

Use the Trinity Exam Practice cards (optional).

- The pupils practise asking and answering questions (see p31).

Review Toby's tongue twister.

▶ *CD3 Track 11 p267*

- Ask **What sound did you practise in Toby's tongue twister? Can you remember the tongue twister?** (*Wally the worm washes windows.*) Play the CD. Practise the tongue twister as a class.
- Talk Partners The pupils practise saying the tongue twister as fast as possible with a Talk Partner. Choose a fast pair to say it for the class.

Review the *It's fun in the park* song.

▶ *CD3 Track 1 p266*

▶ *CD3 Track 2 p266 (optional karaoke version)*

- Put the playground objects and nature flashcards on the board in the order they appear in the song. Divide the class into three groups. Play the CD (or use the karaoke version). Each group sings a verse. They change roles and repeat.

Set learning outcomes using the task flashcards.

- Say **Today we're going to learn about parks in Britain.**
- Hold up the task flashcards in turn and elicit the activities. Stick them on one side of the board. Point to them during the lesson to reinforce your instructions.

Pupil's Book Activity 1

Listen and read. Answer.

▶ *CD3 Track 14 p267*

- (Books open.) Focus the pupils on the photos. Ask **What can you see?** Read the speech bubble at the top of the page.
- Play the CD, pausing after each piece of information to check understanding. The pupils listen and look at the photos.
- Play the CD again. The pupils listen and read. Encourage them to repeat some of the sentences.

Suggested comprehension questions

- Photo 1: **What game are they playing?** (*Cricket.*)
- Photo 2: **What animals can you see?** (*Ducks.*)
- Photo 3: **Are they riding a bike?** (*No, they're riding on a train.*)
- Photo 4: **Where are they now?** (*At the playground.*)

Pupil's Book Think about your culture

What do you do at the park?

- Read out the question.
- The pupils tell you what they do at the park.
- Ask additional questions, e.g. **Is there a park near your house? Do you like the slides and swings? Do you play football in the park? Are there any ducks?**

Activity Book

Activity 1

Listen and match.

▶ *CD3 Track 15 p267*

- (Books open.) Focus the pupils on the pictures. Elicit what they can see.
- Play the CD, pausing after each text. The pupils listen and match the names to the pictures.
- Play the CD again to check the answers.

Answers: **1** feeding the ducks **2** playing on the zip wire **3** riding on a train **4** playing cricket

Activity 2: Think about your culture

Read and tick (✓). Draw and write.

- Read out the question in the speech bubble. Elicit the pupils' answers.
- Read out the first sentence. The pupils tick the box if they do this activity at the park.
- Repeat with the other sentences.
- The pupils draw one of the activities they do.
- Invite different pupils to show the class their drawing and say what they do at the park.

Recycled vocabulary

- The pupils look at the picture and say the word. Then they trace the word.

Ending the lesson

Review the lesson.

- (Books closed.) Say **Today we've learnt about parks in Britain. What activities can you do in a park?** Elicit answers from the pupils.

Review the task flashcards.

- Point to the task flashcards. Say **Look at the activities you've done today. Which activity was your favourite?** Elicit the pupils' favourite activities.

Extra activities

Reinforcement

- Play *Clever parrots* (see p23) with the unit flashcards.

Extension

- Find information about a nearby park. The pupils say five things they can do there and five things they can see.

Key Competences and Key Learning Outcomes

- Read and understand instructions for growing flowers
- Order and draw instructions
- Identify what plants need to survive (optional)

Key language

- *grow, plants, pot, seeds, soil, sun, sunny place, watch, water*
- *Put the (pot in a sunny place). Push the seeds (into the soil). Water the seeds.*

Recycled: *book; frog; finger; flowers, garden*

Materials

- Pupil's Book p67; Activity Book p64; Class CD3; Teacher's App on Navio
- Teacher's Resource Bank: Task flashcards: *think, circle, listen, read, match*

Optional materials

- Teacher's Resource Bank: Playground objects and nature word cards
- Teacher's Resource Bank: Five Trinity Exam Practice cards (selected from the Starter Unit and Units 1, 2, 3, 4 and 5)
- Pots, soil, packet of seeds

At a Glance Lesson Plan

Starting the lesson

- Use the Trinity Exam Practice cards (optional).
- Review the culture lesson.
- Set learning outcomes using the task flashcards.

Before you read

- Say if you've got a garden.

Activity 1

- What do you need to grow flowers?
- Think and circle.

Activity 2

- Listen and read the instructions.

▶ *CD3 Track 16 p267*

After you read

Go to page 64 in your Activity Book.

Pupil's Book

Ending the lesson

- Review the lesson.
- Review the task flashcards.

Extra activities

Reinforcement

- Play *Bit by bit.*

Extension

- Grow flowers from seeds.

Link to Science

- **Plants:** Review what plants need to survive.

Activity Book

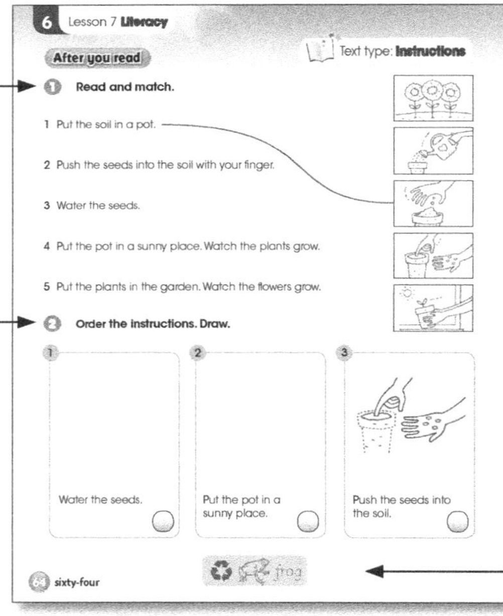

Activity Book

After you read: Activity 1

- Read and match.

Activity 2

- Order the instructions. Draw.

Recycled vocabulary

- Look, say and trace the word.

Digital resources

Teacher's Digital: Don't forget you can teach this lesson using the Teacher's App on Navio.

Pupil's Digital: Encourage your pupils to use the Pupil's App on Navio to practise the vocabulary from this lesson.

Powered By NAVIO

Detailed Lesson Plan

Starting the lesson

Use the Trinity Exam Practice cards (optional).
- The pupils practise asking and answering questions (see p31).

Review the culture lesson.
- Review the activities that British children do at the park.
- Elicit *play cricket*, *play on a zip wire*, *ride on a train* and *feed the ducks*.

Set learning outcomes using the task flashcards.
- Say **Today we're going to read some instructions.**
- Hold up the task flashcards in turn and elicit the activities. Stick them on one side of the board. Point to them during the lesson to reinforce your instructions.

Before you read

Say if you've got a garden.
- Ask **Have you got a garden? Have you got flowers in your garden?**
- Elicit answers from the pupils.

Pupil's Book Activity 1

What do you need to grow flowers? Think and circle.
- Focus the pupils on the photos. Read out the question.
- Elicit answers from the pupils. Then they circle the pictures.

Answers: soil, seeds, water, sun

Pupil's Book Activity 2

Listen and read the instructions.

▶ *CD3 Track 16 p267*
- Focus the pupils on Activity 2. Say **Let's read and listen to the instructions.**
- Play the CD, pausing after each instruction. The pupils point to the correct picture and mime the action.
- Play the CD again. The class repeats the instructions.
- Ask volunteers to read the instructions aloud.

Activity Book

After you read: Activity 1

Read and match.
- (Books open.) Focus the pupils on the first sentence. Read out the instructions and ask the pupils to follow the line.
- Ask a volunteer to do the same for the second sentence.
- The pupils work on their own to complete the activity.

Answers: **1** third picture **2** fourth picture **3** second picture **4** fifth picture **5** first picture

Activity 2

Order the instructions. Draw.
- Read out the instructions in the boxes. Ask the pupils to tell you the order of the instructions.
- The pupils number the instructions in the correct order.
- In boxes 1 and 2, they draw a picture to illustrate the instructions.

Answers: **1** Push the seeds into the soil. **2** Water the seeds. **3** Put the pot in a sunny place.

Recycled vocabulary
- The pupils look at the picture and say the word. Then they trace the word.

Ending the lesson

Review the lesson.
- (Books closed.) Say **Today we've read some instructions in English. What were they?** Elicit the instructions from the pupils.

Review the task flashcards.
- Point to the task flashcards. Say **Look at the activities you've done today. Which activity was your favourite?** Elicit the pupils' favourite activities.

Extra activity

Reinforcement
- Play *Bit by bit* (see p23) with the playground and nature objects word cards.

Extension
- Grow flowers from seeds in the classroom. Bring in some soil in pots and some seeds. The pupils plant the seeds, water them and put them in a sunny place. Remind the class to water the seeds regularly. Watch the flowers grow.

Link to Science

- If you are studying the Science topic of **Plants** in English, you could review what plants need to survive before you do the **Pupil's Book Activity 1: Before you read**. Elicit 'sunlight', 'air', 'water' and 'soil'.

Key Competences and Key Learning Outcomes

- Review language in the unit
- Reflect on own learning
- Sing a cooperative learning song

Key language

- *behind, between, in front of, near, next to; bush, flower, grass, rock, tree; climbing frame, roundabout, seesaw, slide, swing; cats, cow, frogs*
- *Where's (Beth)? (She's) on the (slide). Where are (Beth and Molly)? They're (on the climbing frame). (Molly) is (in front of) (the bush).*

Recycled: *cats, cow, frogs*

Materials

- Pupil's Book p68; Activity Book p65; Class CD3; Teacher's App on Navio
- Playground objects and nature flashcards
- Teacher's Resource Bank: Task flashcards: *listen, number, sing, stick, read, match, think, Talk Partners*
- Teacher's Resource Bank: Traffic light cut-out
- *Give Me Five!* sticker

Optional materials

- Teacher's Resource Bank: Five Trinity Exam Practice cards (selected from the Starter Unit and Units 1, 2, 3, 4 and 5)

At a Glance Lesson Plan

Pupil's Book

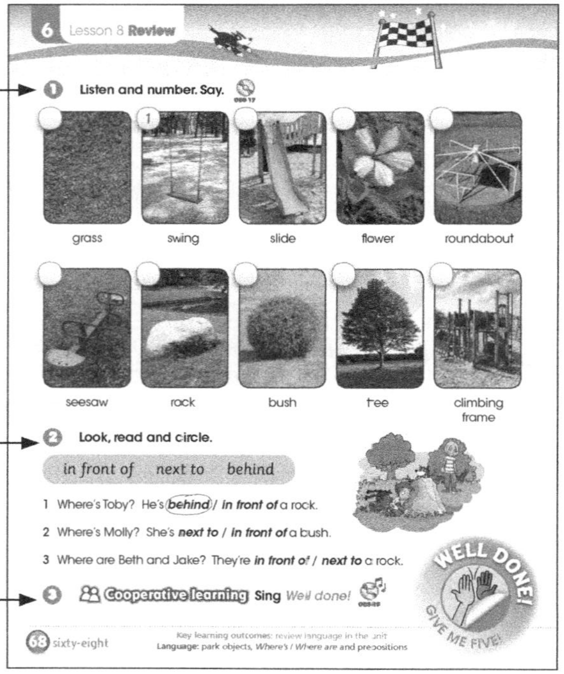

Starting the lesson

- Use the Trinity Exam Practice cards (optional).
- Review the unit vocabulary.
- Set learning outcomes using the task flashcards.

Activity 1

- Listen and number.
- ▶ ***CD3 Track 17 p267***
- Say.

Activity 2

- Look, read and circle.

Activity 3
Cooperative learning

- Sing *Well done!*
- ▶ ***CD3 Track 18 p268***
- Stick the *Give Me Five!* sticker.
- Go to the Activity Book.

Ending the lesson

- Review the task flashcards.

Activity Book

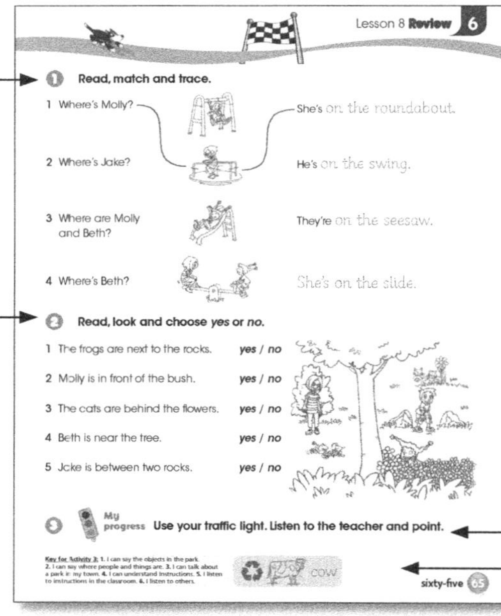

Activity Book

Activity 1

- Read, match and trace.

Activity 2

- Read, look and choose *yes* or *no*.

Activity 3 My progress

- Use your traffic light. Listen to the teacher and point.

Recycled vocabulary

- Look, say and trace the word.

Digital resources

Teacher's Digital: Don't forget you can teach this lesson using the Teacher's App on Navio.

Pupil's Digital: Encourage your pupils to use the Pupil's App on Navio to practise the vocabulary from this lesson.

Powered By NAVIO

Detailed Lesson Plan

Starting the lesson

Use the Trinity Exam Practice cards (optional).

- The pupils practise asking and answering questions (see p31).

Review the unit vocabulary.

- Hold up a playground objects and nature flashcard and elicit the word. Stick the flashcard face down on the board. Repeat with all the flashcards.
- Ask **Where's the (slide)?** Invite a pupil to turn over a flashcard. If it's the correct flashcard, he / she says *It's here*. If it isn't the correct flashcard, another pupil has a turn. Repeat with different words.

Set learning outcomes using the task flashcards.

- Say **Today we're going to remember what we've learnt in Unit 6.**
- Hold up the task flashcards in turn and elicit the activities. Stick them on one side of the board. Point to them during the lesson to reinforce your instructions.

Pupil's Book Activity 1

Listen and number. Say.

▸ *CD3 Track 17 p267*

- (Books open.) Point to the pictures and ask different pupils to name the park objects.
- Play the CD, pausing after each sentence. The pupils point to the park objects.
- Play the CD again. The pupils write the correct number for each picture.
- The pupils say the words under each picture.

Answers: **1** swing **2** grass **3** roundabout **4** slide **5** bush **6** tree **7** seesaw **8** rock **9** climbing frame **10** flower

Pupil's Book Activity 2

Look, read and circle.

- The pupils look at the picture in Activity 2. Read out the first question. Elicit the answer.
- Read out the other questions and sentences. The pupils circle the correct prepositions on their own.
- Ask volunteers to read out the questions and answers.

Answers: **1** behind **2** in front of **3** next to

Pupil's Book Activity 3: Cooperative learning

Sing *Well done!*

▸ *CD3 Track 18 p268*

- Praise the pupils for their hard work and encourage them to praise each other. Play the *Well done!* song. The pupils sing and do the actions.

Stick the *Give Me Five!* sticker.

- The pupils stick the *Give Me Five!* sticker on the Pupil's Book page.
- Variation: Sing the *Well done!* song and stick the *Give Me Five!* sticker after the class has also completed the Activity Book Lesson 8 Review.

Activity Book

Activity 1

Read, match and trace.

- (Books open.) The pupils say what they can see in the pictures.
- Read out the first question. The pupils follow the matching line to the picture and then the answer. Read out the answer.
- Repeat with all the questions.
- The pupils trace the answers.

Answers: **1** She's on the roundabout. **2** He's on the swing. **3** They're on the seesaw. **4** She's on the slide.

Activity 2

Read, look and choose *yes* or *no*.

- Ask **What can you see in the picture?** The pupils describe the picture.
- Read out the sentences for the pupils to say *yes* or *no*.
- The pupils read the sentences again and circle *yes* or *no*.

Answers: **1** no **2** yes **3** no **4** yes **5** yes

Activity 3: My progress My progress

Use your traffic light. Listen to the teacher and point.

- (Books closed.) Ask the class to take out their traffic light cut-out. Say **Let's think about our work in this unit.** Point to the green circle, nod your head, smile a lot, and say **I can say the objects in the playground. Yes, I can do this very well.** Point to the yellow circle, move your head a little, smile a little and say **Yes, I can do this.** Then point to the red circle, shake your head and say **No, I can't do this.**
- Read the different statements. For each one, the pupils point to the colour on their traffic light that shows how they feel about their own learning.

Self-assessment statements

1. I can say the objects in the park.
2. I can say where people and things are.
3. I can talk about a park in my town.
4. I can understand instructions.
5. I listen to instructions in the classroom.
6. I listen to others.

Recycled vocabulary

- The pupils look at the picture and say the word. Then they trace the word.

Ending the lesson

Review the task flashcards.

- Point to the task flashcards. Say **Look at the activities you've done today. Which activity was your favourite?** Elicit the pupils' favourite activities.

Video and 21st Century Skills

Key Competences and Key Learning Outcomes

- Watch and understand a video about playgrounds
- Understand the importance of being careful in the playground
- Think about what you do in the playground

Key language

- *climbing frame, go up, in front of, next to, one/two hands, roundabout, sit down, slide, stand up, wait, zip wire*

Materials

- Pupil's Book p69; Activity Book p66; Class CD3; Video; Teacher's App on Navio
- Teacher's Resource Bank: Task flashcards: *tick, read, circle, listen, match, think, draw, say, Talk Partners*

Optional materials

- Teacher's Resource Bank: Trinity Exam Practice cards (selected from Unit 6)
- Playground and nature words flashcards

At a Glance Lesson Plan

Starting the lesson

- Use the Trinity Exam Practice cards (optional).
- Review playground objects by ranking
- Set learning outcomes and use the task flashcards.

Pre-watching activity

- Predict what playground objects they are going to see.

Activity 1

- Watch the video.
  Unit 6 video p278
- Tick (✓) or cross (✗). Are these playgrounds in the video?

Activity 2

- Watch the video again.
  Unit 6 video
- Read and circle.

Activity 3

- Read and circle.
- Go to the Activity Book.

Pupil's Book

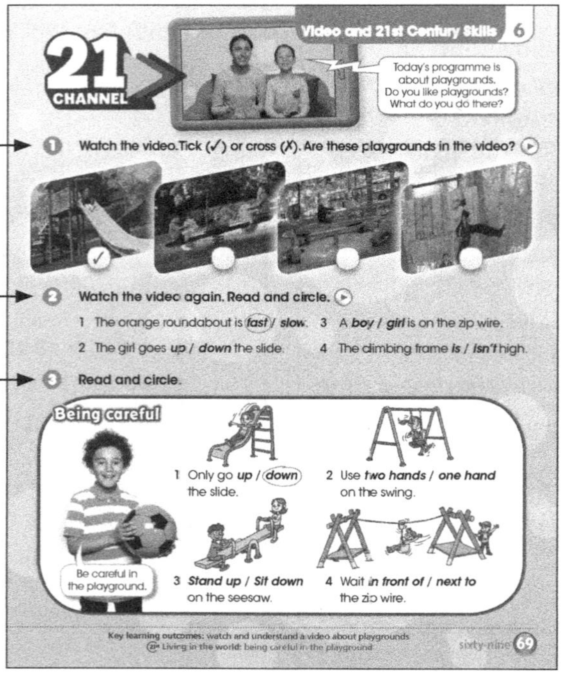

Ending the lesson

- Review the lesson.
- Review the task flashcards. Elicit the pupils' favourite activities.

Extra activity

- Pupils work together in groups to do an activity.

Activity Book

Activity Book

Activity 1

- Read, listen and match.
- ▶ *CD3 Track 19 p268*

Activity 2

- Read and think. Draw and say.

Recycled vocabulary

- Look, say and trace the word.

Digital resources

Teacher's Digital: Don't forget you can teach this lesson using the Teacher's App on Navio.

Pupil's Digital: Encourage your pupils to use the Pupil's App on Navio to practise the vocabulary from this lesson.

Powered By NAVIO

Detailed Lesson Plan

Starting the lesson

Use the Trinity Exam Practice cards (optional).

- The pupils practise asking and answering questions.

Review playground objects.

- Stick the playground objects flashcards on the board. Invite different pupils to the front and give them a playground object word card to match to the picture.
- Ask a few pupils which their number one favourite playground activity is. Write one to three on the board and ask the pupils to rank the activities.
- **Think-Pair-Share** Pupils compare their ranking with their partner.

Set learning outcomes and use the task flashcards.

- Say **Today we're going to watch a video and then ask and answer questions about playgrounds**.
- Point to the task flashcards throughout to elicit activities and reinforce your instructions.

Pre-watching activity

- **Think-Pair-Share** Ask the pupils what playground objects they have in their local playground. Write their answers on the board.

Pupil's Book Activity 1

Watch the video. Tick (✓) or cross (✗). Are these playgrounds in the video? *p278*

- Play Part 1, pausing to elicit the answers. Ask **Do Sophie and Tom like playgrounds? Why?**
- On the board stick four playground flashcards. Tell the pupils to listen and tell you which object you don't say. Say three of the objects. Ask a pupil to come to the board and write a cross under the playground object flashcard you didn't say. Repeat with different playground object flashcards.
- Focus the pupils' attention on the video stills. Ask **What can you see?**
- Explain that the pupils cross the playground object that is not in the video like the previous flashcard activity. Play Part 2 of the video. Pause the video after the first video still. Ask the pupils to point to the corresponding photo in their book.
- Play the rest of Part 2 for pupils to point to the photos in the order they see the playground objects.
- Play Part 2 again for pupils to write the cross. The pupils then tick the playground objects that are in the video.
- Ask **Which playground activity looks the most fun?**

Answers: ✓, ✗, ✓, ✓

Pupil's Book Activity 2

Watch the video again. Read and circle.

- Play Part 2 again. Pause after the orange roundabout. Read out the first sentence in Activity 2. Ask **Is the orange roundabout fast or slow?** *(Fast.)*
- Play Part 2 for pupils to circle the words.
- Ask general questions to check understanding.
  Which playground objects are high? *(Slide, zip line, climbing frame.)*
  Which playground object is slow? *(The red roundabout.)*
  What does Sophie say is important to do on the swing and climbing frame? *(Use two hands.)*
  What are the children doing next to the climbing frame? *(Waiting for their turn.)*
  What nature features do you see? *(Grass, bush, tree.)*
  Why is it important to be careful at the playground? *(Play safely so you don't get hurt or hurt other children.)*

Answers: **1** fast **2** down **3** boy **4** is

Pupil's Book Activity 3

Read and circle.

- Stick the slide, swing and seesaw flashcards on the board. Ask the pupils to tell you how they can play safely on each object.
- Explain that the pictures show how to be safe in the playground and they have to circle the correct words.

Answers: **1** down **2** two hands **3** sit down **4** next to

Activity Book

Activity 1

Read, listen and match.

▶ *CD3 Track 19 p268*

- Tell the pupils they have to mime the actions. Say **I use two hands on the climbing frame. I wait next to the swing. I sit down on the zip wire. I only go down the slide.**
- Play the first exchange on the CD. Show the matching line. In pairs, the pupils read the other sentences and match them to the pictures.
- Play the rest of the CD, pausing after each exchange, for pupils to check their answers.

Answers: **1** climbing frame **2** swing **3** zip wire **4** slide

Activity 2

Read and think. Draw and say.

- Read out the speech bubble. Elicit responses from the pupils.
- The pupils read the instructions and choose what they do in the playground. They draw pictures to illustrate the instructions. They show their partner their pictures and read out the instructions.

Recycled vocabulary

- The pupils looks at the picture and say the word. Then they trace the word.

Ending the lesson

Review the lesson.

- Ask **Which activity was easy / difficult?**

Review the task flashcards.

- Say **Look at the activities you've done today. Which activity was your favourite?**

Extra activity

Extension

- Divide the class into small groups. On the board write the heading *Be careful in the playground*. The groups work together to create a poster, giving instructions on how to stay safe in the playground. If possible, stick the posters in the school playground.

My project 2: Spring

Key Competences and Key Learning Outcomes

- Identify and talk about spring animals and plants
- Count items in a picture
- Identify weather conditions in spring
- Prepare to make a class spring wall display

Key language

- *butterflies, chicks, lambs, rabbits; spring; cloudy, rainy, snowy, stormy, sunny, windy*
- *How many (lambs) can you see? I can see (three lambs). What's the weather like today? It's (windy). Is it (rainy) today? Yes, it is. No, it isn't.*

Recycled: numbers 1–10; *birds, bushes, flowers, trees*

Materials

- Pupil's Book p70; Activity Book p68; Class CD3; Teacher's App on Navio
- Teacher's Resource Bank: Task flashcards: *listen, find, write, Talk Partners, plan*

Optional materials

- Teacher's Resource Bank: Five Trinity Exam Practice cards (selected from the Starter Unit and Units 1, 2, 3, 4, 5 and 6)

At a Glance Lesson Plan

Starting the lesson

- Use the Trinity Exam Practice cards (optional).
- Review weather vocabulary.
- Set learning outcomes using the task flashcards.

Learn: Activity 1

- Listen and say.
- ▶ *CD3 Track 20 p268*
- Read, count and write.

Activity 2

- Listen.
- ▶ *CD3 Track 21 p268*
- Talk Partners Ask and answer.

Plan your project

- Prepare to make a spring wall display.
- Go to page 68 in your Activity Book.

Pupil's Book

Ending the lesson

- Review the lesson.
- Review the task flashcards.

Link to Science

Water and Air: Living things

Activity Book

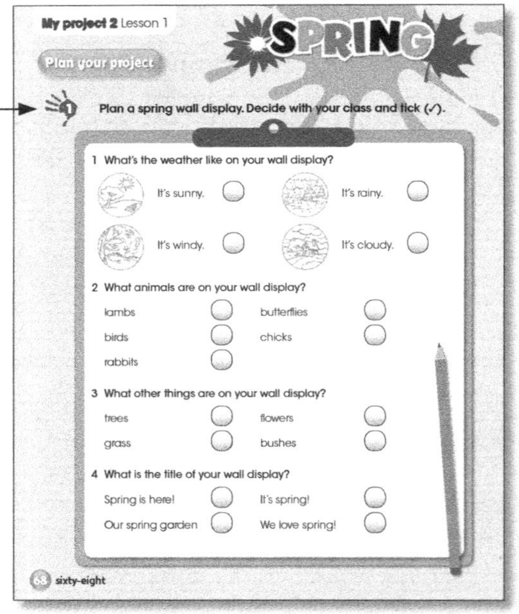

Activity Book: Plan your project

Activity 1

- Plan a spring wall display. Decide with your class and tick (✓).

Digital resources

Teacher's Digital: Don't forget you can teach this lesson using the Teacher's App on Navio.

Pupil's Digital: Encourage your pupils to use the Pupil's App on Navio to practise the vocabulary from this lesson.

Powered By NAVIO

Starting the lesson

Use the Trinity Exam Practice cards (optional).

- The pupils practise asking and answering questions (see p31).

Review weather vocabulary.

- If the pupils already know some weather vocabulary, quickly review the words they know. Ask **What's the weather like today?**

Set learning outcomes using the task flashcards.

- Say **Today we're going to learn about spring and the weather.**
- Hold up the task flashcards in turn and elicit the activities. Stick them on one side of the board. Point to them during the lesson to reinforce your instructions.

Learn: Pupil's Book Activity 1

Listen and say. Read, count and write.

▶ *CD3 Track 20 p268*

- (Books open.) Focus the pupils on the picture. Ask **What can you see?** The pupils name the animals and plants that they already know (*flowers, birds, trees, bushes, grass*). Introduce the new vocabulary *butterflies, rabbits, chicks, lambs*.
- Play the CD. The pupils listen and then say the words.
- Say **Let's count the lambs.** The class finds and counts the lambs in the picture. The pupils then work on their own to find and count the other items. Check the answers as a class.

Answers: 3 lambs, 7 flowers, 4 birds, 2 rabbits, 6 chicks, 8 butterflies

Pupil's Book Activity 2

Listen. Ask and answer.

▶ *CD3 Track 21 p268*

- Play the CD, pausing after each sentence. The pupils listen and repeat. Encourage the class to verify the answer by looking at the picture and their answer in Activity 1. Elicit similar questions and answers about the things in the picture.
- Talk Partners The pupils ask and answer similar questions about the picture in Activity 1.

Digital tip!

- Ask the pupils to look for pictures of spring on the Internet. Elicit what they can see.

Activity Book: Plan your project

Activity 1

Plan a spring wall display. Decide with your class and tick (✓).

- (Books open.) If possible, organise the class into a large circle. Explain to the class that they are going to work together to plan a spring wall display for the classroom. Read out each question in turn and the possible answers. The pupils vote on the answers by raising their hands. When the class has made a decision, all the pupils tick the same relevant box(es) on the page.
- Finally, each pupil chooses and circles one of the animals to make in the next lesson: lamb, butterfly, bird, chick, rabbit. Make sure that all the animals are chosen. You will need to make photocopies of the animal cut-outs before the next lesson (available on the Teacher's Resource Bank.)

Ending the lesson

Review the lesson.

- (Books closed.) Say **Today we've learnt about spring and the weather. What animals can you see in spring?** Elicit the animals from the pupils.

Review the task flashcards.

- Point to the task flashcards on the board. Say **Look at the activities you've done today. Which activity was your favourite?** Elicit the pupils' favourite activities.

Link to Science

- If you are studying the Science topic of **Living things** in English, you could review additional farm animals words, e.g. *goat, rooster, goose, turkey.*

My project 2: Spring

Key Competences and Key Learning Outcomes

- Present a class spring display
- Follow instructions
- Think about your project
- Sing a cooperative learning song
- Work together to make a display
- Make a spring animal

Key language
- *It's got (big) ears.*

Recycled: *animals, bird, butterfly, chick, flowers, lamb, rabbit; ears;* colours; numbers

Recycled: *This is (my butterfly). It's (blue). My (bird) is near (a bush).*

Materials
- Pupil's Book p71; Activity Book p69; Class CD3; Teacher's App on Navio
- Teacher's Resource Bank: Task flashcards: *sing, read, listen, cut out, stick, think, Talk Partners*

Optional materials
- Teacher's Resource Bank: Five Trinity Exam Practice cards (selected from the Starter Unit and Units 1, 2, 3, 4, 5 and 6)
- Teacher's Resource Bank: My Project 2 cut-outs
- Tissue paper (different colours); crayons or coloured pencils; glue; overalls / old shirts

At a Glance Lesson Plan

Starting the lesson
- Use the Trinity Exam Practice cards (optional).
- Review weather vocabulary.
- Set learning outcomes using the task flashcards.

Create: Activity 1 – Cooperative learning
- Sing *What do I need to do?*
- ▶ *CD3 Track 22 p268*

Create: Activity 2
- Read.
- Make a spring animal.

Activity 3
- Create your wall display. Listen.
- ▶ *CD3 Track 23 p268*
- Tell the class about your animal and stick it on the wall display.

Pupil's Book

Think about your project
- Go to page 69 in your Activity Book.

Ending the lesson
- Review the lesson.
- Sing *Well done!*
- ▶ *CD3 Track 18 p268*

Activity Book

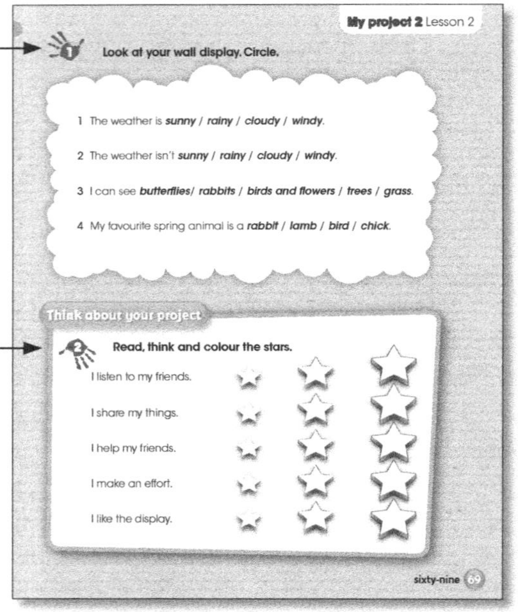

Activity Book

Activity 1
- Look at your wall display. Circle.

Activity 2: Think about your project
- Read, think and colour the stars.

Digital resources

Teacher's Digital: Don't forget you can teach this lesson using the Teacher's App on Navio.

Pupil's Digital: Encourage your pupils to use the Pupil's App on Navio to practise the vocabulary from this lesson.

Powered By NAVIO

Starting the lesson

Use the Trinity Exam Practice cards (optional).
- The pupils practise asking and answering questions (see p31).

Review weather vocabulary.
- Ask **What's the weather like today? Is it (sunny)?**
- Talk Partners The pupils ask and answer with a Talk Partner.

Set learning outcomes using the task flashcards.
- Say **Today we're going to make a spring animal wall display for the classroom.**
- Hold up the task flashcards in turn and elicit the activities. Stick them on one side of the board. Point to them during the lesson to reinforce your instructions.

Create: Pupil's Book Activity 1: Cooperative learning

Sing *What do I need to do?*
▶ *CD3 Track 22 p268*
- Explain that instructions are important. When the teacher gives instructions, the class needs to listen carefully. Highlight that we also read instructions in our Pupil's Books. We need to concentrate in order to understand what we have to do. Explain that pupils can ask for instructions when they don't understand an activity. Teach the question **What do I need to do?**
- Play the CD. The pupils listen and do the actions.
- Play the CD again. The pupils sing and do the actions.

Create: Pupil's Book Activity 2

Read. Make a spring animal.
- (Books open.) Say **We need to read some instructions carefully.**
- Read the instructions. The pupils look at the corresponding photos and follow the text.
- Give each pupil a photocopiable cut-out of the animal that they chose in the previous lesson and a pair of scissors.
- Hold up the tissue paper and elicit the colours. Each pupil chooses one or more colours, tears up the paper and rolls it into balls.
- Variation: crayons or coloured pencils can be used instead.
- The pupils glue the tissue paper balls onto their animal.

Pupil's Book Activity 3

Create your wall display. Listen. Tell the class about your animal and stick it on the wall display.
▶ *CD3 Track 23 p268*
- Play the CD. The pupils listen and follow the conversation.
- Invite different pupils to present their completed animal to the class, describing the size, colour and parts of the body. Extra words: *wings*, *beak* and *fur*.
- When the pupils have described their animal, they stick it on the wall display.

Activity Book

Activity 1
Look at your wall display. Circle.
- (Books open.) Read out the sentences and ask the class to look at their wall display for the answers. Highlight that there is more than one possible answer.
- The pupils read the sentences again and circle the words.

Activity 2: Think about your project
Read, think and colour the stars.
- Say **Let's think about how we work together.** Read out each sentence. The pupils think and colour the corresponding star (small star: sometimes; medium-sized star: usually; big star: always).

Ending the lesson

Review the lesson.
- Say **Today we've worked together. What have we made?** Elicit answers from the pupils.

Sing *Well done!*
▶ *CD3 Track 18 p268*
- (Books closed.) Praise the class for working together and for following instructions well. Play the CD. The pupils sing and do the actions.

Date: ______________ Unit: ______________

1 **What did my pupils learn in this unit?**

2 **How did my pupils work? (✓)**

individually ☐ in pairs ☐ in small groups ☐

in large groups ☐ as a class ☐

3 **Which key competences did my pupils develop?**

Competence in linguistic communication ☐

Competence in mathematics, science and technology ☐

Digital competence ☐

Learning to learn ☐

Social and civic competences ☐

Sense of initiative and entrepreneurship ☐

Cultural awareness and expression ☐

4 **Which lessons / activities were the most successful and why?**

5 **Which lessons / activities did my pupils find the most difficult and why?**

6 **What did I try in the classroom for the first time? How did it go?**

7 **Which resources did I find most useful? (including webpages)**

8 **What could I do differently next time I teach this unit?**

Unit 7

Let's explore my town!

Unit overview

Key Competences and Key Learning Outcomes

- Identify and say places in town (Lesson 1)
- Say the vocabulary chant (Lesson 1)
- Use *There's …* and *There are …* in a conversation (Lesson 2)
- Recognise and say different forms of transport (Lesson 4)
- Watch and understand a video about transport (Video and 21st Century Skills)

- Recognise and use numbers up to 20 (Lesson 4)
- Ask and say how many objects there are (Lesson 4)

- Use the Pupil's App on Navio
- Read and understand digital maps (Video and 21st Century Skills)

- Practise spelling (Lesson 1)
- Say a tongue twister to practise the sound /z/ (Lesson 5)
- Review language in the unit and reflect on own learning (Lesson 8)
- Practise activity types found in the Cambridge English Young Learners Exams: Pre A1 Starters

- Understand the importance of taking care when crossing the road (Lesson 3)
- Draw, say and write places near where you live (Video and 21st Century Skills)

- Work with a Talk Partner to practise and reinforce learning (all lessons)
- Play a communication game about transport (Lesson 5)

- Sing three songs (Lessons 1, 4 and 8)
- Understand and act out a story (Lesson 3)
- Read about cycling in Britain (Lesson 6)
- Think about how you travel where you live (Lesson 6)
- Read and understand a fable (Lesson 7)

Vocabulary

Core vocabulary:
bookshop, café, cinema, hospital, restaurant, sweet shop, swimming pool, supermarket, toyshop, zoo; boat, bus, helicopter, lorry, motorbike, train

Extension vocabulary (optional)
bus stop, crossing, pavement, roundabout, square, street; metro, plane, ship, taxi

Other vocabulary
bone, count, cross the road, steps, sweets, treasure map; bad, cheese, country, fantastic, life, quiet; by bike, by bus, by car, on foot; on the metro; numbers 1–20 (in words and figures)

Recycled vocabulary
bush, flower, grass, tree; roundabout, playground, rock, seesaw, slide, swing; animal, cats; bike, scooter; town; wheels; cake, ice cream; delicious; cousin; days of the week; numbers 1–10

Structures

Core structures
There's a (zoo) in my town. There are (two cafés).
How many (cars) are there? There are (ten) cars.

Other structures
Let's go (to town). Welcome to (my town). Stand up.
Sit down. There's a (tree) (next to / in front of) the (swimming pool). How many (cars) are there? There are (20) cars. I live in the (country). I eat (apples) and (cheese). Where is (Nick)? He's in the (bookshop). How do you go to school? I go to school (by car). Where do you live? I live in (Madrid). How many (girls) are there in your class? There are (twelve) (girls).

Recycled structures
I love (sweets). I don't like (cats). I like (a quiet life).

Phonics

Consonant sound 'z' (**l**a**z**y, **z**ebra, **z**oo)

British Culture

Cycling

Literacy

Text type: a fable (text to entertain and educate)
Reading skills: using visual clues; understanding the order of events; extracting key information; understanding the moral of a story

21st Century Skills

Digital skills: learn to read digital maps

Cooperative learning

Song: *Well done!* (Lesson 8)
Skills: Working together and supporting each other (Lesson 1); Discovering similarities (Lesson 2); Listening to others (Lesson 4); Think-Pair-Share (Lesson 8)

Values

Understanding the importance of crossing the road safely

Cross-curricular links

Links to Science

My neighbourhood: features in their neighbourhood; the importance of road safety rules; identifying and categorising types of transport

Suggested Arts and Crafts concepts

Buildings: identifying symmetry in architecture and in the environment; using symmetry to create a neighbourhood

Key Competences and Key Learning Outcomes

- Identify and say ten places in town
- Say the vocabulary chant
- Stick the places in the town stickers
- Review features of a neighbourhood (optional)
- Practise spelling
- Sing a song about the town

Key language

- *bookshop, café, cinema, hospital, restaurant, sweet shop, swimming pool, supermarket, toyshop, zoo; town*
- *Let's go (to town).There's a (hospital). Stand up. Sit down.*
- Extension: *bus stop, crossing, pavement, roundabout, square, street*

Recycled: *flower; roundabout*

Materials

- Pupil's Book p72; Activity Book pp70 and 79; Class CD3; Teacher's App on Navio
- Places in the town flashcards; Unit 7 stickers
- Teacher's Resource Bank: Places in the town word cards
- Teacher's Resource Bank: Task flashcards: *listen, sing, read, match, stick, say, think, Talk Partners, write*

Optional materials

- Teacher's Resource Bank: Five Trinity Exam Practice cards (selected from the Starter Unit and Units 1, 2, 3, 4, 5 and 6).

At a Glance Lesson Plan

Starting the lesson

- Use the Trinity Exam Practice cards (optional).
- Review instructions.
- Set learning outcomes using the task flashcards.

Vocabulary presentation

- Present the new vocabulary.

Activity 1

- Listen and point.
- ▶ *CD3 Track 24 p268*
- Sing *Let's go to town.*

Word cards

- Read the word cards.
- Match them to the flashcards.

Activity 2

- Read and stick the ten stickers.
- Listen and say the chant.
- ▶ *CD3 Track 26 p268*
- Go to the Activity Book.

Pupil's Book

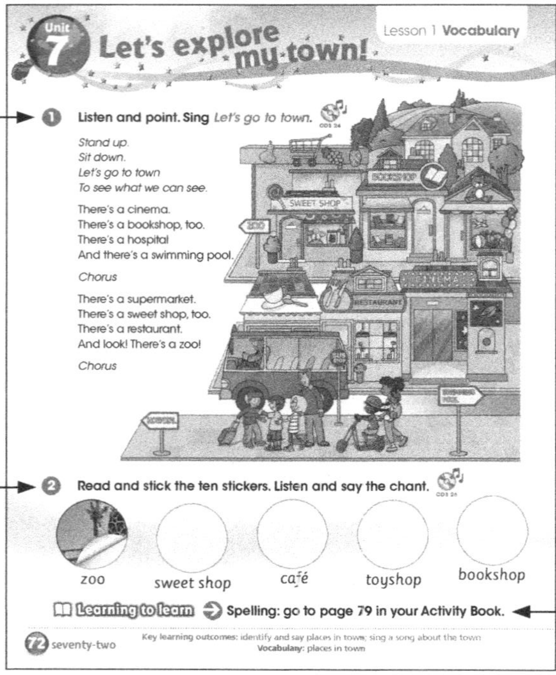

Ending the lesson

- Review the lesson.
- Review the task flashcards.

Extra activity

Vocabulary Extension

- Present six additional vocabulary items.

Cooperative learning

Working together and supporting each other

- Talk Partners Ask and answer *What's this?*

Link to Science

- **My neighbourhood:** Review the main features of a neighbourhood.

Learning to learn

Spelling

- Practise spelling at any time during this unit (Activity Book p79).

Digital resources

Teacher's Digital: Don't forget you can teach this lesson using the Teacher's App on Navio.

Pupil's Digital: Encourage your pupils to use the Pupil's App on Navio to practise the vocabulary from this lesson.

Powered By NAVIO

Activity Book

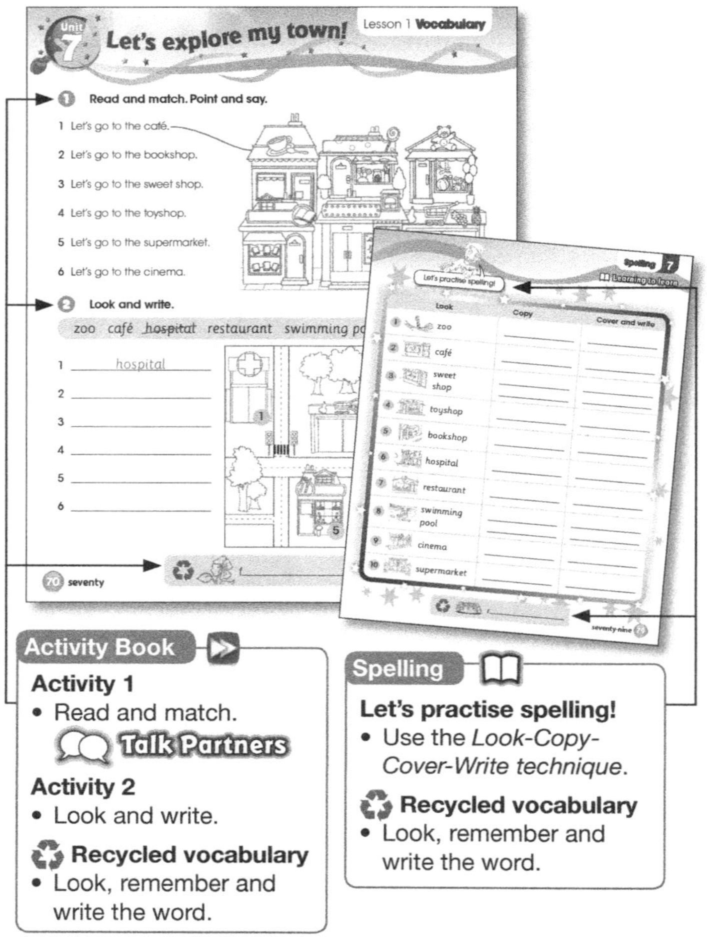

Activity Book

Activity 1

- Read and match.

Talk Partners

Activity 2

- Look and write.

Recycled vocabulary

- Look, remember and write the word.

Spelling

Let's practise spelling!

- Use the *Look-Copy-Cover-Write technique*.

Recycled vocabulary

- Look, remember and write the word.

Detailed Lesson Plan

Starting the lesson

Use the Trinity Exam Practice cards (optional).
- The pupils practise asking and answering questions (see p31).

Review instructions.
- Say **Stand up. Sit down. Point to the (board). Touch your (head).** The pupils listen and do the actions.
- Repeat in random order. Say the instructions at a faster speed as the pupils become more confident.

Set learning outcomes using the task flashcards.
- Say **Today we're going to learn the names of places in a town.**
- Hold up the task flashcards in turn and elicit the activities. Stick them on one side of the board. Point to them during the lesson to reinforce your instructions.

Vocabulary presentation

Present the new vocabulary.
- (Books closed.) Say **Let's go to town, everyone.** The pupils stand up and mime walking on the spot with you. Ask **Where are we now?**
- Hold up a places in the town flashcard and ask **Do you like the (zoo)?** Stick it on the board and repeat with the other places in the town flashcards.
- Point to each flashcard on the board. The pupils mime going to the places and they say the word.

Pupil's Book Activity 1

Listen and point. Sing *Let's go to town.*
▶ *CD3 Track 24 p268*
- (Books open.) Ask **Where are Molly, Jake and Beth? What places can you see?**
- Play the CD. The pupils point to the places.
- Play the CD again. The pupils sing and do the actions. Stick the flashcards on the board in the order of the song, if necessary.

Word cards

Read the word cards. Match them to the flashcards.
- (Books closed.) Hold up the places in the town word cards in turn, and say or elicit each word.
- Ask different pupils to come to the front and stick the word cards with the corresponding flashcards.

Pupil's Book Activity 2

Read and stick the ten stickers. Listen and say the chant.
▶ *CD3 Track 26 p268*
- (Books open.) Ask a pupil to read the first place in the town. The pupils stick the corresponding sticker. Repeat with the other stickers.
- Play the CD. The pupils listen and say the chant, pointing to the stickers in turn.

Activity Book

Activity 1

Read and match. Point and say.
- (Books open.) Different pupils read out the sentences.
- The pupils match the sentences to the places.
- Point to different places in the picture. The pupils say the name of the places.
- Talk Partners The pupils point and say with a Talk Partner.

Activity 2

Look and write.
- Read the words in the box. Look at the signs and name the places. The pupils write the words.

Answers: **1** hospital **2** supermarket **3** café **4** swimming pool **5** restaurant **6** zoo

Recycled vocabulary
- The pupils look at the picture and write the word. If necessary, they look back at the previous unit.

Answer: flower

Ending the lesson

Review the lesson.
- (Books closed.) Say **Today we've learnt the names of places in a town. What words do you remember?** Elicit the words from the pupils.

Review the task flashcards.
- Point to the task flashcards. Say **Look at the activities you've done today. Which activity was your favourite?** Elicit the pupils' favourite activities.

Extra activities

Vocabulary Extension
- Use the Vocabulary Booster on Navio to present and practise six additional words to describe places in the town: *bus stop, crossing, pavement, roundabout, square, street.*

Cooperative learning

Working together and supporting each other
- Talk Partners Pupil A points to a place in the town sticker and asks *What's this?* Pupil B answers using *It's a ...* If Pupil B can't remember, Pupil A helps him / her. Encourage the pupils to help each other to remember vocabulary. When Pupil B has named all ten they swap roles and repeat.

Link to Science

- If you are studying the Science topic of **My neighbourhood** in English, ask the pupils to review places they like and don't like in their neighbourhood.

Spelling (Activity Book page 79)

Let's practise spelling!
- The pupils can practise spelling the ten places in the town using the *Look-Copy-Cover-Write* technique at any time during this unit before the Lesson 8 Review.

Recycled vocabulary
- The pupils look at the picture and write the word. If necessary, they look back at the previous unit.

Answer: roundabout

Key Competences and Key Learning Outcomes

- Use *There's …* and *There are …*
- Complete and practise a conversation
- Listen for specific information

Key language
- *sweets*
- *There are (two cinemas). Welcome to (my town).*

Recycled: *bookshop, café, cinema, hospital, restaurant, sweet shop, swimming pool, supermarket, toyshop, zoo; tree; animals*; numbers 1–10

Recycled: *There's a (hospital). I love (sweets).*

Materials
- Pupil's Book p73; Activity Book p71; Class CD3; Teacher's App on Navio
- Places in the town flashcards
- Teacher's Resource Bank: Task flashcards: *listen, act out, think, write, draw*

Optional materials
- Teacher's Resource Bank: Five Trinity Exam Practice cards (selected from the Starter Unit and Units 1, 2, 3, 4, 5 and 6)

At a Glance Lesson Plan

Starting the lesson
- Use the Trinity Exam Practice cards (optional).
- Review the *Let's go to town* song.
- ▶ ***CD3 Track 24 p268***
- ▶ ***CD3 Track 25 p268 (optional karaoke version)***
- Set learning outcomes using the task flashcards.

Activity 1
- Listen and repeat.
- ▶ ***CD3 Track 27 p268***
- Act out.

Activity 2
- How many are there?
- Listen and write the number.
- ▶ ***CD3 Track 28 p268***
- Go to the Activity Book.

Pupil's Book

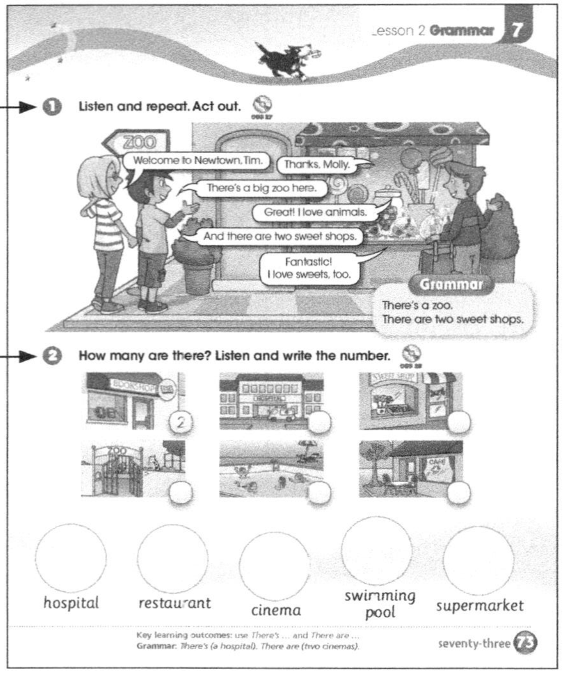

Ending the lesson
- Review the lesson.
- Review the task flashcards.

Extra activity
Reinforcement
- Create a word chain with places in the town.

Extension
- Play a mime game.

Cooperative learning
Discovering similarities
- Play *Me too.*

Activity Book

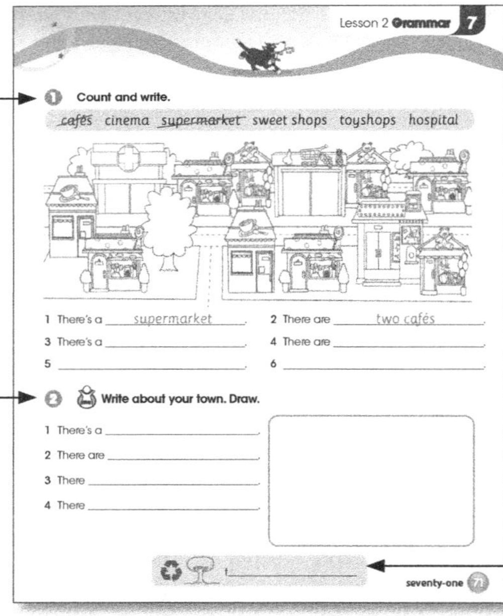

Activity Book
Activity 1
- Count and write.

Activity 2
- Write about your town.
- Draw.

Recycled vocabulary
- Look, remember and write the word.

Digital resources

Teacher's Digital: Don't forget you can teach this lesson using the Teacher's App on Navio.

Pupil's Digital: Encourage your pupils to use the Pupil's App on Navio to practise the vocabulary from this lesson.

Powered By NAVIO

Starting the lesson

Use the Trinity Exam Practice cards (optional).

- The pupils practise asking and answering questions (see p31).

Review the *Let's go to town* song.

▶ *CD3 Track 24 p268*

▶ *CD3 Track 25 p268 (optional karaoke version)*

- Use the places in the town flashcards to quickly review the ten places in the town. Then stick the cards in different places around the classroom. Say **Let's go to the (bookshop)!** The pupils face and point to the corresponding card. Repeat with the other cards. As the pupils become more confident, increase the speed of your delivery.
- Play the CD (or use the karaoke version). The class sing the song and do the actions, facing and pointing to each flashcard in turn as it appears in the song.

Set learning outcomes using the task flashcards.

- Say **Today we're going to talk about places in a town.**
- Hold up the task flashcards in turn and elicit the activities. Stick them on one side of the board. Point to them during the lesson to reinforce your instructions.

Pupil's Book Activity 1

Listen and repeat. Act out.

▶ *CD3 Track 27 p268*

- (Books open.) The pupils look at the picture. Ask **Can you see Molly? Who's the other boy?** Tell the pupils it's Molly's cousin Tim and she and Jake are taking him round the town.
- Play the CD. The pupils listen and read the conversation.
- Ask **What's in the town?**
- Play the CD again, pausing after each sentence for the pupils to repeat.
- Ask different pupils to come to the front and act out the conversation.

Pupil's Book Activity 2

How many are there? Listen and write the number.

▶ *CD3 Track 28 p268*

- Focus the class on the second activity and name the different places. Point to the bookshop and say **There are two bookshops in the town. Let's listen.**
- Play the CD, pausing after the first conversation. Ask **How many hospitals are there in the town?** Play the CD, pausing to check the pupils' answers and to allow them to write the number. Repeat with the other pictures.

Answers: 2 bookshops, 1 hospital, 2 sweet shops, 1 zoo, 1 swimming pool, 4 cafés

Activity Book

Activity 1

Count and write.

- (Books open.) Elicit what the pupils can see in the picture.
- Focus the pupils on the sentences beginning 'There's …' and 'There are …'. Read out the examples and elicit other sentences from the pupils.
- Then the pupils complete the sentences on their own.

Answers: **1** There's a supermarket. **2** There are two cafés. **3** There's a hospital/cinema. **4** There are four sweet shops/three toyshops. **5** There's a cinema/hospital. **6** There are three toyshops/four sweet shops.

Activity 2

Write about your town. Draw.

- Focus the pupils on Activity 2. The pupils name different places in their town.
- The pupils complete the sentences about their town and then draw a picture.
- Encourage different pupils to read out their sentences.

Recycled vocabulary

- The pupils look at the picture and write the word. If necessary, they look back at the previous unit.

Answer: tree

Ending the lesson

Review the lesson.

- (Books closed.) Say **Today we've acted out a conversation together and learnt how to use 'There is …' and 'There are …'. Did you work well?** Elicit answers from the pupils.

Review the task flashcards.

- Point to the task flashcards. Say **Look at the activities you've done today. Which activity was your favourite?** Elicit the pupils' favourite activities.

Extra activities

Reinforcement

- Create a word chain with places in the town. Say **In my town, there are two sweet shops.**
- A pupil continues with *In my town, there are two sweet shops and (four) (hospitals).*
- Continue with other pupils. Encourage them to use their imagination.

Extension

- Mime being in one of the places in town. Ask **Where am I?** The pupils ask *Are you at the (cinema)?*
- When a pupil guesses correctly, he / she takes your part.

Cooperative learning

Discovering similarities

- Discovering similarities helps develop a positive classroom atmosphere.
- Invite a pupil to come to the front of the class. He / She says a place in a town that he / she likes, e.g. *I like sweet shops.*
- The pupils who feel the same say *Me too.*
- Repeat with other pupils and places in the town.

Key Competences and Key Learning Outcomes

- Read, listen and understand a story about a treasure map
- Read the story with some fluency
- Learn safety rules for crossing the road (optional)
- Become familiar with the story through a pre-reading task
- Understand the importance of crossing the road safely
- Understand and act out the story
- Give an opinion on the story

Key language

- *bone, count, cross the road, steps, treasure map*
- *There's (a tree) next to the (swimming pool). There are (two rocks) in front of the (zoo). How many (steps) are there?*

Recycled: *bush, rocks, tree; old*

Materials

- Pupil's Book pp74–75; Activity Book p72; Class CD3; Teacher's App on Navio
- Places in the town flashcards
- Teacher's Resource Bank: Task flashcards: *think, listen, read, act out, write, circle, draw*
- Teacher's Resource Bank: Unit 7 Lesson 3 Animated Story

Other materials

- Teacher's Resource Bank: Five Trinity Exam Practice cards (selected from the Starter Unit and Units 1, 2, 3, 4, 5 and 6)

At a Glance Lesson Plan

Starting the lesson

- Use the Trinity Exam Practice cards (optional).
- Review the language from Lesson 2.
- Set learning outcomes using the task flashcards.

Before you read

- Explain the story title.
- Read and answer the question.

Activity 1

- Listen and read.
- ▶ *CD3 Track 29 p268*
- Act out.
- ***Now watch the animated story!***

After you read: Activity 2

- Go to page 72 in your Activity Book.
- Values: Read and write.

Pupil's Book

Ending the lesson

- Review the lesson.
- Review the task flashcards.

Link to Science

- **My neighbourhood:** Safety rules for crossing the road.

Digital resources

Teacher's Digital: Don't forget you can teach this lesson using the Teacher's App on Navio.

Pupil's Digital: Encourage your pupils to use the Pupil's App on Navio to practise the vocabulary from this lesson.

Powered By NAVIO

Activity Book

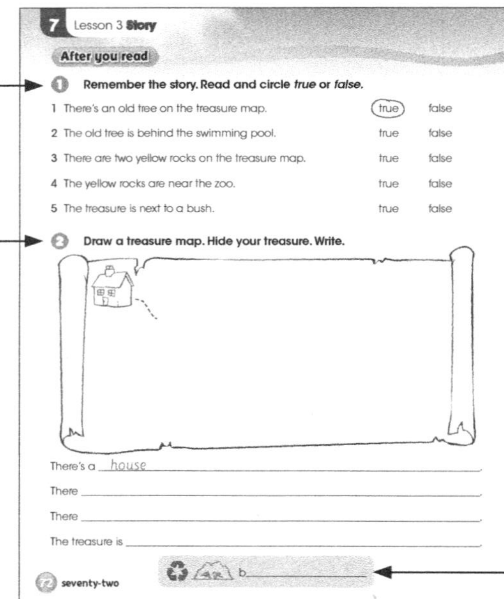

Activity Book

After you read: Activity 1

- Remember the story. Read and circle *true or false.*

Activity 2

- Draw a treasure map.
- Hide your treasure.
- Write.

Recycled vocabulary

- Look, remember and write the word.

Detailed Lesson Plan

Starting the lesson

Use the Trinity Exam Practice cards (optional).

- The pupils practise asking and answering questions (see p31).

Review the language from Lesson 2.

- Take a places in the town flashcard and hold it so the pupils can't see it. Say **In this place, there are (animals).** The pupils guess the place (*zoo*).
- Repeat with different flashcards. Ask the more confident pupils to come to the front to take over your role.

Set learning outcomes using the task flashcards.

- Say **Today we're going to listen to a story**.
- Hold up the task flashcards in turn and elicit the activities. Stick them on one side of the board. Point to them during the lesson to reinforce your instructions.

Before you read

Explain the story title.

- (Books open.) Focus on the story title. Draw a pirate's treasure map on the board to help the pupils understand the title.

Read and answer the question.

- Read the speech bubble. The pupils scan the story to find the places. Ask them to say them.

Answers: a swimming pool, a zoo

Pupil's Book Activity 1

Listen and read. Act out.

▸ *CD3 Track 29 p268*

- The pupils place their 'magic finger' on the first frame of the story.
- Play the CD. The pupils point to the different frames as the story progresses. Pause the CD after each frame to check that all the pupils are following. Ask questions about each story frame to help and check understanding.
- Play the CD again.

Suggested comprehension questions

- Frame 1: **Where are the children?** (*In the garden.*) **Who wants to explore the town?** (*Tim.*)
- Frame 2: **What has Toby got?** (*A treasure map.*)
- Frame 3: **Where is the old tree?** (*Next to the swimming pool.*)
- Frame 4: **Where are the two big rocks?** (*In front of the zoo.*)
- Frame 5: **The children need to take 20 steps.** Mime taking steps. **Can they cross the road?** (*No.*)
- Frame 6: **Can the magic bike help?** (*Yes.*)
- Frame 7: **What do they see?** (*A green man.*) **Can they cross the road now?** (*Yes.*)
- Frame 8: **What is the treasure?** (*A big bone.*) **Is Toby happy?** (*Yes.*)
- Finally, ask the pupils **Is this a good story?** The pupils give their opinion through gesture (thumbs up / down) or orally *(yes / no).*
- Organise the class into four groups (Beth, Molly, Jake and Tim) to act out the story.
- Play the CD. Each group joins in when their character speaks. If the pupils need extra support, pause the CD after each utterance and ask them to repeat the phrase.
- The groups swap roles and join in with their new character.

Now watch the animated story

After you read

Go to page 72 in your Activity Book.

Activity Book

After you read: Activity 1

Remember the story. Read and circle *true* or *false*.

- (Books open.) Ask **Do you remember the story?**
- Invite different pupils to read out the sentences. Elicit if the sentences are true or false.
- The pupils remember the story and circle *true* or *false*.

Answers: **1** true **2** false **3** true **4** false **5** true

Activity 2

Draw a treasure map. Hide your treasure. Write.

- Explain that the pupils are going to draw their own treasure map. Draw an example on the board and describe it. Draw a cross where the treasure is.
- The pupils complete their maps and write sentences.

Recycled vocabulary

- The pupils look at the picture and write the word. If necessary, they look back at the previous unit.

Answer: bush

Pupil's Book Activity 2

Values: Read and circle.

- The pupils look at the photo on the right. Read out the sentence in the speech bubble and prompt the class to tell you the correct answer. The pupils then write the answer.
- Highlight the importance of crossing the road when the man is green.

Answer: green

Ending the lesson

Review the lesson.

- (Books closed.) Say **Today we've listened to a story about a treasure map.** Ask **What happened in the story?** Elicit the story from the pupils.
- Then say **Today you've learnt that it's important to cross the road safely.**

Review the task flashcards.

- Point to the task flashcards. Say **Look at the activities you've done today. Which activity was your favourite?** Elicit the pupils' favourite activities.

Link to Science

- If you are studying the Science topic of **My neighbourhood** in English, you could review basic road safety rules. Remind the pupils to look right, left and right again before crossing the road. Mime doing this with them.

Key Competences and Key Learning Outcomes

- Identify and name different forms of transport
- Practise asking questions
- Recognise and use numbers up to 20
- Ask and say how many objects there are
- Sing a song

Key language

- *boat, bus, helicopter, lorry, motorbike, train;* numbers 1–20 (in words and figures)
- *What is it? It's a (helicopter).*
- Extension: *metro, plane, ship, taxi*

Recycled: numbers 1–10; *grass*

Recycled: *How many (cars) are there? There are (20) cars.*

Materials

- Pupil's Book p76; Activity Book p73; Class CD3; Teacher's App on Navio
- Teacher's Resource Bank: Task flashcards: *listen, sing, Talk Partners, think, write*

Optional materials

- Teacher's Resource Bank: Five Trinity Exam Practice cards (selected from the Starter Unit and Units 1, 2, 3, 4, 5 and 6)

At a Glance Lesson Plan

Starting the lesson

- Use the Trinity Exam Practice cards (optional).
- Review the Lesson 3 story.
- Set learning outcomes using the task flashcards.

Vocabulary presentation

- Present the new vocabulary.

Activity 1

- Listen, point and say.
- ▶ *CD3 Track 30 p269*

Activity 2

- Listen and point.
- ▶ *CD3 Track 31 p269*
- Sing *How many?*

Activity 3

- Listen and repeat.
- ▶ *CD3 Track 32 p269*
- Talk Partners Play a memory game.

Go to the Activity Book.

Pupil's Book

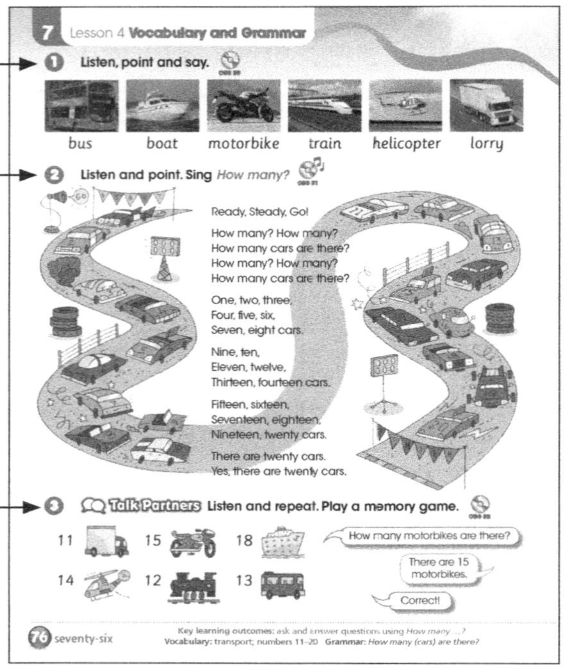

Ending the lesson

- Review the lesson.
- Review the task flashcards.

Extra activity

Vocabulary Extension

- Present four additional vocabulary items.

Cooperative learning

Listening to others

- Practise listening to classmates using a counting chain.

Digital resources

Teacher's Digital: Don't forget you can teach this lesson using the Teacher's App on Navio.

Pupil's Digital: Encourage your pupils to use the Pupil's App on Navio to practise the vocabulary from this lesson.

Powered By NAVIO

Activity Book

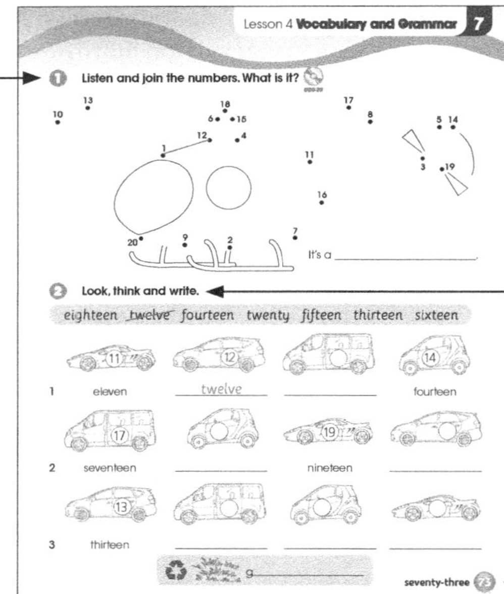

Activity Book

Activity 1

- Listen and join the numbers.
- ▶ *CD3 Track 33 p269*
- What is it?

Activity 2

- Look, think and write.

Recycled vocabulary

- Look, remember and write the word.

Detailed Lesson Plan

Starting the lesson

Use the Trinity Exam Practice cards (optional).

- The pupils practise asking and answering questions (see p31).

Review the Lesson 3 story.

- Give the pupils two minutes to look at the story. Then summarise, prompting the class for the key information. Say **Toby finds a …** *(map)*. **The children look for an …** *(old tree)*. Continue to the end of the story.

Set learning outcomes using the task flashcards.

- Say **Today we're going to learn to count to twenty, sing a song and play a game about transport.**
- Hold up the task flashcards in turn and elicit the activities. Stick them on one side of the board. Point to them during the lesson to reinforce your instructions.

Vocabulary presentation

Present the new vocabulary.

- (Books open.) Point to the first photo on the Pupil's Book and read the word. Say **Look at the bus. Let's drive a bus.** Mime driving a bus and the pupils do the same. Say the word and the pupils repeat.
- Repeat with the other forms of transport.

Pupil's Book Activity 1

Listen, point and say.

▸ *CD3 Track 30 p269*

- (Books open.) The pupils look at the photos. Say **Let's listen and say the words.**
- Play the CD. The pupils say the words and point to the pictures.
- Play *What's missing?* (without the flashcards). Read out the words but miss one out each time. Elicit the missing word.

Pupil's Book Activity 2

Listen and point. Sing *How many?*

▸ *CD3 Track 31 p269*

- Focus the pupils on Activity 2. Say **Let's count the cars**. Count as a class up to ten, then elicit / say the numbers 11–20. Ask the pupils to repeat each number with you.
- Play the CD. The pupils listen to the song and point to and count the cars.
- Play the CD again and the pupils join in with the song.

Pupil's Book Activity 3

Listen and repeat. Play a memory game.

▸ *CD3 Track 32 p269*

- Focus the class on the activity and read out the three speech bubbles. Then ask **How many helicopters are there?** Encourage the pupil who answers to answer with a full sentence. *There are fourteen.* Repeat, asking about the different vehicles and choosing a different pupil to answer each time. Then, prompt a confident pupil to ask you a question about the transport. Repeat with different pupils.
- Play the CD. The pupils listen and read.
- **Talk Partners** The pupils ask and answer with a Talk Partner, with one pupil closing the book and answering from memory. They swap roles and repeat.

Activity Book

Activity 1

Listen and join the numbers. What is it?

▸ *CD3 Track 33 p269*

- (Books open.) Explain that the pupils are going to join numbers to make a picture but the numbers aren't in order. Tell the pupils to place their pencil over number 1.
- Play the CD, pausing after each number. The pupils listen and draw a line to the next number they hear. Continue until the picture is finished. Elicit what it is.

Answer: helicopter

Activity 2

Look, think and write.

- Focus the pupils on Activity 2 and read out the numbers with the class. Point out that the number has been written on the car and on the line each time.
- Elicit the numbers that are missing for each line of cars.
- The pupils work on their own and write the missing numbers on the cars and on the lines.

Answers: **1** twelve, thirteen **2** eighteen, twenty **3** fourteen, fifteen, sixteen

Recycled vocabulary

- The pupils look at the picture and write the word. If necessary, they look back at the previous unit.

Answer: grass

Ending the lesson

Review the lesson.

- (Books closed.) Say **Today we've learnt to count to 20, sung a song and asked questions about forms of transport. What questions did we ask?** Elicit the answers from the pupils.

Review the task flashcards.

- Point to the task flashcards. Say **Look at the activities you've done today. Which activity was your favourite?** Elicit the pupils' favourite activities.

Extra activity

Vocabulary Extension

- Use the Vocabulary Booster on Navio and present and practise four additional words to describe transport: *metro, plane, ship, taxi.*

Cooperative learning

Listening to others

- Do a counting chain with the class. Say **Number 1** and prompt a pupil to say the next number. A second pupil continues the chain. Continue round the class until you reach 20. Then start again.

Key Competences and Key Learning Outcomes

- Say a tongue twister with the 'z' sound
- Listen for specific information
- Play a communication game about transport

Key language

Recycled: *bike, car, boat, bus, helicopter, lorry, motorbike, train; scooter; tree; seesaw*

Recycled: *There are (fourteen cars). There's (one helicopter).*

Materials

- Pupil's Book p77; Activity Book p74; Class CD3; Teacher's App on Navio
- Teacher's Resource Bank: Task flashcards: *listen, say, cut out, write, colour, think, Talk Partners*
- Scissors, crayons or coloured pencils
- Coloured paper
- Teacher's Resource Bank: Unit 7 Lesson 5 Activity 3 cut-outs

Optional materials

- Teacher's Resource Bank: Five Trinity Exam Practice cards (selected from the Starter Unit and Units 1, 2, 3, 4, 5 and 6)

At a Glance Lesson Plan

Starting the lesson

- Use the Trinity Exam Practice cards (optional).
- Review the vocabulary from Lesson 4.
- Review the *How many?* song
- ▶ *CD3 Track 31 p269*
- Set learning outcomes using the task flashcards.

Activity 1

- Listen and say.
- ▶ *CD3 Track 34 p269*
- Go to Magic Phonics.
- Go to the Activity Book.

Activity 2

- Listen and cross out the transport.
- ▶ *CD3 Track 35 p269*
- Say *Bingo.*

Activity 3

- Talk Partners Make the cards. Play *Bingo.*

Pupil's Book

Ending the lesson

- Review the lesson.
- Review the task flashcards.

Extra activity

Reinforcement

- Continue the pronunciation wall display.

Digital resources

Teacher's Digital: Don't forget you can teach this lesson using the Teacher's App on Navio.

Pupil's Digital: Encourage your pupils to use the Pupil's App on Navio to practise the vocabulary from this lesson.

Powered By NAVIO

Activity Book

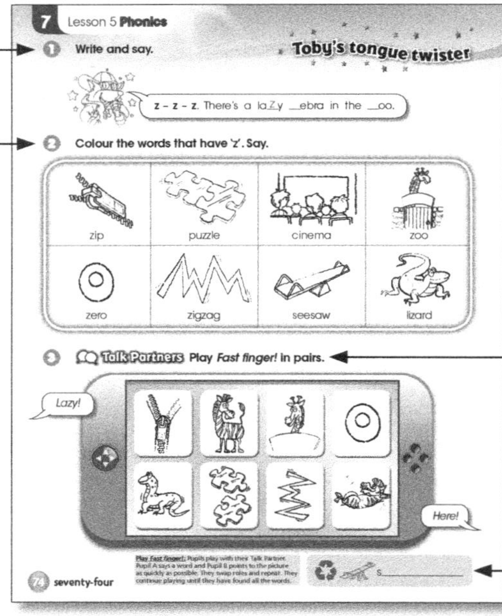

Activity Book

Activity 1

- Write and say.

Activity 2

- Colour the words that have 'z'.
- Say.

Go to Magic Phonics.

Activity 3

- Talk Partners Play *Fast finger!* in pairs.

Recycled vocabulary

- Look, remember and write the word.

Detailed Lesson Plan

Starting the lesson

Use the Trinity Exam Practice cards (optional).

- The pupils practise asking and answering questions (see p31).

Review the *How many?* song.

▸ *CD3 Track 31 p269*

- Count from 1 to 20 around the class. Allocate a number from one to twenty to each pupil. Say **Hands up number (six).**
- Next, ask the class to stand up and mime driving a car.
- Play the CD. The pupils stand up and sing. When they hear their number they sit down.

Set learning outcomes using the task flashcards.

- Say **Today we're going to practise saying a tongue twister and make and play a speaking game.**
- Hold up the task flashcards in turn and elicit the activities. Stick them on one side of the board. Point to them during the lesson to reinforce your instructions.

Pupil's Book Activity 1

Listen and say.

▸ *CD3 Track 34 p269*

- (Books open.) Write the target sound 'z' in letters on the board and say it. The pupils repeat.
- Say **It's time for Toby's tongue twister. What animal can you see? Where is the zebra? What is it doing?** Tell the class it's a lazy zebra.
- Play the CD. The pupils read the tongue twister.
- Play the CD again. The pupils say the tongue twister.

Go to Magic Phonics.

Activity Book

Activity 1

Write and say.

- (Books open.) The pupils write the letter 'z' in the tongue twister.

Answer: There's a lazy zebra in the zoo.

Activity 2

Colour the words that have 'z'. Say.

- Ask the pupils to say the words that have the 'z' sound in them. The pupils colour and say these words.

Answers: zip, puzzle, zoo, zero, zigzag, lizard

Go to Magic Phonics.

Activity 3

Play *Fast finger!* in pairs.

- Demonstrate the activity. Say a word, e.g. **lazy**.
- The pupils point to the correct picture as quickly as possible.
- Talk Partners The pupils play the game with a Talk Partner.

Recycled vocabulary

- The pupils look at the picture and write the word. If necessary, they look back at the previous unit.

Answer: seesaw

Pupil's Book Activity 2

Listen and cross out the transport. Say *Bingo*.

▸ *CD3 Track 35 p269*

- Ask **What can you see in the pictures?**
- Tell the pupils they are going to play 'Bingo'.
- Play the CD, pausing after each sentence. The pupils listen and cross out the transport they hear. When they have crossed out all the pictures, they say *Bingo!*
- Play the CD again.

Pupil's Book Activity 3

Make the cards. Play *Bingo*.

- Focus the pupils on Activity 3. Tell the class that they are going to make and play the same game.
- The pupils cut out and colour the cards and then place them on their desks.
- The pupils choose six of the ten cards. Say a sentence, e.g. **There are five buses.** If the pupils have that card, they turn it over. The winner is the first pupil to turn over all six cards. He / She shouts *Bingo!*
- Different pupils take over your role. Repeat several times.

Ending the lesson

Review the lesson.

- (Books closed.) Say **Today we've practised a tongue twister and played a game in pairs.** Elicit the tongue twister from the pupils.

Review the task flashcards.

- Point to the task flashcards. Say **Look at the activities you've done today. Which activity was your favourite?** Elicit the pupils' favourite activities.

Extra activity

Reinforcement

- Continue the pronunciation wall display. Cut out the letter 'z' in coloured paper. Stick it on a piece of differently coloured paper to make a wall display. Elicit words that begin with that letter and write them on the wall display.
- Encourage the pupils to add new words that have the letter 'z' in them during the year. They can either tell you the new word for you to add or write the word themselves if they can.

Key Competences and Key Learning Outcomes

- Classify forms of transport according to how they move (optional)
- Listen for general information
- Read about cycling in Britain
- Think about how you travel where you live

Key language
- *exercise; rickshaw; travel*
- *How do you travel in your town? I travel by (bus).*

Recycled: *bike, boat, bus, car, train; playground; town; wheels; slide;* days of the week

Recycled: *There's a (cycling class). There are (lots of bikes).*

Materials
- Pupil's Book p78; Activity Book p75; Class CD3; Teacher's App on Navio
- Places in the town flashcards
- Teacher's Resource Bank: Task flashcards: *listen, read, think, number, tick, draw, write*

Optional materials
- Teacher's Resource Bank: Five Trinity Exam Practice cards (selected from the Starter Unit and Units 1, 2, 3, 4, 5 and 6).

At a Glance Lesson Plan

Starting the lesson
- Use the Trinity Exam Practice cards (optional).
- Talk Partners Review Toby's tongue twister.
- ▶ *CD3 Track 34 p269*
- Review the *Let's go to town* song.
- ▶ *CD3 Track 24 p268*
- ▶ *CD3 Track 25 p268 (optional karaoke version)*
- Set learning outcomes using the task flashcards.

Activity 1
- Listen and read.
- ▶ *CD3 Track 36 p269*
- Answer.

Think about your culture
- How do you travel in your town?

Go to the Activity Book.

Pupil's Book

Ending the lesson
- Review the lesson.
- Review the task flashcards.

Extra activity
Reinforcement
- Review the ten places in the town.

Link to Science
- **My neighbourhood:** Review and classify forms of transport according to where and how they move.

Activity Book

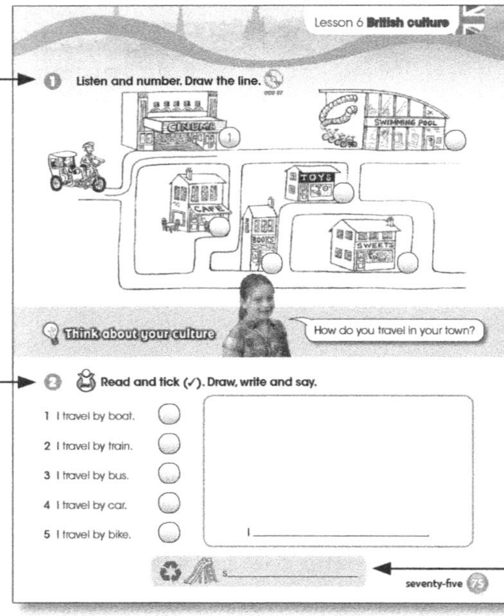

Activity Book

Activity 1
- Listen and number.
- ▶ *CD3 Track 37 p269*
- Draw the line.

Activity 2: Think about your culture
- Read and tick (✓).
- Draw, write and say.

Recycled vocabulary
- Look, remember and write the word.

Digital resources

Teacher's Digital: Don't forget you can teach this lesson using the Teacher's App on Navio.

Powered By NAVIO

Detailed Lesson Plan

Starting the lesson

Use the Trinity Exam Practice cards (optional).

- The pupils practise asking and answering questions (see p31).

Review Toby's tongue twister.

▶ *CD3 Track 34 p269*

- Ask **What sound did you practise in Toby's tongue twister? Can you remember the tongue twister?** (*There's a lazy zebra in the zoo.*)
- Play the CD. Practise the tongue twister as a class.
- **Talk Partners** The pupils practise saying the tongue twister as fast as possible in pairs. Choose a fast pair to say it for the class.

Review the *Let's go to town* song.

▶ *CD3 Track 24 p268*

▶ *CD3 Track 25 p268 (optional karaoke version)*

- Put the places in the town flashcards on the board in the order they appear in the song. Divide the class into two groups. Play the CD (or use the karaoke version). Each group sings a verse. They swap roles and repeat.

Set learning outcomes using the task flashcards.

- Say **Today we're going to learn about travelling in a town in Britain.**
- Hold up the task flashcards in turn and elicit the activities. Stick them on one side of the board. Point to them during the lesson to reinforce your instructions.

Pupil's Book Activity 1

Listen and read. Answer.

▶ *CD3 Track 36 p269*

- (Books closed.) Ask the class **How do you travel in your town? Do you travel by (car / bike / motorbike / on foot)?** Encourage the class to name the types of transport they use. Highlight the prepositions to use with each type of transport. Then say **Let's find out about cycling.**
- (Books open.) Focus the pupils on the photos and ask **What transport can you see?** Read the speech bubble.
- Say **Let's read and listen.** Play the CD, pausing after each piece of information to check understanding by asking the comprehension questions. Highlight the prepositions '<u>by</u> bike', '<u>in</u> a rickshaw'.

Suggested comprehension questions

- Photo 1: **Where are they?** (*In the school playground.*) **What class are they having?** (*A cycling class.*)
- Photo 2: **Who is on a bike? Where are they?** (*Alex, Lucy and their mum. In the town centre.*)
- Photo 3: **What is the name of this special bike?** (*A rickshaw.*) **How many wheels has it got?** (*Three.*)
- Photo 4: **Can she see her bike?** (*No.*)

Pupil's Book Think about your culture

How do you travel in your town?

- Read out the question.
- The pupils tell you how they travel in their town.
- Ask additional questions, e.g. **Do you like travelling by bike? How do you go to school? What's your favourite form of transport?**

Activity Book

Activity 1

Listen and number. Draw the line.

▶ *CD3 Track 37 p269*

- (Books open.) Focus the pupils on the map.
- Play the CD, pausing after each conversation. The pupils listen and number the pictures.
- Then they draw the line that the rickshaw takes.

Answers: **1** cinema **2** café **3** bookshop **4** sweet shop **5** toyshop **6** swimming pool

Activity 2: Think about your culture

Read and tick (✓). Draw, write and say.

- Read out the question in the speech bubble. Elicit the pupils' answers.
- Read out the first sentence. The pupils tick the box if they travel by boat in their town.
- Repeat with the other sentences.
- The pupils draw themselves on the form of transport they use and they write a sentence.
- Different pupils show the class their drawings and read their sentences.

Recycled vocabulary

- The pupils look at the picture and write the word. If necessary, they look back at the previous unit.

Answer: slide

Ending the lesson

Review the lesson.

- (Books closed.) Say **Today we've talked about travelling in a town. How do you travel? What's your favourite way to travel?** Elicit answers from the pupils.

Review the task flashcards.

- Point to the task flashcards. Say **Look at the activities you've done today. Which activity was your favourite?** Elicit the pupils' favourite activities.

Extra activity

Reinforcement

- Use the places in the town flashcards to review the ten places in the town. Then, stick the cards in different places around the classroom. Say **Let's go to the bookshop!** The pupils face and point to the corresponding flashcard. Repeat with the other flashcards. As the pupils become more confident, increase the speed of your delivery.

Link to Science

- If you are studying the Science topic of **My neighbourhood** in English, you could review the names of some common forms of transport. Review whether they travel on land, on water or in the air. Create a transport concept map on the board.

Key Competences and Key Learning Outcomes

- Write a short, personalised text
- Read for specific information
- Read and understand a fable

Key language

- *apples, bad, cheese, country, fantastic, good, life, quiet*
- *I live in the (country). I eat (apples) and (cheese).*

Recycled: *cake, ice cream; delicious; town; swing; cats; cousin*

Recycled: *I don't like (cats). I like (a quiet life).*

Materials

- Pupil's Book p79; Activity Book p76, Class CD3; Teacher's App on Navio
- Teacher's Resource Bank: Task flashcards: *think, write, listen, read, circle, draw*

Optional materials

- Farm animals flashcards; Places in the town flashcards
- Teacher's Resource Bank: Five Trinity Exam Practice cards (selected from the Starter Unit and Units 1, 2, 3, 4, 5 and 6)

At a Glance Lesson Plan

Starting the lesson

- Use the Trinity Exam Practice cards (optional).
- Review the culture lesson.
- Review farm animals vocabulary.
- Set learning outcomes using the task flashcards.

Before you read

- What is a fable?

Activity 1

- Where do you think the mice live?
- Write.

Activity 2

- Listen and read the fable.

▶ *CD3 Track 38 p269*

After you read

Go to page 76 in your Activity Book.

Pupil's Book

Ending the lesson

- Review the lesson.
- Review the task flashcards.

Extra activities

Reinforcement

- Play *Disappearing flashcards*.

Extension

- Perform the fable.

Digital resources

Teacher's Digital: Don't forget you can teach this lesson using the Teacher's App on Navio.

Pupil's Digital: Encourage your pupils to use the Pupil's App on Navio to practise the vocabulary from this lesson.

Powered By NAVIO

Activity Book

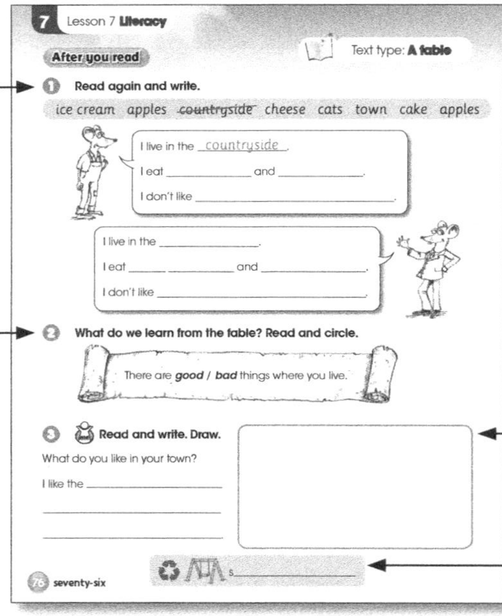

Activity Book

After you read: Activity 1

- Read again and write.

Activity 2

- What do we learn from the fable?
- Read and circle.

Activity 3

- Read and write.
- Draw.

Recycled vocabulary

- Look, remember and write the word.

Detailed Lesson Plan

Starting the lesson

Use the Trinity Exam Practice cards (optional).

- The pupils practise asking and answering questions (see p31).

Review the culture lesson.

- Mime riding a bike and elicit the form of transport.
- Ask **Do Lucy and Alex travel by helicopter in the town? By boat? How do they travel in the town? How do you travel in the town?**

Review farm animals vocabulary.

- Use the farm animals flashcards to review the names of the different animals. Describe each animal in turn and ask **What animal is it?**

Set learning outcomes using the task flashcards.

- Say **Today we're going to read a fable.**
- Hold up the task flashcards in turn and elicit the activities. Stick them on one side of the board. Point to them during the lesson to reinforce your instructions.

Before you read

What is a fable?

- Say **Today we're going to read a fable.** Explain to the class that a fable is a short story which teaches you to be good. Fables often have animals in them and the animals talk and behave like humans.

Pupil's Book Activity 1

Where do you think the mice live? Write.

- (Books open.) Point to one of the mice and ask **What animal is it?** (*A mouse*.) Highlight the irregular plural and ask the pupils to repeat the two words with you: *one mouse / two mice.* Then read out the pre-reading question and encourage the class to predict where the mice live. Confirm that the first mouse lives in the country and ask **What does this mouse eat? Where does this mouse live?** Praise the pupils for their ideas and then repeat the questions about the town mouse.
- The pupils write their answers on the lines.

Answers: country, town

Pupil's Book Activity 2

Listen and read the fable.

▶ *CD3 Track 38 p269*

- Say **Let's read a fable about a town mouse and a country mouse.** The pupils point to the title.
- Play the CD and ask the pupils to follow the text with their finger as they're reading. If necessary, pause the CD between each section of the story and scan the room to check that all the pupils are on task. Ask questions to check understanding.
- Play the CD again. The pupils listen and read.
- Optional: Play the CD again, pausing for volunteers to repeat parts of the conversation. Then, if your pupils are able to read independently, ask them to read the fable on their own.

Suggested comprehension questions

- Picture 1: **What do mice in the country eat?** (*Cheese, apples.*) **Does Town Mouse like this food?** (*No.*)
- Picture 2: **What do mice in the town eat?** (*Chocolate cake and ice cream.*) **Does Country Mouse like this food?** (*Yes.*)
- Picture 3: **What other animal lives in the house?** (*A cat.*) **Does Country Mouse like cats?** (*No.*)
- Picture 4: **Where does Country Mouse go?** (*To the country.*) **Does he like the country?** (*Yes.*)

Activity Book

After you read: Activity 1

Read again and write.

- (Books open.) Read out the words in the word box as a class. Point to the pictures and elicit who the mice are.
- The pupils write the correct words in the spaces. They can refer back to the Pupil's Book if necessary.

Answers: **1** Country Mouse: countryside, cheese, apples, cats **2** Town Mouse: town, ice cream, cake, don't like apples

Activity 2

What do we learn from the fable? Read and circle.

- Tell the pupils that a fable teaches us to be good.
- Read the sentence. The pupils remember the good things where they live and circle the word.
- Encourage the pupils to talk about the good things where they live.

Answer: good

Activity 3

Read and write. Draw.

- The pupils read the question and complete the sentence. They then draw what they like in their town.

Recycled vocabulary

- The pupils look at the picture and write the word. If necessary, they look back at the previous unit.

Answer: swing

Ending the lesson

Review the lesson.

- (Books closed.) Say **Today we've read a fable in English. Can you remember the story?** Elicit the story.

Review the task flashcards.

- Point to the task flashcards. Say **Look at the activities you've done today. Which activity was your favourite?** Elicit the pupils' favourite activities.

Extra activity

Reinforcement

- Play *Disappearing flashcards* (see p23) with the places in the town flashcards.

Extension

- The pupils perform the fable from Pupil's Book Activity 2. Divide the class into two groups, one for each mouse.
- Read out the speech bubbles and the pupils repeat their part.
- Set up the scenes in the classroom. Ask two volunteers to act out the fable whilst you or a confident pupil reads the narrative.

Key Competences and Key Learning Outcomes

- Review language in the unit
- Reflect on own learning
- Sing a cooperative learning song

Key language

Recycled: *bookshop, café, cinema, hospital, restaurant, sweet shop, swimming pool, supermarket, toyshop, zoo; wheels; rock*; numbers 11–20

Recycled: *There's a (café) in the town. There are (sixteen) wheels. How many (cinemas) are there? There are (three cinemas).*

Materials

- Pupil's Book p80; Activity Book p77; Class CD3; Teacher's App on Navio
- Places in the town flashcards
- Teacher's Resource Bank: Task flashcards: *listen, number, write, think, read, sing*
- Teacher's Resource Bank: Traffic light cut-out
- *Give Me Five!* sticker

Optional materials

- Teacher's Resource Bank: Five Trinity Exam Practice cards (selected from the Starter Unit and Units 1, 2, 3, 4, 5 and 6)

At a Glance Lesson Plan

Starting the lesson

- Use the Trinity Exam Practice cards (optional).
- Review the unit vocabulary.
- Set learning outcomes using the task flashcards.

Activity 1

- Listen and number.
- ▶ *CD3 Track 39 p269*
- Write and say.

Activity 2

- What can you see in your classroom?
- Read, count and answer.

Activity 3 Cooperative learning

- Sing *Well done!*
- ▶ *CD3 Track 40 p270*
- Stick the *Give Me Five!* sticker.
- Go to the Activity Book.

Pupil's Book

Ending the lesson

- Review the task flashcards.

Cooperative learning

- **Think-Pair-Share** Review places in the town.

Activity Book

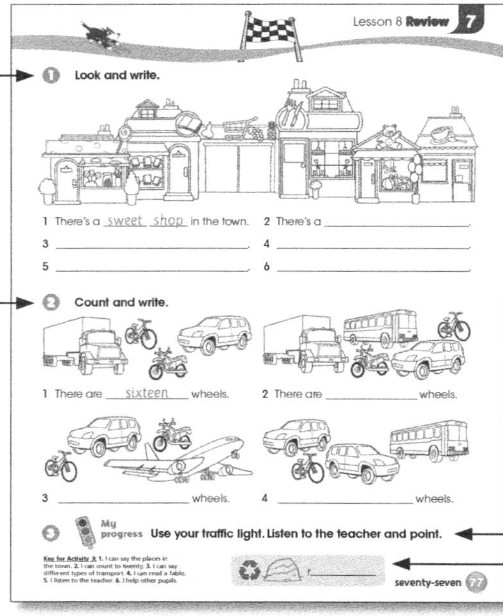

Activity Book

Activity 1
- Look and write.

Activity 2
- Count and write.

Activity 3 My progress
- Use your traffic light. Listen to the teacher and point.

Recycled vocabulary
- Look, remember and write the word.

Digital resources

Teacher's Digital: Don't forget you can teach this lesson using the Teacher's App on Navio.

Pupil's Digital: Encourage your pupils to use the Pupil's App on Navio to practise the vocabulary from this lesson.

Starting the lesson

Use the Trinity Exam Practice cards (optional).
- The pupils practise asking and answering questions (see p31).

Review the unit vocabulary.
- Hold up a places in the town flashcard and elicit the word. Stick the flashcard face down on the board. Repeat until all the flashcards are on the board.
- Ask **Where's the (sweet shop)?** Ask a pupil to come to the front and turn over one of the flashcards. If it's the correct flashcard, he / she says *It's here*. If it isn't the correct flashcard, another pupil has a turn. Repeat with different places in the town words and different pupils.
- Variation: Play the game in two teams. The teams take it in turns to remember the places in a town.

Set learning outcomes using the task flashcards.
- Say **Today we're going to remember what we've learnt in Unit 7.**
- Hold up the task flashcards in turn and elicit the activities. Stick them on one side of the board. Point to them during the lesson to reinforce your instructions.

Pupil's Book Activity 1

Listen and number. Write and say.
▶ *CD3 Track 39 p269*
- (Books open.) Focus the pupils on the photos.
- Play the CD, pausing after each sentence. The pupils listen and write the correct numbers in the circles.
- Play the CD again. This time the pupils write the words under the photos.
- To check answers, point to a picture and ask different pupils to read out the words they have written.

Answers: **1** restaurant **2** swimming pool **3** supermarket **4** toyshop **5** cinema **6** hospital **7** sweet shop **8** bookshop **9** zoo **10** café

Pupil's Book Activity 2

What can you see in your classroom? Read, count and answer.
- Focus the pupils on the questions in Activity 2.
- Ask a pupil to count the items in the classroom and complete the first answer.
- The pupils complete the sentences on their own.

Pupil's Book Activity 3: Cooperative learning

Sing *Well done!*
▶ *CD3 Track 40 p270*
- Praise the pupils for their hard work and encourage them to praise each other. Play the *Well done!* song. The pupils sing and do the actions.

Stick the *Give Me Five!* sticker.
- The pupils stick the *Give Me Five!* sticker on the Pupil's Book page.
- Variation: Sing the *Well done!* song and stick the *Give Me Five!* sticker after the class has also completed the Activity Book Lesson 8 Review.

Activity Book

Activity 1
Look and write.
- The pupils look at the picture. Elicit the places in the town.
- The pupils write and read out the sentences on their own.

Answers: **1** sweet shop **2** bookshop in the town **3** There's a supermarket in the town. **4** There's a restaurant in the town. **5** There's a toyshop in the town. **6** There's a café in the town.

Activity 2
Count and write.
- Draw a wheel on the board and say the word **wheel.**
- The pupils complete the sentences.

Answers: **1** sixteen **2** twenty **3** There are eighteen **4** There are fourteen

Activity 3: My progress

My progress

Use your traffic light. Listen to the teacher and point.
- (Books closed.) Ask the class to take out their traffic light cut-out. Say **Let's think about our work in this unit.** Point to the green circle, nod your head, smile a lot, and say **I can say the places in the town. Yes, I can do this very well.** Point to the yellow circle, move your head a little, smile a little and say **Yes, I can do this.** Then point to the red circle, shake your head and say **No, I can't do this.**
- Read the different statements. For each one, the pupils point to the colour on their traffic light that shows how they feel about their own learning.

Self-assessment statements
1. I can say the places in the town.
2. I can count to twenty.
3. I can say different types of transport.
4. I can read a fable.
5. I listen to the teacher.
6. I help other pupils.

Recycled vocabulary
- The pupils look at the picture and write the word. If necessary, they look back at the previous unit.

Answer: rock

Ending the lesson

Review the task flashcards.
- Point to the task flashcards. Say **Look at the activities you've done today. Which activity was your favourite?** Elicit the pupils' favourite activities.

Cooperative learning

Think-Pair-Share
- Ask **Can you remember the ten places in the town?** The pupils think on their own for one minute.
- **Talk Partners** The pupils work with a Talk Partner to name all ten flashcards. Ask a pair to say one of the places in the town. Hold up the corresponding flashcard and prompt the class to repeat the word.

Key Competences and Key Learning Outcomes

- Watch and understand a video about transport
- Read and understand digital maps
- Draw, say and write what places are near to where you live

Key language
- *behind, bike, bus, café, cinema, hospital, near, next to, on, park, playground, restaurant, rickshaw, supermarket, swimming pool, zoo*

Materials
- Pupil's Book p81; Activity Book p78; Class CD3; Video; Teacher's App on Navio
- Teacher's Resource Bank: Task flashcards: *number, read, tick, circle, listen, think, draw, Talk Partners*

Optional materials
- Teacher's Resource Bank: Trinity Exam Practice cards (selected from Unit 7)

At a Glance Lesson Plan

Pupil's Book

Starting the lesson
- Use the Trinity Exam Practice cards (optional).
- **Think-Pair-Share** Grouping types of transport.
- Set learning outcomes and use the task flashcards.

Pre-watching activity
- Predict the types of transport in the video.

Activity 1
- Watch the video.
  Unit 7 video p278
- Number the pictures.

Activity 2
- Watch the video again.
  Unit 7 video
- Read and tick (✓) or cross (✗).

Activity 3
- Read and circle.
  Go to the Activity Book.

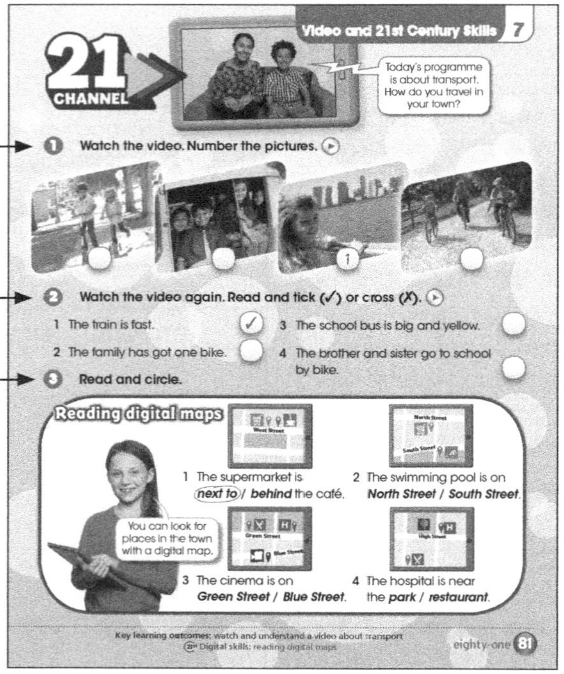

Ending the lesson
- Review the lesson.
- Review the task flashcards. Elicit the pupils' favourite activities.

Extra activity
- Pupils work in pairs to say where places in a town are.

Digital resources

Teacher's Digital: Don't forget you can teach this lesson using the Teacher's App on Navio.

Pupil's Digital: Encourage your pupils to use the Pupil's App on Navio to practise the vocabulary from this lesson.

Powered By NAVIO

Activity Book

Activity Book

Activity 1
- Listen and number the places on the digital map.
- ▶ *CD3 Track 41 p270*

Activity 2
- Read, think and write. Draw a map. Say.

Recycled vocabulary
- Look, remember and write the word.

Starting the lesson

Use the Trinity Exam Practice cards (optional).

- The pupils practise asking and answering questions.

Review types of transport.

- Write the heading Types of transport on the board. Ask pupils to tell you all the types they know and write them under the heading.
- **Think-Pair-Share** In pairs, the pupils think about how they can group the types of transport for example ones with two wheels. Invite pairs to share their groupings to the class and explain why.

Set learning outcomes and use the task flashards.

- Say **Today we're going to watch a video and then ask and answer questions about transport**.
- Point to the task flashcards throughout to elicit activities and reinforce your instructions.

Pre-watching activity

- Ask the pupils to read the speech bubble. Ask **How do you travel in your town?** Elicit answers from the pupils and write them on the board.

Pupil's Book Activity 1

Watch the video. Number the pictures. *p278*

- Play Part 1. Pause after Abby says, *Let's see how other children travel*. Ask **How do Tom and Sophie travel to school?** *(Bus and bike.)*
- Focus the pupils' attention on the video stills. Ask **Which types of transport do you use?**
- Play Part 2 of the video, pausing after the first video still. Ask the pupils to point to the corresponding photo in their book.
- Play the rest of the video for pupils to point to the photos in order.
- Play Part 2 again for pupils to write the numbers in order of the photos.
- Ask **Do the children all travel to school the same way? Which way is the most unusual way to travel? How do you travel to school?**

Answers: 3, 4, 1, 2

Pupil's Book Activity 2

Watch the video again. Read and tick (✓) or cross (✗).

- Read out the first sentence. Ask **Is the train fast?**
- Play the video. Pupils tick or cross the sentences.
- Ask the pupils to look at the sentences they crossed and ask them to correct them.
- Ask general questions to check understanding.
  Who travels by boat? *(A girl.)*
  What has the boy on the train got? *(A computer game.)*
  Are the children on the bus sad? *(No, happy.)*
  How many wheels are there on the rickshaw? *(Four.)*
  What is on the phone? *(A map.)*
  Has Abby got a map on her tablet? *(Yes.)*

Answers: 1 ✓ 2 ✗ 3 ✓ 4 ✗

Pupil's Book Activity 3

Read and circle.

- On the board copy the icons for the hospital, swimming pool, cinema and supermarket. Ask **What are these places in town?** To review directions, draw a simple map and stick three of the places in town flashcards on the map. Ask the pupils to describe where they are, make sure you include near, on, next to and behind.
- The pupils read the sentences and circle the words.

Think-Pair-Share Read out the speech bubble. Ask **Do you use digital maps?**

- Ask **If you want to find a place in town, and you don't have a map, what can you do?** *(Ask for directions, get a map from the tourist office.)*

Answers: **1** next to **2** South Street **3** Blue Street **4** park

Activity Book

Activity 1

Listen and number the places on the digital map.

▶ *CD3 Track 41 p270*

- The pupils look at the digital map. Ask **Where's the playground / restaurant / supermarket / swimming pool / zoo?** Encourage the pupils to use the prepositions of place. Ask the pupils to listen to the CD and point to places as they hear them.
- Play the first exchange on the CD. Ask **What place are they talking about?** Play the rest of the CD, pausing after each exchange, for pupils to number the pictures.

Answers: **1** zoo in the park **2** cinema next to swimming pool **3** toy shop next to the supermarket **4** bookshop near the restaurant

Activity 2

Read, think and write. Draw a map. Say.

- Ask a few pupils **What places are near your house?**
- On the board, write three sentences about places that are near your house, for example, *There's a park behind my house.* Stick the places in town word cards on the board as an additional reference. The pupils write sentences about the places near their house and then draw a map.
- **Talk Partners** Pupils take turns to talk about which places are close to their house.

Recycled vocabulary

Answers: climbing frame

Ending the lesson

Review the lesson.

- Ask **Which activity was easy / difficult?**

Review the task flashcards.

- Say **Which activity was your favourite?**

Extra activity

Extension

- Ask the pupils to look at the map again in Activity 1 in their Activity book. Tell them to choose three more places in town and draw icons for the places on the map. Divide the pupils into pairs and assign them A and B. Tell A to close their book and B to look at the map in Activity 1. Explain that pupil A has to describe where their three new places are for pupil B to draw them on the map.

Date: ______________ Unit: ________

1 **What did my pupils learn in this unit?**

____

____

____

____

2 **How did my pupils work? (✓)**

individually ☐ in pairs ☐ in small groups ☐

in large groups ☐ as a class ☐

3 **Which key competences did my pupils develop?**

- Competence in linguistic communication ☐
- Competence in mathematics, science and technology ☐
- Digital competence ☐
- Learning to learn ☐
- Social and civic competences ☐
- Sense of initiative and entrepreneurship ☐
- Cultural awareness and expression ☐

4 **Which lessons / activities were the most successful and why?**

____

____

____

____

5 **Which lessons / activities did my pupils find the most difficult and why?**

____

____

____

____

6 **What did I try in the classroom for the first time? How did it go?**

____

____

____

____

7 **Which resources did I find most useful? (including webpages)**

____

____

____

____

____

8 **What could I do differently next time I teach this unit?**

____

____

____

____

Unit 8

Camping fun!

Key Competences and Key Learning Outcomes

- Identify and say ten items of clothing (Lesson 1)
- Say the vocabulary chant (Lesson 1)
- Use present continuous in a conversation (Lesson 2 and Lesson 4)
- Read and complete a postcard (Lesson 7)
- Watch and understand a video about camping (Video and 21st Century Skills)
- Say what the weather is like (Video and 21st Century Skills)

- Recognise which clothes we wear when it's hot or cold (Lesson 2)

- Use the Pupil's App on Navio

- Practise spelling (Lesson 1)
- Say a tongue twister to practise the 'v' sound (Lesson 5)
- Review language from the unit and reflect on own learning (Lesson 8)
- Practise activity types found in the Cambridge English Young Learners Exams: Pre A1 Starters

- Understand the importance of safety near water (Lesson 3)
- Understand the importance of thinking before choosing (Video and 21st Century Skills)

- Work with a Talk Partner to practise and reinforce learning (all lessons)
- Play a communication game about what people are doing (Lesson 5)

- Sing four songs (Lessons 1, 4, 6 and 8)
- Understand and act out a story (Lesson 3)
- Read about camping in Britain (Lesson 6)
- Sing and enjoy a traditional camp song (Lesson 6)
- Think about what activities you do (Lesson 6)

Vocabulary

Core vocabulary:
shirt, shoes, shorts, skirt, sweater, swimsuit, sun hat, trainers, trousers, T-shirt; play the guitar, play volleyball, ride a horse, sail a boat, sing songs

Extension vocabulary (optional)
dress, coat, jacket, jeans, scarf, tracksuit; draw a picture, play games on my tablet, play the piano, watch television

Other vocabulary
dangerous, flag, forest, lake; camel, camp, ghost stories, go camping, hump, funny, scary, sea, sleeping bag, tent; beautiful, campsite, postcard; paint a picture

Recycled vocabulary
bookshop, café, cinema, hospital, restaurant, sweet shop, supermarket, toyshop, zoo; fun, lake, swim

Structures

Core structures
What are you wearing? I'm wearing (shorts) and (a T-shirt). What is he / she wearing? He / She is wearing (a T-shirt). What's he / she doing? He's / She's (sailing a boat).

Other structures
He's / She's (riding a horse). It's dangerous. I'm sorry. He's having fun! Camping is great. We sleep in our sleeping bags. We camp in the garden. We sing songs. We tell ghost stories.

Recycled structures
Let's (swim in the lake). You can / can't (swim today). There are (lots of fun activities). There's a (lake). What colour (is / are) your (sweater / trousers)? (It / They) (is / are) purple. Where (is the dog)? It's (near the tree). How many (flowers) are there? There are (five flowers).

Phonics

Consonant sound 'v' (**V**icky, **v**et, lo**v**es, **v**olleyball)

British Culture

Camping in the garden

Literacy

Text type: a postcard (text to express)
Reading skills: using visual clues; reading for specific information

21st Century Skills

Ways of thinking: learn to think before you choose

Cooperative learning

Song: *Well done!* (Lesson 8)
Skills: Working together and supporting each other (Lesson 1); Raising your hand (Lesson 4); Think-Pair-Share (Lesson 8)

Values

Understanding the importance of safety near water

Cross-curricular links

Links to Science
Landscapes: human and physical elements in the environment; the importance of suitable clothing in different weather

Suggested Arts and Crafts concepts
Landscapes: creating landscapes

Key Competences and Key Learning Outcomes

- Identify and say ten items of clothing
- Ask and say what people are wearing
- Say the vocabulary chant
- Stick the clothes stickers

- Identify human and physical elements in a landscape (optional)

- Practise spelling

- Sing a song about clothes

Key language
- *shirt, shoes, shorts, skirt, sweater, swimsuit, sun hat, trainers, trousers, T-shirt*
- *What are you wearing? I'm wearing (shorts) and (a T-shirt).*
- Extension: *dress, coat, jacket, jeans, scarf, tracksuit*
- **Recycled:** colours; *cinema, zoo*

Materials
- Pupil's Book p82; Activity Book pp80 and 89; Class CD3; Teacher's App on Navio
- Clothes flashcards; Unit 8 stickers
- Teacher's Resource Bank: Clothes word cards
- Teacher's Resource Bank: Task flashcards: *listen, sing, read, match, stick, Talk Partners, colour, find, circle, write*

Optional materials
- Teacher's Resource Bank: Five Trinity Exam Practice cards (selected from the Starter Unit and Units 1, 2, 3, 4, 5, 6 and 7).

At a Glance Lesson Plan

Starting the lesson
- Use the Trinity Exam Practice cards (optional).
- Review parts of the body.
- Set learning outcomes using the task flashcards.

Vocabulary presentation
- Present the new vocabulary.

Activity 1
- Listen and point.
- ▶ *CD3 Track 42 p270*
- Sing *What are you wearing?*

Word cards
- Read the word cards.
- Match them to the flashcards.

Activity 2
- Read and stick the ten stickers.
- Listen and say the chant.
- ▶ *CD3 Track 44 p270*
- Go to the Activity Book.

Learning to learn
Spelling
- Practise spelling at any time during this unit (Activity Book p89).

Pupil's Book

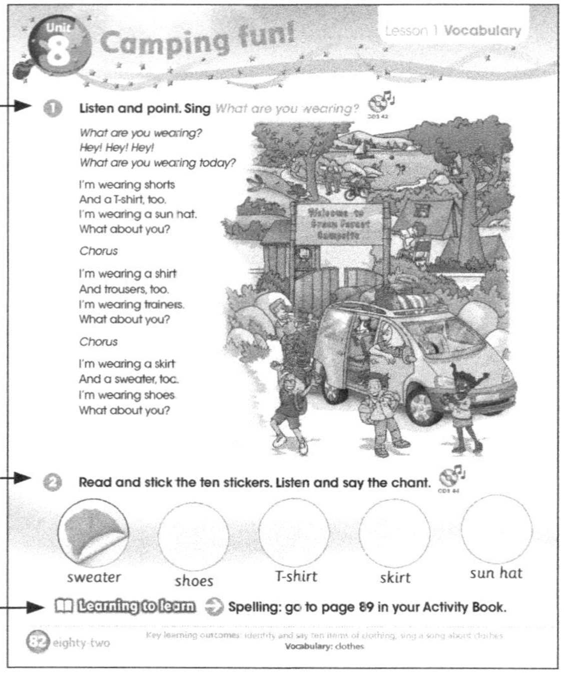

Ending the lesson
- Review the lesson.
- Review the task flashcards.

Extra activity
Vocabulary Extension
- Present six additional vocabulary items.

Cooperative learning
Working together and supporting each other
- Talk Partners Ask and answer *What's this?*

Link to Science
- **Landscapes:** Identify and differentiate between human and physical elements in a landscape.

Digital resources

Teacher's Digital: Don't forget you can teach this lesson using the Teacher's App on Navio.

Pupil's Digital: Encourage your pupils to use the Pupil's App on Navio to practise the vocabulary from this lesson.

Powered By NAVIO

Activity Book

Activity Book
Activity 1
- Read, match and colour.

Activity 2
- Find and circle.
- Write.

Recycled vocabulary
- Look, remember and write the word.

Spelling
Let's practise spelling!
- Use the *Look-Copy-Cover-Write* technique.

Recycled vocabulary
- Look, remember and write the word.

Detailed Lesson Plan

Starting the lesson

Use the Trinity Exam Practice cards (optional).

- The pupils practise asking and answering questions (see p31).

Review parts of the body.

- Say **Touch your (head), (legs) and (toes).** The pupils listen and do the actions.
- Repeat several times and in random order, increasing the speed as the pupils become more confident.

Set learning outcomes using the task flashcards.

- Say **Today we're going to learn the names of clothes.** Hold up the task flashcards in turn and elicit the activities. Stick them on one side of the board. Point to them during the lesson to reinforce your instructions.

Vocabulary presentation

Present the new vocabulary.

- (Books closed.) Hold up the *shoes* flashcard without the pupils seeing the picture. Say **I wear these on my feet.** Elicit the word and the class repeats.
- Say **Put on our shoes.** The class mimes the action. Stick the flashcard on the board and repeat with the other clothes flashcards.
- When all the clothes flashcards are on the board, point to each one. The pupils say the word.

Pupil's Book Activity 1

Listen and point. Sing *What are you wearing?*

▶ *CD3 Track 42 p270*

- (Books open.) Ask **Where are the children? What clothes is (Molly) wearing?**
- Play the CD. The pupils listen and point to the different clothes in the picture.
- Play the CD again. The pupils sing and do the actions.

Word cards

Read the word cards. Match them to the flashcards.

- (Books closed.) Hold up the clothes word cards in turn, and say or elicit each word.
- Different pupils come to the front and stick the word cards with the corresponding flashcards.

Pupil's Book Activity 2

Read and stick the ten stickers. Listen and say the chant.

▶ *CD3 Track 44 p270*

- (Books open.) Ask a pupil to read the first item of clothing. The pupils stick the corresponding sticker. Repeat with the other stickers.
- Play the CD. The pupils listen and say the chant, pointing to the stickers in turn.

Activity Book

Activity 1

Read, match and colour.

- (Books open.) Different pupils read out the phrases.
- The pupils match the phrases with the correct part of the picture. Then they colour the clothes.

Activity 2

Find and circle. Write.

- Point to the example circled in the word search. Read out the word and point to the picture.
- The pupils find and circle the words. Then they write the words under the correct pictures.

Answers: **1** sun hat **2** trousers **3** skirt **4** sweater **5** swimsuit **6** shoes

Recycled vocabulary

- The pupils look at the picture and write the word. If necessary, they look back at the previous unit.

Answer: zoo

Ending the lesson

Review the lesson.

- (Books closed.) Say **Today we've learnt the names of clothes. What words do you remember?**

Review the task flashcards.

- Point to the task flashcards. Say **Look at the activities you've done today. Which activity was your favourite?** Elicit the pupils' favourite activities.

Extra activity

Vocabulary Extension

- Use the Vocabulary Booster on Navio to present and practise six additional words describing clothes: *dress, coat, jacket, jeans, scarf, tracksuit.*

Cooperative learning

Working together and supporting each other

- **Talk Partners** Pupil A points to a clothes sticker and asks *What's this?* Pupil B answers using *It's a …* If Pupil B can't remember, Pupil A helps him / her.
- When Pupil B has named the ten items of clothing, they swap roles and repeat.

Link to Science

- If you are studying the Science topic of **Landscapes** in English, you could ask the pupils to look through the unit and find examples of human and physical elements in a landscape. They will be able to see a forest, a lake and a mountain.

Spelling (Activity Book page 89)

Let's practise spelling!

- The pupils can practise spelling the ten items of clothing using the *Look-Copy-Cover-Write* technique at any time during this unit before the Lesson 8 Review.

Recycled vocabulary

- The pupils look at the picture and write the word. If necessary, they look back at the previous unit.

Answer: cinema

Key Competences and Key Learning Outcomes

- Use present continuous
- Complete and practise a conversation
- Ask and say what people are wearing

- Listen for specific information

Key language

- *cold, hot*
- *Is it (cold)? Yes, it is. No, it isn't. What's the weather like today? It's (hot).*

Recycled: *shirt, shoes, skirt, sun hat, swimsuit, trainers, trousers, T-shirt; café*

Recycled: *What are you wearing? I'm wearing (shorts) and (a T-shirt).*

Materials

- Pupil's Book p83; Activity Book p81; Class CD3; Teacher's App on Navio
- Clothes flashcards
- Teacher's Resource Bank: Task flashcards: *listen, act out, match, read, follow, write, draw, Talk Partners*

Optional materials

- Teacher's Resource Bank: Five Trinity Exam Practice cards (selected from the Starter Unit and Units 1, 2, 3, 4, 5, 6 and 7)

At a Glance Lesson Plan

Starting the lesson

- Use the Trinity Exam Practice cards (optional).
- Review the clothes vocabulary.
- Review the *What are you wearing?* song.
- ▶ ***CD3 Track 42 p270***
- ▶ ***CD3 Track 43 p270 (optional karaoke version)***
- Set learning outcomes using the task flashcards.

Activity 1

- Listen and repeat.
- ▶ ***CD3 Track 45 p270***
- Act out.

Activity 2

- Listen and match.
- ▶ ***CD3 Track 46 p270***
- Go to the Activity Book.

Pupil's Book

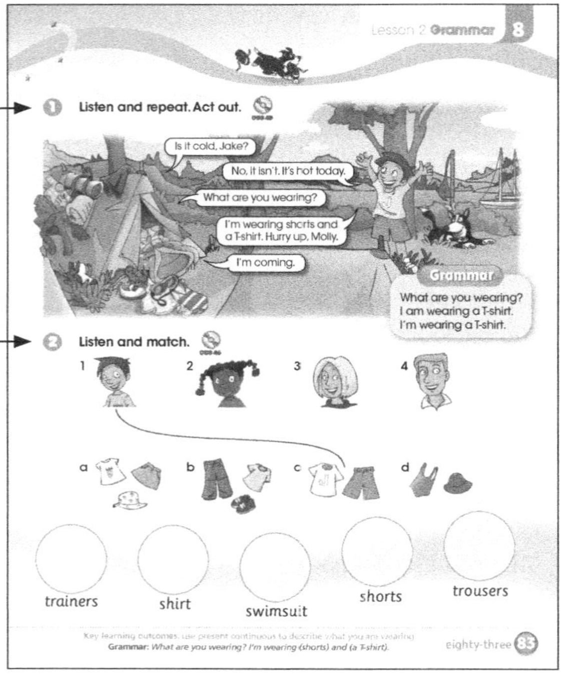

Ending the lesson

- Review the lesson.
- Review the task flashcards.

Extra activities

Reinforcement

- Do a classification activity.
- Play a moving game.

Digital resources

Teacher's Digital: Don't forget you can teach this lesson using the Teacher's App on Navio.

Pupil's Digital: Encourage your pupils to use the Pupil's App on Navio to practise the vocabulary from this lesson.

Powered By NAVIO

Activity Book

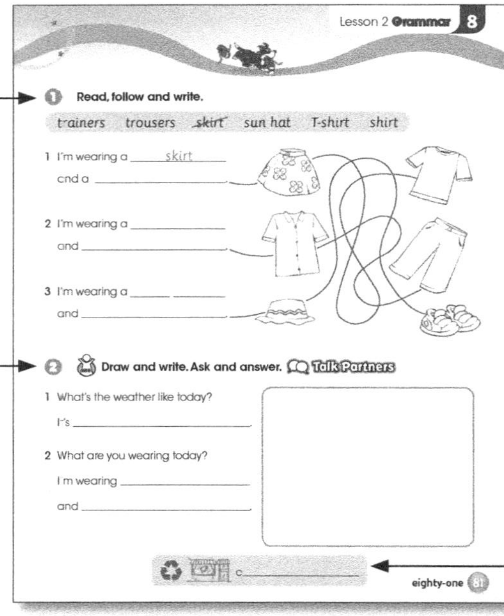

Activity Book

Activity 1

- Read, follow and write.

Activity 2

- Draw and write.
- Talk Partners Ask and answer.

Recycled vocabulary

- Look, remember and write the word.

Detailed Lesson Plan

Starting the lesson

Use the Trinity Exam Practice cards (optional).

- The pupils practise asking and answering questions (see p31).

Review the clothes vocabulary.

- Use the clothes flashcards to review the clothes. Play *Silent words* with the class (see p23).

Review the *What are you wearing?* song.

▶ *CD3 Track 42 p270*

▶ *CD3 Track 43 p270 (optional karaoke version)*

- Ask three pupils to come to the front of the class. Give each pupil the flashcards that correspond to a verse. Play the CD (or use the karaoke version). The pupils hold up the flashcards when they hear the words. Repeat several times.

Set learning outcomes using the task flashcards.

- Say **Today we're going to talk about the clothes you are wearing.**
- Hold up the task flashcards in turn and elicit the activities. Stick them on one side of the board. Point to them during the lesson to reinforce your instructions.

Pupil's Book Activity 1

Listen and repeat. Act out.

▶ *CD3 Track 45 p270*

- (Books open.) Point to the characters in the picture. Ask **Where are Molly and Jake?** (*At a campsite.*) **What is Jake wearing?** (*Shorts and a T-shirt.*)
- Play the CD. The pupils listen and read the conversation.
- Ask **What's the weather like?** (*It's hot.*)
- Play the CD again, pausing after each sentence for the pupils to repeat.
- Ask different pupils to come to the front and act out the conversation.

Pupil's Book Activity 2

Listen and match.

▶ *CD3 Track 46 p270*

- Focus the pupils on Activity 2. Point to the characters and say **Let's listen to what they say.**
- Play the CD. The pupils listen and draw lines from the characters to the clothing. Pause the CD after each conversation to allow the pupils time to do the activity.
- Play the CD again. The pupils say the answers.

Answers: **1** c **2** a **3** d **4** b

Activity Book

Activity 1

Read, follow and write.

- (Books open.) Read the words in the box as a class. Then focus the pupils on the pictures.
- Read the first sentence and ask the pupils to follow the line with their finger to find the second item of clothing.
- Then ask a pupil to complete the sentence with the correct word.
- The pupils complete the activity on their own.

Answers: **1** skirt, T-shirt **2** shirt, trousers **3** sun hat, trainers

Activity 2

Draw and write. Ask and answer.

- The pupils say what the weather is like today and what they are wearing. Write new vocabulary on the board.
- The pupils work on their own and complete the sentences. Then they draw a picture of themselves in the clothes they are wearing.
- **Talk Partners** The pupils ask and answer the questions with a Talk Partner and show each other their drawings.

Recycled vocabulary

- The pupils look at the picture and write the word. If necessary, they look back at the previous unit.

Answer: café

Ending the lesson

Review the lesson.

- (Books closed.) Say **Today we've talked about the clothes you are wearing and acted out a conversation. Did you work well today?** Elicit answers from the pupils.

Review the task flashcards.

- Point to the task flashcards. Say **Look at the activities you've done today. Which activity was your favourite?** Elicit the pupils' favourite activities.

Extra activities

Reinforcement

- Divide the board into two sections and hand out the clothes flashcards. Tell the pupils to place the flashcards of the clothes they wear on the top half of their bodies on the right-hand side of the board. On the left-hand side, they place the flashcards of the clothes they wear on the bottom half of their bodies.
- Play a moving game with the class. Say **Are you wearing (trousers)? Stand up!**
- Repeat with different clothes and different actions each time.

Key Competences and Key Learning Outcomes

- Read, listen and understand a story about an activity camp
- Read the story with some fluency
- Review the importance of safety rules on holiday (optional)
- Become familiar with the story through a pre-reading task
- Understand the importance of safety near water
- Understand and act out the story
- Give an opinion on the story

Key language

- *bookshop; fun, swim; cold, hot*
- *He's (sailing a boat). She's (riding a horse). I'm wearing (trousers). What's the weather like? It's (raining). Let's (swim in the lake). You can / can't (swim today).*

Recycled: *activities, dangerous, flag, lake, ride a horse, sail a boat; raining, sunny, windy*

Materials

- Pupil's Book pp84–85; Activity Book p82; Class CD3; Teacher's App on Navio
- Teacher's Resource Bank: Task flashcards: *think, listen, read, act out, write, circle, colour*
- Teacher's Resource Bank: Unit 8 Lesson 3 Animated Story
- Crayons or coloured pencils

Optional materials

- Teacher's Resource Bank: Five Trinity Exam Practice cards (selected from the Starter Unit and Units 1, 2, 3, 4, 5, 6 and 7)

At a Glance Lesson Plan

Pupil's Book

Starting the lesson

- Use the Trinity Exam Practice cards (optional).
- Talk Partners Review the language from Lesson 2.
- Set learning outcomes using the task flashcards.

Before you read

- Explain the story title.
- Read and answer the question.

Activity 1

- Listen and read.
- ▶ *CD3 Track 47 p270*
- Act out.
- ▶ ***Now watch the animated story!***

After you read: Activity 2

- Go to p82 in your Activity Book.
- Values: Read and write.

Ending the lesson

- Review the lesson.
- Review the task flashcards.

Link to Science

- **Landscapes:** Review the importance of basic safety rules on holiday.

Activity Book

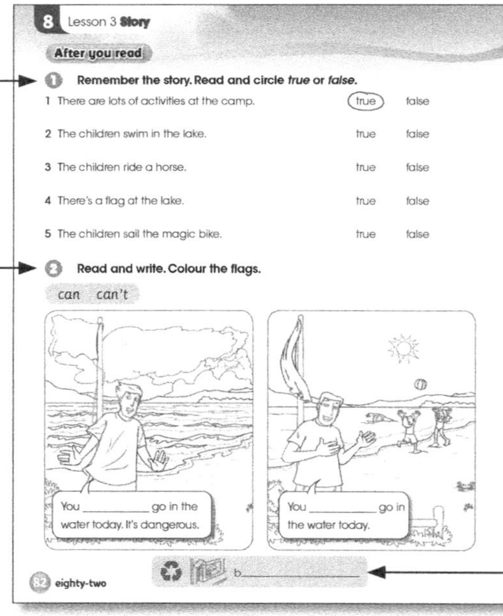

Activity Book

After you read: Activity 1

- Remember the story. Read and circle *true* or *false*.

Activity 2

- Read and write.
- Colour the flags.

Recycled vocabulary

- Look, remember and write the word.

Digital resources

Teacher's Digital: Don't forget you can teach this lesson using the Teacher's App on Navio.

Pupil's Digital: Encourage your pupils to use the Pupil's App on Navio to practise the vocabulary from this lesson.

Powered By NAVIO

Detailed Lesson Plan

Starting the lesson

Use the Trinity Exam Practice cards (optional).

- The pupils practise asking and answering questions (see p31).

Review the language from Lesson 2.

- Ask **What are you wearing today?** The pupils answer in complete sentences.
- Talk Partners The pupils ask and answer the question with a Talk Partner.

Set learning outcomes using the task flashcards.

- Say **Today we're going to listen to a story in English.**
- Hold up the task flashcards in turn and elicit the activities. Stick them on one side of the board. Point to them during the lesson to reinforce your instructions.

Before you read

Explain the story title.

- (Books open.) Focus on the story title. Elicit what activities you can do at an activity camp.

Read and answer the question.

- Read the speech bubble. The pupils scan the story to find the different types of weather.

Answers: **Frame 1:** sunny **Frame 2:** hot **Frame 3:** windy **Frame 4:** cold and raining **Frame 5:** raining **Frames 6–8:** hot and sunny

Pupil's Book Activity 1

Listen and read. Act out.

▶ *CD3 Track 47 p270*

- The pupils place their 'magic finger' on the first frame of the story.
- Play the CD. The pupils point to the different frames as the story progresses. Pause the CD after each frame to check that all the pupils are following and ask questions to help and check understanding.
- Play the CD again.

Suggested comprehension questions

- Frame 1: **Where are the children?** (*At an activity camp.*) **Can they go horse riding?** (*Yes.*) **Can they go sailing?** (*Yes.*)
- Frame 2: **Does Beth want to swim in the lake?** (*Yes.*) **What does she need?** (*Her swimsuit.*)
- Frame 3: **Can the children swim in the lake?** (*No.*) **Why not?** (*It's dangerous.*)
- Frame 4: **What does Jake want to do?** (*Ride a horse.*)
- Frame 5: **Can the children ride a horse?** (*No.*) **Why not?** (*It's raining.*)
- Frame 6: **What's the weather like the next day?** (*Hot and sunny.*) **What does Jake want to do?** (*Sail a boat.*)
- Frame 7: **Can the children sail a boat?** (*No.*) **Why not?** (*It isn't windy.*)
- Frame 8: **Does the magic bike help the children?** (*Yes.*) **Can they sail now?** (*Yes.*)
- Finally, ask the pupils **Is this a good story?** The pupils give their opinion through gesture (thumbs up / down) or orally (*yes / no*).
- Organise the class into four groups (Beth, Molly, Jake and the man at the camp) to act out the story.
- Play the CD. Each group joins in with their character. If the pupils need extra support, pause the CD and ask them to repeat the phrase instead.
- The groups swap roles and join in with their new character.

Now watch the animated story

After you read

Go to page 82 in your Activity Book.

Activity Book

After you read: Activity 1

Remember the story. Read and circle *true* or *false*.

- (Books open.) Ask **Do you remember the story?**
- Ask different pupils to read out the sentences. Elicit if the sentences are true or false.
- The pupils circle the correct words.

Answers: **1** true **2** false **3** false **4** true **5** true

Activity 2

Read and write. Colour the flags.

- Focus the pupils on Activity 2. Ask a pupil to read out the first speech bubble and to complete it. Repeat with the second speech bubble.
- The pupils write the words and colour the flags.

Answers: **1** red flag: can't **2** green flag: can

Recycled vocabulary

- The pupils look at the picture and write the word. If necessary, they look back at the previous unit.

Answer: bookshop

Pupil's Book Activity 2

Values: Read and write.

- The pupils look at the photo on the right. Read out the sentence in the speech bubble and prompt the class to tell you the correct answer.
- Highlight the importance of being careful near water.

Answer: red

Ending the lesson

Review the lesson.

- (Books closed.) Say **Today we've listened to a story about a camp.** Ask **What happened in the story?** Elicit the story from the pupils.
- Then say **Today you've learnt that it's important to be careful near water.**

Review the task flashcards.

- Point to the task flashcards. Say **Look at the activities you've done today. Which activity was your favourite?** Elicit the pupils' favourite activities.

Link to Science

- If you are studying the Science topic of **Landscapes** in English, you could review basic safety rules on holiday, especially near water. Review the meaning of the different coloured flags you can see on the beach (red, yellow, green and purple).

Key Competences and Key Learning Outcomes

- Use present continuous in a conversation
- Sing a song

Key language

- *play the guitar, play volleyball, sing songs; in the sun; forest*
- *What's (Jake) doing? He's (sailing a boat). He's having fun! Camping is great. He's / She's (playing the guitar).*
- Extension: *draw a picture, play games on my tablet, play the piano, watch television*

Recycled: *ride a horse, sail a boat; supermarket; lake*

Materials

- Pupil's Book p86; Activity Book p83; Class CD3; Teacher's App on Navio
- Teacher's Resource Bank: Task flashcards: *listen, sing, number, write, Talk Partners*

Optional materials

- Clothes flashcards
- Teacher's Resource Bank: Five Trinity Exam Practice cards (selected from the Starter Unit and Units 1, 2, 3, 4, 5, 6 and 7)

At a Glance Lesson Plan

Pupil's Book

Starting the lesson

- Use the Trinity Exam Practice cards (optional).
- Review the Lesson 3 story.
- Set learning outcomes using the task flashcards.

Vocabulary presentation

- Present the new vocabulary.

Activity 1

- Listen, point and say.
- ▶ *CD3 Track 48 p270*

Activity 2

- Listen and point.
- ▶ *CD3 Track 49 p270*
- Sing *Camping is great!*

Activity 3

- Listen and repeat.
- ▶ *CD3 Track 50 p271*
- Talk Partners
- Ask and answer.
- Go to the Activity Book.

Ending the lesson

- Review the lesson.
- Review the task flashcards.

Extra activity

Vocabulary Extension

- Present four additional vocabulary items.

Cooperative learning

Raising your hand

- Play *What is it?*

Digital resources

Teacher's Digital: Don't forget you can teach this lesson using the Teacher's App on Navio.

Pupil's Digital: Encourage your pupils to use the Pupil's App on Navio to practise the vocabulary from this lesson.

Powered By NAVIO

Activity Book

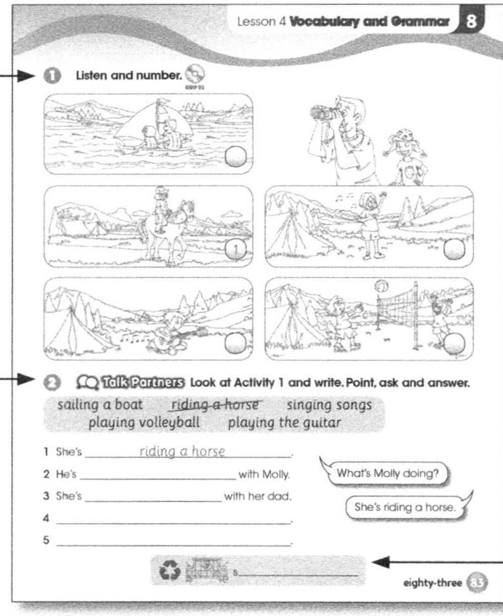

Activity Book

Activity 1

- Listen and number.
- ▶ *CD3 Track 51 p271*

Activity 2

- Look at Activity 1 and write.
- Talk Partners Point, ask and answer.

Recycled vocabulary

- Look, remember and write the word.

Detailed Lesson Plan

Starting the lesson

Use the Trinity Exam Practice cards (optional).

- The pupils practise asking and answering questions (see p31).

Review the Lesson 3 story.

- Give the pupils two minutes to look at the story. Then ask **Who wants to swim in the lake? Who wants to ride a horse? Who wants to sail a boat?** Elicit the answers.

Set learning outcomes using the task flashcards.

- Say **Today we're going to learn about the activities we do at an activity camp, sing a song and practise a conversation.**
- Hold up the task flashcards in turn and elicit the activities. Stick them on one side of the board. Point to them during the lesson to reinforce your instructions.

Vocabulary presentation

Present the new vocabulary.

- (Books open.) Point to the first photo in Activity 1 and say the activity. Mime sailing a boat and the pupils do the same. Say the activity again and the pupils repeat.
- Repeat with the other activities.

Pupil's Book Activity 1

Listen, point and say.

▶ *CD3 Track 48 p270*

- (Books open.) The pupils look at the photos. Say **Let's listen and say the words.**
- Play the CD. The pupils say the words and point to the photos.
- Play *What's missing?* (without the flashcards). Read out the activities but miss one out each time. Elicit the missing activity.

Pupil's Book Activity 2

Listen and point. Sing *Camping is great!*

▶ *CD3 Track 49 p270*

- Focus the pupils on Activity 2. Ask **What is Beth doing?** Repeat the question for the other characters.
- Play the CD. The pupils listen and do the actions.
- Play the CD again and the pupils join in with the song.

Pupil's Book Activity 3

Listen and repeat. Talk Partners **Ask and answer.**

▶ *CD3 Track 50 p271*

- Focus the pupils on Activity 3 and read out the speech bubbles.
- Play the CD. The pupils listen and read.
- Play the CD again. The pupils listen and repeat the question and the answer.
- Ask different pupils to mime different activities. Ask **What's (Anna) doing?** Elicit the answers.

Activity Book

Activity 1

Listen and number.

▶ *CD3 Track 51 p271*

- (Books open.) The pupils say what they can see in the pictures.
- Play the CD, pausing after each conversation. The pupils listen and number the pictures.
- Play the CD again to check the answers.

Answers: 3 sailing a boat, 1 riding a horse, 5 singing songs, 4 playing the guitar, 2 playing volleyball

Activity 2

Talk Partners **Look at Activity 1 and write. Point, ask and answer.**

- Focus the pupils on Activity 2 and read out the activities in the box with the class.
- The pupils look at Activity 1. Point to picture number 1 and ask **What's Molly doing?** Elicit the answer. Repeat with the other pictures.
- The pupils work on their own and write the answers. When they have finished, they point at the pictures and take turns to ask and answer in pairs.

Answers: **1** riding a horse **2** playing volleyball **3** sailing a boat **4** He's playing the guitar. **5** She's singing songs.

Recycled vocabulary

- The pupils look at the picture and write the word. If necessary, they look back at the previous unit.

Answer: supermarket

Ending the lesson

Review the lesson.

- (Books closed.) Say **Today we've learnt about camp activities, sung a song and practised asking and answering questions. What questions did we ask?** Elicit the questions from the pupils.

Review the task flashcards.

- Point to the task flashcards. Say **Look at the activities you've done today. Which activity was your favourite?** Elicit the pupils' favourite activities.

Extra activity

Vocabulary Extension

- Use the Vocabulary Booster on Navio and present and practise four additional phrases to describe activities: *draw a picture, play games on my tablet, play the piano, watch television*.

Cooperative learning

Raising your hand

- For a class to run smoothly, the pupils need to understand that they can't all speak at the same time. Remind them that they need to raise their hands if they have got a question or want to give an answer.
- Play *What is it?* (see p23) with the clothes flashcards, stressing that to have a turn the pupils must raise their hands and wait for you to say they can speak.

Key Competences and Key Learning Outcomes

- Say a tongue twister with the 'v' sound
- Listen for specific information
- Play a communication game about what people are doing

Key language

Recycled: *play the guitar, play volleyball, ride a horse, sail a boat, sing songs; swim; restaurant*

Recycled: *What's (Emma) doing? She's (swimming).*

Materials

- Pupil's Book p87; Activity Book p84; Class CD3; Teacher's App on Navio
- Teacher's Resource Bank: Task flashcards: *listen, say, match, cut out, think, Talk Partners, write, colour*
- Scissors, crayons or coloured pencils
- Teacher's Resource Bank: Unit 8 Lesson 5 Activity 3 cut-outs

Optional materials

- Teacher's Resource Bank: Five Trinity Exam Practice cards (selected from the Starter Unit and Units 1, 2, 3, 4, 5, 6 and 7)
- Coloured paper

At a Glance Lesson Plan

Starting the lesson

- Use the Trinity Exam Practice cards (optional).
- Review the vocabulary from Lesson 4.
- Review the *Camping is great!* song.
- ▶ *CD3 Track 49 p270*
- Set learning outcomes using the task flashcards.

Activity 1

- Listen and say.
- ▶ *CD3 Track 52 p271*
- Go to Magic Phonics.
- Go to the Activity Book.

Activity 2

- Listen and match.
- ▶ *CD3 Track 53 p271*

Activity 3

- Make and play the game. Talk Partners

Pupil's Book

Ending the lesson

- Review the lesson.
- Review the task flashcards.

Extra activity

Reinforcement

- Continue the pronunciation wall display.

Digital resources

Teacher's Digital: Don't forget you can teach this lesson using the Teacher's App on Navio.

Pupil's Digital: Encourage your pupils to use the Pupil's App on Navio to practise the vocabulary from this lesson.

Powered By NAVIO

Activity Book

Activity Book

Activity 1

- Write and say.

Activity 2

- Colour the words that have 'v'.
- Say.
- Go to Magic Phonics.

Activity 3

- Talk Partners Play *What's my word?* in pairs.

Recycled vocabulary

- Look, remember and write the word.

Starting the lesson

Use the Trinity Exam Practice cards (optional).
- The pupils practise asking and answering questions (see p31).

Review the vocabulary from Lesson 4.
- Review the camp activities. Say **You're riding a horse.** The pupils mime the action. Repeat with the other activities.

Review the *Camping is great!* song.
▶ *CD3 Track 49 p270*
- Play the CD. The pupils sing and do the actions.

Set learning outcomes using the task flashcards.
- Say **Today we're going to practise saying a tongue twister and make and play a speaking game.**
- Hold up the task flashcards in turn and elicit the activities. Stick them on one side of the board. Point to them during the lesson to reinforce your instructions.

Pupil's Book Activity 1

Listen and say.
▶ *CD3 Track 52 p271*
- (Books open.) Write the target 'v' sound on the board and say it. The pupils repeat.
- Say **It's time for Toby's tongue twister. What can you see in the picture? What is she doing? What's the girl's name?**
- Play the CD. The pupils listen and repeat the target sound, then the words and then the entire tongue twister, faster and faster.

Go to Magic Phonics.

Activity Book

Activity 1
Write and say.
- (Books open.) The pupils write the letter 'v' in the tongue twister. Remind them that they should use a lower case 'v' and not a capital 'V' as in 'Vicky'.

Answer: Vicky the vet loves volleyball.

Activity 2
Colour the words that have 'v'. Say.
- Ask the pupils to say the words that have 'v'. The pupils colour and say these words.

Answers: drive, love, vegetable, seven, vet, DVD

Go to Magic Phonics.

Activity 3
Play *What's my word?* in pairs.
- Focus the pupils on Activity 3. Point to each picture and elicit the word.
- Think of one of the pictures on the page and ask **What's my word?**
- The pupils ask questions to guess your word.
- Talk Partners The pupils play the game with a Talk Partner.

Recycled vocabulary
- The pupils look at the picture and write the word. If necessary, they look back at the previous unit.

Answer: restaurant

Pupil's Book Activity 2

Listen and match.
▶ *CD3 Track 53 p271*
- Focus the pupils on Activity 2. Ask **What can you see in the picture?**
- Play the CD, pausing after each sentence. The pupils listen and draw matching lines from the name labels to the activities.
- Play the CD again, then ask the pupils to read out complete sentences to check the answers.

Answers: **1** Emma is swimming. **2** Ben is playing the guitar. **3** Tom is sailing a boat. **4** Susan is singing songs. **5** Alex is riding a horse. **6** Mary is playing volleyball.

Pupil's Book Activity 3

Make and play the game.
- Focus the pupils on Activity 3. Tell them that they are going to make and play the same game.
- The pupils cut out and colour the cards and place them on their desks.
- Say a sentence, e.g. **Ben's playing the guitar.** The pupils match the name card with the activity.
- Different pupils take over your role. Repeat several times.
- Talk Partners The pupils play the game with a Talk Partner.

Ending the lesson

Review the lesson.
- (Books closed.) Say **Today we've practised a tongue twister and played a game in pairs.** Elicit the tongue twister from the pupils.

Review the task flashcards.
- Point to the task flashcards. Say **Look at the activities you've done today. Which activity was your favourite?** Elicit the pupils' favourite activities.

Extra activity

Reinforcement
- Continue the pronunciation wall display. Cut out the letter 'v' in coloured paper. Stick it on a piece of differently coloured paper to make a wall display. Elicit words that begin with that sound and write them on the wall display.
- Encourage the pupils to add new words beginning with the letter 'v' during the year. They can either tell you the new word for you to add or write the word themselves if they can.

Key Competences and Key Learning Outcomes

- Listen for general information

- Read about camping in Britain
- Sing and enjoy a traditional camp song
- Think about what activities you do

Key language
- *camel, camp, ghost stories, go camping, hump, funny, scary, sea, sleeping bag, tent*
- *We sleep in our sleeping bags. We camp in the garden. We sing songs. We tell ghost stories.*

Recycled: *sweet shop; forest, lake; volleyball*

Materials
- Pupil's Book p88; Activity Book p85; Class CD3 and 4; Teacher's App on Navio
- Teacher's Resource Bank: Task flashcards: *listen, read, sing, think, number, write, tick, draw*

Optional materials
- Teacher's Resource Bank: Five Trinity Exam Practice cards (selected from the Starter Unit and Units 1, 2, 3, 4, 5, 6 and 7)
- Video recorder

At a Glance Lesson Plan

Pupil's Book

Starting the lesson
- Use the Trinity Exam Practice cards (optional).
- Talk Partners Review Toby's tongue twister.
- ▶ *CD3 Track 52 p271*
- Set learning outcomes using the task flashcards.

Activity 1
- Listen and read.
- ▶ *CD4 Track 1 p271*
- Answer.

Activity 2
- Listen and sing *Alice the camel*.
- ▶ *CD4 Track 2 p271*

Think about your culture
- Do you go camping?
- What activities do you do?
- Go to the Activity Book.

Ending the lesson
- Review the lesson.
- Review the task flashcards.

Extra activity

Extension
- Record a song.

Digital resources

Teacher's Digital: Don't forget you can teach this lesson using the Teacher's App on Navio.

Powered By NAVIO

Activity Book

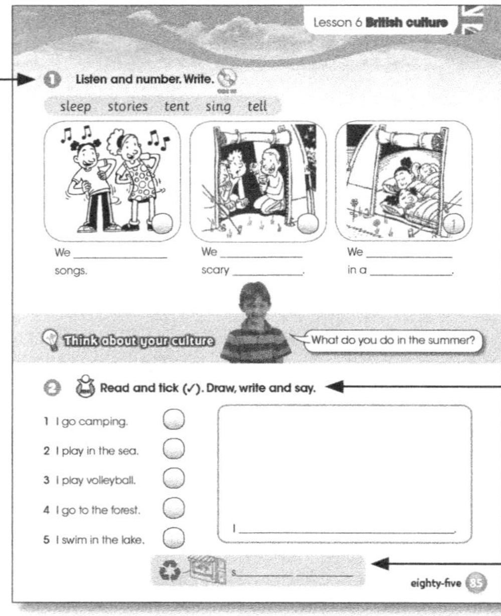

Activity Book

Activity 1
- Listen and number.
- ▶ *CD4 Track 3 p271*
- Write.

Activity 2: Think about your culture
- Read and tick (✓).
- Draw, write and say.

Recycled vocabulary
- Look, remember and write the word.

Detailed Lesson Plan

Starting the lesson

Use the Trinity Exam Practice cards (optional).

- The pupils practise asking and answering questions (see p31).

Review Toby's tongue twister.

▶ *CD3 Track 52 p271*

- Ask **What sound did you practise in Toby's tongue twister? Can you remember the tongue twister?** (*Vicky the vet loves volleyball.*)
- Play the CD. Practise the tongue twister as a class.
- Talk Partners The pupils practise saying the tongue twister as fast as possible with a Talk Partner. Choose a fast pair to say it for the class.

Set learning outcomes using the task flashcards.

- Say **Today we're going to learn about camping in the garden in Britain.**
- Hold up the task flashcards in turn and elicit the activities. Stick them on one side of the board. Point to them during the lesson to reinforce your instructions.

Pupil's Book Activity 1

Listen and read. Answer.

▶ *CD4 Track 1 p271*

- (Books open.) Focus the pupils on the photos. Read the speech bubble.
- Play the CD, pausing to check understanding and ask questions.

Suggested comprehension questions

- Initial photo: **Where do some children camp?** (*In the garden.*)
- Photo 1: **What does Dad play?** (*The guitar.*) **What song do they sing?** (*Alice the camel.*)
- Photo 2: **Do they sleep in sleeping bags in a tent?** (*Yes.*)
- Photo 3: **What stories do they tell at night?** (*Ghost stories.*)

Pupil's Book Activity 2

Listen and sing *Alice the camel*.

▶ *CD4 Track 2 p271*

- Point to the children in photo 1 and ask **What are the children doing?** (*Singing.*) Explain that they are singing a traditional camp song. Explain that it is a funny song. The song is about a camel called Alice.
- Point to the drawing of the camel and ask **Why is Alice special?** (*Because she has got five humps.*) Say **Alice the camel has five humps.** Ask the class to repeat the sentence with you several times.
- Ask the pupils to stand up. Play the first verse of the song and encourage the pupils to hold up five fingers each time the number appears. The children should bump their bottoms with their neighbour when the sing *BOOM! BOOM! BOOM!* Play the rest of the song, encouraging the class to sing and hold up the corresponding fingers for each verse.

Pupil's Book Think about your culture

Do you go camping? What activities do you do?

- Read out the questions.
- The pupils tell you if they go camping and what activities they do.
- Ask additional questions, e.g. **Do you go camping with your family? Do you like sleeping in a tent?**

Activity Book

Activity 1

Listen and number. Write.

▶ *CD4 Track 3 p271*

- (Books open.) Focus the pupils on the pictures. Elicit what they can see.
- Play the CD. The pupils listen and number the pictures.
- Read the words in the word box with the class. Then they complete the sentences with the words from the box.

Answers: **1** We sleep in a tent. **2** We sing songs. **3** We tell scary stories.

Activity 2: Think about your culture

Read and tick (✓). Draw, write and say.

- Read out the question in the speech bubble. Elicit the pupils' answers.
- Read out the first sentence. Then the pupils tick the box if they do this activity in the summer.
- Repeat with the other sentences. Then the pupils draw themselves doing one of the activities and they write a sentence.
- Different pupils show the class their drawings and read their sentences.

Recycled vocabulary

- The pupils look at the picture and write the word. If necessary, they look back at the previous unit.

Answer: sweet shop

Ending the lesson

Review the lesson.

- (Books closed.) Say **Today we've talked about camping in the garden. Do you sleep in a tent? Do you tell ghost stories?** Elicit answers.

Review the task flashcards.

- Point to the task flashcards. Say **Look at the activities you've done today. Which activity was your favourite?** Elicit the pupils' favourite activities.

Extra activity

Extension

- If you have a video recorder, record your class singing a song. The video could be posted on the school website, with consent from the pupils' parents.

Key Competences and Key Learning Outcomes

- Complete a postcard
- Extract key information from a text
- Read and understand a postcard

Key language

- *beautiful, campsite, mountain, postcard, rainy, river*

Recycled: *boats, farm, forest, horses, lake, playground, swimming pool, town; swimsuit; play the guitar, ride a horse, sail a boat, sing songs, swim; fantastic; hot, sunny, windy;* colours

Recycled: *There are (lots of fun activities). There's a (lake). I'm wearing (my new swimsuit). It's (hot and sunny).*

Materials

- Pupil's Book p89; Activity Book p86; Class CD4; Teacher's App on Navio
- Teacher's Resource Bank: Task flashcards: *think, circle, listen, read, write*
- A selection of postcards

Optional materials

- Teacher's Resource Bank: Five Trinity Exam Practice cards (selected from the Starter Unit and Units 1, 2, 3, 4, 5, 6 and 7)
- Clothes flashcards
- Examples of British stamps

At a Glance Lesson Plan

Starting the lesson

- Use the Trinity Exam Practice cards (optional).
- Review the culture lesson.
- Review the *Alice the camel* song.
- ▶ *CD4 Track 2 p271*
- Set learning outcomes using the task flashcards.

Before you read

- Look at different postcards.

Activity 1

- What can you see on the postcard?
- Circle and say.

Activity 2

- Listen and read the postcard.
- ▶ *CD4 Track 4 p271*

After you read

Go to page 86 in your Activity Book.

Pupil's Book

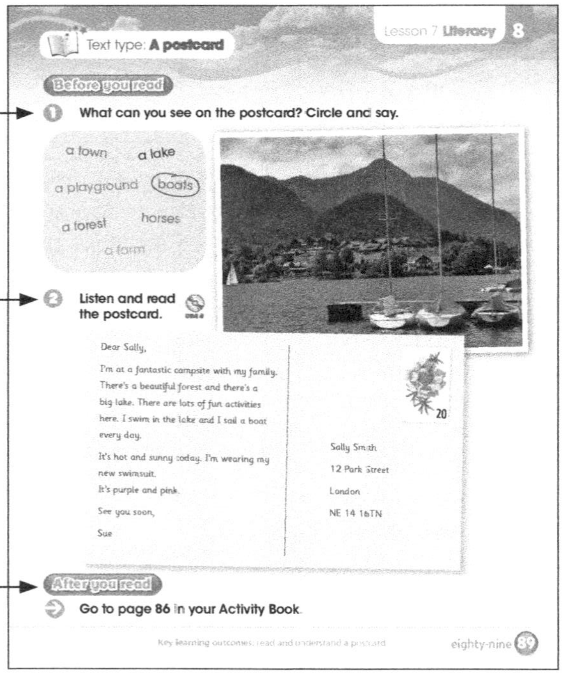
Lesson 7 Literacy 8

Text type: A postcard

Before you read

1 What can you see on the postcard? Circle and say.

a town, a lake, a playground, boats, a forest, horses, a farm

2 Listen and read the postcard.

Dear Sally,

I'm at a fantastic campsite with my family. There's a beautiful forest and there's a big lake. There are lots of fun activities here. I swim in the lake and I sail a boat every day.

It's hot and sunny today. I'm wearing my new swimsuit. It's purple and pink.

See you soon,

Sue

Sally Smith
12 Park Street
London
NE 14 1bTN

After you read

Go to page 86 in your Activity Book.

eighty-nine 89

Ending the lesson

- Review the lesson.
- Review the task flashcards.

Extra activities

Reinforcement

- Play *What's missing?*

Extension

- Look at different types of stamps.

Digital resources

Teacher's Digital: Don't forget you can teach this lesson using the Teacher's App on Navio.

Pupil's Digital: Encourage your pupils to use the Pupil's App on Navio to practise the vocabulary from this lesson.

Powered By NAVIO

Activity Book

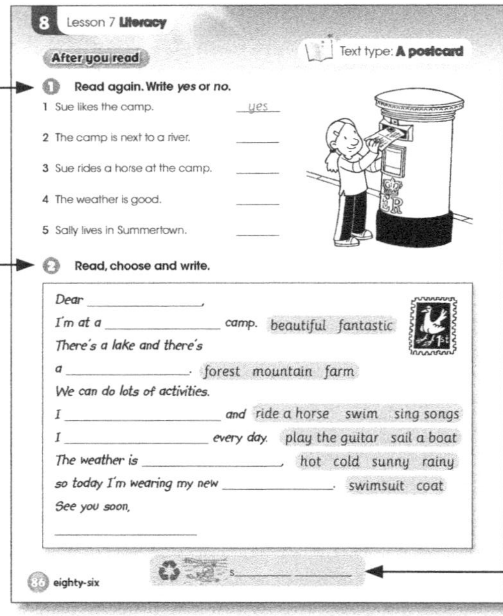
8 Lesson 7 Literacy

Text type: A postcard

After you read

1 Read again. Write yes or no.

1 Sue likes the camp. yes
2 The camp is next to a river.
3 Sue rides a horse at the camp.
4 The weather is good.
5 Sally lives in Summertown.

2 Read, choose and write.

Dear ______,
I'm at a ______ camp. (beautiful, fantastic)
There's a lake and there's a ______. (forest, mountain, farm)
We can do lots of activities.
I ______ and ______ every day. (ride a horse, swim, sing songs, play the guitar, sail a boat)
The weather is ______, (hot, cold, sunny, rainy)
so today I'm wearing my new ______. (swimsuit, coat)
See you soon,
______

86 eighty-six

Activity Book

After you read: Activity 1

- Read again.
- Write *yes* or *no*.

Activity 2

- Read, choose and write.

Recycled vocabulary

- Look, remember and write the word.

Starting the lesson

Use the Trinity Exam Practice cards (optional).

- The pupils practise asking and answering questions (see p31).

Review the culture lesson.

- Review the activities that British children do when they go camping.
- Elicit *sing songs, sleep in sleeping bags in a big tent, tell ghost stories*.

Review the *Alice the camel* song.

▶ *CD4 Track 2 p271*

- Review the numbers 1 to 20 with the class. Then ask **Do you remember the camp song *Alice the camel?*** Say **Let's sing it again!**
- Play the CD. The pupils sing and do the actions.

Set learning outcomes using the task flashcards.

- Say **Today we're going to read a postcard.**
- Hold up the task flashcards in turn and elicit the activities. Stick them on one side of the board. Point to them during the lesson to reinforce your instructions.

Before you read

Look at different postcards.

- Show the postcards you have brought in (alternatively, you can find some examples online).
- Hold up one postcard and ask the pupils what they can see on the front. Then show them the address, stamp and message on the back.
- Explain that people send postcards to family and friends when they go on holiday.
- If possible, pass the postcards around the class so that the pupils can look at them more closely.

Pupil's Book Activity 1

What can you see on the postcard? Circle and say.

- (Books open.) Invite different pupils to read the words on the left.
- Tell the class to look at the photo. Ask **Are there (boats)?** The pupils say if they can see the objects in the picture.
- The pupils circle the words if the objects appear on the postcard.

Answers: boats, a forest, a town, a lake

Pupil's Book Activity 2

Listen and read the postcard.

▶ *CD4 Track 4 p271*

- Say **Let's listen to and read the postcard.** Ask the pupils to place their finger on the postcard. Play the CD and ask the pupils to follow the text with their finger as they're reading. If necessary, pause the CD and ask questions to check understanding.
- Play the CD again. The pupils listen and read.
- Then, if your pupils are able to read independently, ask them to read the postcard on their own.

Suggested comprehension questions

Where's Sue? (*At a campsite.*) **Is the campsite fun?** (*Yes.*) **What activities does she do?** (*Swim in the lake, sail a boat.*) **What's the weather like?** (*Hot and sunny.*) **What's she wearing?** (*A new swimsuit.*)

Activity Book

After you read: Activity 1

Read again. Write *yes* or *no*.

- (Books open.) Ask a pupil to read out the first sentence and point out the answer.
- Different pupils read out the other sentences. Elicit the answer each time.
- The pupils write the answers on their own.

Answers: **1** yes **2** no **3** no **4** yes **5** no

Activity 2

Read, choose and write.

- Tell the pupils that they are going to write a postcard for a family member or a friend.
- Read out the postcard as a class. The pupils write the missing words each time.
- Then the pupils complete their postcards.
- Invite different pupils to read their postcards to the class.

Recycled vocabulary

- The pupils look at the picture and write the word. If necessary, they look back at the previous unit.

Answer: swimming pool

Ending the lesson

Review the lesson.

- (Books closed.) Say **Today we've read and written a postcard in English. Can you remember what you wrote?** Elicit answers.

Review the task flashcards.

- Point to the task flashcards on the board. Say **Look at the activities you've done today. Which activity was your favourite?** Elicit the pupils' favourite activities.

Extra activities

Reinforcement

- Play *What's missing?* (see p23) with the clothes flashcards.

Extension

- Bring in some examples of British stamps and show them to the class or find some examples on the internet.
- Encourage the pupils to describe what they see.

Key Competences and Key Learning Outcomes

- Review language in the unit
- Reflect on own learning
- Sing a cooperative learning song

Key language

Recycled: *shirt, shoes, shorts, skirt, sweater, sun hat, swimsuit, trainers, trousers, T-shirt; play the guitar, play volleyball, ride a horse, sail a boat, sing songs; at the camp, on the lake; hospital*

Recycled: *What (are you) wearing? (I'm) wearing (a skirt). What's he / she wearing? He's / She's wearing a (skirt).*

Materials

- Pupil's Book p90; Activity Book p87; Class CD4; Teacher's App on Navio
- Clothes flashcards
- Teacher's Resource Bank: Task flashcards: *listen, number, write, read, sing, think, stick, circle*
- Teacher's Resource Bank: Traffic light cut-out
- *Give Me Five!* sticker

Optional materials

- Teacher's Resource Bank: Five Trinity Exam Practice cards (selected from the Starter Unit and Unit 1, 2, 3, 4, 5, 6 and 7)

At a Glance Lesson Plan

Pupil's Book

Starting the lesson

Use the Trinity Exam Practice cards (optional).
Review the unit vocabulary.
Set learning outcomes using the task flashcards.

Activity 1

Listen and number.
▶ ***CD4 Track 5 p271***
Write and say.

Activity 2

Look, read and complete.

Activity 3 – Cooperative learning

Sing *Well done!*
▶ ***CD4 Track 6 p272***
Stick the *Give Me Five!* sticker.
Go to the Activity Book.

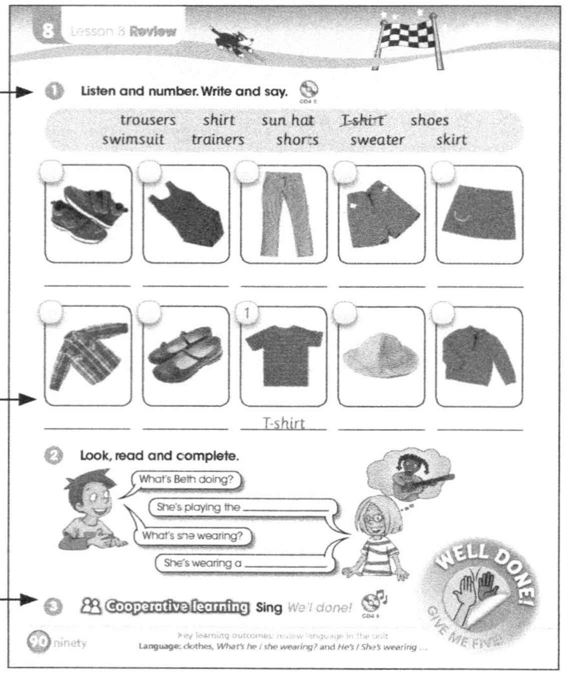

Ending the lesson

Review the task flashcards.

Cooperative learning

- **Think-Pair-Share** Review clothes vocabulary.

Activity Book

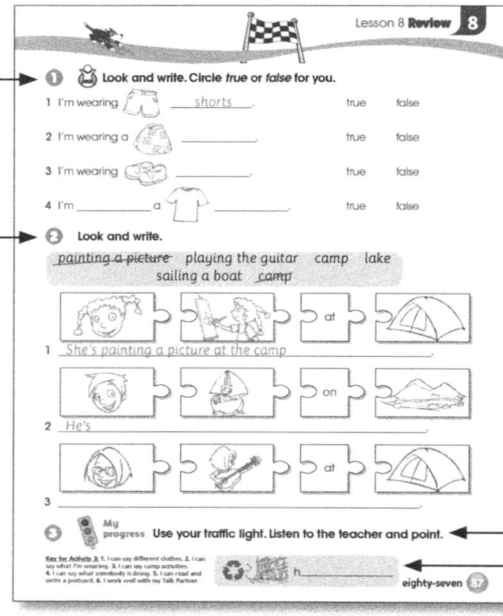

Activity Book

Activity 1
Look and write.
Circle *true or false* for you.

Activity 2
Look and write.

Activity 3 My progress
Use your traffic light. Listen to the teacher and point.

Recycled vocabulary
Look, remember and write the word.

Digital resources

Teacher's Digital: Don't forget you can teach this lesson using the Teacher's App on Navio.

Pupil's Digital: Encourage your pupils to use the Pupil's App on Navio to practise the vocabulary from this lesson.

Powered By NAVIO

Starting the lesson

Use the Trinity Exam Practice cards (optional).

- The pupils practise asking and answering questions (see p31).

Review the unit vocabulary.

- Hold up a clothes flashcard and elicit the word. Stick the flashcard face down on the board. Repeat until all the clothes flashcards are on the board.
- Ask **Where's the (T-shirt)?** Ask a pupil to come to the front and turn over one of the cards. If it's the correct flashcard, he / she says *It's here*. If it isn't the correct flashcard, another pupil has a go. Repeat with different clothes words and different pupils.
- Variation: Play the game in two teams. The teams take it in turns to remember the items of clothing.

Set learning outcomes using the task flashcards.

- Say **Today we're going to remember what we've learnt in Unit 8.**
- Hold up the task flashcards in turn and elicit the activities. Stick them on one side of the board. Point to them during the lesson to reinforce your instructions.

Pupil's Book Activity 1

Listen and number. Write and say.

▶ *CD4 Track 5 p271*

- (Books open.) Focus the pupils on the photos.
- Play the CD, pausing after each conversation. The pupils listen and write the correct numbers in the circles.
- Play the CD again. This time the pupils write the words under the photos.
- To check answers, point to a picture and ask different pupils to read out the words they have written.

Answers: **1** T-shirt **2** shorts **3** trainers **4** skirt **5** sun hat **6** shirt **7** sweater **8** swimsuit **9** shoes **10** trousers

Pupil's Book Activity 2

Look, read and complete.

- Focus the pupils on the pictures in Activity 2.
- Ask two pupils to read and complete the speech bubbles.

Answers: She's playing the guitar. She's wearing a sweater.

Pupil's Book Activity 3: Cooperative learning

Sing *Well done!*

▶ *CD4 Track 6 p272*

- Praise the pupils for their hard work and encourage them to praise each other. Play the *Well done!* song. The pupils sing and do the actions.

Stick the *Give Me Five!* sticker.

- The pupils stick the *Give Me Five!* sticker on the Pupil's Book page.
- Variation: Sing the *Well done!* song and stick the *Give Me Five!* sticker after the pupils have also completed the Activity Book Lesson 8 Review.

Activity Book

Activity 1

Look and write. Circle *true* or *false* for you.

- (Books open). Read the first sentence.
- The pupils complete the other sentences.
- The pupils then circle *true* or *false*, according to the clothes they are wearing.

Answers: **1** shorts **2** skirt **3** shoes **4** wearing, T-shirt

Activity 2

Look and write.

- Read out the words in the word box with the class.
- The pupils write sentences with the words from the box.

Answers: **1** She's painting a picture at the camp. **2** He's sailing a boat on the lake. **3** She's playing the guitar at the camp.

Activity 3: My progress

Use your traffic light. Listen to the teacher and point.

- (Books closed.) Ask the class to take out their traffic light cut-out. Say **Let's think about our work in this unit.** Point to the green circle, nod your head, smile a lot, and say **I can say different clothes. Yes, I can do this very well.** Point to the yellow circle, move your head a little, smile a little and say **Yes, I can do this.** Then point to the red circle, shake your head and say **No, I can't do this.**
- Read the different statements. For each one, the pupils point to the colour on their traffic light that shows how they feel about their own learning.

Self-assessment statements

1. I can say different clothes.
2. I can say what I'm wearing.
3. I can say camp activities.
4. I can say what somebody is doing.
5. I can read and write a postcard.
6. I work well with my Talk Partner.

Recycled vocabulary

- The pupils look at the picture and write the word. If necessary, they look back at the previous unit.

Answer: hospital

Ending the lesson

Review the task flashcards.

- Point to the task flashcards. Say **Look at the activities you've done today. Which activity was your favourite?** Elicit the pupils' favourite activities.

Cooperative learning

Think-Pair-Share

- Ask **Can you remember the ten clothes words?** The pupils think on their own for one minute.
- **Talk Partners** The pupils work with a Talk Partner to name all ten items. Ask a pair to say one of the clothes words. Hold up the corresponding flashcard and prompt the class to repeat the word.
- Repeat until all ten clothes words have been named.

Key Competences and Key Learning Outcomes
- Watch and understand a video about camping
- Say what the weather is like
- Understand the importance of thinking before choosing

Key language
- *forest, lake, playing the guitar, sailing, sun hat, sweater, swimming, T-shirt, volleyball, wear, windy*

Materials
- Pupil's Book p91; Activity Book p88; Class CD4; Video; Teacher's App on Navio
- Teacher's Resource Bank: Task flashcards: *tick, read, circle, think, listen, write, draw, say, Talk Partners*

Optional materials
- Teacher's Resource Bank: Trinity Exam Practice cards (selected from Unit 8)

At a Glance Lesson Plan

Pupil's Book

Starting the lesson
- Use the Trinity Exam Practice cards (optional).
- Review camping activities and weather.
- Set learning outcomes and use the task flashcards.

Pre-watching activity
- Check if camping activities they like are in the video.

Activity 1
- Watch the video.
  Unit 8 video p279
- Tick (✓) or cross (✗). Are these activities in the video?

Activity 2
- Watch the video again.
  Unit 8 video
- Read and circle.

Activity 3
- Read, think and circle.
  Go to the Activity Book.

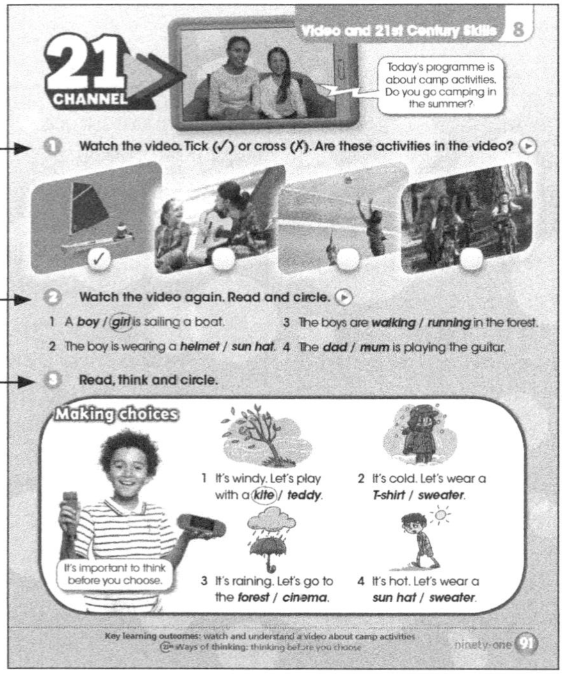

Ending the lesson
- Review the lesson.
- Review the task flashcards. Elicit the pupils' favourite activities.

Digital resources

Teacher's Digital: Don't forget you can teach this lesson using the Teacher's App on Navio.

Pupil's Digital: Encourage your pupils to use the Pupil's App on Navio to practise the vocabulary from this lesson.

Powered By NAVIO

Activity Book

Activity Book

Activity 1
- What do the children choose? Listen and tick (✓).
- ▶ *CD4 Track 7 p272*

Activity 2
- Think and write. Draw and say.

Recycled vocabulary
- Look, remember and write the word.

Detailed Lesson Plan

Starting the lesson

Use the Trinity Exam Practice cards (optional).

- The pupils practise asking and answering questions.

Review camping activities and weather.

- On the board write sunny, cold, raining, windy in four columns. To the left of the columns write activity, clothes.
- In pairs, pupils work together to make a list of activities and clothes for the different types of weather. Do the first one as an example with the whole class: sunny – swimming in the lake, swimsuit.

Set learning outcomes and use the task flashcards.

- Say **Today we're going to watch a video about camping activities**
- Point to the task flashcards throughout to elicit activities and reinforce your instructions.

Pre-watching activity

- **Think-Pair-Share** Ask the pupils what camping activities they like.

Pupil's Book Activity 1

Watch the video. Tick (✓) or cross (✗). Are these activities in the video? *p279*

- Ask **Do Sophie and Tom like camping?** Play Part 1, pausing to elicit the answers.
- Focus the pupils' attention on the video stills. Ask **What are the people doing?**
- Explain that the pupils cross the photo that is not in the video. Play Part 2 of the video. Pause the video after the first video still. Ask the pupils to point to the corresponding photo in their book.
- Play the rest of Part 2 for pupils to point to the photos in the order they see the activities.
- Play Part 2 again for pupils to write the cross. The pupils then tick the activities that are in the video.

Answers: ✓, ✓, ✗, ✓

Pupil's Book Activity 2

Watch the video again. Read and circle.

- Play Part 1 again. Pause after Abby says, *Let's watch a video about camping activities*. Read out the first sentence in Activity 2. Ask **Is it a boy or girl sailing the boat?** (a girl).
- Play Part 2 all the way through for pupils to circle the words.
- Ask general questions to check understanding.

  When do children usually go camping? *(In the summer.)*

  What weather is good for sailing? *(Sunny and windy.)*

  What is the boy riding a horse wearing? *(Trousers, a T-shirt and a helmet.)*

  What is the little sister doing? *(Singing.)*

  Where does Sophie want to go camping? *(In the garden.)*

  Why is it not a good idea? *(It's raining.)*

  Which activity is a good idea? *(Play computer games.)* **Why?** *(It's indoors.)*

Answers: **1** girl **2** helmet **3** walking **4** dad

Pupil's Book Activity 3

Read, think and circle.

- Say. **Look out the window.** Ask **What's the weather like today? What activities are good to do today?**
- Read out the first sentence including both options. Ask **Which activity is good to do and why?**
- Read out the rest of the sentences for the pupils to follow. Pupils circle the correct word.
- Ask **Why is it important to think before you choose?** (It's important to think about all the choices and options so you can make the right choice).

Answers: **1** kite **2** sweater **3** cinema **4** sun hat

Activity Book

Activity 1

What do the children choose? Listen and tick (✓).

CD4 Track 7 p272

- Look at each pair of pictures and ask **What do you think the people are going to talk about for each picture?** As questions such as **When do you wear shorts / trousers? Which food is healthy?**
- Play the first exchange on the CD. Ask **What's the weather like? What clothes do they choose?** Show trousers ticked.
- Play the rest of the CD, pausing after each exchange, to ask questions to guide the pupils to choose the correct picture.

  Suggested questions:

  Why is fruit a good choice?

  Why isn't it a good idea to go on the slide?

  Why isn't sailing a good choice?

Answers: **1** trousers **2** fruit **3** swing **4** volleyball

Activity 2

Think and write. Draw and say.

- Ask **Where can you go and what can you do in this weather?** Think of good choices.
- The pupils complete the sentences with good choices. The pupils draw pictures to illustrate their choices.

Recycled vocabulary

Answers: toyshop

Ending the lesson

Review the lesson.

- Ask **Which activity was easy / difficult?**

Review the task flashcards.

- Say **Look at the activities you've done today. Which activity was your favourite?**

Date: ______________________ Unit: __________

1 **What did my pupils learn in this unit?**

____

____

____

____

2 **How did my pupils work? (✓)**

individually ☐ in pairs ☐ in small groups ☐

in large groups ☐ as a class ☐

3 **Which key competences did my pupils develop?**

- Competence in linguistic communication ☐
- Competence in mathematics, science and technology ☐
- Digital competence ☐
- Learning to learn ☐
- Social and civic competences ☐
- Sense of initiative and entrepreneurship ☐
- Cultural awareness and expression ☐

4 **Which lessons / activities were the most successful and why?**

____

____

____

____

5 **Which lessons / activities did my pupils find the most difficult and why?**

____

____

____

____

6 **What did I try in the classroom for the first time? How did it go?**

____

____

____

____

7 **Which resources did I find most useful? (including webpages)**

____

____

____

____

____

____

8 **What could I do differently next time I teach this unit?**

____

____

____

____

Unit 9

Day and night

Unit overview

Key Competences and Key Learning Outcomes

- Identify and say ten daily routines (Lesson 1)
- Say the vocabulary chant (Lesson 1)
- Use present simple in a conversation (Lesson 2)
- Identify and say the three meals a day (Lesson 4)
- Say when you have meals (Lesson 4)
- Watch and understand a video about teeth (Video and 21st Century Skills)
- Say what you do to look after your teeth (Video and 21st Century Skills)

- Think about what you can see in the day or at night (Lesson 7)

- Use the Pupil's App on Navio

- Practise spelling (Lesson 1)
- Say a tongue twister to practise the 'th' sound (Lesson 5)
- Review language in the unit and reflect on own learning (Lesson 8)
- Practise activity types found in the Cambridge English Young Learners Exams: Pre A1 Starters

- Understand the importance of looking after your teeth (Lesson 3,Video and 21st Century Skills)

- Work with a Talk Partner to practise and reinforce learning (all lessons)
- Play a communication game about daily routines (Lesson 5)

- Sing three songs (Lessons 1, 4 and 8)
- Understand and act out a story (Lesson 3)
- Read about the Tooth Fairy in Britain (Lesson 6)
- Think about what happens to teeth where you live (Lesson 6)
- Read and understand a poem (Lesson 7)

Vocabulary

Core vocabulary:
brush my teeth, comb my hair, get dressed, get up, go to bed, go to school, have a shower, make my bed, sleep, wash my face; breakfast in the morning, lunch in the afternoon, dinner in the evening, a snack at night

Extension vocabulary (optional)
do my homework, get undressed, have a bath, put my pyjamas on, read a book, wake up; fork, knife, plate, spoon

Other vocabulary
breakfast, dinner; champion, incredible, magic, pillow, tomorrow, wobbly tooth; hungry; garden, letter, lunch, money, pillow, Tooth Fairy; children, cockerel, moon, owl, stars in the day; animal noises

Recycled vocabulary
shirt, shoes, skirt, sweater, sun hat, swimsuit, T-shirt, trainers, trousers; play, sleep; sun; days of the week

Structures

Core structures
I (brush my teeth) every day. Me, too. I (have breakfast) every (morning).

Other structures
It's a beautiful day. I (wash my face). What's the matter? I've got (a wobbly tooth). Are you hungry (in the morning)? Yes, I am. The Tooth Fairy (comes at night). I put the box (under my pillow). I find (a letter).

Recycled structures
Are you ready? Yes, I am. Me too. Let's play. Can you (see my tooth)? No, I can't. Have you got (a wobbly tooth)? Yes, I have. No, I haven't. Yes, that's right. That isn't right. My turn.

Phonics

Consonant sound 'th' (**th**ree, **th**in, ba**th**, **Th**ursday)

British Culture

The Tooth Fairy

Literacy

Text type: a poem (text to express)
Reading skills: using visual clues; reading for specific information; using rhyme when reading

21st Century Skills

Living in the world: learn to look after your teeth

Cooperative learning

Song: *Well done!* (Lesson 8)
Skill: Working together and supporting each other (Lesson 1)

Values

Understanding the importance of looking after your teeth

Cross-curricular links

Links to Science

The Sun: daytime and night-time activities; elements seen in the sky at night and during the day; understanding that the pattern of day and night affects some animals

Suggested Arts and Crafts concepts

Colours: identifying warm and cool colours in Art and in the environment; using warm and cool colours to represent day and night

Key Competences and Key Learning Outcomes

- Identify and say ten daily routines
- Say the vocabulary chant
- Stick the daily routines stickers

- Review day and night-time activities (optional)

- Practise spelling

- Sing a song about daily routines

Key language
- *brush my teeth, comb my hair, get dressed, get up, go to bed, go to school, have a shower, make my bed, sleep, wash my face*
- *It's a beautiful day. I (wash my face).*
- Extension: *do my homework, get undressed, have a bath, put my pyjamas on, read a book, wake up*

Recycled: *shirt, trainers*

Materials
- Pupil's Book p92; Activity Book pp90 and 99; Class CD4; Teacher's App on Navio
- Daily routines flashcards; Unit 9 stickers
- Teacher's Resource Bank: Daily routines word cards
- Teacher's Resource Bank: Task flashcards: *listen, sing, read, match, stick, say, think, Talk Partners, write*

Optional materials
- Teacher's Resource Bank: Five Trinity Exam Practice cards (selected from the Starter Unit and Units 1, 2, 3, 4, 5, 6, 7 and 8)

At a Glance Lesson Plan

Starting the lesson
- Use the Trinity Exam Practice cards (optional).
- Review clothes vocabulary.
- Set learning outcomes using the task flashcards.

Vocabulary presentation
- Present the new vocabulary.

Activity 1
- Listen and do the actions.
- ▶ ***CD4 Track 8 p272***
- Sing *It's a beautiful day.*

Word cards
- Read the word cards.
- Match them to the flashcards.

Activity 2
- Read and stick the ten stickers.
- Listen and say the chant.
- ▶ ***CD4 Track 10 p272***
- Go to the Activity Book.

Pupil's Book

Ending the lesson
- Review the lesson.
- Review the task flashcards.

Extra activity
Vocabulary Extension
- Present six additional vocabulary items.

Cooperative learning
Working together and supporting each other
- **Talk Partners** Ask and answer *What's this?*

Link to Science
- **The Sun:** Review day and night-time activities.

Learning to learn
Spelling
- Practise spelling at any time during this unit (Activity Book p99).

Digital resources

Teacher's Digital: Don't forget you can teach this lesson using the Teacher's App on Navio.

Pupil's Digital: Encourage your pupils to use the Pupil's App on Navio to practise the vocabulary from this lesson.

Powered By NAVIO

Activity Book

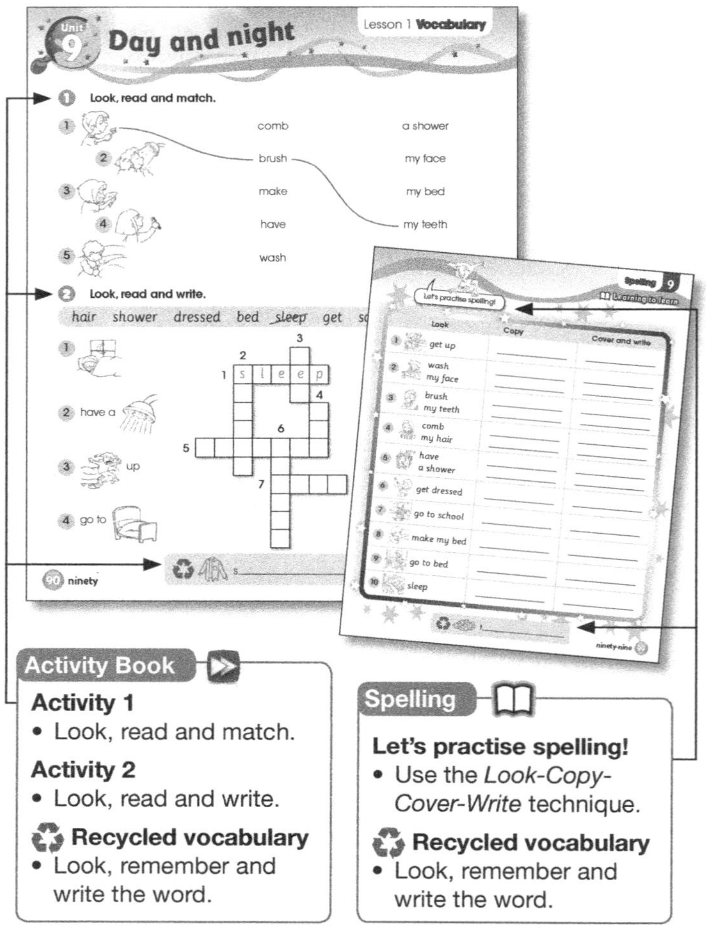

Activity Book
Activity 1
- Look, read and match.

Activity 2
- Look, read and write.

Recycled vocabulary
- Look, remember and write the word.

Spelling
Let's practise spelling!
- Use the *Look-Copy-Cover-Write* technique.

Recycled vocabulary
- Look, remember and write the word.

Detailed Lesson Plan

Starting the lesson

Use the Trinity Exam Practice cards (optional).
- The pupils practise asking and answering questions (see p31).

Review clothes vocabulary.
- Ask **What are you wearing today?** The pupils respond.
- Play *Who am I?* Describe what a pupil is wearing and the rest of the class guesses who it is. Say **I'm wearing a (white shirt). Who am I?**

Set learning outcomes using the task flashcards.
- Say **Today we're going to learn about the actions we do every day.**
- Hold up the task flashcards in turn and elicit the activities. Stick them on one side of the board. Point to them during the lesson to reinforce your instructions.

Vocabulary presentation

Present the new vocabulary.
- (Books closed.) The pupils put their heads on their desks and pretend to go to sleep. Say **Cock-a-doodle-do. It's morning.** Hold up the *get up* flashcard and say **Get up.** The pupils repeat the word and do the action.
- Stick the flashcard on the board and repeat the procedure with the other daily routines flashcards. The pupils say each word.

Pupil's Book Activity 1

Listen and do the actions. Sing *It's a beautiful day.*
▶ *CD4 Track 8 p272*
- (Books open.) Focus on the picture. Ask **Who can you see? Where are they? What's the weather like?**
- Play the CD and mime the daily routines. The pupils listen and watch.
- Play the CD again. The pupils sing and do the actions.

Word cards

Read the word cards. Match them to the flashcards.
- (Books closed.) Hold up the daily routines word cards in turn, and say or elicit each word.
- Different pupils come to the front and stick the word cards on the board with the corresponding flashcards.

Pupil's Book Activity 2

Read and stick the ten stickers. Listen and say the chant.
▶ *CD4 Track 10 p272*
- (Books open.) Ask a pupil to read the first action. The pupils stick the corresponding sticker. Repeat with the other stickers.
- Play the CD. The pupils listen and say the chant, pointing to the stickers in turn.

Activity Book

Activity 1
Look, read and match.
- (Books open.) The pupils look at the pictures and then match them to the two halves of the corresponding phrases.

Answers: **1** brush my teeth **2** have a shower **3** wash my face **4** comb my hair **5** make my bed

Activity 2
Look, read and write.
- Read out the words in the word box with the class.
- The pupils find the missing word from each daily routine and write it in the crossword.

Answers: **1** sleep **2** shower **3** get **4** bed **5** dressed **6** school **7** hair

Recycled vocabulary
- The pupils look at the picture and write the word. If necessary, they look back at the previous unit.

Answer: shirt

Ending the lesson

Review the lesson.
- (Books closed.) Say **Today we've learnt the names of activities we do every day. What activities do you remember?** Elicit the daily routines.

Review the task flashcards.
- Point to the task flashcards. Say **Look at the activities you've done today. Which activity was your favourite?** Elicit the pupils' favourite activities.

Extra activity

Vocabulary Extension
- Use the Vocabulary Booster on Navio to present and practise six additional phrases to describe daily routines: *do my homework, get undressed, have a bath, put my pyjamas on, read a book, wake up.*

Cooperative learning

Working together and supporting each other
- **Talk Partners** Pupil A points to a daily routines sticker and asks *What's this?* Pupil B answers using *It's …* If Pupil B can't remember, Pupil A helps him / her.
- When Pupil B has named all ten, they swap roles.

Link to Science

- If you are studying the Science topic of **The Sun** in English, review day and night activities. Draw a sun and a moon on the board. Point to each and ask **Do you (get up) in the day or at night?** The children point and say 'day' or 'night'. Elicit other day and night activities.

Spelling (Activity Book page 99)

Let's practise spelling!
- The pupils can practise spelling the ten daily routines using the *Look-Copy-Cover-Write* technique at any time during this unit before the Lesson 8 Review.

Recycled vocabulary
- The pupils look at the picture and write the word. If necessary, they look back at the previous unit.

Answer: trainers

Key Competences and Key Learning Outcomes

- Use present simple
- Complete and practise a conversation
- Listen for specific information

Key language

- *I (wash my face) every day. Me too. Are you ready? Yes, I am. Let's play!*

Recycled: *brush my teeth, comb my hair, get dressed, get up, go to bed, go to school, have a shower, make my bed, sleep, wash my face; skirt;* days of the week

Materials

- Pupil's Book p93; Activity Book p91; Class CD1 and 4; Teacher's App on Navio
- Daily routines flashcards
- Teacher's Resource Bank: Task flashcards: *listen, act out, tick, read, write, sing*

Optional materials

- Teacher's Resource Bank: Five Trinity Exam Practice cards (selected from the Starter Unit and Units 1, 2, 3, 4, 5, 6, 7 and 8)

At a Glance Lesson Plan

Starting the lesson

- Use the Trinity Exam Practice cards (optional).
- Review daily routines.
- Review the *It's a beautiful day* song.
- ▶ ***CD4 Track 8 p272***
- ▶ ***CD4 Track 9 p272 (optional karaoke version)***
- Set learning outcomes using the task flashcards.

Activity 1

- Listen and repeat.
- ▶ ***CD4 Track 11 p272***
- Act out.

Activity 2

- Listen and tick (✓).
- ▶ ***CD4 Track 12 p272***
- Go to the Activity Book.

Pupil's Book

Ending the lesson

- Review the lesson.
- Review the task flashcards.

Extra activities

Reinforcement

- Sing *Seven days a week.*
- ▶ ***CD1 Track 7 p256***

Extension

- Play a mime game.

Activity Book

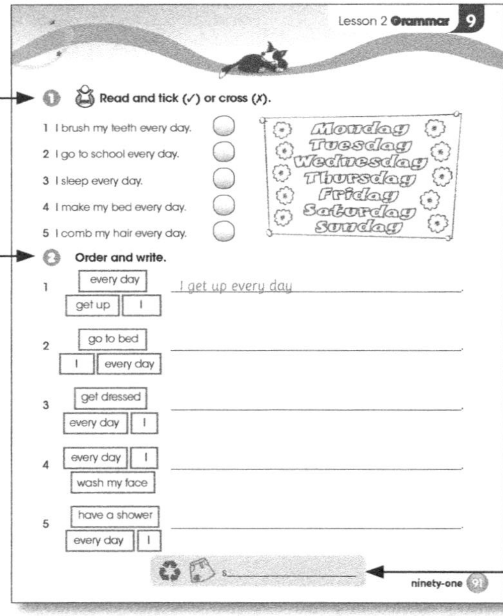

Activity Book

Activity 1

- Read and tick (✓) or cross (✗).

Activity 2

- Order and write.

Recycled vocabulary

- Look, remember and write the word.

Digital resources

Teacher's Digital: Don't forget you can teach this lesson using the Teacher's App on Navio.

Pupil's Digital: Encourage your pupils to use the Pupil's App on Navio to practise the vocabulary from this lesson.

Powered By NAVIO

Detailed Lesson Plan

Starting the lesson

Use the Trinity Exam Practice cards (optional).

- The pupils practise asking and answering questions (see p31).

Review daily routines.

- Use the daily routines flashcards to review the daily routines. Play *Simon says* with the class. Give the pupils an instruction. If you say 'Simon says' before the action, the pupils do the action. If you don't say 'Simon says', they do nothing. Say **Simon says 'Go to sleep!'** The pupils mime sleeping. Say **Get up!** They remain sitting down.

Review the *It's a beautiful day* song.

▶ *CD4 Track 8 p272*

▶ *CD4 Track 9 p272 (optional karaoke version)*

- Play the CD (or use the karaoke version). The pupils sing and do the actions.

Set learning outcomes using the task flashcards.

- Say **Today we're going to talk about the activities we do every day.**
- Hold up the task flashcards in turn and elicit the activities. Stick them on one side of the board. Point to them during the lesson to reinforce your instructions.

Pupil's Book Activity 1

Listen and repeat. Act out.

▶ *CD4 Track 11 p272*

- (Books open.) Point to the characters in the picture. Ask **What is Molly doing? What is Beth doing?**
- Play the CD. The pupils listen and read the conversation.
- Ask **Do Molly and Beth brush their teeth / wash their face every day?**
- Play the CD again, pausing after each sentence for the pupils to repeat.
- Ask different pupils to come to the front and act out the conversation.

Pupil's Book Activity 2

Listen and tick (✓).

▶ *CD4 Track 12 p272*

- Focus the pupils on Activity 2. Point to the characters and say **Let's listen to what Beth and Jake do every day.**
- Play the CD. The pupils listen and tick the correct boxes. Pause the CD after each sentence to allow the pupils time to do this.
- Play the CD again. The pupils say what Beth and Jake do every day.

Answers: **1** Beth: brush my teeth, comb my hair, have a shower, get dressed, sleep **2** Jake: brush my teeth, comb my hair, get dressed, sleep

Activity Book

Activity 1

Read and tick (✓) or cross (✗).

- (Books open.) Elicit the days of the week from the class. Then say that if you do something on every day of the week it means that you do it every day.
- Ask the pupils to read out the sentences in their Activity Books.
- The pupils tick the sentences that are true for them and write a cross for the sentences that aren't true.
- Ask volunteers to read out their sentences.

Activity 2

Order and write.

- Focus the pupils on Activity 2. Ask a volunteer to read the jumbled words and then to say the correct sentence.
- The pupils work on their own to order the words and write the correct sentences.

Answers: **1** I get up every day. **2** I go to bed every day. **3** I get dressed every day. **4** I wash my face every day. **5** I have a shower every day.

Recycled vocabulary

- The pupils look at the picture and write the word. If necessary, they look back at the previous unit.

Answer: skirt

Ending the lesson

Review the lesson.

- (Books closed.) Say **Today we've talked about the activities we do every day and acted out a conversation. Did you work well today?** Elicit answers from the pupils.

Review the task flashcards.

- Point to the task flashcards. Say **Look at the activities you've done today. Which activity was your favourite?** Elicit the pupils' favourite activities.

Extra activities

Reinforcement

▶ *CD1 Track 7 p256*

- Sing *Seven days a week* with the class.

Extension

- Practise the new daily routines vocabulary. Play a mime game with the class. Call out daily routines at random and the pupils mime the action.

Key Competences and Key Learning Outcomes

- Read, listen and understand a story about a lost tooth
- Read the story with some fluency
- Become familiar with the story through a pre-reading task
- Understand the importance of looking after your teeth
- Understand and act out the story
- Give an opinion on the story

Key language:
- *breakfast, champion, dinner, incredible, magic, pillow, tomorrow, wobbly tooth*
- *I (have breakfast every morning). What's the matter? I've got (a wobbly tooth).*

Recycled: *hungry; sweater; garden*

Recycled: *Can you (see my tooth)? No, I can't. Have you got (a wobbly tooth)? Yes, I have. No, I haven't.*

Materials
- Pupil's Book pp94–95; Activity Book p92; Class CD4; Teacher's App on Navio
- Daily routines flashcards
- Teacher's Resource Bank: Task flashcards: *think, read, listen, act out, write, number, Talk Partners*
- Teacher's Resource Bank: Unit 9 Lesson 3 Animated Story

Optional materials
- Teacher's Resource Bank: Five Trinity Exam Practice cards (selected from the Starter Unit and Units 1, 2, 3, 4, 5, 6, 7 and 8)

At a Glance Lesson Plan

Pupil's Book

Starting the lesson
- Use the Trinity Exam Practice cards (optional).
- Review the language from Lesson 2.
- Set learning outcomes using the task flashcards.

Before you read
- Explain the story title.
- Read and answer the question.

Activity 1
- Listen and read.

▶ *CD4 Track 13 p272*
- Act out.

Now watch the animated story!

After you read: Activity 2
- Go to page 92 in your Activity Book.
- Values: Read and write.

Ending the lesson
- Review the lesson.
- Review the task flashcards.

Activity Book

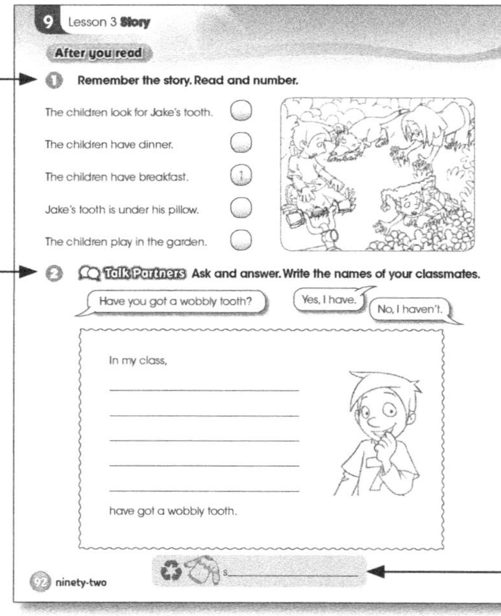

Activity Book

After you read: Activity 1
- Remember the story. Read and number.

Activity 2
- **Talk Partners** Ask and answer.
- Write the names of your classmates.

Recycled vocabulary
- Look, remember and write the word.

Digital resources

Teacher's Digital: Don't forget you can teach this lesson using the Teacher's App on Navio.

Pupil's Digital: Encourage your pupils to use the Pupil's App on Navio to practise the vocabulary from this lesson.

Powered By NAVIO

Detailed Lesson Plan

Starting the lesson

Use the Trinity Exam Practice cards (optional).
- The pupils practise asking and answering questions (see p31).

Review the language from Lesson 2.
- Ask a volunteer to come to the front of the class. Hold up a daily routines flashcard so the pupil can't see it but the rest of the class can. The class mimes the activity and the pupil guesses what it is.
- Repeat with other pupils and other activities.

Set learning outcomes using the task flashcards.
- Say **Today we're going to listen to a story**.
- Hold up the task flashcards in turn and elicit the activities. Stick them on one side of the board. Point to them during the lesson to reinforce your instructions.

Before you read

Explain the story title.
- (Books open.) Focus on the story title. Mime having a wobbly tooth. Say **I've got a wobbly tooth.** Check understanding and ask the pupils to repeat the expression.

Read and answer the question.
- Read the speech bubble. The pupils scan the story to find the magic bike (frames 7 and 8).

Pupil's Book Activity 1

Listen and read. Act out.

▶ *CD4 Track 13 p272*
- The pupils place their 'magic finger' on the first frame of the story.
- Play the CD. The pupils point to the different frames as the story progresses. Pause the CD after each frame to check that all the pupils are following. Ask questions about each story frame to help and check understanding.
- Play the CD again.

Suggested comprehension questions
- Frame 1: **What's on the table?** (*Breakfast, cereal, fruit, eggs, toast.*)
- Frame 2: **Has Jake got a wobbly tooth?** (*Yes.*)
- Frame 3: **Where are the children?** (*In the garden.*) **Is Jake wobbling his tooth?** (*Yes.*)
- Frame 4: **What does Jake say?** (*I win! I'm the champion.*) **What's missing?** (*His tooth.*)
- Frame 5: **Can the children see Jake's tooth?** (*No.*)
- Frame 6: **Who's hungry?** (*Beth.*) **Can the children see the tooth?** (*No.*)
- Frame 7: **Is it day or night?** (*Night.*) **What is the magic bike doing?** (*Looking for the tooth.*)
- Frame 8: **What's under the pillow?** (*Jake's tooth.*) **How did it get there?** (*The magic bike.*)
- Finally, ask the pupils **Is this a good story?** The pupils give their opinion through gesture (thumbs up / down) or orally (*yes* / *no*).
- Organise the class into four groups (Beth, Molly, Jake and Mum / Dad) to act out the story.
- Play the CD. Each group joins in when their character speaks. If they need extra support, pause the CD and ask them to repeat the phrase instead.
- The groups swap roles and join in with their new character.

Now watch the animated story

After you read

Go to page 92 in your Activity Book.

Activity Book:

After you read: Activity 1

Remember the story. Read and number.
- (Books open.) Ask **Do you remember the story?**
- Ask different pupils to read out the sentences. Elicit which is the first sentence and point to the number 1.
- The pupils remember the story and number the other sentences in the correct order.

Answers: 3, 4, 1, 5, 2

Activity 2

Ask and answer. Write the names of your classmates.
- Focus the pupils on the speech bubbles in Activity 2. Ask the pupils if they've got a wobbly tooth. They answer *Yes, I have* or *No, I haven't*.
- **Talk Partners** The pupils ask and answer the question with a Talk Partner. Then they write the names of all the children in the class with a wobbly tooth.

Recycled vocabulary
- The pupils look at the picture and write the word. If necessary, they look back at the previous unit.

Answer: sweater

Pupil's Book Activity 2

Read and write.
- The pupils look at the photo on the right. Read out the sentence in the speech bubble and prompt the class to tell you the correct answer.
- Highlight the importance of brushing your teeth regularly.

Answer: teeth

Ending the lesson

Review the lesson.
- (Books closed.) Say **Today we've listened to a story about a wobbly tooth.** Ask **What happened in the story?** Elicit the story from the pupils.
- Then say **Today you've learnt that it's important to look after your teeth.**

Review the task flashcards.
- Point to the task flashcards. Say **Look at the activities you've done today. Which activity was your favourite?** Elicit the pupils' favourite activities.

Key Competences and Key Learning Outcomes

- Identify and say the three meals a day
- Say when you have meals
- Write about what you do at different times of the day

- Sing a song

Key language

- *breakfast in the morning, lunch in the afternoon, dinner in the evening, a snack at night*
- *I have (dinner) in the (evening). Are you hungry (in the morning)? Yes, I am.*
- Extension: *fork, knife, plate, spoon*
- **Recycled:** *play; T-shirt; I get up. I brush my teeth.*

Materials

- Pupil's Book p96; Activity Book p93; Class CD4; Teacher's App on Navio
- Teacher's Resource Bank: Task flashcards: *listen, sing, Talk Partners, circle, read, write*

Optional materials

- Teacher's Resource Bank: Five Trinity Exam Practice cards (selected from the Starter Unit and Units 1, 2, 3, 4, 5, 6, 7 and 8).
- Daily routines flashcards

At a Glance Lesson Plan

Starting the lesson

- Use the Trinity Exam Practice cards (optional).
- Review the Lesson 3 story.
- Set learning outcomes using the task flashcards.

Vocabulary presentation

- Present the new vocabulary.

Activity 1

- Listen, point and say.
- ▶ *CD4 Track 14 p272*

Activity 2

- Listen and point.
- ▶ *CD4 Track 15 p272*
- Sing *Are you hungry?*

Activity 3

- Listen and repeat.
- ▶ *CD4 Track 16 p273*
- Talk Partners Play a game.

Go to the Activity Book.

Pupil's Book

Ending the lesson

- Review the lesson.
- Review the task flashcards.

Extra activities

Reinforcement

- Play *How many can you remember?*

Vocabulary Extension

- Present four additional vocabulary items.

Digital resources

Teacher's Digital: Don't forget you can teach this lesson using the Teacher's App on Navio.

Pupil's Digital: Encourage your pupils to use the Pupil's App on Navio to practise the vocabulary from this lesson.

Powered By NAVIO

Activity Book

Activity Book

Activity 1

- Listen and circle.
- ▶ *CD4 Track 17 p273*

Activity 2

- Read and write.
- Say.

- Talk Partners Play *Me too!*

Recycled vocabulary

- Look, remember and write the word.

Detailed Lesson Plan

Starting the lesson

Use the Trinity Exam Practice cards (optional).

- The pupils practise asking and answering questions (see p31).

Review the Lesson 3 story.

- Describe one of the story frames, e.g. **Jake, Beth and Molly are in the garden. They are playing volleyball. Which frame is it?** Continue with all the other frames.

Set learning outcomes using the task flashcards.

- Say **Today we're going to learn about the meals we eat, sing a song and practise a conversation.**
- Hold up the task flashcards in turn and elicit the activities. Stick them on one side of the board. Point to them during the lesson to reinforce your instructions.

Vocabulary presentation

Present the new vocabulary.

- (Books open.) Point to the first picture in the Pupil's Book and ask **Are you hungry? This is breakfast. What's for breakfast? We have breakfast in the morning.** Repeat with the other meals.

Pupil's Book Activity 1

Listen, point and say.

▶ *CD4 Track 14 p272*

- (Books open.) The pupils look at the pictures.
- Play the CD. The pupils point to the pictures and say the phrases.
- Play *What's missing?* Read out the phrases but miss one out each time. Elicit the missing phrase.

Pupil's Book Activity 2

Listen and point. Sing *Are you hungry?*

▶ *CD4 Track 15 p272*

- Focus the pupils on Activity 2. Ask **What are the children doing?** Elicit the meals and food.
- Play the CD. The pupils listen to the song and do the actions.
- Play the CD again and the pupils join in with the song.

Pupil's Book Activity 3

Listen and repeat. Play a game.

▶ *CD4 Track 16 p273*

- Focus the pupils on the activity and read out the speech bubbles. Remind them of when they have different meals.
- Play the CD. The pupils listen and read.
- Play the CD again. The pupils listen and repeat the statements and the responses. Repeat with more examples.
- Talk Partners The pupils play the game with a Talk Partner.

Activity Book

Activity 1

Listen and circle.

▶ *CD4 Track 17 p273*

- (Books open.) Elicit what the pupils can see in the pictures.
- Play the CD, pausing after each conversation. The pupils listen and circle the correct phrase.
- Play the CD again to check the answers.

Answers: **1** in the morning **2** in the afternoon **3** in the evening **4** at night

Activity 2

Read and write. Say.

- Focus the pupils on Activity 2. Read out the activities, encouraging different pupils to finish the sentences.
- The pupils work on their own to complete the sentences about their daily routines.
- Talk Partners The pupils play *Me too!* with a Talk Partner. They say *Me too!* when they both do the activity at the same time of day.

Recycled vocabulary

- The pupils look at the picture and write the word. If necessary, they look back at the previous unit.

Answer: T-shirt

Ending the lesson

Review the lesson.

- (Books closed.) Say **Today we've learnt about the meals we have, sung a song and practised saying sentences. What meals do we have?** Elicit the answers from the pupils.

Review the task flashcards.

- Point to the task flashcards. Say **Look at the activities you've done today. Which activity was your favourite?** Elicit the pupils' favourite activities.

Extra activities

Reinforcement

- Play *How many can you remember?* (see p23) with the daily routines flashcards.

Vocabulary Extension

- Use the Vocabulary Booster on Navio and present and practise four additional words to describe cutlery: *fork, knife, plate, spoon*.

Key Competences and Key Learning Outcomes

- Say a tongue twister with the 'th' sound
- Listen for specific information
- Play a communication game about daily routines

Key language

- *I (have a shower) (in the morning). I (sleep) at night.*

Recycled: *shorts; in the morning, in the afternoon, in the evening, at night*

Recycled: *Yes, that's right. That isn't right. My turn.*

Materials

- Pupil's Book p97; Activity Book p94; Class CD4; Teacher's App on Navio
- Teacher's Resource Bank: Task flashcards: *listen, say, write, colour, Talk Partners, match, cut out, think*
- Scissors, crayons or coloured pencils
- Teacher's Resource Bank: Unit 9 Lesson 5 Activity 3 cut-outs

Optional materials

- Teacher's Resource Bank: Five Trinity Exam Practice cards (selected from the Starter Unit and Units 1, 2, 3, 4, 5, 6, 7 and 8)
- Coloured paper

At a Glance Lesson Plan

Starting the lesson

- Use the Trinity Exam Practice cards (optional).
- Review the vocabulary from Lesson 4.
- Review the *Are you hungry?* song.

▶ *CD4 Track 15 p272*

- Set learning outcomes using the task flashcards.

Activity 1

- Listen and say.

▶ *CD4 Track 18 p273*

Go to Magic Phonics.

Go to the Activity Book.

Activity 2

- Listen and match.

▶ *CD4 Track 19 p273*

Activity 3

- Talk Partners
  Make and play the game.

Pupil's Book

Ending the lesson

- Review the lesson.
- Review the task flashcards.

Extra activity

Reinforcement

- Continue the pronunciation wall display.

Activity Book

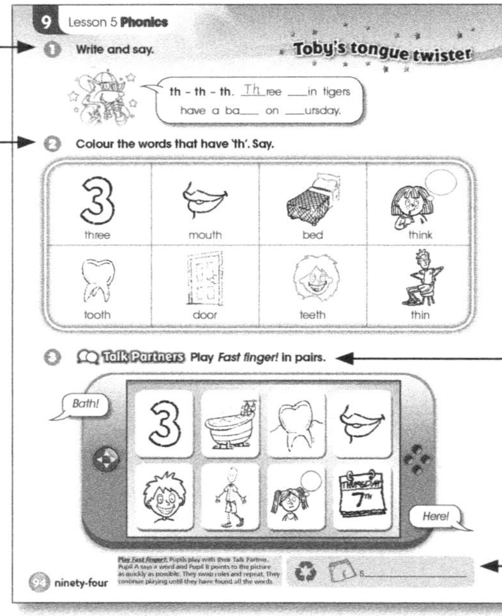

Activity Book

Activity 1

- Write and say.

Activity 2

- Colour the words that have 'th'.
- Say.

Go to Magic Phonics.

Activity 3

- Talk Partners
  Play *Fast finger!* in pairs.

Recycled vocabulary

- Look, remember and write the word.

Digital resources

Teacher's Digital: Don't forget you can teach this lesson using the Teacher's App on Navio.

Pupil's Digital: Encourage your pupils to use the Pupil's App on Navio to practise the vocabulary from this lesson.

Powered By NAVIO

Starting the lesson

Use the Trinity Exam Practice cards (optional).
- The pupils practise asking and answering questions (see p31).

Review the vocabulary from Lesson 4.
- Review the three meals of the day and the times of the day.

Review the *Are you hungry?* song.
▶ *CD4 Track 15 p272*
- Play the CD. The pupils sing and do the actions.

Set learning outcomes using the task flashcards.
- Say **Today we're going to practise saying a tongue twister and make and play a speaking game.**
- Hold up the task flashcards in turn and elicit the activities. Stick them on one side of the board. Point to them during the lesson to reinforce your instructions.

Pupil's Book Activity 1

Listen and say.
▶ *CD4 Track 18 p273*
- (Books open.) Write the target 'th' sound on the board and say it. The pupils repeat.
- Say **It's time for Toby's tongue twister. What can you see in the picture? Where are the tigers? What are they doing?**
- Play the CD. The pupils listen and repeat the target sound, then the words and then the entire tongue twister, faster and faster.

Go to Magic Phonics.

Activity Book

Activity 1
Write and say.
- (Books open.) The pupils write the letter 'th' in the tongue twister. Remind them that they should use a lower case 't' and not a capital 'T' as in 'Three' or 'Thursday'.

Answer: Three thin tigers have a bath on Thursday.

Activity 2
Colour the words that have 'th'. Say.
- Ask the pupils to say the words that have the letters 'th'. The pupils colour and say these words.

Answers: three, mouth, think, tooth, teeth, thin

Go to Magic Phonics.

Activity 3
Play *Fast finger!* in pairs.
- Demonstrate the activity. Say a word, e.g. **bath.** The pupils point to the correct picture as quickly as possible.
- Talk Partners The pupils play the game with a Talk Partner.

Recycled vocabulary
- The pupils look at the picture and write the word. If necessary, they look back at the previous unit.

Answer: shorts

Pupil's Book Activity 2

Listen and match.
▶ *CD4 Track 19 p273*
- Ask **What can you see in the pictures?**
- Explain to the pupils that they are going to listen to two children playing a memory game.
- Play the CD, pausing after each sentence. The pupils listen and draw a matching line to join the different items.
- Play the CD again and check the answers.

Answers: **1** in the morning, happy face **2** at night, unhappy face, **3** in the evening, happy face

Pupil's Book Activity 3

Make and play the game.
- Focus the pupils on Activity 3. Tell them that they are going to make and play the same game.
- The pupils cut out and colour the picture cards and place all 12 of them on their desks.
- When the pupils have cut out the cards, play the game with the class. Place 12 cards face down on a table at the front of the room. Invite a pupil to turn over two of the cards and say the corresponding sentence. Ask the rest of the class **Is that right?** If the cards are a pair, the pupil keeps the cards and has another turn. If not, the pupil places the cards face down on the table with the other cards and another pupil has a turn.
- Talk Partners The pupils play the game with a Talk Partner.

Ending the lesson

Review the lesson.
- (Books closed.) Say **Today we've practised a tongue twister and played a game in pairs.** Elicit the tongue twister from the pupils.

Review the task flashcards.
- Point to the task flashcards. Say **Look at the activities you've done today. Which activity was your favourite?** Elicit the pupils' favourite activities.

Extra activity

Reinforcement
- Continue the pronunciation wall display. Cut out the letters 'th' in coloured paper. Stick them on a piece of differently coloured paper to make a wall display. Elicit words that begin with these letters and write them on the wall display.
- Encourage the pupils to add new words that have the letters 'th' during the year. Introduce the alternative way of reading this sound, e.g. as in 'father'. They can either tell you the new word for you to add or write the word themselves if they can.

Key Competences and Key Learning Outcomes

- Listen for general information

- Read about the Tooth Fairy in Britain
- Think about what happens to teeth where you live

Key language

- *box, letter, lunch, money, money box, pillow, Tooth Fairy*
- *The Tooth Fairy (comes at night). I put the box (under my pillow). I find (a letter).*

Recycled: *trousers; at night, in the morning; breakfast; tooth*

Materials

- Pupil's Book 98; Activity Book p95; Class CD4; Teacher's App on Navio
- Teacher's Resource Bank: Task flashcards: *listen, read, think, write, tick, draw*

Optional materials

- Teacher's Resource Bank: Five Trinity Exam Practice cards (selected from the Starter Unit and Units 1, 2, 3, 4, 5, 6, 7 and 8)
- Teacher's Resource Bank: Daily routines word cards
- sheets of A4 paper

At a Glance Lesson Plan

Starting the lesson

- Use the Trinity Exam Practice cards (optional).
- Talk Partners Review Toby's tongue twister.
- ▶ ***CD4 Track 18 p273***
- Review the *It's a beautiful day* song.
- ▶ ***CD4 Track 8 p272***
- ▶ ***CD4 Track 9 p272 (optional karaoke version)***
- Set learning outcomes using the task flashcards.

Activity 1

- Listen and read.
- ▶ ***CD4 Track 20 p273***
- Answer.

Think about your culture

- Have you got a Tooth Fairy in your country?

Go to the Activity Book.

Pupil's Book

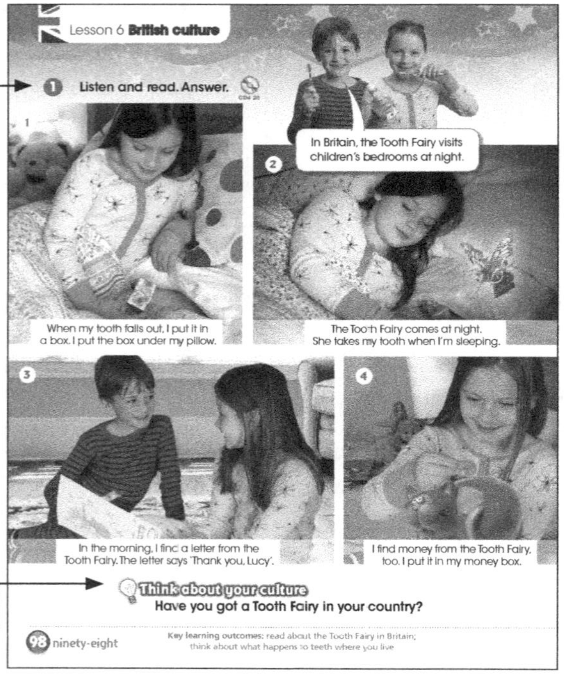

Ending the lesson

- Review the lesson.
- Review the task flashcards.

Extra activities

Reinforcement

- Play *Splat!*

Extension

- Make a class wall display.

Digital resources

Teacher's Digital: Don't forget you can teach this lesson using the Teacher's App on Navio.

Powered By NAVIO

Activity Book

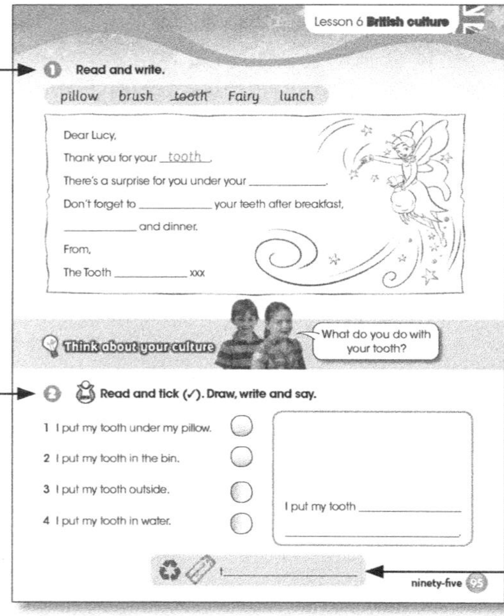

Activity Book

Activity 1

- Read and write.

Activity 2: Think about your culture

- Read and tick (✓).
- Draw, write and say.

Recycled vocabulary

- Look, remember and write the word.

Starting the lesson

Use the Trinity Exam Practice cards (optional).
- The pupils practise asking and answering questions (see p31).

Review Toby's tongue twister.
▶ *CD4 Track 18 p273*
- Ask **What sound did you practise in Toby's tongue twister? Can you remember the tongue twister?** (*Three thin tigers have a bath on Thursday.*)
- Play the CD. Practise the tongue twister as a class.
- Talk Partners The pupils practise saying the tongue twister as fast as possible with a Talk Partner. Choose a fast pair to say it for the class.

Review the *It's a beautiful day* song.
▶ *CD4 Track 8 p272*
▶ *CD4 Track 9 p272 (optional karaoke version)*
- Play the CD (or use the karaoke version). The pupils sing the song and do the actions.

Set learning outcomes using the task flashcards.
- Say **Today we're going to learn about the Tooth Fairy in Britain.**
- Hold up the task flashcards in turn and elicit the activities. Stick them on one side of the board. Point to them during the lesson to reinforce your instructions.

Pupil's Book Activity 1

Listen and read. Answer.
▶ *CD4 Track 20 p273*
- Say to the class **Show me your teeth.** Encourage the class to give a wide smile to display their front teeth. Say **Hands up if you've got a wobbly tooth.** These pupils raise their hands. Then ask **Has a tooth fallen out?** Use mime to clarify the meaning and ask the pupils to put their hands up if any of their teeth have fallen out. Ask **How many teeth have fallen out?** Encourage the pupils to tell you the number and show the class the gaps in their teeth. (On average pupils have lost between two and eight teeth by the time they are seven.) Then say **Let's find out what happens to children's teeth in Britain.**
- (Books open.) Focus the pupils on the picture of the Tooth Fairy. Ask **Who's this?** Elicit comments. Read the speech bubble.
- Play the CD, pausing after each piece of information to check understanding and ask questions.

Suggested comprehension questions
- Photo 1: **What do the children put in a box under their pillow?** (*A tooth.*)
- Photo 2: **When does the tooth fairy come?** (*At night.*)
- Photo 3: **When do they find a letter and money under their pillow?** (*In the morning.*)
- Photo 4: **What do they put in a money box?** (*Money.*)

Pupil's Book Think about your culture

Have you got a Tooth Fairy in your country?
- Read out the question.
- The pupils tell you if they have a Tooth Fairy in their country. If not, ask what they do have.
- Ask additional questions, e.g. **Where do you put your teeth when they fall out? What do you find in the morning?**

Activity Book

Activity 1
Read and write.
- (Books open.) Read the words in the word box with the class. Then focus the pupils on the letter.
- Ask different pupils to read the letter, completing it with words from the word box.
- The pupils work on their own to complete the letter.

Answers: tooth, pillow, brush, lunch, Fairy

Activity 2: Think about your culture
Read and tick (✓). Draw, write and say.
- Read out the question in the speech bubble. Elicit the pupils' answers.
- Read out the first sentence. The pupils tick the box if this is what happens to their teeth when they fall out.
- The pupils do the same for the other sentences.
- The pupils draw themselves with whoever takes their teeth. They write a corresponding sentence.
- Different pupils show the class their drawings and read their sentences.

Recycled vocabulary
- The pupils look at the picture and write the word. If necessary, they look back at the previous unit.

Answer: trousers

Ending the lesson

Review the lesson.
- (Books closed.) Say **Today we've talked about the Tooth Fairy. Who takes your teeth? Do you find a letter and money in the morning?** Elicit answers.

Review the task flashcards.
- Point to the task flashcards. Say **Look at the activities you've done today. Which activity was your favourite?** Elicit the pupils' favourite activities.

Extra activities

Reinforcement
- Play *Splat!* (see p23) with the daily routines word cards.

Extension
- Make a class wall display of Tooth Fairy letters. Give out a piece of A4 paper to each pupil and ask them to copy the completed letter from page 95 of their Activity Books onto it. They can then draw a picture of the Tooth Fairy, or whoever it is that takes their teeth, and colour it.

Key Competences and Key Learning Outcomes

- Think about what they can see in the day and at night
- Review animal behaviour at different times of the day (optional)
- Read for specific information
- Read and understand a poem

Key language

- animal noises; *children, cockerel, moon, owl, stars; in the day*
- *I can see (the moon). I can hear (a cockerel).*

Recycled: *shoes; at night, sleep; sun*

Materials

- Pupil's Book p99; Activity Book p96, Class CD4; Teacher's App on Navio
- Farm animals flashcards
- Teacher's Resource Bank: Task flashcards: *listen, number, read, act out, write*

Optional materials

- Teacher's Resource Bank: Five Trinity Exam Practice cards (selected from the Starter Unit and Units 1, 2, 3, 4, 5, 6, 7 and 8)
- Daily routines flashcards
- Teacher's Resource Bank: Daily routines word cards
- Video recorder

At a Glance Lesson Plan

Starting the lesson

- Use the Trinity Exam Practice cards (optional).
- Review farm animals.
- Set learning outcomes using the task flashcards.

Before you read

- Learn about daytime and night-time animals.

Activity 1

- Listen and number.
- ▶ *CD4 Track 21 p273*
- Say *day* or *night*.

Activity 2

- Listen and read the poem.
- ▶ *CD4 Track 22 p273*

Activity 3

- Act out the poem.

After you read

Go to page 96 in your Activity Book.

Pupil's Book

Ending the lesson

- Review the lesson.
- Review the task flashcards.

Extra activities

Reinforcement

- Play *Match the word and flashcard*.

Extension

- Record a performance of a poem.

Link to Science

- **The Sun:** Review daytime and night-time elements in the sky and the animals that are awake during those times.

Digital resources

Teacher's Digital: Don't forget you can teach this lesson using the Teacher's App on Navio.

Pupil's Digital: Encourage your pupils to use the Pupil's App on Navio to practise the vocabulary from this lesson.

Powered By NAVIO

Activity Book

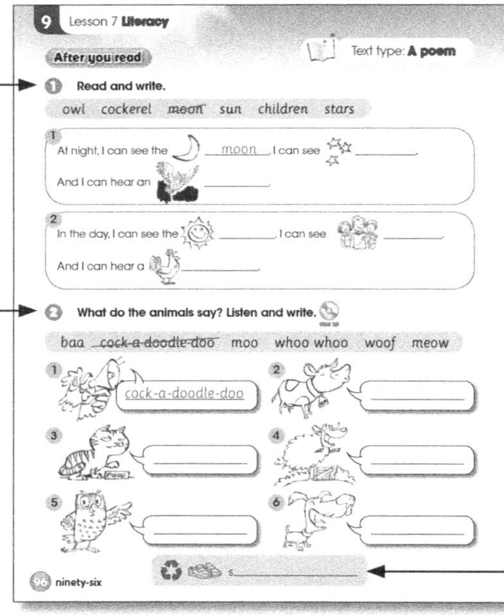

Activity Book

After you read: Activity 1

- Read and write.

Activity 2

- What do the animals say?
- Listen and write.
- ▶ *CD4 Track 23 p273*

Recycled vocabulary

- Look, remember and write the word.

Starting the lesson

Use the Trinity Exam Practice cards (optional).
- The pupils practise asking and answering questions (see p31).

Review farm animals.
- Hold up each farm animal flashcard and elicit the name.
- Hold a farm animals flashcard so it is facing you, describe it and the pupils guess which farm animal it is, e.g. **It's big. It's got four legs. It can run. It's black and white.** (*Cow.*)
- Explain that some animals are awake during the day and others are awake at night.
- Ask **Can we see this animal in the day time or at night time?** (*Daytime.*) Repeat with the other flashcards.
- Elicit some daytime and night-time animals from the pupils and write or draw them on the board.

Set learning outcomes using the task flashcards.
- Say **Today we're going to read and write a poem.**
- Hold up the task flashcards in turn and elicit the activities. Stick them on one side of the board. Point to them during the lesson to reinforce your instructions.

Before you read

Learn about daytime and night-time animals.
- Say **We're going to learn about daytime and night-time animals. Daytime animals come out during the day and sleep at night. Night-time animals come out at night and sleep during the day.**
- Elicit any daytime / night-time animals that pupils know.

Pupil's Book Activity 1

Listen and number. Say *day* or *night*.

▶ *CD4 Track 21 p273*
- (Books open.) Play the CD, pausing for the pupils to say which picture it is.
- Play the CD again and the pupils number the pictures. The pupils say *day* if they hear this sound during the day, and *night* if they hear it at night.

Answers: **1** owl **2** cockerel **3** sleep **4** children

Pupil's Book Activity 2

Listen and read the poem.

▶ *CD4 Track 22 p273*
- Say **Let's listen and read the poem.**
- Play the CD, pausing after each pair of sentences to do the action with the class.
- Play the CD again. The pupils listen and do the actions.
- Play the CD again. The pupils read the poem aloud with the recording.

Suggested comprehension questions
- **What does the owl say?** Elicit an owl's hoots.
- **What does the cockerel say?** Elicit a cockerel crowing.

Pupil's Book Activity 3

Act out the poem.
- Organise the class into groups. Ask a group to come to the front of the class.
- Play the CD. The group acts out the poem.
- Ask different groups to come to the front of the class and act out the poem.

Activity Book

After you read: Activity 1

Read and write.
- (Books open.) Read out the words in the word box with the pupils.
- Read the sentences and ask the pupils to look at the pictures. Elicit the answers.
- The pupils work on their own to write the answers.

Answers: **1** moon, stars, owl **2** sun, children, cockerel

Activity 2

What do the animals say? Listen and write.

▶ *CD4 Track 23 p273*
- Point to and name the animals. Then say the animal noises in the word box with the pupils.
- Play the CD. The pupils listen and write the animal noises in the speech bubbles next to the correct pictures.

Answers: **1** cock-a-doodle-doo **2** moo **3** meow **4** baa **5** whoo whoo **6** woof

Recycled vocabulary
- The pupils look at the picture and write the word. If necessary, they look back at the previous unit.

Answer: shoes

Ending the lesson

Review the lesson.
- (Books closed.) Say **Today we've read and written a poem in English. Can you remember what you wrote?** Elicit answers.

Review the task flashcards.
- Point to the task flashcards. Say **Look at the activities you've done today. Which activity was your favourite?** Elicit the pupils' favourite activities.

Extra activities

Reinforcement
- Play *Match the word and flashcard* (see p23) with the daily routines word cards and flashcards.

Extension
- Record your pupils performing the poem.

Link to Science

- If you are studying the Science topic of **The Sun** in English, you could review the names of some of the elements seen in the night and day sky and day and night time animals. Review these concepts by doing a drawing dictation on the board. Divide the board into two parts: *day* and *night*. Then say **I can see the moon at night.** Invite a pupil to come to the board and draw the moon in the corresponding part of the board. Repeat with other day and night time elements, inviting a different pupil to draw each time.

Key Competences and Key Learning Outcomes

- Review language in the unit
- Reflect on own learning
- Sing a cooperative learning song

Key language

Recycled: *brush my teeth, comb my hair, get dressed, get up, go to bed, go to school, have a shower, make my bed, sleep, wash my face; breakfast in the morning, lunch in the afternoon, dinner in the evening, a snack at night; swimsuit*

Recycled: *I (get up) (in the morning). I (have lunch) (in the afternoon). I (have dinner) (in the evening). I (sleep) (at night).*

Materials

- Pupil's Book p100; Activity Book p97; Class CD4; Teacher's App on Navio
- Daily routines flashcards
- Teacher's Resource Bank: Task flashcards: *listen, number, write, sing, think, stick, match*
- Teacher's Resource Bank: Traffic light cut-out
- *Give Me Five!* sticker

Optional materials

- Teacher's Resource Bank: Five Trinity Exam Practice cards (selected from the Starter Unit and Units 1, 2, 3, 4, 5, 6, 7 and 8)

At a Glance Lesson Plan

Starting the lesson

- Use the Trinity Exam Practice cards (optional).
- Review the unit vocabulary.
- Set learning outcomes using the task flashcards.

Activity 1

- Listen and number.
- ▶ *CD4 Track 24 p273*
- Write and say.

Activity 2

- Look and write.

Activity 3 Cooperative learning

- Sing *Well done!*
- ▶ *CD4 Track 25 p273*
- Stick the *Give Me Five!* sticker.
- Go to the Activity Book.

Pupil's Book

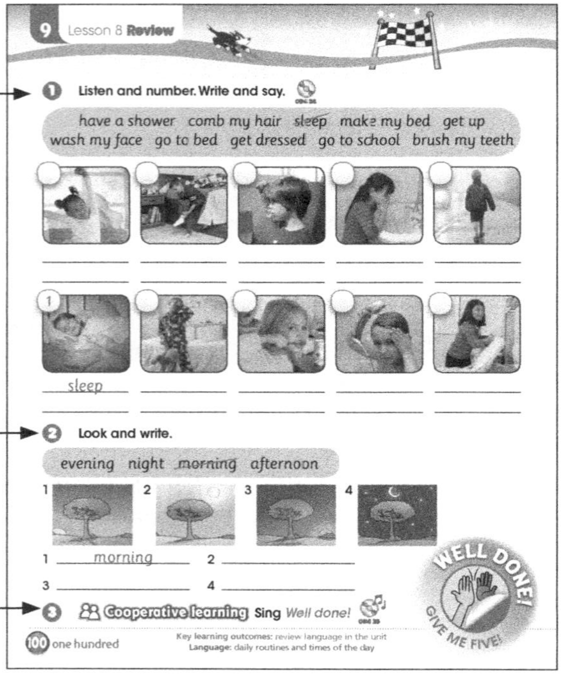

Ending the lesson

- Review the task flashcards.

Digital resources

Teacher's Digital: Don't forget you can teach this lesson using the Teacher's App on Navio.

Pupil's Digital: Encourage your pupils to use the Pupil's App on Navio to practise the vocabulary from this lesson.

Powered By NAVIO

Activity Book

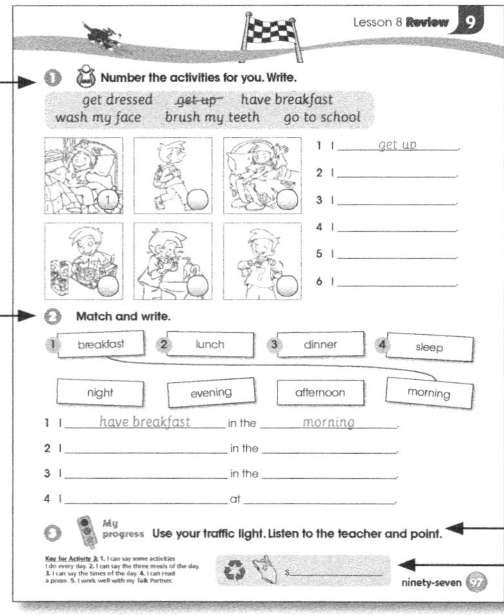

Activity Book

Activity 1

- Number the activities for you.
- Write.

Activity 2

- Match and write.

Activity 3 My progress

- Use your traffic light. Listen to the teacher and point.

Recycled vocabulary

- Look, remember and write the word.

Starting the lesson

Use the Trinity Exam Practice cards (optional).

- The pupils practise asking and answering questions (see p31).

Review the unit vocabulary.

- Hold up a daily routines flashcard and elicit the word. Stick the flashcard face down on the board. Repeat until all the flashcards are on the board.
- Ask **Where's (get up)?** Ask a pupil to come to the front and turn over one of the flashcards. If it's the correct flashcard, he / she says *It's here*. If it isn't the correct flashcard, another pupil has a go. Repeat with different daily routines words and different pupils.
- Variation: Play the game in two teams. The teams take it in turns to remember the daily routines.

Set learning outcomes using the task flashcards.

- Say **Today we're going to remember what we've learnt in Unit 9.**
- Hold up the task flashcards in turn and elicit the activities. Stick them on one side of the board. Point to them during the lesson to reinforce your instructions.

Pupil's Book Activity 1

Listen and number. Write and say.

▶ *CD4 Track 24 p273*

- (Books open.) Focus the pupils on the photos. Elicit the daily routines.
- Play the CD, pausing after each sentence. The pupils listen and write the correct numbers in the circles.
- Play the CD again. This time the pupils write the words under the photos.
- Invite pupils to read out their answers.

Answers: **1** sleep **2** have a shower **3** wash my face **4** go to bed **5** comb my hair **6** get up **7** make my bed **8** brush my teeth **9** go to school **10** get dressed

Pupil's Book Activity 2

Look and write.

- Ask a volunteer to read out the words in the word box.
- The pupils write the words in the correct places.

Answers: **1** morning **2** afternoon **3** evening **4** night

Pupil's Book Activity 3: Cooperative learning

Sing *Well done!*

▶ *CD4 Track 25 p273*

- Praise the pupils for their hard work and encourage them to praise each other. Play the *Well done!* song. The pupils sing and do the actions.

Stick the *Give Me Five!* sticker.

- The pupils stick the *Give Me Five!* sticker on the Pupil's Book page.
- Variation: Sing the *Well done!* song and stick the *Give Me Five!* sticker after the class has also completed the Activity Book Lesson 8 Review.

Activity Book

Activity 1 (me)

Number the activities for you. Write.

- Read out the phrases in the word box with the class.
- Point to the first picture and elicit the daily routine. Repeat for the other pictures.
- Ask the pupils to think about the order in which they do these daily activities. They number the pictures in order.
- Then ask them to write the sentences.

Activity 2

Match and write.

- The pupils match a word in the top row with one in the bottom row.
- Then they complete the sentences with the correct words.

Answers: **1** I have breakfast in the morning. **2** I have lunch in the afternoon. **3** I have dinner in the evening. **4** I sleep at night.

Activity 3: My progress (My progress)

Use your traffic light. Listen to the teacher and point.

- (Books closed.) Ask the class to take out their traffic light cut-out. Say **Let's think about our work in this unit.** Point to the green circle, nod your head, smile a lot, and say **I can say some activities I do every day. Yes, I can do this very well.** Point to the yellow circle, move your head a little, smile a little and say **Yes, I can do this.** Then point to the red circle, shake your head and say **No, I can't do this.**
- Read the different statements. For each one, the pupils point to the colour on their traffic light that shows how they feel about their own learning.

Self-assessment statements

1. I can say some activities I do every day.
2. I can say the three meals of the day.
3. I can say the times of the day.
4. I can read a poem.
5. I work well with my Talk Partner.

Recycled vocabulary

- The pupils look at the picture and write the word. If necessary, they look back at the previous unit.

Answer: swimsuit

Ending the lesson

Review the task flashcards.

- Point to the task flashcards. Say **Look at the activities you've done today. Which activity was your favourite?** Elicit the pupils' favourite activities.

Key Competences and Key Learning Outcomes

- Watch and understand a video about teeth
- Draw and say what you do to look after your teeth

- Understand the importance of looking after your teeth

Key language

- *at night, brush teeth, dentist, in the afternoon, in the evening, in the morning, letter, pillow, Tooth Fairy, wobbly tooth*

Materials

- Pupil's Book p101; Activity Book p98; Class CD4; Video; Teacher's App on Navio
- Teacher's Resource Bank: Task flashcards: *number, read, tick, think, listen, write, draw, say, Talk Partner*

Optional materials

- Teacher's Resource Bank: Trinity Exam Practice cards (selected from Unit 9)

At a Glance Lesson Plan

Starting the lesson

- Use the Trinity Exam Practice cards (optional).
Think-Pair-Share
Review the Tooth Fairy.
- Set learning outcomes and use the task flashcards.

Pre-watching activity

- Predict the words about teeth in the video.

Activity 1

- Watch the video.
Unit 9 video p279
- Number the pictures.

Activity 2

- Watch the video again.
Unit 9 video
- Read and tick (✓) or cross (✗).

Activity 3

- Read and think. Tick (✓) or cross (✗).
Go to the Activity Book.

Pupil's Book

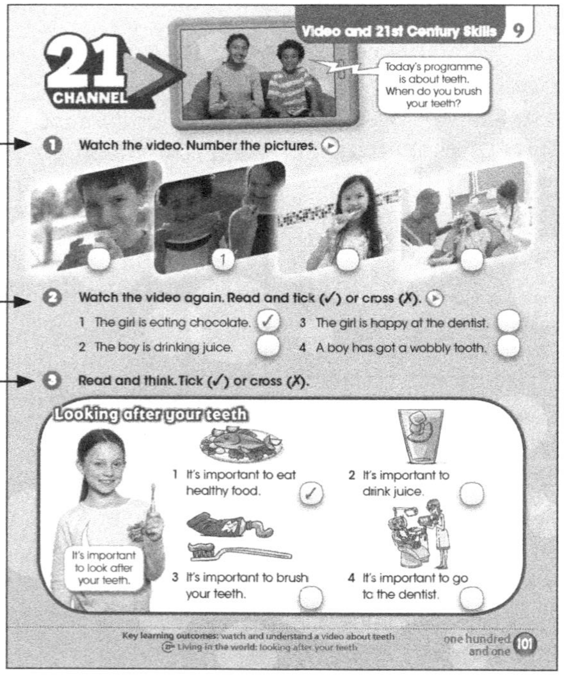

Ending the lesson

- Review the lesson.
- Review the task flashcards. Elicit the pupils' favourite activities.

Extra activity

- Pupils ask their friends about when they brush their teeth.

Digital resources

Teacher's Digital: Don't forget you can teach this lesson using the Teacher's App on Navio.

Pupil's Digital: Encourage your pupils to use the Pupil's App on Navio to practise the vocabulary from this lesson.

Powered By NAVIO

Activity Book

Activity Book

Activity 1

- When do the children brush their teeth? Listen and tick (✓).
▶ *CD4 Track 26 p274*

Activity 2

- Read, think and write. Draw and say.

Recycled vocabulary

- Look, remember and write the word.

Detailed Lesson Plan

Starting the lesson

Use the Trinity Exam Practice cards (optional).

- The pupils practise asking and answering questions.

Review the tooth fairy.

- Write the heading *The Tooth Fairy* on the board. Write the sentences from Lesson 6 on the board in a different order so that they are jumbled.
- In pairs, the pupils copy the sentences in the correct order. Do the first one as a class: 1 The Tooth Fairy visits at night.

Set learning outcomes and use the task flashcards.

- Say **Today we're going to watch a video and then ask and answer questions about teeth**.
- Point to the task flashcards throughout to elicit activities and reinforce your instructions.

Pre-watching activity

- Ask the children **When do you brush your teeth?**

Pupil's Book Activity 1

Watch the video. Number the pictures. *p279*

- Play Part 1. Pause after Sophie says, *Me too.* Ask **When do Sophie and Tom brush their teeth?** *(Every day.)*
- Now focus the pupils' attention on the video stills. Ask **What can you see? What do the children do in each picture?**
- Play Part 2, pausing after the first video still. Ask the pupils to point to the corresponding photo in their book.
- Play the video again for pupils to write the numbers in order of the photos.
- Ask **Do you go to the dentist? When do you go to the dentist?**

Answers: 2, 1, 4, 3

Pupil's Book Activity 2

Watch the video again. Read and tick (✓) or cross (✗).

- Read out the first sentence in Activity 2. Ask **Is the girl eating chocolate?** Show the tick in the circle.
- Play Part 2. Pupils tick or cross the sentences.
- Ask the pupils to look at the sentences they crossed and ask them to correct them.
- Ask general questions to check understanding.
  Why is chocolate bad for your teeth? *(It has got a lot of sugar.)*
  What do Tom and Sophie eat every day? *(Fruit and vegetables.)*
  Is it a good idea to drink milk and water? *(Yes.)*
  What does the dentist teach about brushing your teeth? *(Brush up and down.)*
  How long should you brush your teeth for? *(Two minutes.)*
  Are Tom's teeth healthy and white? *(Yes.)*
  How can you look after your teeth? *(Eat healthy food, visit the dentist, drink milk and water, brush your teeth every day.)*

Answers: 1 ✓ 2 ✗ 3 ✓ 4 ✗

Pupil's Book Activity 3

Read and think. Tick (✓) or cross (✗).

- Read the sentences for the pupils to follow. The pupils read the sentences again and tick or cross.
- **Think-Pair-Share** Read out the speech bubble.
- Ask **Which food isn't good for your teeth? How often do you go to the dentist?**

Answers: 1 ✓ 2 ✗ 3 ✓ 4 ✓

Activity Book

Activity 1

When do the children brush their teeth? Listen and tick (✓).

▶ *CD4 Track 26 p274*

- The pupils look at the table. Ask **When do you brush your teeth?** Play the first exchange on the CD. Ask **When does Jack brush his teeth?** Show the example tick. Ask **Does he brush his teeth in the afternoon, evening or at night?** Pupils tick at night.
- Play the rest of the CD, pausing after each exchange. Play the CD again for the pupils to check their answers.
- Ask **Who is good at looking after their teeth?** *(Jack, Bethany and Paul.)* **What about Anna?** *(No, she only brushes her teeth in the morning.)*

Answers: **1** in the morning, at night **2** morning, afternoon, at night **3** morning **4** morning, afternoon, evening

Activity 2

Read, think and write. Draw and say.

- Read out the speech bubble. Ask a few pupils, **How do you look after your teeth?**
- The pupils write sentences about how they look after their teeth and draw pictures. Then they show the pictures to their partners.

Recycled vocabulary

Answers: sun hat

Ending the lesson

Review the lesson.

- Ask **Which activity was easy / difficult?**

Review the task flashcards.

- Say **Look at the activities you've done today. Which activity was your favourite?**

Extra activity

Extension

- Ask the pupils to copy the table from Activity 1 in their Activity Book. Tell them to choose four of their friends and write their names on the table. On the board write *When do you brush your teeth*? The pupils find their friends and ask when they brush their teeth and tick the correct time of day.

My project 3: Holidays

Key Competences and Key Learning Outcomes

- Identify and talk about holiday places and objects
- Identify places in the world around us
- Prepare to make a holiday list

Key language

- *beach, city, desert, jungle; boots, camera, map, sunglasses, torch, water*
- *Where do you go on holiday? I go to the (beach).*

Recycled: *shorts, swimsuit, sun hat, trainers, T-shirt; country, mountain; sweets*

Recycled: *What's your favourite place? My favourite place is (the mountains). I've got (a map and boots).*

Materials

- Pupil's Book p102; Activity Book p100; Class CD4; Teacher's App on Navio
- Teacher's Resource Bank: Task flashcards: *listen, tick, Talk Partners, plan, read*

Optional materials

- Teacher's Resource Bank: Five Trinity Exam Practice cards (selected from the Starter Unit and Units 1, 2, 3, 4, 5, 6, 7, 8 and 9)

At a Glance Lesson Plan

Starting the lesson

- Use the Trinity Exam Practice cards (optional).
- Set learning outcomes using the task flashcards.

Learn: Activity 1

Listen, point and say.
▶ *CD4 Track 27 p274*
- Where do you go on holiday? Tick (✓).

Activity 2

- Listen.
▶ *CD4 Track 28 p274*
- Talk Partners Ask and answer.

Activity 3

- Listen, point and say.
▶ *CD4 Track 29 p274*
- Circle the things you use on holiday.

Pupil's Book

Plan your project

- Prepare to make a holiday list.
Go to page 100 in your Activity Book.

Ending the lesson

- Review the lesson.
- Review the task flashcards.

Link to Science

- **Continents and oceans:** Identify cardinal points; continents and oceans.

Activity Book

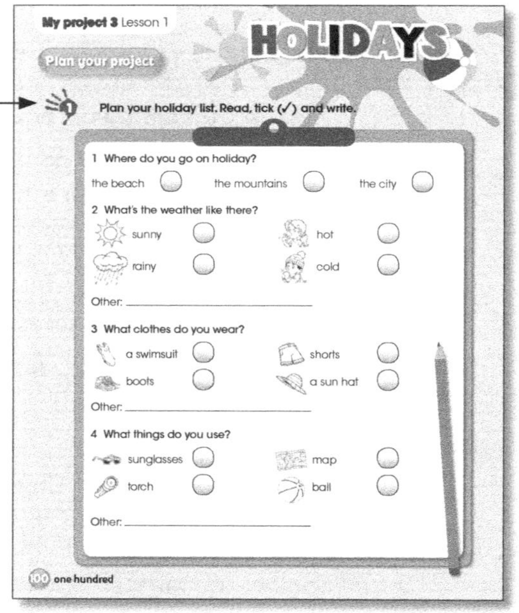

Activity Book

Activity 1: Plan your project
- Plan your holiday list. Read, tick (✓) and write.

Digital resources

Teacher's Digital: Don't forget you can teach this lesson using the Teacher's App on Navio.

Pupil's Digital: Encourage your pupils to use the Pupil's App on Navio to practise the vocabulary from this lesson.

Powered By NAVIO

Starting the lesson

Use the Trinity Exam Practice cards (optional).

- The pupils practise asking and answering questions (see p31).

Set learning outcomes using task flashcards.

- Say **Today we're going to talk about our favourite place for a holiday.**
- Hold up the task flashcards in turn and elicit the activities. Stick them on one side of the board. Point to them during the lesson to reinforce your instructions.

Learn: Pupil's Book Activity 1

Listen, point and say. Where do you go on holiday? Tick (✓).

▶ *CD4 Track 27 p274*

- (Books open.) Play the CD. The pupils listen and point to the photos.
- Play the CD again. The pupils listen and repeat the words.
- The pupils choose and tick their favourite place for a holiday.

Pupil's Book Activity 2

Listen. Ask and answer.

▶ *CD4 Track 28 p274*

- Play the CD, pausing after each sentence for the pupils to repeat.
- Ask different individual pupils the question and encourage them to answer using the full sentence.
- Talk Partners The pupils ask and answer the question with a Talk Partner.

Pupil's Book Activity 3

Listen, point and say. Circle the things you use on holiday.

▶ *CD4 Track 29 p274*

- (Books open.) Ask **What can you see?** Encourage the pupils to name the holiday items they know from previous units (*sweets*, *swimsuit*).
- Play the CD. The pupils listen and point.
- Play the CD again. The pupils point and repeat the words.
- The pupils circle the items they use on holiday. Have a show of hands for each item to see which is the most popular item the class uses on holiday.

Activity Book: Plan your project

Activity 1: Plan your project

Plan your holiday list. Read, tick (✓) and write.

- (Books open.) Explain that in the next lesson, the pupils are going to make a holiday list in a group. But first, today, they have to decide some things individually.
- Read out the first sentence and the options. The pupils work alone to choose one of the places for a holiday and tick the corresponding box. Repeat for the other sentences. Highlight that the pupils can tick more than one option in Questions 2, 3 and 4, and they can also write their own ideas.

Ending the lesson

Review the lesson.

- (Books closed.) Say **Today we've talked about holidays. What places can we go to on holiday? What things do we take with us on holiday?** Elicit answers from the pupils.

Review the task flashcards.

- Point to the task flashcards on the board. Say **Look at the activities you've done today. Which activity was your favourite?** Elicit the pupils' favourite activities.

Link to Science

- If you are studying the Science topic of **Continents and oceans** in English, you could review the names of the continents and where they are. Ask the pupils to identify the seasons in each continent and the clothes they would need for a holiday.

My project 3: Holidays

Key Competences and Key Learning Outcomes

- Describe holiday clothes and holiday things
- Present the holiday list

- Use a computer to make a holiday list and create a class display

- Think about your project

- Work together to make a list
- Sing a cooperative learning song

Key language

- *I go to the (beach). It's (hot) there. I've got a (swimsuit) on my list. Have a nice holiday!*

Recycled: *beach, city, country, desert, jungle, mountains; camera, map, sunglasses, sweets, swimsuit, torch, water*

Materials

- Pupil's Book p103; Activity Book p101; Class CD4; Teacher's App on Navio
- Teacher's Resource Bank: Task flashcards: *read, draw, colour, cut out, stick, listen, Talk Partners, sing, write, think*
- Glue, coloured pencils or crayons, scissors, one large sheet of poster paper or card per group

Optional materials

- Teacher's Resource Bank: Five Trinity Exam Practice cards (selected from the Starter Unit and Units 1, 2, 3, 4, 5, 6, 7, 8 and 9)

At a Glance Lesson Plan

Starting the lesson

- Use the Trinity Exam Practice cards (optional).
- Review the vocabulary from Lesson 1.
- Set learning outcomes using the task flashcards.

Create: Activity 1

- Read.
- Make a holiday list.

Show and tell: Activity 2 Cooperative learning

- Sing *Listen to others.*
- ▶ *CD4 Track 30 p274*

Activity 3

- Create a class display. Listen.
- Tell the class about your holiday list.
- ▶ *CD4 Track 31 p274*

Pupil's Book

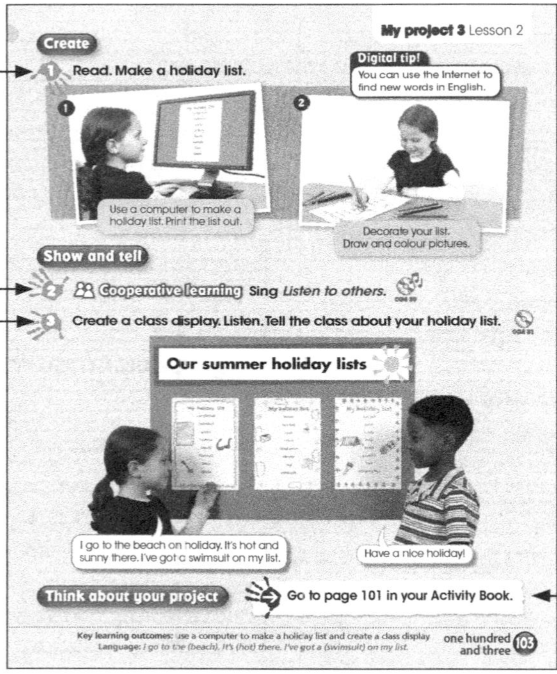

Think about your project

Go to page 101 in your Activity Book.

Ending the lesson

- Sing *Well done!*
- ▶ *CD4 Track 25 p273*
- Review the lesson.

Activity Book

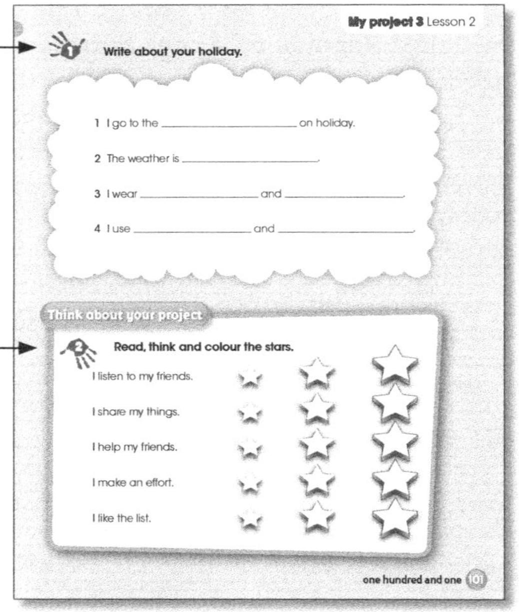

Activity Book

Activity 1

- Write about your holiday.

Think about your project: Activity 2

- Read, think and colour the stars.

Digital resources

Teacher's Digital: Don't forget you can teach this lesson using the Teacher's App on Navio.

Pupil's Digital: Encourage your pupils to use the Pupil's App on Navio to practise the vocabulary from this lesson.

Powered By NAVIO

Detailed Lesson Plan

Starting the lesson

Use the Trinity Exam Practice cards (optional).

- The pupils practise asking and answering questions (see p31).

Review the vocabulary from Lesson 1.

- Ask **What places for a holiday can you remember? What holiday things can you remember?** Elicit answers and write them in two lists on the board.

Set learning outcomes using the task flashcards.

- Say **Today you're going on holiday. You're going to make a holiday list.**
- Hold up the task flashcards in turn and elicit the activities. Stick them on one side of the board. Point to them during the lesson to reinforce your instructions.

Digital tip!

- Ask the pupils to look on the Internet to find new words in English. Elicit some words.

Create: Pupil's Book Activity 1

Read. Make a holiday list.

- Tell the pupils that they are going to make their own holiday list first, and then make a display in groups.
- The pupils use a computer to make their holiday list, based on what they ticked or wrote in their Activity Book (p100). Remind them that they can use an online translator to find new words in English, or they can ask you. Once they are happy with their list they can print it out.
- Focus on the second photo and read the instructions. The pupils decorate their printed list, and draw and colour pictures.

Show and tell: Pupil's Book Activity 2
Cooperative learning

Sing *Listen to others.*

▶ *CD4 Track 30 p274*

- Remind the class that when we work in groups, we need to share the classroom equipment and wait until other pupils have finished using it.
- To reinforce the importance of sharing, play the CD. The pupils listen and do the actions.
- Play the CD again. The pupils sing and do the actions.

Pupil's Book Activity 3

Create a class display. Listen. Tell the class about your holiday list.

▶ *CD4 Track 31 p274*

- Put the pupils into groups of three and have them talk to each other about their holiday lists.
- Give each group a large sheet of paper, glue and coloured pencils. The pupils write the heading 'Our Summer Holiday Lists' and each pupil sticks their list on the large sheet of paper. The groups can add further decoration if they want to.
- Play the CD for the children to listen and repeat.
- Invite groups to come to the front of the class and talk about where they go on holiday, what it's like there, and what they take with them. Encourage the groups listening to say *Have a nice holiday!* when each group has presented their lists.

Activity Book

Activity 1

Write about your holiday.

- (Books open.) Focus the pupils on Activity 1. For each sentence, invite a confident pupil to complete it for their holiday list.
- The pupils work alone to think about their holiday list and answer the questions. Help as necessary.
- As an extra activity, the pupils could copy their text onto a piece of paper and decorate it. Stick the group holiday posters and their accompanying texts on the wall. Invite other classes to come and enjoy the pupils' work.

Activity 2: Think about your project

Read, think and colour the stars.

- Say **Let's think about how we work together.** Read out each sentence. The pupils think about how they work together and colour the corresponding star (small star: sometimes; medium-sized star: usually; big star: always).

Ending the lesson

Sing *Well done!*

▶ *CD4 Track 25 p273*

- (Books closed.) Praise the class for working together and for following instructions well. Play the CD. The pupils sing and do the actions.

Review the lesson.

- (Books closed.) Say **Today we've worked together. What have we made?** Elicit answers from the pupils.

Bonfire Night

Key Competences and Key Learning Outcomes

- Say and do a firework action rhyme

- Read about Bonfire Night in Britain
- Think about fireworks in your country
- Make a firework

Key language

- *bonfire, Bonfire Night, firework, toffee apple*
- *I can see (fireworks). They're (red and yellow).*

Recycled: *blue, brown, orange, purple, red, yellow, sky, stars*

Materials

- Pupil's Book p104; Class CD4; Teacher's App on Navio
- Colours flashcards; Bonfire Night flashcards
- Teacher's Resource Bank: Task flashcards: *listen, find, sing, read, match, think, cut out, draw, colour*
- Scissors, crayons or coloured pencils, cardboard tubes, lollipop sticks, card

At a Glance Lesson Plan

Starting the lesson

- Review colours.
- Set learning objectives using the task flashcards.

Vocabulary presentation

- Present the new vocabulary.

Activity 1

- Read and listen.

▶ *CD4 Track 32 p274*

Activity 2

- Listen and read the action rhyme.

▶ *CD4 Track 33 p274*

- Say and do the rhyme.

Pupil's Book

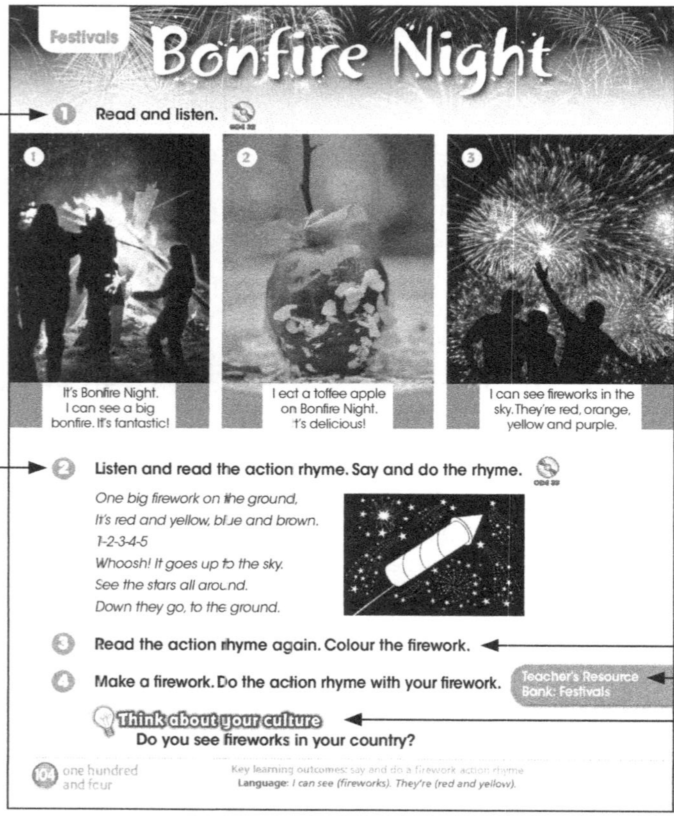
Festivals
Bonfire Night
1 Read and listen.
1 It's Bonfire Night. I can see a big bonfire. It's fantastic!
2 I eat a toffee apple on Bonfire Night. It's delicious!
3 I can see fireworks in the sky. They're red, orange, yellow and purple.
2 Listen and read the action rhyme. Say and do the rhyme.
One big firework on the ground,
It's red and yellow, blue and brown.
1-2-3-4-5
Whoosh! It goes up to the sky.
See the stars all around.
Down they go, to the ground.
3 Read the action rhyme again. Colour the firework.
4 Make a firework. Do the action rhyme with your firework. Teacher's Resource Bank: Festivals
Think about your culture
Do you see fireworks in your country?
104 one hundred and four
Key learning outcomes: say and do a firework action rhyme
Language: *I can see (fireworks). They're (red and yellow).*

Activity 3

- Read the action rhyme again.
- Colour the firework.

Teacher's Resource Bank

- Make a firework.
- Do the action rhyme with your firework.

▶ *CD4 Track 33 p274*

Ending the lesson

- Review the lesson.
- Perform the firework action rhyme.

▶ *CD4 Track 33 p274*

Think about your culture

- Do you see fireworks in your country?

Digital resources

Teacher's Digital: You can also teach this lesson using the Teacher's App on Navio.

Pupil's Digital: Encourage your pupils to use the Pupil's App on Navio to practise the activities from this lesson.

Powered By NAVIO

Detailed Lesson Plan

Starting the lesson

Review colours.

- (Books closed.) Review colours using the flashcards. Play *What's missing?* with the class (see p23).

Set learning outcomes using the task flashcards.

- Say **Today we're going to learn about Bonfire Night and do a firework action rhyme.**
- Hold up the task flashcards in turn and elicit the activities. Stick them on one side of the board. Point to them during the lesson to reinforce your instructions.

Vocabulary presentation

Present the new vocabulary.

- Explain that in Britain in 1605, a man called Guy Fawkes wanted to kill the king so that someone else would rule England instead. Luckily his plan failed and he was caught on 5th November. People celebrate on this date every year by lighting bonfires and setting off fireworks.
- Use the Bonfire Night flashcards to introduce the new vocabulary. Hold up the bonfire flashcard and ask **What's this?** Elicit or say the name and ask the class to repeat. Repeat with the other flashcards.

Pupil's Book Activity 1

Read and listen.

▶ *CD4 Track 32 p274*

- Focus the pupils on Activity 1. Point to the pictures and ask what the pupils can see.
- Play the CD. The pupils listen and point to the pictures as they are mentioned.
- Point to the pictures and ask questions **Have you seen a bonfire? What colours can you see? Have you eaten a toffee apple? What colours are the fireworks in the picture?**
- Play the CD again, pausing after each sentence for the pupils to repeat.

Pupil's Book Activity 2

Listen and read the action rhyme. Say and do the rhyme.

▶ *CD4 Track 33 p274*

- Point to the picture and ask **What's this?** to elicit *A firework.*
- Play the CD. The pupils listen and read the rhyme.
- Play the CD again, pausing after each pair of sentences for the children to repeat.
- Tell the pupils you are going to add actions to the rhyme and demonstrate these for the class. Crouch down for the start of the rhyme and say the first two lines. For the third line, gradually start standing up until you are fully upright at 'Whoosh!' with your hands raised above your head. For the fifth line, move your head as if looking all around you. For the final line, bring your arms back to your sides with a fluttering motion.
- Invite some volunteers to come to the front to perform the actions with you as the class says the rhyme and joins in with the actions.
- Finally, play the CD again and have the whole class say the rhyme and do the actions.

Pupil's Book Activity 3

Read the action rhyme again. Colour the firework.

- As a class, read the action rhyme again, pausing at the end of the second line. Ask **What colours do you need to colour in your firework?**
- The pupils colour in their firework according to the colours given in the rhyme.

Teacher's Resource Bank

Make a firework. Do the action rhyme with your firework.

▶ *CD4 Track 33 p274*

- Give each pupil a cardboard tube and a lollipop stick for them to make their own firework. Show them how to glue the lollipop stick to the bottom of the tube. The pupils then decorate their firework with any colours they like. Alternatively, give each child a sheet of card for them to draw and colour their own firework in any shape or size they like.
- When the pupils have finished, play the CD and have the pupils do the actions holding their fireworks. You can substitute the colours in the rhyme for any other colours the pupils have used if you wish.

Pupil's Book Think about your culture

- Ask **Do you see fireworks in your country? What occasions are fireworks used for?** The pupils answer.

Ending the lesson

Review the lesson.

- Ask the pupils to say what Bonfire Night words they know in English.

Perform the firework action rhyme.

▶ *CD4 Track 33 p274*

- Play the CD. The pupils do the action rhyme one last time with their fireworks. If possible, you may wish to invite parents or another class to see the performance.

Valentine's Day

Key Competences and Key Learning Outcomes

- Read about Valentine's Day
- Think and write about the people you love
- Think about Valentine's Day in your country
- Make a Valentine's Day card

Key language

- *I love (my mother). She (helps me).*

Recycled: *aunt, brother, cousin, family, father, grandfather, grandmother, mother, sister, uncle*

Materials

- Pupil's Book p105; Class CD4; Teacher's App on Navio
- Teacher's Resource Bank: Task flashcards: *read, listen, number, think, cut out, colour*
- Card, crayons or coloured pencils

At a Glance Lesson Plan

Starting the lesson
- **Think-Pair-Share** Review family members.
- Set learning outcomes using the task flashcards.

Activity 1
- Read and listen.
- ▶ *CD4 Track 34 p274*

Activity 2
- Who do you love?
- Write and draw.

Pupil's Book

Teacher's Resource Bank
- Make a Valentine's Day card.

Ending the lesson
- Review the lesson.
- Think of other Valentine's Day ideas.

Think about your culture
- Do you have Valentine's Day in your country?

Digital resources

Teacher's Digital: You can also teach this lesson using the Teacher's App on Navio.

Pupil's Digital: Encourage your pupils to use the Pupil's App on Navio to practise the activities from this lesson.

Powered By NAVIO

Detailed Lesson Plan

Starting the lesson

- **Think-Pair-Share Review family members.**
- Ask **Can you remember the names of family members?** Ask pupils to turn to page 38 in their Pupil's Books and look at the list of family members in Activity 1.
- Give the pupils one minute to to read and reread the list, then ask them to close their books.
- **Talk Partners** The pupils work with a Talk Partner to remember as many family members from the list as they can.
- Invite different pairs to say family members. Write their answers on the board. You can leave the names on the board to help the pupils when they are deciding who to make their Valentine card for.
- Repeat the procedure, asking different pairs of pupils each time, until all nine family members have been named.

Set learning outcomes using the task flashcards.

- Say **Today we're going to learn about Valentine's Day and make a Valentine's Day card.**
- Hold up the task flashcards in turn and elicit the activities. Stick them on one side of the board. Point to them during the lesson to reinforce your instructions.

Pupil's Book Activity 1

Read and listen.

▸ *CD4 Track 34 p274*

- (Books open.) Say **Let's find out about Valentine's Day in Britain.**
- Focus the pupils on the photos. Elicit what they can see. Say **Let's read and listen**.
- Play the CD. The pupils listen and read. Ask questions to check understanding. Ask **What do people think about on Valentine's Day? Who does the girl think about? What does she do with her grandfather? What's her friend's name?**

Pupil's Book Activity 2

Who do you love? Write and draw.

- Ask the pupils to choose two people they love that they want to write about and draw. They complete the sentences, then draw a picture of each person in the picture frames.
- Invite volunteers to read out their sentences and hold up their books to show the class their pictures.

Teacher's Resource Bank

Make a Valentine's Day card.

- Tell the pupils that they are going to make a Valentine's Day card. They can either address it to one of the people they wrote about in Activity 2, or to a different person.
- Write the following model text on the board:

  Dear ________,
  I love you because … ______________________.
  Love from ________

- Talk the pupils through the text for their cards. Say **What should go in the first space?** (*The name of the person they're giving the card to.*) **What should go in the last space?** (*Their own name.*) Ask for suggestions for what can go in the middle space (*… you help me, you're a good friend, we have fun together*, etc.)
- Give each pupil some card and show them how to fold it in half, and where to write their text. Go around the class to check each pupil has written in their card and offer help as needed. When they have finished writing, they can colour and decorate their card as they wish.
- Invite volunteers to come to the front to show and read their card to the class.

Pupil's Book Think about your culture

- Ask **Do you have Valentine's Day in your country?** The pupils answer.

Ending the lesson

Review the lesson.

- Ask **What do people think about on Valentine's Day?**

Think of other Valentine's Day ideas.

- Ask the pupils to think of other things they could do on Valentine's Day as well as giving a card. Elicit suggestions from the class (*being kind to their brother / sister, helping their parents with housework, being nice to a friend*). Point out that the pupils can do this every day, not just on Valentine's Day!

Cambridge Exams Practice and Vocabulary Practice answers

Key Competences and Key Learning Outcomes

- Practise for Starters Listening Part 4 and Speaking Part 3
- Practise for Reading and Writing Parts 2 and 3

Key language

Recycled: *board, book, chair, computer, cupboard, desk, rubber, ruler; black, blue, green, orange, pink, purple, red, white*; numbers 1–10

Recycled: *Find the (computer on the cupboard). Point to the (pencil). What colour is it? It's (black).*

Materials

- Pupil's Book p106; Activity Book pp 102 and 111; Class CD4; Teacher's App on Navio
- Colours and classroom objects flashcards
- Teacher's Resource Bank: Task flashcards: *listen, colour, Talk Partners, read, write, circle*
- Coloured pencils or crayons (red, blue, orange, green, pink)

Optional materials

- Teacher's Resource Bank: External Exams Video

At a Glance Lesson Plan

Starting the lesson

- Review colours, classroom objects and prepositions.
- Set learning outcomes using the task flashcards.

Activity 1

- Listen and colour. There is one example.

▶ *CD4 Track 35 p274*

Activity 2

- Listen and point.

▶ *CD4 Track 36 p274*

- Talk Partners Ask and answer.

Go to the Activity Book.

Ending the lesson

- Review the lesson.
- Review the task flashcards.

External Exams Video

- Additional Cambridge Exams Practice Video: Pre A1 Starters

Pupil's Book

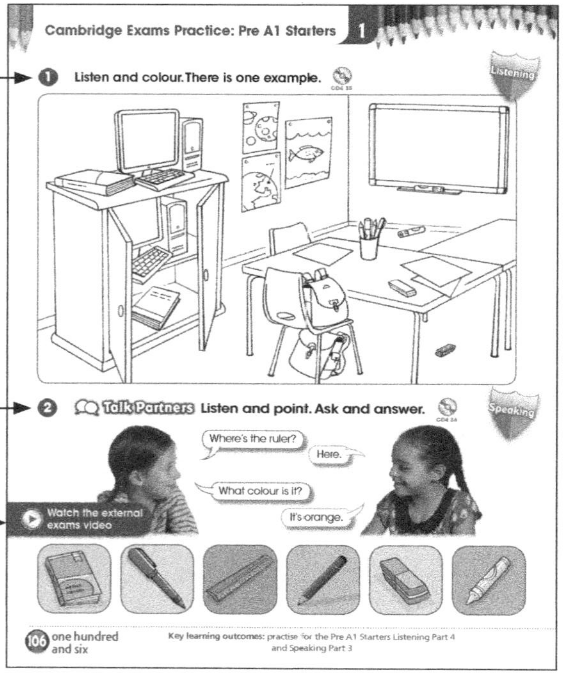

Activity Book

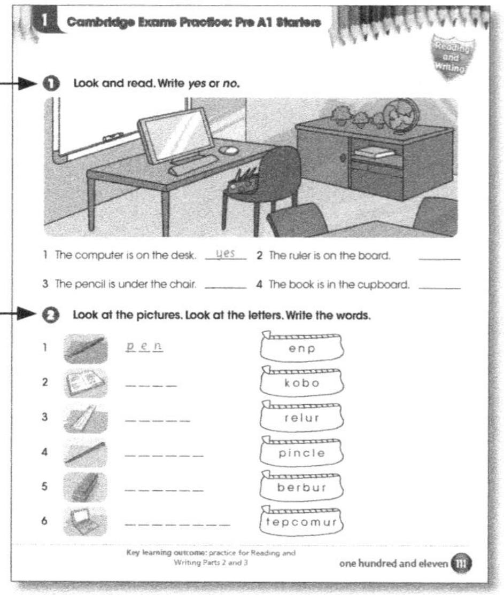

Activity Book

Activity 1

- Look and read.
- Write *yes* or *no*.

Activity 2

- Look at the pictures. Look at the letters.
- Write the words.

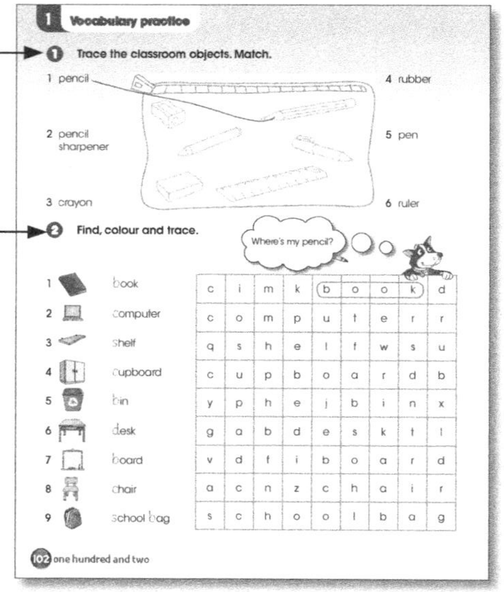

Activity Book

Activity 1

- Trace the classroom objects. Match.

Activity 2

- Find, colour and trace.

Digital resources

Teacher's Digital: You can also teach this lesson using the Teacher's App on Navio.

Pupil's Digital: Encourage your pupils to use the Pupil's App on Navio to practise the activities from this lesson.

Powered By NAVIO

Detailed Lesson Plan

Starting the lesson

Review colours, classroom objects and prepositions.

- Divide the class roughly down the middle and distribute the colours flashcards to pupils in the left half and the classroom objects flashcards to pupils in the right half.
- Point to a pupil in the left half and ask them to hold up their flashcard for the class to see and call out the colour. Repeat with a pupil in the right half and their classroom object flashcard.
- Have both pupils hold up their flashcards and say **What do we have?** Elicit *A* (*blue*) (*ruler*). Repeat with other pupils and flashcards.
- Set out a range of classroom objects at the front of the class. Move one item to a different position and say **The (crayon) is (under) the (chair).** Repeat with several correct prepositions and sentences, then say incorrect sentences. Ask the class to correct you.

Set learning outcomes using the task flashcards.

- Say **Today we're going to practise activities for an external exam.**
- Hold up the task flashcards in turn and elicit the activities. Stick them on one side of the board. Point to them during the lesson to reinforce your instructions.

Pupil's Book Activity 1

Listen and colour. There is one example.

▸ *CD4 Track 35 p274*

- (Books open.) Ask **How many (rubbers) can you see?**
- Point to one of the (rubbers) and ask **Where's this (rubber)?**
- Play the CD, pausing after each conversation. The pupils listen and colour.

Answers: **1** A red rubber under the desk. **2** A blue computer on the cupboard. **3** An orange book in the cupboard. **4** A green pen on the board. **5** A pink school bag under the chair.

Pupil's Book Activity 2

Listen and point. Ask and answer.

▸ *CD4 Track 36 p274*

- Focus the pupils on the conversation.
- Play the CD. The pupils follow in their Pupil's Books.
- Ask two volunteers to read the conversation.
- Place a selection of classroom objects on a desk at the front of the class. Ask two volunteers to demonstrate the activity. Repeat with different pairs.
- Talk Partners The pupils ask and answer with a Talk Partner. Encourage the pupils to change the object and the colour. Repeat several times.

Activity Book

Activity 1

Look and read. Write *yes* or *no*.

- (Books open.) Ask the pupils what they can see in the picture.
- Ask a pupil to read out the first sentence. The class answers *yes* or *no*.
- The pupils read the sentences, look at the picture and write *yes* or *no*.
- Check the answers as a class.

Answers: **1** yes **2** no **3** no **4** yes

Activity 2

Look at the pictures. Look at the letters. Write the words.

- Focus the pupils on Activity 2. Point out the picture of the pen and the jumbled letters on the right. Elicit that the letters can be rearranged to spell *pen*.
- The pupils continue the activity, looking at the pictures and the letters to find the words.

Answers: **1** pen **2** book **3** ruler **4** pencil **5** rubber **6** computer

Ending the lesson

Review the lesson.

- (Books closed.) Say **Today we've practised activities for an exam.** Ask **What questions did you learn?**

Review the task flashcards.

- Point to the task flashcards. Say **Look at the activities you've done today. Which activity was your favourite?** Elicit the pupils' favourite activities.

External Exams Video

Additional Cambridge Exams Practice Video: Pre A1 Starters

- Additional external exams preparation material, including videos, worksheets and practice tests, can be found in the Teacher's Resource Bank on Navio.

Activity Book page 102: Vocabulary Practice

Answers: **1.1** pencil **1.2** pencil sharpener **1.3** crayon **1.4** rubber **1.5** pen **1.6** ruler
2.1 book **2.2** computer **2.3** shelf **2.4** cupboard **2.5** bin **2.6** desk **2.7** board **2.8** chair **2.9** school bag

Key Competences and Key Learning Outcomes

- Practise for Starters Listening Part 1 and Speaking Part 4
- Practise for Reading and Writing Parts 1 and 4

Key language

- *Put the (car in the cupboard). How old are you? I'm (six).*

Recycled: *ball, car, doll, kite, robot, train; big, old; chair, cupboard, desk, shelf; in, on, under; pencil case*

Recycled: *It's a (bike).*

Materials

- Pupil's Book p107; Activity Book pp 103 and 112; Class CD4; Teacher's App on Navio
- Toy flashcards
- Teacher's Resource Bank: Task flashcards: *listen, draw, Talk Partners, read, tick, match*

Optional materials

- Teacher's Resource Bank: External Exams Video

At a Glance Lesson Plan

Starting the lesson

- Review toys and prepositions.
- Set learning outcomes using the task flashcards.

Activity 1

- Listen and tick (✓). There is one example.

▶ *CD4 Track 37 p274*

Activity 2

- Listen and repeat.

▶ *CD4 Track 38 p275*

- Talk Partners Ask and answer.

Go to the Activity Book.

Ending the lesson

- Review the lesson.
- Review the task flashcards.

External Exams Video

- Additional Cambridge Exams Practice Video: Pre A1 Starters

Pupil's Book

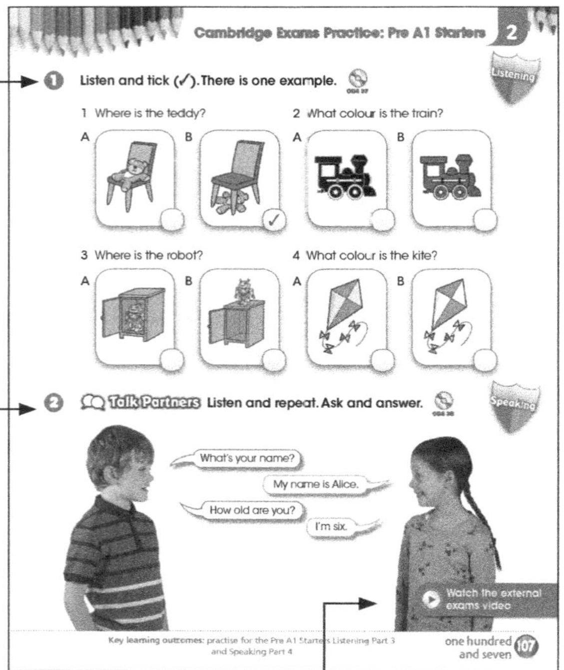

Activity Book

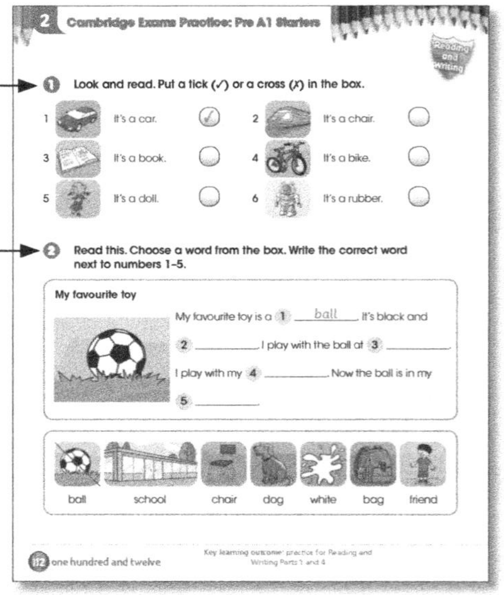

Activity Book

Activity 1

- Look and read.
- Put a tick (✓) or a cross (✗) in the box.

Activity 2

- Read this. Choose a word from the box. Write the correct word next to numbers 1–5.

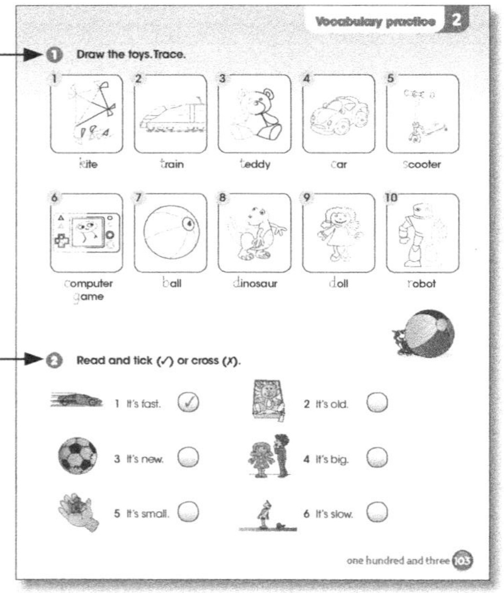

Activity Book

Activity 1

- Draw the toys. Trace.

Activity 2

- Read and tick (✓) or cross (✗).

Digital resources

Teacher's Digital: You can also teach this lesson using the Teacher's App on Navio.

Pupil's Digital: Encourage your pupils to use the Pupil's App on Navio to Practice the activities from this lesson.

Powered By NAVIO

Detailed Lesson Plan

Starting the lesson

Review toys and prepositions.

- Draw a basic room with a chair, a bed, a cupboard and a desk on the board. Take one of the toy flashcards, hold it up and say **A (doll)**. Stick the (doll) flashcard on one of the items on the board and say **The (doll) is (on) the (bed).**
- Ask a pupil to come to the front and repeat the activity. Encourage the pupil to place their toy flashcard anywhere they like on the board, using the correct preposition to describe where the toy is.
- Repeat the activity with other pupils.

Set learning outcomes using the task flashcards.

- Say **Today we're going to practise activities for an external exam.**
- Hold up the task flashcards in turn and elicit the activities. Stick them on one side of the board. Point to them during the lesson to reinforce your instructions.

Pupil's Book Activity 1

Listen and tick (✓). There is one example.

▸ *CD4 Track 37 p274*

- (Books open.) Focus the class on the pictures. Elicit the names of the objects they know in the bedroom and the six toys around the bedroom scene.
- Play the CD, pausing after each conversation to check the answer and to give pupils time to tick the correct boxes.

Answers: **1** the teddy is under the chair **2** the train is red **3** the robot is in the cupboard **4** the kite is blue and white

Pupil's Book Activity 2

Listen and repeat. Ask and answer.

▸ *CD4 Track 38 p275*

- Play the CD. The pupils listen to the conversation.
- Encourage the class to repeat the question *How old are you?* Ask different pupils their age.
- Ask two volunteers to ask and answer the question. Repeat with different pairs.
- Talk Partners The pupils practise the conversation with a Talk Partner, answering with their own age.

Activity Book

Activity 1

Look and read. Put a tick (✓) or a cross (✗) in the box.

- (Books open.) Ask a pupil to read out the first sentence. He / She looks at the picture and says if the sentence is correct. Repeat with the other pictures.
- The pupils complete the activity on their own.

Answers: **1 ✓ 2 ✗ 3 ✓ 4 ✓ 5 ✓ 6 ✗**

Activity 2

Read this. Choose a word from the box. Write the correct word next to numbers 1–5.

- (Books open.) As a class, read out the words in the word box at the bottom of the page. Ask the pupils which of the words they can see in the main picture.
- Ask different pupils to read out the sentences. Elicit the missing words.
- The pupils read and write the missing words.

Answers: **1** ball **2** white **3** school **4** friend **5** bag

Ending the lesson

Review the lesson.

- (Books closed.) Say **Today we've practised activities for an external exam.** Ask **What questions did you learn?**

Review the task flashcards.

- Point to the task flashcards. Say **Look at the activities you've done today. Which activity was your favourite?** Elicit the pupils' favourite activities.

External Exams Video

Additional Cambridge Exams Practice Video: Pre A1 Starters

- Additional external exams preparation material, including videos, worksheets and practice tests, can be found in the Teacher's Resource Bank on Navio.

Activity Book page 103: Vocabulary Practice

Answers: **1.1** kite **1.2** train **1.3** teddy **1.4** car **1.5** scooter **1.6** computer game **1.7** ball **1.8** dinosaur **1.9** doll **1.10** robot

My favourite toy is a big **ball**.

2.1 ✓ 2.2 ✗ 2.3 ✗ 2.4 ✓ 2.5 ✓ 2.6 ✓

Cambridge Exams Practice and Vocabulary Practice answers

Key Competences and Key Learning Outcomes

LEARN
- Practise for Starters Listening Part 1 and Speaking Part 4
- Practise for Reading and Writing Parts 1 and 4

Key language
- *What colour are (your eyes)? My eyes are (brown). What colour is (your hair)? My hair is (black).*

Recycled: *ears, legs, nose, toes; dog; ball, scooter*
Recycled: *How old are you? I'm (seven). What's your favourite toy? It's a (scooter).*

Materials
- Pupil's Book p108; Activity Book pp 104 and 113; Class CD4; Teacher's App on Navio
- Parts of the body flashcards
- Teacher's Resource Bank: Task flashcards: *listen, tick, Talk Partners, read, write*

Optional materials
- Teacher's Resource Bank: External Exams Video

At a Glance Lesson Plan

Starting the lesson
- Review parts of the body and descriptions.
- Set learning outcomes using the task flashcards.

Activity 1
- Listen and draw lines. There is one example.

▶ ***CD4 Track 39 p275***

Activity 2
- Listen and repeat.

▶ ***CD4 Track 40 p275***
- **Talk Partners** Ask and answer.

Go to the Activity Book.

Ending the lesson
- Review the lesson.
- Review the task flashcards.

External Exams Video
- Additional Cambridge Exams Practice Video: Pre A1 Starters

Pupil's Book

Activity Book

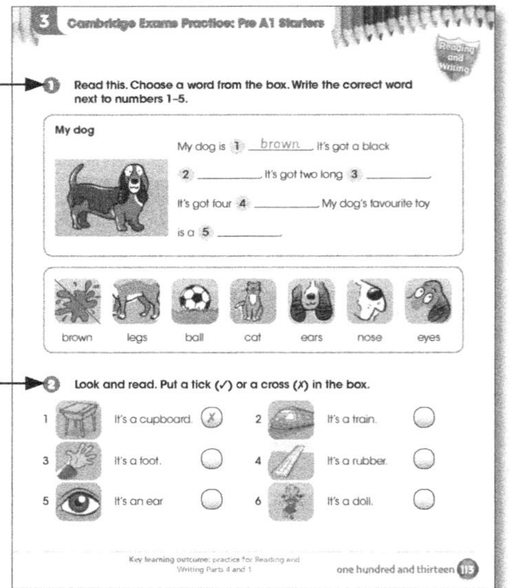

Activity Book

Activity 1
- Read this. Choose a word from the box. Write the correct word next to numbers 1–5.

Activity 2
- Look and read.
- Put a tick (✓) or a cross (✗) in the box.

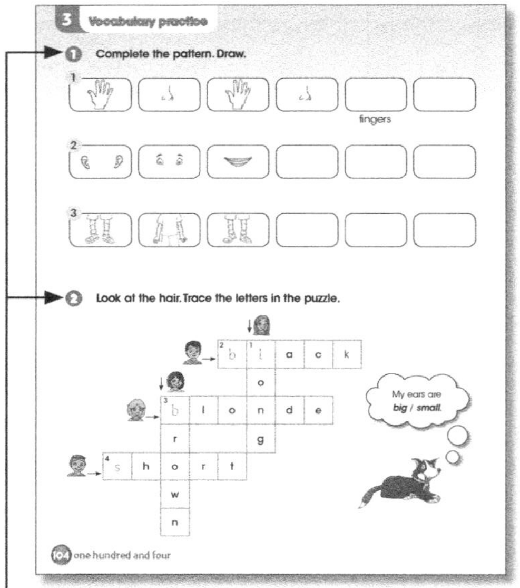

Activity Book

Activity 1
- Complete the pattern. Draw.

Activity 2
- Look at the hair. Trace the letters in the puzzle.

Digital resources

Teacher's Digital: You can also teach this lesson using the Teacher's App on Navio.

Pupil's Digital: Encourage your pupils to use the Pupil's App on Navio to Practice the activities from this lesson.

Powered By NAVIO

Starting the lesson

Review parts of the body and descriptions.

- Draw a large stick person on the board with no features. Say **What's missing?** Have the pupils take turns to name a body part and draw it on the figure on the board. Repeat until all ten body part flashcards have been mentioned.
- Tell the class to imagine they are clowns in a circus with different coloured hair and eyes. Say **I'm (Sally) the clown. I've got (long), (green) hair and (blue) eyes.**
- Ask a confident pupil to give their clown description. Repeat the activity with other pupils.

Set learning outcomes using the task flashcards.

- Say **Today we're going to practise activities for an external exam.**
- Hold up the task flashcards in turn and elicit the activities. Stick them on one side of the board. Point to them during the lesson to reinforce your instructions.

Pupil's Book Activity 1

Listen and draw lines. There is one example.

▶ *CD4 Track 39 p275*

- (Books open.) Play the CD, pausing after each conversation. The pupils listen and draw a line from the name to the correct person.
- Play the CD again if necessary.

Answers: **1** Alice – long green hair **2** Lucy – long blue hair **3** Pat – short red hair and green eyes **4** Hugo – blue hair and brown eyes **5** Eva – short green hair **6** Anna – red hair and blue eyes

Pupil's Book Activity 2

Listen and repeat. Ask and answer.

▶ *CD4 Track 40 p275*

- Play the CD. The pupils listen and read the conversation in their Pupil's Books.
- Ask volunteers to ask and answer the questions.
- Talk Partners The pupils Practice the conversation with a Talk Partner, answering with their own hair and eye colour.

Activity Book

Activity 1

Read this. Choose a word from the box. Write the correct word next to numbers 1–5.

- (Books open.) As a class, read out the words in the word box at the bottom of the page. Ask the pupils which of the words they can see in the main picture.
- Ask different pupils to read out the sentences. Elicit the missing words.
- The pupils read and write the missing words.

Answers: **1** brown **2** nose **3** ears **4** legs **5** ball

Activity 2

Look and read. Put a tick (✓) or a cross (✗) in the box.

- Ask a pupil to read out the first sentence. He / She looks at the picture and says if the sentence is correct. Repeat with the other pictures.
- The pupils complete the activity on their own.

Answers: **1** ✗ **2** ✓ **3** ✗ **4** ✗ **5** ✗ **6** ✓

Ending the lesson

Review the lesson.

- (Books closed.) Say **Today we've practised activities for an external exam. What questions did you learn?**

Review the task flashcards.

- Point to the task flashcards. Say **Look at the activities you've done today. Which activity was your favourite?** Elicit the pupils' favourite activities.

External Exams Video

Additional Cambridge Exams Practice Video: Pre A1 Starters

- Additional external exams preparation material, including videos, worksheets and practice tests, can be found in the Teacher's Resource Bank on Navio.

Activity Book page 104: Vocabulary Practice

Answers: **1.1** fingers, nose **1.2** ears, eyes, mouth **1.3** arms, legs, arms
2.1 long **2.2** black **2.3** (across) blonde, (down) brown **2.4** short
My ears are **small**.

Key Competences and Key Learning Outcomes

LEARN
- Practise for Starters Listening Part 3 and Speaking Part 4
- Practise for Reading and Writing Parts 2 and 3

Key language

- *apple*
- *What is (Sue's) favourite (fruit)? What's for lunch today?*

Recycled: *bananas, coconuts, eggs, grapes, ice cream, lemon, meat, orange juice*

Recycled: *What's your favourite (food)? It's (pasta). My favourite (food) is (ice cream). Do you like (ice cream)? Have you got (a banana in your school bag)? I've got (six eggs in my bag).*

Materials

- Pupil's Book p109; Activity Book pp 105 and 114; Class CD4; Teacher's App on Navio
- Food flashcards
- Teacher's Resource Bank: Task flashcards: *listen, tick, Talk Partners, read, write, match*

Optional materials

- Teacher's Resource Bank: External Exams Video

At a Glance Lesson Plan

Starting the lesson

- Review food items and preferences.
- Set learning outcomes using the task flashcards.

Activity 1

- Listen and tick. There is one example.

▶ ***CD4 Track 41 p275***

Activity 2

- Listen and repeat.

▶ ***CD4 Track 42 p275***

- Talk Partners Ask and answer.

Go to the Activity Book.

Ending the lesson

- Review the lesson.
- Review the task flashcards.

Extra activity

Reinforcement

- Play *Disappearing flashcards*.

External Exams Video

- Additional Cambridge Exams Practice Video: Pre A1 Starters

Pupil's Book

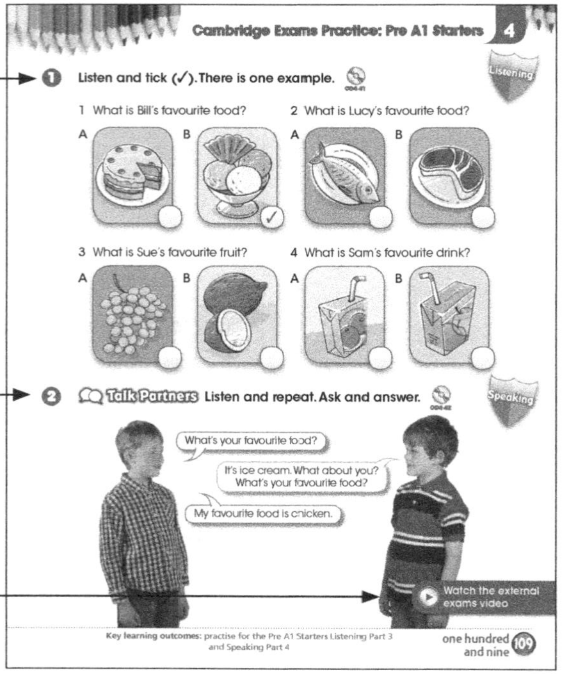

Activity Book

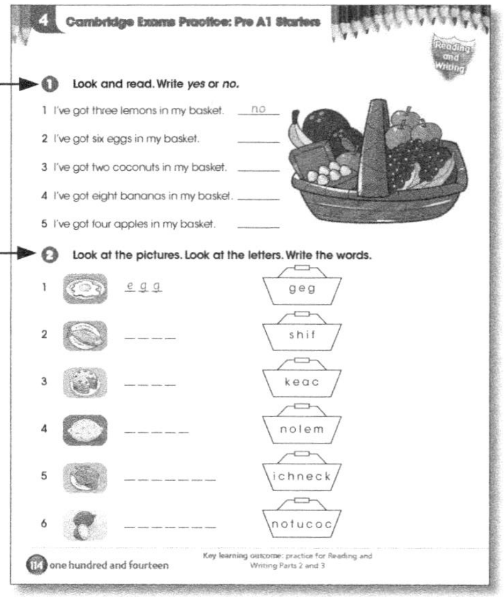

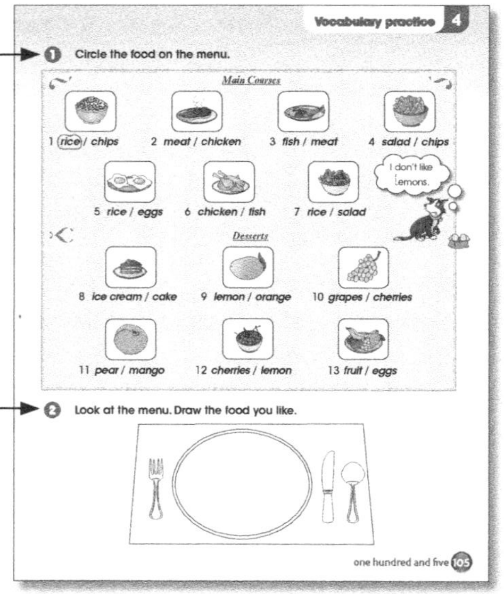

Activity Book

Activity 1

- Look and read.
- Write *yes* or *no*.

Activity 2

- Look at the pictures. Look at the letters. Write the words.

Activity Book

Activity 1

- Circle the food on the menu.

Activity 2

- Look at the menu. Draw the food you like.

Digital resources

Teacher's Digital: You can also teach this lesson using the Teacher's App on Navio.

Pupil's Digital: Encourage your pupils to use the Pupil's App on Navio to Practice the activities from this lesson.

Powered By NAVIO

Detailed Lesson Plan

Starting the lesson

Review food items and preferences.

- Draw a smiley face on one side of the board and a sad face on the other side. Turn over the first food flashcard and Say **(Apple). I like (apples).** Stick the (apple) flashcard under the smiley face on the board.
- Turn over the next flashcard and say **(Fish). I don't like (fish).** Stick the (fish) flashcard under the sad face on the board.
- Invite a pupil to take a food flashcard, say what it is and place it under the appropriate face on the board according to whether or not they like that food. Repeat until all of the food flashcards have been used.
- Point to the flashcards in the smiley face section. Choose one and say **(Chicken) is my favourite food. What about you? What's your favourite food?** Start a chain around the class by having one pupil answer your question in a full sentence, then asking another pupil the question.
- Repeat until all the pupils have asked and answered about their favourite food.

Set learning outcomes using the task flashcards.

- Say **Today we're going to practise activities for an exam.**
- Hold up the task flashcards in turn and elicit the activities. Stick them on one side of the board. Point to them during the lesson to reinforce your instructions.

Pupil's Book Activity 1

Listen and tick (✓). There is one example.

▶ *CD4 Track 41 p275*

- (Books open.) Play the CD, pausing after each conversation. The pupils listen and tick the correct pictures.
- Play the CD again if necessary.

Answers: **1** B **2** B **3** A **4** A

Pupil's Book Activity 2

Listen and repeat. Ask and answer.

▶ *CD4 Track 42 p275*

- Play the CD. The pupils read the conversation in their Pupil's Book.
- Play the CD again for the class to repeat the conversation.
- The class repeats the question **What's your favourite food?** Elicit answers.
- Ask two confident pupils to ask and answer the questions in front of the class.
- **Talk Partners** The pupils ask and answer the questions about their favourite food with a Talk Partner.

Activity Book

Activity 1

Look and read. Write *yes* or *no*.

- (Books open.) Focus the pupils on the picture.
- Invite different pupils to read out the sentences. Elicit whether they are true or false.
- The pupils then write *yes* or *no*.

Answers: **1** no **2** yes **3** yes **4** no **5** yes

Activity 2

Look at the pictures. Look at the letters. Write the words.

- Focus the pupils on Activity 2. Point out the picture of the egg and the jumbled letters on the right. Elicit that the letters can be rearranged to spell *egg*.
- The pupils continue the activity, looking at the pictures and the letters to find the words.

Answers: **1** egg **2** fish **3** cake **4** lemon **5** chicken **6** coconut

Ending the lesson

Review the lesson.

- (Books closed.) Say **Today we've practised activities for an external exam. What questions did you learn?**

Review the task flashcards.

- Point to the task flashcards. Say **Look at the activities you've done today. Which activity was your favourite?** Elicit the pupils' favourite activities.

Extra activity

Reinforcement

- Play *Disappearing flashcards* (see p23) with the food flashcards.

External Exams Video

Additional Cambridge Exams Practice Video: Pre A1 Starters

- Additional external exams preparation material, including videos, worksheets and practice tests, can be found in the Teacher's Resource Bank on Navio.

Activity Book page 105: Vocabulary Practice

Answers: **1.1** rice **1.2** meat **1.3** fish **1.4** chips **1.5** eggs **1.6** chicken **1.7** salad **1.8** cake **1.9** lemon **1.10** grapes **1.11** peach **1.12** cherries **1.13** fruit

I don't like **lemons**.

2 Pupils' own answers

Cambridge Exams Practice and Vocabulary Practice answers

Key Competences and Key Learning Outcomes

- Practise for Starters Listening Part 4 and Speaking Part 3
- Practise for Reading and Writing Parts 1 and 2

Key language

- *What can (Peter) see? This is a (cow).*

Recycled: *chicken, cow, frog; rubber, ruler; doll, robot; ears, toes; grape; jump, fly, ride a bike, swim; juggle*

Recycled: *Can you (swim)? Yes, I can. No, I can't. I can see (a robot).*

Materials

- Pupil's Book p110; Activity Book pp 106 and 115; Class CD4; Teacher's App on Navio
- Farm animal flashcards
- Teacher's Resource Bank: Task flashcards: *listen, tick, Talk Partners, read, circle*

Optional materials

- Teacher's Resource Bank: External Exams Video

At a Glance Lesson Plan

Starting the lesson

- Review farm animals and descriptions.
- Set learning outcomes using the task flashcards.

Activity 1

- Listen and colour. There is one example.
- ▶ *CD4 Track 43 p275*

Activity 2

- Listen and point.
- ▶ *CD4 Track 44 p276*
- **Talk Partners** Ask and answer.
- Go to the Activity Book.

Ending the lesson

- Review the lesson.
- Review the task flashcards.

External Exams Video

- Additional Cambridge Exams Practice Video: Pre A1 Starters

Pupil's Book

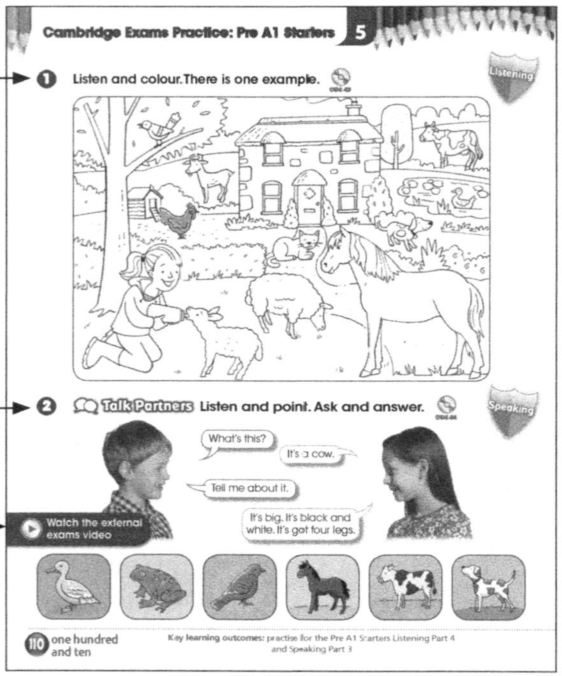

Activity Book

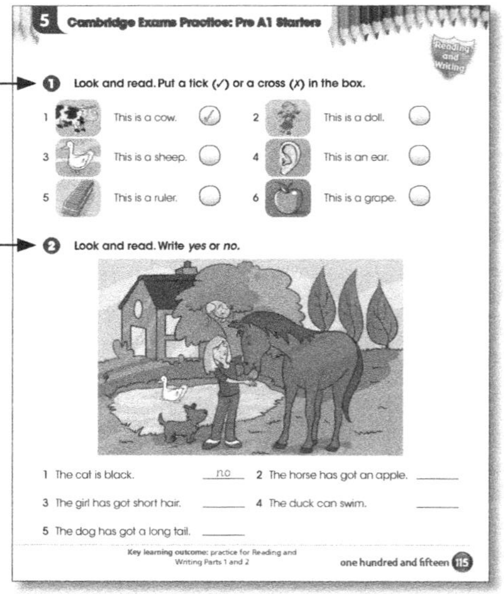

Activity Book

Activity 1

- Look and read.
- Put a tick (✓) or a cross (✗) in the box.

Activity 2

- Look and read. Write *yes* or *no*.

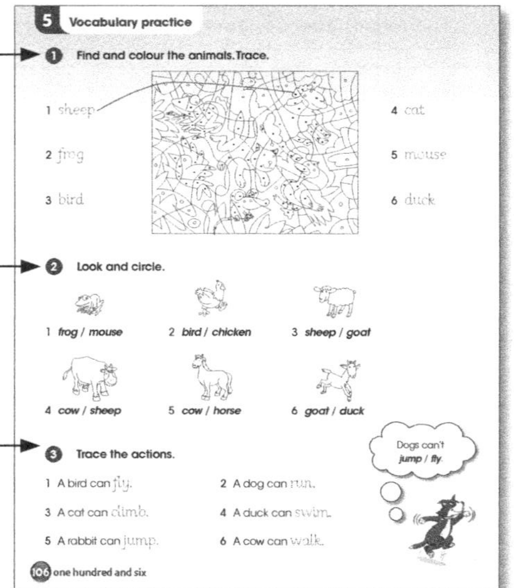

Activity Book

Activity 1

- Find and colour the animals. Trace.

Activity 2

- Look and circle.

Activity 3

- Trace the actions.

Digital resources

Teacher's Digital: You can also teach this lesson using the Teacher's App on Navio.

Pupil's Digital: Encourage your pupils to use the Pupil's App on Navio to Practice the activities from this lesson.

Powered By NAVIO

Detailed Lesson Plan

Starting the lesson

Review farm animals and descriptions.

- Take a farm animal flashcard at random and hold it up to the class so the picture is facing away from you. Ask **What colour is it?** and elicit the answer from one pupil. Ask **Is it big or small?** and elicit the answer from another pupil. Ask **How many legs does it have?** and elicit the answer from another pupil. Say **I know! It's a (cow)**. The pupils clap if your guess is correct and shake their heads if you are incorrect.
- Repeat with more flashcards. Deliberately guess a few incorrectly and ask the pupils to say the name of the correct animal.
- The pupils repeat the activity in pairs, taking turns to ask and answer the questions.

Set learning outcomes using the task flashcards.

- Say **Today we're going to practise activities for an external exam.**
- Hold up the task flashcards in turn and elicit the activities. Stick them on one side of the board. Point to them during the lesson to reinforce your instructions.

Pupil's Book Activity 1

Listen and colour. There is one example.

▶ *CD4 Track 43 p275*

- (Books open.) Play the CD, pausing after each conversation to check comprehension. The pupils listen and colour the animals according to the instructions they hear.
- Play the CD again if necessary.

Answers: **1** chicken – orange **2** horse – brown **3** bird – blue **4** duck – yellow **5** big sheep – black **6** cat – orange

Pupil's Book Activity 2

Listen and point. Ask and answer.

▶ *CD4 Track 44 p276*

- Play the CD. The pupils listen to the conversation.
- Play the CD again. The pupils point to the picture of the cow and repeat the conversation.
- Point out the row of animal pictures. Ask two confident pupils to act out the conversation, with one pupil choosing one of the other animals and changing the details in the fourth speech bubble.
- Talk Partners The pupils ask and answer with a Talk Partner, asking and answering about the different animals.

Activity Book

Activity 1

Look and read. Put a tick (✓) or a cross (✗) in the box.

- (Books open.) Ask a pupil to read out the first sentence. He / She looks at the picture and says if the sentence is correct. Repeat with the other pictures.
- The pupils complete the activity on their own.

Answers: 1 ✓ 2 ✓ 3 ✗ 4 ✓ 5 ✗ 6 ✗

Activity 2

Look and read. Write *yes* or *no*.

- Focus the pupils on Activity 2. Ask them to look at the picture, then read the first sentence. Say **The cat is black. Yes or no?** Elicit answers, and point out the example answer.
- The pupils read the other sentences and write their answers.
- Ask for volunteers to read the sentences and their answers.

Answers: **1** no **2** yes **3** no **4** yes **5** no

Ending the lesson

Review the lesson.

- (Books closed.) Say **Today we've practised activities for an external exam. What questions did you learn?**

Review the task flashcards.

- Point to the task flashcards. Say **Look at the activities you've done today. Which activity was your favourite?** Elicit the pupils' favourite activities.

External Exams Video

Additional Cambridge Exams Practice Video: Pre A1 Starters

- Additional external exams preparation material, including videos, worksheets and practice tests, can be found in the Teacher's Resource Bank on Navio.

Activity Book page 106: Vocabulary Practice

Answers: **1.1** sheep **1.2** frog **1.3** bird **1.4** cat **1.5** mouse **1.6** duck
2.1 frog **2.2** chicken **2.3** sheep **2.4** cow **2.5** horse **2.6** goat
Dogs can't **fly**.
3.1 fly **3.2** run **3.3** climb **3.4** swim **3.5** jump **3.6** walk

Key Competences and Key Learning Outcomes

- Practise for Starters Listening Part 3 and Speaking Part 2
- Practise for Reading and Writing Parts 1 and 5

Key language

Recycled: colours; *in, in front of, near, next to; bird; bush, flower, rocks, tree; bin, books, chair, computer, pencil, rubber, ruler, school bag*

Recycled: *Where's the (rubber)? It's (between) (the books). Where are (the birds)? Put the (pen near the computer).*

Materials

- Pupil's Book p111; Activity Book pp 107 and 116; Class CD4; Teacher's App on Navio
- Nature flashcards
- Teacher's Resource Bank: Task flashcards: *listen, colour, Talk Partners, read, write, draw*
- Crayons or coloured pencils

Optional materials

- Teacher's Resource Bank: External Exams Video

At a Glance Lesson Plan

Starting the lesson

- Review nature words and prepositions.
- Set learning outcomes using the task flashcards.

Activity 1

- Listen and tick (✓). There is one example.
- ▶ *CD4 Track 45 p276*

Activity 2

- Listen and point.
- ▶ *CD4 Track 46 p276*
- Talk Partners Ask and answer.
- Go to the Activity Book.

Ending the lesson

- Review the lesson.
- Review the task flashcards.

External Exams Video

- Additional Cambridge Exams Practice Video: Pre A1 Starters

Pupil's Book

Activity Book

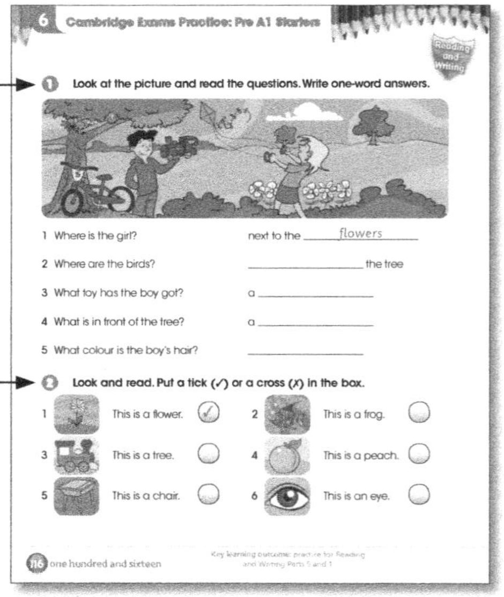

Activity Book

Activity 1

- Look at the picture and read the questions.
- Write one-word answers.

Activity 2

- Look and read. Put a tick (✓) or a cross (✗) in the box.

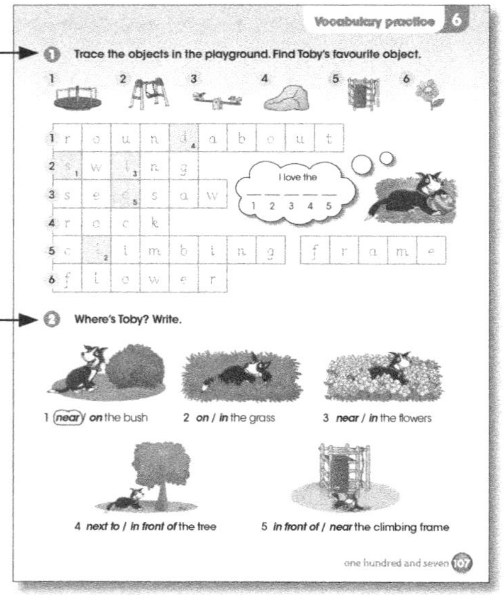

Activity Book

Activity 1

- Trace the objects in the playground. Find Toby's favourite object.

Activity 2

- Where's Toby? Circle.

Digital resources

Teacher's Digital: You can also teach this lesson using the Teacher's App on Navio.

Pupil's Digital: Encourage your pupils to use the Pupil's App on Navio to Practice the activities from this lesson.

Powered By NAVIO

Detailed Lesson Plan

Starting the lesson

Use the Trinity Exam Practice cards (optional).

- The pupils Practice asking and answering questions using the Unit 6 cards.

Review nature words and prepositions.

- Divide the class into two teams and challenge the pupils to think of as many nature words from the unit as they can in one minute.
- Write their answers on the board, or invite volunteers to do so. Add any nature words that the teams didn't think of from the nature flashcards.
- Place a chair at the front of the class and ask for two volunteers to come and demonstrate prepositions. Say **Stand so that the chair is *between* you** for the children to position themselves either side of the chair.
- Ask for three more volunteers, one by one, and repeat the activity to demonstrate *behind*, *next to* and *in front of*.

Set learning outcomes using the task flashcards.

- Say **Today we're going to practise activities for an external exam.**
- Hold up the task flashcards in turn and elicit the activities. Stick them on one side of the board. Point to them during the lesson to reinforce your instructions.

Pupil's Book Activity 1

Listen and colour. There is one example.

▶ *CD4 Track 45 p276*

- (Books open.) Focus the pupils on the picture. Elicit what they can see.
- Play the CD, pausing after each conversation. The pupils listen and tick the correct pictures.
- Play the CD again if necessary.

Answers: **1** B **2** A **3** B **4** B

Pupil's Book Activity 2

Listen and point. Ask and answer.

▶ *CD4 Track 46 p276*

- Focus the pupils' attention on the conversation and play the CD as a model. If necessary, Practice the exchanges as a class several times.
- Then invite two confident pupils to act out the conversation with your support. Place a selection of classroom objects on the desk in front of them (book, pen, pencil, ruler, rubber, sharpener, crayon, pencil case). Prompt them to use these objects in their exchange. Repeat with other pairs of pupils.
- **Talk Partners** The pupils place a selection of classroom objects on their desk and Practice asking and answering the questions with a Talk Partner.

Activity Book

Activity 1

Look at the picture and read the questions. Write one-word answers.

- (Books open.) Focus the pupils on the picture. Ask them what they can see in the picture.
- Read out the first question. The pupils answer the question.
- The pupils work on their own to complete the activity.
- Check answers as a class.

Answers: **1** flowers **2** in **3** train **4** bike **5** black

Activity 2

Look and read. Put a tick (✓) or a cross (✗) in the box.

- Ask a pupil to read out the first sentence. He / She looks at the picture and says if the sentence is correct. Repeat with the other pictures.
- The pupils complete the activity on their own.
- **Talk Partners** The pupils say the sentences with a Talk Partner to Practice the language.

Answers: **1** ✓ **2** ✗ **3** ✗ **4** ✓ **5** ✗ **6** ✓

Ending the lesson

Review the lesson.

- (Books closed.) Say **Today we've practised activities for an external exam. What questions did you learn?**

Review the task flashcards.

- Point to the task flashcards. Say **Look at the activities you've done today. Which activity was your favourite?** Elicit the pupils' favourite activities.

External Exams Video

Additional Cambridge Exams Practice Video: Pre A1 Starters

- Additional external exams preparation material, including videos, worksheets and practice tests, can be found in the Teacher's Resource Bank on Navio.

Activity Book page 107: Vocabulary Practice

Answers: **1.1** roundabout **1.2** swing **1.3** seesaw **1.4** rock **1.5** climbing frame **1.6** flower
I love the **slide**.
2.1 near **2.2** on **2.3** in **2.4** next to **2.5** in front of

Key Competences and Key Learning Outcomes

- Practise for Starters Listening Part 4 and Speaking Part 3
- Practise for Reading and Writing Parts 3 and 4

Key language

- *by bike, by bus, by car, on foot, on the metro*
- *Where is (Nick)? He's in the (bookshop). How do you go to school? I go to school (by car). Where do you live? I live in (Madrid). How many (girls) are there in your class? There are (twelve) (girls).*

Recycled: *bookshop, park, swimming pool, supermarket, toyshop, zoo; boat, bus, lorry, motorbike, train*

Materials

- Pupil's Book p112; Activity Book pp 108 and 117; Class CD4; Teacher's App on Navio
- Teacher's Resource Bank: Task flashcards: *listen, tick, Talk Partners, write, read*

Optional materials

- Teacher's Resource Bank: External Exams Video

At a Glance Lesson Plan

Starting the lesson

- Review forms of transport.
- Set learning outcomes using the task flashcards.

Activity 1

- Listen and colour. There is one example.

▶ *CD4 Track 47 p276*

Activity 2

- Listen and point.

▶ *CD4 Track 48 p276*

- Talk Partners Ask and answer.

Go to the Activity Book.

Ending the lesson

- Review the lesson.
- Review the task flashcards.

External Exams Video

- Additional Cambridge Exams Practice Video: Pre A1 Starters

Pupil's Book

Activity Book

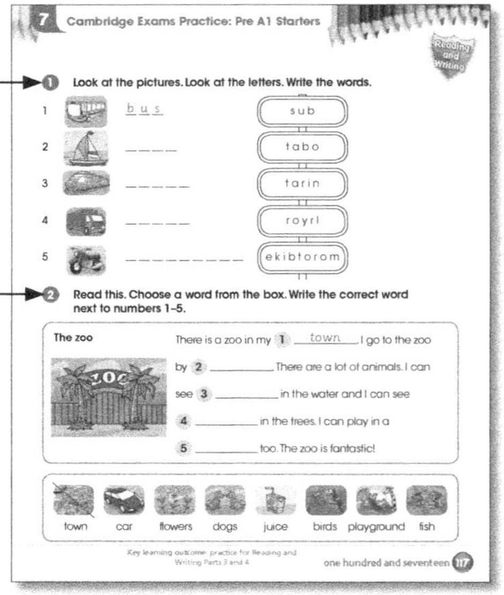

Activity Book

Activity 1

- Look at the pictures. Look at the letters.
- Write the words.

Activity 2

- Read this. Choose a word from the box. Write the correct word next to numbers 1–5.

Activity Book

Activity 1

- Follow and write the places.

Activity 2

- Write the missing letters for the places.

Activity 3

- Match. Write the transport.

Digital resources

Teacher's Digital: You can also teach this lesson using the Teacher's App on Navio.

Pupil's Digital: Encourage your pupils to use the Pupil's App on Navio to Practice the activities from this lesson.

Powered By NAVIO

Detailed Lesson Plan

Starting the lesson

Review forms of transport.

- Describe different forms of transport for the pupils to guess. Say **It has two wheels. You need to wear a helmet** to elicit *motorbike*. Repeat with other forms of transport, or ask for volunteers to describe them for the rest of the class to guess.

Set learning outcomes using the task flashcards.

- Say **Today we're going to practise activities for an external exam.**
- Hold up the task flashcards in turn and elicit the activities. Stick them on one side of the board. Point to them during the lesson to reinforce your instructions.

Pupil's Book Activity 1

Listen and colour. There is one example.

▶ *CD4 Track 47 p276*

- (Books open.) Play the CD, pausing after each conversation to check comprehension. The pupils listen and colour the picture according to what they hear.
- Play the CD again if necessary.

Answers: **1** car – blue **2** teddy bear – pink **3** helicopter – red **4** robot – green **5** ice cream – brown **6** small book – purple

Pupil's Book Activity 2

Listen and point. Ask and answer.

▶ *CD4 Track 48 p276*

- Play the CD. The pupils read the conversation.
- Focus the pupils' attention on the pictures of different forms of transport and say the name of each one as a class.
- The class repeats the question *Do you go to school by boat?* Elicit answers from different pupils.
- Ask two confident pupils to ask and answer the questions in front of the class.
- **Talk Partners** The pupils ask and answer with a Talk Partner, saying the name of different forms of transport and how they go to school.

Activity Book

Activity 1

Look at the pictures. Look at the letters. Write the words.

- Point out the picture of the bus and the jumbled letters on the right. Elicit that the letters can be rearranged to spell *bus*.
- The pupils continue the activity, looking at the pictures and the letters to find the words.

Answers: **1** bus **2** boat **3** train **4** lorry **5** motorbike

Activity 2

Read this. Choose a word from the box. Write the correct word next to numbers 1–5.

- (Books open.) As a class, read out the words in the word box at the bottom of the page. Point out that *town* is crossed out in the box as it is the answer for the first sentence.
- Ask different pupils to read out the sentences. Elicit the missing words.
- The pupils read and write the missing words.

Answer: **1** town **2** car **3** fish **4** birds **5** playground

Ending the lesson

Review the lesson.

- (Books closed.) Say **Today we've practised activities for an exam. What questions did you learn?**

Review the task flashcards.

- Point to the task flashcards. Say **Look at the activities you've done today. Which activity was your favourite?** Elicit the pupils' favourite activities.

External Exams Video

Additional Cambridge Exams Practice Video: Pre A1 Starters

- Additional external exams preparation material, including videos, worksheets and practice tests, can be found in the Teacher's Resource Bank on Navio.

Activity Book page 108: Vocabulary Practice

Answers: **1.1** zoo **1.2** sweet shop **1.3** café **1.4** cinema **1.5** toy shop

I go to the park on my **scooter**.

2.1 hospital **2.2** supermarket **2.3** restaurant **2.4** bookshop **2.5** swimming pool

3.1 train **3.2** motorbike **3.3** lorry **3.4** bus **3.5** boat **3.6** helicopter

Key Competences and Key Learning Outcomes

- Practise for Starters Listening Part 3 and Speaking Part 2
- Practise for Reading and Writing Parts 3 and 5

Key language

- *paint a picture*

Recycled: *shorts, skirt, shoes, sweater, T-shirt, trousers; ride a horse, swim; dog; flowers; tent; toyshop;* colours

Recycled: *What is (Bill) wearing? He's wearing (a T-shirt). What are you wearing today? I'm wearing (a sweater and trousers). What colour is (your sweater)? My (sweater is purple). What colour are (your trousers)? My (trousers are green). Where (is the dog)? It's (near the tree). How many (flowers) are there? There are (five flowers).*

Materials

- Pupil's Book p113; Activity Book pp 109 and 118; Class CD4; Teacher's App on Navio
- Clothes flashcards
- Teacher's Resource Bank: Task flashcards: *listen, tick, Talk Partners, read, write, match*

Optional materials

- Teacher's Resource Bank: External Exams Video

At a Glance Lesson Plan

Starting the lesson

- Review activities and clothes.
- Set learning outcomes using the task flashcards.

Activity 1

- Listen and tick (✓). There is one example.
- ▶ *CD4 Track 49 p276*

Activity 2

- Listen and point.
- ▶ *CD4 Track 50 p276*
- Talk Partners Ask and answer.

Go to the Activity Book.

Ending the lesson

- Review the lesson.
- Review the task flashcards.

External Exams Video

- Additional Cambridge Exams Practice Video: Pre A1 Starters

Pupil's Book

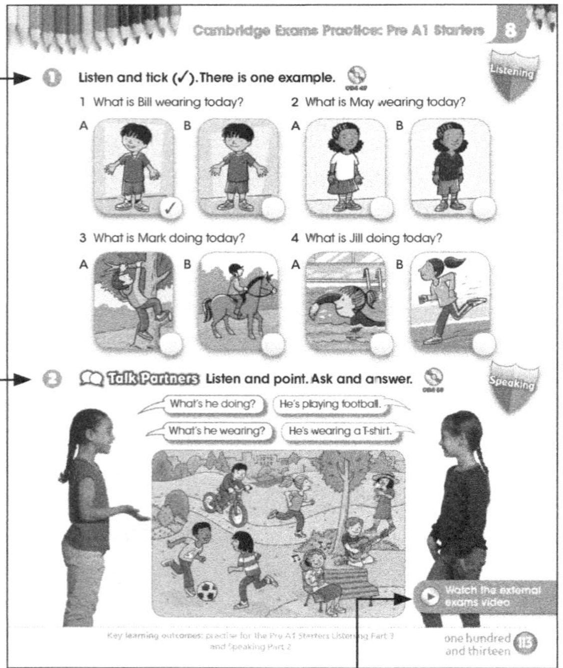

Activity Book

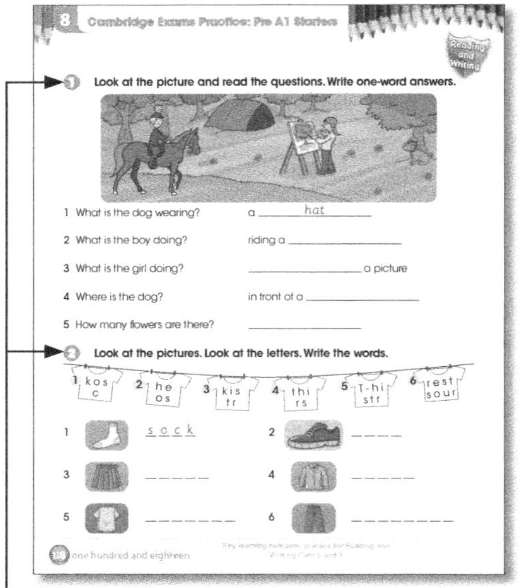

Activity Book

Activity 1

- Look at the picture and read the questions.
- Write one-word answers.

Activity 2

- Look at the pictures. Look at the letters. Write the words.

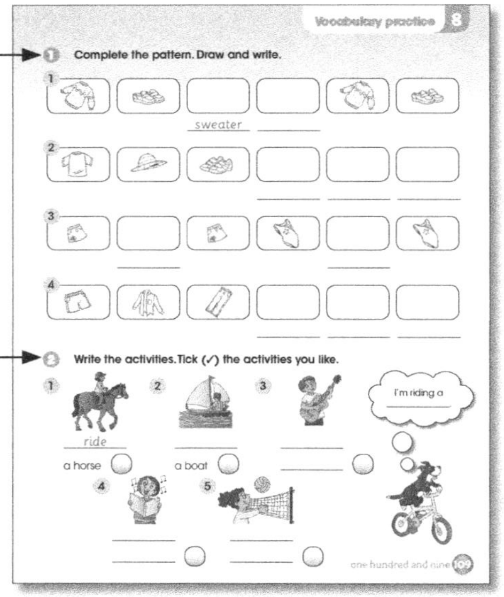

Activity Book

Activity 1

- Complete the pattern. Draw and write.

Activity 2

- Write the activities. Tick the activities you like.

Digital resources

Teacher's Digital: Don't forget you can teach this lesson using the Teacher's App on Navio.

Pupil's Digital: Encourage your pupils to use the Pupil's App on Navio to Practice the vocabulary from this lesson.

Powered By NAVIO

Starting the lesson

Review activities and clothes.

- Distribute the clothes flashcards at random around the class. Say **What are you wearing?** Ask a confident pupil to turn over their flashcard and say *I'm wearing (a T-shirt).*
- Ask the class **What's (Katy) wearing?** to elicit *She's wearing a T-shirt.*
- Repeat with other pupils and flashcards around the class.
- Ask a volunteer to come to the front. Whisper an action for the pupil to mime. Say **What's (Juan) doing?** to elicit *He's (swimming).*
- Repeat with other pupils and actions for the class to guess.

Set learning outcomes using the task flashcards.

- Say **Today we're going to practise activities for an external exam.**
- Hold up the task flashcards in turn and elicit the activities. Stick them on one side of the board. Point to them during the lesson to reinforce your instructions.

Pupil's Book Activity 1

Listen and tick (✓). There is one example.

▶ *CD4 Track 49 p276*

- (Books open.) Look at the first two pictures and elicit what Bill is wearing. Play the CD, pausing after each conversation to check understanding. The pupils listen and tick the correct pictures.
- Play the CD again if necessary.

Answers: **1** A **2** A **3** B **4** A

Pupil's Book Activity 2

Listen and point. Ask and answer.

▶ *CD4 Track 50 p276*

- Play the CD. The pupils listen and read the conversation.
- Play the CD again and the class repeats.
- Ask volunteers to ask and answer the questions.
- **Talk Partners** The pupils ask and answer the questions with a Talk Partner, giving answers about what the people are doing and wearing in the picture.

Activity Book

Activity 1

Look at the picture and read the questions. Write one-word answers.

- (Books open.) Focus the pupils on the picture and elicit what they can see.
- Read out the first question and point out the answer.
- The pupils read the questions and write the answers.

Answers: **1** hat **2** horse **3** painting **4** tree **5** seven

Activity 2

Look at the pictures. Look at the letters. Write the words.

- Point out the picture of the sock and the jumbled letters in the T-shirts on the washing line. Elicit that the letters in the first T-shirt can be rearranged to spell *sock.*
- The pupils continue the activity, looking at the pictures and the letters to find the words.

Answers: **1** sock **2** shoe **3** skirt **4** shirt **5** T-shirt **6** trousers

Ending the lesson

Review the lesson.

- (Books closed.) Say **Today we've practised activities for an exam. What questions did you learn?**

Review the task flashcards.

- Point to the task flashcards. Say **Look at the activities you've done today. Which activity was your favourite?** Elicit the pupils' favourite activities.

External Exams Video

Additional Cambridge Exams Practice Video: Pre A1 Starters

- Additional external exams preparation material, including videos, worksheets and practice tests, can be found in the Teacher's Resource Bank on Navio.

Activity Book page 109: Vocabulary Practice

Answers: **1.1** sweater, shoes **1.2** T-shirt, sun hat, trainers **1.3** swimsuit, skirt **1.4** shorts, shirt, trousers

I'm riding a **bike**.

2.1 ride **2.2** sail **2.3** play the guitar **2.4** sing songs **2.5** play volleyball

Cambridge Exams Practice and Vocabulary Practice answers

Key Competences and Key Learning Outcomes

LEARN
- Practise for Starters Listening Part 1 and Speaking Part 3
- Practise for Reading and Writing Parts 2 and 4

Key language

Recycled: *breakfast, lunch, dinner; at night, in the afternoon, in the evening, in the morning; brush my teeth, get dressed, get up, play, wash my face; cereal, eggs, fish, orange juice, rice; sun hat*

Recycled: *What do you (do in the morning)? I (have breakfast). What do you have for (breakfast)? I have (cereal and milk). I (get up) (in the morning).*

Materials
- Pupil's Book p114; Activity Book pp 110 and 119; Class CD4; Teacher's App on Navio
- Teacher's Resource Bank: Task flashcards: *listen, tick, Talk Partners, read, write, draw*

Optional materials
- Teacher's Resource Bank: External Exams Video

At a Glance Lesson Plan

Starting the lesson
- Review daily routines and meals.
- Set learning outcomes using the task flashcards.

Activity 1
- Listen and draw lines. There is one example.
- ▶ *CD4 Track 51 p276*

Activity 2
- Listen and point .
- ▶ *CD4 Track 52 p277*
- Talk Partners Ask and answer.
- Go to the Activity Book.

Ending the lesson
- Review the lesson.
- Review the task flashcards.

External Exams Video
- Additional Cambridge Exams Practice Video: Pre A1 Starters

Pupil's Book

Activity Book

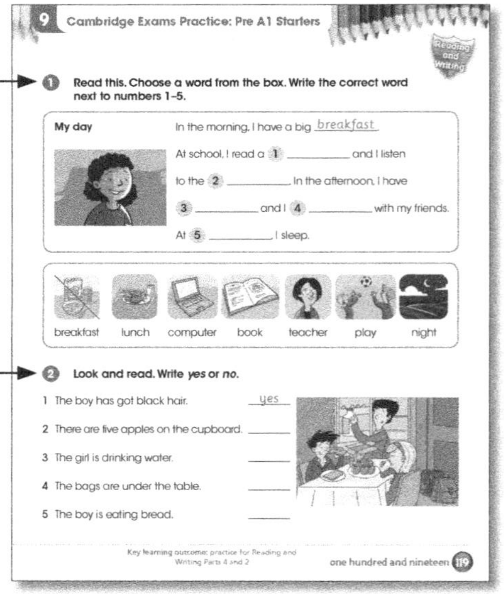

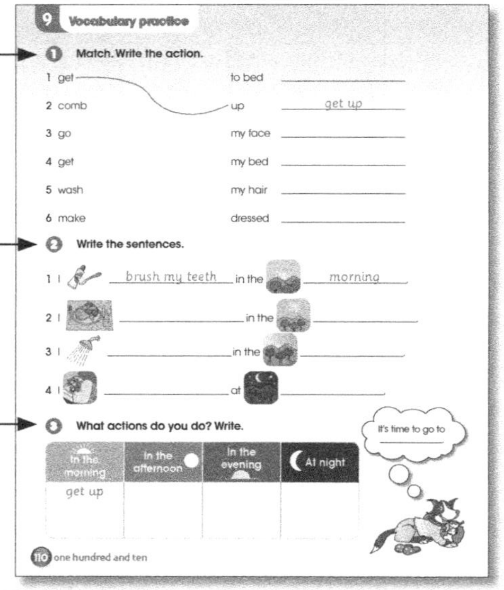

Activity Book

Activity 1
- Read this. Choose a word from the box. Write the correct word next to numbers 1–5.

Activity 2
- Look and read. Write *yes* or *no*.

Activity Book

Activity 1
- Match. Write the action.

Activity 2
- Write the sentences.

Activity 3
- What actions do you do? Write.

Digital resources

Teacher's Digital: You can also teach this lesson using the Teacher's App on Navio.

Pupil's Digital: Encourage your pupils to use the Pupil's App on Navio to Practice the activities from this lesson.

Powered By NAVIO

Detailed Lesson Plan

Starting the lesson

Review daily routines and meals.

- Talk to the class about your daily routine and ask the children to listen out for any errors. If they think you've said something wrong, they shake their heads and put their hands up to tell you the correct sentence. Say **I (get up) in the (morning) and I have (dinner).** A pupil corrects you by saying the full sentence *I get up in the morning and I have breakfast.*
- Repeat the activity with all of the daily routines in the unit.
- Start a food chain around the class. Say **I have fish for dinner.** Point to a confident pupil for them to say *I have fish and chips for dinner.* The next pupil says *I have fish and chips and rice for dinner.* Continue around the class this way until the list gets too long!
- Ask a pupil to start a new chain for breakfast or lunch items.

Set learning outcomes using the task flashcards.

- Say **Today we're going to practise activities for an external exam.**
- Hold up the task flashcards in turn and elicit the activities. Stick them on one side of the board. Point to them during the lesson to reinforce your instructions.

Pupil's Book Activity 1

Listen and draw lines. There is one example.

▶ *CD4 Track 51 p276*

- (Books open.) Play the CD, pausing after each piece of information. The pupils listen and draw a line from the name to the correct person.
- Play the CD again if necessary.

Answers: **1** Alex – boy drinking juice **2** Lucy – girl eating fish and potatoes **3** Anna – girl eating meat and chips **4** Hugo – boy eating rice and fish **5** Sue – girl drinking water **6** May – girl eating fish and chips

Pupil's Book Activity 2

Listen and point. Ask and answer.

▶ *CD4 Track 52 p277*

- Play the CD. The pupils listen and read the conversation.
- Play the CD again and the class repeats.
- Ask volunteers to ask and answer the questions.
- **Talk Partners** The pupils ask and answer with a Talk Partner, giving answers that are true for them.

Activity Book

Activity 1

Read this. Choose a word from the box. Write the correct word next to numbers 1–5.

- (Books open.) As a class, read out the words in the word box at the bottom of the page. Point out that *breakfast* is crossed out in the box as it is the example answer for the first sentence.
- Ask different pupils to read out the sentences. Elicit the missing words.
- The pupils read and write the missing words.

Answers: **1** book **2** teacher **3** lunch **4** play **5** night

Activity 2

Look and read. Write *yes* or *no*.

- Focus the pupils on Activity 2. Ask them to look at the picture, then read the first sentence. Say **The boy has got black hair. Yes or no?** Elicit answers, and point out the example answer.
- The pupils read the other sentences and write their answers.

Answers: **1** yes **2** no **3** yes **4** no **5** yes

Ending the lesson

Review the lesson.

- (Books closed.) Say **Today we've practised activities for an external exam. What questions did you learn?**

Review the task flashcards.

- Point to the task flashcards. Say **Look at the activities you've done today. Which activity was your favourite?** Elicit the pupils' favourite activities.

External Exams Video

Additional Cambridge Exams Practice Video: Pre A1 Starters

- Additional external exams preparation material, including videos, worksheets and practice tests, can be found in the Teacher's Resource Bank on Navio.

Activity Book page 110: Vocabulary Practice

Answers: **1.1** get up **1.2** comb my hair **1.3** go to bed **1.4** get dressed **1.5** wash my face **1.6** make my bed **2.1** 1 brush my teeth in the morning. **2.2** I have lunch in the afternoon. **2.3** I have a shower in the evening. **2.4** I go to bed at night. It's time to go to **bed**.

Audioscript

Starter Unit Lesson 1

Pupil's Book

CD1 Track 1

PB page 4 Activity 1

***What's your name?* song**

Hello! Hello! [Wave your hand.]
What's your name? [Shrug your shoulders.]
I'm Jake.
Come and play! [Beckon with your arm.]
Hello! Hello! [Wave your hand.]
What's your name? [Shrug your shoulders.]
I'm Molly.
Come and play! [Beckon with your arm.]
Hello! Hello! [Wave your hand.]
What's your name? [Shrug your shoulders.]
I'm Beth.
Yes! Let's play! [Beckon with your arm.]

CD1 Track 2

PB page 4 Activity 1

Karaoke version: *What's your name?* song

CD1 Track 3

PB page 4 Activity 2

***Ten balloons* chant**

One, two, three, four, five, six, seven, eight, nine, ten balloons in the sky.

Starter Unit Lesson 2

Pupil's Book

CD1 Track 4

PB page 5 Activity 1

Jake and Molly's Dad: Hello!
Magician: Hello!
Jake and Molly's Dad: What's this?
Magician: It's a bike. It's for two children.
Jake and Molly's Dad: It's perfect!

CD1 Track 5

PB page 5 Activity 2

1
Boy: What's this?
Woman: It's a balloon.
2
Woman: What's this?
Man: It's a hat.
Woman: Oh! It's fantastic.
3
Small boy: What's this?
Market stall owner: It's a banana. Here you are.
Boy: Thank you.
4
Girl: What's this?
Man: It's a book.
Girl: Wow! This book is fantastic!

Starter Unit Lesson 3

Pupil's Book

CD1 Track 6

PB page 6 Activity 1

A big surprise
Frame 1
Jake: What's this, Dad?
Dad: It's a bike. It's for two children.
Molly: Wow! Thank you, Dad.
Frame 2
Jake: Let's clean the bike.
Molly: Good idea!
Beth: Let's clean the bell, too.
Frame 3
Beth: Oops!
Jake: Look! The bike is green and red now.
Molly: It's a magic bike!
Frame 4
Molly: Ring the bell again, Beth.
Jake: Look! It's green, red and orange now!
Frame 5
Beth: What colour is it now?
Jake: Wow! It's green, red, orange and blue!
Frame 6
Beth: Look! The bike is green, red, orange, blue, brown and yellow now!
Molly: This magic bike is fantastic!

Starter Unit Lesson 4

Pupil's Book

CD1 Track 7

PB page 7 Activity 1

***Seven days a week* song**

Monday, Tuesday,
Wednesday, Thursday,
Friday, Saturday and Sunday. [Count a finger on your hands for each day.]
Seven days a week. [Hold up seven fingers.]
Seven days a week. [Hold up seven fingers.]
We ride our magic bike, [Mime riding a bike and ringing bell.]
Seven days a week.

CD1 Track 8

PB page 7 Activity 2

Dan: What day is it today?
Ella: It's Thursday.

Activity Book

CD1 Track 9

AB page 5 Activity 1

1
Molly: Monday, Tuesday, Wednesday, Thursday, … Saturday, Sunday. What's missing?
2
Jake: Monday, … Wednesday, Thursday, Friday, Saturday, Sunday. What's missing?
3
Beth: Monday, Tuesday, Wednesday, Thursday, Friday, … Sunday. What's missing?
4
Jake: Monday, Tuesday, Wednesday, … Friday, Saturday, Sunday. What's missing?
5
Molly: Monday, Tuesday, Wednesday, Thursday, Friday, Saturday, … What's missing?
6
Beth: Monday, Tuesday, … Thursday, Friday, Saturday, Sunday. What's missing?

Unit 1 Lesson 1

Pupil's Book

CD1 Track 10

PB page 8 Activity 1

***I'm ready for school* song**

A pen, a pencil,
A crayon, too.
[Mime putting on school bag and walking.]
I'm ready! I'm ready!
I'm ready for school!
[Mime putting on school bag and walking.]

A rubber, a ruler,
A sharpener, too.
I'm ready! I'm ready!
I'm ready for school!

A book, a school bag,
A pencil case, too.
I'm ready! I'm ready!
I'm ready for school!
Hurray! I'm ready for school!
[Raise arms in the air.]

CD1 Track 11

PB page 8 Activity 1

Karaoke version: *I'm ready for school!* song

CD1 Track 12

PB page 8 Activity 2

Book, pen, rubber, pencil, ruler, crayon, sharpener, computer, school bag, pencil case

Unit 1 Lesson 2

Pupil's Book

CD1 Track 13

PB page 9 Activity 1

Jake: Oh no! Where's my pencil?
Beth: It's here.
Jake: And where's my book?
Beth: It's here, too. Look!
Jake: Oh! Thank you, Beth.

CD1 Track 14

PB page 9 Activity 2

1
Girl: Where's my rubber?
Boy: It's here.
Girl: Oh yes! Thank you.
2
Boy: Where's my pencil?
Girl: It's here. Look!
Boy: Oh yes! Thank you.
3
Boy: Where's my pen?
Girl: It's here. Look!
Boy: Oh yes! Thank you.
4
Girl: Where's my ruler?
Boy: It's here.
Girl: Where?
Boy: Your ruler is here.
Girl: Oh yes! Thank you.

Unit 1 Lesson 3

Pupil's Book

CD1 Track 15

PB pages 10 and 11 Activity 1

Toby goes to school
Frame 1
Molly: Look at Toby. He's sad.
Beth: Poor Toby. Dogs don't go to school.
Frame 2
Jake: Look! Toby is on the magic bike.
Frame 3
Jake: Look! He's in the classroom now.
Beth: Be quiet, Toby. The teacher is here.
Frame 4
Jake: Stop, Toby!
Molly: Oh no! My pencil case!
Frame 5
Jake: Where's my black and white book?
Molly: And where's my purple pencil case?
Frame 6
Jake: Look! The book is in the bin.
Molly: And the pencil case is on the shelf.
Beth: Bad dog, Toby! Tidy up.
Frame 7
Molly: Put the pencil case on the desk, Toby.
Jake: And put the book in the school bag. Good dog!
Frame 8
Teacher: What a tidy desk. Well done, children.
Beth: Thank you.

Unit 1 Lesson 4

Pupil's Book

CD1 Track 16

PB page 12 Activity 1

Shelf, cupboard, bin, desk, board, chair

CD1 Track 17

PB page 12 Activity 2

***Let's tidy up* song**

Put the book on the shelf,
On the shelf, [Clap.] *on the shelf.* [Clap.]
Put the book on the shelf.
Let's tidy up! [Clap, clap.]

Put the paper in the bin, [Clap.]
In the bin, in the bin. [Clap.]
Put the paper in the bin.
Let's tidy up! [Clap, clap.]

Put the chair under the desk, [Clap.]
Under the desk, under the desk. [Clap.]
Put the chair under the desk. [Clap.]
Let's tidy up! [Clap, clap.]

CD1 Track 18

PB page 12 Activity 3

Anna: Put the pencil under the chair.
Anna: Good.

Activity Book

CD1 Track 19

AB page 9 Activity 1

1
Woman: Let's tidy up. Put the bag under the chair.
Boy: Where?
Woman: Under the chair.
Boy: OK.
2
Woman: Now put the pen on the board.
Boy: Where?
Woman: On the board.
Boy: OK.
3
Woman: Put the pencil case on the desk, please.
Boy: Where?
Woman: On the desk.
Boy: OK.
4
Woman: Now put the ruler in the cupboard.
Boy: Where?
Woman: In the cupboard.
Boy: OK.
Woman: Thank you. Well done!

Unit 1 Lesson 5

Pupil's Book

CD1 Track 20

PB page 13 Activity 1

Toby: r – r – r.
Red – rabbit – red – ruler.
A red rabbit on a red ruler.
A red rabbit on a red ruler.
A red rabbit on a red ruler.

CD1 Track 21

PB page 13 Activity 2

1
Girl: Where's the sharpener?
Boy: It's in the cupboard.
Girl: In the cupboard. Thank you.
2
Girl: Where's the computer?
Boy: It's on the shelf.
Girl: On the shelf. Thank you.
3
Girl: Where's the pencil?
Boy: It's under the chair.
Girl: Under the chair. Thank you.
4
Girl: Where's the school bag?
Boy: It's under the desk.
Girl: Under the desk. Thank you.

Unit 1 Lesson 6

Pupil's Book

CD1 Track 22

PB page 14 Activity 1

Alex: Hello! I'm Alex.
Lucy: And I'm Lucy. We go to primary school in England. At school, we have an assembly every day.
Alex: We sit on the floor with all the children in our school. We listen to the head teacher.
Lucy: We play music and we sing songs.
Alex: We clap our hands when boys and girls do good work.

Activity Book

CD1 Track 23

AB page 11 Activity 1

1
Teacher: Are you ready to listen?
Group of children: Yes.
Teacher: Good. Now, this is a story about a boy and a girl …
2
Children: Well done!
3 … If you're happy and you know it and you really want to show it, if you're happy and you know it …
4 [sfx: musical instruments sounding.]

Unit 1 Lesson 7

Pupil's Book

CD1 Track 24

PB page 15 Activity 2

Class rules
Listen to others.
Put your hand up to speak.
Work quietly.
Sit down on your chair.
Walk in the classroom.
Tidy up your things.

Audioscript

Unit 1 Lesson 8 Review

Pupil's Book

CD1 Track 25

PB page 16 Activity 1

1
Boy: Where's my sharpener?
Girl: It's here.
2
Boy: Where's my book?
Girl: It's here.
3
Boy: Where's my pencil?
Girl: It's here.
4
Girl: Where's my rubber?
Boy: It's here.
5
Girl: Where's my pen?
Boy: It's here.
6
Girl: Where's my ruler?
Boy: It's here.
7
Boy: Where's my school bag?
Girl: It's here.
8
Girl: Where's my pencil case?
Boy: It's here.
9
Boy: Where's my crayon?
Girl: It's here.
10
Girl: Where's my computer?
Boy: It's here.

CD1 Track 26

PB page 16 Activity 3

Cooperative learning: Sing *Well Done!*
Well done! [Put left thumb up.]
Well done! [Put right thumb up.]
Well done everyone! [Put right thumb up.]
Let's do a high five! [Do a high five with partner.]
Well done everyone! [Put both thumbs up.]
(Repeat.)

Unit 1 Video and 21st Century Skills

Activity Book

CD1 Track 27

AB page 14 Activity 1

1
Mum: Are you ready for school, Ben?
Boy: Yes, look! Here's my pencil case. Here's my water. Here's my ruler and here's my snack.
Mum: Where's your book?
Boy: Oh. It's in the cupboard.
Mum: It's important to prepare your school bag, Ben.
2
Dad: Are you ready for school, Lisa?
Girl: Yes, look! Here's my snack. Here's my book. Here's my ruler and here's my pencil case.
Dad: Where's your water?
Girl: Oh! It's on the shelf.
3
Mum: Are you ready for school, Tom?
Boy: Yes, look! Here's my book. Here's my pencil case. Here's my snack and here's my water.
Mum: Where's your ruler?
Boy: Oh! It's under the chair.
4
Dad: Are you ready for school, Anna?
Girl: Yes, look! Here's my snack. Here's my water. Here's my ruler and here's my book.
Dad: Where's your pencil case?
Girl: Oh! It's on the desk.
Dad: It's important to prepare your school bag, Anna.

Unit 2 Lesson 1

Pupil's Book

CD1 Track 28

PB page 18 Activity 1

***Happy Birthday!* song**
Happy birthday!
Happy birthday to you!
Here's a present, [Mime passing a present.]
A present for you.

Is it a doll? [Shrug shoulders with each question.]
Is it a train?
Is it a kite?
or a computer game?

Happy birthday!
Happy birthday to you!
Here's a present, [Mime passing a present.]
A present for you.

Is it a robot? [Shrug shoulders with each question.]
Is it a ball?
Is it a scooter?
or a dinosaur?

Happy birthday!
Happy birthday to you!
Here's a present, [Mime passing a present.]
A present for you.

CD1 Track 29

PB page 18 Activity 1

Karaoke version: *Happy Birthday!* song

CD1 Track 30

PB page 18 Activity 2

Ball, train, car, doll, kite, robot, scooter, teddy, dinosaur, computer game

Unit 2 Lesson 2

Pupil's Book

CD1 Track 31

PB page 19 Activity 1
Beth: What is it? Is it a bike?
Jake: No, it isn't.
Beth: Is it a scooter?
Molly: Yes, it is!
Beth: It's a fantastic present. Thank you!

CD1 Track 32

PB page 19 Activity 2

1
Girl: Here's a present for you.
Boy: What is it? Is it ball?
Girl: Yes, it is.
Boy: Thank you.
2
Boy: Here's a present for you.
Girl: What is it? Is it a doll?
Boy: No, it isn't.
Girl: Is it a teddy?
Boy: Yes, it is.
Girl: Brilliant! Thank you.
3
Girl: Oh! A present! Is it a car?
Boy: No, it isn't.
Girl: Is it a train?
Boy: Yes, it is.
Girl: Amazing! Thank you.
4
Boy: Oh! A present! Is it a dinosaur?
Boy: Yes, it is.
Boy: Fantastic! Thank you.

Unit 2 Lesson 3

Pupil's Book

CD1 Track 33

PB pages 20 and 21 Activity 1

The slow scooter
Frame 1
Beth: Let's have a race.
Jake: Good idea!
Molly: Ready, steady … go!

Frame 2
Beth: Oh no! My new scooter is slow. Wait for me!
Frame 3
Jake: What's the matter, Beth?
Beth: My new scooter is slow. The wheels are very small.
Molly: I've got an idea.
Frame 4
Molly: Magic Bike! Magic Bike! Can you help?
Frame 5
Beth: Look! The wheels are big now.
Jake: Ring the bell again, Molly!
Frame 6
Beth: Look! What is it?
Jake: It's a motor.
Molly: Amazing!
Frame 7
Beth: My scooter is fast now. Wheeee!
Jake: Stop! Stop! Wait for us, Beth!
Frame 8
Jake: Well done, Beth.
Molly: You win the race.
Beth: Thank you, Jake and Molly. Thank you, Magic Bike!

Unit 2 Lesson 4

Pupil's Book

CD1 Track 34

PB page 22 Activity 1

Big, small, old, new, fast, slow

CD1 Track 35

PB page 22 Activity 2

***My favourite toy* song**
My favourite toy is a train
My favourite toy is a train
It's fast. It's new.
It's red and blue.
My favourite toy is a train.
[Mime pulling the train's whistle each time the whistle sounds.]
My favourite toy is a teddy.
My favourite toy is a teddy.
It's old. It's big.
It's brown and pink.
My favourite toy is a teddy.
[Hold up your hands like claws each time the bear growls.]

CD1 Track 36

PB page 22 Activity 3

Ella: What's your favourite toy?
Dan: My favourite toy is a ball. It's old.

Activity Book

CD1 Track 37

AB page 19 Activity 1

1
Boy: What's your favourite toy?
Girl: My favourite toy is a ball. Look!
Boy: Wow! It's big.
Girl: Yes, it is. It's amazing!
2
Girl: What's your favourite toy?
Boy: My favourite toy is a bike. Look!
Girl: Is it fast?
Boy: Yes, it is. It's very fast!
3
Girl: What's your favourite toy?
Boy: My favourite toy is a dinosaur. Look!
Girl: It's very small.
Boy: Yes, it is. But it's fantastic!
4
Boy: What's your favourite toy?
Girl: My favourite toy is a doll. Look!
Boy: Is it old?
Girl: Yes, it is. It's old, but I love it!

Unit 2 Lesson 5

Pupil's Book

CD1 Track 38

PB page 23 Activity 1

Toby: s – s – s.
Six – snakes – slow – scooter.
Six snakes on a slow scooter.
Six snakes on a slow scooter.
Six snakes on a slow scooter.

CD1 Track 39

PB page 23 Activity 2

1
Girl: My favourite toy is new.
Boy: Is it a bike?
Girl: No, it isn't.
Boy: Is it a scooter?
Girl: Yes, it is.
2
Boy: My favourite toy is fast.
Girl: Is it a train?
Boy: Yes, it is.
3
Girl: My favourite toy is slow.
Boy: Is it a dinosaur?
Girl: Yes, it is.
4
Boy: My favourite toy is old.
Girl: Is it a ball?
Boy: No, it isn't.
Girl: Is it a doll?
Boy: Yes, it is.

CD1 Track 40

PB page 23 Activity 3

Cooperative learning: Sing *Sharing is a good thing to do.*
Pencils, rubbers, scissors, too. [Pupil A places a hand on the table.]
You share with me. [Pupil B places a hand on top of Pupil A's hand.]
I share with you. [Pupil A places his / her other hand on top of Pupil B's hand.]
Sharing is a good thing to do. [Pupil B places his / her other hand on top of Pupil A's hand.]
Yes! Sharing is a good thing to do. [The pupils leave all four hands on the table.]
(Repeat.)

Unit 2 Lesson 6

Pupil's Book

CD1 Track 41

PB page 24 Activity 1

Alex: It's my birthday today. I'm seven. I have a party on my birthday.
Alex: My party is a fancy dress party. Look! We're pirates today.
Alex: I've got lots of birthday cards. They're fantastic!
Alex: I play party games in the garden with my friends. It's good fun!
Alex: I've got a birthday cake with seven candles.

Activity Book

CD1 Track 42

AB page 21 Activity 1

1
Girl: I've got presents on my birthday. Look at the big present on the table.
2
Boy: It's my birthday today. Look! My favourite birthday card is on the shelf.
3
Girl: I've got a birthday cake on my birthday. My birthday cake has got six candles this year.
4
Boy: I wear fancy dress at my birthday party. Today I am a cowboy!

Unit 2 Lesson 7

Pupil's Book

CD1 Track 43

PB page 25 Activity 2

To Beth,
Happy birthday!
Have a fantastic party with your friends.
Lots of love,
from
Mum and Dad

Audioscript

Unit 2 Lesson 8 Review

Pupil's Book

CD1 Track 44

PB page 26 Activity 1

1
Girl: Is it a dinosaur?
Boy: Yes, it is.
2
Boy: Is it a computer game?
Girl: Yes, it is.
3
Boy: Is it a doll?
Girl: Yes, it is.
4
Girl: Is it a car?
Boy: Yes, it is.
5
Girl: Is it a train?
Girl: Yes, it is.
6
Boy: Is it a teddy?
Boy: Yes, it is.
7
Girl: Is it a scooter?
Boy: Yes, it is.
8
Boy: Is it a ball?
Girl: Yes, it is.
9
Boy: Is it a robot?
Girl: Yes, it is.
10
Girl: Is it a kite?
Boy: Yes, it is.

CD1 Track 45

PB page 26 Activity 3

Cooperative learning: *Well Done!* song
Well done! [Put left thumb up.]
Well done! [Put right thumb up.]
Well done everyone! [Put both thumbs up.]
Let's do a high five! [Do a high five with partner.]
Well done everyone! [Put both thumbs up.]
(Repeat.)

Unit 2 Video and 21st Century Skills

Activity Book

CD1 Track 46

AB page 24 Activity 1

1
Boy: What are your three favourite toys, Emma?
Girl: Hmm … Number 3 is a computer game. Number 2 is a ball. And my number 1 toy is … a bike! My bike is new. And it's fast.
2
Girl: What are your three favourite colours, Sam?
Boy: Hmm … Number 3 is red. Number 2 is yellow. And my number 1 colour is … blue. My school bag is blue. My pencil case is blue, too.
3
Boy: What are your three favourite days, Emma?
Girl: Number 3 is Wednesday. Number 2 is Monday. And my number 1 day is … Sunday. I play with my toys on Sunday.
4
Girl: What are your three favourite animals, Sam?
Boy: Number 3 is a rat.
Girl: A rat?
Boy: Yes, a rat. Number 2 is a rabbit. And my number 1 animal is … a dog. Dogs are great!

Unit 3 Lesson 1

Pupil's Book

CD1 Track 47

PB page 28 Activity 1

***This is me* song**
This is my body, [Gesture from head to toe.]
This is me. [Point to your chest.]
This is my body, [Gesture from head to toe.]
Count with me.

Two feet, [Touch your feet.]
Ten toes, [Touch your toes.]
Two eyes, [Touch your eyes.]
One big nose. [Touch your nose.]

This is my body,
This is me.
This is my body,
Count with me.

Ten fingers, [Touch your fingers together.]
One head, [Touch your head.]
Two arms, [Touch your arms.]
Two long legs. [Touch your legs.]

CD1 Track 48

PB page 28 Activity 1

Karaoke version: *This is me* song

CD1 Track 49

PB page 28 Activity 2

Head, legs, feet, toes, arms, ears, mouth, eyes, nose, fingers

Unit 3 Lesson 2

Pupil's Book

CD1 Track 50

PB page 29 Activity 1

Molly: Look at me! I've got a red nose.
Jake: I've got big ears.
Molly: And I've got a big mouth. I'm a clown.
Jake: I'm a clown, too.

CD1 Track 51

PB page 29 Activity 2

1 Look at me! I've got a big nose. I'm a clown.
2 I've got a small mouth. Look at me!
3 Look at me! I've got big eyes. I'm a clown.
4 I've got big ears. Look at me!

Unit 3 Lesson 3

Pupil's Book

CD1 Track 52

PB pages 30 and 31 Activity 1

Fun at the circus
Frame 1
Beth: I can't juggle.
Jake: Let's make a circus. Magic Bike, can you help?
Frame 2
Circus ringmaster: Welcome to the circus, children.
Beth: Wow! This circus is very big.
Frame 3
Circus ringmaster: Here's Annie the acrobat.
Jake: She's fantastic!
Frame 4
Circus ringmaster: And here's Molly the clown.
Jake and Beth: Wow!
Molly: Look at me! I've got big feet and I've got purple hair.
Frame 5
Circus ringmaster: And now here's amazing Toby!
Beth: Wow! He's very strong!
Frame 6
Circus ringmaster: And now here's Jake and his magic bike.
Jake: Look! I've got one hand on the bike.
Molly: Be careful, Jake!
Frame 7
Jake: I'm not an acrobat. Help!
Molly: Oh no!
Frame 8
Molly: Are you OK, Jake?
Jake: Yes, I am. Look! We're in the garden again.
Beth: But look at Toby! He's got purple hair!

Unit 3 Lesson 4

Pupil's Book

CD2 Track 1

PB page 32 Activity 1

Long hair, short hair, blonde hair, brown hair, black hair, red hair

CD2 Track 2

PB page 32 Activity 2

***My friend* song**

I've got a friend called Jake.
He's got green eyes. [Point to your eyes.]
He's got short hair. [Point to your hair.]
He's fantastic! [Put both thumbs up.]

We're different,
And that's OK.
We're different,
And we're friends.

I've got a friend called Beth.
She's got brown eyes. [Point to your eyes.]
She's got long hair. [Point to your hair.]
She's fantastic! [Put both thumbs up.]

We're different,
And that's OK.
We're different,
And we're friends.

CD2 Track 3

PB page 32 Activity 3

Boy: My friend has got black hair.
Girl: My friend has got green eyes.

Activity Book

CD2 Track 4

AB page 29 Activity 1

1
Boy: My friend has got long hair. She's got brown hair. And she's got green eyes.
2
Girl: My friend has got short hair. He's got red hair. And he's got blue eyes.
3
Girl: My friend has got short hair. She's got black hair. And she's got brown eyes.
4
Boy: My friend has got short hair. He's got black hair. And he's got blue eyes.

Unit 3 Lesson 5

Pupil's Book

CD2 Track 5

PB page 33 Activity 1

Toby: *h – h – h.*
Helen – happy – hippo – hops – hops.
Helen the happy hippo hops and hops.
Helen the happy hippo hops and hops.
Helen the happy hippo hops and hops.

CD2 Track 6

PB page 33 Activity 2

1
Girl: My clown has got yellow hair. My clown has got big eyes and a small nose. My clown has got a big mouth.
Boy: Is this your clown?
Girl: Yes, it is. Well done!
2
Boy: My clown has got orange hair. My clown has got small eyes and a big nose. My clown has got a big mouth.
Girl: Is this your clown?
Boy: Yes, it is. Well done!
3
Boy: My clown has got yellow hair. My clown has got big eyes and a small nose. My clown has got a small mouth.
Girl: Is this your clown?
Boy: Yes, it is. Well done!
4
Girl: My clown has got orange hair. My clown has got small eyes and a big nose. My clown has got a small mouth.
Boy: Is this your clown?
Girl: Yes, it is. Well done!

Unit 3 Lesson 6

Pupil's Book

CD2 Track 7

PB page 34 Activity 1

Alex: 'Circus Day' is a special day at our school. We paint our faces. We do different circus activities, too.
Alex: I spin a plate. It's very difficult! Look!
Lucy: I juggle scarves. It's fun.
Alex: I ride a special bike. My teacher helps me.
Lucy: I walk on stilts. Look! I've got long legs.

Activity Book

CD2 Track 8

AB page 31 Activity 1

1 On Circus Day, I walk on stilts. Look! I've got long legs.
2 I spin a plate. Look … oh dear!
3 I juggle scarves. One scarf … two scarves … ta-daaa! THREE scarves!
4 I paint my face. Look! I'm a clown. I've got a big nose!
5 And I ride a special bike. Circus Day is fantastic!

Unit 3 Lesson 7

Pupil's Book

CD2 Track 9

PB page 35 Activity 2

My feelings

When I'm sad, I sit and cry.
When I'm happy, I laugh and smile.
When I'm angry, I stamp my feet.
When I'm tired, I go to sleep.

CD2 Track 10

PB page 35 Activity 3

Cooperative learning: *We can do it!* song

We can do it! [Roll arms.]
We can do it! [Roll arms.]
Yeah! [Wave both arms in the air.]
We can do it! [Roll arms.]
We can do it! [Roll arms.]
Yeah! [Wave both arms in the air.]
Come on everybody! [Clap to the left.]
Come on everybody! [Clap to the right.]
We can do it! [Roll arms.]
We can do it! [Roll arms.]
Yeah! [Wave both arms in the air.]

Unit 3 Lesson 8 Review

Pupil's Book

CD2 Track 11

PB page 36 Activity 1

1
Girl: I've got one head.
2
Boy: I've got two legs.
3
Girl: I've got two feet.
4
Boy: I've got one mouth.
5
Girl: I've got one nose.
6
Boy: I've got ten fingers.
7
Girl: I've got two ears.
8
Boy: I've got two arms.
9
Girl: I've got two eyes.
10
Boy: I've got ten toes.

CD2 Track 12

PB page 36 Activity 3

Cooperative learning: *Well Done!* song

Well done! [Put left thumb up.]
Well done! [Put right thumb up.]
Well done everyone! [Put both thumbs up.]
Let's do a high five! [Do a high five with partner.]
Well done everyone! [Put both thumbs up.]
(Repeat.)

Audioscript

Unit 3 Video and 21st Century Skills

Activity Book

CD2 Track 13

AB page 34 Activity 1

1
Boy: We juggle together.
Girl: Look! We've got three balls. 1 … 2 … and whoops!
2
Girl: We play music together.
Boy: Listen to this!
3
Girl: We play football together.
Girl: We play in the playground at school. It's fun!
4
Boy: We tidy up the classroom together.
Boy: Yes. It's fast when we work together.

My project 1 Lesson 1

Pupil's Book

CD2 Track 14

PB page 38 Activity 1

1 grandmother
2 grandfather
3 father
4 mother
5 uncle
6 aunt
7 brother
8 sister
9 cousins

CD2 Track 15

PB page 38 Activity 2

Dan: Have you got a brother?
Anna: Yes, I have. I've got two brothers.
Dan: Have you got a sister?
Anna: No, I haven't.

My project 1 Lesson 2

Pupil's Book

CD2 Track 16

PB page 39 Activity 2

Cooperative learning: *It's fun to work together* song

Together, together, [Hold hands with partner and wave arms in the air.]
It's fun to work together,
You and me, [Point to your partner and then yourself.]
Me and you, [Point to yourself and then your partner.]
It's fun to work together.

Together, together.
It's fun to work together.
You and me,
Me and you.
It's fun to work together.

CD2 Track 17

PB page 39 Activity 3

Boy: This is my happy family.
This is my mother. Her name is Marta.
This is my brother. His name is Ben.

Unit 4 Lesson 1

Pupil's Book

CD2 Track 18

PB page 40 Activity 1

***Delicious food* song**

I've got rice and eggs
And chicken today.
Delicious food [Rub stomach and mime eating.]
At the Astro Café!

I've got fish and chips
And salad today.
Delicious food [Rub stomach and mime eating.]
At the Astro Café!

I've got fruit and cake
And ice cream today.
Delicious food [Rub stomach and mime eating.]
At the Astro Café!

CD2 Track 19

PB page 40 Activity 1

Karaoke version: *Delicious food* song

CD2 Track 20

PB page 40 Activity 2

Eggs, meat, fish, chips, rice, fruit, cake, salad, chicken, ice cream

Unit 4 Lesson 2

Pupil's Book

CD2 Track 21

PB page 41 Activity 1

Molly: Mmmm. I like fish.
Jake: I don't like fish. I like chicken.
Molly: I like ice cream, too. What about you?
Jake: Oh yes! I LOVE ice cream. It's delicious!

CD2 Track 22

PB page 41 Activity 2

1
Girl: Mmm. I like eggs.
2
Boy: I don't like meat.
3
Girl: I LOVE chips.
4
Boy: I don't like salad.
5
Girl: I like fruit.
6
Boy: I LOVE ice cream.

Unit 4 Lesson 3

Pupil's Book

CD2 Track 23

PB pages 42 and 43 Activity 1

I'm hungry
Frame 1
Beth: Let's play! Hello, Molly and Jake. Welcome to my restaurant.
Molly: Hello! A table for two, please.
Frame 2
Jake: This food isn't real. I'm hungry.
Molly: I'm hungry, too.
Beth: I know. Let's ring the bell.
Frame 3
Molly: Wow! The food is real now.
Jake: And look! The waiter is a robot!
Beth: I love robots.
Frame 4
Robot: Here you are, Molly. Here you are, Beth.
Beth: Thank you. I like ice cream.
Molly: And I love chocolate cake. It's my favourite.
Frame 5
Robot: And here's an orange for you, Jake.
Jake: But I don't like oranges.
Frame 6
Robot: Do you like peaches?
Jake: No, I don't.
Beth: Do you like grapes?
Jake: No, I don't. I don't like fruit!
Frame 7
Robot: No problem. One minute …
Beth, Jake and Molly: Wow! Robot, you're amazing!
Frame 8
Robot: Here's a delicious fruit juice for you, Jake.
Jake: Mmm. I love fruit juice! Thank you, Robot.

Unit 4 Lesson 4

Pupil's Book

CD2 Track 24

PB page 44 Activity 1

Mango, grape, peach, cherry, lemon, coconut

CD2 Track 25

PB page 44 Activity 2

***Do you like fruit?* song**

I like grapes.
What about you?
Do you like grapes?
Do you like fruit?

I like grapes.
Yes, I do.
Eating fruit is fun to do.

I like peaches.
What about you?
Do you like peaches?
Do you like fruit?

I like peaches.
Yes, I do.
Eating fruit is fun to do.

CD2 Track 26

PB page 44 Activity 3

Anna: Do you like grapes?
Dan: Yes, I do. What about you?
Anna: No, I don't. I don't like grapes.

Activity Book

CD2 Track 27

AB page 41 Activity 1

1
Boy: Do you like fruit?
Girl: Yes, of course.
Boy: Do you like grapes?
Girl: Yes, I do.
Boy: And do you like coconuts?
Girl: Mmm … No, I don't.
Boy: What about pears? Do you like pears?
Girl: Oh. Yes, I do.
Boy: And do you like cherries?
Girl: Yes, I do. Cherries are delicious!
2
Girl: Do you like fruit?
Boy: Yes, I do. I love fruit!
Girl: Do you like lemons?
Boy: Oh no, I don't. I don't like lemons.
Girl: And do you like mangoes?
Boy: Yes, I do.
Girl: Do you like grapes?
Boy: Yes, I do. Grapes are delicious!
Girl: And what about cherries? Do you like cherries?
Boy: Mmm … Yes, I do. Eating fruit is fun!

Unit 4 Lesson 5

Pupil's Book

CD2 Track 28

PB page 45 Activity 1

Toby: j – j – j.
Jim – juggles – jam – juice – jelly.
Jim juggles jam, juice and jelly.
Jim juggles jam, juice and jelly.
Jim juggles jam, juice and jelly.

CD2 Track 29

PB page 45 Activity 2

1
Boy: Do you like chicken?
Girl: Yes, I do.
Boy: Do you like ice cream?
Girl: Yes, I do.
Boy: Do you like chicken ice cream?
Girl: Yuck! No I don't.
2
Girl: Do you like fruit?
Boy: Yes, I do.
Girl: Do you like jelly?
Boy: Yes, I do.
Girl: Do you like fruit jelly?
Boy: Oh! Yes, I do.
3
Boy: Do you like bananas?
Girl: Yes, I do.
Boy: Do you like cake?
Girl: Yes, I do.
Boy: Do you like banana cake?
Girl: Mmm. Yes, I do.

CD2 Track 30

PB page 45 Activity 4

Cooperative learning: *Calm down* song

Let's calm down. [Palms face down, lower hands.]
Let's calm down. [Palms face down, lower hands.]
Breathe in. [Breathe in deeply.]
Breathe out. [Breathe out deeply.]
Now let's count.
1, 2, 3, 4, 5. [Count on your fingers.]
Let's calm down. [Palms face down, lower hands.]

Unit 4 Lesson 6

Pupil's Book

CD2 Track 31

PB page 46 Activity 1

Lucy: It's Sunday morning. Let's make a traditional English breakfast today.
Lucy: Here are the ingredients: eggs, mushrooms, baked beans, tomatoes and bread.
Alex: I mix the eggs. Lucy makes the toast. Dad cuts the tomatoes.
Lucy: Dad cooks the food. We prepare the tray.
Alex: We take the breakfast to Mum. She's in bed. She's very happy.

Activity Book

CD2 Track 32

AB page 43 Activity 1

1
Girl 1: For my breakfast, I've got orange juice, fruit and some bread. It's delicious!
2
Boy 1: Today I've got bread, eggs and orange juice for breakfast. Oh, dear! I don't like eggs.
3
Girl 2: I've got cereal and milk for breakfast. Yummy!
4
Boy 2: For my breakfast, I've got an egg, mushrooms and tomatoes. Mmm … I'm hungry now!

Unit 4 Lesson 7

Pupil's Book

CD2 Track 33

PB page 47 Activity 2

Girl: What's for lunch on Monday?
Boy: On Monday, we've got salad, meat and vegetables, and jelly.
Girl: What's for lunch on Tuesday?
Boy: On Tuesday, we've got carrots, chicken and pasta, and fruit.
Girl: What's for lunch on Wednesday?
Boy: On Wednesday, we've got soup, meat and rice, and ice cream.
Girl: What's for lunch on Thursday?
Boy: On Thursday we've got salad, chicken and potatoes, and fruit salad.
Girl: What's for lunch on Friday?
Boy: On Friday we've got soup, fish and salad, and carrot cake.
Apple: Munch! Munch! Munch! I like a healthy lunch!

Unit 4 Lesson 8 Review

Pupil's Book

CD2 Track 34

PB page 48 Activity 1

1
Girl: I like meat.
2
Boy: I like chicken.
3
Girl: I love ice cream.
4
Boy: I love salad.
5
Girl: I don't like fish.
6
Boy: I don't like rice.

Audioscript

7
Girl: I like cake.
8
Boy: I like fruit.
9
Girl: I love chips.
10
Girl: I love eggs.

CD2 Track 35

PB page 48 Activity 3

Cooperative learning: *Well Done!* song
Well done! [Put left thumb up.]
Well done! [Put right thumb up.]
Well done everyone! [Put both thumbs up.]
Let's do a high five! [Do a high five with partner.]
Well done everyone! [Put both thumbs up.]
(Repeat.)

Unit 4 Video and 21st Century Skills

Activity Book

CD2 Track 36

AB page 46 Activity 1

1
Boy: What's in your lunch box today, Emma?
Girl: I've got pasta, vegetables, grapes and a bottle of water.
Boy: Mmm! That's healthy!
2
Girl: What's in your lunch box today, Charlie?
Boy: I've got salad, chicken, an apple and orange juice.
Girl: Do you like chicken?
Boy: Yes, I do.
3
Boy: What's in your lunch box today, Lucy?
Girl: I've got a sandwich, fruit and a bottle of water.
Boy: What fruit have you got?
Girl: A banana and an apple
4
Girl: What's in your lunch box today, Peter?
Boy: I've got a sandwich, fruit salad and orange juice.
Girl: What a healthy lunch!

Unit 5 Lesson 1

Pupil's Book

CD2 Track 37

PB page 50 Activity 1

***On the farm* song**
Animals, animals.
We love animals.
Animals, animals
On the farm.

Can you see a duck? [Mime looking for an animal to the left.]
Can you see a cat? [Mime looking for an animal to the right.]
Yes, I can. Yes, I can.
The duck is yellow [Mime being a duck.]
And the cat is black [Mime being a cat.]
[Repeat chorus.]

Can you see a horse? [Mime looking for an animal to the left.]
Can you see a cow? [Mime looking for an animal to the right.]
Yes, I can. Yes, I can.
The horse is grey. [Mime being a horse.]
And the cow is brown. [Mime being a cow.]
[Repeat chorus.]

Can you see a sheep? [Mime looking for an animal to the left.]
Can you see a mouse? [Mime looking for an animal to the right.]
Yes, I can. Yes, I can.
The sheep is white. [Mime being a sheep.]
And the mouse is brown. [Mime being a mouse.]
[Repeat chorus.]

CD2 Track 38

PB page 50 Activity 1

Karaoke version: *On the farm* song

CD2 Track 39

PB page 50 Activity 2

Cat, cow, bird, frog, goat, horse, sheep, duck, mouse, chicken

Unit 5 Lesson 2

Pupil's Book

CD2 Track 40

PB page 51 Activity 1

Molly: Can you see Toby?
Jake: No, I can't.
Molly: Can you see the black cat?
Jake: Yes, I can. The cat is here. But where's Toby?

CD2 Track 41

PB page 51 Activity 2

Boy: Can you see a frog?
Girl: Yes, I can.
Boy: What colour is it?
Girl: It's green.

Boy: Can you see a cow?
Girl: Yes, I can.
Boy: What colour is it?
Girl: It's black and white.

Boy: Can you see a horse?
Girl: No, I can't.
Boy: Can you see a bird?
Girl: Yes, I can.
Boy: What colour is it?
Girl: It's yellow.

Boy: Can you see a sheep?
Girl: Yes, I can.
Boy: What colour is it?
Girl: It's black.

Boy: Can you see a duck?
Girl: No, I can't.

Unit 5 Lesson 3

Pupil's Book

CD2 Track 42

PB pages 52 and 53 Activity 1

Animal magic
Frame 1
Jake: Look. Here's Toby.
Molly: Oh no! He can see the cat!
Frame 2
Molly: The cat is on the magic bike. Shoo!
Beth: Stop, Toby!
Frame 3
Narrator: Suddenly …
Beth: Look. Is it a cow?
Jake: Yes, it is. But cows can't fly.
Molly: It's magic!
Frame 4
Jake: And look! Is it a goat?
Molly: Yes, it is. But goats can't swim.
Beth: Amazing!
Frame 5
Beth: Look at the sheep.
Molly: But sheep can't climb trees.
Jake: This sheep can climb trees.
Frame 6
Jake: Ring the bell again, Molly.
Molly: Stop, magic. Stop!
Frame 7
Beth: Can you see the cat now?
Molly: Yes, I can. It's in the tree. Look.
Frame 8
Beth: The cat is happy now.
Molly: Yes. Dogs can't climb trees.
Jake: Bad luck, Toby!

Unit 5 Lesson 4

Pupil's Book

CD2 Track 43

PB page 54 Activity 1

Fly, swim, run, walk, climb, jump

CD2 Track 44

PB page 54 Activity 2

***Cats can't fly* song**

I love cats.
Cats can fly. [Flap your arms like a bird.]
No! No! No! [Wave your finger.]
Cats can't fly
Cats can climb. [Climb like a cat.]

I love frogs.
Frogs can run.
No! No! No! [Wave your finger.]
Frogs can't run.
Frogs can jump. [Jump.]

I love cows.
Cows can talk. [Open and close your hands like a mouth.]
No! No! No! [Wave your finger.]
Cows can't talk
Cows can walk.

CD2 Track 45

PB page 54 Activity 3

Anna: Cats can fly.
Ella: No!
Ella: Cats can swim.
Anna: Yes!

Activity Book

CD2 Track 46

AB page 51 Activity 1

1
Boy: Cats can climb trees.
2
Girl: Goats can't climb trees.
3
Boy: Horses can swim.
4
Girl: Ducks can fly.

Unit 5 Lesson 5

Pupil's Book

CD2 Track 47

PB page 55 Activity 1

Toby: sh – sh – sh.
Shush – shout – sheep.
Shush! Don't shout, sheep.
Shush! Don't shout, sheep.
Shush! Don't shout, sheep.

CD2 Track 48

PB page 55 Activity 2

1
Girl: Cat – swim – Cats can swim.
Boy: Yes. Well done.
2
Boy: It's my turn now. Frog – fly – Frogs can´t fly.
Girl: Yes. Well done.
3
Girl: It's my turn now. Horse – run – Horses can run.
Boy: Yes. Well done.
4
Boy: It's my turn now. Cow – jump – Cows can´t jump
Girl: Yes. Well done.

CD2 Track 49

PB page 55 Activity 3

Cooperative Learning: *Let's take turns* song

Let's take turns
Let's take turns
Come on everybody. [Beckon.]
Let's take turns
It's my turn. [Point to yourself.]
It's your turn. [Point to your partner.]
Let's have fun! [Put your hands in the air.]
(Repeat.)

Unit 5 Lesson 6

Pupil's Book

CD2 Track 50

PB page 56 Activity 1

Alex: There's a farm in our town. Schools and families can visit the farm. It's very interesting.
Lucy: I love the goats on the farm. I can feed them. Look. This goat is very hungry.
Alex: I love the horses. This horse is small and it's got lots of hair. Its name is Bob.
Alex: We can see chickens on the farm. I help the farmer to collect the eggs.
Lucy: I like the garden. Fruit and vegetables grow here. Look. Here are some delicious carrots.

Activity Book

CD2 Track 51

AB page 53 Activity 1

1
Girl: I like this farm.
Boy: I like this farm, too. Look. I can see some chickens.
Girl: Fantastic! Let's help the farmer collect the eggs.
2
Boy: I like horses.
Girl: OK! Let's look at the horse.
Boy: Good idea.
3
Girl: Look at the garden.
Boy: Wow! There are lots of fruit and vegetables.
Girl: Can you see the carrots in the garden?
Boy: Yes, I can. Mmm, delicious.
4
Boy: I love the baby animals.
Girl: Me, too. Let's feed the goat now.
Boy: Good idea! The goats are hungry.

Unit 5 Lesson 7

Pupil's Book

CD2 Track 52

PB page 57 Activity 2

I've got two legs
I can swim.
I can fly.
I'm small and brown.
What am I?

I've got four legs.
I can walk
I can't climb.
I'm big.
I'm black and white.
What am I?

Unit 5 Lesson 8 Review

Pupil's Book

CD2 Track 53

PB page 58 Activity 1

1
Girl: Can you see a chicken?
Boy: Yes, I can.
2
Girl: Can you see a bird?
Boy: Yes, I can.
3
Girl: Can you see a frog?
Boy: Yes, I can.
4
Girl: Can you see a horse?
Boy: Yes, I can.
5
Girl: Can you see a duck?
Girl: Yes, I can.
6
Boy: Can you see a cow?
Boy: Yes, I can.

Audioscript

7
Girl: Can you see a cat?
Boy: Yes, I can.
8
Girl: Can you see a mouse?
Boy: Yes, I can.
9
Girl: Can you see a sheep?
Boy: Yes, I can.
10
Girl: Can you see a goat?
Boy: Yes, I can.

CD2 Track 54

PB page 58 Activity 3

Cooperative learning: *Well Done!* song
Well done! [Put left thumb up.]
Well done! [Put right thumb up.]
Well done everyone! [Put both thumbs up.]
Let's do a high five! [Do a high five with partner.]
Well done everyone! [Put both thumbs up.]
(Repeat.)

Unit 5 Video and 21st Century Skills

Activity Book

CD2 Track 55

AB page 56 Activity 1

1
Boy: Look at this group. All the animals eat grass.
Girl: Oh yes. Horses, cows and sheep eat grass.
2
Boy: All the animals can run in this group.
Girl: You're right. Cats, dogs and horses can run.
3
Boy: All the animals have got short tails in this group. Look!
Girl: You're right. Goats, sheep and birds have got short tails.
4
Boy: Look! All the animals can climb in this group.
Girl: You're right. Mice, cats and goats can climb.

Unit 6 Lesson 1

Pupil's Book

CD3 Track 1

PB page 60 Activity 1

***It's fun in the park* song**
We can climb a tree. [Mime climbing.]
We can jump and run. [Jump / Run on the spot.]
We can play on the swing. [Swing your arms.]
The park is fun.

It's fun, fun, fun in the park. [Dance.]
Yes, it's fun, fun, fun in the park.

We can play on the slide. [Make a slide motion with your arm.]
We can jump and run.
We can play on the roundabout. [Turn around.]
The park is fun.

It's fun, fun, fun in the park.
Yes, it's fun, fun, fun in the park.

We can play on the grass. [Point to the floor.]
We can jump and run. [Jump / Run on the spot.]
We can play on the seesaw. [Bob down and up again.]
The park is fun.

It's fun, fun, fun in the park.
Yes, it's fun, fun, fun in the park.

CD3 Track 2

PB page 60 Activity 1

Karaoke version: *It's fun in the park* song

CD3 Track 3

PB page 60 Activity 2

Swing, slide, seesaw, roundabout, climbing frame, grass, flower, tree, bush, rock

Unit 6 Lesson 2

Pupil's Book

CD3 Track 4

PB page 61 Activity 1

Boy: I'm lost. Where's my big sister?
Beth: She's on the swing. Look!
Boy: And where's my big brother?
Beth: He's on the roundabout. Come on. Let's play, too.

CD3 Track 5

PB page 61 Activity 2

1
Molly: Where's Beth?
Jake: She's on the rocks.
Molly: Oh yes! I can see her now.
2
Jake: Where's Molly?
Beth: She's on the climbing frame.
Jake: Oh yes! I can see her now.
3
Beth: Where's Jake?
Molly: He's on the roundabout.
Beth: Oh yes! I can see him now.
4
Molly: Where's Toby?
Jake: He's under the tree.
Molly: Oh yes! I can see him now.

Unit 6 Lesson 3

Pupil's Book

CD3 Track 6

PB pages 62 and 63 Activity 1

Hide and seek
Frame 1
Beth: Let's play hide and seek.
Jake: Good idea, Beth.
Molly: Sorry, Toby. You can't play in here.
Frame 2
Beth: 8, 9, 10! Ready or not, here I come! Where are they?
Frame 3
Beth: Where are Jake and Molly?
Boy: They're behind the tree.
Beth: Thank you.
Frame 4
Beth: Got you!
Molly: Aaargh!
Frame 5
Narrator: Later …
Beth: Oh no! Where's Toby?
Jake: I don't know. Toby! Toby!
Molly: I can't see him in the park.
Frame 6
Jake: He isn't under the bush.
Beth: And he isn't in the long grass.
Molly: Magic Bike, can you help?
Frame 7
Molly: Now I can see Toby.
Jake: Where is he?
Molly: He's on the slide!
Frame 8
Molly: You can't go in the playground, Toby.
Jake: But you can have a ride on the magic bike. Let's go!

Unit 6 Lesson 4

Pupil's Book

CD3 Track 7

PB page 64 Activity 1

Behind the tree, near the grass, in front of the flowers, next to the bush, between the rocks

CD3 Track 8

PB page 64 Activity 2

***Hide and seek* song**
Hide, hide, [Hide your face behind your hands.]
Hide everyone
Ready or not.
Here I come! [Remove hands from in front of face.]

Where are Jake and Molly? [Shade eyes and peer around classroom.]
Where are they?
They're next to the tree. [Point to the flashcard.]
Let's play again!

Hide, hide, [Hide your face behind your hands.]
Hide everyone.
Ready or not.
Here I come! [Remove hands from in front of face.]

Where are Beth and Molly? [Shade eyes and peer around classroom.]
Where are they?
They're near the rocks. [Point to the flashcard.]
Let's play again!

Hide, hide, [Hide your face behind your hands.]
Hide everyone
Ready or not.
Here I come! [Remove hands from in front of face.]

Where are Jake and Beth? [Shade eyes and peer around classroom.]
Where are they?
They're behind the bush. [Point to the flashcard.]
Let's play again!

CD3 Track 9

PB page 64 Activity 3

Dan: Where are Anna and David?
Ella: They're in front of the desk.

Activity Book

CD3 Track 10

AB page 61 Activity 1

1
Boy: Where are Beth and Molly?
Girl: They're in front of the flowers.
Boy: Pardon?
Girl: They're in front of the flowers.
Boy: Oh, yes. I can see them now.
2
Girl: Where are Jake and Toby?
Boy: They're between the rocks?
Girl: Behind the rocks?
Boy: No, between the rocks. Look!
Girl: Oh, yes. Thank you.
3
Boy: Where are Jake and Molly?
Girl: They're next to the tree?
Boy: In the tree?
Girl: No, next to the tree.
Boy: Oh, yes. I can see them now.
4
Girl: Where are Beth and Toby?
Boy: They're near the bush.
Girl: Pardon?
Boy: They're near the bush.
Girl: Oh, yes. I can see them. Thanks.

Unit 6 Lesson 5

Pupil's Book

CD3 Track 11

PB page 65 Activity 1

Toby: w – w – w.
Wally – worm – washes – windows.
Wally the worm washes windows.
Wally the worm washes windows.
Wally the worm washes windows.

CD3 Track 12

PB page 65 Activity 2

1
Girl: Where are Molly and Toby?
Boy: They're between the bushes.
2
Girl: Where's Jake?
Boy: He's near the roundabout.
3
Girl: Where's the Magic Bike?
Boy: It's next to the tree.
4
Girl: Where's Beth?
Boy: She's in front of the flowers.

CD3 Track 13

PB page 65 Activity 3

Cooperative learning: *Listen to others* song
Listen to others.
Listen, please.
Listen with your ears.
Listen, please.
Listen to others.
Listen, please.
Listen, everybody.
(Repeat.)

Unit 6 Lesson 6

Pupil's Book

CD3 Track 14

PB page 66 Activity 1

Lucy: I love the park in my town. It's very big. I go with my family on Saturday. We do lots of fun activities.
Alex: We play cricket on the grass. Look. I can hit the ball.
Lucy: We feed the ducks on the pond. They love bread.
Lucy: We ride on the train. It's great!
Alex: We love the playground. The zip wire is very fast.

Activity Book

CD3 Track 15

AB page 63 Activity 1

1
Ann: Hi! I'm Ann. I love the park! I can see lots of animals here. Look! I can feed the ducks on the pond.
2
Tom: Hi! I'm Tom. I'm in the play area. I'm on the zip wire now. It's fast!
3
Bill: Hi! I'm Bill. I love the train in the park. It's very fast. I'm on the train with my friend now. Whee!
4
Tony: Hi! I'm Tony.
Alex: And I'm Alex.
Tony: We play cricket in the park.
Alex: Look! I can hit the ball.
Tony: Well done, Alex!

Unit 6 Lesson 7

Pupil's Book

CD3 Track 16

PB page 67 Activity 2

1 Put the soil in a pot.
2 Push the seeds into the soil with your finger.
3 Water the seeds.
4 Put the pot in a sunny place. Watch the plants grow.
5 Put the plants in the garden. Watch the flowers grow.

Unit 6 Lesson 8 Review

Pupil's Book

CD3 Track 17

PB page 68 Activity 1

1
Girl: I can play on the swing in the park.
2
Boy: I can see grass in the park.
3
Girl: I can play on the roundabout in the park.
4
Boy: I can play on the big slide in the park.
5
Girl: I can see a bush in the park.
6
Boy: I can see a big tree in the park.
7
Girl: I can play on the seesaw in the park.
8
Boy: I can see a rock in the park.
9
Girl: I can play on the climbing frame in the park.
10
Boy: I can see a flower in the park.

Audioscript

CD3 Track 18

PB page 68 Activity 3

Cooperative learning: *Well done!* song

Well done! [Put left thumb up.]
Well done! [Put right thumb up.]
Well done everyone! [Put both thumbs up.]
Let's do a high five! [Do a high five with partner.]
Well done everyone! [Put both thumbs up.]
(Repeat.)

Unit 6 Video and 21st Century Skills

Activity Book

CD3 Track 19

AB page 66 Activity 1

1
Adult: Be careful, Ben! That climbing frame is very high.
Child: It's OK, Mum. I use two hands on the climbing frame.
Adult: That's good.
2
Adult: That swing is fast, Susan. Be careful!
Child: It's OK, Dad. I wait next to the swing.
Adult: Good.
3
Adult: The zip wire is very fast. Be careful!
Child: It's OK, Mum. I sit down on the zip wire.
Adult: Good.
4
Adult: Don't go up the slide, Sam.
Child: No, Dad. I only go down the slide.
Adult: Excellent.

My project 2 Lesson 1

Pupil's Book

CD3 Track 20

PB page 70 Activity 1

lambs
flowers
birds
rabbits
chicks
butterflies

CD3 Track 21

PB page 70 Activity 2

Girl: How many lambs can you see?
Boy: I can see three lambs.

My project 2 Lesson 2

Pupil's Book

CD3 Track 22

PB page 71 Activity 1

Cooperative learning: *What do I need to do?* song

What do I need to do? [Shrug shoulders.]
What do I need to do? [Shrug shoulders.]
Read instructions. [Mime reading.]
They help you. [Point finger at partner.]

What do I need to do? [Shrug shoulders.]
What do I need to do? [Shrug shoulders.]
Listen to instructions. [Mime listening.]
They help you. [Point finger at partner.]

CD3 Track 23

PB page 71 Activity 3

Girl: This is my butterfly. It´s brown, pink, orange and blue.
Boy: My bird is near a bush.

Unit 7 Lesson 1

Pupil's Book

CD3 Track 24

PB page 72 Activity 1

***Let's go to town* song**

Stand up.
Sit down.
Let's go to town.
To see what we can see. [Shade eyes and peer around.]

There's a cinema. [Point to the flashcards in turn.]
There's a bookshop, too.
There's a hospital.
And there's a swimming pool.

Stand up.
Sit down.
Let's go to town.
To see what we can see. [Shade eyes and peer around.]

There's a supermarket. [Point to the flashcards in turn.]
There's a sweet shop, too
There's a restaurant.
And look! There's a zoo!

Stand up.
Sit down.
Let's go to town
To see what we can see. [Shade eyes and peer around.]

CD3 Track 25

PB page 72 Activity 1

Karaoke version: *Let's go to town* song

CD3 Track 26

PB page 72 Activity 2

Zoo, sweet shop, café, toyshop, bookshop, hospital, restaurant, cinema, swimming pool, supermarket

Unit 7 Lesson 2

Pupil's Book

CD3 Track 27

PB page 73 Activity 1

Molly: Welcome to Newtown, Tim.
Tim: Thanks, Molly.
Jake: There's a big zoo here.
Tim: Great! I love animals.
Jake: And there are two sweet shops.
Tim: Fantastic! I love sweets, too.

CD3 Track 28

PB page 73 Activity 2

Girl: There are two bookshops in my town. They're fantastic!
Boy: There's a big hospital in my town.
Girl: There are two sweet shops in my town. I love sweets!
Boy: There's a zoo in my town. I can see amazing animals there.
Girl: There's a big swimming pool in my town. It's good fun.
Boy: There are four cafés in my town.

Unit 7 Lesson 3

Pupil's Book

CD3 Track 29

PB pages 74 and 75 Activity 1

The treasure hunt

Frame 1
Tim: Can we explore your town today?
Jake: Yes, of course.
Molly: Look! Toby has got something in his mouth.
Frame 2
Molly: What is it?
Tim: It's a treasure map!
Jake: Well done, Toby! Let's look for the treasure!
Frame 3
Tim: First, look for a big, old tree.
Molly: There's a big, old tree next to the swimming pool.
Jake: Let's go!

Frame 4
Molly: Look! There's the old tree.
Tim: Now look for two yellow rocks.
Beth: There are two yellow rocks in front of the zoo. Come on!
Frame 5
Molly: What's next, Tim?
Tim: Count twenty steps.
Beth: We can't cross the road here.
Frame 6
Jake: Magic Bike, can you help?
Beth: WOW! Now we can cross the road.
Frame 7
Jake: The man is green. Let's cross.
Molly: How many steps are there, Tim?
Tim: There are twenty.
Beth: 1, 2, 3, …
Frame 8
Beth: … 18, 19, 20! What can you see, Molly?
Molly: It's a big bone!
Tim: Of course! It's a dog's treasure map!

Unit 7 Lesson 4

Pupil's Book

CD3 Track 30

PB page 76 Activity 1

Bus, boat, motorbike, train, helicopter, lorry

CD3 Track 31

PB page 76 Activity 2

***How many?* song**

Ready, Steady, Go!

How many? How many?
How many cars are there?

One, two, three,
Four, five, six,
Seven, eight cars.

Nine, ten,
Eleven, twelve,
Thirteen, fourteen cars.

Fifteen, sixteen,
Seventeen, eighteen,
Nineteen, twenty cars.

There are twenty cars.
Yes, there are twenty cars.

CD3 Track 32

PB page 76 Activity 3

Boy: How many motorbikes are there?
Girl: There are fifteen motorbikes.
Boy: Correct!

Activity Book

CD3 Track 33

AB page 73 Activity 1

1, 12, 6, 10, 13, 18, 17, 8, 15, 4, 11, 3, 5, 14, 19, 16, 7, 2, 9, 20

Unit 7 Lesson 5

Pupil's Book

CD3 Track 34

PB page 77 Activity 1

Toby: z – z – z.
Lazy – zebra – zoo.
There's a lazy zebra in the zoo.
There's a lazy zebra in the zoo.
There's a lazy zebra in the zoo.

CD3 Track 35

PB page 77 Activity 2

There are fourteen cars.
There are twelve trains.
There are five buses.
There is one helicopter.
There are nineteen motorbikes.
There are seventeen lorries.

Unit 7 Lesson 6

Pupil's Book

CD3 Track 36

PB page 78 Activity 1

Alex: Lots of people travel by bike in our town. Cycling is fun and it's good exercise, too. We love our bikes!
Lucy: On Monday, there's a cycling class in the school playground.
Alex: On Saturday, we go shopping. We go to the town centre by bike with Mum.
Alex: This is a rickshaw. It's got three wheels. You can see our town in a rickshaw. There are lots of things to see!
Lucy: There are lots of bikes in our town. Oh no! Where's my bike?

Activity Book

CD3 Track 37

AB page 75 Activity 1

1
Girl: Let's ride on a rickshaw.
Boy: Good idea. There are lots of things to see in our town.
Girl: Look! There's a cinema.
Boy: Oh yes. I love the cinema.
2
Boy: Can you see the café?
Girl: Yes, I can.
Boy: I'm hungry.
Girl: We can't stop. Sorry.
3
Girl: Look! There's a bookshop.
Boy: I can see lots of books.
Girl: Me too.
4
Boy: Can you see the sweet shop?
Girl: Yes, I can.
Boy: Can we stop, please?
Girl: No. Sorry.
5
Girl: Look! There's a fantastic toyshop.
Boy: I can see a ball.
Girl: And I can see a scooter.
6
Boy: There's the swimming pool.
Girl: There are lots of bikes, too.
Boy: That's right.

Unit 7 Lesson 7

Pupil's Book

CD3 Track 38

PB page 79 Activity 2

Town Mouse and Country Mouse

Narrator: Town Mouse travels to the country. He visits his cousin, Country Mouse. They eat cheese and apples.
Town Mouse: I don't like apples. The country is horrible.
Narrator: Country Mouse travels to the town with his cousin, Town Mouse. They eat chocolate cake and ice cream.
Country Mouse: This food is delicious. The town is fantastic.
Narrator: Suddenly, Country Mouse hears a noise.
Country Mouse: What's that noise?
Town Mouse: Don't worry. It's only a cat. It lives in the house, too.
Country Mouse: I don't like cats!
Narrator: Country Mouse is scared. He runs and he runs and he runs.
Narrator: Soon, he is in the country again. Country Mouse: The food is good in the town, but I like a quiet life.

Unit 7 Lesson 8 Review

Pupil's Book

CD3 Track 39

PB page 80 Activity 1

1
Girl: There's a restaurant in my town.
2.
Boy: There's a swimming pool in my town.
3
Girl: There's a supermarket in my town.
4
Boy: There's a toyshop in my town.
5
Girl: There's a cinema in my town.
6
Boy: There's a hospital in my town.

Audioscript

7
Girl: There's a sweet shop in my town.
8
Boy: There's a bookshop in my town.
9
Girl: There's a zoo in my town.
10
Boy: There's a café in my town.

CD3 Track 40

PB page 80 Activity 3

Cooperative learning: *Well done!* song
Well done! [Put left thumb up.]
Well done! [Put right thumb up.]
Well done everyone! [Put both thumbs up.]
Let's do a high five! [Do a high five with partner.]
Well done everyone! [Put both thumbs up.]
(Repeat.)

Unit 7 Video and 21st Century Skills

Activity Book

CD3 Track 41

AB page 78 Activity 1

1
Boy: Where's the zoo, Emma?
Girl: I don't know. Let's look on the digital map.
Boy: Good idea … Look. It's in the park.
Girl: Oh yes.
2
Girl: There's a new cinema in town.
Boy: Where is it?
Girl: It's in King Street. Look!
Boy: Oh yes. It's next to the swimming pool.
3
Boy: Where's the new toyshop?
Girl: One minute … It's in North Street.
Boy: Oh yes. It's next to the supermarket.
4
Boy: And where's the new bookshop?
Girl: It's in James Street. Look!
Boy: Oh yes. It's near the restaurant.
5
Boy: Where's the new playground?
Girl: Let's look on the digital map.
Boy: Look. It's next to the park.
Girl: Oh yes. I can see it.

Unit 8 Lesson 1

Pupil's Book

CD3 Track 42

PB page 82 Activity 1

***What are you wearing?* song**
What are you wearing?
Hey! Hey! Hey! [Punch arm in the air three times.]
What are you wearing today?

I'm wearing shorts [Touch your legs.]
And a T-shirt, too.
I'm wearing a sun hat. [Touch your head.]
What about you?

What are you wearing?
Hey! Hey! Hey! [Punch arm in the air three times.]
What are you wearing today?

I'm wearing a shirt [Touch your body.]
And trousers, too. [Touch your legs.]
I'm wearing trainers.
What about you?

What are you wearing?
Hey! Hey! Hey!
What are you wearing today?

I'm wearing a skirt [Touch your legs.]
And a sweater, too.
I'm wearing shoes. [Touch your feet.]
What about you?

CD3 Track 43

PB page 82 Activity 1

Karaoke version: *What are you wearing?* song

CD3 Track 44

PB page 82 Activity 2

Sweater, shoes, T-shirt, skirt, sun hat, trainers, shirt, swimsuit, shorts, trousers

Unit 8 Lesson 2

Pupil's Book

CD3 Track 45

PB page 83 Activity 1

Molly: Is it cold, Jake?
Jake: No, it isn't. It's hot today.
Molly: What are you wearing?
Jake: I'm wearing shorts and a T-shirt. Hurry up, Molly.
Molly: I'm coming.

CD3 Track 46

PB page 83 Activity 2

1
Molly: What are you wearing Jake?
Jake: I'm wearing shorts and a T-shirt. I'm ready to play.
2
Molly: What are you wearing Beth?
Beth: I'm wearing a skirt and a T-shirt. I'm wearing a sun hat, too. I'm ready to walk.
3
Molly: What are you wearing Mum?
Molly and Jake's Mum: I'm wearing a swimsuit and a sun hat. I'm ready to swim.
4
Molly: What are you wearing Dad?
Molly and Jake's Dad: I'm wearing trousers and a T-shirt. I'm wearing trainers, too. I'm ready to play football.

Unit 8 Lesson 3

Pupil's Book

CD3 Track 47

PB pages 84 and 85 Activity 1

Fun at the camp
Frame 1
Molly: Wow! There are lots of fun activities here.
Beth: Look! She's riding a horse.
Jake: And he's sailing a boat. I love boats.
Frame 2
Jake: It's hot! Let's swim in the lake.
Beth: Good idea. Now, where's my swimsuit?
Frame 3
Lifeguard: I'm sorry, children. You can't swim today. It's dangerous.
Molly: Bad luck.
Frame 4
Narrator: The next day …
Beth: It's cold.
Jake: I'm not cold. I'm wearing trousers and a shirt. Come on! Let's ride a horse.
Molly: But it's raining, too.
Frame 5
Riding instructor: I'm sorry, children. You can't ride today. It's raining.
Molly: Oh no! What a pity.
Frame 6
Narrator: The next day …
Molly: Hurray! It's hot and sunny today.
Jake: Perfect! Let's sail a boat.
Frame 7
Lifeguard: You can go in the water today, children.
Molly: Yes, but we can't sail a boat. It isn't windy.
Beth: Magic Bike, can you help?
Frame 8
Molly: Wheeee! This is fantastic!
Jake: Yes! We can't sail a boat …
Beth: … but we can sail the Magic Bike!

Unit 8 Lesson 4

Pupil's Book

CD3 Track 48

PB page 86 Activity 1

Sail a boat, ride a horse, play the guitar, play volleyball, sing songs

CD3 Track 49

PB page 86 Activity 2

***Camping is great!* song**
Jake, Molly, Beth: *We're in a forest* [Dance to the chorus.]
Near a lake.
Camping is great!
Yes! Camping is great!

Jake: *What's Beth doing in the sun?* [Point to the sky.]
Molly: *She's sailing a boat.* [Pull the ropes of a sailing boat.]
She's having fun! [Put both hands in air.]
Chorus

Beth: *What's Molly doing in the sun?* [Point to the sky.]
Jake: *She's riding a horse.* [Ride a horse.]
She's having fun! [Put both hands in air.]
Chorus

Molly: *What's Jake doing in the sun?* [Point to the sky.]
Beth: *He's playing the guitar.* [Play the guitar.]
He's having fun! [Put both hands in air.]
Chorus

CD3 Track 50

PB page 86 Activity 3
David: What's Dan doing?
Ella: He's swimming.

Activity Book

CD3 Track 51

AB page 83 Activity 1

1
Beth: What's Molly doing?
Lifeguard: She's riding a horse.
Beth: Oh yes. There she is.
2
Beth: What's Jake doing?
Lifeguard: He's playing volleyball with Molly.
Beth: Oh yes. I can see him now.
3
Beth: What's Molly doing?
Lifeguard: She's sailing a boat with her dad.
Beth: Oh yes. I can see them now.
4
Beth: What's Jake doing?
Lifeguard: He's playing the guitar.
Beth: Oh yes. I can see him now.
5
Beth: What's Molly doing?
Lifeguard: She's singing songs.
Beth: Oh yes. There she is.

Unit 8 Lesson 5

Pupil's Book

CD3 Track 52

PB page 87 Activity 1
Toby: v – v – v.
Vicky – vet – loves – volleyball.
Vicky the vet loves volleyball.
Vicky the vet loves volleyball.
Vicky the vet loves volleyball.

CD3 Track 53

PB page 87 Activity 2

1
Boy: What's Emma doing?
Girl: She's swimming.
2
Girl: What's Ben doing?
Boy: He's playing the guitar.
3
Boy: What's Tom doing?
Girl: He's sailing a boat.
4
Girl: What's Susan doing?
Boy: She's singing songs.
5
Boy: What's Alex doing?
Girl: He's riding a horse.
6
Girl: What's Mary doing?
Boy: She's playing volleyball.

Unit 8 Lesson 6

Pupil's Book

CD4 Track 1

PB page 88 Activity 1
Alex: In the summer we camp in the garden. It's good fun.
Lucy: Dad plays the guitar, and we sing songs. My favourite song is 'Alice the camel'. It's funny.
Alex: We sleep in our sleeping bags in big tents.
Lucy: At night, we tell stories. They're scary!

CD4 Track 2

PB page 88 Activity 2

***Alice the camel* song**
Alice the camel has five humps.
Alice the camel has five humps.
Alice the camel has five humps.
So go, Alice, go!
BOOM! BOOM! BOOM!

Alice the camel has four humps.
Alice the camel has four humps.
Alice the camel has four humps.
So go, Alice, go!
BOOM! BOOM! BOOM!

Alice the camel has three humps.
Alice the camel has three humps.
Alice the camel has three humps.
So go, Alice, go!
BOOM! BOOM! BOOM!

Alice the camel has two humps.
Alice the camel has two humps.
Alice the camel has two humps.
So go, Alice, go!
BOOM! BOOM! BOOM!

Alice the camel has one hump.
Alice the camel has one hump.
Alice the camel has one hump.
So go, Alice, go!
BOOM! BOOM! BOOM!

Alice the camel has no humps.
Alice the camel has no humps.
Alice the camel has no humps.
Now Alice is a horse!

Activity Book

CD4 Track 3

AB page 85 Activity 1

1
Girl 1: Good night!
Boy and Girl 2: Good night!
2
Girl 1 and girl 2:
Alice the camel has five humps.
Alice the camel has five humps.
Alice the camel has five humps.
So go, Alice, go!
BOOM! BOOM! BOOM!

3
Boy: The boy is in the forest. It's dark. He hears a noise … Woooooo!

Unit 8 Lesson 7

Pupil's Book

CD4 Track 4

PB page 89 Activity 2
Dear Sally,
I'm at a fantastic campsite with my family. There's a beautiful forest and there's a big lake. There are lots of fun activities here. I swim in the lake and I sail a boat every day.

It's hot and sunny today. I'm wearing my new swimsuit. It's purple and pink. See you soon,

Sue

Unit 8 Lesson 8 Review

Pupil's Book

CD4 Track 5

PB page 90 Activity 1

1
Girl: What are you wearing?
Boy: I'm wearing a T-shirt.
2
Girl: What are you wearing?
Boy: I'm wearing shorts.
3
Girl: What are you wearing?
Boy: I'm wearing trainers.
4
Boy: What are you wearing?
Girl: I'm wearing a skirt.
5
Boy: What are you wearing?
Girl: I'm wearing a sun hat.
6
Girl: What are you wearing?
Boy: I'm wearing a shirt.

Audioscript

7
Boy: What are you wearing?
Girl: I'm wearing a sweater.
8
Boy: What are you wearing?
Girl: I'm wearing a swimsuit.
9
Boy: What are you wearing?
Girl: I'm wearing shoes.
10
Girl: What are you wearing?
Boy: I'm wearing trousers.

CD4 Track 6

PB page 90 Activity 3

Cooperative Learning: Sing *Well done!*
Well done! [Put left thumb up.]
Well done! [Put right thumb up.]
Well done everyone! [Put both thumbs up.]
Let's do a high five! [Do a high five with partner.]
Well done everyone! [Put both thumbs up.]
(Repeat.)

Unit 8 Video and 21st Century Skills

Activity Book

CD4 Track 7

AB page 88 Activity 1

1
Girl: Let's wear shorts today.
Girl: It isn't a good idea. It's cold and it's raining today.
Girl: OK. Let's wear trousers.
Girl: Good idea.
2
Boy: Let's eat cake at lunch time.
Girl: Cake isn't very healthy. It isn't a good idea
Boy: OK. Let's eat fruit.
Girl: Great. Fruit is very healthy.
3
Girl: Let's go on the slide.
Boy: It isn't a good idea. Look! The slide is very old.
Girl: Oh yes. Let's go on the swing.
Boy: Good idea.
4
Boy: Let's sail a boat.
Girl: It isn't windy today. It isn't a good idea.
Boy: OK. Let's play volleyball.
Girl: Good idea! I love volleyball.

Unit 9 Lesson 1

Pupil's Book

CD4 Track 8

PB page 92 Activity 1

***It's a beautiful day* song**
I get up. [Mime getting up.]
I get dressed. [Mime getting dressed.]
I open the window and I say
It's a beautiful day. [Wave right hand.]
It's a beautiful day today. [Wave left hand.]

I wash my face. [Mime washing your face.]
I brush my teeth. [Mime brushing your teeth.]
I open the window and I say
It's a beautiful day. [Wave right hand.]
It's a beautiful day today. [Wave left hand.]

I comb my hair. [Mime combing your hair.]
I make my bed. [Mime making your bed.]
I open the window and I say
It's a beautiful day. [Wave right hand.]
It's a beautiful day today. [Wave left hand.]

CD4 Track 9

PB page 92 Activity 1

Karaoke version. *It's a beautiful day* song

CD4 Track 10

PB page 92 Activity 2

Get up, wash my face, brush my teeth, comb my hair, have a shower, get dressed, make my bed, go to school, go to bed, sleep

Unit 9 Lesson 2

Pupil's Book

CD4 Track 11

PB page 93 Activity 1

Molly: I wash my face every day.
Beth: Me too.
Molly: And I brush my teeth every day.
Beth: Me too.
Molly: Are you ready?
Beth: Yes, I am. Let's play!

CD4 Track 12

PB page 93 Activity 2

Beth: I do lots of things every day. I brush my teeth and I comb my hair. I have a shower and I get dressed every day. Oh yes! I sleep every day, too.
Jake: I do lots of things every day, too. I brush my teeth and I comb my hair every day. I get dressed and I sleep every day, too.

Unit 9 Lesson 3

Pupil's Book

CD4 Track 13

PB pages 94 and 95 Activity 1

The wobbly tooth
Frame 1
Molly and Jake's Dad: Good morning. Are you ready for breakfast?
Molly: Yes, I am. I have breakfast every morning.
Beth: Great!
Frame 2
Molly: What's the matter, Jake?
Jake: I've got a wobbly tooth. Look!
Beth: Wow! It's very wobbly.
Frame 3
Molly: Let's play in the garden.
Beth: Good idea! Let's play volleyball.
Jake: Wait for me!
Frame 4
Narrator: Later …
Jake: I win! I'm the champion!
Beth: Jake, where's your tooth?
Frame 5
Jake: Can you see my tooth?
Molly: No, I can't. It isn't in the grass.
Beth: And it isn't in the flowers. Sorry, Jake.
Frame 6
Molly and Jake's Mum: It's time for dinner. Come in and wash your hands, please.
Beth: Great! I'm hungry.
Molly: Don't worry, Jake. We can look for your tooth tomorrow.
Frame 7
Narrator: After dinner …
Molly: Look at the magic bike. What's it doing?
Beth: It's looking for your tooth, Jake.
Frame 8
Beth: Look, Jake! There's magic under your pillow.
Jake: Wow! It's my tooth! Magic Bike, you're incredible.

Unit 9 Lesson 4

Pupil's Book

CD4 Track 14

PB page 96 Activity 1

Breakfast in the morning, lunch in the afternoon, dinner in the evening, a snack at night

CD4 Track 15

PB page 96 Activity 2

***Are you hungry?* song**
Are you hungry in the morning? [Shrug shoulders.]
Yes, I am. Yes, I am. [Nod head.]
I have breakfast in the morning. [Mime eating meal.]
Yum, yum, yum. [Rub stomach.]

Are you hungry in the afternoon? [Shrug shoulders.]
Yes, I am. Yes, I am. [Nod head.]
I have lunch in the afternoon [Mime eating meal.]
Yum, yum, yum. [Rub stomach.]

Are you hungry in the evening? [Mime eating meal.]
Yes, I am. Yes, I am. [Nod head.]
I have dinner in the evening. [Mime eating meal.]
Yum, yum, yum. [Rub stomach.]

CD4 Track 16

PB page 96 Activity 3

Ella: I have lunch in the morning.
Anna: No!
Anna: I have lunch in the afternoon.
Ella: Yes!

Activity Book

CD4 Track 17

AB page 93 Activity 1

1
Girl: I have breakfast in the morning. I have orange juice and cereal every day.
2
Boy: I have lunch in the afternoon. My favourite lunch is fish and salad. It's delicious!
3
Boy: I have a shower in the evening. I wash my hair and my body.
4
Girl: I go to bed at night. I love my teddy.

Unit 9 Lesson 5

Pupil's Book

CD4 Track 18

PB page 97 Activity 1

Toby: th – th – th.
Three – thin – bath – Thursday.
Three thin tigers have a bath on Thursday.
Three thin tigers have a bath on Thursday.
Three thin tigers have a bath on Thursday.

CD4 Track 19

PB page 97 Activity 2

1
Boy: I get up in the morning
Girl: Yes, that's right.
2
Boy: I have lunch at night.
Girl: That isn't right.
3
Girl 1: I have dinner in the evening.
Girl 2: Yes, that's right.

Unit 9 Lesson 6

Pupil's Book

CD4 Track 20

PB page 98 Activity 1

Alex: In Britain, the Tooth Fairy visits children's bedrooms at night.
1
Lucy: When my tooth falls out, I put it in a box. I put the box under my pillow.
2
Lucy: The Tooth Fairy comes at night. She takes my tooth when I'm sleeping.
3
Lucy: In the morning, I find a letter from the Tooth Fairy. The letter says, 'Thank you, Lucy'.
4
Lucy: I find money from the Tooth Fairy, too. I put it in my money box.

Unit 9 Lesson 7

Pupil's Book

CD4 Track 21

PB page 99 Activity 1

1 [sfx: an owl hooting]
2 [sfx: a cockerel crowing]
3 [sfx: snores]
4 [sfx: children laughing and playing a clapping game in pairs]

CD4 Track 22

PB page 99 Activity 2

Morning time
It's morning time.
The sun is in the sky. [Draw a circle in the air with your hands.]
The moon and the stars
Say goodbye. [Wave goodbye.]

The owl goes to sleep
With a whoo whoo. [Mime going to sleep.]
And the cockerel crows
Cock-a-doodle-doo. [Puff out chest like a cockerel.]

Get up, children,
It's a new day. [Stand up.]
Get up, children,
It's time to play. [Raise hands in the air.]

Activity Book

CD4 Track 23

AB page 96 Activity 2

1
Boy: What does the cockerel say?
Girl: Cock-a-doodle-doo.
2
Girl: What does the cow say?
Boy: Moo.
3
Boy: What does the cat say?
Girl: Meow.
4
Girl: What does the sheep say?
Boy: Baa.
5
Boy: What does the owl say?
Boy: Whoo whoo.
6
Girl: What does the dog say?
Girl: Woof.

Unit 9 Lesson 8 Review

Pupil's Book

CD4 Track 24

PB page 100 Activity 1

1
Girl: I sleep at night.
2
Boy: I have a shower in the evening.
3
Girl: I wash my face in the morning.
4
Boy: I go to bed at night.
5
Boy: I comb my hair in the morning.
6
Girl: I get up in the morning.
7
Girl: I make my bed in the morning.
8.
Girl: I brush my teeth in the morning.
9
Boy: I go to school in the morning.
10
Boy: I get dressed in the morning.

CD4 Track 25

PB page 100 Activity 3

Cooperative learning: *Well done!* song
Well done! [Put left thumb up.]
Well done! [Put right thumb up.]
Well done everyone! [Put both thumbs up.]
Let's do a high five! [Do a high five with partner.]
Well done everyone! [Put both thumbs up.]
(Repeat.)

Audioscript

Unit 9 Video and 21st Century Skills

Activity Book

CD4 Track 26

AB page 98 Activity 1

1
Girl: Do you brush your teeth every day, Jack?
Boy: Yes. I brush my teeth in the morning and at night.
Girl: That's good.
2
Boy: Do you brush your teeth every day, Bethany?
Girl: Yes, I brush my teeth in the morning, in the afternoon and at night.
Boy: That's excellent!
3
Boy: What about you, Anna?
Girl: I brush my teeth in the morning.
Boy: Anna! It's important to look after your teeth!
4
Girl: What about you, Paul?
Boy: Oh! I brush my teeth in the morning, in the afternoon and in the evening.
Girl: Fantastic!

My Project 3 Lesson 1

Pupil's Book

CD4 Track 27

PB page 102 Activity 1

beach
mountains
city

CD4 Track 28

PB page 102 Activity 2

Girl: Where do you go on holiday?
Boy: I go to the beach. What about you?

CD4 Track 29

PB page 102 Activity 3

boots
swimsuit
sunglasses
sweets
torch

My Project 3 Lesson 2

Pupil's Book

CD4 Track 30

PB page 103 Activity 2

Cooperative learning: *Listen to others* song

Listen to others.
Listen, please.
Listen with your ears.
Listen, please.
Listen to others.
Listen, please.
Listen, everybody.
(Repeat.)

CD4 Track 31

PB page 103 Activity 3

Girl: I go to the beach on holiday. It's hot and sunny there. I've got a swimsuit on my list.
Boy: Have a nice holiday!

Festivals: Bonfire Night

Pupil's Book

CD4 Track 32

PB page 104 Activity 1

Girl: It's Bonfire Night. I can see a big bonfire. It's fantastic!
Girl: I eat a toffee apple on Bonfire Night. It's delicious!
Girl: I can see fireworks in the sky. They're red, orange, yellow and purple.

CD4 Track 33

PB page 104 Activity 2

One big firework on the ground,
It's red and yellow, blue and brown.
1-2-3-4-5
Whoosh! It goes up to the sky.
See the stars all around.
Down they go to the ground.

Festivals: Valentine's Day

Pupil's Book

CD4 Track 34

PB page 105 Activity 1

Girl: On Valentine's Day people think about the people they love.
I love my mother. Her name is Amanda. She helps me every day.
I love my grandfather. His name is Tony. We read books together.
I love my friend. Her name is Anna. We play in the playground at school.

Unit 1 Cambridge Exams Practice: Starters

Pupil's Book

CD4 Track 35

PB page 106 Activity 1

1
Female adult: Find the rubber under the desk.
Boy: Here it is.
Female adult: Good. Colour it red.
Boy: OK. The rubber under the desk is red.
2
Female adult: Find the computer on the cupboard.
Boy: Here it is.
Female adult: Good. Colour it blue.
Boy: OK. The computer on the cupboard is blue.
3
Female adult: Find the book in the cupboard.
Boy: Here it is.
Female adult: Good. Colour it orange.
Boy: OK. The book in the cupboard is orange.
4
Female adult: Find the pen on the board.
Boy: Here it is.
Female adult: Good. Colour it green.
Boy: OK. The pen on the board is green.
5
Female adult: Find the school bag under the chair.
Boy: Here it is.
Female adult: Good. Colour it pink.
Boy: OK. The school bag under the chair is pink.

CD4 Track 36

PB page 106 Activity 2

Girl 1: Where's the ruler?
Girl 2: Here.
Girl 1: What colour is it?
Girl 2: It's orange.

Unit 2 Cambridge Exams Practice: Starters

CD4 Track 37

PB page 107 Activity 1

1
Boy's mum: Pick up your toys, please.
Boy: OK, mum.
Boy's mum: Put the car in the cupboard.
Boy: Where?
Boy's mum: In the cupboard.
Boy: OK
2
Boy's mum: Now put the train on the cupboard.
Boy: Where?
Boy's mum: On the cupboard.
Boy: OK

3
Boy's mum: Put the kite under the desk, please.
Boy: Where?
Boy's mum: Under the desk.
Boy: OK
4
Boy's mum: Now put the doll on the chair.
Boy: Where?
Boy's mum: On the chair.
Boy: OK.
5
Boy's mum: Put the ball under the chair, please.
Boy: Where?
Boy's mum: Under the chair.
Boy: OK.
6
Boy's mum: Put the robot on the desk, please.
Boy: Where?
Boy's mum: On the desk.
Boy: OK.
Boy's mum: Thank you, Hugo.

Pupil's Book

CD4 Track 38

PB page 107 Activity 2
Boy: What's your name?
Girl: My name is Alice.
Boy: How old are you?
Girl: I'm six.

Unit 3 Cambridge Exams Practice: Starters

Pupil's Book

CD4 Track 39

PB page 108 Activity 1
1
Female child: Look! This is a photo of my friends.
Male adult: It's very funny
Female child: Yes. Can you see Alice? She's got long hair.
Male adult: What colour is her hair?
Female child: It's green.
Male adult: Ah yes! Here's Alice.
2
Female child: Can you see Lucy? She's got long hair.
Male adult: What colour is her hair?
Female child: It's blue.
Male adult: Ah yes! Here's Lucy.
3
Female child: Can you see Pat? She's got short hair.
Male adult: What colour is her hair?
Female child: It's red. And her eyes are green.
Male adult: Ah yes! Here she is.
4
Female child: Can you see Hugo? He's got blue hair.
Male adult: What colour are his eyes?
Female child: Brown.
Male adult: Ah yes! Here's Hugo.
5
Female child: Can you see Eva? She's got short hair.
Male adult: What colour is her hair?
Female child: It's green.
Male adult: Ah yes! Here she is.
6
Female child: Can you see Anna? She's got red hair.
Male adult: What colour are her eyes?
Female child: Blue.
Male adult: Ah yes! Here's Anna.

CD4 Track 40

PB page 108 Activity 2
Dan: What colour is your hair?
Anna: My hair is black.
Dan: What colour are your eyes?
Anna: My eyes are brown.

Unit 4 Cambridge Exams Practice: Starters

Pupil's Book

CD4 Track 41

PB page 109 Activity 1
1
Girl: What is your favourite food, Bill?
Boy: My favourite food is ice cream.
Girl: Oh yes, ice cream is delicious!
2
Boy: What is your favourite food, Lucy?
Girl: My favourite food is meat?
Boy: Yes, I like meat, too.
3
Boy: What is your favourite fruit, Sue?
Girl: My favourite fruit is grapes.
Boy: Really? I don't like grapes.
4
Girl: What's your favourite drink, Sam?
Boy: My favourite drink is orange juice. I love it.
Girl: Mmm I love orange juice, too

CD4 Track 42

PB page 109 Activity 2
Boy 1: What's your favourite food?
Boy 2: It's ice cream. What about you? What's your favourite food?
Boy 1: My favourite food is chicken.

Unit 5 Cambridge Exams Practice: Starters

Pupil's Book

CD4 Track 43

PB page 110 Activity 1
1
Female adult: Look at this picture, Sam.
Male child: That's nice. Can I colour the animals?
Female adult: OK. Colour the chicken.
Male child: What colour?
Female adult: Colour the chicken orange.
2
Male child: Can I colour the horse?
Female adult: OK. Have you got a brown pencil?
Male child: Yes, I have.
Female adult: Good. Colour the horse brown.
Male child: Brown?
Female adult: Yes, please. Colour the horse brown.
3
Female adult: Can you see the bird?
Male child: Yes, I can. It's in the tree.
Female adult: Good. Colour the bird blue.
Male child: Blue?
Female adult: Yes, please.
4
Male child: Can I colour the duck?
Female adult: Yes.
Male child: What colour?
Female adult: Colour the duck yellow.
Male child: OK. My duck is yellow.
5
Male child: What animal can I colour now?
Female adult: You can colour a sheep.
Male child: The big sheep or the small sheep?
Female adult: The big sheep. Colour the big sheep black.
Male child: OK. The big sheep is black now.
6
Male child: Can I colour the cat?
Female adult: Yes.
Male child: What colour?
Female adult: Colour the cat orange.
Male child: OK. I like orange cats.
Female adult: Me too.

Audioscript

CD4 Track 44

PB page 110 Activity 2

Male child: What's this?
Female child: It's a cow.
Male child: Tell me about it.
Female child: It's big. It's black and white. It's got four legs.

Unit 6 Cambridge Exams Practice: Starters

Pupil's Book

CD4 Track 45

PB page 111 Activity 1

1
Male adult: Can you see the cats, Lucy?
Female child: No, I can't. Where are they?
Male adult: They're in the tree.
Female child: In the tree? Oh yes!
2
Male child: Where's the duck, Mum?
Female adult: It's between the flowers.
Male child: Behind the flowers?
Female adult: No. It's between the flowers. Look!
3
Male adult: Can you see the birds, Alice?
Female child: No, I can't. Where are they?
Male adult: They're next to the tree.
Female child: Oh yes!
4
Female adult: Where's the dog, Sam?
Male child: It's behind the flowers.
Female adult: Oh yes. I can see it.
Male child: Good.

CD4 Track 46

PB page 111 Activity 2

Boy: Where's the blue bird?
Girl: It's on the bike.
Boy: Where are the red birds?
Girl: They're between the flowers.

Unit 7 Cambridge Exams Practice: Starters

Pupil's Book

CD4 Track 47

PB page 112 Activity 1

1
Male adult: This picture's nice, Eva.
Female child: It's a picture of my street. Can I colour it?
Male adult: Yes. Have you got a blue pencil?
Female child: Yes, I have.
Male adult: Good. Colour the car blue.
Female child: The car? OK.
2
Female child: Can I colour a toy?
Male adult: Good idea. Colour the teddy bear.
Female child: What colour?
Male adult: You can colour the teddy bear pink.
Female child: Great!
3
Male adult: Look. There's a plane in the picture.
Female child: There's a helicopter, too. Can I colour the helicopter?
Male adult: Yes. Colour it red.
Female child: Thank you.
4
Male adult: Look! There's a robot in the shop.
Female child: Can I colour it?
Male adult: OK. What colour?
Female child: Green. Yes, this robot is green.
5
Female child: Look. The boy has got an ice cream.
Male adult: You can colour the ice cream.
Female child: Great. What colour?
Male adult: Brown
Female child: Mmm. It's chocolate ice cream. My favourite!
6
Male adult: There are four books in this shop.
Female child: Yes. Can I colour one?
Male adult: OK. Colour the small book purple.
Female child: Purple?
Male adult: Yes. Colour the small book purple.
Female child: OK.

CD4 Track 48

PB page 112 Activity 2

Girl 1: What's this?
Girl 2: It's a boat.
Girl 1: Do you go to school by boat?
Girl 2: No, I don't.

Unit 8 Cambridge Exams Practice: Starters

Pupil's Book

CD4 Track 49

PB page 113 Activity 1

1
Girl: What is Bill wearing today?
Boy: He's wearing a red T-shirt and blue shorts.
Girl: A red T-shirt and blue shorts … Oh yes, I can see him now.
2
Boy: What is May wearing today?
Girl: She's wearing a pink skirt and a white T-shirt.
Boy: Sorry. What colour is the skirt?
Girl: The skirt is pink and the T-shirt is white.
Boy: Oh yes. I can see her now.
3
Girl: What is Mark doing today?
Boy: He's riding a horse.
Girl: Oh yes. Thank you.
4
Boy: What is Jill doing today?
Girl: She's swimming.
Boy: OK. Thank you.

CD4 Track 50

PB page 113 Activity 2

Girl 1: What's he doing?
Girl 2: He's playing football.
Girl 1: What's he wearing?
Girl 2: He's wearing a T-shirt.

Unit 9 Cambridge Exams Practice: Starters

Pupil's Book

CD4 Track 51

PB page 114 Activity 1

1
Female child: Look at this photo of my friends.
Male adult: That's nice. Are they having lunch?
Female child: Yes. Can you see Alex?
Male adult: What's he doing?
Female child: He's drinking juice.
Male adult: Ah yes! Here's Alex.
2
Female child: Can you see Lucy?
Male adult: What's she doing?
Female child: She's eating fish and potatoes.
Male adult: Mmm … I like fish and potatoes.
3
Female child: Can you see Anna?
Male adult: What's she doing?
Female child: She's eating chips.
Male adult: Fish and chips?
Female child: No, she's eating meat and chips.
Male adult: Oh yes. Here's Anna.
4
Female child: Can you see Hugo? He's eating fish.
Male adult: Rice and fish?
Female child: Yes.
Male adult: I can see Hugo. He's happy.
5
Female child: Look at Sue.
Male adult: What's she doing?
Female child: She's drinking water.
Male adult: Aha. I can see Sue.
6
Female child: Can you see May?
Male adult: What's she doing?
Female child: She's eating fish and chips.
Male adult: Mmm … fish and chips. My favourite!

CD4 Track 52

PB page 114 Activity 2

Male child: What's this?
Female child: Juice.
Male child: Do you have juice for breakfast?
Female child: Yes, I do.

Videoscript

Unit 1 21st Century Video

PB page 17 Activities 1 and 2

Abby: Hello everyone. Welcome to Channel 21. My name's Abby. This is Sophie …
Sophie: Hello!
Abby: … and this is Tom.
Tom: Hi!
Sophie: Today's programme is about our school.

Sophie: This is our classroom.
Tom: And this is our teacher.
Sophie: Look! We put our hands up to speak.

Tom: At school, we listen to stories.
Sophie: It's great. We sit on the floor and listen to the teacher.

Sophie: We read stories, too.
Tom: The teacher helps us.

Tom: At break time we go to the playground.

Tom: We run and we play there.
Sophie: It's fun!

Tom: And on Monday and Wednesday we play music.
Sophie: We sing songs, too.

Tom: At home time we tidy up the classroom.
Sophie: We put the toys in the box.
Tom: And we put the books on the shelf.

Abby: What do you take to school, Sophie?
Sophie: My school bag. Look! Here's my book and here's my pencil case. I'm ready for school.
Tom: I'm ready for school, too. Oh! Where's my pencil case? And where's my book?
Sophie: Here's your pencil case and … here's your book.
Tom: Thanks Sophie.
Abby: Remember! It's important to prepare your school bag. Bye everyone.
Tom: Bye!
Sophie: Goodbye.

Unit 2 21st Century Video

PB page 27 Activities 1 and 2

Abby: Hello again. Welcome back to Channel 21.
Sophie: Hello!
Tom: Hi!
Abby: Today's programme is about toys.
Tom: It's about our five favourite toys.
Sophie: Let's watch the video.

Sophie: Number five on the favourite toy list is … a teddy!
Tom: This teddy is grey.
Sophie: Aww … It's cute!

Tom: Number four is … a dinosaur!

Sophie: These dinosaurs are small and green.
Tom: Look at the boy. Dinosaurs are fun. ROAR!!!

Sophie: What's number three, Tom?
Tom: Number three is … a robot!
Sophie: This robot is red.
Tom: It walks and it turns around. Fantastic!

Tom: Here's another robot.
Sophie: Wow! It's fast!

Tom: What's number two, Sophie?
Sophie: Number two is … a scooter! Look! This scooter is pink.

Tom: It's a race.
Sophie: Ready, steady … GO!
Tom: The scooter is fast!

Sophie: Are you ready for the number 1 toy? It's a …
Tom and Sophie: … video game!
Tom: This video game is fun. Look!
Sophie: Is this a car video game?
Tom: Yes, it is. It's my favourite. It's fantastic!

Abby: What a great video.
Sophie: What's your favourite toy, Abby?
Abby: Hmm … that's a difficult question.
Tom: Is your favourite toy a video game?
Abby: No, it isn't.
Sophie: Is your favourite toy a ball?
Abby: No, it isn't. My favourite toy is … a kite.
Children: A kite!
Abby: Yes. Everybody is different. And that's OK. See you next time!
Tom: Bye!
Sophie: Goodbye.

Unit 3 21st Century Video

PB page 37 Activities 1 and 2

Abby: Hello everyone. Welcome back to Channel 21. Today's programme is about …
Girl and Tom: … the circus!
Abby: Sophie - you've got red hair!
Sophie: Yes, I've got big eyes and a red nose, too.
Tom: And look at me. I've got yellow hair and a big mouth.
Abby: Let's watch a video about the circus.

Sophie: This circus is blue and yellow.
Tom: It's fantastic.

Sophie: Look! This clown juggles balls.
Tom: He's got three balls … oh dear!

Sophie: And this man spins plates. He's got a green plate and a yellow plate …
Tom: … and now he's got a red plate.

Abby: Children learn circus skills, too.
Tom: This girl has got a plate on her head!

Sophie: These girls walk on stilts. What long legs!
Tom: This boy is a clown. He's got a big, red nose.

Sophie: This boy is a clown, too. He's got a small red nose.

Sophie: Wow! Look at this man on a special bike.
Tom: He's amazing!

Tom: These girls are on bikes, too. They work together. Look!

Sophie: This boy and girl work together, too. It's fun!

Abby: What a great video.
Sophie: Circus skills are fun.
Tom: Yes, but it's difficult to juggle.

Videoscript

Abby: You can juggle together. Like in the video.
Sophie: Great idea.
Abby: Well done! It's good to work together.
Tom: It's fun, too!
Abby: See you next time!
Sophie: Bye!
Tom: Goodbye.

Unit 4 21st Century Video

PB page 49 Activities 1 and 2

Abby: Hello again. Welcome back to Channel 21.
Tom and Sophie: Hello! Hi!
Tom: Are you hungry, Abby?
Abby: Yes, I am.
Tom: Today's programme is about food.
Sophie: It's about school lunches
Abby: Great. Let's watch the video.

Sophie: Some children have a hot lunch at school.
Tom: They put the lunch on a tray.
Abby: Look! The children like the lunch today.

Tom: The children eat lunch together.
Sophie: It's fun!
Sophie: Some children take a lunch box to school.
Tom: This lunch box has got a sandwich, fruit and water.

Tom: Look at this lunch. It's a happy face!
Sophie: The face is spaghetti. That's funny!

Tom: This lunch is a bird. Look at the big eyes!
Sophie: Mmm! I like the fruit.
Sophie: And here's a rabbit!
Tom: The body is rice.

Sophie: Do you like this lunch, Abby?
Abby: Yes, I do. It's very healthy.
Tom: It's a teddy bear! It's got small eyes.
Tom: This lunch is healthy, too.
Sophie: The sandwich has got orange and green hair.

Abby: What fantastic lunches.
Tom: What's in your lunch box today, Abby?
Abby: Let's see … I've got biscuits, crisps and chocolate.
Sophie: Abby!!
Tom: That's not healthy!!
Abby: That isn't my lunch box. Here's my lunch box. I've got a sandwich and an apple.
Children: Oh Abby!!
Abby: Bye everyone and remember to eat a healthy lunch.
Tom: Yes, bye!
Sophie: Goodbye.

Unit 5 21st Century Video

PB page 59 Activities 1 and 2

Abby: Hello everybody! Welcome back to Channel 21.
Tom and Sophie: Hello!
Sophie: Today's programme is about animals.
Abby: What's your favourite animal, Tom?
Tom: Hmmm. My favourite animal is a horse.
Abby: What about you, Sophie?
Sophie: Oh! My favourite animal is a duck. I love ducks!
Abby: Me too! Let's watch a video about farm animals.

Tom: This horse has got brown and black hair.
Sophie: It's got a long tail, too.
Abby: Horses eat grass. Look! It's hungry.

Abby: Cows eat grass, too.
Sophie: Look! It's got big, black ears.
Abby: Can you hear the goats?
Sophie: Yes, I can. They're funny!

Tom: Look at this sheep. It's got long ears.
Sophie: And it's got a long nose.

Abby: Here's a baby sheep – a lamb.
Sophie: Aww! The lamb is tired.

Sophie: This chicken is on the farm.
Tom: Can it fly?
Abby: No, it can't.

Sophie: Ducks can fly.
Abby: That's right. They can swim and they can fly.

Tom: And here are baby ducks – ducklings.
Sophie: They're cute! I love ducklings!

Sophie: The animals on the farm are different.
Abby: Yes, but look. These animals are similar.
Tom: A chicken, a duck and a bird … Can they fly?
Abby: No! Chickens can't fly.
Sophie: I know! They've got two legs.
Abby: That's right. Putting things in groups is a good idea. It helps you to think more.
Tom: It's fun, too! Bye!
Sophie: Bye!

Unit 6 21st Century Video

PB page 69 Activities 1 and 2

Abby: Hello everybody. Welcome to Channel 21.
Tom and Sophie: Hello!
Abby: Do you like the playground, Sophie?
Sophie: Yes, I do.
Tom: Me too.
Abby: Great! Today's programme is about playgrounds. Let's watch the video.

Tom: It's fun to go to the playground. Look at the children.
Sophie: The children are on a roundabout.
Tom: I don't like this roundabout. It's slow!

Sophie: This roundabout isn't slow. It's fast.
Tom: Yes. It's fantastic!
Sophie: The girl is on a slide.
Tom: Oh! It's high. 1 … 2 … 3 … down she goes!

Tom and Sophie: Wow!
Sophie: What a great swing.
Abby: It's important to use two hands on the swing.

Sophie: Look at this zip wire.
Tom: It's high in the trees!

Tom: This climbing frame is high, too.
Abby: The children wait next to the climbing frame. That's good.

Sophie: Look at these children.
Abby: Oh dear! It's important to use two hands on the climbing frame.

Tom: And look at this boy on the swing.
Sophie: Oh! Is he OK?
Abby: Yes, he is.

Tom: Those playgrounds are fun!
Abby: Yes. But be careful at the playground.
Sophie: It's important to sit on the swing.
Tom: And use two hands on the climbing frame.
Abby: That's right. Bye everyone. See you next time.
Tom and Sophie: Bye!

Unit 7 21st Century Video

PB page 81 Activities 1 and 2

Sophie: Hello everybody!
Tom: Hi!
Abby: Welcome to Channel 21.
Sophie: Today's programme is about transport.
Abby: How do you travel in town, Tom?
Tom: I travel by bus.
Abby: What about you, Sophie?
Sophie: I travel by bike.
Abby: Great! Let's see how other children travel in their town.

Abby: This girl travels by boat in her town.
Sophie: It's windy on the boat.

Abby: And this boy travels by train.
Sophie: He's got a computer game.
Tom: I love the train. It's fast!

Abby: Look at this family. They travel by bike!
Tom: There are 2, 4, 6 wheels!

Abby: These children go to school by bus.
Sophie: They're happy.
Tom: It's a big, yellow bus.

Abby: This brother and sister go to school by scooter.
Sophie: That's nice.
Tom: It's good exercise, too.

Abby: And these children go to school by car.
Tom: It's a big car!

Abby: What's this?

Girl and Tom: It's a rickshaw!
Abby: Yes. These children go to school by rickshaw.
Tom and Sophie: Wow!

Sophie: Rickshaws are very slow.
Tom: This rickshaw isn't slow. It's fast!

Tom: Look at this phone! It's got a map.
Abby: Yes – you can look for places in the town.
Sophie: Cool!

Sophie: What a fantastic video!
Tom: Have you got a map on your phone, Abby?
Abby: Yes, I have. Why?
Tom: There's a new bookshop in town. Where is it, please?
Abby: One moment … It's near to the Channel 21 studio! We can go there on foot!
Tom: Hurray! Let's go!
Abby: Goodbye everyone.
Tom: Bye!
Sophie: See you next time.

Unit 8 21st Century Video

PB page 91 Activities 1 and 2

Abby: Hello everybody. Welcome back to Channel 21.
Tom and Sophie: Hello!
Abby: Today's programme is about camping. Do you go camping in the summer, Sophie?
Sophie: Yes, I do.
Tom: Me too. It's fun!
Abby: Great! Let's watch a video about camp activities.

Sophie: Some children go camping in the summer.
Tom: Camping is fun!

Sophie: Look! This boy is swimming.
Tom: He's swimming in a lake. Fantastic!

Sophie: And this girl is sailing a boat.
Abby: It's sunny and windy. Perfect for sailing!

Tom: This boy is riding a horse.
Sophie: He's wearing trousers and a shirt.
Abby: He's wearing a helmet on his head, too. That's good.

Sophie: Look at the family.
Tom: They're riding bikes in the forest.
Sophie: Wow! What a big tree!

Tom: These boys are walking in the forest.
Sophie: It's a cold day. Brrrr!

Tom: This family is camping in the forest.
Sophie: Dad is playing the guitar

Sophie: Look at the big sister. She's playing the guitar, too.
Tom: And the little sister is singing.

Sophie: Camping is fantastic. Let's camp in the garden today.
Abby: It isn't a good idea, Sophie. It's raining.
Sophie: OK. Let's play a computer game. This game is fun.
Tom: Good idea.
Sophie: Bye everyone!
Abby: See you next time.

Unit 9 21st Century Video

PB page 101 Activities 1 and 2

Sophie: Hello everybody!
Tom: Hello!
Abby: Welcome to Channel 21.
Sophie: Today's programme is about teeth.
Abby: Do you brush your teeth, Tom?
Tom: Yes, I do. I brush my teeth every day.
Sophie: Me too!
Abby: Great! Let's watch the video.

Sophie: This girl is eating chocolate. Yum!
Abby: Chocolate has got sugar. It's bad for your teeth. Don't eat a lot.

Abby: It's important to eat healthy food.
Sophie: I eat fruit and vegetables every day.
Tom: Me too!

Abby: It's a good idea to drink milk and water.
Tom: I drink milk in the morning and in the evening.

Abby: And it's important to go to the dentist.
Sophie: This dentist is nice.

Tom: The dentist looks in your mouth.
Sophie: Open your mouth, please!

Abby: The dentist teaches you to brush your teeth.
Sophie: You brush up and down, up and down,

Tom: This girl is brushing her teeth. Look!
Abby: Brush your teeth for two minutes.

Sophie: Look at this girl. She's got a wobbly tooth!
Tom: She can put the tooth under her pillow …
Sophie: … for the tooth fairy!

Sophie: It's important to look after your teeth.
Tom: My teeth are white and healthy.
Abby: I know. Look at these photos!
Tom: Channel 21 is fun.
Abby: But now it's time to say goodbye.
Sophie: Bye everyone.
Tom: Bye!
Sophie: Have a good holiday and see you next year.